www.wadsworth.com

wadsworth.com is the World Wide Web site for Wadsworth and is your direct source to dozens of online resources.

At wadsworth.com you can find out about supplements, demonstration software, and student resources. You can also send email to many of our authors and preview new publications and exciting new technologies.

wadsworth.com
Changing the way the world learns®

A History of Russia, the Soviet Union, and Beyond

Russia
and the USSR
in the Twentieth Century

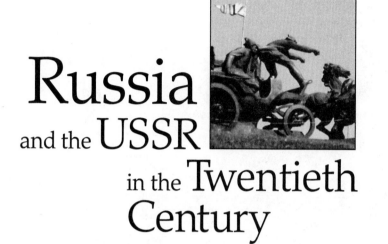

Century

Fourth Edition

David MacKenzie
The University of North Carolina at Greensboro

Michael W. Curran
The Ohio State University

WADSWORTH

THOMSON LEARNING   Australia • Canada • Mexico • Singapore • Spain • United Kingdom • United States

WADSWORTH

THOMSON LEARNING ™

Editorial Director: Clark G. Baxter
Senior Developmental Editor: Sue Gleason
Assistant Editor: Jennifer Ellis
Editorial Assistant: Jonathan Katz
Executive Marketing Manager: Diane McOscar
Marketing Assistant: Kasia Zagorski
Project Manager: Dianne Jensis Toop
Print/Media Buyer: Robert King

Permissions Editor: Joohee Lee
Production Service: Johnstone Associates
Photo Researcher: Susie Friedman
Cover Designer: Lisa Devenish
Cover Image: © Amelia Kunhardt/The Image Works
Cover Printer: R.R. Donnelley, Willard
Compositor: TBH Typecast, Inc.
Printer: R.R. Donnelley, Willard

Printed in the United States of America
1 2 3 4 5 6 7 05 04 03 02 01

For permission to use material from this text, contact us:
Web: http://www.thomsonrights.com **Fax:** 1-800-730-2215
Phone: 1-800-730-2214

Library of Congress Cataloging-in-Publication Data
MacKenzie, David, 1927–
    Russia and the USSR in the 20th Century / David MacKenzie, Michael W. Curran.—4th ed.
       p. cm.
    Includes bibliographical references and index.
    ISBN 0-534-57195-6
    1. Soviet Union—History. I. Title: Russia and the USSR in the twentieth century. II. Curran, Michael W. III. Title.
DK266 M22 2002
947—dc21

                2001026964

Wadsworth/Thomson Learning
10 Davis Drive
Belmont, CA 94002-3098
USA

For more information about our products, contact us:
Thomson Learning Academic Resource Center
1-800-423-0563
http://www.wadsworth.com

International Headquarters
Thomson Learning
International Division
290 Harbor Drive, 2nd Floor
Stamford, CT 06902-7477
USA

UK/Europe/Middle East/South Africa
Thomson Learning
Berkshire House
168-173 High Holborn
London WC1V 7AA
United Kingdom

Asia
Thomson Learning
60 Albert Street, #15-01
Albert Complex
Singapore 189969

Canada
Nelson Thomson Learning
1120 Birchmount Road
Toronto, Ontario M1K 5G4
Canada

To Bruce, Bryan, and Brendan MacKenzie
To Sara and Elizabeth Curran
And in memory of Peter F. Curran

Preface to the Fourth Edition

OVER THE PAST DECADE monumental changes have occurred in Russia (or the Russian Federation) and the now-independent countries that formerly belonged to the Soviet Union. In this edition we provide a succinct history of Russia and its associated lands from the late imperial tsarist regimes to the current Russia of President Vladimir Putin and the countries of the "near abroad." We attempt to balance the history of the Great Russian people centering in Moscow with that of the chief national minorities of the former Soviet Union now belonging to the loosely organized Commonwealth of Independent States.

Why have the authors, some readers might ask, devoted considerable space to the late imperial period of Russian history? Simply because there are many elements of continuity in political, economic, cultural, and national development throughout the imperial, Soviet, and post-Soviet eras. The Revolution of 1917, along with Soviet and recent Russian policies, cannot be adequately understood without carefully examining pre-revolutionary Russian institutions and ideologies. The close connection between Russia's defeat by

Japan and the reforms of the subsequent Duma monarchy can be compared significantly with the troubled post-Soviet transition. Since the Crimean War, Russia and its neighbors have had to confront the perplexing problems of modernization and the challenges posed by a more advanced western Europe and the United States. The Slavophile-Westernizer debate of the 1840s over Russia's past and proper future path persists in that somewhat shrunken but still giant country. For these reasons it seemed inadvisable to begin the textbook with 1917.

Marxist-Leninist theories, now mostly repudiated in both Russia and eastern Europe, fail to explain the troubled history of Russia and its neighbors, although they contain some useful insights. We question whether socioeconomic change, the key in Marxism, necessarily precedes or determines political and cultural change. Soviet viewpoints and scholarship, although still included in this volume, now appear less valuable and relevant than previously. To introduce college and university students to major controversies among various historical schools, notably those among Soviet, post-Soviet, and Western historians, we have included a series of problems presenting contrasting views and interpretations of key events. We hope that these problems will encourage students to think about major historical issues, to probe further, and to reach their own conclusions based on examining the evidence. After all, history is not primarily concerned with memorizing facts and dates; it is about analyzing and arranging specific data into general and meaningful patterns.

In this fourth edition of *Russia and the USSR in the Twentieth Century,* we have sought to present a balanced view of a rapidly changing Russia and its neighbors. In addition to political, socioeconomic,

military, and diplomatic history (written mainly by David MacKenzie), several chapters (primarily by Michael W. Curran) explore Russian and Soviet culture and environmental problems. Our aim has been to write directly and straightforwardly for college students, and to include material from recent events. We hope that this volume will attract other readers interested in learning about the Russian and Soviet past. We welcome suggestions for improvement.

David MacKenzie
Michael W. Curran

Acknowledgments

TO ALL THOSE WHO KINDLY introduced me to the study of Russian history, language, and culture, profound thanks; without their inspiration I could not have written this book. To Boris Miller of Stuttgart, Germany, my first teacher of Russian language and history, who encouraged me to devote myself to lifelong study of the Russian and Slavic experience, heartfelt thanks. At the Russian Institute of Columbia University I had the good fortune to study under professors Philip E. Mosely, Geroid T. Robinson, Henry L. Roberts, and John Hazard, all of whom contributed greatly to my training in the field of Slavic studies. Extended visits to the USSR in 1958–1959 and 1966 under the auspices of the Inter-University Committee on Travel Grants, and shorter sojourns in the Soviet Union in 1969, 1974, and 1990, provided me with essential firsthand exposure to Russia and the opportunity to travel widely and to conduct research in Soviet libraries and archives. At Moscow State University, I received valuable advice and encouragement from the eminent Soviet historians S. A. Nikitin and P. A. Zaionchkovskii. During these sojourns, I visited historic cities in the USSR and took photographs, some of which appear in this book. This text derives, in part, from lectures for my students at the University of North Carolina at Greensboro; I thank them for their interest and support. Without the patience and self-sacrifice of my wife, Patricia, I could neither have traveled to the Soviet Union nor had the time needed to complete this volume.

DM

WHILE IT IS NOT POSSIBLE to acknowledge all those who have contributed to this endeavor, I do wish to recognize some of the most important. I owe a very special debt of gratitude to those who first introduced me to Russia and Russian history: the late Michael B. Petrovich of the University of Wisconsin, and the late Werner Philipp of the Free University of Berlin. Their knowledge of Russia and their scholarly enthusiasm have been a source of inspiration over many years. My brief association with the late George C. Soules did much to shape my views of Russian history. Special thanks are due my colleagues at The Ohio State University: Arthur E. Adams,

Charles Morley, Allan Wildman, and Eve Levin. Their criticisms, helpful suggestions, encouragement, and constant intellectual stimulation are reflected in this volume. I am particularly indebted to my graduate students whose enthusiasm and intellectual curiosity have contributed significantly to the evolution of this book. I hasten to add, however, that any shortcomings and errors contained in this study are entirely my own. I also wish to express my thanks to the Inter-University Committee on Travel Grants and to the Ministry of Higher and Specialized Secondary Education of the USSR, which together provided me with two periods of extended study and research in the USSR in 1962–1963 and 1966. The Ohio State University has supported a number of additional trips to the Soviet Union—the most recent in 1993. The contributions of my two daughters, Sara and Elizabeth, who are just discovering the powerful magnetic qualities of Russian history and the Soviet Union, are too numerous to recount, as are the contributions of my wife, Ann M. Salimbene; suffice it to say that without their support and encouragement and their understanding patience this work would never have been completed.

MWC

WE WOULD BOTH LIKE to thank the following reviewers for their helpful comments on this and previous editions: Steve D. Boilard, Western Kentucky University; Sharyl Cross, University of California, San Jose; David Edwards, University of Arkansas; Thomas Fiddick, University of Evansville; Stephen Frank, University of California, Los Angeles; David M. Griffiths, University of North Carolina, Chapel Hill; Michael C. Hickey, Bloomsburg University; Yanni Kotsanis, New York University; Donald Ostrowski, Harvard University; Roger V. Paxton, University of Utah; Geraldine Phipps, University of Massachusetts; Gerald Surh, North Carolina State University; Kate Transchel, California State University, Chico; Theodore R. Weeks, Southern Illinois University, Carbondale; and William Wood, Point Loma Nazarene University.

DM
MWC

A Note on Russian Dates, Names, Measures, and Money

DATING RUSSIAN EVENTS has been complicated by the use in Russia until 1918 of "Old Style" dates of the Julian calendar, which in the 18th century were 11 days behind those of the Gregorian calendar employed in the West. In the 19th century the lag was 12 days, and in the 20th, 13 days. Early in 1918 the Soviet regime adopted the "New Style" Gregorian calendar. Generally, dates have been rendered here according to the calendar used in Russia at the time, except that we have shifted to "New Style" dates beginning with 1917.

Transliterating Russian names into English likewise presents some peculiar problems. We have adhered largely to the Library of Congress system, but have omitted diacritical marks for the sake of simplicity. Most Russian first names have been replaced with English equivalents, such as Peter, Alexander, and Catherine, but not John and Basil instead of Ivan and Vasili.

Russian weights, measures, and distances have been rendered in their English equivalents for the convenience of English-speaking readers. However, Russian rubles have been retained with indications of their dollar value. The ruble, containing 100 kopeks, was worth about 50 cents in 1914. The official value of the Russian Ruble in 2000 was about 28 to the dollar.

Contents

LIST OF FIGURES

LIST OF TABLES

LIST OF MAPS

1

Background and Early History

Is Russia, despite the collapse of the Soviet Union in 1991 and its own numerous current problems, still expansionist? Is Soviet Communism truly dead, or might it revive in the future? Will the Russian Federation, containing many different ethnic groups, remain unified, or dissolve into its component national parts? Will Russia reassert political, economic, and even military control over the newly independent countries formerly parts of the USSR? Such questions are being raised currently about Russia and the Commonwealth of Independent States (CIS) consisting of the former Soviet republics. These cannot, of course, be answered definitively, nor even satisfactorily. However, we can uncover clues to the answers by examining the Russian and Soviet past and its institutions.

This volume aims to introduce the serious reader to 20th-century Russia and the Soviet Union through a factual survey of events and a number of problems that suggest the widely divergent views held both inside and outside Russia and the CIS. This text on 20th-century Russia and the USSR, based on the last portion of

our *A History of Russia, the Soviet Union, and Beyond* (6th ed., Wadsworth, 2002), includes a summary of major developments in Russian history down to about 1900 for those who have not studied those earlier periods. We have sought to steer a difficult passage between excessive factual detail and facile generalization.

A history of modern Russia cannot properly begin in 1917 if it hopes to explain the Bolshevik Revolution or the institutions and policies of the subsequent Soviet and post-Soviet regimes. First we will look at basic factors and controversies in Russian history and then summarize historical developments to 1855. Chapter 2 will examine major developments in most fields, 1855 to 1904. Political trends from the Revolution of 1905 until World War I will be treated in Chapter 3, and major cultural developments in Chapter 4. The following chapter explores political developments from the Revolution of 1905 until World War I. These aim to provide some background for studying the Russian and Soviet experience since 1917. While concentrating on the Great Russian core of the former Soviet empire, we have sought also to indicate the roles of major national, ethnic, and religious groups that until 1991 composed the Union of Soviet Socialist Republics.

A basic controversy between Soviet and non-Soviet scholars[1] throughout Russian history is whether external or internal factors and influences have predominated in shaping the course followed by Russian and Soviet peoples. Generally, Soviet scholars who lived and worked in Soviet Russia from November 1917 to December 1991—basing their views necessarily upon the Marxist-Leninist scheme—argued the primacy of *internal* factors in Russia's historical development from the formation of the first significant Russian state until 1991. Internal socioeconomic change, they argued, produced political change in an evolution from primitive communism through feudalism and capitalism to Soviet socialism. External factors such as migrations of peoples, wars, conquest, and alien rule, they agreed, at times had a significant impact, but invariably remained subsidiary to the inexorable laws of internal development and the maturation and decline of institutions.

Among non-Soviet historians, Normanist and Eurasian scholars especially have asserted that *external* influences upon Russia have been preeminent in influencing the development of its peculiar institutions, attitudes, and the character of its people since the dawn of history.[2] Thus, the Normanists—chiefly Scandinavian and German scholars—have asserted that the Varangians, or Vikings, allegedly invited into Russia by its Slavic tribes about A.D. 850 to rule over them, created the

first cohesive Russian state and a basis for Russian civilization. These claims have been rejected vehemently by Soviet and some Western scholars. Nonetheless, it seems clear that the Varangian impact on early Russian development, as on western Europe, was significant, although by no means as great as the Normanists have affirmed. Less questionable, though also controversial, are Byzantine influences upon Kievan and subsequent Muscovite Russia. The late British historian B. H. Summer described as Byzantine "gifts" to nascent Kievan Rus religion, the alphabet, the arts, and law, suggesting Russia's profound debt to Constantinople, or Tsargrad (the imperial city), as Russians called it. Thus some Byzantinists and Western scholars consider Kievan Rus a political and economic satellite of the Byzantine Empire. The Soviet view, on the other hand, emphasized that Kievan Rus, described as a powerful and independent feudal Slavic state, was a native product evolving from previous tribal confederations living under primitive communism. Agriculture, they affirmed, predominated over foreign trade in the Kievan era, suggesting independence from external influences.

Likewise, interpretations differ widely over the Asiatic impact on Russia, notably over the great Mongol invasion (1237–1241) that destroyed Kievan Rus and established Asiatic control over most parts of the Russian land for 200 to 250 years. The Eurasian school, viewing that cataclysmic event rather positively, regards Moscow as the political successor of the Golden Horde, stresses the growth and advantages of Eurasian trade, and considers the Mongol era as vital to an emergent Russian autocracy and empire. Soviet views of the Mongol conquest, however, based on ancient Russian chronicle accounts, emphasized its terrible destructiveness and claimed that the Mongol yoke was primarily responsible for centuries of Russian backwardness relative to a more fortunate western Europe.

Over the past three centuries the chief and most pervasive influence upon Russia and its neighbors unquestionably has been western European, and still more recently American. Nonethe-

---

[1] The latter may be subdivided into non-Russian "Western" scholars living throughout the world, prerevolutionary Russian historians who lived in Imperial Russia, émigré Russian scholars who left Soviet Russia after 1917, and Russian scholars after the collapse of the Soviet Union in 1991. Each of these groups has its own peculiar ax to grind in assessing Russian history; the dates and places of publication of their works often provide clues to their biases.
[2] On Normanism see D. MacKenzie and M. Curran, *A History of Russia, the Soviet Union, and Beyond,* 6th ed. (Belmont, CA, 2002), pp. 23–26 and on the Eurasian school, pp. 89–90.

less, Soviet, Russian, and Western scholars have disagreed sharply over its extent and impact on Russian institutions. An outstanding prerevolutionary Russian historian V. O. Kliuchevskii (1841–1911) discerned even in 17th-century Muscovy a profound cultural conflict between Greco-Byzantine traditional elements and values in Russian life associated with the Orthodox Church and Latin-Western values introduced into Muscovy by European travelers, merchants, and officers. What had been in Kliuchevskii's view merely casual contacts with the West prior to 1600 became subsequently genuine influence upon Russian institutions, beginning with the army.[3] Under Peter I, "the Great" (1672–1725), this Western influence deepened and broadened. Most Western scholars agree that western Europe served as the chief model for the partial modernization of Russian institutions under Peter I, Catherine II, and Alexander I and II, from roughly 1700 to 1881. However, Soviet scholars, while granting that Western influences were undoubtedly present, affirm that the reforms by these monarchs originated primarily in Russian needs and were derived from the Russian past. Similarly, Western economic historians dispute whether Russia represented a backward European country following belatedly in western Europe's footsteps or a unique entity between Europe and Asia pursuing its own distinctive development. Did Russia after 1860 undergo "modernization" (C. E. Black) —a process faced by all modern societies—or "Westernization" (T. von Laue), adapting its institutions to a western European model? Finally, after Stalin, American influences, notably cultural and economic, became significant.

Challenge and Response

Location, climate, and topography have confronted the Russian people with severe challenges during a difficult and turbulent history.

---

[3] V. O. Kliuchevskii, *Course of Russian History* (New York, 1911–1931), III.

Traditionally, Russia (and the USSR) was a relatively poor country where most people extracted a precarious living from the soil or worked for low wages. Poverty, vulnerability to attack, and poor interior communications helped produce responses distinguishing Russian history and culture in important ways from those of western Europe and the United States. The chief responses to peculiar Russian conditions and problems seem to have been autocracy, collectivism, and mysticism. The first two, especially, persisted regardless of regime or ideology until very recently as vital elements of the Russian experience.

Autocracy, or statism, conspicuously absent during early Russian history, began to develop during the unification of Great Russia about 1500. It persisted until late 1991 as a centralized monarchical or communist state with a virtual monopoly of power, except for a few brief "times of trouble" (1598–1613, 1725–1730, and 1917–1921). During the 16th and 17th centuries autocracy grew as limitations on the tsar's powers, such as an independent hereditary aristocracy, representative institutions like the assembly of the lands, and an autonomous church, withered. Although of Greek origin, autocracy in Russia derived more from the practice of the Mongol Golden Horde than from Byzantine political theory. Russian tsars, such as Ivan IV, "the Terrible," Peter the Great, and Nicholas I, wielded awesome authority that resembled Oriental despotism more closely than western European monarchy.

Unlike western Europe, Russia did not experience prolonged or complete feudalism and fell increasingly under strong, centralized monarchical power. People and property became possessions of the Muscovite state, as they had been in the Mongol Golden Horde. Institutions that challenged state authority were gradually stripped of influence. Autocracy grew more powerful and pervasive over time, mobilized Russia's natural and human resources in order to resist external invasions, and conquered contiguous areas; in the Soviet period it created formidable industrial and military power. Absorbing parts of the Byzantine and Mongol political traditions, autocracy used the principle of service to the state to subordinate to its dictates both the bodies and minds of individuals, not protected as in western Europe by corporate groups with inherent rights.

Collectivism, which contrasts with the individualism of western Europe and the United States, has been another peculiar Russian response linked closely with autocracy. For centuries, under tsars and commissars alike, most land in Russia was held and worked in common, and taxes were gathered and paid collectively by village communities, long after these practices died out in western Europe. Collectivism aided Muscovy, the Russian Empire, and the USSR to mobilize resources to combat severe external and internal challenges. The collectivism inherent in the Great Russian repartitional commune of the 18th and 19th centuries foreshadowed that of Soviet collective and state farms. About 1600, autocracy subjected a semifree Russian peasantry to the collective bondage of serfdom, a degrading but vital feature of Russian life until the 1860s.

Finally, the prevalent mysticism of the Russian Orthodox tradition, increasing church subordination to the state, and a relative lack of intellectual inquiry within the church differed greatly from the rationalism and questioning in western Catholic and Protestant faiths. In Muscovite Russia, matters such as the spelling of Jesus's name and elements of ritual and tradition acquired vast significance for an unsophisticated populace. The prevalent belief that Russia was the center of the only true faith tended to intensify suspicion of foreigners and their institutions. In a sense Soviet communism, despite a theoretically antithetical ideology, continued this mystical tradition. Until World War II, Soviet spokesmen reiterated that the USSR was the only land of socialism and center of the true Marxist-Leninist faith. Xenophobia—extreme fear of foreigners and suspicion of their motives—persisted and was reinforced deliberately by the Soviet regime. Like Russian Orthodoxy under tsarism, with the passing years Soviet Marxist-Leninist ideology degenerated into a sterile dogmatism incapable of inspiring or convincing the young.

To be sure, the roles and personalities of tsarist and Soviet rulers have been important in shaping Russian history, providing a convenient, if not always revealing, method of dividing it into periods. Such major figures as Ivan IV, Peter, and Catherine the Great in the tsarist era, and Lenin, Stalin, and Khrushchev in the Soviet period stand out above the flood of events. But unless one accepts the "great man" (or woman) theory of history, to view an era through the career and character of the ruler exaggerates individual leadership and oversimplifies complex trends. Instead, tracing such themes as autocracy, collectivism, and mysticism through history should prove more effective in clarifying how Russia and its neighbors have evolved.

Geography

The Soviet Union, of which Russia comprised about three-fourths the area and about half the population, was a huge empire almost three times the size of the United States and about equal in area to all of North America. Spanning most of eastern Europe and northern Asia, it extended about 6,000 miles east to west and more than 3,000 miles north to south to include about one-sixth the land area of the globe. By its vastness and location the Soviet Union was in a position to dominate the combined land mass of Europe and Asia called Eurasia. During 1991 the USSR fragmented into 15 allegedly independent countries of which Russia is by far the largest, but with frontiers in the west and south resembling those of the early 17th century.

Most of the USSR was a huge plain extending eastward from Poland almost to the Pacific Ocean. Narrowing as one moves across Siberia, it runs out in the plateau and mountainous terrain of eastern Siberia. This expanse is barely interrupted by the low, worn Ural Mountains (maximum height 6,214 feet), which divide Europe from Asia only in part. Until the 13th century, through the gap of some 800 miles between the Urals and the Caspian Sea, successive waves of Asiatic invaders poured into Europe. Impressive mountain ranges are limited to the frontiers of the former Russian Empire and USSR: the Carpathians in the southwest, the Caucasus to the south, and the Pamir, Tien-Shan, and Altai mountains on the borders of Afghanistan, India, and China. European Russia, where the main drama of Russian history has been played, is mostly flat and low. The Valdai Hills, a plateau in the northwest where the great European Russian rivers rise, reaches a maximum elevation of only 1,000 feet above sea level.

Flowing slowly through the European Russian plain, the rivers have served throughout history as arteries of communication and commerce. The Northern Dvina and Pechora flow northward into the Arctic basin, most of the others southward: the Dniester, Bug, Dnieper, and Don into the Black Sea and the Sea of Azov, and the majestic "mother" Volga, comparable in breadth and importance to the Mississippi, into the Caspian Sea. These rivers and their tributaries form an excellent water communications system, greatly improved in modern times by connecting canals. In Siberia (the region east of the Urals and north of Central Asia) the Ob, Lena, Enisei, and Kolyma rivers, moving northward into the frozen Arctic, are of limited commercial value. Only the Amur, part of the modern boundary with China, moves eastward into the Pacific.

The climate of Russia and its neighbors is continental—that is, marked by extremes of heat and cold. Most of Russia lies in the latitudes of Canada and Alaska. The Gulf Stream, which moderates the climate of the east coast of the United States and the northwest coast of western Europe, affects only the western part of the north Russian coast from Murmansk to Archangel. Extremes of temperature generally increase as one moves eastward, but even in European Russia there are no internal mountain barriers to keep icy winds from sweeping to the Black Sea. Northeast Siberia is one of the world's coldest regions: temperatures as low as −90° F have been recorded in Verkhoiansk region. However, heat waves occur in European Russia, and even Siberia, during the summer. In the Central Asian deserts temperatures of 120° F are not uncommon. Precipitation in Russia, partly

because of the continental climate, is generally moderate or light and often greatest in summer.

There are five major soil and vegetation zones in Russia and the Commonwealth, stretching generally northeast to southwest. About 15 percent of these countries in the extreme north is level or undulating treeless plain, called tundra, and 47 percent of it has permanently frozen subsoil. (See Map 1.1.) The tundra, a virtually uninhabited wasteland, has many lakes and swamps, with moss and low shrubs the only vegetation. South of it lies the taiga, or coniferous forest, in the north and mixed coniferous and deciduous forest farther south. This vast forest belt, the largest in the world, extends across all Russia and covers more than half its territory. The poor ashy soils, called *podzol*, of the boggy coniferous forest with their low acid content are mostly unfit for crops. Agriculture is possible only in cleared portions of the southern forest region. The mixed forest zone to the south, the heart of Muscovite Russia, has richer gray and brown soils. Below this the forest shades into wooded steppe or meadow, mostly with very fertile black soil (*chernozem*), excellent for grains wherever there is sufficient rainfall. Still farther south is mostly treeless prairie like the American Great Plains, extending monotonously for hundreds and hundreds of miles, also a fertile black soil region. East of the Caspian Sea this black soil shades into semidesert, then true desert to the south and east. In the Crimea and along the Caucasian shore of the Black Sea lies a small subtropical region, Russia's Riviera. Early frosts, a short growing season, and barren or frozen soil mean that only about 10 percent of the former Soviet Union is under cultivation, although one-third is potentially arable. In some regions with rich soil, rainfall is often insufficient for crops. Even the black soil region of the southern steppe has a shorter growing season than the American plains.

How has geography affected Russia's history? Until the late 19th century, chiefly European Russia should be considered. Siberia remained sparsely populated, its great resources unexploited; Central Asia and the Caucasus were

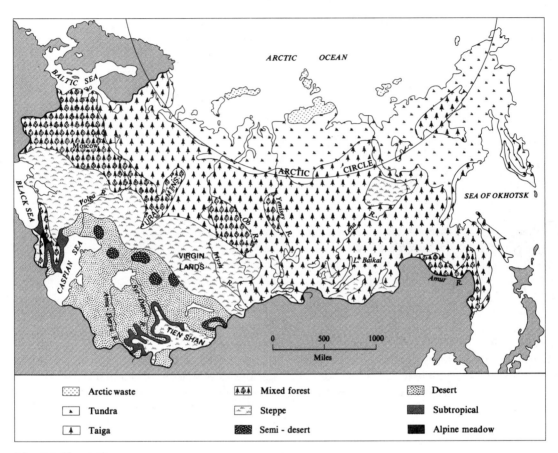

Map 1.1 Vegetation zones

acquired only in the 19th century. European Russia's flat plains fostered colonization and expansion, persistent themes in Russian history for almost 1,000 years. Unworried by waste, Russians cleared forest glades and ploughed up virgin steppe lands. In the 19th century, a continental colonialism developed as the Russians occupied areas next to their borders.

Geography has provided Russia with natural ocean frontiers on the north and east and mountain boundaries in the south and southwest. These frontiers were attained after centuries of struggle with Asian invaders and by Russian expansion. In the west such natural barriers were lacking. In modern history foreign invasions of Russia have

come from the west, and Russian efforts at expansion have focused there. Until recently, Russia was largely landlocked without ready access to warmwater ports or to foreign markets. Some historians, such as R. J. Kerner, have interpreted Russian expansion as a drive to secure such ports and unfettered access to the Pacific Ocean and Baltic, Black, and Mediterranean seas. Vast distances, while contributing to the eventual defeat or absorption of invaders, have complicated the achievement or maintenance of unity and perhaps have promoted highly centralized, authoritarian regimes. The severe climate of the north and Siberia contributed to sparse population and easy Russian conquest.

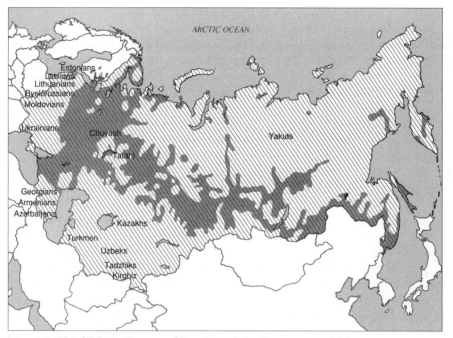

Map 1.2 Chief Ethnic Groups of Russia and the Commonwealth*

*Predominantly Russian areas are shown in gray.

SOURCE: Joe LeMonnier, *NYT Magazine*, Jan. 28, 1990. Copyright 1990 by The New York Times Company. Reprinted by permission.

The Peoples

The former Russian Empire, then the Soviet Union—multinational and multiethnic lands—contained almost 180 distinct nationalities and tribes, speaking about 125 languages and dialects, and practicing 40 different religions. Ninety-five groups numbered over 100,000 persons each; 54 had their own national territories. About three-fourths of the Soviet population were eastern Slavs who began as a single people, then separated after the Mongol invasion of 1237–1241 into three major groups: Russians, Ukrainians, and Byelorussians.

Russians, or Great Russians, the most numerous group, number about 143 million or 51 percent of the former USSR's population. (See Map 1.2.) They have played a dominant historical and political role in the Russian Empire, the Soviet Union, and now the Commonwealth of Independent States. About five-sixths of ethnic Russians resided in the RSFSR (Russian Republic), which occupied almost three-fourths of the entire USSR. The remaining 25 million Russians, living in other union republics, mostly in large cities, often held key political and economic positions. Since 1991 many of these have emigrated back into Russia. The roughly 45 million Ukrainians are descended directly from the people of Kievan Rus. In the 17th century they were reunited with the Great Russians, initially received autonomy, then were subjected to direct Russian rule. About 85 percent of Ukrainians now live in Ukraine, comprising about three-fourths of its population. More than 3.5 million Ukrainians reside in Russia. Byelorussians, or "White Russians," number over 10 million and comprise about 80 percent of the populace of Belarus; some 1.6 million live elsewhere. Byelorussia was absorbed into the Russian Empire in the

17th and 18th centuries. Most of the one million Poles of the former USSR, the fourth largest Slavic group within it, entered the Soviet Union involuntarily in 1939 after Soviet annexation of eastern Poland.

The Baltic peoples—some 5.5 million—mostly inhabit the newly independent countries of Latvia, Lithuania, and Estonia on Russia's western border. After enjoying independence from 1919 to 1940, they were forcibly annexed to the USSR under the Nazi-Soviet Pact of 1939. The 3 million Lithuanians had a proud heritage of independence as a Grand Duchy, then were linked with Poland until annexed to the Russian Empire in 1795. Latvian and Lithuanian are Baltic Indo-European languages; Estonian is a Uralic tongue closely related to Finnish. All three peoples use the Latin alphabet, are strongly European in outlook, and are mostly Catholic or Lutheran.

The leading peoples of the Caucasus are Armenians, Georgians, and Azerbaijani, and their three independent countries contain about 15 million people. Many of the 4.4 million Armenians live outside Armenia, where they represent almost 90 percent of the population. Armenians, like Georgians and Azerbaijani, are heirs to an ancient and proud civilization; their language is Indo-European. Annexed to the Russian Empire in 1828, Armenia enjoyed a brief independence from 1918 to 1920, as did Georgia and Azerbaijan, before being forcibly incorporated into the Soviet Union. Neighboring Georgia with about 5 million people, two-thirds of them Georgians who are mostly Eastern Orthodox, have an alphabet and language totally different from Russian. Georgia was annexed to Russia in 1801. Unlike their Christian neighbors, most of the Muslim Azerbaijani, who speak a Turkic language, live in independent Azerbaijan; others live in neighboring Iran. The mountainous Caucasus region also contains many smaller groups, such as the militant Chechens, some possessing autonomous status.

The more than 50 million Muslims were the second largest religious group in the USSR after the Orthodox. In the Volga River basin live smaller Turko-Tatar peoples, including the Kazan Tatars,

Bashkirs, and Chuvash; the Crimean Tatars returned only recently to their homeland. All are descended from Mongol and Turkic warriors who conquered Russia in the 13th century only to be overrun in the subsequent Russian eastward and southward expansion. Farther east lies Central Asia with some 50 million people, now comprising five independent countries: Uzbekistan, Kazakhstan, Tajikistan, Kyrgyzstan, and Turkmenistan. Their inhabitants are chiefly Muslims speaking Turkic languages. Between 1730 and 1885 Russian armies conquered Central Asia and renamed it Russian Turkestan. It was absorbed into the USSR by the early 1920s and remained within it until late 1991. Two other significant minorities in Russia and Ukraine have recently emigrated in large numbers. Germans, settling mostly along the Volga River in the 18th century, were scattered during World War II; many have left for Germany. Jews, residing chiefly in cities of European Russia and Ukraine, have been greatly reduced in numbers by emigration since 1970.

Summary of Russian History to 1855

Ancient Rus[4] (to about A.D. 850)

Because of a lack of written Russian sources, the era prior to the mid-ninth century, often called ancient or prehistoric Russia, remains obscure despite many 20th-century archeological discoveries. Where the Slavs originated and when they settled western Russia and Ukraine remain disputed issues. No central political, military, or economic organizations existed among these rather primitive pagan people, who lacked a written alphabet and worshipped local or regional deities often associated with natural forces. Early Slav tribes were constantly exposed to incursions by new waves of Asiatic invaders sweeping across the

---

[4] The term *Rus* refers to much of the territory that would later become Russia and Ukraine. We will use *Rus* until about 1300, when the process of unification of Great Russia under the aegis of Moscow began.

steppes. Following the Marxian scheme, Soviet historians designated this period primitive communism when most land and goods were held collectively. The Slavs gradually prevailed over non-Slavic Asiatic intruders. The first Russian state, insisted Soviet scholars, arose in today's western Ukraine in the sixth or seventh century A.D.; by the mid-ninth century feudalism had triumphed in both eastern and western Europe.

Kievan Rus (about 850–1240)

Controversy persists among Soviet, Normanist, and Western scholars over the formation of Kievan Rus in the mid-ninth century,[5] but the results are evident. During the late ninth century, a federation emerged of about a dozen Slav-Varangian principalities, ruled by princes belonging to a single dynasty, generally called the House of Riurik, and centered in Kiev in the south and Novgorod in the north. Unity was forged partly by several Varangian-Slav attacks upon the Byzantine capital, Constantinople. Normally, the prince of Kiev was senior in this ruling family, exercising limited and uncertain control over other principalities. Politically, Kievan Rus comprised a federation, later a confederation, lacking a single army or administration. Soviet scholars viewed it as a powerful feudal state with a definite sense of national purpose. Within Kievan Rus political power was divided among ruling princes, noble advisory councils (*boyar duma*), and town councils (*vieche*), reflecting monarchical, aristocratic, and democratic principles, respectively. At its peak in the 10th and 11th centuries, Kievan Rus traded extensively with nearby Byzantium, although most of its population engaged in subsistence agriculture. Kievan society was diverse and mobile: Middle-class freemen (*liudi*) were significant, and its peasantry was mostly free, although there were indentured groups and slaves. Thus it does not appear to fit the feudal patterns of contemporary western Europe.

---

[5] See MacKenzie and Curran, *A History of Russia, the Soviet Union, and Beyond,* 6th ed. (Belmont, CA, 2002).

Internationally, Kievan Rus's chief relations were with the Byzantine Empire, and some scholars even consider it a Byzantine satellite. Following a series of attacks from Kievan Rus upon Constantinople, regular commercial relations were established as well as close links between Kievan and Byzantine rulers. During the 12th century Kievan Rus's commercial and political ties with central and western Europe increased. There was little contact between Kievan Rus and the Arab world to the south.

Culturally, Kievan Rus relied heavily on Byzantium, deriving its alphabet, religion, art, church architecture, and iconography (paintings on wood portraying religious themes) from Constantinople. Thus the Greek brothers Saints Cyril and Methodius created a written alphabet for the Slavs, fostering the translation of Greco-Byzantine religious works into Church Slavonic. In 988, Kievan Rus converted to Orthodox Christianity under Prince Vladimir I, though paganism survived for centuries in remote areas. Greco-Byzantine clergy dominated an Orthodox Church directly subordinate to the Patriarchate of Constantinople. The cultural traditions that emerged during Kievan times—notably those of the Orthodox Church—would play a very significant role in the development of Russian culture into the 18th century and beyond.

Both internal and external factors contributed to the decline and fall of the Kievan Rus federation: political disintegration, rising civil strife, economic decline, vulnerability to nomadic attacks from the east, and inability to resist the great Mongol onslaught of the mid-13th century. Nonetheless, the Kievan epoch represented a diversified, relatively free, and prosperous beginning to Russian history.

Appanage or Mongol Era (1240 to about 1450)

The relative unity of the early Kievan era yielded to disunity and fragmentation after 1139, accelerated a century later by the Mongol conquest. Kiev's politicoeconomic decline was accompanied by outward migration and emergence of three separate centers of life in Rus, all subject to much foreign control or influence between 1200 and 1450. The southwestern principalities of Galicia and Volhynia retained their former Kievan culture and prosperity until falling victim first to Mongol conquest, then Lithuanian and Polish rule. In the 12th and early 13th centuries, the cities of Suzdal and Vladimir, in the northeastern mesopotamia formed by the Volga and Oka rivers, flourished briefly before succumbing to Mongol conquest. From 1157 to 1240, Vladimir served as unofficial capital of all Rus, replacing declining Kiev. In the northwest, the virtually independent commercial city-republics of Novgorod and Pskov, resembling by their institutions the German Hansa towns, continued Kievan traditions of diversity and freedom well into the 15th century. Developing an extensive empire to the north and east, Novgorod in the 13th century under Prince Alexander Nevskii repelled invaders from the west (Teutonic Knights, Swedes, and Lithuanians), but felt compelled to submit to Mongol overlordship.

In the midst of this fragmentation of Rus came the devastating Mongol invasion (1237–1241), the final Asiatic assault on Rus. The triumphant Mongols, under Khan Batu, grandson of Chingis-khan, established the Golden Horde, a separate state centered at Sarai on the Volga. From there they administered the conquered country through Rus vassal princes who supplied their Mongol overlords with tribute money and army recruits. The khans of the Golden Horde were Oriental despots claiming total authority and ownership of all land; they were emulated subsequently by their faithful servitors and tax collectors, the princes of Moscow.

Moscow's initial rise occurred during this Mongol or appanage era. Founded in the mid-12th century in the northeastern mesopotamia, Moscow enjoyed a favorable location for trade, settlement, and colonization. In the early 14th century, the Golden Horde bestowed the grand princely title on Moscow; it also became the seat of the Orthodox Church, which the Mongols generally did not persecute. In 1380, Moscow's Prince Dmitri "Donskoi" (of the Don), heading an army of Russian princely contingents, inflicted the first serious defeat on the Horde. By the mid-15th century, as the Horde fragmented into several warring khanates, an expanded Moscow, or Muscovy, constituted one of several major Russian principalities contending for territory and power in central Russia.

The culture of Rus under Mongol rule, cut off from most outside contacts, was forced inward. Byzantine forms in art and architecture adopted during the Kievan era were internalized, and in the process much of the refined Byzantine subtlety and sophistication was lost. Many skilled crafts, such as pottery making, elaborate enamel work, and intricate gold and silver work, practiced in the towns declined or disappeared altogether. However, Orthodox Byzantine Christianity helped preserve the national identity and the nucleus for a national Russian culture.

Muscovite Era (1450–1689)

During the 15th century Mongol disintegration yielded to increasing integration and unification of Great Russia under Muscovite princes. Ivan III, "the Great" (1462–1505), defeated and incorporated Novgorod, Tver, and lesser rivals, then established diplomatic relations with leading European states. Ivan III set for Moscow the aim of securing control over all territories that had once belonged to Kievan Russia. After marrying the niece of the last Byzantine emperor, whose remaining domains had fallen to the Ottoman Turks, Ivan III asserted that Moscow was the true successor to Byzantine imperial traditions, claimed equality with European rulers, and refused further subservience or tribute to the fragmented Mongol Golden Horde. Internally, he undermined the power of his brothers and other appanage princes, built a more centralized army, issued a national law code, and increased church dependence on the crown. The centralizing policies and military victories of this so-called gatherer of the Russian lands created a powerful but primitive Muscovite monarchical state.

Ivan III's grandson, Ivan IV, "the Terrible" (ruled 1533–1584), was crowned as the first Muscovite tsar (Caesar) in 1547. Conquering the Mongol khanates along the Volga River in the 1550s, he inaugurated an eastward expansion across the Urals, which by 1640 had brought Russian Cossacks (frontiersmen) and fur trappers to the forbidding shores of the northern Pacific. Claiming full autocratic powers, Ivan IV launched a reign of terror—the Oprichnina (1564–1572)—against titled boyars, churchmen, and other domestic opponents. Defeated in the lengthy Livonian War by a western coalition of Sweden, Lithuania, and Poland, and driven from the shores of the Baltic Sea, Ivan created near chaos at home with his unbridled Oprichnina and then accidentally killed his eldest son, Ivan Ivanovich. In 1598 the death of Fedor, his imbecile second son, ended the old Muscovite dynasty and helped produce a "time of troubles" (1598–1613). This involved a struggle for the throne, won initially by the able boyar, Boris Godunov, depicted in perhaps the greatest of Russian operas (see below). Exploiting disorder and famine, the Poles occupied Moscow, setting up briefly a "false Dmitri." This bloody, confused era ended with the expulsion of foreign invaders and restoration of unity under the new Romanov dynasty (ruled 1613–1917), elected by a representative assembly of the land *(zemskii sobor)*.

Early Romanov tsars (1613–1689) were mediocre and physically weak, but royal power, supported by a growing central bureaucracy, prevailed over the hereditary aristocracy (boyars), the church, and poorly organized representative bodies. Serfdom and a virtual caste system enslaved more than 90 percent of the Russian people and bound them to their residences and occupations. By mid-century serfs on private estates were under the absolute power of noble landowners, who controlled their lives and exacted increasing rents and forced labor services. There developed a profound schism in the Russian Orthodox Church: Millions of Russian peasants remained "Old Believers," worshipping from traditional Muscovite church books; they were anathematized by the official Church and persecuted by the state.

Under the early Romanovs the conquest of Siberia was completed and the eastern Ukraine was incorporated after lengthy warfare with a disorganized and disintegrating Poland.

The cultural traditions of northeast Russia received a powerful impetus from Moscow's emergence in the 15th century as a major political, economic, and cultural center with the support of the Orthodox Church. A sense of religious superiority emerged, especially after Constantinople's fall to the Ottoman Turks in 1453, which fostered the subsequent concept of Moscow as "the Third Rome"—that is, the successor to Rome and Constantinople as the center of "true" Christianity. Russians now viewed Moscow as the capital of an independent Muscovite state and the spiritual capital of Orthodox Christendom. Historical chronicles and cultural attitudes began to reflect the enhanced stature of an independent Muscovy. However, the progressive centralization of Russian political and economic institutions under Moscow produced a rigid, immobile, and Church-dominated culture that severely restricted individual initiative and creativity. The unfortunate results were cultural stagnation and a very defensive attitude toward non-Russian cultures. The monolithic Byzantine cultural tradition of the Orthodox Church was finally shattered during its 17th-century struggle with the tsarist state over liturgy and ritual. The triumph of the state prepared the way for a reorientation and secularization of Russian culture.

Early Imperial Era (about 1700–1855)

The first energetic Romanov ruler and unchallenged Russian autocrat was huge and dynamic Peter I, "the Great" (ruled 1689–1725). During a turbulent youth, Peter developed a passionate interest in the army, navy, and European technology. After almost a year studying technology and recruiting experts in western Europe, Peter returned home, crushed the opposition of the conservative palace guard (*streltsi*), and launched the Great Northern War (1699–1721) against imperial Sweden. Eventual victory in that conflict

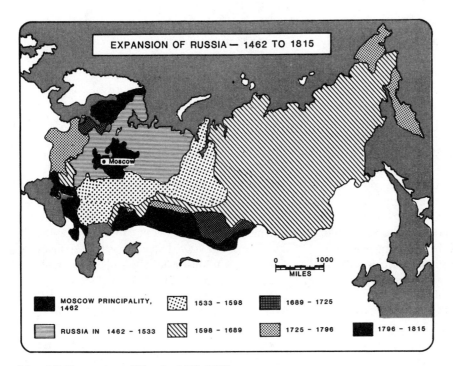

EXPANSION OF RUSSIA — 1462 TO 1815

Moscow

0   1000
MILES

| | MOSCOW PRINCIPALITY, 1462 | | 1533 – 1598 | | 1689 – 1725 |

| | RUSSIA IN 1462 – 1533 | | 1598 – 1689 | | 1725 – 1796 | | 1796 – 1815 |

Map 1.3 Expansion of Russia, 1462–1815

ended Russia's virtual isolation from Europe, gave it control of the eastern Baltic shores (his "window to the West"), and enabled Peter to construct a new capital—St. Petersburg—near the Baltic Sea. (See Map 1.3.) During that war Peter transformed an ill-disciplined, inefficient armed force into a large regular standing army of conscripts. By now a vast Eurasian multinational empire, Russia became a great European power, recognized as such by the others: Great Britain, France, the Austrian Empire, and a rising Prussia. Requirements for war underlay most of Peter I's far-reaching domestic reforms: a centralized administration, headed by a Senate and organized by a Table of Ranks into parallel hierarchies for the military, civil service, and the court; a more efficient and onerous system of taxation of the masses; and a superficially educated and westernized upper-class elite. The Petrine reforms harnessed all elements of a highly stratified Russian society, resting on a bonded peasantry paying the poll tax and a nobility pressed into lifelong service to the state. Peter's

mercantilistic economic policies laid the foundation for Russian heavy industry but did little to promote the growth of towns or an urban middle class so important for economic development in western Europe. Russia remained overwhelmingly rural, peasant, and illiterate, scarcely affected by Petrine reforms of dress and beard shaving. In 1725, Peter I died suddenly without designating a successor.

Following an interlude often called the "Era of Palace Revolutions" when a series of minors and four women were enthroned and manipulated by the nobility in Peter's Guards regiments, a remarkable German woman married to the immature ruler, Peter III, usurped power as Catherine II, "the Great" (ruled 1762–1796). She ruled through a series of official favorites who shared her bed but rarely her power. Posing as a legitimate, enlightened despot like Frederick II of emergent Prussia, the superbly educated Catherine continued Peter the Great's expansion at the expense of Poland— thrice partitioned—and the Ottoman Empire—

twice defeated. By the end of her reign Russia had solved the Swedish, Polish, and Turkish "problems." Millions of Poles and Jews had been subjected involuntarily to Russian rule, which now extended over the entire Baltic region, Byelorussia, the entire Ukraine, and the northern shores of the Black Sea. Initially aligned with Prussia in a northern bloc, Russia later allied with Austria; they were opposed by France especially because of their partitions of Catholic Poland. Russia began to exert influence over Christian peoples in the Balkans, subject to a corrupt and disintegrating Ottoman Empire. At home, Catherine reformed provincial and local government, crushed the massive Pugachev Revolt of peasants and Cossacks, and rewarded her loyal nobility with rights and privileges. Catherine continued the Petrine policies of westernization and cultural and economic development. Exploiting a freer intellectual atmosphere, liberal noblemen like Nikolai Novikov and Alexander Radishchev criticized serfdom and autocracy, only to be imprisoned when the aging empress grew fearful that the ideas of the French Revolution would prove contagious.

The last period of an old regime resting on serfdom and autocracy (1796–1855) was an age of bureaucratic monarchy as rulers and their ministers gradually reasserted control over the nobility. The autocratic Paul I (ruled 1796–1801), Catherine's disgruntled son, ended the rule of women with his primogeniture, decreed in 1797. He stressed Prussian-style discipline even over the nobility and Guards. Predictably, he was murdered by a palace conspiracy, which placed in power his enigmatic son, Alexander I (ruled 1801–1825). Aided by the able Mikhail Speranskii, Alexander partially reformed the central administration, replacing Petrine administrative colleges with European-style ministries, and restricted serfdom, avoiding fundamental political and social change for fear it might undermine his autocratic powers. Thus he refused to implement Speranskii's reform plan of 1809, which proposed a monarchy based on law with strict separation of functions and several levels of elected assemblies culminating in

a national assembly (State Duma). Drawn into abortive coalition wars against Napoleon (1805–1807), Alexander felt compelled to conclude an unpopular alliance with the French emperor and join his Continental System directed against Britain. In 1812, Napoleon launched a massive invasion of Russia (paralleled by Hitler's invasion in 1941) and reached Moscow, only to be defeated by Russian national resistance, a severe climate, and bad roads. Russia then joined the other European great powers to destroy the Napoleonic empire. The Congress of Vienna (1814–1815), ending the Napoleonic wars, confirmed Russia's predominance in eastern Europe and its annexation of most of Poland, Finland, and Bessarabia, adding millions more non-Russians to its empire. For the next 40 years a conservative and satiated Russian Empire aligned itself with equally conservative and legitimist Prussian and Austrian monarchies. All three feared liberal ideas emanating from western Europe, notably Britain and France, and national feeling of subject peoples.

Alexander I's reign ended in political reaction, public disillusionment, and revolt by liberal noblemen. Forming secret societies that spread across Europe after 1815, the so-called Decembrists mostly favored constitutional monarchy, liberal reforms, and abolition of serfdom. However, Pavel Pestel, leader of their Southern Society, whom some consider Russia's first professional revolutionary, advocated a Jacobin-type unitary republic and confiscation of much noble land. After Alexander I's sudden death (1825), the Northern Society tried to seize power with the slogan "Constantine and Constitution!" Constantine, Alexander's younger brother, ordinarily would have become tsar, but had secretly renounced his claims in favor of his younger brother Nicholas. Some soldiers in regiments supporting Constantine apparently believed "constitution," which has a feminine ending in Russian, was Constantine's wife! In any case, Nicholas quickly quelled the poorly planned Decembrist Revolt, hanged the ringleaders, and sent many others to Siberia, creating martyrs for the incipient revolutionary movement.

John Massey Stewart

Tsar Nicholas I, 1825–1855, known as the "Iron Tsar" for his repressive policies.

Assuming power was Nicholas I (ruled 1825–1855), dubbed the "Iron Tsar" for his stern military image and conservative, repressive policies. Nicholas viewed Russia as a vast fortress, which under his determined command would withstand the winds of change sweeping eastward from Paris across Europe. Wrote a French visitor, Marquis de Custine: "The Emperor of Russia is a military commander and each one of his days is a day of battle." The official ideology of Nicholas's regime, announced by his Minister of Education, Count Uvarov, in 1833, was autocracy, orthodoxy, and nationality—one emperor, one faith, and one dominant language and people (Russian). To supplement the regular state machinery, Nicholas elaborated a powerful personal chancellery whose

Third Section, or political police, exercised surveillance over foreigners, dissidents, and suspected persons and reported on public moods and opinions. Although Nicholas's system became synonymous with despotism, repression, censorship, rampant bureaucracy, and brutal punishments, it employed some capable, dedicated ministers who sought to improve efficiency and reform abuses. Thus his Second Section under Count Speranskii codified Russian civil and military law; the Fifth Section, led by the able Count P. D. Kiselev, reformed and improved conditions of the state peasantry.

The so-called marvelous decade (1838–1848) began a great debate between Slavophiles and Westernizers, small groups of intellectuals, over Russia's past and future, which has persisted ever since. The Slavophiles were Russia-firsters, mostly conservative nationalists who idealized pre-Petrine Orthodoxy and traditional Muscovite institutions like the Assembly of the Land and the peasant commune as distinctly Russian and superior. The Westernizers, mostly liberal or radical critics like V. G. Belinskii, castigated the Orthodox Church and were ardent individualists. With a strong faith in civil liberties, science, and education, Westernizers believed Russian development should follow western European paths and methods, as under Peter I. The European revolutions of 1848 cut short this promising intellectual evolution as the fearful Nicholas responded to its ideas of liberalism and nationalism with iron-fisted repression and censorship.

Nicholas's despotism rested on the powerful pillars of bureaucracy, church, police, and army. Upon his beloved army Nicholas lavished resources and attention. Suspicious after the Decembrist Revolt of innovative, educated officers, Nicholas relied instead on harsh discipline, seniority, the bayonet, and precise parade-ground drill. The Russian army was Europe's largest (some 860,000 men in peacetime) but also the least literate and the poorest equipped and prepared for battle. After easy victories over Persians, Turks, Poles, and Hungarians, its commanders were overconfident and complacent, believing in Russian omnipotence. When severely tested in the Crimean War (1853–1856), Nicholas's army, the product of a backward agrarian economy based upon serfdom, failed even to defend Russian soil. The Crimean conflict, fueled by deep suspicions in western Europe about Russian intentions and grave miscalculations by both Nicholas and the western powers, pitted an isolated Russia against the declining Ottoman Empire backed by Britain, France, and Piedmont-Sardinia. In the midst of that bloody and futile war, Nicholas I died a broken, discouraged man. After the fall of Sevastopol, his son and successor, Alexander II, wisely accepted the Treaty of Paris (1856), which prescribed the demilitarization of Russia's Black Sea coast and naval bases, restored Bessarabia to Turkish control, and ended Russia's vague protectorate over the Balkan Christians. This marked the demise of the old regime in imperial Russia.

In the realm of culture, Peter the Great's Western-influenced reforms initiated a totally new direction. At first affecting only the noble elite, this cultural change became institutionalized as the Russian Empire mastered Western cultural forms, much as Kievan artisans and scholars had absorbed Byzantine forms earlier. The culture that emerged from the 17th-century Church-state conflict was largely emancipated from Orthodox religious traditions and became secularized. Art, literature, music, and architecture at first imitated Western cultural forms, then gained confidence and originality by drawing on native Russian traditions.

Symbolic of Russia's cultural reorientation was the city of Sankt Peterburg (St. Petersburg), founded by Peter the Great as his new capital on the Gulf of Finland with easy access to the West. Peter's famous "window on Europe," St. Petersburg was the antithesis of traditionalist, clerical, and obscurantist Moscow. Carefully planned and contemporary, St. Petersburg epitomized Russia's cultural integration into Europe. Its broad avenues and thoroughfares, its neoclassical and rococo buildings, glittering palaces, bustling commercial activity, and foreign languages gave it a cosmopolitan atmosphere in sharp contrast with other Russian towns. St. Petersburg welcomed foreigners of all kinds, who helped reshape Russian culture. During the early imperial period, the magnificent imperial court at St. Petersburg came to resemble closely other European royal courts, and in some ways it outshone its Western rivals.

This "Westernization" process symbolized by St. Petersburg drove a deep cultural wedge between upper and lower classes, divided now by profound political and socioeconomic differences. The "Westernized" noble elite, speaking mostly French and German, created a vast cultural gulf between itself and lower classes speaking only Russian; this gulf deepened thereafter, contributing to a growing impasse between state and society.

From the late 18th century, Western values and education, theories of the Enlightenment and the French Revolution, and gradual socioeconomic change all contributed to a growing disillusionment with autocracy and serfdom, the pillars of the Russian old regime. Well-educated Westernized Russian aristocrats, beginning with Nikolai Novikov and Alexander Radishchev, began to expose the basic injustices of a system that granted almost unlimited power to the few and virtually enslaved the many.

Meanwhile Russian culture in the early 19th century was emancipating itself from slavish dependence on Western models. In literature the age was dominated by giants such as Alexander Pushkin, Mikhail Lermontov, and Nicholas Gogol. In music the chief innovators were Mikhail Glinka and Alexander Dargomyzhskii, who established bases for a Russian national school with their operas. In painting Karl Briullov and Alexander Ivanov were original artists who placed their personal stamps on a developing Russian school of art. By the mid-19th century Russian culture was bursting forth in a flurry of creative activity that propelled it into the forefront of European culture.

Suggested Additional Reading

GEOGRAPHY AND GEOPOLITICS

ADAMS, ARTHUR, et al. *An Atlas of Russian and East European History* (New York, 1967).

CHEW, ALLEN. *An Atlas of Russian History* (New Haven, CT, 1970).

DEWDNEY, JOHN C. *A Geography of the Soviet Union*, 2d ed. (New York, 1971).

GILBERT, MARTIN. *Russian History Atlas*, 2d ed. (New York, 1993).

LYDOLPH, PAUL E. *Geography of the USSR*, 3d ed. (New York, 1977).

PARKER, W. H. *An Historical Geography of Russia* (London, 1968).

SUMNER, B. H. "The Frontier," in *A Short History of Russia* (New York, 1949).

TREADGOLD, DONALD. "Russian Expansion in the Light of Turner's Study of the American Frontier," *Agricultural History, 26*, pp. 147–152.

WESSON, R. G. *The Russian Dilemma: A Political and Geopolitical View* (New Brunswick, NJ, 1974).

WIECZYNSKI, J. L. *The Russian Frontier: The Impact of the Borderlands upon the Course of Early Russian History* (Charlottesville, VA, 1976).

PEOPLES AND NATIONALITIES

ALLEN, W. E. D. *A History of the Georgian People* (New York, 1971).

ALLWORTH, EDWARD. *The Modern Uzbeks: A Cultural History* (Stanford, CA, 1990).

BARTOLD, V. V. "Slavs," in *Encyclopedia of Islam,* vol. 4 (Leiden, Holland, 1978).

BLUM, DIETER. *Russia, the Land and People of the Soviet Union* (New York, 1980).

CLYMAN, TOBY W., and JUDITH VOWLES, eds. *Russia through Women's Eyes: Autobiographies from Tsarist Russia* (New Haven, CT, 1996).

DVORNIK, FRANCIS. *The Slavs in European History and Civilization* (New Brunswick, NJ, 1962).

GOLDHAGEN, ERICH. *Ethnic Minorities in the Soviet Union* (New York, 1968).

GREENBERG, L. S. *The Jews in Russia*, 2 vols. (New Haven, CT, 1944, 1951).

GROUSSET, R. *The Empire of the Steppes: A History of Central Asia*, trans. N. Walford (New Brunswick, NJ, 1970).

HOOSON, DAVID. *The Soviet Union: People and Regions* (London, 1966).

HORAK, S., ed. *Guide to the Study of the Soviet Nationalities* (Littleton, CO, 1982).

HOSKING, GEOFFREY. *Russia: People and Empire 1552–1917* (Cambridge, MA: 1997).

HRUSHEVSKYI, M. *A History of the Ukraine* (New Haven, CT, 1941).

KOLARZ, WALTER. *The People of the Soviet Far East* (Camden, CT, 1969).

LAND, DAVID M. *The Armenians: A People in Exile.* (Winchester, MA, 1989).

LANG, D. M. *A Modern History of Georgia* (London, 1962).

MALIA, MARTIN. *Russia under Western Eyes: From the Bronze Horseman to the Lenin Mausoleum* (Cambridge, MA: 2000).

OLCOTT, MARTHA. *The Kazakhs* (Stanford, CA, 1987).

PIERCE, R. A. *Russian Central Asia, 1867–1917: A Study in Colonial Rule* (Berkeley, CA, 1960).

PUSHKAREVA, NATALIA. Trans. and ed. Eve Levin. *Women in Russian History: From the Tenth to the Twentieth Century* (Armonk, NY, 1997).

RAUN, TOIVO. *Estonia and the Estonians* (Stanford, CA, 1987).

SENN, A. R. *The Emergence of Modern Lithuania* (New York, 1959).

SUNY, ROBERT G. *The Making of the Georgian Nation* (Stanford, CA, 1988).

VAKAR, N. *Belorussia: The Making of a Nation* (Cambridge, MA, 1956).

WHEELER, G. *The Modern History of Soviet Central Asia* (London, 1964).

HISTORY TO 1855

ANISIMOV, EVGENII. *The Reforms of Peter the Great* (Armonk, NY, 1993).

BILLINGTON, JAMES. *The Icon and the Axe: Interpretive History of Russian Culture* (New York, 1970).

BLACK, C. E. *Understanding Soviet Politics: The Perspective of Russian History* (Boulder, CO, 1986).

BLUM, JEROME. *Lord and Peasant in Russia* (Princeton, NJ, 1961).

CRUMMEY, ROBERT O. *The Formation of Muscovy, 1304–1613* (London and New York, 1987).

CUSTINE, A. L. L. *Journey for Our Times* (New York, 1951).

EGAN, DAVID, and M. EGAN. *Russian Autocrats from Ivan the Great to the Fall of the Romanov Dynasty: An Annotated Bibliography of English Language Sources* (Metuchen, NJ, 1987).

FENNELL, J. L. *Ivan the Great of Moscow* (London, 1961).

GREY, IAN. *Ivan the Terrible* (London, 1964).

HELLIE, R. *Enserfment and Military Change in Muscovy* (Chicago, 1971).

KEEP, JOHN H. *Soldiers of the Tsar: Army and Society in Russia, 1462–1874* (Oxford, 1985).

KLUCHEVSKII, V. O. *Peter the Great* (New York, 1961).

LEDONNE, JOHN. *Ruling Russia: Politics and Administration in the Age of Absolutism* (Princeton, NJ, 1985).

LIKHACHEV, D. S. *The Great Heritage* (Moscow, 1982).

LINCOLN, W. B. *Nicholas I* (Bloomington, IN, 1978).

MACKENZIE, D., and M. CURRAN. *A History of Russia, the Soviet Union, and Beyond*, 6th ed. (Belmont, CA, 2002).

MADARIAGA, ISABEL. *Russia in the Age of Catherine the Great* (New Haven, CT, 1981).

MASSIE, ROBERT. *Peter the Great: His Life and World* (New York, 1980).

MILIUKOV, PAVEL N. *Outlines of Russian Culture*, 3 vols. (Philadelphia, 1942).

PASKIEWICZ, H. *The Making of the Russian Nation* (London, 1963).

PIPES, RICHARD. *Russia Under the Old Regime* (London, 1974).

PLATONOV, S. *The Time of Troubles* (Lawrence, KS, 1970).

PRESNIAKOV, A. E. *The Formation of the Great Russian State* (Chicago, 1970).

PUSHKAREV, SERGEI. *The Emergence of Modern Russia, 1801–1917* (New York, 1963).

RAEFF, MARC. *The Decembrist Movement* (Englewood Cliffs, NJ, 1966)

——. *Imperial Russia 1682–1825. The Coming of Age of Modern Russia* (New York, 1971).

RIASANOVSKY, NICHOLAS V. *A History of Russia*, 5th ed. (New York, 1994).

——. *A Parting of the Ways: Government and the Educated Public in Russia, 1801–1855* (Oxford, 1976).

ROBERTS, IAN W. *Nicholas I and the Russian Intervention in Hungary*. (New York, 1991).

ROBINSON, GEROID T. *Rural Russia Under the Old Regime* (New York, 1949).

RYBAKOV, BORIS. *Early Centuries of Russian History* (Moscow, 1965).

SAWYER, P. H. *The Age of Vikings* (London, 1962).

SETON-WATSON, HUGH. *The Russian Empire, 1801–1917* (Oxford, 1967).

SPULER, BERTOLD. *The Mongols in History* (New York, 1971).

SUMNER, B. H. *A Short History of Russia* (New York, 1949).

TREADGOLD, DONALD. *The Great Siberian Migration* (Princeton, NJ, 1957).

VERNADSKY, G., and M. KARPOVICH. *A History of Russia*, 5 vols. (New Haven, CT, 1943–1969). (The most complete survey in English to 1689.)

VOYCE, ARTHUR. *Moscow and the Roots of Russian Culture* (Norman, OK, 1964).

WARE, T. *The Orthodox Church* (Baltimore, 1963).

WITTFOGEL, KARL. *Oriental Despotism* (New Haven, CT, 1957).

WREN, MELVIN. *The Western Impact upon Russia* (Chicago, 1971).

2

Reform and Reaction, 1855–1904

Following defeats in major wars Russia has generally undergone significant reform or revolution. The Crimean defeat revealed that traditional serf Russia could not compete militarily or economically with more advanced western European nations and spurred the far-reaching reforms of Alexander II. The death of the "Iron Tsar" in 1855 marked the end of a conservative old regime based upon serfdom, unlimited autocracy, and repressive censorship. Although his successor, Alexander II, was conservative by nature and training, his new regime undertook major changes in many aspects of Russian life. Of these the emancipation of the serfs was the greatest and most difficult. (*Note:* For more on the reasons for the Emancipation see Problem 1 at the end of this chapter.)

The Great Reforms

Emancipation was accompanied by basic reforms in Russia's economy, army, and society. Alexander II's Great Reforms, although incomplete, espe-cially in the political sphere (see Figure 2.1), began to transform Russia into a more modern country. In many respects the Great Reforms are compara-ble with the manifold changes instituted by Mikhail S. Gorbachev in the USSR after 1985. (See Chapter 18.)

Serfdom, established legally in 1649, had bound some 85 percent of Russia's population to the land as private serfs or state peasants, con-demning them to eke out a precarious and depen-dent existence focused on agriculture. The realization was growing among intellectuals and enlightened bureaucrats and landowners that serfdom had outlived all usefulness. In 1860, some 60 percent of private serfs were mortgaged to state banks by an ever more indebted nobility. Alexan-der II, otherwise often indecisive and uncertain, played a vital role in preparing and carrying through the Emancipation, which represented the most far-reaching reform undertaken by any Euro-pean government in the 19th century. Soon he realized that Russia could not remain a great European power or generate needed military and economic strength unless serfs and state peasants were liberated. Dmitrii A. Miliutin, subsequently

Library of Congress

Tsar Alexander II, ruled 1855–1881, known for "the Great Reforms," including emancipation of Russia's serfs.

his Minister of War, viewed serfdom as the chief obstacle to a modern army: "Serfdom does not allow us either to reduce the term of service or increase the number of unlimited leaves so as to diminish the present number of troops." Increasing numbers of bureaucrats tended to place interests of state and reform ahead of their personal concerns as landowners. Saddled with heavy debts and dependent upon state aid, most serf owners could not effectively resist governmental action. Roughly 70 years of criticism and condemnation of serfdom by the Russian intelligentsia had helped prepare the way for its abolition. Finally, there had been rising peasant discontent and rural violence during the first half of the century, which Soviet scholars stress as the chief cause of emancipation. However, there is inadequate evidence to prove that Alexander II freed the serfs mainly out of fear of peasant revolution.

To guard his autocratic powers, Alexander had the Emancipation prepared secretly and bureaucratically, but pushed the nobility and his officials along and warned he would not tolerate delay. The Emancipation Act of 1861 granted private serfs personal freedom, but the servile economy persisted for many years because the process of providing them with land proved lengthy and complex. The state advanced about three-fourths of the redemption cost directly to the landowners in interest-bearing bonds, deducting the landowners' debts. The peasants had to pay the remaining fourth as well as repaying the state over 49 years. This compromise settlement, still incomplete in 1905, satisfied neither party completely and left the Russian peasantry, hampered by ignorance and low yields per acre, with inadequate land. In the rich Black Soil region of the south, peasants lost about one quarter of the land they had worked before the Emancipation. Peasant land allotments varied in size by region—Black Soil, non-Black Soil, and steppe. Maximum and minimum norms were set for each province, but the landowner was, in any case, guaranteed at least one-third of his estate. Extensive police powers hitherto wielded by the landowner were mostly transferred to the peasant community (*mir*), which was thus retained for fiscal and administrative reasons and to maintain rural order and stability. Initially elated at their emancipation, many former serfs soon wondered whether their economic status had really been improved because they now had to pay for services they had formerly received from their lords. Imperial and state peasants were freed in 1863 and 1866, respectively, receiving lands they had worked before the Emancipation in return for higher rents. Strip farming with traditional techniques and primitive plows and periodic redistribution of the land persisted in Russia proper, while between 1860 and 1914 the rural population roughly doubled. Despite universal conscription, some schooling, and the abolition of the poll tax (1886), peasants tended to remain at the bottom of the Russian social pyramid until 1917.

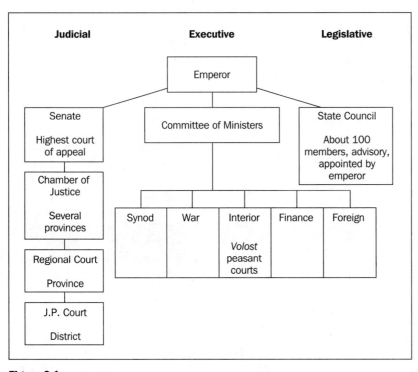

Figure 2.1
Russian Imperial Government (1855–1905)

Other highly significant changes accompanied the Emancipation. Alexander II's government promptly relaxed censorship and travel restrictions, which promoted freer contacts with Europe and spurred a great growth in the towns of newspapers and periodicals expressing a variety of viewpoints. However, a capricious and limiting censorship of the press persisted. Universities were freed from most of the severe restrictions imposed under Nicholas I and were opened, along with secondary schools, to all social groups. The important *zemstvo* reform, necessitated by the gentry's loss of direct control over the peasantry, introduced limited provincial and district self-government in European Russian provinces that possessed an organized nobility. Zemstvo assemblies were to be elected by landowners, peasants, and townspeople according to the land and real property they held, allowing the nobility to dominate them, especially at the provincial level. With

money raised from property taxes, but with severely limited budgets, *zemstva* were to establish and operate primary schools, build roads and bridges, erect prisons, and found clinics. However, zemstva were denied permission to operate in *volosti* (townships) or above the provincial level. Decisions of their executive boards could be vetoed by the regular provincial bureaucracy, and accounts of their proceedings could be censored. Serving initially as schools of self-government, the zemstva, despite many shortcomings, gradually undermined the autocratic principle and agitated for liberal reform and national representation. Similarly, the municipal law of 1870 established a measure of urban self-rule and greatly improved city services.

A women's movement for emancipation and access to education arose in Russia in the 1860s, simultaneously with those in western Europe. In both areas, the rise of feminism was stimulated by the heritage of the Enlightenment, the French Revolution, and Utopian Socialism. As emancipation of the serfs neared, the liberalized Russian press of the late 1850s voiced ideas of liberating women from their traditional bondage to men. The legal basis for women's subservience in 19th-century Russia was a declaration in the Code of Russian Laws (1836): "The woman must obey her husband, reside with him in love, respect, and unlimited obedience, and offer him every pleasantness and affection as the ruler of the household."[1] The few women educated in Russia before 1860 were prepared for motherhood and domesticity in a few secondary schools open mostly to daughters of the gentry. Even before the Emancipation gentry women began to petition and agitate for access to higher education. In 1859, women were admitted to university lectures, only to be barred once again from attending lectures in 1861. Access to education and employment were to be the initial focuses of the Russian feminist movement, led by gentry women.

The court system, harsh and inequitable under Nicholas I, was greatly altered by the law of November 1864, which set up independent regular courts of a western European type, initially free from administrative controls, with irremovable, trained judges and jury trials for major cases. Justice of the peace courts, established in district centers for lesser cases, proved efficient, popular, and fair. However, cases concerning peasants alone were still tried by separate peasant courts under police supervision; ecclesiastical courts handled all divorces and cases affecting the clergy. Later, political cases as well were removed from the purview of the new regular courts.

Finally, able and liberal War Minister Dmitrii A. Miliutin (1861–1881) transformed the Russian army over powerful aristocratic opposition. First, Miliutin reduced the term of service from 25 to 15 years and abolished most corporal punishments. Regional military districts largely replaced Nicholas's overcentralized and overstaffed army

administration. Military gymnasia with a broad curriculum and open to all classes superseded exclusive cadet corps; primary schools were set up in the army to make many recruits literate. The principles of the judicial reform were extended to army courts. Finally, the law of 1874 introduced universal military training, with a maximum term of six years, decreasing according to educational attainment. "The defense of the fatherland," declared the law, "forms the sacred duty of *every* Russian [male] citizen." Universal service allowed Russia to establish trained reserves, reduced social barriers, and raised army morale.

Despite limitations and bureaucratic opposition, the Great Reforms changed Russia fundamentally. The all-class principle, at the heart of most of them, reduced noble privilege and increased rights of other groups. The masses could now be educated and gradually integrated into society. Concepts of equality before the law, universal military service, local self-government, and greater press freedom weakened autocracy. The reforms, noted Soviet historians, marked Russia's transition from feudalism to capitalism, though there were many feudal survivals and persisting inequalities. However, legally, Alexander II remained an autocrat and blocked any move toward a constitution or national parliament. He controlled the executive branch, where no cabinet was permitted to develop, by appointing and dismissing all ministers. An appointed State Council of some 100 officials debated prospective laws, but its decisions lacked binding force because the emperor and his ministers initiated all legislation. Failure to achieve real political change at the top would prove fateful for tsarism.

Trends toward liberal change were strongest from 1856 to 1861, when most of the Great Reforms were conceived. A subsequent conservative countertrend was reinforced by D. V. Karakozov's attempt on the life of Alexander II in 1866. Count P. A. Shuvalov, chief of gendarmes and former large serf owner, dominated Alexander II for the next seven years and helped block completion of the reforms.

[1] Richard Stites, *The Women's Liberation Movement in Russia* (Princeton, NJ, 1978), pp. 6–7.

Foreign Affairs, 1815–1881

Shifting Policies Toward Europe

Imperial Russia 1815–1914 remained mostly defensive toward other European powers, largely abandoning the aggressive expansionism of previous centuries that had brought her deep into central Europe; 19th-century Russian leaders sought to preserve and defend the generous European boundaries secured in 1815 at the Congress of Vienna. After absorbing Finland, most of Poland, and Bessarabia during the Napoleonic era, Russia, without further legitimate or pressing territorial claims in Europe, became there essentially a satiated power. Backward economically and socially relative to western Europe, Russia aimed to consolidate its gains and, except for the Crimean debacle, avoided armed conflicts with other great powers. Until 1890, Russia often cooperated with Austria, Prussia, and later Germany, states with similar political and social systems. Russia was linked with Europe by dynastic marriages, common diplomatic use of French, and manifold ties with European aristocracies. During its final century, Imperial Russia, unlike Soviet Russia later, sought generally to uphold the European order created by the Vienna settlement, which benefited and protected her. Russia sought to guard its preeminence in eastern Europe by perpetuating the partitions of Poland (in which the German powers had shared) and to uphold conservative, legitimate monarchy throughout Europe against the challenges of nationalism, liberalism, and socialism. Russia sought to achieve limited aims by cautious diplomacy, adjustment, and compromise.

From the Congress of Vienna until the Crimean War, Russia espoused a defensive conservatism. Remaining the dominant European land power, it cooperated with equally conservative Austrian and Prussian monarchies. Threats to the Vienna settlement and European peace were resolved by periodic meetings of great power leaders that produced compromise solutions. Alexander and Nicholas I departed occasionally from support of legitimate monarchy to provide sporadic backing to Serbian and Greek national movements in the Balkans.

The Crimean defeat altered Russian policies toward Europe. No self-respecting power could acquiesce indefinitely in the defenseless Black Sea coast and absence of naval bases imposed by the Paris Treaty. Nor could the Romanov dynasty feel secure until its prestige and European role, shaken in the Crimea, had been reaffirmed. For centuries Russian foreign policy had been essentially that of the tsar, who could determine it at will—making war or peace, signing treaties, and hiring and firing his ministers without having to accept advice from anyone. However, with less grasp of foreign affairs and less self-confidence than his immediate predecessors, Alexander II left everyday policy to subordinates. Frequently indecisive and susceptible to various influences, he displayed strong loyalty toward his uncle, King William I of Prussia. Alexander promptly selected A. M. Gorchakov, a native Russian, as foreign minister. Advocating revival of Russia's leading diplomatic role in Europe, Gorchakov with his fluent French and close ties with European aristocrats, favored negotiation and peace, essential policies for an impoverished Russia absorbed with domestic reform.

After the Crimean War, Russia cooperated with France, especially in Italy and the Balkans, until the Polish Revolt of 1863 induced her to seek Prussia's support instead. Russia's benevolent neutrality in 1866 and 1870 aided the outstanding Prussian statesman, Otto von Bismarck, to unify Germany under Prussian leadership. During the Franco-Prussian War (1870–1871), Gorchakov, with German support, scored his greatest personal triumph: Denouncing the Black Sea clauses of the Paris Treaty, he regained for Russia the right to fortify its coastline. For this Russia paid an exorbitant price: the formation on its western frontier of a powerful Germany which would invade Russia during two world wars. In 1873, on Bismarck's initiative, the rulers of Russia, Germany, and

Austria-Hungary formed the Three Emperors' League, an entente to preserve the status quo in eastern Europe.

Balkan Policies

In the Balkans Gorchakov sought to rebuild Russia's influence and safeguard its traditional interests. These were to protect and lead its Christian, especially Orthodox, peoples; to ensure free passage through the Turkish Straits for Russian commerce, and eventually to dominate those waterways; and to establish a Balkan client state or states. However, a group of bellicose Pan-Slavs and Russia-firsters exerted increasing influence on Russia's Balkan policies. Pan-Slavism, a movement to unite the Slav peoples resembling efforts to unify Italians and Germans, had developed initially among Austrian Slavs as a cultural movement to resist Germanization. Russian Pan-Slavism of the 1860 and 1870s, the offspring of Slavophilism and militant nationalism, advocated a forceful national imperialism. Regarding Russia as a superior "big brother" for smaller, weaker Slav peoples, some Russian noblemen, journalists, and army officers expounded doctrines laced with social Darwinism and racism. N. Ia. Danilevskii's *Russia and Europe* (1872), dubbed "the Bible of Pan-Slavism," predicted victory for Russia and its Slav allies in an "inevitable conflict" with the German world and formation of an all-Slav federation centering in Constantinople. R. A. Fadeev, a retired major general, proclaimed that Russia must "extend her preeminence to the Adriatic," leading Orthodox Slavs in a war against Germans until "the Russian reigning house covers the liberated soil of eastern Europe with its branches under the supremacy of the tsar of Russia."[2] In western Europe, Fadeev's provocative pamphlet raised the spectre of Russian imperial rule over eastern European satellite states. Such nationalistic views were shared widely in the Foreign Ministry's Asiatic Department whose talented director, N. P. Ignatiev, became Russian ambassador to Constantinople (1864–1877). Favoring a unilateral Russian solution of the "Eastern Question" involving the future of the Ottoman Empire, Turkish Straits, and Balkan Christians, Ignatiev advocated forceful Russian policy in the Balkans and Near East, opposing Gorchakov's pacific, pro-European orientation.

These divergent policies—one pro-European, the other unilateralist—were tested in the Balkan Crisis (1875–1878). In July 1875 Orthodox Serbs in Turkish-ruled Bosnia and Herzegovina revolted and received support, at first unofficially, from Serbia, Montenegro, and Russian Slav Committees (See Map 2.1.) Officially, Russia proclaimed nonintervention, but Russian Pan-Slavs encouraged Balkan Slavs to aid the insurgents and organized financial and medical aid for them. Early in 1876, the Moscow Slav Committee, sending retired General M. G. Cherniaev to Serbia, recruited several thousand Russian volunteers to serve under his command in the ensuing Serbo-Turkish War. When the Turks defeated Cherniaev's motley Serbo-Russian army, official Russia was soon drawn into a Russo-Turkish War (1877–1878), which ended in a Russian victory. Upon defeated Turkey, Count Ignatiev imposed the Treaty of San Stefano (March 1878) that envisioned a Big Bulgaria under Russian military occupation. When Great Britain and Austria-Hungary threatened war, Alexander II, to prevent another disastrous conflict with a European coalition, submitted that treaty to the Congress of Berlin (June–July 1878). Directed by Germany's Bismarck as "honest broker," the Berlin Treaty reduced Russian gains and alienated the frustrated Pan-Slavs. Austria-Hungary occupied Bosnia and Herzegovina and dominated the western Balkans; Russian influence was confined to a shrunken, divided, and autonomous Bulgaria.

---

[2] R. A. Fadeev, *Opinion on the Eastern Question* (London, 1876).

Map 2.1 Russia and the Balkans, 1876–1885

Asia and America

Russia's policies in Asia were more dynamic and successful as it acted as an imperialist European power toward more backward, weaker neighbors. (See Map 2.2.) By 1863, guerrilla resistance by Muslim mountaineers in the Caucasus had been broken and the region pacified. The Caucasus provided Russia with secure natural boundaries in the south and bases for expansion into Central Asia. Most of that vast area, lying east of the Caspian Sea and south of Siberia, was annexed to the Russian Empire by 1895. Between 1730 and 1850, the broad Kazakh steppe (now Kazakhstan) was occupied. Then for reasons resembling those of European overseas neoimperialism, Russia moved southward deep into the Muslim oasis region. The War Ministry favored filling a major power vacuum; frontier generals and governors, seeking promotion and glory, spurred the process.

The imperial family, tempted by easy victories, sanctioned most conquests and rewarded those responsible; the Foreign Ministry sought to justify military advances as absolutely essential. Beginning in 1864, small Russian forces seized northern Turkestan from weak, feuding Muslim khanates, culminating in the assault on Tashkent by General Cherniaev (June 1865). In 1867, Alexander II appointed General K. P. Kaufman as the first governor-general of Turkestan; he built an administration, won native respect, and began developing its silk and cotton resources. Kaufman greatly expanded Russian Turkestan, a process completed in 1895, giving Russia natural frontiers in the Pamir Mountains with Afghanistan and India. By 1905, railroad lines had linked this vast Central Asian colony firmly with the Russian motherland.

Simultaneously, Russia was liquidating its Alaskan holdings and establishing a firmer

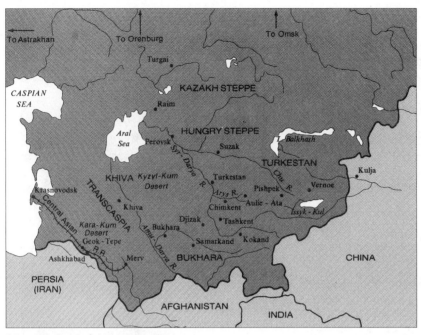

Map 2.2 Central Asia, 1850–1914

foothold on the shores of the Pacific. In Alaska, the fur trade was dwindling, the inefficient Russian-America Company continued to pile up debts, and the region had become indefensible. Thus the Russian government in 1867 sold Alaska to a reluctant United States for a paltry $7.2 million. Meanwhile in the Far East, exploiting the weakness and disintegration of Manchu China in the face of Western imperialism, Governor-General M. N. Muraviev (Amurskii) of eastern Siberia seized the Amur and Ussuri river valleys and founded the city of Vladivostok ("Ruler of the East") in July 1860. That December, Count Ignatiev negotiated the Treaty of Peking with helpless China, superseding the Treaty of Nerchinsk (1689), which had held left the Amur region to China, and confirming Russia's possession of what became the Maritime Province. A century later Communist China would claim that these territories had been seized illegally at gunpoint.

Domestic Affairs, 1881–1904
Counterreform
Under the Last Two Tsars

Alexander II's assassination in March 1881 by terrorists of the People's Will inaugurated two decades of reaction and political stagnation. To combat terrorism, the government in February 1880 set up a Supreme Executive Commission under Count M. T. Loris-Melikov, a former war hero, with full police powers. That August, with terrorism apparently checked, Loris-Melikov urged creation of a legislative commission with representatives appointed by zemstva and by cities to advise the State Council on legislation. Dubbed the Loris-Melikov constitution, this innocuous proposal was approved by Alexander II the day of his assassination. However, the unimaginative new ruler, Alexander III (1881–1894), at the demand of his tutor and chief adviser, Constantine Pobedonostsev, shelved Loris-Melikov's scheme; liberal ministers resigned. Alexander III, rabidly religious and nationalistic, relied chiefly upon Pobedonostsev, who as procurator of the Holy Synod and tutor to his son, largely determined the last two tsars' outlooks and policies.

Pobedonostsev elaborated a complete theory of autocracy, gentry rule, and status quo conservatism derived from Uvarov's triad of autocracy, orthodoxy, and nationality. As the "gray eminence" of moribund tsarism, Pobedonostsev contributed heavily to a "dogma of autocracy," which blocked essential political change and provoked radical opposition. He believed that people by nature were unequal, weak, and vicious. Russians, he argued, as shown by their history, required firm leadership and control. Western institutions, he warned, could not be grafted onto the Russian tree. Favoring concentrating political power in the tsar and central administration, he opposed self-government as divisive and counted on traditional bonds of tsar and people. To him, constitutional government would poison the Russian organism. A distinguished jurist, Pobedonostsev nonetheless rejected the rule of law and civil liberties as restrictions on autocracy. Orthodoxy, he declared, was the only true faith; only one religion was tolerable in an autocratic state. Rigid censorship by the Holy Synod must shield Russians from false Western doctrines; the Orthodox Church would imbue them with correct ideas. Unity was indispensable—one tsar, one faith, one language; national and religious minorities should be converted, assimilated, or expelled by ruthless Russification. Pobedonostsev's program was mainly negative, designed to preserve paternalistic noble, bureaucratic, and clerical authority and the status quo. To a remarkable extent, he persuaded his imperial pupils to accept and implement these outdated principles.

Thus Alexander III sought obediently to nullify the Great Reforms of his father with bureaucratic counterreforms. The land captain law of 1889 abolished most justice of the peace courts and transferred their functions to judges appointed by the Interior Ministry. Land captains, usually influential hereditary noblemen, were to supervise peasant affairs and could rescind decisions of

Tsarina Alexandra with Tsar Nicholas II, who ruled 1894–1917 as last tsar of Russia.

village assemblies and peasant courts. In 1890, peasant representation in zemstva assemblies was reduced, and the Interior Ministry's authority over them was tightened. City electorates were drastically reduced. The central authorities sought to curtail local self-government and stifle local initiative. Nonetheless, zemstva and city assemblies continued to achieve much, and tension persisted between the bureaucracy and institutions of local government.

Alexander III's sudden death by stroke in 1894 brought his son Nicholas II to the throne amid hopes of liberal change. Though more intelligent than his father and privately charming, Nicholas was irresolute and wholly ignorant of the forces shaping the modern world. Shortly before his accession, he married Alexandra of Hesse, "Alix," a deeply religious German woman who dominated him and reinforced his own pious conservatism. Sincerely devoted to wife and family, Nicholas became increasingly isolated from Russian reality.

He never visited factories and blamed social unrest on Jews and revolutionaries. His chief interests, reflected in a carefully kept diary, were military reviews, hunting, tennis, and yachting. Early in 1895, he dashed hopes for change at a reception warning liberals to abandon "senseless dreams" about an increased role for zemstva: "I, devoting all my strength to the welfare of the people, will uphold the principle of autocracy as firmly and unflinchingly as my late unforgettable father." Dominated by Pobedonostsev and the reactionary Prince V. P. Meshcherskii, Nicholas believed that constitutions and parliaments were evil. At first he displayed reasonable judgment in state affairs and retained capable men like Sergei Witte in office, but increasingly he listened to irresponsible adventurers and reactionaries. Although the first decade of Nicholas II's reign was outwardly calm and uneventful, beneath the surface opposition movements germinated.

Active discrimination against the Russian Empire's numerous national and religious minorities intensified from 1881 to 1905. Favoring Great Russians and the Orthodox church everywhere and fueled by Pobedonostsev's reactionary theories, the regime discriminated severely against non-Russians. Fostered by an intolerant central bureaucracy and police, Russification was supported by the Orthodox clergy and military. Among those who suffered severely were Baltic Germans, Finns, and Armenians, who had displayed unswerving loyalty toward the imperial regime. In Finland, which formerly had enjoyed broad autonomy as a grand duchy, the independent postal service was abolished in 1890, and Russian was introduced forcibly into certain Finnish institutions. Under a narrow-minded governor-general, A. I. Bobrikov (1898–1904), the separate Finnish army was abolished, and sessions of the Finnish Senate had to be conducted in Russian. In 1903, the Finnish Constitution was suspended. The governor-general's assassination by a Finn in 1904 produced strong animosity between Finland and Russia. In Russian Poland, all school subjects except Polish had to be taught in Russian. Alexander III and Nicholas II, both anti-Semitic and tutored by Pobedonostsev, enacted harsh laws against Jews. Pogroms— unofficial mob violence against Jews and their shops—intensified and were often condoned by the police. "Temporary Rules" of 1882, enforced until 1905, forbade Jews to live outside towns or large villages and forced them into business and certain professions. Strict Jewish quotas were established for secondary schools and universities. Jewish responses to such persecution were to emigrate, especially to the United States, or enter the revolutionary movement. Bigoted decrees undermined the loyalty of minorities, especially in the western borderlands, and helped stimulate revolutions in 1905 and 1917.

Economic and Social Development

The Crimean defeat began the development of a capitalist economy in Russia. Soviet historians, regarding 1861 to 1917 as a capitalist phase, asserted that Russia was transformed swiftly into a capitalist country. Most Western scholars regard 1861–1890 as a period of slow growth preparatory to more rapid development after 1890. First, numerous obstacles blocking industrialization had to be overcome: shortage of investment capital, an inadequate transportation system, lack of a skilled labor force, and a weak internal market. The state's role would prove crucial in removing the first two barriers. Sobered by the Crimean defeat, to which the lack of railroads south of Moscow had contributed, Alexander II's government promptly recognized the military value of railroads and later their economic benefits. Finance Minister Mikhail Reutern wrote Alexander: "Without railways and mechanical industries Russia cannot be considered secure in her boundaries. Her influence in Europe will fall to a level inconsistent with her international power and her historic significance."[3] Because the impoverished treasury could not then finance railroad construction, foreign loans were sought and private companies encouraged. After

---

[3] T. von Laue, *Sergei Witte and the Industrialization of Russia* (New York, 1963), p. 9.

1865, the government provided subsidies and guarantees for construction of lines the state deemed essential. An orgy of construction and speculation ensued, but many small concerns went bankrupt in the depression of 1873–1876, and others became heavily indebted to the state. In the 1880s, the government constructed major lines itself, bought up many private railways, and created an expanding state-owned system. By 1880, major economic regions had been interconnected and linked with major ports as the railway network grew from only 600 miles in 1857 to 11,730 in 1876 and more than 22,000 miles in 1890.

The Finance Ministry became the key agency promoting Russian economic development. Under Reutern (1861–1878), it faced complex and inter-related problems of stabilizing the currency, bal-ancing the budget, achieving an active trade balance, and attracting foreign investment. One step forward was to create a new State Bank with branches throughout Russia. Another was to establish (1862) a unified state budget, enabling the Finance Ministry to coordinate economic activities and develop some state planning. An extraordinary budget, financed by foreign loans, was set up to pay for industrial equipment, arms, and railway construction. Lowered tariffs encour-aged an influx of foreign products and capital, and sharply increased Russian grain exports paid for foreign loans. However, neither Reutern nor his immediate successors could find the formula to overcome Russia's persisting poverty, and their progress was slowed by heavy expenditures on the Russo-Turkish War.

Until 1890, industrial growth proceeded at a modest pace. At first, the emancipation settlement did little to assist it, contributing instead to an industrial slump in the early 1860s, especially in Ural metallurgy, which had employed mostly serf labor. Meanwhile, the mir (peasant commune) blocked permanent migration of peasant labor to the cities. However, relaxation of restrictions on importing foreign capital and goods and judicial and administrative reforms of the 1860s created a better climate for business activity. The govern-ment, gradually losing its fear of industrializa-tion, began to consider it necessary in order to strengthen Russia's role in world affairs. Among domestic manufacturers, textiles alone had an assured and expanding home market as per capita consumption of cotton goods roughly doubled between 1860 and 1880. Sugar refining expanded markedly. During the 1880s, the Donets Basin became an important iron and steel producing region with factories owned mostly by foreign capitalists. Large factories, like that built at Iuzovka by John Hughes, an English capitalist, were more modern and productive than Ural enterprises. Private capitalism flourished as joint-stock companies were formed with government encouragement.

These achievements during the preparatory era brought significant financial gains and fostered the industrial boom of the 1890s, both attributable largely to Finance Minister Sergei Iu. Witte (1893–1903). Self-confident and dynamic, Witte had forged a brilliant career in private business before entering state service as a railway expert. He soon reformed the Finance Ministry into an efficient general staff for economic development. In his first budget report, Witte affirmed govern-ment responsibility for the whole economy and warned: "International competition does not wait." Unless Russian industry developed swiftly, foreign concerns would predominate, and Russia would become an economic colony of the West: "Our economic backwardness may lead to politi-cal and cultural backwardness as well." His work, therefore, was filled with a sense of urgency: Rus-sia's industrialization was viewed as a race against time. The "Witte System" called for stimulating private enterprise and exploiting domestic resources through a vast state-sponsored program of railway construction, which would trigger expansion of heavy industry, notably metallurgy and fuels. Their development would spark light industry, and eventually agriculture would prosper as growing industrial cities demanded more food-stuffs. General prosperity would raise tax yields and recompense the government for heavy initial capital outlays.

Witte's program, concentrating on heavy industry and substituting the role of the state for inadequate private capital, foreshadowed Stalin's more ruthless Five Year Plans. (See Chapter 11.) An experiment in state capitalism, it might enable a backward country to overtake the industrial leaders. To fuel Russia's first industrial boom, Witte channeled about two-thirds of government revenues into economic development. His most ambitious project was building the Trans-Siberian Railroad. Besides constructing this vital transcontinental line, he promoted peasant colonization of Siberia and envisioned the railroad as a means to penetrate and dominate Asian markets. Russia's European railroads were doubletracked and lines built to more seaports. From 1898 through 1900, almost 2,000 miles of railroads were constructed annually, fueling a boom in the Donets Basin's iron and steel industry. The Witte upsurge produced an average industrial growth rate for the 1890s of some 8 percent annually, the highest of any major European country. During that decade, pig iron output trebled, oil production rose two and one-half times, and coal output doubled.

Witte financed his program chiefly with a state liquor monopoly and other indirect taxes, which fell largely on peasants and townspeople. The high tariff of 1891 also brought large sums into the treasury. For railway construction he relied mainly on foreign loans. Witte was favored by abundant foreign private funds seeking investment and the Franco-Russian Alliance of 1893, which induced the French government to foster private investment in Russia. Witte had to borrow heavily abroad to balance the budget overall, but his prompt payment of dividends in gold maintained a high Russian credit rating. To preserve a favorable trade balance, he pushed grain exports and curtailed imports. In 1897, after stabilizing the paper ruble and building state gold reserves, he finally put Russia on the gold standard, enhancing her international prestige and encouraging further foreign investment. However, Witte's vast authority and advocacy of further reforms such as abolition of the mir aroused opposition from conservatives, notably Pobedonostsev, who accused

him of causing growing foreign economic influence and supposed agricultural decline. They and Nicholas II, opposing Witte's efforts to adapt Russian autocracy to 20th-century needs, blamed him for the economic slump of 1900–1903. Nonetheless, his system laid a sound basis for subsequent Russian industrial development and proved that rapid economic growth was possible in a backward country by state mobilization of its resources.

Under the impact of the Great Reforms and industrialization, Russia's social structure underwent profound change after 1860. Officialdom continued for census purposes to use the old legal categories of the estate (*soslovie*) system, but new elements emerged that rejected the old patterns: a professional middle class of lawyers, doctors, and journalists; a better-off peasant element; and an industrial working class. Industrialization, urbanization, and reform legislation promoted social mobility. The new courts largely disregarded estate, title, and wealth while universal military service, abolition of the poll tax (1886), schools, and participation in zemstva lessened peasant isolation. Increasing sales of noble lands to merchants and peasants reduced the nobility's economic power and social prestige. However, after 1881, the rise of new social groupings was hampered by a conservative regime anxious to preserve the traditional order and by the failure of new groups to form economic organizations to promote their interests.

Among the peasantry, still the overwhelming bulk of the Russian population, differentiation was proceeding, spurred by the developing money economy, causing much controversy. Between 1877 and 1905, the average land allotment per peasant household in European Russia declined by about one-third. Whereas Populists (see Chapter 3) affirmed that the mir remained unshaken and that Russian peasants were still fundamentally equal in land and wealth, V. I. Ulianov (Lenin) asserted in his *Development of Capitalism in Russia* (1899) that about one-sixth had become kulaks ("rural bourgeoisie"), and more than one-tenth "rural proletarians" without arable land or livestock. Communal agriculture, he concluded, was disintegrating and doomed. Western scholars concur that the Emancipation, by leaving some 4 million peasants landless or with dwarf allotments, had fostered differentiation.[4] Nevertheless, the collective traditions of the mir remained predominant because even in 1905 almost three-fourths of peasant allotments in European Russia were subject to periodic repartition. However, kulaks, a small minority of thrifty, hardworking peasants, were acquiring livestock, renting and buying more land, and hiring impoverished peasants to work for them.

Industrial workers, still listed as peasants in the 1897 census, were slow to become genuine proletarians in the Marxist sense. But Soviet accounts claimed that the working class was far larger than tsarist statistics suggested. Workers employed in manufacturing, mining, and transportation in European Russia, according to Lenin, grew from 706,000 (1865) to 2,208,000 (1900–1903). Recent Western studies, on the other hand, portray tsarist Russian industrial workers as still half peasant in 1905. Migrating to new industrial centers nearby, peasants were slow to master industrial skills or become integrated into urban life. As late as 1905, 90 percent of Russian urban workers still belonged to communes, sent money to families or relatives in villages, and returned there periodically themselves. Low industrial wages and miserable living conditions delayed formation of a hereditary proletariat. Some 60 percent of workers, noted the 1897 census, lived alone, many in filthy barracks owned by their employers. Johnson states: "The typical worker had one foot in the village and one in the factory, but showed little inclination to commit himself irrevocably to either alternative."[5] The state acted belatedly to protect industrial workers and regulate factory conditions. The law of 1897 set an 11½ hour maximum for all workers and 10 hours for night work, but many manufac-

turers evaded the law. Before 1905, few Russian workers were unionized, they lacked rights to strike or bargain collectively, and their wages were far lower than those of workers in western Europe.

Russian women also were struggling to escape their traditional inferior status. Developing after 1860 were parallel movements of feminism, nihilism, and political radicalism. Seeking solutions within the bounds of existing tsarist society, liberal feminism aimed at gradual, peaceful reforms to improve women's status, especially in education and employment. Reformist feminists, mostly well-educated gentry women led by Maria Trubnikova, Nadezhda Stasova, and Anna Filosofova, attacked patriarchal social mores; by petitions and through the press, they campaigned for women's education. During the 1860s, some 150 women's secondary schools with some 10,000 students were opened. In the 1870s, feminist victories in higher education, despite opposition from conservatives and the Education Ministry, were aided by a favorable public and by official fears that if denied education in Russia, women would study abroad. In 1872, university courses for women were created in Moscow and soon after at other Russian universities. A Russian medical school for women opened in St. Petersburg in 1872. By 1880, in quality and range of women's university education, Russia was unequaled in Europe (though behind the United States) and had the most practicing women doctors on the continent.

Alexander III's accession in 1881 undermined this promising movement as Pobedonostsev conservatives equated feminism with revolution. Medical facilities and women's university courses (except in St. Petersburg) were closed, and the institutional weakness of Russian feminism was revealed. An impassioned appeal by Maria Tsebrikova to Alexander III denouncing "bureaucratic anarchism" and urging him to eliminate poverty, hunger, and disease in the villages brought her banishment to a remote province. A halting revival began about 1895, but Russian feminism, lacking

---

[4] Lenin emphasized differentiation to discredit the Populists and justify Marxist predictions.

[5] Robert Johnson, *Peasant and Proletarian* (New Brunswick, NJ, 1979), p. 50.

suffrage societies, remained largely apolitical, disorganized, and ineffectual until 1905.

Foreign Affairs, 1881–1904

A rare generation of peace—1878 to 1904—fostered Russia's internal economic development. With Alexander III rarely interfering directly in foreign affairs, policy was directed ably by Foreign Minister N. K. Girs, a prudent professional diplomat, who restrained nationalists and militarists and until 1890 kept Russia firmly aligned with the German powers. Alexander's lone foray into foreign policy making in the Bulgarian crisis (1885–1887) proved a fiasco. After Bulgaria's unification in 1885 without his authorization, Alexander removed its prince as Russian officers assumed control of Bulgaria. Eventually, Bismarck and Girs surmounted the resulting crisis, which threatened to embroil Russia with Austria-Hungary, by negotiating the Reinsurance Treaty of 1887. However, three years later when Emperor William II of Germany refused to renew it and fired Bismarck, Russo-German relations deteriorated rapidly. That fostered rapprochement between France and Russia, despite profound differences in their regimes, policies, and ideologies. This produced the crucial Franco-Russian Alliance of 1893, in which longstanding rivals, facing growing German military power, buried the hatchet. At a stroke this ended Russia's traditional alignment with the German powers. If either France or Russia were attacked by Germany, the other pledged to assist its partner with all its forces. Their defensive alliance opposed the Triple Alliance (1882) of Germany, Austria-Hungary, and Italy, splitting Europe into two formidable power blocs. Meanwhile, after 1887 Russia adopted a pacific, low-profile policy in the Balkans culminating in Austro-Russian agreements (1897, 1903) to preserve the status quo. Only if the moribund Ottoman Empire collapsed would they divide its European lands. Absorbed elsewhere, the major Balkan imperial rivals agreed to keep that region quiet and the Turkish Straits closed to foreign warships.

Anglo-Russian rivalry in the Middle East persisted until the settlement of 1907. Tension between them had almost resulted in war during the Afghan Crisis of 1885, then gradually subsided. Britain and Russia competed for influence in corrupt and prostrate Persia (now Iran), where military and civilian agents steadily extended Russian influence, and a Cossack Brigade (founded in 1879) served as an anti-British spearhead. Whereas London considered Persia an outpost in the defense of British India, Russia viewed it as ripe for the plucking. "The entire northern part of Persia," declared Count Witte, "was intended, as if by nature, to turn in the future . . . into a country under our complete protectorate." In Persia, the British, whose chief interests lay in the south and west, were losing ground to Russia in competition for trade, influence, and railway building.

After acquiring the Amur region and Vladivostok by 1860, Russia emerged as a Pacific power. Until the late 1890s, Russian interests there remained limited. The Treaty of St. Petersburg (1875) with emerging Japan provided Russia with the large offshore island of Sakhalin, but Siberia's settlement lagged, and Russian naval facilities and overland communications remained inadequate. A group of Russian scholars, journalists, and military men known as Vostochniki (Easterners), like the Pan-Slavs for the Balkans, advocated imperial expansion in Asia. Russia, with its essentially non-European culture, they asserted, was destined to develop or incorporate much of Asia and protect Europe against the "yellow peril." Mongolia and Sinkiang longed to join Russia, affirmed the explorer, M. N. Przhevalskii. Prince E. E. Ukhtomskii, a journalist who influenced Nicholas II, believed that once opened by modern communications, Siberia would become Russia's Eldorado. Count Witte translated such vague imperial dreams into a degree of reality by inducing the government, in 1891, to begin constructing the Trans-Siberian Railroad; he envisioned it as the spearhead of Russian economic expansion in the Far East.

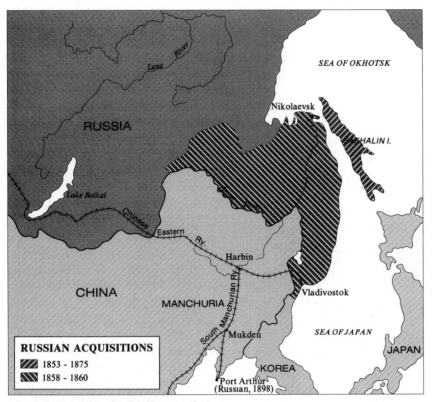

Map 2.3 Russia in the Far East until 1914

By revealing China's helplessness, the Sino-Japanese War of 1894 stimulated European imperial powers, including Russia, to press forward. In 1895, Witte, with Franco-German diplomatic support, compelled a reluctant Japan to return the Liaotung Peninsula with its warm-water ports to China. In 1896, the Li-Lobanov Agreement authorized a Russian-controlled corporation to build and operate a Chinese Eastern Railroad across northern Manchuria. (See Map 2.3.) In 1898, Nicholas II, urged on by military and naval leaders, and over Witte's strong objections, ordered seizure of strategic Port Arthur, the naval base on the Liaotung Peninsula, and forced China to lease to Russia the very region she had compelled Japan to renounce! Construction of a South Manchurian Railroad, northward from Port Arthur to a junction with the Chinese Eastern, allowed Russia to dominate all of Manchuria. After the Boxers, a national-ist Chinese society, attacked Russian railway properties in 1900, War Minister A. N. Kuropatkin dispatched troops to occupy Manchuria; he told Witte that it would become a Russian protectorate.

Its government gravely divided over Far Eastern policy, Russia embarked on a reckless, aggressive course in the Orient. While Witte and the Foreign Ministry favored continued peaceful economic penetration of China and an alliance with her, adventurers led by a former Guards officer, A. M. Bezobrazov, obtained the Yalu River timber concession on the Manchurian-Korean border, a move toward eventual Russian annexation of Korea. Japan sought a compromise settlement with Russia, which Witte repeatedly urged Nicholas II to accept, but Interior Minister V. K. Pleve declared that bayonets had made Russia, not diplomats: "In order to restrain revolution [at home], we need a little victorious war." Nicholas

At the Portsmouth Peace Conference in August 1905. Left to right:
Count Sergei Iu. Witte, Russia's chief delegate; Baron Roman Rosen,
second delegate; U.S. President Theodore Roosevelt; Foreign
Minister Baron J. Komura; and K. Takahira of Japan.

II, blissfully confident, wrote William II, emperor of Germany: "There will be no war [with Japan] because I do not wish it." Thus Russia rejected reasonable Japanese peace offers and blundered ill prepared into a needless and disastrous war.

The Russo-Japanese War (1904–1905) began in January 1904 with sudden Japanese attacks on the scattered Russian fleet. Invading Manchuria from Korea, the Japanese besieged Port Arthur, the chief Russian naval base in the Far East. In Manchuria, Japanese armies repeatedly defeated General Kuropatkin and drove him north; Port Arthur surrendered ignominiously to them. Seeking to redress the military balance, Russia's Baltic Fleet sailed around Africa, only to suffer virtual annihilation by Admiral Togo's main fleet in Tsushima Strait. With Japan nearing the end of its limited resources and Russia engulfed by revolution, both sides willingly allowed President Theodore Roosevelt of the United States to mediate their conflict. The Treaty of Portsmouth, New Hampshire, ending the war, transferred southern Manchuria to Japan and confirmed its preeminence in Korea; Russia retained northern Manchuria and the Chinese Eastern Railroad. The Russo-Japanese War, halting Russia's imperial drive in the Far East and weakening the Franco-Russian Alliance, ended British fears of Russian imperialism and naval power. Japan's victory, its first over a great European power and the initial defeat for white imperialism in Asia, discredited the tsarist regime at home and helped induce it to grant important concessions to the Russian people.

Problem 1

Why Did Alexander II Free the Serfs?

Emancipation of the Russian private serfs in 1861 and of the court and state peasants in 1863 and 1866, respectively, constitutes the most significant and controversial act of Alexander II's reign. Some scholars consider it the greatest reform by a European government in the 19th century. It affected roughly 85 percent of Russia's population and began to transform its peasant masses from virtual slaves bound to the land into free citizens and property holders. Some historians still describe the struggle over emancipation as one between "liberals" and "planters," though it is difficult to find avowed liberals or planters involved in the legislative process. During the working out of the reform legislation the reformers held secondary and tenuous positions, whereas their detractors held high offices. Most of the nobility revealed its opposition and resentment toward emancipation but demonstrated less cohesion and political capacity than one might expect from an elite class. Because senior bureaucrats involved in the reform lacked requisite skills, lower officials and outsiders were able to play key roles in drawing up the reform legislation. Writes Daniel Field:

> The manifest inadequacy of the government's nebulous and moderate program of 1857, coupled with a formal, public commitment to a reform of serfdom, impelled the regime to adopt a far more venturesome program in 1858 and enact it with substantial modifications in 1861.[6]

Why did Alexander II take this fateful step, which his predecessors (including his strong-willed father, Nicholas I, who had denounced serfdom as immoral) had refused to do? Is there a single explanation of the decision to emancipate?

---

[6] D. Field, *The End of Serfdom* (Cambridge, MA, 1976), pp. 3–5.

The official tsarist view depicted emancipation as a personal and generous decision by the new sovereign. Prerevolutionary liberal historians, on the other hand, stressed the role of an aroused public opinion directed by abolitionist writers (reform was "in the air"), which exerted decisive pressure on the government.

The Official Tsarist View

Tatishchev's official biography of Alexander II presents the Emancipation as the personal decision of an emperor convinced that serfdom was a great social evil and that the Crimean defeat had made a reorganization of the state administration imperative. Tatishchev emphasizes Alexander's concern that the nobility agree to and cooperate with his efforts at reform:

> The Crimean War revealed the unsatisfactory condition of many branches of state administration whose improvement Alexander II considered his immediate task. The young sovereign considered serfdom a great social evil whose elimination his predecessors had already repeatedly thought about and about which all the best Russian minds had long dreamed. From the first day of his reign Alexander Nikolaevich [Alexander II] firmly resolved to implement the noble intentions of Empress Catherine II and Emperors Alexander I and Nicholas I, to achieve what they had backed away from because of the difficulties associated with implementing an act affecting and changing all aspects of the state and social order of Russia. He planned to undertake it only with the consent and the active participation of the nobility, not doubting its readiness to waive its rights to own souls [serfs] and to make this sacrifice voluntarily for the benefit and dignity of the country. This was the meaning of his first address to the nobility of Petersburg immediately after he mounted the throne, when, receiving their delegation, he expressed the hope that "the nobility will be in the full sense of the word a truly noble class, in the forefront of all that is good."

. . . Meanwhile from the first days of the reign vague rumors about the desire of the new sovereign to emancipate the peasants from serfdom began to spread in society both among the landowners and among the peasants, causing among both groups agitation so strong that Emperor Alexander considered it essential, at the first opportunity, to explain to the nobles the true meaning of his intentions. Soon after the conclusion of the Treaty of Paris on March 30, 1856, the emperor utilized a brief stay in Moscow in order, while receiving representatives of the nobility of Moscow province, to address them as follows: "I have learned, gentlemen, that among you have spread rumors of my intention to destroy serfdom. In refuting various unfounded reports on such an important matter, I consider it essential to declare to all of you that I do not intend to do this now. But, of course, you yourselves understand that the existing order of owning souls cannot remain unchanged. It is better to begin to destroy serfdom from above than to await the time when it begins to destroy itself from below. I ask you, gentlemen, to consider how all this can be carried out. Pass on my words to the nobility for their consideration."

In the tsar's speech to the Moscow nobility was clearly stated both the sovereign's personal view of serfdom and the wish for the nobility to take upon itself the initiative in the matter of its destruction. The emperor considered it a necessary condition for success that nowhere would the legal order be violated and that prior to the issuance of the new legislation, private serfs not express impatience and remain wholly obedient to their masters.[7]

Soviet Views

Until the 1960s Soviet historians, quoting extensively from the works of Marx, Lenin, and Stalin, placed overwhelming emphasis on peasant discontent as a cause of emancipation. They asserted that emancipation had been enacted reluctantly by a fearful tsarist regime vulnerable during a "revolutionary situation" of 1859–1861.[8]

P. A. Zaionchkovskii Later Soviet scholarship shifted to a multicausational explanation of the abolition of serfdom. Here is an outstanding example from the pen of one of the pioneers, Zaionchkovskii, taken from the introduction to *The Abolition of Serfdom in Russia*:

The abolition of serfdom in Russia was a precondition ensuring the consolidation of capitalism. The reason that induced the government to undertake this reform was the crisis of the feudal-serf system. The existence of serfdom dictated the economic and political backwardness of Russia. As long as serfdom was retained, the development of industry and the rise of agriculture were impossible. The crisis of the feudal-serf system provoked the sharpening of class contradictions, finding expression in the growth of antifeudal ideology and the rise of the peasant movement, especially during the 1850s. Therefore, the question of serfdom and its liquidation was the central problem of social and ideological struggle in the first half of the nineteenth century.

The Crimean War, revealing with utmost clarity all the backwardness of the serf-holding state, compelled the government of Alexander II to undertake reform. The fear of peasant uprising played a major role. However, under existing circumstances, the abolition of serfdom by revolutionary means was impossible. The peasant movement represented a spontaneous struggle unilluminated by any political consciousness. There were no other forces capable of fighting against autocracy. The bourgeoisie, economically dependent on tsarism, although favoring the liquidation of serfdom, lacked the decisiveness with which the Third Estate in France had entered the struggle against the feudal regime [in 1789]. The Russian bourgeoisie was incapable of revolutionary struggle against the autocracy. . . . Revolutionary democrats, reflecting the aspirations of the peasantry, were very few and did not represent any real force. As a

---

[7] S. S. Tatishchev, *Imperator Aleksandr II* . . . , 2 vols. (St. Petersburg, 1903), vol. 1, pp. 300–303.

[8] M. V. Nechkina, "Reforma 1861 goda kak pobochnyi produkt revoliutsionnoi borby," in *Revoliutsionnaia situatsiia v Rossii v 1859–1861 gg.* (Moscow, 1962), pp. 7, 9, 10. On Marxism, see Chapter 3; on Lenin's ideology, see Chapter 3.

result the revolutionary situation . . . could not develop into a revolution.[9]

L. G. Zakharova In a recent article Professor Zakharova of Moscow State University, basing her findings chiefly on Soviet archives without reference to the "classics of Marxism-Leninism," emphasizes the positive roles in the emancipation process of public opinion, Alexander II, and liberal bureaucrats. Reflecting the "new thinking" of the Gorbachev era, her multi-causational approach resembles that of Western interpretations.

The removal of serfdom in Russia in 1861 and the resultant reforms . . . was the greatest event or "turning point" in Russian history. . . . On the eve of reform, the year, 1856, was the thaw, or: why the serf monarchy undertook the removal of serfdom . . . Prince D. A. Obolenskii, serving in the Navy Ministry . . . left in his diary characteristic entries. October 16, 1856: "In general there is a force upon which I am beginning to lay great hopes. . . . People are beginning to breathe freely; that in itself is a powerful prescription for recovery." . . .

The first powerful blow to the Nicholaevian system was delivered from outside. Defeat in the Crimean War (1853–1856) revealed the true condition of serf Russia. It not only emerged from the war defeated but in international isolation. The reactionary Holy Alliance of Russia, Prussia and Austria, created after the Napoleonic Wars, had fallen apart. The foreign policy of Nicholas I had turned out bankrupt. Concern about the prestige of the country in European public opinion . . . was revealed by the first steps of the government of Alexander II, even before the peasant question was raised. . . .

Dissatisfaction gripped every layer of society inspiring a flood of accusatory handwritten statements and plans of reform, "an underground literature." It seemed as if all thinking Russia had taken

up the pen. . . . Returning at this time from exile M. E. Saltykov-Shchedrin [a leading satirical writer], coming to Moscow, then to St. Petersburg . . . , was amazed by the freedom with which everyone talked everywhere about everything. . . . *Glasnost* (openness) arose spontaneously from below. The government followed in the wake of events, renouncing extraordinary censorship prohibitions, but then utilized *glasnost* as a weapon. . . . In Russia, "like mushrooms after a rain," as [Leo] Tolstoy expressed it, were issued publications embodying the thaw. . . . *Glasnost* . . . carried a charge of optimism and bright hopes, inducing the government and society to act, and drove away fear which had permeated the Nicholaevian system. The emancipation of the moral forces of society preceded the reforms and were their precondition.

A powerful economic stimulus operated also. The realization that free labor was more advantageous than serf, that serfdom, as the government had known earlier, was hampering the development of agriculture and commercial production of grain, incited the removal of serfdom. . . . Already in January 1857 was revealed to the ruling circles and to Alexander II the true and extremely grave and threatening financial situation. . . . A well-known economist L. V. Tengoborskii in a memorandum in the tsar's name concluded: "It is essential to take immediately the most decisive measures to curtail expenditures . . . ; otherwise state bankruptcy is inevitable." The threatening financial crisis stimulated the leadership to seek reforms and especially aroused Alexander II. . . . "The former system has outlived its age," was the verdict of one of its ideologists, M. P. Pogodin. . . .

Alexander II . . . already as heir to the throne had participated in state affairs, in the work of secret committees on the peasant question. He was neither a liberal nor a fanatical reactionary. Prior to ascending the throne he lacked a program of his own. . . . But coming to the throne during the crisis of the old system and the awakening of public opinion which demanded reform, he was able to realize this and began seeking new solutions and new men. . . . In the Interior Ministry the activity of liberal bureaucrats was manifested especially. . . . From this ministry came the leader of the liberal bureaucracy, N. A. Miliutin, who in 1856 . . . was already prepared to solve the basic issue: the peas-

---

[9] P. A. Zaionchkovskii, *Otmena krepostnogo prava v Rossii*, 3d ed. (Moscow, 1968), pp. 3–4.

Problem 1 continued

ant question. . . . His memorandum served as a model for the reform of 1861. It was important that in the apparatus of authority were new people with their own program. They united and were prepared under favorable circumstances to take the matter of reforms into their hands. Among the nobility were also some adherents of liberal reforms although they comprised a clear minority. . . .

The role of peasant movements in the preparation of ending serfdom has ever since the 1930s generally been exaggerated by Soviet sources, but while overcoming that exaggeration, one need not go to the other extreme. . . . Although there was no direct threat of an insurrection, memories of the Pugachov Revolt . . . increased fears of the leadership.[10]

Western Views

During the post–World War II era European and American scholars have debated whether economic, political, military, or personal factors were decisive in Alexander II's decision to free the Russian serfs.

Alexander Gerschenkron A leading American economist of Russian origin, Alexander Gerschenkron, emphasizes economic considerations.

The question of whether, on the eve of the reform, the system of serfdom was disintegrating for economic reasons or whether its vitality and viability were still essentially unimpaired has been the subject of much controversy. But even those who, like the present writer, tend toward the latter view must admit that the development of the non-agrarian sectors of the economy was virtually premised upon the abolition of serfdom.

To say this, however, does not at all imply that promotion of economic development was a paramount objective of the emancipation. . . . The authors of the Russian reform either considered industrialization undesirable or, at best, were indif-

ferent to it. The actual procedures chosen reflected these attitudes. In many ways they were bound to hamper rather than facilitate economic growth. . . . Over wide parts of the country (and particularly in the black-earth belt) the peasants received a good deal less land than had been customarily assigned to them prior to the reform. Second, there was the question of the magnitude of the quitrents (*obrok*) to be paid by the peasants as compensation for land allotments. . . . It might be argued that the two features of the Russian reform just mentioned should have provided a favorable climate for subsequent industrialization; the inadequacy of the peasants' landholdings in conjunction with the considerable financial obligations imposed upon the peasants' households could have been expected to favor the flight from the country and thus to provide a large reservoir of labor supply to the nascent industry. Such might have been the consequences indeed, if the reform and the later legislative measures had not erected considerable barriers to land flight by strengthening the *obshchina*, the village commune, wherever it existed.[11]

W. Bruce Lincoln The late American historian, W. Bruce Lincoln, argued that Alexander II initiated reform for a complex set of reasons that included restoring the nation's power status and role in European affairs.

Defeat in the Crimean War immediately challenged Russia's single claim to membership in the community of great powers. As the quality of armaments technology began to counterbalance the number of armed forces in determining a nation's power, Russians began to debate how to prevent any further erosion of their nation's international standing. No one doubted that Russia must move decisively into the industrial age, for a nation without heavy industry and railroads could not hope to be counted among the great powers of the West. At the same time, the young Alexander II and his advisers knew that Russia no longer could afford to support an army of more than a million men in peacetime.

[10] L. G. Zakharova, "Samoderzhavie, biurokratiia i reformy 60-kh godov XIX v. v Rossii," *Voprosy istorii*, no. 10 (1989): 3–8.

[11] A. Gerschenkron, "Problems and Patterns . . . ," in *The Transformation of Russian Society*, ed. C. E. Black (Cambridge, MA, 1960), pp. 42–43. Reprinted by permission.

Problem 1 continued

European nations had begun to experiment with small standing armies that could be supplemented by a large system of ready reserves in time of war. Yet, as General Dmitrii Miliutin stated flatly in a memorandum in March 1856, no nation that drew its soldiers from a servile population dared to return them to bondage after training them in the use of arms.

Dangerously weakened finances, a local administration that had failed to connect her people with their government, a pre-modern system of law in which semiliterate judges still presided over catastrophically backlogged law courts, the problems of developing modern industrial and transportation networks in a society that had not yet entered the industrial age, and an army in which a term of military service was akin to a sentence of penal servitude all had to be considered in plotting Russia's course after the Crimean War. Across all of these, serfdom continued to cast its retrograde shadow, for modern armies and modern industry required a free citizenry and a mobile labor force.

Serfdom's was not the only dark shadow that lay upon the Russian political and social landscape when the Crimean War ended in 1856. Although the army could not be modernized and industry could not be developed so long as serfdom remained, emancipation posed other problems whose resolution seemed fully as complex as serfdom itself. Emancipation would free Russia's nobility of its responsibilities for collecting taxes, assembling recruits, and administering justice to more than 20 million peasants. At one liberating stroke of the tsar's pen, these responsibilities would shift to the shoulders of the government, yet there were no current institutions that could integrate so many new citizens into the fabric of Russia's national life. Nor could the nearly bankrupt imperial treasury finance an emancipation.

Not only did the Crimean defeat challenge Russia's claim to great power status but it called into question the principles that had directed her national life and government since the time of Peter the Great. To develop Russia's traditional institutions along the lines followed by Nicholas I and his predecessors—to bring them to the level of perfection implied by Uvarov's slogan "Orthodoxy, Autocracy, and Nationality" and proclaimed as truth by defenders of Official Nationality—meant, in fact, to weaken Russia, not to strengthen her ability to confront the disconcerting challenges of the Crimean defeat. "Orthodoxy, Autocracy, and Nationality" articulated a political outlook that no longer had a place in Europe's experience, just as it described a social order that could not hope to survive among modern nations that had entered the industrial age. Even though Peter the Great had used them to win membership in the European great power community for Russia, such principles now could only carry Russia further away from the West.[12]

Conclusion

Both Russian and Western scholars have been moving toward multicausational explanations of the decision to emancipate. Undoubtedly, both the regime and the nobility feared growing peasant discontent, but that fear increased most *after* the decision to emancipate had been reached. There may have been a "crisis of the servile economy," but the serf owners do not appear to have realized it at the time, and they feared economic ruin and peasant upheaval if the serfs were emancipated. Nor is there much evidence in primary sources that the Crimean defeat convinced contemporary Russian leaders that serfdom must be abolished. And whereas Alexander's personal role in deciding on emancipation was crucial, one should not view him as a benevolent liberal. He came to power in 1855 as a profoundly conservative and traditionally minded man who was linked powerfully with the past. Thus the decision to free the serfs involved a variety of complex, interacting factors and considerations. ■

---

[12] W. Bruce Lincoln, *The Great Reforms* . . . (DeKalb, IL, 1990), pp. 37–39. Copyright ©1990 Northern Illinois University Press. Used by permission of the publisher.

Suggested Additional Reading

BALMUTH, DANIEL. *Censorship in Russia, 1865–1905* (Washington, DC, 1979).

BAUMGART, WINFRIED. *The Crimean War, 1853–1856* (London, 1999).

BLACK, E. E., ed. *The Transformation of Russian Society . . . since 1861* (Cambridge, MA, 1960).

BLACKWELL, WILLIAM. *The Industrialization of Russia,* 2d ed. (Arlington Heights, IL, 1982).

BRADLEY, JOSEPH. *Muzhik and Muscovite: Urbanization in Late Imperial Russia* (Berkeley, CA, 1985).

BROWER, DANIEL R. *The Russian City Between Tradition and Modernity, 1850–1900* (Berkeley, CA, 1990).

CLEMENTS, BARBARA E., et al. *Russia's Women: Accommodation, Resistance, Transformation* (Berkeley, CA, 1991).

CRACRAFT, JAMES, ed. *Major Problems in the History of Imperial Russia* (Lexington, MA, 1994).

CRANKSHAW, EDWARD. *The Shadow of the Winter Palace . . . 1825–1917* (New York, 1976).

CRISP, OLGA. *Studies in the Russian Economy Before 1914* (New York, 1976).

DALY, JONATHAN W. *Autocracy under Siege: Security Police and Opposition in Russia, 1866–1905* (DeKalb, IL, 1998).

EMMONS, TERENCE. *The Emancipation of the Russian Serfs* (New York, 1970).

ENGEL, BARBARA A. *Mothers and Daughters: Women of the Intelligentsia in 19th-Century Russia.* (Evanston, IL, 2000).

FIELD, DANIEL. *The End of Serfdom* (Cambridge, MA, 1976).

FISCHER, G. *Russian Liberalism* (Cambridge, MA, 1958).

FITZPATRICK, ANNE L. *The Great Russian Fair: Nizhnii-Novgorod, 1840–90* (New York, 1989).

FRIERSON, CATHY. *Peasant Icons: Representations of Rural People in Late Nineteenth Century Russia* (New York, 1993).

GADDIS, JOHN. *Russia, the Soviet Union, and the United States* (New York, 1978).

GATRELL, PETER. *The Tsarist Economy, 1850–1917* (New York, 1986).

GEYER, DIETRICH. *Russian Imperialism . . . 1860–1914* (New Haven, CT, 1987).

GRANT, JONATHAN A. *Big Business in Russia: The Putilov Company in Late Imperial Russia, 1868–1917* (Pittsburgh, PA, 1999).

GREENBURG, LOUIS. *The Jews in Russia,* 2 vols. (New Haven, CT, 1951).

HAUNER, MILAN. *What Is Asia to Us? Russia's Asian Heartland Yesterday and Today* (London and New York, 1992).

KAZEMZADEH, FIRUZ. *Russia and Britain in Persia, 1864–1914* (New Haven, CT, 1968).

KEEP, J. L. H. *The Rise of Social Democracy in Russia* (Oxford, 1963).

KOLCHIN, PETER. *Unfree Labor: American Slavery and Russian Serfdom* (Cambridge, MA, 1987).

LE DONNE, JOHN. *The Russian Empire and the World, 1700–1917. The Geopolitics of Expansion and Containment* (New York, 1997).

LENIN, V. I. *The Development of Capitalism in Russia* (Moscow, 1956).

MACKENZIE, DAVID. *Imperial Dreams, Harsh Realities: Tsarist Russian Foreign Policy, 1815–1917* (Fort Worth, TX, 1994).

———. *The Lion of Tashkent: The Career of General M. G. Cherniaev* (Athens, GA, 1974).

MALOZEMOFF, A. *Russian Far Eastern Policy, 1881–1904* (Berkeley, CA, 1958).

MCNEAL, ROBERT. *Tsar and Cossack, 1855–1914* (New York, 1987).

MENNING, BRUCE W. *Bayonets Before Bullets: The Imperial Russian Army, 1861–1914.* (Bloomington, IN, 2000).

MILLER, MARTIN. *Freud and the Bolsheviks: Psychoanalysis in Imperial Russia and the Soviet Union* (New Haven, 1998).

MOSSE, W. E. *Alexander II and the Modernization of Russia* (New York, 1962).

NEUBERGER, JOAN. *Hooliganism, Crime, Culture and Power in St. Petersburg, 1900–1914.* (Berkeley, CA, 1993).

OLYMAN, TOBY, and JUDITH VOWLES, eds. *Russia through Women's Eyes: Autobiographies from Tsarist Russia* (New Haven, 1996).

OWEN, T. C. *Capitalism and Politics in Russia . . . 1855–1905* (Cambridge, 1981).

PEARSON, THOMAS S. *Russian Officialdom in Crisis: Autocracy and Local Self-Government, 1861–1900* (Cambridge and New York, 1989).

PINTNER, W. M., and D. K. ROWNEY, eds. *Russian Officialdom* (Chapel Hill, NC, 1980).

RAGSDALE, HUGH, ed. *Imperial Russian Foreign Policy* (New York and Cambridge, 1993).

RIEBER, ALFRED, ed. *The Politics of Autocracy* . . . (Paris, 1966).

ROBINSON, G. T. *Rural Russia Under the Old Regime* (New York, 1949).

ROGGER, HANS. *Russia in the Age of Modernisation and Revolution, 1881–1917* (London and New York, 1983).

ROMANOV, B. A. *Russia in Manchuria, 1892–1906*, trans. S. Jones (Ann Arbor, MI, 1952).

RUUD, CHARLES, and SERGEI A. STEPANOV. *Fontanka 16: The Tsar's Secret Police* (Montreal, 1999).

SIMMS, J. Y. "The Crisis in Russian Agriculture at the End of the 19th Century: A Different View," *Slavic Review, 36* (September 1977), pp. 377–398.

SOLOMON, PETER H., ed. *Reforming Justice in Russia, 1864–1996* (Armonk, NY, 1997).

STITES, RICHARD. *The Women's Liberation Movement in Russia* . . . (Princeton, NJ, 1978).

SUMNER, B. H. *Russia and the Balkans, 1870–1880* (Oxford, 1937).

THADEN, E. C. *Conservative Nationalism in 19th Century Russia* (Seattle, 1964).

TUGAN-BARANOVSKY, M. I. *The Russian Factory in the 19th Century*, trans. A. Levin ET AL. (Homewood, IL, 1970).

VON LAUE, T. H. *Sergei Witte and the Industrialization of Russia* (New York, 1963).

VUCINICH, W. S., ed. *The Peasant in Nineteenth Century Russia* (Stanford, CA, 1968).

WESTWOOD, J. N. *A History of Russian Railways* (London, 1964).

WIRTSCHAFTER, E.K. *Social Identity in Imperial Russia* (DeKalb, IL, 1997).

WITTE, S. Iu. *The Memoirs of Count Witte* (New York, 1921).

WOROBEC, CHRISTINE D. *Peasant Russia: Family and Community in the Post-Emancipation Period* (Princeton, NJ, 1991).

WORTMAN, RICHARD. *Scenarios of Power: From Alexander II to the Abdication of Nicholas II*, vol. 2 (Princeton, 2000).

ZAIONCHKOVSKII, P. A. *The Russian Autocracy Under Alexander III*, trans. D. D. Jones (Gulf Breeze, FL, 1976).

ZELNICK, REGINALD E., ed. *Workers and Intelligentsia in Late Imperial Russia: Realities, Representation, Reflections* (Berkeley, 1999).

3

The Revolutionary Movement to 1904

The Russian people have not always remained docile under a repressive regime. Although modern Russian history has featured the growth of political autocracy, serfdom, and repression, it has also witnessed several massive peasant revolts and great revolutions in 1905 and 1917. Whenever autocratic government weakened or controls were relaxed, popular upheavals erupted, virtually unmatched in violence and destructiveness. To suggest Russia's ideologies and forces of dissent, we will now trace movements against tsarism, notably from 1855 to the 1905 Revolution.

During the 17th and 18th centuries, provoked by serfdom and a centralized autocratic state, several major peasant and Cossack revolts erupted. Lacking cohesion and disciplined armies, they were all doomed to eventual suppression by the Muscovite tsardom.[1] In 1773–1774 occurred the Pugachev Revolt, the greatest rural upheaval in Russia and Europe before 1905. Led by a Don Cossack, Emelian Pugachev, who claimed to be

Peter III, the legitimate tsar, it spread like wildfire through the Ural and Volga regions until defeated by Catherine II's army. "The entire populace was for Pugachev," wrote the great poet Alexander Pushkin. "Only the nobility openly supported the government."[2] These uprisings were suppressed brutally by a tsarist regime that, rather than remedy popular grievances, fastened ever tighter controls over an enslaved people.

Educated leaders would be required before successful warfare could be waged against tsarism and serfdom. Such leadership arose with the emergence under Catherine II in the 1780s of a Russian intelligentsia, defined by a Populist historian, Ivanov-Razumnik, as an hereditary group, outside estate and class, seeking the physical, mental, social, and personal emancipation of the individual from oppression. Under Catherine it comprised only a handful of enlightened noblemen led by Nikolai Novikov and Alexander Radishchev, but its ideas circulated among the elite of Moscow and St. Petersburg. They were

---

[1] On these see MacKenzie and Curran, *Russia, the Soviet Union, and Beyond* (Belmont, CA, 2002).

[2] A. S. Pushkin, *Istoriia Pugacheva* (Moscow, 1835).

passed on to the Decembrists, who drew up extensive programs of reform and revolution, and attempted unsuccessfully to overturn autocracy and serfdom in 1825. The intelligentsia movement broadened during the Slavophile–Westernizer debate of 1838–1848 to include middle-class leaders such as the radical literary critic Vissarion Belinskii, who in 1847 from Austrian exile excoriated the autocratic system of the "Iron Tsar":

> Russia sees her salvation not in mysticism, not in asceticism, not in pietism, but in the achievement of civilization, enlightenment and humanitarianism . . . , an awakening in her people of the sense of human dignity.

Belinskii and other Westernizers pointed the way forward toward the goal of a new, free Russia:

> The most topical, the most vital national questions in Russia today are the abolition of serfdom, the repeal of corporal punishment, and the introduction as far as possible, of the strictest application of at least those laws which are already on the books.[3]

Alexander Herzen (1812–1870), the founder of Populism and the first important Russian socialist, combined Slavophile and Westernizer tenets into a radical ideology. From the Slavophiles, Herzen derived his passion for Russian institutions and values. Rejecting European industrialism and urban life, he viewed the Russian peasant commune (mir) as the basis for a decentralized peasant Russian socialism. Going into exile in 1847, Herzen published in London (1857–1867) the biweekly *Bell* (*Kolokol*). This highly influential Russian émigré newspaper attacked the evils of the old regime and called for freedom and emancipation. A vibrant new intellectual climate marked the first decade of Alexander II's reign as numerous liberal and radical newspapers and periodicals appeared. "Everyone is talking, everyone is studying, including people who never before read anything in their lives," wrote the historian K. D. Kavelin. Contacts with Europe,

severed by Nicholas I, were renewed; hopes for drastic change soared.

In the post-Crimean epoch, a diversified liberal and radical opposition against the autocracy developed. Liberals, aiming at peaceful reform, competed with revolutionaries who sought to overthrow the regime. Liberals were hampered by governmental repression and the absence of a parliament. Determined radicals, often using despotic methods and organizations, answered police repression with terrorism, secrecy, and ruthlessness. Before 1890 they looked to the peasantry as their army of revolution; afterward, Marxism grew rapidly, and its adherents wooed a rising urban working class. Soviet historians stressed the role of Marxist Social Democrats, claiming that only a workers' party could have taken Russia to socialism. Recent Western scholars have emphasized more the role of agrarian socialists and liberals.

The relaxation of censorship increased contacts with Europe, and government overtures stimulated liberal gentry to advocate reform. In Tver province, liberal gentry leaders, in a memorandum criticizing the bureaucracy and official reform proposals, advocated immediate emancipation with land and an equal role for gentry committees in working it out.

The Tver provincial gentry assembly appealed early in 1862 to the regime to "gather representatives from the entire people without distinction as to class." Renouncing its class privileges, it requested the tsar's permission "to take upon ourselves a part of state taxes and obligations."[4] Refusing to meet with the Tver leaders or grant their requests, Alexander II ordered their arrest.

After 1865 gentry liberalism centered in the new zemstva. Their leaders aimed to convert them into a school of self-government, and by this means prepare the way for a constitutional state order. They aimed to expand zemstva activities and take most control over rural affairs. The liberals sought a society where the individual would be

---

[3] "Letter to N. V. Gogol," in Marc Raeff, *Russian Intellectual History: An Anthology* (New York, 1966), p. 254.

[4] Emmons, pp. 341–343.

Nikolai Gavrilovich Chernyshevskii, 1828–1889, leading radical of the 1860s and author of *What Is to Be Done?*

central and self-governing, private property would be guaranteed, and law would reign supreme. Zemstva liberals strove to persuade the regime to accept their "small deeds" in raising popular cultural and material well-being, hoping eventually it would grant a national constitution.

Meanwhile young intellectuals, led by N. G. Chernyshevskii, determined to remake the world through reason, turned enthusiastically to radicalism. Some were priests' sons estranged from existing values and institutions and convinced that partial reforms were useless. Radicals gathered around a journal, *The Contemporary*. Soviet scholars regarded Chernyshevskii, a leading contributor, as the chief precursor of Bolshevism and praised his materialism and scorn for liberalism. Dreaming of changing history's course by building a perpetual motion machine to abolish poverty, Chernyshevskii stressed the intellectual's duty to educate and lead the toiling masses. Viewing the

mir (peasant commune) as the basis for decentralized agrarian socialism, Chernyshevskii affirmed that Russia, avoiding capitalism, could move directly to socialism. In a novel, *What Is to Be Done?* (1863), Chernyshevskii described a socialist utopia achieved by relentless, practical revolutionaries who would "impose their character on the pattern of events, and hurry their course." Now few, they would multiply rapidly, and "in a few years . . . people will call unto them for rescue, and what they say will be performed by all." Although his "toiler's theory" asserted that labor was entitled to all it produced, he derived his socialism more from Fourier than from Marx. Twenty years in Siberian exile made him a revolutionary martyr.

Dmitri Pisarev (1840–1868) reflected the uncompromising radicalism of intelligentsia "sons" of the 1860s, attacking the values and beliefs of the "fathers" of the 1840s. "Here is the ultimatum of our camp: what can be smashed should be smashed; what will stand the blow is good; . . . . at any rate hit out left and right."[5] This thrilled rebellious adolescents fighting the establishment. The writer Ivan Turgenev dubbed their ideology nihilism, and Bazarov, the hero of his novel *Fathers and Sons* (1862), was Pisarev thinly disguised. A convinced Westernizer, Pisarev believed that an educated elite with modern science and European technology would uplift the masses and destroy autocracy.

In the mid-1860s, a small group of Moscow intelligentsia, led by Nikolai Ishutin, a follower of Chernyshevskii, plotted direct, violent action. A secret terrorist band known as Hell was to destroy autocracy. In April 1866 a student, Dmitri Karakozov, Ishutin's cousin, shot at but missed the tsar (and apologized to Alexander II before being executed!); the Ishutin circle was broken up.

Russian exiles, too, developed conspiratorial ideas. In 1869 Sergei Nechaev, a Moscow University student in Geneva, Switzerland, and the romantic revolutionary Mikhail Bakunin composed *Catechism of a Revolutionary*, which stressed

---

[5] Cited in A. Yarmolinsky, *Road to Revolution* (London, 1957), p. 120.

that revolutionaries must be professional, dedicated, and disciplined:

> The revolutionary is a doomed man. He has no interests, no affairs, no feelings, no attachments of his own. . . . Everything in him is wholly absorbed by one sole, exclusive interest . . . revolution. He must train himself to stand torture, and be ready to die. . . . The laws, the conventions, the moral code of civilized society have no meaning for him. . . . To him whatever promotes the triumph of the revolution is moral, whatever hinders it is criminal.[6]

Later Lenin, praising the *Catechism* highly, patterned his Bolshevik party upon it. Nechaev returned briefly to Russia in 1870 and set up a small organization, the People's Reckoning (*Narodnaia Rasprava*), which murdered a member believed planning to betray it to the authorities.[7]

Revolutionary Populism

In the 1870s, a broader movement of revolutionary intelligentsia heeded Herzen's appeal: "Go to the people." Populism (*Narodnichestvo*) combined idealistic faith in the peasantry with determination to overthrow the old social and political order by force. Lacking central organization or a cohesive ideology, Populism advocated a peasant socialism derived largely from Herzen. The Populists regarded factory industry as degrading and dehumanizing, denied that an industrial revolution must precede socioeconomic progress, and believed that only agriculturalists led the good and natural life. Using intelligence and free will, Russians could avoid European errors. Like Rousseau, Populists believed that bad institutions had corrupted people, that the state had fostered inequality, injustice, and oppression. Popular revolution, not parliaments, would produce a decentralized socialist order. Populists idealized the people

(*narod*), chiefly the peasantry, as a mystical, irresistible, and virtuous force whose traditional institutions—the mir and the primitive producers' cooperative (*artel*) with their collective landholding and quasi self-government—would become socialist once the old order was destroyed. Convinced that peasants in the mir were practicing rudimentary socialism, Populists disregarded clear signs of its disintegration before an advancing money economy. While emphasizing ethical values and faith in collective institutions, they disagreed about revolutionary organization, the intelligentsia's relationship to the people, and how and when to achieve revolution. In the early 1870s, émigrés Bakunin and Lavrov had small followings of socialist youth; later P. N. Tkachev's conspiratorial views tended to prevail.

Mikhail Bakunin, a founder of anarchism with long experience in tsarist prisons, urged an immediate, spontaneous mass peasant uprising (*bunt*). Regarding the intelligentsia as largely a privileged elite that despised the people, Bakunin appealed to emotion, feeling, and mass instincts: "The Russian peasantry are socialists by instinct and revolutionary by nature. . . . We must not act as schoolmasters for the people; we must lead them to revolt." The existing state must be totally destroyed and replaced by a free federation. A romantic apostle of freedom, Bakunin opposed "the authoritarian communism of Marx and the entire German school." He helped inspire the "going to the people" movement of 1874, but no true Bakuninist organization ever emerged in Russia. When anticipated popular uprisings failed to erupt, Bakunin's following in Russia dwindled.[8]

P. L. Lavrov's more moderate, cautious approach won some support. A mathematics professor, Lavrov achieved prominence with his legally published *Historical Letters* (1870). For their education, intellectuals owed a debt to the people and should repay it by preparing them for revolution: a "critically thinking" elite should propagandize and agitate among the people. Abroad, in his

---

[6] Yarmolinsky, *Road to Revolution* (London, 1957, reprinted Princeton, NJ, 1986), pp. 156–157.

[7] Fyodor Dostoevsky based his novel *The Possessed* on this incident and the character Peter Verkhovenskii on Nechaev.

[8] Franco Venturi, *Roots of Revolution* (New York, 1960), pp. 429–436.

journal, *Forward!*, Lavrov developed a complete Populist program borrowing some Marxian tenets. He remained uncertain whether revolution in Russia would precede or follow full capitalist development. He stressed careful intelligentsia preparation of a peasant revolution. Dedicated revolutionaries were to explain socialism to the masses and recruit members from their ranks. (Lavrov worked it all out mathematically!) Local uprisings, directed by a revolutionary organization, would fuse in a nationwide revolution. Afterward, a strong central government would rule temporarily, yielding later to a federation.

P. N. Tkachev, the heir of nihilism and Ishutin, led a small Jacobinist faction that rejected Lavrov's patient approach. His views in the émigré newspaper *The Tocsin* combined Populism, Marxism, and Blanquism.[9] Urging immediate action like Bakunin, Tkachev believed that a centralized, elite organization of revolutionaries must lead the masses and impose its will. His writing was filled with urgency: Unless revolution comes soon, capitalism will destroy the mir. "This is why we cannot wait. This is why we insist that a revolution in Russia is indispensable . . . at the present time."[10] A temporary dictatorship would follow armed overthrow of the old order, withering away once the people had been educated in socialism. Appealing desperately for immediate revolution, Tkachev finally went insane. Later, Lenin described his plan for seizing power as majestic.

Populism's practical achievements were few. Its main early organization, the Chaikovskii Circle (Lavrovist), was broken up by arrests. In 1873–1874, after a famine in the Volga region, more than 3,000 young urban intellectuals "went to the people" to spread socialist ideas and prepare revolution. Peasants responded to this naive "children's crusade" by turning over ragged agitators to the police; the rest returned home disillusioned. The failure of this movement, discrediting Lavrovism,

dissipated some of the Populists' naive idealism. In 1876, a broader Populist organization, the second Land and Liberty, split mainly over terrorism. Moderates founded an organization and newspaper, *Black Repartition*, which repudiated terrorism and violence, but soon its leaders (Plekhanov, Deutsch, and Zasulich) fled abroad. An extremist, proterrorist element created the People's Will (*Narodnaia Volia*), based on ideas of Nechaev and Tkachev. Its secret Executive Committee plotted to assassinate the tsar and other high officials in order to disorganize the regime and trigger popular revolution. In March 1881, the People's Will murdered Alexander II. Within two years the police had destroyed it, breaking the revolutionary movement.

Before the 1860s few women engaged in revolutionary activity. Under Alexander II, female radicalism at first involved only individual defiance and participation in radical circles. Revolutionary proclamations of the 1860s mostly failed to mention women's rights. However, Zaichnevskii's pamphlet *Young Russia* (1862) demanded complete women's emancipation, civil and political equality, and abolition of marriage and the family. Becoming the Bible for Russian feminists and revolutionaries, Chernyshevskii's novel *What Is to Be Done?* described the development of Vera Pavlovna, the new socialist woman, who frees herself from family control and escapes an arranged marriage. Love and sexual fulfillment, she concludes, are less important for women than economic independence. The few women among Russian revolutionaries of the 1860s entered radical circles such as Ishutin's and workshops such as the Ivanova sisters' Dressmaking Shop in Chernyshevskii's novel where educated women and lower-class seamstresses lived, worked, and read radical authors together.

Women comprised about one-eighth of revolutionary Populists of the 1870s, reflecting a growing women's movement. As revolutionaries, women could achieve equality and occupy top leadership posts, achieving things undreamed of by traditional society. About one-third of the Executive Committee of People's Will was female; they were

---

[9]Named after Auguste Blanqui, a mid-19th-century French revolutionary who advocated armed insurrection and dictatorship by a revolutionary minority.

[10] Cited in Venturi, p. 412.

later incarcerated in the worst prisons alongside male terrorists. Vera Figner (1852–1942), a prominent People's Will leader, was an aristocratic woman who studied medicine and worked among the peasantry as a Bakuninist. Concluding that only violent revolution could overturn tsarism, she joined the Executive Committee and held People's Will together for two years after Alexander II's assassination. Betrayed to the police, she served 22 years' solitary confinement, then was exiled, returning to Soviet Russia after 1917. Another prominent revolutionary was Sofia Perovskaia, daughter of the St. Petersburg governor-general. As a leader of the Executive Committee, she prepared the tsar's assassination, placed the bomb throwers, and gave the signal. She was the first Russian female political prisoner to be hanged.

Women played a vital and growing role in the revolutionary movement, both in its Populist and Marxist phases. Setting examples of dedication to violent struggle, they created precedents for numerous women participants in the 1905 and 1917 revolutions. Wrote V. I. Lenin in 1918: "From the experience of all liberation movements, it can be noted that the success of revolution can be measured by the extent of women's involvement in it."[11]

Karl Marx, 1818–1883, founder of "scientific socialism."

economic trends. Some found the answer in Marxism, which attracted intellectuals and linked them with the new working class.

The Development of Marxism

By 1881 naive, idealistic intelligentsia elements had mostly been eliminated or discredited. The Populist movement lay in disarray. Urban-bred revolutionaries, still idealizing the peasantry, had not bridged the gulf in education, attitudes, and lifestyles with the rural masses. As economic conditions changed, an industrial working class emerged with more revolutionary potential. Alexander III's stifling autocracy, allied with rising business, heightened radical despair and isolation. Youth of the 1880s, dismayed by Populist defeats, searched for a new theory to explain disturbing

Fundamentals of Marxian Theory

Karl Marx (1818–1883), descended from Jewish rabbis, and Friedrich Engels (1820–1895), son of a wealthy German manufacturer, derived their cohesive theory of "scientific socialism" from many sources, weaving others' ideas ingeniously into a system to explain history. Their complex and sometimes contradictory theory embodied European ideas of progress and human perfectibility. Marx, the philosopher, and Engels, the publicist, formed a unique intellectual partnership. Owing much to the system of dialectical idealism of G. F. Hegel, an outstanding German philosopher, Marx accepted his method of reasoning (dialectic) and his belief that conflict of opposites and a resulting synthesis produces progress, unfolding in stages

---

[11] V. I. Lenin, *Polnoe sobranie sochinenii*, 5th ed. (Moscow, 1960), vol. 36, p. 186.

and culminating in perfection. Rejecting Hegel's conservative political and social views and his belief that ideas create reality, Marx adopted Ludwig Feuerbach's atheism and materialism: How people earn their daily bread determines their actions and outlook ("Man is what he eats"). Antagonistic social classes (such as bourgeoisie versus proletariat), affirmed Marx, contend over the means of production (land, factories, tools). Economic elements (means and relations of production), he argued, comprise society's substructure and basically determine its superstructure (government, law, religion, ideas). A person's economic and social status largely determines what he or she does, writes, and thinks. Nonetheless, Marx believed strongly in human dignity and the goal of freedom.

Applying their philosophy to history (historical materialism), Marx and Engels shared Hegel's view of human evolution by inexorable laws through a series of stages toward freedom. Each successive historical stage—primitive communism, slavery, feudalism, capitalism, and socialism—reflects a more mature form of production. Passage to the next stage results inevitably from conflict between a class owning the means of production (in capitalism, the bourgeoisie) and the one it exploits (proletariat). As one mode of production yields to a more advanced one and the exploited class achieves greater freedom, a new stage develops, usually by revolution.

Capitalism, explained Marx, is the historical stage in western Europe when the bourgeoisie (especially factory owners) exploits the proletariat. At first, with numerous small, competing firms, capitalism is revolutionary and dynamic, and unprecedentedly productive. However, the worker, the creator of value, receives in wages only a fraction of the value his labor creates; the capitalist pockets the rest ("surplus value") as profit. As weaker firms succumb, competitive capitalism will evolve into its opposite—monopoly. The industrial workforce will absorb much of the peasantry and lesser bourgeoisie until the proletariat becomes the vast majority of the population. As overpro-

duction and unemployment grow, so will worker dissatisfaction and class consciousness. Fully developed capitalism will produce mountains of goods, which miserably paid workers cannot buy.

Revolutions, predicted Marx, would occur first in advanced capitalist countries, led by communists—class-conscious workers and intellectuals, thus "the most advanced and resolute section of the working-class parties of every country . . . which pushes forward all others."[12] In 1848, Marx believed revolutions would mostly be violent because ruling capitalists and feudal lords would not yield wealth and power voluntarily, but they would be democratic as the vast oppressed majority would dispossess the few exploiters. In 1872, Marx declared there were countries, such as the United States, England, and perhaps Holland, where workers might achieve their goal peacefully. These differing views on the need for revolution would be reflected later in a split between European democratic socialists and Russian Bolsheviks.

After capitalism's collapse, a transitional era of unspecified length—the dictatorship of the proletariat (which Marx never defined clearly)—would prevail. Workers the world over would unite to cast off their chains and establish socialism everywhere. A workers' state would run the government and economy, distribute goods fairly to the people, and educate them in socialist values. Coercing only former exploiters, it would be more democratic than "bourgeois democracy" because it would represent the workers, the vast majority. Achieving its purposes, the workers' state—at least its coercive aspects—would wither away. Private property, class struggle, and exploitation would disappear, producing a perfect socialist order of abundance and freedom called *communism*. In 1875, Marx described this utopia:

> After the subordination of the individual to the division of labor, and therewith also the antithesis between mental and physical labor has vanished . . . ; after the productive forces

---

[12] K. Marx and F. Engels, *The Communist Manifesto* (New York, 1948), pp. 22–23.

have also increased with the all-round development of the individual, and all the springs of cooperative wealth flow more abundantly— only then can the narrow horizon of bourgeois right be crossed in its entirety and society inscribe on its banner: From each according to his ability, to each according to his needs![13]

Did Marxian theory, conceived for western Europe with its liberal, humanitarian traditions, apply to backward, autocratic Russia? Marx learned Russian, read Chernyshevskii, and corresponded with Russian socialists, but his views on Russia were uncertain and inconsistent. In 1877, he suggested that Russia could escape capitalism and move directly from feudalism to socialism *if* capitalist elements within the mir were eliminated and *if* proletarian revolutions erupted soon in western Europe. In 1881, anxious to see tsarism overthrown, Marx replied to Vera Zasulich, a leading Russian Populist, that he was convinced the mir would be "the mainspring of Russia's social regeneration," provided it could "eliminate the deleterious influences which assail it from every quarter."[14] However, after Marx's death Engels lamented that these conditions had not been fulfilled; Russia was doomed after all to undergo capitalism. On Russia, Marx and Engels proved to be hesitant Marxists.

From Das Kapital to What Is to Be Done?

In the 1870s Marxist ideas began circulating in Russia. The abstruse, technical *Das Kapital* (1867) and other nonpolitical Marxist works were published openly. In 1875, the first significant worker organization in Russia—the South Russian Workers' Alliance—opened in Odessa, but soon its leaders were arrested. Three years later, the Northern Alliance of Russian Workers, with more

than 200 active members, arose in St. Petersburg, but until the mid-1880s Russia had few Marxists and no Marxist movement.

George Plekhanov (1856–1918), of noble origin, "reared a whole generation of Russian Marxists," stated Lenin. Earlier, Plekhanov had sought to create scientific Populism while stressing the industrial workers' revolutionary potential. As editor of *Black Repartition*, the moderate Populist newspaper, he became discouraged by the failure of its agitation among the peasantry. In 1880 he fled into Swiss exile. Realizing that the Russian commune was disintegrating and industry was developing, Plekhanov in Geneva converted to Marxism, attracted by its orderliness and by Marx's claim to have discovered the laws of history. In Switzerland he, Paul Akselrod, and Vera Zasulich set up an independent Marxist group, the Liberation of Labor (1883), which for the next two decades acted as an embryo Russian social democratic party. Its members translated Marxist works and sent pamphlets into Russia; at first Russians remained apathetic. In *Our Differences* (1885), Plekhanov denounced the People's Will for urging terrorism and minority insurrection. As industry grew in Russia, he wrote: "We must recognize that in this sphere the present as much as the [near] future belongs to capitalism in our country." Like western Europe, Russia too must pass through capitalism to reach socialism; only the proletariat, sparked by the intelligentsia, could organize a true socialist revolution. He balanced between voluntarist and determinist aspects of Marxism: the proletariat needed knowledge and organization, but history's laws would surely bring defeat to the bourgeoisie. "The Social Democrats," he exulted, "are swimming along the current of history."

The Russian intelligentsia viewed Marxism and Populism as separate, competing movements. In 1885, a Bulgarian student, D. Blagoev, set up the first Marxist study group in Russia; soon these became popular among university students and workers. The 1891 famine, revealing peasant helplessness, stimulated Marxism's growth as younger intellectuals such as V. I. Ulianov, later known as Lenin, rejected Populism and turned to the work-

---

[13] Quoted in Robert Tucker, *The Marx-Engels Reader*, 2d ed. (New York, 1978), p. 531. For more on Marxism see R. N. Carew-Hunt, *The Theory and Practice of Communism* (New York, 1958) and *Marxism: Past and Present* (New York, 1954).
[14] Tucker, *Marx-Engels Reader*, p. 675.

ers. In St. Petersburg, a Central Workers Circle linked workers and Marxist intellectuals. In 1893, Ulianov, joining one of them, began an illustrious revolutionary career. Marxist literature then mostly stressed determinism: Capitalist development, undermining the mir, was proving Populism wrong. In 1895, major strikes in the textile industry revealed the workers' revolutionary energy and dispelled naive faith in Marxist study circles. However, many Marxist leaders, including Ulianov, were arrested and exiled to Siberia.

Some Russian Marxists, influenced by European currents, renounced revolution. Eduard Bernstein, a German Social Democrat, attacking some of Marx's main premises, claimed that socialism could be reached by gradual, democratic means. In Russia, Peter Struve and S. Bulgakov argued that capitalism would evolve gradually into socialism. The movement of Economism developed, stressing "spontaneous" development and peaceful agitation to encourage workers to demand economic benefits from employers. Many Russian workers seemed more interested in shorter hours and higher pay than in revolution. An attempt by Russian Marxist "politicals" to form a national social democratic party failed when leaders of the initial secret congress of the Social Democrats (SDs) of 1898 in Minsk were arrested.

Returning from exile, the youthful Lenin (Ulianov), insisting on the need for violent revolution to achieve socialism, helped reinvigorate Russian Marxism. Vladimir Ilich Ulianov had been raised in the disciplined, religious household of Ilia N. Ulianov, teacher and provincial school inspector, in Simbirsk on the mid-Volga River. At age three, Vladimir Ilich became a nobleman when his father, promoted to school superintendent, acquired hereditary nobility (his Soviet biographers omitted this fact). He and his older brother, Alexander, whom Vladimir greatly admired, were both top students and avid readers. In 1887, Alexander was executed for conspiring with remnants of the People's Will to assassinate Alexander III. His brother's death and Alexander's favorite author, Chernyshevskii, influenced Vladimir Ilich profoundly. Chernyshevskii's *What*

Vladimir Ilich Lenin (1870–1924), founder of the Bolshevik Party, leader of the Bolshevik Revolution (November 1917), and first Soviet leader.

Is to Be Done? convinced him that "strong personalities" impose their patterns on history. Admitted in 1887 to the law faculty of Kazan University, Ulianov was expelled months later after a student demonstration. After private study, he passed the bar examination in St. Petersburg and practiced law briefly in Samara. Though admiring dedicated members of the People's Will, his disciplined mind was attracted to Marxism, and by 1892 he had become a convert. In an early pamphlet, *Who Are the Friends of the People?* (1894), Ulianov attacked the Populists, insisting that Russia was irrevocably committed to capitalist development. This thesis emerged fully in his major work written in exile, *The Development of Capitalism in Russia* (1899), arguing that peasant differentiation into a rural proletariat and rural bourgeoisie (kulaks) proved the disintegrating peasant commune was doomed to disappear.

After his exile, Lenin along with Plekhanov became orthodox Marxism's chief spokesmen against revisionism. Restating Plekhanov, Lenin affirmed that revolution was absolutely essential in Russia and urged Social Democrats to lead an organized, class-conscious working class. Attacking the Economists' view that workers could develop cohesion spontaneously while improving their economic status, he argued that the working class by itself could develop only trade unionism. Marxists must provide conscious leadership, not trail behind the masses. In 1900, Lenin and Martov joined older émigrés of the Liberation of Labor (Plekhanov, Akselrod, and Zasulich) to found the newspaper *Iskra (The Spark)* in Stuttgart, Germany, to combat revisionism and consolidate Marxist ideology and organization. In its first issue, using his pseudonym for the first time, Lenin stressed active political work.

> The task of Social Democracy is to instill social democratic ideas and political consciousness into the mass of the proletariat and to organize a revolutionary party unbreakably tied to the spontaneous labor movement. . . . We must train people who will dedicate to the revolution not a free evening but the whole of their lives.

What Is to Be Done? (1902), a lengthy pamphlet derived from his lead articles for *Iskra*, contained Lenin's main ideas on the nature and organization of the party. In it he stressed the need for discipline and cohesive organization to combat the Russian autocracy.

> We are marching in a compact group along a precipitous and difficult path, firmly holding each other by the hand. We are surrounded on all sides by enemies, and we have to advance almost constantly under their fire.

Frequent use of military metaphors characterized the writings of Lenin and other Bolsheviks. Lenin argued that a small, centralized body of professional revolutionaries from the intelligentsia must serve as the vanguard of the working class in its struggle to achieve socialism. "Class political consciousness can be brought to the workers *only from without*." Lenin further defined the party:

> The organization of the revolutionaries must consist first and foremost of people who make revolutionary activity their profession. . . . Such an organization must perforce not be very extensive and must be as secret as possible.

With such a party, success would be assured: "Give us an organization of revolutionists and we will overturn the whole of Russia."[15]

Iskra's leaders moved to reorganize Russian social democracy. In July 1903, a Second Congress (the abortive 1898 Minsk meeting was designated the first) convened in Brussels, Belgium. Because *Iskra* controlled 33 of the 43 delegates, some with more than one vote, its program was mostly approved. After the congress was forced to move to London, a severe struggle developed within the *Iskra* group between Lenin and Martov over party membership and organization. Arguing for an elite party, Lenin insisted membership be limited to active participants in a party organization. Martov advocated a broad, mass party: "The more widely the title of party member is extended the better." That would inundate the party with opportunists, objected Lenin. Plekhanov, the party's elder statesman, sided with Lenin, but at first Martov's more democratic formula prevailed, 28 to 22. After the congress rejected the Jewish Bund's demand for autonomy, the Bundists walked out, soon joined by the defeated Economists. These walkouts, engineered by Lenin, gave his "hard" faction a majority of 2 over Martov's "softs." Lenin promptly dubbed his group Bolsheviks (majority men) and won a psychological edge over Martov's group, which meekly accepted the name Mensheviks (minority men). Lenin sought to exploit his slim majority to impose his views and make the party a centralized organization of professional revolutionaries. The Second Congress split the Social Democrats irreconcilably. Soon afterward, the Mensheviks took over *Iskra* and won a majority on the central committee. Less

---

[15] V. I. Lenin, *What Is to Be Done?* (New York, 1969), pp. 11, 78–79, 109.

disciplined and united than the Bolsheviks, the Mensheviks believed Russia's first revolution must be bourgeois and create a democratic republic. Menshevik differences with the Bolsheviks, at first over seemingly minor matters of party organization, widened steadily. Mensheviks favored a broad, democratic workers' party, not a narrow conspiratorial elite of intellectuals. In 1905, Akselrod, a leading Menshevik, urged Russian workers to form their own trade unions and party and draft their own program rather than accept dictation from professional revolutionaries like Lenin. As Bolsheviks and Mensheviks feuded and his former *Iskra* colleagues accused Lenin of dictatorial methods and of creating a state of siege within the SD party, young Leon Trotskii (Lev Bronstein), a brilliant polemicist and orator standing between the factions, sought to mediate their differences.

From Populism to the Socialist Revolutionaries

Populism recovered slowly from the demise of the People's Will. Populist ideologists of the early 1890s denounced capitalism, arguing it must never come to Russia. However, younger Populists, calling themselves Socialist Revolutionaries (SRs), agitated among new factory workers of peasant origin. In the capitals the Marxists outdid them, but in provincial centers the SRs won much support. Some Populist exiles returned, including Catherine Breshko-Breshkovskaia, known later as "the grandmother of the revolution."

In the 1890s, three centers of SR activity emerged. In 1896, the Union of Socialist Revolutionaries was founded in Saratov and won followers in the Moscow and Volga regions. *Our Tasks* (1898) proclaimed: "Propaganda, agitation, and organization . . . , such are the tasks of preparatory work at present." Emphasizing winning political freedom, it deferred revolution to an indefinite future. A southern element from Voronezh and the Ukraine advocated a constitution, agitation among the peasantry, strikes by agricultural workers, and boycotts against landlords. A third group, formed in Minsk by Breshko-Breshkovskaia and A. Gershuni, a young Jewish scientist, advocated terror as its chief weapon against autocracy. In 1900, an underground SR organization and newspaper, *Revolutionary Russia*, were set up in Kharkov. Two years later, elements from the various SR groups met in Berlin to establish the Socialist Revolutionary Party.

Its chief ideologist, Victor Chernov (1876–1952), an SR organizer in Tambov province, accepted some Marxist doctrines and recognized capitalist development in Russia. Urging SRs to agitate in factories and to include workers in "the people," Chernov admitted that the proletariat would lead the revolution against capitalism, but the peasantry would be "the fundamental army." In the new society, socialized enterprise in the towns would complement reorganized socialist rural communes. Like the Populists but unlike the Marxists, Chernov stressed free will, passion, and creativity, but he was ready to collaborate with Marxists and urban workers to overturn capitalism.

In contrast to the Social Democrats, the rapidly growing SR party never had a large or disciplined formal membership. Forming many local groups around various leaders, they propagandized vigorously among peasants and factory workers. Unlike their Populist forbears, SRs enjoyed considerable support from workers and white-collar people in provincial towns, though they remained peasant oriented. Never producing a truly outstanding leader, the SRs lacked the cohesion to link a massive peasant following with a town-bred intellectual leadership. Within the party, but actually independent, was the small, disciplined Combat Detachment, led by terrorists A. Gershuni and Evno Azev. Between 1902 and 1905, it assassinated two interior ministers, the Moscow governor-general, and other officials. Thus the tsarist police considered the SRs more dangerous than the more academic SDs.

On the Eve

On the eve of the 1905 Revolution, Russian liberalism, reinforced with former revolutionaries, became a vigorous, effective national movement seeking a national union of zemstva, a constitution, and civil liberties. At the turn of the century, Russian liberals acquired a press and a more cohesive political program. Liberal gentry set up Beseda, a private discussion group, including Slavophiles and constitutionalists. After 1896, zemstvo liberals of all shadings met irregularly to agitate for a national zemstvo union. In May 1902, the first congress of zemstvo officials—52 leaders from 25 provinces—met without official authorization at the home of D. N. Shipov, chairman of the Moscow provincial zemstvo board. This semilegal action set a pattern for liberals during 1905. The founding in 1902 in Stuttgart of the periodical *Osvobozhdenie* (*Liberation*), edited by Struve, with money from a Moscow landowner, established a militant liberal press organ. Adopting a radical constitutionalist line, it became almost as influential as Herzen's *Bell*. In 1903, a Union of Liberation, designed to unite the entire non-Marxist intelligentsia, was formed in Switzerland with many outstanding theorists and activists. In January 1904, its leaders, meeting privately in St. Petersburg, pledged to work to abolish autocracy, establish constitutional monarchy, and achieve universal, secret, and direct suffrage in equal constituencies—a "four-tailed" suffrage—for a national parliament. The Union's national council met regularly until the 1905 Revolution.

Before 1905, opposition movements developed greater cohesion and clearer programs. The liberals, led by pro-Western intellectuals such as Paul Miliukov, were supported by a growing professional middle class and some provincial zemstvo gentry. Generally agreeing on the need to overthrow the tsarist autocracy by force and establish a less rigidly centralized popular government, Russian socialists differed sharply over timing and means, how their parties should be organized, and which elements should constitute and lead them. The SRs, with an urban intellectual leadership and mainly peasant rank and file, opposed a Marxist workers' party, the SDs, itself split among Bolsheviks, Mensheviks, and smaller factions. Both liberal and radical opposition to the imperial regime was rising on the eve of the 1905 Revolution.

Suggested Additional Reading

ANDERSON, T. *Russian Political Thought* (Ithaca, NY, 1967).

ASCHER, A. *Pavel Axelrod and the Development of Menshevism* (Cambridge, MA, 1972).

BALABANOFF, ANGELICA. *My Life as a Rebel* (New York, 1938).

BARON, S. H. *Plekanov: The Father of Russian Marxism* (Stanford, CA, 1963).

BILLINGTON, JAMES. *Mikhailovsky and Russian Populism* (New York, 1958).

BYRNES, R. F. *Pobedonostsev: His Life and Thought* (Bloomington, IN, 1969).

CARR, E. H. *Mikhail Bakunin* (New York, 1961).

CHERNYSHEVSKY, N. G. *What Is to Be Done?* (New York, 1961).

DAN, FEDOR. *The Origins of Bolshevism*, trans. and ed. by Joel Carmichael (New York, 1970).

EMMONS, T. *The Russian Landed Gentry* (Cambridge, 1968).

ENGEL, B. A. *Mothers and Daughters: Women of the Intelligentsia of 19th Century Russia* (Cambridge, MA, 1983).

FIGNER, VERA. *Memoirs of a Revolutionist* (New York, 1927).

FISCHER, GEORGE. *Russian Liberalism* (Cambridge, MA, 1958).

FRÖHLICH, K. *The Emergence of Russian Constitutionalism, 1900–1904* (The Hague, 1982).

GELFMAN, ANNA. *Thou Shalt Kill: Revolutionary Terrorism in Russia, 1894–1917* (Princeton, NJ, 1993).

GETZLER, J. *Martov* (New York, 1967).

GLEASON, ABBOTT. *Young Russia: The Genesis of Russian Radicalism in the 1860s* (New York, 1980).

GOOD, JANE. *Babushka: The Life of the Russian Revolutionary Ekaterina K. Bresko-Breshkovskaia (1844–1934)* (Newtonville, MA, 1991).

GOTTLIEB, ROGER, S. *Marxism 1844–1990: Origins, Betrayal, Rebirth* (New York and London, 1992).

HAIMSON, LEOPOLD. *The Russian Marxists* . . . (Cambridge, MA, 1955).

HARE, RICHARD. *Pioneers of Russian Social Thought* (New York, 1964).

HERZEN, A. I. *My Past and Thoughts*, 6 vols. (New York, 1924–1928 and reprints).

KEEP, J. L. *The Rise of Social Democracy in Russia* (Oxford, 1963).

KROPOTKIN, PETER. *Memoirs of a Revolutionist* (New York, 1927 and reprints).

LAMPERT, E. *Sons Against Fathers* . . . (London, 1965).

———. *Studies in Rebellion* (London, 1957).

LANE, DAVID. *The Roots of Russian Communism* (University Park, PA, 1968).

LAVROV, P. L. *Historical Letters*, ed. J. Scanlan (Berkeley, CA, 1967).

MAXWELL, MARGARET. *Narodniki Women* (New York, 1990).

MILLER, MARTIN. *The Russian Revolutionary Émigrés, 1825–1870* (Baltimore, 1986).

OFFORD, DEREK. *The Russian Revolutionary Movement in the 1880s* (London and New York, 1986).

PIPES, RICHARD, ed. *The Russian Intelligentsia* (New York, 1961).

POMPER, PHILIP. *The Russian Revolutionary Intelligentsia* (New York, 1970).

———. *Sergei Nechaev* (New Brunswick, NJ, 1979).

RANDALL, F. N. *N. G. Chernyshevskii* (New York, 1967).

REESE, ROGER R. *The Soviet Military Experience: A History of the Soviet Army, 1917–1991* (New York, 1999).

SAKWA, RICHARD. *The Rise and Fall of the Soviet Union, 1917–1991* (New York, 1999).

SCHAPIRO, LEONARD. *Rationalism and Nationalism in Nineteenth Century Russian Thought* (New Haven, CT, 1967).

SEDDON, J. H. *The Petrashevtsy* . . . (Manchester, England, 1985).

SETON-WATSON, HUGH. *The Russian Empire 1801–1917* (Oxford, 1967).

THADEN, E. C. *Conservative Nationalism in Nineteenth Century Russia* (Seattle, 1964).

TIMBERLAKE, CHARLES, ed. *Essays on Russian Liberalism* (Columbia, MO, 1972).

TREADGOLD, DONALD. *Lenin and His Rivals, 1898–1906* (New York, 1955).

TURGENEV, IVAN. *Fathers and Sons*, trans. Constance Garnett (New York, 1950).

VENTURI, FRANCO. *Roots of Revolution* . . . *(New York, 1960)*.

WALICKI, A. *Marxism and the Leap to the Kingdom of Freedom: The Rise and Fall of the Communist Utopia* (Stanford, CA, 1995).

WILDMAN, A. K. *The Making of a Workers' Revolution* (Chicago, 1967).

WOLFE, BERTRAM. *Three Who Made a Revolution* (New York, 1964).

WORTMAN, RICHARD. *The Crisis of Russian Populism* (London, 1967).

YARMOLINSKY, A. *Road to Revolution* (London, 1957).

ZAIONCHKOVSKY, P. A. *The Russian Autocracy in Crisis, 1878–1882*, trans. and ed. G. M. Hamburg (Gulf Breeze, FL, 1979).

4

Revolution, Reaction, and Reform, 1905–1914

The decade 1905–1914 witnessed a crucial race in Russia between reform and revolution and alternating periods of radicalism and reaction. The major revolution, which erupted in 1905, brought masses of workers and peasants, under intelligentsia leadership, for the first time into a broad, popular movement against the autocracy. Although the revolution failed and was succeeded by ironhanded political reaction, the tsarist system was altered significantly. A semiconstitutional monarchy with a national parliament sought, albeit hesitantly, to grapple with Russia's perplexing problems. Important agrarian reform was undertaken, and industrialization resumed. While the armed forces were being reorganized and modernized, a weakened Russia sought simultaneously to recover prestige abroad and avoid conflict. By 1914, a measure of success seemed to have crowned these efforts. Partially industrialized Russia, though plagued by social turmoil, was moving ahead economically and maturing politically.

Why did the Revolution of 1905 break out? Why did it fail to overthrow tsarism? How genuine was the constitutional monarchy that suc-

ceeded unlimited autocracy? Was Russia in 1914 truly moving toward parliamentary government, prosperity, and social harmony or toward imminent, massive social revolution?

The Revolution of 1905

Historians differ widely over the meaning of the Revolution of 1905. Most Western scholars regard it, like the European revolutions of 1848, as a liberal-democratic movement in which workers and peasants acted largely spontaneously. Early Soviet accounts, such as Pokrovskii's, agreed, but Stalinist historians dramatized and glorified Bolshevik leadership of the proletariat in a "bourgeois-democratic revolution." Most scholars affirm that 1905 was the dress rehearsal for the greater 1917 revolutions because similar parties and mass elements participated, though with less cohesion and militancy in the first case.

Revolution occurred in 1905 because industrial workers, intellectuals, peasants, and ethnic minorities found their repressive, unresponsive government unbearable. Supporting the government, on the other hand, were a large and cohesive bureaucracy, a vast police network, the nobility, the church, and the army, but until Witte was returned to office (October 1905), the regime used these still powerful elements ineptly. The depression of 1900–1903 and bad harvests had brought hard times to Russia, and an increasingly articulate opposition sought political freedom, civil liberties, and social reform. Spurring the revolution were Japanese victories in the Far East, which discredited the government, eroded its prestige, inflated prices, and caused rising disaffection in the armed forces. Each setback in Asia reinforced dissatisfaction and opposition in European Russia.

The assassination (July 1904) of Interior Minister V. K. Pleve had removed the only dynamic government figure. Replacing him with the mild Prince Peter Sviatopolk-Mirskii, Nicholas II made minor concessions to the public. In Paris in October 1904, the Liberation movement and socialists agreed to agitate for the replacement of autocracy with a democratic regime based on universal suffrage, and by December most educated Russians were criticizing the regime. In many cities, political banquets were held similar to those before the Paris revolution of 1848.

The revolution began on "Bloody Sunday" (January 9, 1905). With police cooperation, the priest Father George Gapon had organized St. Petersburg factory workers to deflect them from revolutionary ideas. When news came of Port Arthur's fall, a strike of locomotive workers spread through the giant Putilov plant and several other St. Petersburg factories. Gapon urged the workers to petition the tsar to end the war, convene a constituent assembly, grant civil rights, and establish an eight-hour workday, all also goals of the Liberationists. On January 9, a snowy Sunday morning, Gapon led one of several columns of workers from various parts of the city toward the Winter Palace. The marchers—men, women, and children—bore icons, sang hymns, and clearly intended no violence. When they disregarded orders to halt, the tsar's uncle, Grand Duke Vladimir Aleksandrovich, ordered troops to fire on the crowd, and hundreds of the unarmed workers were slaughtered.

Bloody Sunday united the Russian people against the autocracy and undermined its faith in the tsar. During January, half a million workers struck, and assemblies of nobles and zemstva issued sharp protests. As students and professional people joined the workers, St. Petersburg became the center of nationwide agitation. Except for Socialist Revolutionary terrorists, however, there was relatively little violence. At their congress in March, the Liberationists demanded a constituent assembly, universal suffrage (including women), separation of church and state, autonomy for national minorities, transfer of state and crown lands to the peasants, an eight-hour workday, and the right to strike. Revolutionary socialists, mostly in exile, squabbling over tactics, played little part in this movement.

In May and June, the opposition organized, the strike movement expanded, and a naval mutiny erupted. Fourteen unions of professional people established the Union of Unions to coordinate their campaign for a constituent assembly. Paul Miliukov, head of the Union of Liberation, was elected its president, giving liberals in 1905 a unity that socialists and conservatives lacked. Although Bolsheviks and many Socialist Revolutionaries favored armed insurrection, other socialists cooperated with the Union. At the textile center of Ivanovo-Voznesensk, virtually the entire workforce struck, some 70,000 workers. Their strike committee, calling itself a soviet (council), took on governmental functions such as price regulation. On June 14, the crew of the new battleship *Potemkin* mutinied under a red flag and forced the government to deactivate the Black Sea Fleet.

Some minority nationalities of the Empire, notably in Russian Poland, the Baltic provinces, Finland, and the Caucasus, took uncoordinated but sometimes violent action during 1905, aiming chiefly to win autonomy within the Russian Empire. At the same time, Ukrainian nationalism emerged for the first time as a considerable force, combining intelligentsia and peasantry. In August 1905, Muslims organized politically at Nizhnii-Novgorod, demanding elimination of all legal discrimination against their faith.

Bloody Sunday (January 9, 1905) touched off the Revolution of 1905.
The demonstrators, led by Father Gapon, are attacked by the tsar's
cavalry in St. Petersburg.

Nicholas II's response to all this was to announce the Bulygin Duma (named after the new Minister of Interior, A. G. Bulygin), a consultative assembly to be elected by a limited suffrage favoring rural elements. It would be able to speak but not act, and autocracy would be preserved. This temporarily split the opposition three ways: zemstvo moderates favored participating in such elections, the Union of Unions urged a boycott and agitation for a constituent assembly, and revolutionaries advocated an armed uprising.

The spreading mass unrest forced greater governmental concessions. Peasant disorders grew in many regions. Radical demands by the Peasant Union, formed in July, revealed that contrary to official expectations, the peasantry had joined the opposition. The workers forced the government's hand: History's first general strike began spontaneously September 19 with a walkout by Moscow printers, who were then joined by bakers and factory workers. Spreading to St. Petersburg, the strike halted railroad, telegraph, and telephone service completely. In all Russia, only one newspaper, a conservative Kiev daily, was published, and in mid-October mobs controlled the streets of

leading cities. The workers' strike committee in St. Petersburg became a soviet and selected a 22-man executive committee under Leon Trotskii and a Menshevik, G. Khrustalev-Nosar.

Powerless to halt the strike, the regime fell into panic and virtual paralysis. Count Witte advised either a military dictatorship or a constitution. Unable to find a dictator and faced with general revolt in town and countryside, the tsar yielded. His October Manifesto (October 17 old style) promised a constitution, civil liberties, and a national parliament (Duma) elected by a broad suffrage without whose consent no bill was to become law. It also legalized most strikes and ended peasant redemption payments. Two days later, Nicholas revived the Council of Ministers, creating a unified executive branch, and named Witte premier. Nicholas was in despair because he had broken his pledge to maintain autocracy unaltered.

The tsar replaced reactionary ministers, but liberal leaders refused to join the government, and socialists and left liberals spurned the Manifesto. The two months after it was issued were the most disorderly of 1905. In those "days of free-

Bloody Sunday. Taking refuge behind a hastily assembled barricade,
the demonstrators fire on the tsar's troops.

dom," the St. Petersburg Soviet, coordinating a
growing soviet movement, decreed the end of
censorship, newspapers ignored censorship
restrictions, and the public began exercising rights
that the Manifesto had promised. In October and
November, rural violence reached its peak, and
national minorities agitated for autonomy or independence. Naval mutinies broke out at Kronstadt,
Vladivostok, and Sevastopol, and in November
postal and telegraph workers struck, touching
off new railroad strikes. Government troops suppressed peasant revolts and arrested the St.
Petersburg Soviet's leaders, but the Soviet, supported by the Peasant Union and the socialists,
proclaimed economic war against the regime and
called for another general strike. In December, the
Moscow Soviet led a weeklong armed workers'
rebellion, but it was suppressed after bitter street
fighting reminiscent of the Paris "June Days" of
1848; thousands of Moscow workers were shot or
deported. The regime had now recovered its
nerve, and after the Moscow Soviet called off its

faltering general strike, the Revolution gradually
subsided. Opposition newspapers were closed,
and the "days of freedom" ended.

Tsarism survived 1905 for reasons not present
in the fatal crisis of 1917. Quick and honorable
conclusion of the Russo-Japanese war in August
localized disaffection in the armed forces, and
mutinies were suppressed; most peasant soldiers
remained loyal. The timely political and economic
concessions of the October Manifesto satisfied
most moderates, isolated radical elements, and
divided advocates of social change from advocates
of political change. Many top revolutionaries were
in exile. Mass groups were uncoordinated and
lacked good leadership, and their protest movements peaked at different times. On the other
hand, the bureaucracy and police backed the
regime solidly. Finally, at a crucial time Witte
secured a large loan from France, which was anxious to prop up its ally, Russia, so it would not
have to face Germany alone. Nonetheless, the
Revolution of 1905 aroused the Russian people

Heller model 1:400 constructed by Bruce MacKenzie

The battleship *Potemkin,* named after Catherine II's influential favorite and launched in 1900, was the last Russian predreadnought ship to be built. Constructed in Nikolaev shipyard, it combined French and German designs. The *Potemkin* weighed 13,000 tons and was 378 feet long. The mutineers who took over the ship in June 1905 later surrendered to Romanian authorities.

politically and gave them a taste of freedom. The government restored order but not the awe it had formerly inspired in the masses. Tsarism had a last chance but under altered conditions.

Creation of the Duma Monarchy, 1905–1906

The most dangerous time for a bad government, noted the 19th-century French writer Alexis de Tocqueville, is when it begins to change for the better. Bloody Sunday had shattered the myth of the tsar as a benevolent, omniscient father. A new principle of political authority was needed, but as the revolution ebbed, Nicholas II salvaged most of his autocratic powers, fired Witte, and blocked creation of a true parliamentary regime. Further trouble portended between "society" and the government as the Manifesto's promises were hedged with restrictions, infuriating the left liberals and making them into defiant obstructionists.

Decrees and acts of the next six months laid the foundation for a regime satisfying neither side. To the liberals' dismay, an imperial manifesto of February 1906 created a bicameral legislature. (See Figure 4.1.) The hitherto wholly appointive State Council was reorganized as a conservative upper chamber, half of it appointed by the emperor, half of it elected by various social bodies (including zemstva, municipal dumas, the nobility, and universities). Though most males over the age of 25 could vote for deputies to the lower house, the State Duma, the electorate was divided into the traditional classes: landowners, peasants, and townspeople. A weighted, indirect franchise favored landowners and peasants and excluded many workers. It represented the belated realization of Speranskii's scheme of 1809,[1] not the "four-tailed" suffrage of liberal demands. The government expected the Duma to be a conservative assembly.

The Duma's powers were very limited. Russia's constitution, the Fundamental Laws of April 1906, described the emperor now as "autocrat" instead of "unlimited autocrat." He retained power to declare war and appoint and dismiss ministers of

---

[1] As chief adviser to Alexander I, M. Speranskii proposed comprehensive political reforms to give Russia representative bodies and the rule of law.

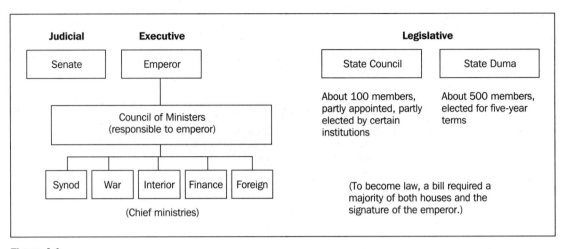

Figure 4.1
Russian Imperial Government (1906–1917)

state, who were responsible to him alone. Duma members could question ministers, but the latter did not have to give satisfactory replies, and the crown retained all powers not specifically given to the legislature. To become law, a measure had to pass both houses, and the emperor retained absolute veto power. Article 87 of the Fundamental Laws further restricted Duma authority by authorizing ministers to govern by decree during Duma recesses, provided the Duma approved such decrees subsequently. The Duma's ability to obstruct the executive was slight because the emperor determined the duration of its sessions and could prorogue it at will if he set a date for new elections. The Duma could not overturn the ministry nor revise the Fundamental Laws, and its control of the purse was severely restricted. (It had no control over court expenses and little over the army or state debt.) Could any legislature operate effectively under such limitations?

Amid continuing revolutionary disturbances, the electoral campaign for the First Duma began in December 1905. Excitement and expectancy gripped Russia as for the first time political parties, though still not legal, contended in national elections. (See Table 4.1) The SRs, deciding at their first open congress in Finland to boycott the elec-

tions and promote violent revolution, demanded socialization of the land, its issuance to peasants on the basis of need, and a federal system with full national self-determination for non-Russians. At their Fourth Congress in Stockholm (spring 1906), the SDs restored surface unity, but serious Bolshevik–Menshevik differences persisted. Initially most SDs favored boycotting the elections, but then the Mensheviks decided to participate. Arguing that Bolsheviks could use the Duma to denounce tsarism, Lenin shocked his colleagues by voting with the Mensheviks. As revolutionary parties scarcely competed in the elections, peasants voted mostly for the Trudovik (Labor) group, largely SR in ideology but peaceful in tactics. Among the nonrevolutionary parties, the most radical was the Constitutional Democrats (Kadets, KD), ably led by Miliukov and Struve from the Union of Liberation and Petrunkevich from the zemstva. Abandoning temporarily their call for a constituent assembly, the Kadets campaigned for full parliamentary rights for the Duma, alienation of large estates with compensation, and more rights for labor. The Octobrist Party, led by A. I. Guchkov, representing moderate zemstvo leaders, business, and liberal bureaucrats, accepted the October Manifesto. Aiming to strengthen constitutional

Table 4.1 Russian political parties and programs, 1905–1917

Party	Program
RSDLP (Social Democrats), 1898. Splits 1903 into:	Marxist (overthrow of tsarism; establishment of a workers' state)
1. Bolsheviks (majority faction)	1. Stress violent revolution
2. Mensheviks (minority faction)	2. Orthodox Marxists; move toward nonviolent, parliamentary socialism
SRs (Socialist Revolutionaries), 1900	Peasant socialism (violent overthrow of tsarism; establishment of federal state; confiscation of estates without compensation)
KD (Constitutional Democrats), 1905	Liberal-democratic (constitutional monarchy or a republic; all civil rights; ministerial responsibility; land reform)
Trudoviks (Labor faction), 1906	Radical groups favor drastic land reform; national autonomy for minority peoples; civil liberties
Octobrists, 1905	Conservatives (program of "October Manifesto"; limited monarchy; mild reform; rule of law)
United Nobility, 1906	Faction or pressure group to promote noble interests; mainly conservative
Union of the Russian People, 1905	Extreme conservatives ("orthodoxy, autocracy, and nationalism"; racist)

monarchy and civil liberties, it opposed real land reform and national self-determination. The extreme Right, especially the ultranationalist Union of the Russian People, denounced the Duma and the Jews and demanded restoration of unlimited autocracy.

The election revealed Russia's radical mood and dismayed the government. The Kadets (180 seats) with their allies organized and dominated the First Duma, and the peasant Trudoviks had about 100 deputies. There were 18 Menshevik Social Democrats, 17 Octobrists, 15 extreme Rightists, and about 100 deputies from national and religious minorities.

In the Winter Palace's elegant St. George's room, the tsar opened the First Duma on May 10, 1906. He, his court, and ministers, magnificent and bejeweled, occupied one side of the hall. Opposite sat the staid State Council, and behind them crowded the 500 Duma delegates: bearded peasants, Mensheviks in worker blouses, and minority groups in national costume. The contrast between the elite and popular representatives resembled that at the French Estates-General of 1789. In a brief, colorless "Address from the Throne," Nicholas II, like Louis XVI, gave the legislature no directives.

Organizing the Duma, the Kadets elected one of their own, Sergei Muromtsev, as speaker. Their reply to the tsar's "Address" demanded fully democratic suffrage, abolition of the State Council as an upper house, ministerial responsibility to the Duma, and amnesty for all political prisoners, but Nicholas and his ministers refused such exorbitant demands. Obsessed by European precedents and blind to Russian realities, Miliukov spurned compromise. I. L. Goremykin, the faded and servile bureaucrat who had replaced Witte as premier, responded for the tsar that the Duma's requests were all "inadmissible." The Duma promptly declared no confidence in the government, which simply ignored it. Because the Kadets failed to use existing Duma powers, vital issues such as land reform, minority rights, and education were neglected. Secret Duma discussions with the tsar on a Kadet or coalition ministry proved fruitless. The Kadets' doctrinaire approach, the pressure of P. A. Stolypin on the tsar, and Nicholas's suspicion doomed the First Duma and ultimately the constitutional experiment. When the Duma appealed directly to the public on the land question, Nicholas dissolved it without ordering new elections.

The Kadets responded with illegal defiance. When troops closed the Duma, some 180 delegates, mostly Kadets and Trudoviks, went to Vyborg, Finland, where Muromtsev proclaimed it reconvened. Miliukov drew up the Vyborg Manifesto, which urged Russians not to pay taxes or supply army recruits until the Duma met again, but there was little public response and the Manifesto's signers were tried, jailed briefly, and disfranchised. Losing many talented leaders, the Kadets never fully recovered their political leadership.

Originally dedicated to promoting the broad, liberal development of Russia into a parliamentary democracy, the Kadets gradually became a narrower party of the professional middle class confined largely to towns and increasingly suspicious of the masses. After 1906, the Kadets began to hedge on their democratic aims, tending to prefer constitutional monarchy. To many workers and peasants the Kadets were "bourgeois," a party favoring gradual change while preserving upper-class privilege and social order.

After the Duma's dissolution, Stolypin, since July 1906 premier and minister of the interior, made frequent use of Article 87, which allowed the executive to rule by decree. This last statesman of imperial Russia dominated the political scene for the next five years. Stolypin, a well-to-do landowner, had been a provincial marshal of nobility who in 1905, as governor of Saratov province, had ruthlessly repressed peasant disorders. He was an impressive orator, thoroughly convinced of his rectitude, who favored bold measures and strong-arm tactics. A Russian nationalist, Stolypin viewed repression as the prelude to reform by an enlightened autocracy. Proclaiming a state of emergency, he instituted field courts-martial against SR terrorists, who were killing hundreds of police, priests, and officials. By the spring of 1907, the trials had effectively broken the revolutionary movement.

To the government's chagrin, the short-lived Second Duma (February–June 1907) was more extreme and less constructive than the first. Both SDs and SRs participated in the elections, but Stolypin declared leftist parties illegal and forbade their campaign literature. Almost half those elected were socialists, but they failed to form a bloc and disdained collaboration with the Kadets, who had lost ground. The Duma debated Stolypin's agrarian reforms (see pp. 74–75) heatedly, then refused to approve them. Violent SD attacks on the army infuriated the tsar who, urged on by the Union of the Russian People, dissolved the Duma. The first constitutional phase ended in complete deadlock between the Duma and the executive.

Political Development, 1907–1914

Stolypin's decree of June 1907, dubbed a coup d'état, altered the original electoral laws arbitrarily to produce a Duma "Russian in spirit." Declared Stolypin: "We don't want professors, but men with roots in the country, local gentry, and the like." Blatantly violating the Fundamental Laws, his measure ensured that subsequent elections would be far from democratic. The government reduced peasant representation drastically, guaranteeing that noblemen would choose almost half the electors: Non-Russians lost most of their seats. Only about 2.5 percent of the population voted for the Third Duma, in which the Octobrists emerged as the largest party, the Right was greatly strengthened, and the Kadets were further weakened. On the Left, Trudoviks and Social Democrats each had 14 deputies. This "Masters' Duma" proved so satisfactory to the government that it was allowed to serve out its full five-year term. Though the State Council blocked many progressive laws, the Duma nonetheless approved Stolypin's agrarian reforms, promoted universal education, extended local self-government and religious freedom, and expanded its control of the budget. Even the Third Duma marked an advance over the Pobedonostsev era: All political points of view were represented, political parties operated openly, and newspapers debated public issues. Whenever possible, the Duma protected and broadened civil liberties by drawing public attention to government abuses.

Outwardly, the Fourth Duma (1912–1917), more than half noblemen, seemed still more conservative. The strengthening of Right and Left at the expense of the political center revealed dangerous political polarization, but even many conservative deputies defended the Duma and observed parliamentary forms. The Duma's tragedy, notes Thomas Riha, was that "too few were learning too slowly" in a political oasis far from the masses. The government often treated it as a mere department, and the emperor, until dissuaded by his ministers, considered making the Duma merely advisory.

Non-Russian elements were strongly represented in the First Duma of 1906. There were 51 Polish deputies united in a Polish Circle, about 40 Ukrainian nationalists, and 30 Muslims, most of whom cooperated with the Kadets. Under this pressure the imperial government restored the Finnish Diet as a single chamber of 200 members elected for a three-year term by a system of proportional representation and virtual universal suffrage of both sexes. Finland thus became the first country in eastern Europe to grant the vote to women.

From this atmosphere of reluctant concessions to the nationalities by a beleaguered imperial regime in 1905, their situation deteriorated sharply during the years 1907–1914. They faced a conservative imperial government and hostility by most of the Russian people. Polish schools reverted to their pre-1905 Russified condition and the Ukrainian nationalist movement was subjected to vigorous repression. Baltic Germans were favored by the Russian regime, whereas other Baltic peoples (Estonians, Latvians, and Lithuanians) were suppressed. A law of the Russian Duma in 1910 reduced the Finnish Diet to the status of a provincial assembly before dissolving it altogether; Fin-

land was then governed dictatorially by decree as an occupied and hostile country. Simultaneously, persecution of the Jews was intensified. The policies of the Russian imperial government generally alienated most national minorities completely, preparing the way for their common revolt against Russian rule in 1917–1918.

Until late in 1911, Stolypin ran the executive branch capably, if high-handedly. He used Article 87 to bypass the legislature whenever it obstructed his measures. At first he enjoyed Nicholas II's confidence and support; later he offended the imperial family. In September 1911, Stolypin was assassinated in the Kiev opera house by a double agent who received a ticket from the chief of police! Succeeding him as premier was Finance Minister V. N. Kokovtsov, who was able and moderate but lacked his predecessor's independence and dynamism. In late 1913, the emperor removed him under pressure from the empress and Grigori Rasputin, whose influence Kokovtsov had consistently opposed. The aged and incompetent Goremykin replaced him.

The revolutionary movement, though plagued by police infiltration, recovered somewhat after 1912 from its eclipse under Stolypin. The SRs were appalled by the exposure of Evno Azev, head of their Combat Detachment, as a police agent. Arrests and double agents also weakened the SDs. According to Trotskii, Bolshevik membership had shrunk to 10,000 in 1910. Early in 1914, Roman Malinovskii, Bolshevik leader in the Duma, was exposed as a police spy. Abroad, Lenin maintained his own organization and blocked efforts to reunite the party. In 1912, he convened a conference in Prague and set up a separate Bolshevik party. Later that year the so-called August Bloc under Martov and Trotskii held a separate Menshevik conference, and in 1913 separate Menshevik and Bolshevik factions were formed in the Duma. The Bolsheviks retained their revolutionary fervor while the Mensheviks tried to create a legal, trade-union-oriented labor movement run by the workers themselves.

How were the Bolsheviks faring in 1914? Some Western accounts, emphasizing their demoralization, cite declining circulation of *Pravda* (their party newspaper), Lenin's isolation in SD ranks, a small, weak party in Russia, and loss of popularity among Russian workers. Only the outbreak of World War I, claims British scholar Leonard Schapiro, prevented the Bolsheviks' demise. A Soviet source, however, asserts that by July 1914 the Bolsheviks had the support of four-fifths of Russian workers and were leading a militant strike movement in St. Petersburg.[2] Leopold Haimson, an American historian, agrees that Bolsheviks were outdoing Mensheviks in the capitals because their revolutionary program and tactics appealed to many new workers. Bolshevik success, if success it was, reflected worker militancy more than skillful, perceptive leadership.

Economic and Social Development

Important economic and social change occurred between 1906 and 1914. Industrial growth was lifting Russia out of backwardness, and the Stolypin agrarian reforms were creating a basis for a new class of independent farmers. Social inequality was lessening as workers and peasants obtained higher incomes, greater mobility, and more rights.

Stolypin agreed with the socialists that a communal peasantry was potentially revolutionary. His government's aim, therefore, was to abolish the mir (peasant commune), free the peasant from it, and foster individual farming. Stolypin explained to the Duma in 1908: "The government has put its wager not on the drunken and the weak but on the sober and the strong—on the sturdy individual proprietor."[3] In November 1906, he decreed after the First Duma that in communes without a general repartition since 1882, a householder could claim ownership of all plow land worked in 1906. In case of a repartition, he could

demand land held before 1882, plus land received in a repartition provided he paid the commune the original redemption price. This policy encouraged peasants to shift from repartitional to hereditary tenure. The law of June 1910 dissolved all communes with no general repartition since 1861. After one peasant in such a commune applied for an ownership deed, all land in it became private. In repartitional and hereditary communes, the head of the household received ownership of the land, a policy that encouraged or even forced younger males to go to the city. Stolypin's ultimate objective was consolidation of scattered strips into Western-style farms.

How successful were these land reforms? Stolypin stressed the need for 20 years of peace to implement them, but they were halted in 1915. Though the government appointed many surveyors and exerted great pressure, results were inconclusive. By 1915, more than half of Russian peasant households had hereditary ownership of their allotments, but less than 10 percent were fully consolidated individual farms.[4] Agricultural techniques and output improved considerably on such farms, but village collectivism, though weakened, remained prevalent. Many communes, supposedly dissolved by the law of 1910, never were. After a big initial push, state enforcement lagged. Thus, in 1917, most Russian peasant households still lived in the traditional mir.

Who benefited from the reforms? According to Soviet accounts, only a minority of wealthy peasants. Stolypin sought to end strip farming and carry through an agricultural revolution, reply recent Western accounts. Viewing the process as a race against time, Lenin feared that Stolypin's reforms would transform the dissatisfied peasantry,

---

[2] *History of the Communist Party of the Soviet Union* (Moscow, 1960), pp. 169–170.

[3] Cited in M. Florinsky, *Russia: A History and an Interpretation* (New York, 1953), *vol. II, p. 1220.*

[4] In 1915, of some 14 million peasant allotments, some 5 million remained under repartitional tenure. About 1.3 million were subject to automatic dissolution but had not actually been dissolved, and 1.7 million had been affected to some degree. About 4.3 million holdings had fully hereditary title in scattered strips, and more than 1.3 million had been partially or completely consolidated into farms. Geroid T. Robinson, *Rural Russia* (New York, 1949), pp. 215–216.

upon which he counted in the future, into a class of loyal, conservative peasant proprietors.

The government encouraged colonization of Siberia to absorb dispossessed younger peasants and to increase farm output. About half of Siberian wheat was exported abroad or to other parts of Russia. Siberia, however, lacking a local nobility, promoted rugged individualism and a bourgeois ethos that distressed conservatives. After a visit in 1910, Stolypin called Siberia "an enormous, rudely democratic country which will soon throttle European Russia."[5] The government also promoted peasant land purchases through the Peasant Bank. In 1914, the European Russian peasantry owned more than four times as much land as the nobility (460 to 108 million acres). The vast state and imperial holdings (390 million acres) were mostly unsuited to agriculture. By 1917, most Russian crop land was already in peasant hands.

After 1905, significant industrial progress occurred, though the government did not promote it with Witte's single-minded determination. The economy now was more mature, and the official role less marked. The Finance Ministry, despite creation of a separate Ministry of Trade and Industry, still controlled the keys to industrial development but used them more cautiously. Finance Minister Kokovtsov (1906–1913), stressing balanced growth, sought to maintain the gold standard and a high tariff to uphold Russia's foreign credit and to balance the budget. Thanks to a spurt in new railroad building, the growth rate almost equaled that of the Witte period. Excellent harvests, large exports, and wider prosperity enhanced Russia's overall economic performance, although in 1914 it still had the lowest per capita wealth of the major powers and its industry trailed that of England, Germany, the United States, and France.[6] Industrial progress now, instead of impoverishing the population, was combined with agricultural growth and modest prosperity. Russia had overcome its backwardness, claimed Kokovtsov, and only the Bolshevik Revolution interrupted its "swift and powerful development."

The geographical distribution of Russian industry changed little, but consolidation and foreign ownership increased. In 1912, the central industrial region produced more than one-third of all manufactures, followed by the Ukraine, the northwest, and the Urals. In manufacturing, the largest labor force was in metalworking, cottons, and other textiles. Soviet accounts stress that foreign interests initiated most industrial combinations in this "era of imperialism." In 1902, French capitalists fostered creation in southern Russia of Prodameta, a metallurgical cartel; by 1910, its member firms produced about three-fourths of the empire's iron products and almost half its rails. The Duma, however, prevented it from becoming a full-fledged trust, a circumstance that revealed big industry's limited influence in imperial Russia. Other combinations formed in sugar (1887) and oil (1904). Foreign influence and investment in Russian industry were considerable, but Soviet claims that Russia had become a semicolonial appendage of Western capitalism seem exaggerated. A tsarist source estimated foreign investment in Russia in 1916 at 2,243 million rubles, more than half of it in mining, metallurgy, and metalworking, with the French holding almost one-third of this total, followed by the British, Germans, and Belgians.

Railroad construction remained the key to Russian industrial booms. The 6,600 miles of line built between 1902 and 1911 triggered an annual industrial growth rate of almost 9 percent between 1909 and 1913 and overall economic growth of about 6 percent annually between 1906 and 1914. Private railroad lines were more efficient, but the state owned about two-thirds of the network; rising revenues from its lines enabled the government to pay interest on railroad loans and still have a surplus. Nonetheless, in 1914, Russia's external debt (5.4 billion rubles) was one of the world's largest.

---

[5]Cited in Florinsky, *Russia.*
[6]In total volume of industrial production in 1913, France exceeded Russia 2.5 times, England 4.6, Germany 6, and the United States 14.3. P. Liashchenko, *History of the Russian National Economy* (New York, 1949), p. 674.

Russia's foreign trade increased considerably in volume, but its direction and structure changed little. In 1913, exports were worth more than 1.5 billion rubles, and imports nearly 1.4 billion. Russia still exported mostly agricultural goods: grain, 44 percent, livestock and forest products, 22 percent). Industrial exports (10 percent) went mostly to backward Asian lands. Germany bought about 30 percent of Russian exports and supplied 47 percent of its imports; Britain stood second with 17.5 percent and 13 percent, respectively.

The empire's population rose by almost one-third between 1897 and 1913, to more than 165 million (excluding Finland). Mainly responsible were a birthrate much higher than in western Europe and a declining death rate. The east had the highest growth rates, but three-fourths of the population resided in European Russia. Despite industrialization and urban growth, cities in 1913 contained only 16 percent of the population.

Russian society in 1914, undergoing transition and with numerous inequities and frictions, remained dominated by a nobility that guarded its privileges jealously against the bourgeoisie. Impoverished lesser gentry were selling their lands rapidly, but large landowners retained much wealth and strengthened their influence at court. After 1906, a pressure group, the Council of the United Nobility, protected their interests. Within the Church, the elite black (monastic) clergy remained in control and blocked needed reform. In an expanding bourgeoisie, Moscow entrepreneurs led the commercial and industrial elements; St. Petersburg remained the financial center. Outside the capitals, the bourgeoisie was often cautious and stodgy and engaged mainly in local trade and industry. Within the Russian middle class, liberal professions exceeded industrial and commercial elements in numbers and influence.

Among the peasantry, slow differentiation was speeded somewhat by the Stolypin reforms, but the mass of middle peasantry was still growing numerically. There were tensions in the village between an upper crust of kulaks and proletarian and semiproletarian elements, but the basic rural rivalry pitted peasant against noble. Peasant isola-tion was diminishing, and with freedom of movement gained after 1906, many younger peasants migrated to the cities. Peasant inferiority and poverty were lessening, but remained potential dangers to the regime.

Far from suffering increasing misery, as Marx had predicted, Russian industrial workers after 1905 found their status and economic position improving. Sharply reduced summertime departures for the village revealed growth of a largely hereditary proletariat. By 1914, more than 3 million workers labored in mines and factories, about one-half in enterprises with over 1,000 employees. Such large factories enhanced worker consciousness and solidarity and facilitated agitation by socialists and union organizers. Real wages rose considerably, but still lagged far behind those in western Europe because of a plentiful labor supply and low labor productivity. Increasingly unionized skilled and semiskilled workers were now usually paid enough to maintain a normal family life. Working conditions were also improving. After 1912, the 10-hour day prevailed, accident and sickness compensation, partly paid by employers, was instituted, and factory inspection increased. Theoretically legalized in 1905, strikes remained virtually prohibited, and unions were barred from organizing public meetings. Strikes were few in 1907–1910, but an industrial revival and a massacre of workers in the British-owned Lena goldfields (April 1912) sparked a resurgence: some 700,000 workers struck in 1912, 900,000 in 1913, and about 1.5 million in the first half of 1914. St. Petersburg metalworkers, the most literate, highest paid workers, were also the most militant.

Wage levels and living conditions, bad enough for working men, remained far worse for women, who generally received only about two-thirds the pay of males. Many working women remained below a normal subsistence level as conditions in small sweatshops were appalling and unregulated. Nonetheless, the poorly educated working women in tsarist Russia were mostly docile and obedient and proved difficult to organize in unions or politically. Women's education and literacy lagged far behind that of men: In 1903–1905, only 13.7

percent of Russian women were literate, compared with 32.6 percent of men.

No genuine Russian women's movement emerged until the 1905 Revolution, which brought women consciousness and organization but few tangible benefits. Two separate movements developed: a feminist women's suffrage organization and a socialist movement sharply opposed to it in methods and goals. Early in 1905, the feminist All-Russian Union for Women's Equality was formed, seeking "freedom and equality before the law without regard to sex." Centering in St. Petersburg, it developed branches all across Russia. In April in the capital, the first political meeting for women in Russian history convened, drawing about 1,000 people and laying a basis for the Union's first congress in Moscow in May. The Union demanded an immediate constituent assembly elected without distinctions of sex, nationality, or religion; equality of the sexes under law; protection of women workers; and equal educational opportunity for women at every level. In July it joined the Union of Unions. During and after 1905, the feminist movement focused on the issue of women's suffrage, which was denied by the October Manifesto but supported increasingly by liberal and radical political parties. However, in 1908, under pressure of political reaction, the Women's Union collapsed as antagonism escalated between feminists and socialists. In 1910, feminist activity revived around the weekly *Women's Cause*. The largest feminist organization in Russia had under 1,000 members by 1917, minuscule compared to the West. Most feminists came from the middle class and were led chiefly by nongentry university graduates. Confronting powerful foes on left and right, Russian feminism failed to persuade the Duma to give women the vote.

Also emerging from the 1905 Revolution was a small women's socialist movement, which encountered hostility or indifference from male workers and most Social Democratic leaders. Its outstanding leader was Alexandra Kollontai, born in 1872, an energetic nonconformist who began as a Populist before becoming a Marxist follower of Plekhanov. The Revolution of 1905 turned Kollontai into a dedicated revolutionary who wrote and distributed socialist literature, raised money, and marched with workers. Women and their fate had occupied her entire life, she recalled later. Finding support in the Union of Textile Workers, mostly women, she gave Marxist lectures and organized public meetings that emphasized the themes of exploitation and social liberation. After spending the years of reaction abroad, Kollontai returned to lead a revival of the women's socialist movement (1912–1914), remaining its chief link with the European International Socialist Women's Movement. In March 1913, Kollontai promoted the first celebration of International Women's Day in Russia.

Foreign Affairs, 1906–1914

Defeat in the war with Japan, the 1905 Revolution, and indebtedness restricted Russia's freedom of action abroad, and dreams of an expanded Asian empire lay shattered. Settling outstanding disputes in the Far and Near East, Russia concentrated again on Europe and the Balkans in an effort to regain lost prestige. The Foreign Ministry's task was to prevent exploitation of Russia's military weakness by other powers. Until 1914, it averted disaster by repeated diplomatic retreats under German pressure.

In the Far East, relations between Russia and Japan were transformed as Russian leaders learned from their defeat. Both powers were anxious to protect their mainland interests and moved toward partnership. The United States' Open Door policy, an apparent screen for economic penetration of Manchuria, fostered a series of Russo-Japanese agreements. In 1910, Russia recognized Japan's special interests in Korea and south Manchuria in return for Japan's pledge to respect Russian domination of northern Manchuria and Outer Mongolia. Russia encouraged Mongolia to escape Chinese control; in 1912, it proclaimed its "independence" and became de facto a Russian protectorate. On the eve of World War I, Russia's position in the Far East was secure.

Powerful imperial Germany absorbed much of Russia's attention. In 1904–1905, William II, to undermine the Franco-Russian Alliance, had offered the tsar the defensive Björkö Treaty. Although the naive tsar signed it, Foreign Minister Lamsdorf and Count Witte persuaded him to ignore it and stick to Russia's alliance with France. When Germany sought to humiliate France in Morocco (1905–1906), Russia backed France loyally at the Algeciras Conference in return for a large French loan. The French alliance remained the cornerstone of Russian foreign policy until the end of the empire, and growing German military and naval strength fostered rapprochement between Russia and England. German leaders believed that Anglo-Russian imperial rivalries were insoluble, but Japan's defeat of Russia caused London to abandon fears of Russian expansionism. The friendship of Russia and England with France encouraged the British Liberal cabinet, realizing that it could not defend Persia, to seek agreement with Russia. Foreign Secretary Lord Grey wrote: "An entente between Russia, France, and ourselves would be absolutely secure. If it is necessary to check Germany, it could then be done."[7]

Serious obstacles had to be overcome on the Russian side. Foreign Minister Alexander Izvolskii (1906–1910), who reasserted his ministry's role (sometimes rashly), had to neutralize pro-German feeling at court and overcome the old Turkestan military men who coveted all of Persia. The Anglo-Russian Convention of August 1907 left Afghanistan and Tibet in the British sphere, while unfortunate Persia was partitioned into a British sphere in the southeast and a huge Russian zone in the north, separated by a neutral area. Anglo-Russian rivalry in Persia continued, but became tolerable and peaceful. By 1914, Russia dominated most of it, but England accepted this as the price of containing Germany.

Izvolskii hoped that Britain would now assist him to revise the Straits Convention to let Russian warships pass through the Bosporus, but he was disappointed. His interest in the Straits coincided with Austria's more dynamic Balkan policies. Conrad von Hötzendorf, Austrian chief of staff, wished to crush Serbia by preventive war, while Alois von Aehrenthal, the Foreign Minister, aimed to annex Bosnia and Herzegovina, which Austria had occupied since 1878. (See Map 4.1.) At Buchlau (September 1908), Aehrenthal and Izvolskii agreed that Russia would support their annexation by Austria in return for Austrian backing to revise the Straits Convention. Austria annexed Bosnia and Herzegovina, but Izvolskii could not win the other power's consent on the Straits question. Angered by Austria's absorption of two Serbian-speaking provinces, Serbia demanded territorial compensation, but because Germany backed Austria, Russia dared not support Serbia's claims. Russia and Serbia had to back down before the German powers. The Bosnian crisis discredited Izvolskii and gave warning of a general war over the Balkans.

Succeeding Izvolskii as foreign minister was S. D. Sazonov (1910–1916), a conscientious diplomat who lacked firm control over his subordinates. As Pan-Slav tendencies revived, Russian consuls N. G. Hartvig in Belgrade and A. Nekliudov in Sofia advocated a forward policy. In 1912, with their warm encouragement, a Balkan League of Serbia, Bulgaria, Montenegro, and Greece was formed. In October, disregarding official Russian and Austrian warnings, the League attacked Turkey and conquered Macedonia. Austria, however, blocked Serbia's aspiration to Adriatic ports, and Russia yielded again to German threats. In a second Balkan war of 1913, Bulgaria, seeking control of Macedonia, attacked the Serbs and Greeks, but they, aided by Romania and Turkey, defeated Bulgaria and seized Bulgarian Macedonia. This victory smashed the Balkan League, turned embittered Bulgaria toward the Central Powers (Germany, Austria-Hungary, and Italy), and damaged Russian prestige. Serbian nationalism intensified further as the Austrian military awaited an opportunity to crush Serbia completely.

In the Balkans before 1914, Russian and Austrian imperialism clashed and Russo-German

---

[7] Memorandum of February 20, 1906, cited in A. J. P. Taylor, *The Struggle for Mastery in Europe, 1848–1918* (Oxford, 1954), pp. 441–442.

Map 4.1 Russia and the Balkans, 1912–1914

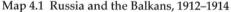
Countries with Austrian and German influence against Russia
Russia's Balkan allies

tension was sometimes severe, but war between Russia and the Central Powers was far from inevitable. Russo-German friction over the Berlin-to-Baghdad Railway and over German attempts to dominate the Straits was settled peacefully. The Romanovs remained pro-German, supported by the Duma Right, which sought to buttress autocracy against Western liberal parliamentarism.

Suggested Additional Reading

BOCK, MARIA. *Reminiscences of My Father, Peter A. Stolypin* (Metuchen, NJ, 1970).

BYRNES, ROBERT. *V. O. Kliucheskii, Historian of Russia* (Bloomington, IN, 1995).

CHARQUES, RICHARD. *The Twilight of Imperial Russia* (London, 1958, 1974).

EDELMAN, R. *Gentry Politics on the Eve of the Russian Revolution: The Nationalist Party, 1907–1917* (New Brunswick, NJ, 1980).

———. *Proletarian Peasants: The Revolution of 1905 in Russia's Southwest* (Ithaca, NY, 1987).

EDMONDSON, L. H. *Feminism in Russia, 1900–17* (Stanford, CA, 1984).

FLORINSKY, MICHAEL. *The End of the Russian Empire* (New York, 1931, 1961).

GAPON, GEORGE. *The Story of My Life* (London, 1905).

GURKO, V. I. *Features and Figures of the Past . . .* (Stanford, CA, 1939).

HAIMSON, LEOPOLD. "The Problem of Social Stability in Urban Russia, 1905–1917," *Slavic Review, 23,* pp. 619–642; and *24,* pp. 1–22. Comments by Mendel and von Laue in *24,* pp. 23–46.

HARCAVE, SIDNEY. *The Russian Revolution of 1905* (London, 1970).

HEALY, A. E. *The Russian Autocracy in Crisis: 1905–1907* (Hamden, CT, 1976).

HENNESSY, R. *The Agrarian Question in Russia, 1905–1917: The Inception of the Stolypin Reform* (Giessen, W. Germany, 1977).

HOSKING, GEOFFREY. *The Russian Constitutional Experiment . . . 1907–1914* (New York, 1973).

IZVOLSKY, A. P. *Recollections of a Foreign Minister* (New York, 1921).

KOKOVTSOV, V. N. *Out of My Past* (Stanford, CA, 1935).

LINCOLN, W. BRUCE. *In War's Dark Shadow: The Russians Before the Great War* (New York, 1983).

MAKLAKOV, V. A. *The First State Duma* (Bloomington, IN, 1964).

MANNING, R. T. *The Crisis of the Old Order in Russia* (Princeton, NJ, 1983).

MCCAULEY, M., and P. WALDRON, eds. *Octobrists to Bolsheviks . . . Documents . . .* (Baltimore, 1984).

MCDONALD, DAVID M. *United Government and Foreign Policy in Russia, 1900–1914* (Cambridge, MA, 1992).

MCNEAL, ROBERT, ed. *Russia in Transition, 1905–1914* (New York, 1970).

MEHLINGER, H. D., and J. M. THOMPSON. *Count Witte and the Tsarist Government in the 1905 Revolution* (Bloomington, IN, 1972).

MILIUKOV, PAUL. *Political Memoirs, 1905–1917,* ed. A. Mendel (Ann Arbor, MI, 1967).

———. *Russia and Its Crisis* (Chicago, 1905, 1962).

MILLER, M. S. *Economic Development of Russia, 1905–1914,* 2d ed. (London, 1967).

OBERLANDER, E., et al. *Russia Enters the Twentieth Century . . .* (New York, 1971).

OWEN, L. A. *The Russian Peasant Movement, 1906–1917* (London, 1937; reprint New York, 1963).

PALLOT, JUDITH. *Land Reform in Russia, 1906–1917* (New York and Oxford, 1999).

PARES, BERNARD. *Russia Between Reform and Revolution* (New York, 1962).

POSPIELOVSKY, D. *Russian Police Socialism: Experiment or Provocation?* (London, 1971).

RAWSON, DON L. *Russian Rightists and the Revolution of 1905* (New York, 1995).

REICHMAN, HENRY. *Railwaymen and Revolution: Russia, 1905* (Berkeley, CA, 1987).

RICE, CHRISTOPHER. *Russian Workers and the Socialist-Revolutionary Party Through the Revolution of 1905–07* (New York, 1988).

RIHA, THOMAS. *A Russian European: Paul Miliukov . . .* (Notre Dame, IN, 1968).

"The Russian Revolution of 1905–07: 80th Anniversary," *Russian History, 12,* no. 1 (Spring 1985).

ROOSA, RUTH A. ed. Thomas C. Owen. *Russian Industrialists in an Era of Revolution: The Associations of Industry and Trade, 1906–1917* (Armonk, NY, 1997).

SABLINSKY, WALTER. *The Road to Bloody Sunday* (Princeton, NJ, 1976).

SCHLEIFMAN, NURIT. *Undercover Agents in the Russian Revolutionary Movement: The SR Party, 1902–14* (New York, 1988).

SCHWARZ, S. M. *The Russian Revolution of 1905 . . . ,* trans. G. Vakar (Chicago, 1967).

STAVROU, T. G., ed. *Russia Under the Last Tsar* (Minneapolis, 1969).

SZEFTEL, MARC. *The Russian Constitution of April 23, 1906* (Brussels, 1976).

THADEN, EDWARD. *Russia and the Balkan Alliance of 1912* (University Park, PA, 1965).

TROTSKY, L. D. *1905,* trans. A. Bostock (New York, 1972).

VERNER, ANDREW M. *The Crisis of Russian Autocracy: Nicholas II and the 1905 Revolution* (Princeton, NJ, 1990).

WALDRON, PETER. *Between Two Revolutions: Stolypin and the Politics of Renewal in Russia* (DeKalb, IL, 1998).

WEINBERG, ROBERT. *The Revolution of 1905 in Odessa: Blood on the Steps* (Bloomington, IN, 1993).

WILLIAMS, ROBERT C. *The Other Bolsheviks: Lenin and His Critics, 1904–1914* (Bloomington, IN, 1986).

ZENKOVSKY, A. V. *Stolypin: Russia's Last Great Reformer,* trans. M. Patoski (Princeton, NJ, 1986).

5

Cultural Developments, 1855–1917

The late 19th century witnessed a spectacular flowering of Russian culture. Nicholas I's death removed an oppressive weight from Russian life and ushered in a relatively liberal era that, combined with a powerful national upsurge, produced remarkable cultural creativity. Individuals in literature, art, music, and architecture began to experiment with new modes of expression. Frank discussion of the plight of the peasantry and emancipation focused attention on this long-neglected segment of society. The daily lives of commoners and the drama and pathos of peasant life captured the imagination of Russian artists.

Literature

Russian literature entered a Golden Age associated primarily with Turgenev, Dostoevsky, and Tolstoy, all among the world's greatest novelists. This triumvirate, building upon the legacy of Pushkin, Lermontov, and Gogol, became the most consummate practitioners of literary realism. Under their tutelage, Russian literature achieved great international recognition and acclaim.

Turgenev (1818–1883)

Ivan Turgenev, a nobleman well educated by private tutors, studied at Russian and German universities and became an ardent Westerner. Through his works this most Western of Russia's major writers taught Europeans to appreciate Russian literature. His short stories about peasant life, based on personal observation, appeared in *The Contemporary,* a leading journal of literature and criticism and were later published as *A Sportsman's Sketches* (1852), winning him recognition as a leading author. The stories denounced serfdom while portraying the serf as compassionate and dignified. Publication that same year of his laudatory obituary of Nicholas Gogol, who had satirized official corruption and social injustice, brought brief imprisonment and banishment. In 1853, pardoned and having returned to the capital with an enhanced reputation, Turgenev became literary Russia's chief spokesman.

Turgenev embodied the new spirit pervading Russian life. In his first novels, *Rudin* (1856) and *Nest of Gentlefolk* (1859), he depicted the well-intentioned but unrealistic idealism of the older

Library of Congress

Ivan Sergeevich Turgenev 1818–1883. The most "western" of Russia's 19th-century writers, Turgenev brought Russian literature to Europeans.

generation. In the novel *On the Eve* (1860), he described aspirations of the new generation, tried to reveal life as it really was, and faced the toughest issues of the day. In these novels the critics found beauty, truth, simplicity, and sensitivity, hailing his descriptive powers, portrayal of character, and insight.

Fathers and Sons (1862), Turgenev's most famous novel, described the generational conflict between men of the 1860s—Arkadi and the nihilist Bazarov—and men of the 1840s—Arkadi's father and uncle. Conservative critics condemned Turgenev for apparently approving radicalism by depicting Bazarov too positively. The left criticized Bazarov as a caricature of the younger generation's aspirations. Except for Dmitri Pisarev (on whom

Bazarov was based), who praised the novel, most radical critics claimed Turgenev had exhausted his talent. The general rejection of *Fathers and Sons* crushed Turgenev's ego. Settling in western Europe, he visited Russia rarely. His novel *Smoke* (1867), revealing his disillusionment with Russia, stressed the arrogance and deceitfulness of Russian aristocrats and émigrés.

Turgenev's last novel, *Virgin Soil*, which analyzed the "going to the people" movement of the 1870s, revealed that as his fame in Europe grew, he had lost touch with Russian life. With his international reputation, Turgenev was more at ease among Europe's literary elite than among Russians. Unreconciled with his beloved Russia, he died in a village near Paris.

Dostoevsky (1821–1881)

If Turgenev was the stylistic master of realism, Fedor Dostoevsky strove to be "a realist in a higher sense," plumbing the depths of humanity's soul and laying bare conflicts within human nature. His metaphysical realism dealt with the meaning and purpose of life. For him ideas had a tangible, palpable quality. Seeking to overcome divisions in Russian life, he discovered that only by surmounting the division between humans and God could Russian life be restored to wholeness. Dostoevsky wrote:

> I am a child of the age, a child of unbelief and skepticism. I have been so far, and shall be I know to the grave. . . . If anyone proved to me that Christ was not the truth, and it really was a fact that the truth was not in Christ, I would rather be with Christ than with the truth.[1]

Throughout his life he sought to know and understand Christ. Believing deeply in Russia and its people, he tried similarly to believe in God. A character in *The Possessed* blurts out: "I believe in Russia. I believe in Orthodoxy. . . . I believe that

---

[1] Quoted in E. H. Carr, *Dostoevsky* (New York, 1931), pp. 281–82.

Library of Congress

Fedor Mikhailovich Dostoevskii, 1821–1881.
A contemporary photograph from the 1870s
reveals the inner intensity of the author whose
works probe the psychology of human beings as
they struggle with life.

exchange of letters between a young girl and an
aging government clerk exposes the pathos and
constant struggle of the downtrodden for human
dignity. The novel revealed Dostoevsky's intense
concern with psychological torment, self-sacrifice,
and alienation—key themes of his later great
novels. At 23 he was already recognized as a leading Russian author, but the cool response to his
second novel, *The Double* (1846), gravely wounded
his vanity. He attended the radical Petrashevskii
Circle partly from boredom and curiosity. But
Nicholas I's regime equated nonconformity with
treason, and Dostoevsky was arrested in April
1849. Convicted of crimes against the state, Dostoevsky was sentenced to death, but at the execution
site his sentence was commuted to eight years of
Siberian exile. Being snatched from the jaws of
death stimulated his deep interest in human psychology and torments of the mind.

Dostoevsky recorded his prison sojourn vividly
in *Notes from the House of the Dead* (1861), a work
that resembles Alexander Solzhenitsyn's *Gulag
Archipelago* (see Chapter 19). His imprisonment, a
turning point in his life, caused an intellectual
reorientation affecting his entire outlook. He discovered two sources of inspiration for his later
views: the New Testament and "the people" of
Russia.

Allowed to return to St. Petersburg in 1859,
Dostoevsky and his brother, Mikhail, entered
journalism as partners, but suppression by the
authorities and financial failure resulted in disaster. In 1864 the deaths of his wife and beloved
brother plunged him into grief; his debts brought
him close to bankruptcy. In that disastrous year
Dostoevsky ventured into philosophy in *Notes
from Underground*. Releasing his despair, he sought
to answer Chernyshevskii's utopian novel, *What Is
to Be Done?* Chernyshevskii believed people were
inherently good and rational; Dostoevsky argued
that people could use their free will to choose
between good and evil, and he presented people
as irrational and contradictory. A man's ability to
choose, claimed Dostoevsky, was the root of his

Christ will come again in Russia." This was Dostoevsky's own conviction, proclaimed in his writings.

The son of a well-to-do but miserly doctor,
Dostoevsky was an engineering student in St.
Petersburg when he learned of his father's murder
by peasants. With his inheritance he soon resigned his army commission to devote himself to
literature.

"We have all sprung from Gogol's 'Overcoat,'"[2]
Dostoevsky once remarked. Indeed, his first novel,
Poor Folk (1845), is related to "The Overcoat." An

---

[2] A famous short story written by Gogol in 1842.

freedom. He developed these ideas further in his major novels.

The great novels *Crime and Punishment* (1866), *The Idiot* (1869), *The Possessed* (1871–1872), and his profound final work, *The Brothers Karamazov* (1879–1880), constitute a related cycle dealing with contemporary Russian issues, reflecting stages in Dostoevsky's elaboration of Christianity, and portraying the "underground man." *Crime and Punishment* reveals the tragic failure of Raskolnikov, a poor student, to assert his individuality "without God" by senselessly murdering a pawnbroker and her sister. Raskolnikov succeeds only in denying his humanity and Christian spirit. In *The Idiot* Dostoevsky portrays saintly idiocy—a long revered Russian trait—in Christlike Prince Myshkin, an impotent epileptic, long confined in mental institutions. Returning to society, he becomes enmeshed in the lives of "ordinary" people who find him amusing and wholly gullible. Exploiting his kind generosity, they turn him into a real madman. By his actions Myshkin fosters Christian compassion and, like Christ, is ridiculed and abused.

The Possessed depicts socialism's alleged destructiveness. A ruthless nihilist, Peter Verkhovenskii, persuades followers to murder a fellow conspirator for planning to squeal to the police. Reacting to the "Nechaev Affair," a contemporary event, Dostoevsky was convinced that socialism was morally bankrupt. In *The Possessed* he depicts the alienation resulting from rejecting Christianity. The theater of the struggle between good and evil is all Russia which, Dostoevsky feared, socialism threatened with destruction. A powerful indictment of the revolutionary movement, the novel provoked criticism from radicals and conservatives. Undaunted, he continued his quest for personal spiritual peace and salvation for Russia.

In his greatest novel, *The Brothers Karamazov*, Dostoevsky tried to resolve issues that had long tormented him. Old Feodor Karamazov is murdered by one of his four sons, provoking a great theological debate between Ivan Karamazov and his younger brother Alyosha over the existence of God. The debate culminates in the famous "Legend of the Grand Inquisitor," portraying in parable form the human conflict between material well-being and belief in God. Christ reappears in Spain during the Inquisition and is recognized by the Grand Inquisitor, who threatens to burn him at the stake because Christ asks people to grant Him allegiance freely without coercion. Freedom of choice, warns the Grand Inquisitor, threatens the happiness of people who beg for authoritarianism in order to be free of the responsibility of freedom. Like the Grand Inquisitor, socialist revolutionaries offered people material well-being at the cost of their freedom, contended Dostoevsky. Society was doomed unless it embodied Christ's ideal; the Russian people possessed a Christlike harmony that could redeem humanity. Russia's and humanity's salvation were to be found in spiritual rebirth by voluntary acceptance of Christ's spirit.

Tolstoy (1828–1910)

From a prosperous noble family south of Moscow, Leo Tolstoy was tutored at home, attended Kazan University, then left it to open a school for peasant children on his estate. Joining the army in 1851, he served in the Caucasus, beginning his literary career there with a widely acclaimed autobiographical trilogy, *Childhood, Boyhood,* and *Youth* (1852–1857). In *Sevastopol Stories* he recorded his impressions of Sevastopol's siege in the Crimean War. After the war Tolstoy resigned from the army and traveled in Europe. Returning to his estate in 1862, he married and devoted himself to writing and his family.

His great novels, *War and Peace* and *Anna Karenina,* stem from this tranquil period. *War and Peace* (1869), a vast literary canvas of the Napoleonic era, probes lives of people from all social groups. Vast panoramas, great battles, agonizing retreats, and Napoleon's historic encounter with General Kutuzov serve as backdrop for Tolstoy's historical and moral philosophy. The novel's heroine and Tolstoy's ideal woman is Natasha Rostova,

Library of Congress

Count Lev Nikolaevich Tolstoi, 1828–1910, photographed in his study at Iasnaia Poliana (Bright Glade), his beloved estate outside of Moscow.

whose experiences mirror mighty historical forces. Ordinary people move history, not vaunted leaders like Napoleon, he believed. Tolstoy viewed Napoleon as a mere puppet, manipulated by forces beyond his control. To Tolstoy history had an inner logic that worked itself out through people as agents, not creators. Despite numerous characters and varied human experiences, *War and Peace* is a remarkably unified masterpiece perfectly integrating Tolstoy's philosophy with his artistry.

In *Anna Karenina*, an outstanding social novel (1877), Tolstoy discusses family issues, emancipation, the role of women, and the nobility's economic decline. The focus is the triangle of Anna, her husband, and her lover, Count Vronskii. Contrasting with Anna and Vronskii's tempestuous affair is her friend Kitty's marriage to the idealistic landowner, Levin. Anna and Vronskii struggle against social conventions that deny them happiness. Bitterness and guilt corrupt their relationship until Anna, to find peace, commits suicide and Vronskii's life is ruined.

Tolstoy's later works lack the intensity and depth of these masterworks. In the late 1870s he

underwent a religious conversion dramatically recounted in *A Confession* (1882). Rejecting conventional Orthodoxy for a rationalistic Christianity based on nonresistance to evil, he urged rejection of all coercive institutions: church, state, and private property. His critique of contemporary society brought his public excommunication in 1901.* Tolstoy's denunciation of the nobles' greed and his repudiation of private property caused conflict with them while the state viewed him as a dangerous revolutionary. His unconventional views on marriage and the family expressed in *The Kreutzer Sonata* (1889) and *The Devil*, published posthumously, provoked bitter family dissension. At 82, signing over his property to his estranged wife, Tolstoy set out on a pilgrimage and died a few days later at a house in Riazan province. Justifiably, he is known as the last "true giant of the reformist aristocratic intelligentsia." He searched restlessly for answers to the meaning of life and history.

Chekhov (1860–1904)

Anton Chekhov was the last great figure of 19th-century Russian literature. Born in Taganrog on the Sea of Azov, son of a greengrocer and grandson of a serf, he grew up in poor health amidst provincial boredom, middle-class piety, and straitened finances. When his family moved to Moscow, Anton remained in Taganrog, supporting himself by tutoring and running errands. He was a carefree youth with an extraordinary sense of humor, evident in his later stories. His literary career began in 1880 with stories hastily written for pulp magazines under a pseudonym. Besides paying for medical school, his writings gave him the reputation of a prolific but mediocre writer. When one story was noticed by the literary elite upon its publication in 1885, Chekhov was invited to St. Petersburg and met Alexis Suvorin, editor of

---

* In February 2001, Vlademir Tolstoy, the writer's great-great-great grandson, asked the Orthodox Church to lift the ban of excommunication in the name of "national reconcilation." The church has refused.

Anton Pavlovich Chekhov, 1860–1904, physician, playwright, short-story writer, and chronicler of the declining Russian nobility.

New Times, a prominent daily. Impressed with Chekhov's ability, Suvorin urged him to make writing his career. Much flattered, Chekhov continued writing short stories whose quality improved as their quantity decreased. In 1888 the Academy of Sciences gave him the prestigious Pushkin Prize. Amidst this growing success came warnings of tuberculosis, which would end his life prematurely. Foreseeing death, Chekhov wrote between 1889 and 1897 many fine stories reflecting personal restlessness and a belief that Russia required sweeping changes. Recurrent themes are human vanity, weaknesses, and melancholia. His characters often yearn for a richer, more beautiful future.

Always fascinated by the theater, Chekhov in 1895 wrote a serious play, *The Sea Gull,* but its first performance flopped because the director and actors misunderstood it. Two years later it was presented by a new theatrical company formed by K.S. Stanislavskii and V.I. Nemirovich-Danchenko: the famous Moscow Art Theater. Its directors (Stanislavskii and Nemirovich-Danchenko) and actors understood its subtleties, and *The Sea Gull* became a sensation. In close association with Stanislavskii's theater, Chekhov from 1899 to 1903 wrote the immortal plays *Uncle Vania, The Three Sisters,* and *The Cherry Orchard.* Lacking clear plots or dramatic climaxes, they are studies in human psychology. Understatement, lack of suspense, little action—Chekhov's literary characteristics—succeed brilliantly on stage. Chekhov wrote with great enthusiasm for life and unfaltering optimism about the future. He lived in a Russia entering a century of momentous change.

Chekhov died in the summer of 1904 while taking a health cure in Germany, leaving a rich legacy of plays, stories, letters, and essays that deeply influenced writers in Russia and abroad. He brought the Golden Age to a close, though Russian literature continued to be creative and original. The last tsarist decades witnessed another outburst of creative energy, called the Silver Age. The transitional figure was Maxim Gorkii (1868–1936), whose literary credo evolved from classical realism through neoromanticism to socialist realism.

Gorkii (1868–1936)

From a lower-middle-class family, Maxim Gorkii (born A. M. Peshkov) saw his modest social status deteriorate rapidly after his father's premature death. On the streets at a tender age, he was educated by surviving in hostile Nizhnii-Novgorod. Gorkii wandered ceaselessly through southern Russia, learning much from those he met and gaining insight into life's problems. (The pseudonym Gorkii means "bitter," and for him it was a constant reminder of his miserable childhood as a street urchin.) He gained sympathy for the downtrodden. Gorkii's first published work was *Makar Chudra* (1892), a tale of love, passion, and violence among gypsies. His realistic early works reflect

Library of Congress (Alice Boughton)

Maksim Gorkii (pseudonym of Aleksei Maksimovich Peshkov), 1868–1936, photographed at his desk shortly after the turn of the century. His career as a writer spanned the late tsarist period and extended well into the Soviet era.

preference for broad social themes and reveal his humanitarianism. Portraying vividly a little-known world, Gorkii's stories were well received. His collected stories, issued in two popular volumes in 1898, made his reputation as a forceful writer. In 1902 he was elected an honorary member of the Academy of Sciences; when the government annulled this award on political grounds, Gorkii's popularity soared. On close terms with revolutionaries, he often supported the Bolsheviks after 1903.

In 1902 Stanislavskii's Moscow Art Theater staged with limited success his drama *The Lower Depths,* an unconventional play set in a decaying boardinghouse filled with drunks, prostitutes, and thieves. Translated, it soon became a hit in western Europe. In this call for freedom, Gorkii defended the dignity of people ground down by tsarism. The authorities banned it in the provinces and branded Gorkii a dangerous radical.

Gorkii's tendentious novels were less successful artistically. One, *Mother* (1907), was written on an

ill-fated visit to the United States. Participating in the 1905 Revolution, Gorkii had been arrested and then released, provided he left Russia. Disillusioned with the United States, he bitterly criticized American society in *The City of the Yellow Devil* (1907), a collection of stories about New York. He finally settled in Italy, where his villa on the Isle of Capri became a haven for political exiles and an artists' and writers' colony. In his absence his reputation in Russia dwindled, but the great autobiographical work, *Childhood* (1913), and *Among Strangers* (1915) restored it. During the Romanovs' tercentenary in 1913, he returned to Russia, wrote for the Bolshevik press, and edited a Marxist journal, *Annals.* Gorkii rejoiced at tsarism's collapse but was unenthusiastic about the Bolshevik coup in November. Quarreling frequently with Lenin, Gorkii eventually made peace with him and continued writing in the Soviet era.

Decadence and Symbolism

Other writers criticized Gorkii for continued commitment to a literary realism they considered outmoded. Many grew preoccupied with form and beauty. A general European romantic revival influenced these new trends in Russia, where it was called the Decadent movement and later Symbolism. Such writers stressed aesthetics and "art for art's sake." Mysticism, individualism, sensualism, and demonism were its hallmarks. Language became vague and obscure to create symbolic images and sounds; poetry revived. Younger Symbolists included the great Alexander Blok, Andrei Bely, and Nicholas Gumilev. These poets formed a closely knit group that contributed to the same journals and created poetry of technical perfection, pure tonal harmony, and sheer beauty. Little affected at first by World War I and Russia's social crisis, most welcomed the March but not the November Revolution. Afterward some sought exile abroad; others remained in Russia hoping to influence the new regime. Taking their toll on Russian culture, war and revolution pointed in uncharted directions.

Music, painting, and architecture paralleled, though belatedly, developments in literature. Painting and music responded favorably after the Crimean War and were influenced by realistic aesthetics. Architecture was less affected until the turn of the 20th century.

Music

The Russian Music Society, founded in 1859, fostered musical activity, promoted conservatory training, and encouraged public music appreciation. Anton Rubinstein, a leading pianist and composer, and his younger brother, Nicholas, established branches in Moscow and some 30 provincial centers. Conservatories were founded in leading Russian cities to provide musical education. The Society organized several symphony orchestras and smaller performing ensembles and sponsored concerts all over Russia. Conservative in musical taste and theory, the Society followed the Rubinsteins, who viewed German schools of composition as models to emulate.

The Five

Despite the Society's remarkable popular success and rising interest in music, its conservative credo was challenged. A small group of composers—the famous "Five" or "Mighty Handful"—sought to initiate a revolution in Russian music and direct it along new paths. These men seemed an unlikely revolutionary group. Its leader and organizer was Mily Balakirev, its only trained musician, an excellent pianist and conductor, but only a mediocre composer. Cesar Cui, trained as an engineer, later became a general of army engineers. Modest Musorgskii was a Guards officer and later an official in the Transport Ministry. Alexander Borodin, trained as a medical doctor, eventually became a chemistry professor. Nicholas Rimskii-Korsakov became a naval officer and later a music professor at the St. Petersburg Conservatory. From diverse backgrounds and with differing professional interests, they did not always agree but shared common musical ideals and attitudes.

The Five, as successors of Glinka, aimed to create a Russian national school of music based on native folk and church music. Rejecting strict Western rules of technical form, they preferred a freer, more flexible style associated with folk music. They abhorred imitation of foreign models and scorned Italian opera as devoid of content and dramatic effect. Bitter polemics erupted between Rubinstein's conservatives and Balakirev's musical nationalists, which publicized and popularized music. In 1862, to counter Rubinstein's Music Society, the Five organized the Free School of Music to promote their musical theories and perform their works. Their great champion and defender of the nationalist musical trend was the distinguished art and music critic Vasili V. Stasov (1824–1906), whose caustic polemics and enthusiastic reviews won for the Five a large and loyal following.

Balakirev and Borodin were the creators of the Russian symphony and contributed much to symphonic theory. Musorgskii, Rimskii-Korsakov, and Borodin were geniuses of Russian opera, and their works remain in the repertoire throughout the world. Borodin worked 18 years on his great opera, *Prince Igor,* first performed in 1890 with great success. Based on the disputed 12th-century epic *The Tale of the Host of Igor,* it is a heroic national saga.

Modest Musorgskii is renowned for his monumental music drama, the opera *Boris Godunov,* one of Russia's greatest works of art. The composer studied carefully the history and language of the 16th century and was influenced by old Russian church music. The opera's hero was not Tsar Boris but the suffering Russian people, epitomized by a simpleton. Adapting Pushkin's play, Musorgskii wrote much of the libretto and stated: "My music must reproduce the people's language even in the most insignificant nuances."[3] *Boris Godunov,* in its original stark, tense version with no female lead, was rejected as insufficiently operatic by St. Petersburg's Mariinsky Theater. Completely

---

[3] V. Seroff, *Modeste Moussorgsky* (New York, 1968), p. 90.

Library of Congress

Modest Petrovich Musorgskii, 1839–1881. Portrait painted in the year of Mussorgskii's death by Russia's well-known painter Ilia Repin.

revising the score, Musorgskii added a "Polish" third act with Marina as prima donna and a revolutionary scene. The new version was performed successfully until 1882, when it was withdrawn under pressure from Alexander III's regime, which disliked its revolutionary implications. Rimskii-Korsakov, Musorgskii's friend, completely reorchestrated *Boris Godunov,* and his polished version scored triumphs in Europe and the United States. Musorgskii also composed most of *Khovan-shchina,* a second folk opera based on the Moscow *streltsy* (musketeers') revolt of 1682. Completed and revised by Rimskii-Korsakov, it has remained a favorite in Russia. *Pictures at an Exhibition,* a piano suite also composed by Musorgskii, is best known in Maurice Ravel's orchestral version. Rimskii-Korsakov's operas, little known outside Russia, include *Sadko,* an old folktale of Novgorod, and *The Golden Cockerel,* also based on a fairy tale.

Tchaikovsky (1840–1893)

Among the first students at the St. Petersburg Conservatory, opened in 1862, was Peter I. Tchaikovsky, destined to become the best-known Russian composer. Like many of his contemporaries, Tchaikovsky was trained not for a musical career but for the civil service, serving briefly in the Ministry of Justice. After studying music privately, he enrolled in the Conservatory. He was such an excellent student that he was invited to join the faculty of the new Moscow Conservatory in 1866, and he worked and taught there for 12 years. His association with the Rubinsteins, and with Moscow, fostered enmity with the Five in St. Petersburg, which obscured how much they shared and how close they were in musical tastes and attitudes. Some critics describe Tchaikovsky's music as cosmopolitan and Western while calling that of the Five nationalist and Russian, but this dichotomy ignores their common origins and national feelings.

Tchaikovsky composed some of his finest music in Moscow. Despite recurring mental crises, he completed four symphonies; several operas, including *Eugene Onegin* (adapted from Pushkin); concertos; and his greatest ballet, *Swan Lake.* Then a period of acute depression and nervous tension prevented his composing so intensely and creatively. In 1889 another creative burst began with his second major ballet, *The Sleeping Beauty,* soon followed by a third, *The Nutcracker,* one of his most popular compositions. Then he composed his Sixth Symphony ("Pathetique"), often considered his masterpiece. First performed in St. Petersburg in 1893 under the composer's direction, it was soon acclaimed as one of the greatest of Russian musical works.

Tchaikovsky acquired an international reputation even in his lifetime. In his last years he traveled extensively, conducting his music all over the world, and was specially honored at the opening of Carnegie Hall in New York City in 1891. Nationalists criticized his music as too Western and imitative of foreign models, but Igor Stravinsky, his worthy successor, stressed repeatedly its uniquely Russian qualities.

By 1900 Russian music had achieved great maturity, international recognition, and general respect. A group of brilliant teachers took up the cause in Russian conservatories, molding a new generation of composers that carried on the traditions of the Five and Tchaikovsky. Among the most talented were Sergei Rakhmaninov, a great pianist whose romantic compositions won plaudits worldwide, and Alexander Glazunov, composer and teacher. A pair of innovative Russian composers, Alexander Scriabin and Igor Stravinsky, like the Symbolists in poetry, opened up entirely new vistas. Alexander Scriabin (1871–1915), enrolled in the Moscow Conservatory at age 16, revealed prodigious ability as pianist and composer. He dabbled in mysticism, devoured Decadent poetry, and wrote poetry himself. Influenced by the Symbolists, Scriabin rejected the musical realism of the Five and Tchaikovsky's academicism to chart a new musical course. Inspired by romanticism, the occult, and the Decadents, Scriabin concluded that art must transform life, overcoming pain, ugliness, and evil and realizing the Kingdom of God on earth. He viewed the artist as a new messiah to redeem humankind and infuse life with new creative energy. His *Poem of Ecstasy* had eerie, haunting qualities, music he characterized as mysticoreligious, the basis for a new harmonic system. Scriabin's compositions, notably his piano music, influenced Stravinsky, Sergei Prokoviev, and Dmitri Shostakovich, the Russian giants of the 20th century, and have experienced a revival in the West.

Stravinsky (1882–1971)

Igor Stravinsky represents the first tide of musical influence flowing *from* Russia *into* Europe. Unlike most of his contemporaries, Stravinsky was self-taught, until he was tutored by Rimskii-Korsakov. His early career was closely associated with the famous Russian impresario, Serge Diagilev

Igor Stravinsky, 1882–1971. Stravinsky left Russia at the time of World War I, returning for the first time in 1963 for a triumphant concert tour.

(1872–1929), who was impressed by his early works. Preparing the program for the first season of the revolutionary Ballet Russe de Monte Carlo in Paris, Diagilev asked Stravinsky to orchestrate two Chopin pieces for the ballet. Thus began a revolutionary and highly productive association—Diagilev, the organizer and man of ideas; Stravinsky, the innovator whose scores would revolutionize music; Mikhail Fokine, the choreographer whose ballets would become modern classics; Leon Bakst, a brilliant set and costume designer; and Vaslav Nijinsky, a great ballet dancer. Together in 1910 they created a stunning and opulent production of *The Firebird,* based on an old Russian folktale. The result was a great international triumph. In 1911 the same company staged *Petrushka,* a ballet teeming with new ideas and musical forms.

Stravinsky's radical orchestral style and boldly innovative music shocked many listeners. In 1913 Diagilev staged Stravinsky's revolutionary ballet, *The Rite of Spring,* whose brutal realism, violence, and extraordinary vitality created a public scandal. In these early works, Stravinsky was a musical descendant of Musorgskii's realism and nationalism, utilizing the rich tradition of Russian folk music. Before World War I he lived in France and Switzerland and adopted a neoclassical style reflected especially in the ballet *Pulcinella* (1919), based on themes by Pergolesi. Although he became a French citizen in 1934, Stravinsky was attracted increasingly to the United States. One of the first major foreign composers to use jazz in his works, he moved to the United States at the outbreak of World War II. He revisited Russia, triumphantly, only in his final years. The creativity of Russian music in the twilight of the tsarist monarchy, epitomized by Stravinsky, parallels the flowering of Russian literature in its Silver Age.

Painting

Russian painting developed rapidly during the late 19th century, finally emancipating itself from neoclassicism, long imposed by the Academy of Arts. Younger artists challenged old artistic conventions and strove to develop realism and nationalism. In 1863 the entire graduating class of the Academy defied its rigid policies after "The Festival of the Gods in Valhalla" was decreed as compulsory subject matter for a competition to determine who would be selected to continue their studies in Italy. Refusing to participate, the students demanded the right to select their own subjects freely. When the authorities demurred, 14 students resigned from the Academy to form their own artistic cooperative (*artel*), soon becoming the Society of Traveling Art Exhibitions; it dominated Russian art into the 1890s. The Society's young nationalist artists rejected the Academy's cosmopolitan and neoclassical approach. Annual exhibitions were organized in St. Petersburg and then toured throughout Russia. Exhibitions of the so-called Itinerants (artists of the Society) acquainted audiences with recent works by Russia's best artists. The critic Vasili V. Stasov staunchly defended the Itinerants, who promoted artistic realism based on portrayals and interpretations of real Russian life. Emphasizing content over form and composition, they were by no means indifferent to color and design. Often protesting against injustice, inequality, and exploitation, they realized that in order to make serious social statements their art had to display sound form, too. They considered themselves artists first, not mere propagandists.

The moving forces behind the Society of Traveling Art Exhibitions were Ivan Kramskoi and Vasili Perov, who were organizers and entrepreneurs as well as skillful artists. Kramskoi was a fine painter whose portraits of prominent leaders reveal great psychological insight and understanding. Perov, of humble origin, depicted lower-class life and problems. His searching criticism of the hypocrisy and moral turpitude among Orthodox clergy brought him into conflict with the authorities.

The most famous and successful 19th-century Russian artist was Ilia Repin (1844–1930). Though of humble origin, he studied at the Academy of Arts and won a prestigious traveling fellowship to study in Italy. *The Volga Boatmen* (1870–1873), designed as a group portrait of the human beasts of burden who hauled heavy barges up the Volga River, won him a reputation throughout Europe. This painting revealed a brutal exploitation widespread in Russia. Repin knew each of the people depicted in the painting and recorded their tragic lives in his memoirs. Another devastating social critique was his *Religious Procession in Kursk Province* (1880–1883), suggesting the clergy's arrogance and aloofness, police brutality, and quiet suffering of the peasantry. In the 1880s, turning to history, Repin in *Tsar Ivan and the Body of His Son* (1881–1885) showed Ivan IV moments after he had clubbed his eldest son to death, suggesting the corrupting influence of unlimited autocracy. Repin won greater recognition for Russian art, but after the Bolshevik Revolution he retired to his country house in Finland and refused to return to Soviet Russia.

Library of Congress

Ilia Efimovich Repin, 1844–1930. A self-portrait completed in 1878, after a sojourn in Paris (1873–76), at a time when the artist was beginning to be recognized at home and abroad as a gifted painter.

Beginning in the 1890s, the Russian art world too revolted against the canons of realism and nationalism. Younger artists such as Mikhail Vrubel (1856–1911) broke with the Itinerants' realism. His abbreviated and tragic career contributed much to turning Russian art away from traditional approaches. After studying philosophy, he enrolled in the Academy of Arts and became a successful designer and mural painter skilled at church decoration. In an artwork every element was important to him: form, line, color, design, and subject matter. Vrubel advocated "art for art's sake"—art created for aesthetic purposes—an idea the realists considered outrageous. Suffering from serious mental stress, Vrubel was obsessed by demons, particularly after illustrating Lermontov's story "The Demon." Vrubel produced a powerful, brooding devil, but still unsatisfied, he finally produced a huge figure with contorted features

and an expression of terrible despair that mirrored his own accelerating breakdown. He placed this figure against a background of dark swirling colors reminiscent of European Impressionism. Then he went insane and was confined in an asylum until his death. In his short career Vrubel helped shake Russian art loose from crystallized forms of realism and influenced poets and composers.

The foundations of a new direction in Russian art were firmly established in 1898 by the group *Mir Iskusstva* (World of Art), named after the journal it published (1898–1904). This group of young, cosmopolitan aristocrats was led by Serge Diagilev, Alexander Benois, Leon Bakst, and Dmitri Filosofov. Diagilev, the moving force and impresario, began with successful exhibitions of advanced Russian and European art. The journal attracted talented, avant-garde artists, essayists, and poets who wrote daring articles on various topics. The journal advocated "art for art's sake" and publicized new artistic trends. The success of *Mir Iskusstva* encouraged similar publications, such as *Byloe* (Past Years) and *The Golden Fleece*, which informed their readers of new European trends and attempted to integrate Russian and European art. Movements such as Symbolism, Futurism, and Cubism all found supporters and practitioners in Russia. The best-known Russian artists of this period included young Marc Chagall, Vasily Kandinskii, and Kazimir Malevich, who helped shape the development of modern art.

Architecture

Russian architecture lacked the originality and striving for national forms of expression revealed in literature, music, and painting; it was dominated largely by foreign architects and styles. But about 1900 some Russian architects sought consciously to create a new national style based on Russian medieval structures. The Slavic Revival, a rebirth of interest in Russia's past, affected all aspects of Russian culture. Iconography was rediscovered as a developed art form, and its carefully prescribed principles influenced and inspired many architects. The Slavic Revival caused architects to turn to traditional Russian wooden structures for inspiration and to translate them into innovative stone and brick structures. Slavic Revival architecture, found all over Russia, centered in Moscow, as epitomized by the Historical Museum. A leader in this movement was A. V. Shchusev (1873–1949), who designed several Orthodox churches in traditional Novgorod and Pskov style and built Moscow's Kazan Railroad Station in the style of 17th-century Muscovy.

Thus Russian culture between the Crimean War and World War I revealed to the world tremendous vitality and originality in most fields. For the first time Russian culture, notably in Stravinsky's music, began to influence international standards rather than responding to or imitating Western trends. On the eve of World War I, Russian culture was extraordinarily dynamic and diverse, exciting and energetic. War and revolution dampened but failed to destroy the creative impulses of the Russian intelligentsia.

Popular Culture

The achievements of Russian high culture—literature, art, drama, and music—were undeniably world-class by the end of the 19th century, but it was only a small minority of urban, educated society that was engaged by this high culture. The vast majority of the population, especially the rural peasantry, was denied access to the accomplishments of the creative energies of Russian high culture. The basic obstacle was a lack of literacy among large portions of the population. Gradually, however, literacy would spread, opening up new opportunities for many to become aware of the achievements of the Russian Silver Age.

Just over 20 percent of the Russian Empire's population were registered as literate in the 1897 census. This number would double to 40 percent by the beginning of World War I, a positive development for the old regime. At the mid-19th century, however, rural literacy was in single digits— a mere 6 percent in 1860—rising rapidly with the spread of rural schooling in the post-emancipation period in the second half of the century. Over half of Russian peasant children of school age (8- to 11-year-olds) were enrolled in primary schools by 1910. The transformation of peasant life in the decades after emancipation included a growing recognition by peasants themselves of the value of literacy.

As Jeffrey Brooks has argued in a groundbreaking study, there were a number of reasons for promoting the spread of literacy in post-reform Russia.[4] Expanded literacy was necessary if peasants were to assume greater responsibility for management of their own affairs. Literacy became a means to greater independence and economic opportunity for peasants. Military authorities recognized that literate recruits made better soldiers. Shorter terms of service were offered to those able to read and write. The clergy understood that increased peasant literacy contributed to fuller participation in and understanding of religious services and practices. Peasants themselves came to recognize that literacy opened up greater social and economic opportunities and offered new avenues for pleasure and entertainment in their lives.

What had most illiterate peasants done with what little leisure time they had before emancipation? The village offered few opportunities for entertainment besides the consumption of vodka with friends and relatives and various community activities in village streets or in a local tavern. The oral tradition of storytelling and the reciting of folktales also were important sources of entertainment and enlightenment, but the printed word played little role in peasant life. Family occasions —weddings, christenings, funerals—and religious holidays and festivals associated with the church calendar were among the few opportunities to escape the unchanging monotony of subsistence agricultural labor. The expansion of literacy in the 1870s and 1880s gave rise to a new village reading public, which in turn stimulated a growth in the variety and availability of printed materials for a

---

[4] Jeffrey Brooks, *When Russia Learned to Read: Literacy and Popular Literature,* 1861–1917, pp. 3–34, passism.

rural audience. Peasant life acquired a whole new dimension.

Collectively, these printed materials are known as *lubok* literature, a term derived from the popular prints or broadsheets, which were the first printed materials widely disseminated in the countryside. Printed from wood blocks or copper plates, and sold for a pittance in villages by peddlers, the *lubok* (plural, *lubki*) was a lively printed illustration, usually with a small amount of text. *Lubki* communicated religious stories, parables about daily life, scenes from popular folklore, occasionally jokes and proverbs, and scenes from history. Many *lubki* had religious content. Peasant huts were often decorated with an assortment of *lubki,* which were cheaper and easier to obtain than icons. The widespread distribution of *lubki* prepared the way for the appearance of more sophisticated printed materials.

Among the published materials available in increasing numbers to a rural reading audience were commercial works published for profit, and materials prepared by individuals and groups wishing to promote a message or program—religious groups, propagandists, educators. The number of titles published for a newly literate rural audience skyrocketed, doubling between 1887 and 1895, and tripling again between 1895 and 1914.[5]

At first, religious subjects predominated in this new *lubok* literature, but secular subjects quickly emerged as the more popular. "Once the spiritual books do their job, they are quickly replaced by secular ones."[6] Stories from folklore, travel accounts, humorous stories, battle stories, tales of chivalry and adventure, as well as self-help books on how to get rich were written in easy-to-understand vernacular language and they quickly found an eager audience among common readers. Gradually other types of popular literature competed for common readership—romance fiction and tales of banditry, crime and adventure. Many of the authors were of peasant origin themselves

and consciously tailored their writings for the peasant world, whether in the countryside or among the growing number of peasants migrating to urban industrial centers in the late 19th and early 20th centuries. These works were designed to appeal to an entirely different audience than works of *belles letters* or serious literature. This was literature for the common reader, for ordinary readers who sought escape from the rigors of life. Despite the spread of literacy, Ben Eklof, in a study of Russian peasant schools, argues that: "Peasants . . . were learning to read, but not yet learning from reading. Peasant reading habits were simply an extension of traditional oral readings, with a marked preference for entertainment, popular narrative, and hagiography, and with little regard for self-help literature or tracts on science, hygiene, or agriculture."[7] In this sense, the Russian reading public's tastes began to resemble those of Western countries. Brooks suggests: "Each country is in many respects unique, but the social structure of Russia in the last half-century of the old regime was rapidly becoming more like that of the West, and so was its popular culture."[8] This popular literature was an important factor in shaping attitudes about the world among the growing literate population.

The increasing movement of peasants from the village to industrial centers generated interplay between rural and urban cultural attitudes and habits of social interaction. Peasants carried village cultural attitudes to urban centers, where they were confronted with a new, alien, and complex world. Peasant attitudes influenced the evolving cultural attitudes of the emerging working class. Urban cultural forms confronted the peasant worker as he entered the industrial work force. The focus of the urban peasant worker's life was the factory.

Workers quickly bonded in factory units, tended to maintain ties with others from their village or locale, and developed social solidarity in

[5] Ibid. p. 60.

[6] N. Rubakin, *"Knizhyi potok," Russkaia mysl,* no. 12 (1903), p. 166. Cited in Brooks, p. 67.

[7] Ben Eklof, *Russian Peasant Schools: Officialdom, Village Culture, and Popular Pedagogy,* 1861–1914, p. 481.

[8] Brooks, *op. cit.,* p. 355.

communal living arrangements and in neighborhoods. They found themselves confronting common problems of adjustment in an alien world. One environment was especially important to peasant/workers as a venue for leisure-time activities: the tavern. In conditions of rapid social change, urban subcultures emerged that often fostered anti-social behavior: drunkenness, fighting, petty criminal activity. In an alien environment, group activity was important for young men and groups—actually gangs—formed that provided a cultural milieu for social interaction. Groups of young men spent their free time on the streets, flirting with young women, singing, dancing, often carousing and brawling when vodka was available.

Urban popular culture drew heavily on the traditions of the countryside. Carnivals, folk festivals, traveling minstrel companies, song-and-dance ensembles, puppet shows, dancing bears, and other trained animals were popular in both countryside and urban centers. Beginning in the 1880s, sites for popular cultural activities were established—the People's House (narodnyi dom). These institutions became educational and entertainment centers. They were the models for later Soviet palaces of culture. Folk ensembles made up of both professional and peasant musicians and dancers became sleek purveyors of an idealized, romantic folk culture far removed from village life.

By the turn of the century, the moving picture on film became the most powerful and popular form of mass entertainment. Relatively cheap and easy to produce, films filled an important void in urban cultural life. Foreign films predominated until the first decade of the 20th century, when Russians began to produce their own films. An historian of popular culture, Richard Stites, states: "Cinema made foreign culture and Russian classics in vulgarized form directly available to the mass public for the first time in Russian history."[9]

[9] Richard Stites, *Russian Popular Culture: Entertainment and Society Since 1900*, p. 28.

Film appealed to all classes in society, and by 1914 more people in Russia were viewing films than any other form of popular entertainment. The most popular early films were based on folk tales and the popular pulp fiction of the *lubok* literature tradition—stories of crime, banditry, detective stories, and romance melodramas. By 1917, the Russians had firmly established a sophisticated, creative, and energetic film industry.

A wide gulf, however, continued to separate popular culture from the high culture of the educated elite. Cultured urban society was often suspicious of and even hostile toward the "unwashed" masses. They were viewed as "dark, dangerous and drunken." Richard Stites writes:

> The intelligentsia assaulted all the varieties of popular culture in the last decades of the Old Regime partly because of greater awareness of it and partly because of its wider dissemination. Intellectuals, censors, priests, physicians, revolutionaries—however sharply they differed among themselves—were often united in their animosity to the new culture which they linked directly to vice.[10]

Crude and vulgar, addressed to the lowest common denominator, popular culture was viewed by the Russian intelligentsia as being associated with backward, uneducated, and untrustworthy masses, incapable of appreciating refined culture. What they railed against was a new urban culture hewn out of the crudity of the peasant village combined with the filthy factory, the overcrowded slum, and the dingy tavern. Life for the lower classes was often cruel, intolerant, harsh, and violent, offering little time or energy for refined culture.

After the October Revolution, however, the Bolsheviks attempted to reshape the country in the image of their ideals. To that end they took over the publishing industry and proceeded quickly to restrict the choice of popular reading material for the general public, including both the *lubok* literature and more serious *belles lettres*. In addition, they would try to shape Russian popular culture to fit their image of the socialist future.

[10] Ibid. p. 12.

InfoTrac® College Edition Search Terms

Enter the search term *Dostoevsky* in Keywords.
Enter the search term *Tolstoy* in Keywords.
Enter the search term *Chekhov* in Keywords.
Enter the search term *Stravinsky* in Keywords.

Suggested Additional Reading

ANDREW, J. *Women in Russian Literature* (New York, 1988).

ASAFIEV, B. *Russian Music from the Beginning of the Nineteenth Century,* trans. A. Swan (Ann Arbor, MI, 1953).

BACKLER, J. A. *The Literary Lorgnette: Attending Opera in Imperial Russia* (Stanford, CA, 2000).

BERESFORD, MICHAEL. *Gogol's The Government Inspector* (London, 1997).

BERLIN, I. *The Hedgehog and the Fox: An Essay on Tolstoy's View of History* (New York, 1953).

BROOKS, J. *When Russia Learned to Read* (Princeton, NJ, 1985).

BOROVSKY, V., and R. LEACH, eds. *A History of Russian Theatre* (Cambridge, England, 1999).

BOUSOVA, E., and G. STERNIN. *Russian Art Nouveau* (New York, 1988).

BOWLT, J. E., and O. MATICH, eds. *Laboratory of Dreams: The Russian Avant-Garde and Cultural Experiment* (Stanford, CA, 1996).

COSTLOW, J. T. *Worlds Within Worlds: The Novels of Ivan Turgenev* (Princeton, 1989).

DONSKOV, A., and J. WOODSWORTH. *Leo Tolstoy and the Concept of Brotherhood* (New York, 1966).

EIKHENBAUM, B. M. *The Young Tolstoy,* trans. G. Kern (Ann Arbor, MI, 1972).

EMERSON, C. *Boris Godunov: Transpositions of a Russian Theme* (Bloomington, IN, 1987).

———. *Modest Musorgsky and Boris Godunov* (Cambridge, 1994).

EMERSON, C. *The Life of Musorgsky* (Cambridge, England, 1999).

ENGEL, B. A. *Mothers and Daughters: Women of the Intelligentsia in 19th-Century Russia* (Evanston, IL, 2000).

FANGER, D. L. *Dostoevsky and Romantic Realism* (Cambridge, MA, 1965).

FAUCHEREAU, S. *Moscow, 1900–1930* (New York, 1988).

FRANK, J. *Dostoevsky,* 3 vols. (Princeton, NJ, 1980–1987).

GRAY, C. *The Great Experiment: Russian Art 1863–1922* (London, 1962).

GRIERSON, R., ed. *Gates of Mystery: The Art of Holy Russia* (Fort Worth, 1993).

GROSSMAN, L. *Dostoevsky: A Biography,* trans. M. Mackler (New York, 1975).

GUSTAFSON, R. F. *Leo Tolstoy: Resident and Stranger* (Princeton, 1986).

HELDT, B. *Terrible Perfection: Women and Russian Literature* (Bloomington, IN, 1987).

HINGLEY, R. *Chekhov: A New Biography* (New York, 1976).

HOISINGTON, S. *A Plot of Her Own: The Female Protagonist in Russian Literature* (Evanston, IL, 1995).

JAHN, G. R., ed. *Tolstoy's The Death of Ivan Il'ich: A Critical Companion* (Evanston, IL, 1999).

KELLY, A. M. *Views from the Other Shore: Essays on Herzen, Chekhov, and Bakhtin* (New Haven, CT, 1999).

KNAPP, L. *The Annihilation of Inertia: Dostoevsky and Metaphysics* (Evanston, IL, 1996).

LAYTON, S. *Russian Literature and Empire: Conquest of the Caucasus from Pushkin to Tolstoy* (New York, 1994).

LEONARD, R. *A History of Russian Music* (New York, 1968).

MALIA, M. *Russia under Western Eyes: From the Bronze Horseman to the Lenin Mausoleum* (Cambridge, MA, 1999).

MAUDE, A. *The Life of Tolstoy,* 2 vols. (Oxford, 1987).

NEUBERGER, J. *Hooliganism: Crime, Culture and Power in St. Petersburg, 1900–1914* (Berkeley, 1993).

OBOLENSKY, C. *The Russian Empire: A Portrait in Photographs* (New York, 1979).

PYMAN, A. *A History of Russian Symbolism* (New York, 1994).

RABINOWITZ, S., ed. *The Noise of Change: Russian Literature and the Critics (1891–1917)* (Ann Arbor, MI, 1986).

RAYFIELD, D. *Understanding Chekhov: A Critical Study of Chekhov's Prose and Drama* (London, 1999).

SALMOND, W. *Arts and Crafts in Late Imperial Russia* (Cambridge, 1996).

SEELEY, F. F. *Turgenev: A Reading of His Fiction* (New York, 1991).

SIMMONS, E. J. *Chekhov: A Biography* (Boston, 1962).

STITES, R. *Russian Popular Culture: Entertainment and Society Since 1900* (New York, 1992).

TERRAS, V. *Reading Dostoevsky* (Madison, WI, 1998).

THOMPSON, D. O. *The Brothers Karamazov and the Poetics of Memory* (New York, 1991).

TROYAT, H. *Tolstoy* (Garden City, NY, 1967).

VALKENIER, E. *Ilyia Repin* (New York, 1990).

———. *Russian Realist Art: The State and Society: The Peredvizniki and Their Tradition* (Ann Arbor, MI, 1977).

WALSH, S. *Stravinsky, A Creative Spring: Russia and France 1882–1934* (New York, 1999).

WARTENWEILER, D. *Civil Society and Academic Debate in Russia, 1905–1914* (New York, 1999).

YARMOLINSKY, A. *Turgenev. The Man, His Art and His Age* (New York, 1959).

6

War and Revolution, 1914–1917

In August 1914 imperial Russia, its armed forces still being reorganized, refused to yield to Austro-German pressure and entered World War I. Initially, the war produced unity, patriotic resolve, and predictions of quick victory. As it dragged on, it revealed Russia's bureaucratic ineptitude, disunity in the army and government, and financial disarray. Military defeats and the regime's incompetence undermined morale among soldiers and civilians alike. In March 1917, in the midst of this great conflict, the tsarist regime was overthrown by a popular revolution. What caused the sudden collapse of the Romanov regime, which had ruled Russia for more than 300 years? Was it economic backwardness, social conflicts, bureaucratic bungling, or incompetent military leadership—or a combination of these—that accounted for Russia's defeat in World War I? This chapter probes the complex relationship between the war and the coming of revolution in March 1917.

Russia Enters World War I

On June 28, 1914, a Bosnian student linked with the Serbian national movement assassinated Archduke Francis Ferdinand, heir to the Austrian throne, in Sarajevo, Bosnia, sparking war among the European powers, Japan, and later the United States. The assassination alone did not cause the war. World War I resulted from increasingly rigid alliance systems that divided Europe between the Triple Alliance (Germany, Austria-Hungary, and Italy) and the Triple Entente (Great Britain, France, and Russia) and involved the prestige of all powers; from a precipitous growth of armaments and militarism; from intense nationalism, especially in Serbia and France, expressed in hatred of their national enemies, Austria and Germany; and from imperial rivalries. In this tense, intolerant atmosphere, diplomats could not reach reasonable compromises.

Russian leaders, at first not unduly alarmed by the Sarajevo murder, went on vacation. The Russian public and press, although mostly anti-Austrian and pro-Serbian, were not violently so. In mid-July the Russian government even sent the quartermaster-general on a routine mission to the Caucasus. By July 20, Russian leaders had returned to St. Petersburg to greet President Poincaré of France, who spent three days there on a previously arranged state visit. French and Russian chiefs reaffirmed their solemn obligation under the Franco-Russian Alliance.

No sooner had Poincaré departed than Austria-Hungary issued an ultimatum to Serbia that was so framed as to be unacceptable. Russian Foreign Minister S. D. Sazonov exclaimed, "That means European war!" but he urged Serbia to make a conciliatory reply, appeal to the powers, and not resist Austria militarily. He requested Austria to give the Serbs more time to answer, but Russia, assured of French support, resolved not to back down.

The mobilization of Russia's army became a vital factor in the last days before war broke out. On July 24 the Council of Ministers empowered War Minister V. A. Sukhomlinov to mobilize only districts facing Austria. Sazonov saw this as mainly a diplomatic move to back Serbia. Sukhomlinov and Chief of Staff N. N. Ianushkevich agreed to this partial mobilization, though subordinates objected that there were no plans for it and that to improvise them might disrupt full mobilization later. On July 25 the tsar and his ministers, learning that Serbia's reply had not satisfied Austria, agreed to support Serbia at any cost. Austria mobilized and, on July 28, declared war on Serbia, and Sazonov announced that Russia would carry out partial mobilization.

Meanwhile, Russian staff officers had convinced their chiefs, and finally Nicholas II and Sazonov, that partial mobilization was impractical. On July 29, with the Austrians bombarding Belgrade, the Russian chief of staff issued the decree of Nicholas II, authorizing full mobilization. Nicholas, receiving the Kaiser's telegram warning of the consequences, rescinded this order, but on July 30 Sazonov and the military chiefs persuaded him to authorize general mobilization. Germany demanded that Russia demobilize; when it refused, Germany declared war on Russia, then on France. After Germany violated Belgian neutrality, England joined France and Russia on August 4. The Central Powers (Germany and Austria-Hungary) now faced a coalition of Serbia, Russia, France, and England.

Russia's responsibility for World War I remains debatable. German and Western revisionist historians argue that its general mobilization doomed German and British efforts to head off conflict. But the tsar and Sazonov, who opposed war, concluded that partial mobilization would disorganize the Russian army. Another retreat in the Balkans, they believed, might destroy Russia's credibility as a great power. Also, Austria was the first to mobilize, declare war, and begin hostilities against Serbia, a protégé of Russia. Like all great European powers in 1914, Russia bore some responsibility, but its leaders went to war reluctantly after failing to find a peaceful solution. Soviet historians, following Lenin, considered World War I a clash of rival imperialist powers, with Germany and Austria-Hungary bearing primary responsibility.

War Aims and Wartime Diplomacy

Russia entered the war without clear aims except to protect itself and Serbia. At first no specific territorial claims were made against Germany, and Sazonov merely denounced German militarism and pledged to restore a "free" Poland. In September 1914 he told the French and British ambassadors that Russia advocated reorganizing Austria-Hungary into a triple monarchy, ceding Bosnia, Hercegovina, and Dalmatia to Serbia and restoring Alsace-Lorraine to France. As an afterthought he requested free passage for Russian warships through the Turkish Straits. Grand Duke Nicholas, Russia's commander in chief, urged the peoples of Austria-Hungary to overthrow Habsburg rule and achieve independence, but other Russian leaders did not pursue this nationalist tack. Like other members of the Entente, Russian leaders expected victory to provide them with a program of war aims.

Early defeats and Turkish entry into the war ended official Russian reticence. After Germany persuaded the Ottoman Empire to join the Central Powers (November 1, 1914), the tsar favored expelling it from Europe and solving "the historic task bequeathed to us by our forefathers on the shores of the Black Sea." Nationalists and liberals in the Duma and press took up the refrain. Only securing Constantinople, Professor Trubetskoi of Moscow University declared, would guarantee Russia's independence. P. N. Miliukov, leader of the Kadets and the liberal opposition in the Duma, echoing the general nationalist euphoria, demanded that Russia seize the Straits and Constantinople, and to do so became the principal Russian war aim.

The Entente powers pledged, in September 1914, not to conclude a separate peace and to consult on peace terms, but they disagreed over war plans and aims. As a basis for a future peace they concluded secret treaties and agreements. In December 1914 Grand Duke Nicholas, lacking forces to capture or garrison the Straits, urged Sazonov to obtain them by diplomacy. London, to keep Russia fighting, responded warmly. "As to Constantinople, it is clear that it must be yours," the English king told the Russian ambassador.[1] In 1915 the British undertook a Dardanelles campaign to force open the Straits and develop a supply line to Russia; its failure helped doom Russia instead to eventual defeat. In March 1915 Sazonov insisted that if the Entente won, the Straits and environs go to Russia; England, then France, agreed. The tsar told the French ambassador, Maurice Paléologue: "Take the left bank of the Rhine, take Mainz; go further if you like."[2] Later, secret inter-Allied agreements arranged a partition of the Ottoman Empire. Russia would obtain the Straits, eastern Anatolia, and part of the southern coast of the Black Sea. The former Crimean powers promised this, knowing that without Russia they would lose the war. Thus the Russian government and liberals were committed to an imperialistic peace, which aroused no popular enthusiasm at home.

---

[1] Quoted in Maurice Paléologue, *An Ambassador's Memoirs* (London, 1923), vol. 1, p. 297.
[2] Paléologue, *Ambassador's Memoirs*, vol. 1, p. 297.

The Army and the Fronts

Russia began World War I with unity, optimism, and loyalty to the Crown, a situation unlike the public apathy prevalent at the beginning of the Japanese war. Domestic quarrels and differences seemed forgotten, and the strike movement, so threatening in July, ended abruptly. Virtually the entire Duma pledged to support the war effort, except for a few socialists who refused to vote war appropriations. The enthusiasm was largely defensive; the Russian people believed that the war was being fought to defend Russia and Serbia. In the cities this spontaneous patriotism became anti-German: The name of St. Petersburg was changed to Petrograd, and there were anti-German riots. The villages, however, remained ominously silent.

At first the generals and nationalist press proclaimed that the Russian "steamroller" would move to Berlin and end the war in a few weeks. In the West, this myth of Russian invincibility was widely believed. Actually, the army, its leadership split between "patricians" and "praetorians" (aristocratic and professional elements), reflected the deep rifts in Russian government and society. Though contemporaries claimed that the army had been unprepared, the military *was* prepared for a replay of the Russo-Japanese War. As the German General Staff realized, the Russian army had recovered completely from that defeat and possessed more infantry and mobile guns on the eastern front than the Germans did. What hampered the Russian army in 1914 was divided command, incompetent leadership, and failure to mobilize industry. Grand Duke Nicholas, the impressive-looking six-foot-six commander in chief appointed at the last moment, lacked real authority and knew neither his subordinates nor military plans. In General A. A. Polivanov's words, he "appeared entirely unequipped for the task and . . . spent much time crying because he did not know how to approach his new duties."[3] His military bearing made him popular with the men,

---

[3] Quoted in M. T. Florinsky, *Russia: A History and an Interpretation* (New York, 1953), vol. 2, p. 1320.

who mistook his severity for competence. In August 1915 Nicholas II, who knew even less, replaced him, continuing a disastrous Romanov tradition of placing members of the imperial family in top military posts. War Minister Sukhomlinov, who had put through needed reforms before the war, succumbed to intrigues by his political and military foes.[4] High army commands, despite Sukhomlinov, were filled largely by seniority, not proven ability. Abler company-grade officers, killed in large numbers in the first months, could not be replaced, producing a grievous officer shortage.

General conscription swelled a peacetime force of 1.35 million men to almost 6.5 million, with no comparable increase in trained officers. During the war, more than 15 million men were called up— some 37 percent of all Allied soldiers—but only a fraction could be equipped; they were poorly led and early in the war were inadequately supplied. The rank and file were mostly illiterate peasants ignorant of why they fought. Red tape and lack of a unified command or agreed war plan produced much confusion. Shortages of shells and rifles soon developed, mainly from lack of planning and failure to mobilize industry. The autocracy was unprepared for the overwhelming complexity of total war, which necessitated mobilizing the entire population to support it, but other belligerents also proved ill-prepared.

Within the army command, prewar controversies between those favoring an offensive against weaker Austria-Hungary and others advocating an invasion of Germany remained unresolved. The army was split among competing fronts, strategies, and generals jealous of one another; men and resources were wasted. Appeals for help from the hard-pressed French and British in the west

persuaded the Russian high command to dispatch two armies under Generals P. K. Rennenkampf and A. V. Samsonov (personal enemies) into East Prussia. Inadequate maps, inaccurate intelligence, and poor coordination between the armies and their commanders produced defeat. The Germans rushed in reinforcements from France, and General von Hindenburg trapped Samsonov's army at Tannenberg. Some 300,000 men were lost, Samsonov apparently shot himself, and Russian morale was seriously damaged. Revealing German tactical superiority and ending Russian dreams of a march to Berlin, Tannenberg proved "that armies will lose battles if they are led badly enough."[5] However, a Russian offensive against the smaller, poorly armed, and unreliable Austro-Hungarian army led to occupation of Galicia and heavy Austrian losses and ended hopes by the Central Powers for quick victory in the east.

Unlike the positional trench warfare in France, a war of maneuver persisted on the eastern front. In April 1915 the Germans, reinforcing their armies, scored a breakthrough in Russian Poland. A devastating four-hour artillery bombardment smashed Russian trenches and scared their ill-trained defenders from their posts. Galicia was reconquered, and the Russians retreated hastily, abandoning Poland and part of the Baltic provinces. An unwise Russian scorched-earth policy produced swarms of refugees who poured into Russian cities and demoralized the population. Severe shortages of war matériel and even food plagued the Russian forces. Their artillery had few shells while German guns fired ceaselessly; many Russian soldiers even lacked rifles. Losses and desertions soared, officers lost faith in their men, and morale plummeted. Rumors spread: "Britain will fight to the last drop of Russian blood." Commented one Russian soldier: "We throw away our rifles and give up because things are dreadful in our army, and so are the officers."[6] Only swampy terrain, overextended German supply lines, and the heroism of the

---

[4] Sukhomlinov, notes Norman Stone in his revisionist treatment of Russia in World War I, was hated by Duma liberals for his autocratic methods and by old guard, aristocratic military elements for his reforms. Accused of corruption, he was imprisoned by the tsarist and Provisional governments, though the charges were never proven. Norman Stone, *The Eastern Front* (New York, 1975), pp. 24–32.

[5] Stone, *Eastern Front*, p. 59.
[6] Stone, p. 170.

Russian soldier prevented utter collapse. During 1915, while the western front had a long breathing spell, Russia bore the main pressure of the Central Powers.

In the winter of 1915–1916 began a surprising recovery. Though few of the promised war supplies came from Russia's allies, Russian industry in a great effort produced more than 11 million shells during 1915, proving its capacity to support a modern war. Unofficial efforts by *zemstva*, Duma deputies, and other public-spirited groups left the army far better equipped and supplied. By mid-1916, the Russian army enjoyed a considerable superiority in both men and matériel over the Central Powers. The new war minister, A. A. Polivanov, and Chief of Staff M. Alekseev were abler than their predecessors. General A. A. Brusilov's sudden but carefully prepared attack in Galicia (May 1916) shattered Austrian lines and forced the Germans to send reinforcements (see Map 6.1). This action revealed Russia's renewed ability to fight and induced Romania to join the Allies. In the Caucasus, Russian forces prevailed against poorly organized Turkish armies, capturing Erzurum and Trebizond in 1916 and penetrating deep into Anatolia.

Thus the Russian army, despite poor command and organization, played a vital part in World War I. It tied down much of the Central Powers' strength and repeatedly saved the western front from disaster. However, the cost to Russia was staggering: more than 3 million soldiers killed and wounded and 2.7 million captured and missing. Though they coped well with Austrians and Turks, Russian forces were usually defeated by the Germans. These defeats, speeding deterioration of relations between Russian officers and their men, demoralized the army and contributed greatly to the downfall of the tsar's regime.

The Home Front

Modern war, the supreme test of a nation's soundness, reveals both strengths and hidden weaknesses. Few had foreseen before 1914 that in an age of industrialization and technology war would require a total mobilization of a nation's resources. Russia proved most inadequately prepared to face such a total conflict. On the one hand, World War I triggered rapid growth of Russian machine-tool and chemical industries and swelled the industrial proletariat. On the other hand, it ruthlessly exposed Russia's inadequate transportation system, fumbling government, and chaotic finances. It revealed the tsar's incompetence and isolation, heightening the problems of a disintegrating regime and a disgruntled public. The terrible weaknesses on the home front, more than military shortcomings, produced defeat and revolution. Interior Minister Peter Durnovo's memorandum to Nicholas II in February 1914 proved prophetic:

> A war involving all of Europe would be a mortal danger for Russia and Germany regardless of which was the victor. In the event of defeat . . . social revolution in its most extreme form would be inevitable in our country.[7]

The Economy

Agriculture suffered less than industry from the ill-considered mobilization of Russian manpower. Because of rural overpopulation and prewar wastage of labor, peasant farms were able to operate almost normally, despite the loss of most male laborers. In some unoccupied provinces, acreage under cereal crops actually increased as women, children, and old men took up the slack. Large estates, which had produced most of the surplus for home and foreign markets, were harder hit because they could not obtain hired laborers, machinery, or spare parts. Despite increased demand, the total Russian grain and potato harvest and meat production fell by about one-third during the war. At first peasant soldiers ate better in the army than they had at home, but by 1917 the front was receiving less than half the grain it required. As commanders searched for food, their soldiers grew hungry and dissatisfied.

---

[7] Quoted in M. Heller and A. Nekrich, *Utopia in Power . . .*, trans. P. Carlos (New York, 1986).

SWEDEN

Helsingfors •   Viborg •

Petrograd •

Reval •   Vologda •

Baltic Sea   Pskov •   *Volga*   Tver •

Libau •   Riga •   Moscow •

Danzig •   Dvinsk •

Tannenberg Aug. 1914   Vilna •   Riazan •

Sept. 1914 Masurian Lakes   Smolensk •   Penza •

GERMANY   Minsk •   Mogilev •   R U S S I A

Bug   **POLAND**   Gomel •

Front in November 1917

Voronezh •

Kiev •   *Don*   *Volga*

GALICIA   Kharkov •   Tsaritsyn •

Brusilov Offense 1916

AUSTRIA   U K R A I N E

Budapest •   Ekaterinoslav •

HUNGARY   **Rumanian and Russian Forces 1916**

Belgrade •   Odessa •   Rostov-on-Don •

Kuban

Sarajevo •   **RUMANIA**   *Terek*

Bucharest •   Sevastopol •   *Caucasus*

Danube   **CRIMEA**

SERBIA   **BULGARIA**   *Black Sea*

Sofia •   *Kura*

ALBANIA   Batum •

Bosporus •   Kars •

Constantinople   Trebizond •

Gallipoli •   *Farthest Russian Advance 1916*

Dardanelles   Tabriz •

GREECE   **TURKEY**

Allies, 1915–16

✸ Major battle sites   **+++++ Major Russian railways**   **—··— Farthest Russian advance 1916**

▄▄▄ Russian border 1914   **ꓥꓥꓥ Farthest Russian advance in Germany and Austria, 1914**

Map 6.1 Russia in World War I, 1914–1918

SOURCE: Adapted from *A History of Russia,* Sixth Edition, by Nicholas V. Riasanovsky. Copyright © 1963, 1977, 1984, 1993, 2000 by Oxford University Press, Inc. Used by permission.

Hungry Petrograd in World War I. Bread lines were a common occurrence in the capital as food supplies dwindled.

Even in 1917 Russia possessed enough food for both civilians and soldiers. The virtual cessation of food exports and diminished use of grain to manufacture vodka roughly balanced production declines. Government policy contributed to shortages: Artificially low state prices for grain deprived farmers of production incentives while prices of manufactured goods they desired rose rapidly. Peasants, therefore, consumed more grain and brewed their own alcohol while speculators hoarded grain and awaited higher prices. Because shipping foodstuffs to the cities was complicated by a worsening transportation crisis, by 1917 the cities in the northern consuming provinces were hungry while in Ukraine and Siberia food was relatively abundant.

Transportation, the economy's weakest link, was nearing breakdown by 1917. The railroad system, which had barely met ordinary peacetime needs, had a low carrying capacity and inferior connections with seaports. (Only a narrow-gauge line went to Archangel, and not until 1916 was a railroad built to the new port of Murmansk.) Wartime needs virtually monopolized a railway system further overburdened by the retreat in Poland and massive evacuation of civilians. Railroad cars and spare parts, formerly obtained largely in western Europe, became critically short. The government spent 1.5 billion rubles to improve the network and build additional lines; it ordered American railway equipment, but it did not arrive until late in 1917. On the eve of the March Revolution, a crisis in railroad transport worsened the problems of industry and food supply.

Because at first the government had no deferment system, industry was crippled by mobilization of irreplaceable skilled labor. Much of the labor force came to be composed of women, children, and war prisoners. The war halted a burgeoning strike movement. Initially, many factory owners pursued "business as usual," and some curtailed production because of mobilization, disruption of foreign business connections, and expected decreases in domestic demand. Unprecedented need for munitions and war supplies placed an intolerable burden on industry, which could not get essential raw materials and fuel. (More shells were used in a month than in a year of the Russo-Japanese War.) The loss in 1915 of Russian Poland, the Empire's most industrialized region, reduced production by about one-fifth. To be sure, certain branches of industry, spurred by war demand, grew rapidly: Metalworking trebled in 1916, and chemicals expanded 250 percent. Rifle production in August 1916 was 11 times that of 1914 but was still insufficient.

Red tape and lack of government planning further complicated industry's problems. The official hands-off policy lasted until appalling munitions shortages spurred public action. During 1915 industrialists, Duma members, *zemstva,* and municipalities formed military-industrial committees, which improved the supply picture greatly. But government action was too little and too late. By 1917 industrial production was falling sharply in a growing economic crisis.

The war badly disrupted Russian foreign trade. In the first year exports fell to about 15 percent of the prewar level and later recovered to only 30 percent. Imports, dropping sharply at first in 1916, were double the prewar value in 1917—mainly war supplies and equipment sent by the Allies through Siberian ports. Instead of the 47 million ruble export surplus of 1913, the wartime Russian trade deficit totaled some 2.5 billion rubles. Incompetent government wartime financing damaged the Russian economy. At the outset Russia

seemed in better financial shape than in the Russo-Japanese War, but the Treasury expended as much in a month of World War I as in a year of the war against Japan. A drastic fall in customs and railway receipts cut Treasury revenues, and an incredible blunder robbed it of the liquor tax. The finance minister ordered state liquor stores closed during mobilization and introduced legislation to raise liquor prices to combat drunkenness. A decree of August 1914 kept liquor stores closed throughout the war. Such pioneering in prohibition cost the Treasury about 700 million rubles annually—about 25 percent of its total revenue. Peasants brewed their own liquor, and illicit vodka sales brought huge profits to dealers but nothing to the Treasury. New wartime taxes barely covered this loss, and state revenues fell far short of war expenditures. Income and war profits taxes were low and introduced too late. Huge domestic and foreign loans and massive use of the printing press financed the war. Foreign nations, chiefly Great Britain, loaned Russia some 8 billion rubles, accelerating a sharp decline in the ruble's exchange value, which produced rampant inflation, loss of confidence in the currency, and a rapid rise in living costs. Russia grew ever more dependent financially upon its allies.

The serious economic strain of the war helped bring on revolution and made it more profound. The basic economic framework, especially of peasant agriculture, remained sound, but food supplies in the swollen cities of Petrograd and Moscow became increasingly inadequate as the overstrained railway system deteriorated. With paper rubles losing their value, there was little incentive for peasants to ship their grain to the cities. Although the masses' purchasing power rose, people found little to buy. Russian resources were wasted and misused by incompetent officials.

The Government

During the war the tsarist regime revealed its inability to govern the country and disintegrated rapidly. Nicholas II, retaining his faith in autocracy,

Orthodoxy, and nationality, failed to supply leadership; he believed that constitutional government was evil and that the public could not be allowed to help run Russia. Though interfering little with the Duma, he largely ignored it and absorbed himself in family affairs and problems. Ever more dominated by Empress Alexandra, he and his family were estranged from the public and the bureaucracy. "The characteristic feature of the imperial family," noted a trusted minister, "is their inaccessibility to the outside world, and their atmosphere of mysticism." Empress Alexandra, who hated the Duma and liberal ministers with a passion, was largely responsible for this isolation, and as Rasputin's hold over her grew, she interfered more and more in state affairs. The most influential of several "men of God" to influence the superstitious empress, Rasputin had been introduced at court in November 1905. She found this semiliterate, debauched (his motto was "Redemption through sin"!), but dynamic Siberian peasant indispensable to preserving her hemophiliac son, Alexis (born 1904), and the dynasty. Rasputin managed, apparently through hypnotism, to stop the tsarevich's bleeding, and to the imperial couple he apparently embodied the Russian people.

When Nicholas II took command of the army in September 1915, control over the government passed to the empress and Rasputin. Believing that she could save Russia from revolution, Alexandra relied completely on Rasputin, who lacked clear political aims; she was surrounded with unscrupulous, greedy adventurers. When the more competent, liberal ministers, appointed under public pressure early in 1915, protested Nicholas's decision to become army chief, the empress, to preserve autocracy, removed them from office. A nonentity, Boris Stürmer, was named premier. "A country cannot be lost whose sovereign is guided by a man of God," Alexandra wrote Nicholas. "Won't you come to the assistance of your hubby now that he is absent . . . ?" Nicholas queried. "You ought to be my eyes and ears there in the capital. . . . It rests with you to

keep peace and harmony among the ministers."[8] The final disgraceful year of Romanov rule was marked by "ministerial leapfrog" as the empress and Rasputin shifted ministers with bewildering speed. The last premier, Prince N. D. Golitsyn, begged to be relieved of his tasks, which he did not know how to perform. Late in 1916 Rasputin's behavior became intolerable even to loyal monarchists. An ultraconservative Duma delegate, V. M. Purishkevich, and two grand dukes invited Rasputin to a banquet, fed him cake laced with cyanide, shot him, and finally drowned him in a canal. This was a terrible blow to the empress, but she and A. D. Protopopov continued to rule and hold seances to recall Rasputin from the dead. On the eve of the March Revolution, the government was inactive, divided, and in an advanced state of decay.

Meanwhile, the Duma had risen to unprecedented national leadership. After the war began, the Duma set up a provisional committee to aid the wounded and war sufferers and to coordinate its war work. At first, the Duma supported the government unconditionally, but early in 1915 it agitated with *zemstvo* and municipal representatives for a responsible ministry. That summer, about two-thirds of the Duma, excluding the extreme left and right, formed a Progressive Bloc led by Kadets and Octobrists, which advocated a government capable of winning public confidence, political amnesty, religious freedom, and freedom for trade unions. Though most of the ministers accepted this program, Premier Goremykin stubbornly rejected it as an illegal attempt to limit the autocrat's power. During 1916 the Duma's relations with the executive branch deteriorated sharply when deputies led by Miliukov accused the government and the tsarina of conspiring with the Germans. Censorship deleted the sharpest Duma attacks, but its debates were widely publicized and it was winning a public following. The fatal weakness that prevented the Duma from

---

[8] Bernard Pares, *The Letters of the Tsar to the Tsaritsa, 1914–1917* (London, 1929) and *Letters of the Tsaritsa to the Tsar, 1914–1916* (London, 1923).

representing and leading the Russian people in 1917 was an electoral process of indirect and weighted voting that favored the landed nobility. Thus the majority of Russians were still not politically represented.

The Revolutionary Movement

The government's ineffectiveness and inability to win liberal support provided revolutionaries with a rare opportunity. In 1915, after the defeat in Galicia, strikes grew more numerous and continued to mount until the March Revolution, but the socialist parties in Russia remained too disorganized and fragmented to prepare a revolution. Their leaders mostly remained in exile in Siberia or Europe, out of touch with Russia. Initially, the SDs in the Duma denounced the war as the product of aggressive capitalism and urged the proletariat to oppose it. The Bolshevik deputies, more aggressively antiwar than the Mensheviks, were soon arrested, tried, and exiled to Siberia. Social Democrats abroad were divided by the war. Plekhanov, splitting with Lenin and the majority, urged Russian workers to fight against Prussian imperialism and with the Western democracies to final victory. Lenin, in his *Theses on War* (1914), written in Switzerland, denounced World War I as imperialist and exhorted Russian workers to help defeat tsarism, to turn the conflict into a civil war, and to prepare revolution. Lenin accused the Second International and its leader, Karl Kautsky, of betraying the proletariat by voting for a fratricidal war. At international socialist conferences at Zimmerwald (1915) and Kienthal (1916), the minority Leninist left urged a civil war of workers against all capitalist governments, but most European socialists supported their governments in World War I.

The Bolsheviks' Russian rivals were likewise divided. The Menshevik organizational committee in Switzerland, including Martov, Akselrod, and A. S. Martynov, denounced the war and advocated eventual revolution but sought to restore unity to international socialism. Rather than favor Russia's defeat, they exhorted workers to exert pressure on all governments to conclude a democratic peace without annexations and indemnities. In Russia, an important Menshevik group around the publication *Our Dawn (Nasha Zaria)* advocated noncooperation with the regime without hampering the war effort; later it favored defense of Russia against invasion. The SRs, still dispirited, were split among a right actively supporting the war effort, Chernov's pacifist center, and a sizable left internationalist wing favoring defeat of tsarism. In Russia and abroad, socialists divided into three main groupings: patriots, centrists (defensists and pacifists), and defeatists advocating revolution.

Bolshevik organizations in Russia were tougher and more resilient than their rivals. The British scholar Leonard Schapiro claims that Bolshevik wartime activity was intermittent and ineffective, but Soviet accounts asserted that the Bolsheviks led the workers' struggle against the war from the start, steadily expanded their organization, and followed Lenin's instructions. Although the police "liquidated" the Petrograd Committee 30 times and arrested more than 600 Bolsheviks, the party nonetheless expanded its membership and activities. By late 1916 the Bolsheviks, numbering perhaps 10,000, were led by A. G. Shliapnikov (Lenin's man), V. M. Molotov, and P. A. Zalutskii. Though Soviet historians exaggerated Bolshevik strength and leadership of the workers, the party represented a considerable force ready, unlike Mensheviks and SRs, to exploit a revolutionary situation.

The March Revolution

In five days—March 8–12, 1917 (February 23–27 Old Style)[9]—a mass movement in Petrograd overturned the tsarist government. The eyewitness accounts of N. N. Sukhanov, a moderate socialist, and French ambassador Maurice Paléologue stress that it was spontaneous and not led by a party or

---

[9] New Style dates, like those used in western Europe, will be used from this point onward instead of Old Style dates of the Julian calendar, which by the 20th century were 13 days behind the New Style dates.

organization. Western historians and early Soviet accounts, such as Trotskii's *History of the Russian Revolution,* accept this view, whereas Stalinist historians overstate Bolshevik leadership of the masses.

In previous months the Petrograd strike movement had steadily gathered momentum. A strike by some workers at the Putilov factory, Russia's largest, became general, and on March 7 the management locked out the workers. Though the government and tsar had received numerous warnings of impending revolution (from foreign ambassadors and Duma president M. V. Rodzianko), they made no concessions. Nicholas II, confident that nothing unusual was afoot, left his palace at Tsarskoe Selo near Petrograd on March 7 for military headquarters at Mogilev. The authorities had a detailed plan for suppressing an uprising: First the 3,500 police were to be used, then Cossacks with whips, and finally troops from the 150,000-man garrison. The plan, though later implemented, proved ineffective.

Revolution began in Petrograd on March 8, International Women's Day. In the large factories of Vyborg district, women in bread lines and strikers began spontaneous demonstrations, which spread to the Petersburg side. (See Chapter 7, Map 7.1.) Women textile workers, the most downtrodden segment of the Petrograd proletariat, supplied the impetus. In the streets appeared placards with slogans: "Down with the war!" "Give us bread!" and "Down with autocracy!" That day, notes Sukhanov, "the movement in the streets became clearly defined, going beyond the limits of the usual factory meetings. . . . The city was filled with rumors and a feeling of 'disorders.'" Fearing conflict with the authorities while the party was weak, the Bolsheviks, who controlled Vyborg Borough Committee, relegated revolution to the indefinite future, not realizing that one was in progress. In March, noted Trotskii, the higher the revolutionary leaders, the further they lagged behind the masses. Next day (March 9), continued Sukhanov, "the movement swept over Petersburg like a great flood. Nevskii Prospect [the main street] and many squares in the center were crowded with workers." Mounted police

were sent to disperse the demonstrations, then Cossacks were ordered out. They charged the crowds halfheartedly and often chatted amicably with the workers.

By March 10 "the entire civil population felt itself to be in one camp united against the enemy —the police and the military." Proclamations of the garrison commander, General S. S. Khabalov, threatening stern punishment for demonstrators, were torn down, police were disarmed or vanished from their posts, and factories and streetcars halted operation. Khabalov sent in troops, but the crowds, avoiding clashes with them, sought to win them over.

Early on Sunday, March 11, workers advanced from outlying districts toward Petrograd's center. Stopped at the bridges, they poured across the solidly frozen Neva River, dodging bullets. At the tsar's orders, Khabalov sent thousands of infantry into the streets. On Nevskii Prospect, soldiers fired on crowds, killing many and terrorizing the rest; that afternoon the Vyborg Borough Committee considered calling off the strike. The critical moment of the revolution had come. In the evening, after police fired on a crowd, soldiers of the passing Pavlovskii Regiment mutinied, fired on the police, then returned to barracks, resolved not to fire again at strikers, and appealed to their comrades to join them. This was the military's first revolutionary act of 1917.

On the fifth day (March 12) workers streamed into the factories and in open meetings resolved to continue the struggle. Armed insurrection grew irresistibly from events while the Bolshevik headquarters staff looked on despondently, leaving the districts and barracks to their own devices. Soldiers mutinied in growing numbers and joined crowds of workers.

New centers of authority sprang up before old ones had disappeared. The government had ordered the Duma prorogued, but on March 12 some members elected a Provisional Committee under the Duma president, Rodzianko, representing all groups except the right, "to restore order in the capital and establish contact with public organizations and institutions." Reflecting views of the

Progressive Bloc, the Committee sought to save the dynasty with a responsible ministry. Simultaneously, the Petrograd Soviet was reborn while mutinous troops freed worker and socialist leaders from the city's prisons. Proceeding with the troops to the Tauride Palace and aided by the trade union leaders, they created the Provisional Executive Committee of the Soviet of Workers' Deputies. At the Petrograd Soviet's first meeting that evening some 250 delegates were present, but new ones kept entering the noisy, chaotic session. No political party proposed a definite plan or took decisive leadership. When soldier deputies asked to join, the organization became the Soviet of Workers' and Soldiers' Deputies. Henceforth, this spontaneous fusion of popular elements led the revolution.

The tsarist government and dynasty came to a swift, unlamented end. By March 14 the entire garrison of Petrograd had defected, and the tsarist ministers were arrested. The Duma's Provisional Committee selected a Provisional Government from liberal members of the Progressive Bloc, the "government having public confidence," which the bourgeoisie had long sought. Learning of the deteriorating situation in Petrograd, Nicholas II decided to rejoin his family at Tsarskoe Selo, but railroad workers halted his train and forced him to return to Pskov, headquarters of the northern front. Behind events as usual, he agreed now to a responsible ministry, but his commanders unanimously advised abdication. On March 15 delegates Guchkov and V. V. Shulgin, sent to Pskov by the Provisional Committee, secured Nicholas's abdication in favor of his brother, Grand Duke Mikhail. Rumors of Mikhail's impending rule caused such indignation among the workers that he wisely renounced his claims, and on March 15, 1917, Romanov rule ended in Russia.

Problem 2

Did World War I Cause the Collapse of Tsarism?

What is the relationship between the defeat of a regime in war and its overthrow? What is the connection between war and revolution? Did Germany's defeat of the Russian imperial army cause or trigger the collapse of tsarism in March 1917? Without war, was it likely that the regime could have survived in liberalized form, turning perhaps into something resembling the British constitutional monarchy? Or, conversely, did the war delay tsarist collapse by generating a final outburst of Russian patriotism? Was the regime's disintegration so far advanced in 1914 that it would soon have collapsed in any case? Were social and political tensions rising or declining in Russia in 1914? Finally, could either the tsarist regime, without war, or a liberal successor have confronted 20th-century problems successfully?

The Soviet Position

An official Soviet account, written during the rule of N. S. Khrushchev, emphasizes the approaching collapse of tsarist Russia and the revolutionary upsurge just before World War I, as well as the growing strength and cohesion of the Bolsheviks in leading the discontented masses:

> The cost of living was rising, and the position of the worker was deteriorating. An official industrial survey revealed that while annual wages averaged 246 rubles, annual profit per worker averaged 252 rubles. . . . Incredible poverty reigned in the countryside. Stolypin's agrarian policy had, as its direct result, the mass impoverishment of the peasants and enrichment of the kulak [better-off peasants]

Tsar Nicholas II and family. The tsar is seated second from left, and his wife
Alexandra stands behind him. Photograph taken just after the turn of the century.

Library of Congress

Problem 2 continued

bloodsucker. . . . The Russian countryside presented a picture of omnipotent feudal landlords,
bigger and richer kulak farms, the impoverishment
of a vast mass of middle peasants, and a substantially increased mass of landless peasants. . . . The
situation left no doubt whatever that the Stolypin
policy had collapsed.

Its collapse brought out more saliently than ever
the profound contradictions throughout Russia's
social and political system. It demonstrated anew
that the tsarist government was incapable of
solving the country's basic social and economic
problems. . . . Poverty, oppression, lack of human
rights, humiliating indignities imposed on the
people—all this, Lenin emphasized, was in crying
contradiction to the state of the country's productive forces and to the degree of political understanding and demands of the masses. . . . Only a
new revolution could save Russia. . . .

The Bolsheviks' prediction that a new revolutionary upsurge was inevitable proved to be true. Everywhere there was growing discontent and indignation

among the people. The workers saw in the Bolshevik revolutionary slogans a clear-cut expression of
their own aspirations. . . . Of all the political parties
then active in Russia, only the Bolsheviks had a
platform that fully accorded with the interests of the
working class and the people generally. . . .

The workers' movement continued to grow in
scope and strength. There were over one million
strikers in 1912, and 1,272,000 in 1913. Economic
struggles were intertwined with political ones and
culminated in mass revolutionary strikes. The
working class went over to the offensive against
the capitalists and the tsarist monarchy. . . . In
1910–1914, according to patently minimized figures, there were over 13,000 peasant outbreaks, in
which many manor houses and kulak farmsteads
were destroyed. . . . The unrest spread to the tsarist
army. . . . Mutiny was brewing in the Baltic and
Black Sea fleets. A new revolution was maturing in
Russia.

Together with the rise of the working-class movement, the party of the working class, the Bolshevik
Party, grew and gained in strength. . . . Amidst the
difficulties created by their illegal status, the

Bolsheviks *reestablished a mass party,* firmly led and guided by its Central Committee. . . . Everywhere—in mass strikes, street demonstrations, factory gate meetings—the Bolsheviks emphasized that revolution was the only way out, and put forward slogans expressing the people's longings: a democratic republic, an eight-hour working day, confiscation of the landed estates in favor of the peasants.

Meanwhile the waves of the working-class movement rose higher and higher. In the first half of 1914 about 1,500,000 workers were involved in strikes. . . . On July 3 the police opened fire on a workers' meeting at the Putilov Works in St. Petersburg. A wave of indignation swept over the country. The St. Petersburg Bolshevik committee called for immediate strike action. . . . Demonstrations began in protest against the actions of the tsarist authorities and the war, which everyone felt was about to break out. The strike wave spread to Moscow; barricades were thrown up in St. Petersburg, Baku, and Lodz.

Russia was faced with a revolutionary crisis. The landlords and capitalists were accusing each other of inability to put out the flames of revolution. . . . The tsarist government adopted "emergency" measures, the capital was turned into a veritable military camp. . . . The advance of the revolution was interrupted by the outbreak of the world war.[10]

The Pessimists' View

Leopold Haimson, writing in *Slavic Review* in 1965, presents an interesting analysis of conditions in Russia on the eve of World War I, in some ways refuting and in others supporting the preceding Soviet assertions:

The four-day interval between the last gasps of the Petersburg strike and the outbreak of war may not altogether dispose of the thesis of Soviet historians that only the war prevented the strike movement of July, 1914, from turning into a decisive attack against the autocracy. . . . Yet surely much of the

conviction of this argument pales in the light of the two glaring sources of political weakness that the strike revealed from its very inception . . . the failure of the clashes in St. Petersburg to set off anything like the all-national political strike, which even the Bolshevik leaders had considered . . . a necessary condition for the armed assault against the autocracy . . . [and] the inability of the Petersburg workers to mobilize, in time, active support among other groups in society. . . . No demonstrations, no public meetings, no collective petitions—no expressions of solidarity even barely comparable to those that Bloody Sunday had evoked were now aroused. . . . Thus, . . . the most important source of the political impotence revealed by the Petersburg strike was precisely the one that made for its "monstrous" revolutionary explosiveness: the sense of isolation, of psychological distance, that separated the Petersburg workers from educated, privileged society.

. . . The crude representations to be found in recent Soviet writings of the "revolutionary situation" already at hand in July, 1914, can hardly be sustained. Yet when one views the political and social tensions evident in Russian society in 1914 in a wider framework and in broader perspective, any flat-footed statement of the case for stabilization appears at least equally shaky. . . .

By July, 1914, along with a polarization between workers and educated, privileged society . . . , a second process of polarization—this one between the vast bulk of privileged society and the tsarist regime—appeared almost equally advanced. Unfolding largely detached from the rising wave of the labor movement, this second process could not affect its character and temper but was calculated to add a probably decisive weight to the pressure against the dikes of existing authority. By 1914, this second polarization had progressed to the point where even the most moderate spokesmen of liberal opinion were stating publicly, in the Duma and in the press, that an impasse had been reached between the state power and public opinion, which some argued could be resolved only by a revolution of the left or of the right. . . .

Indeed, by the beginning of 1914 any hope of avoiding a revolutionary crisis appeared to be evaporating even among the more moderate representatives of liberal opinion. Under the impact of

---

[10] *History of the Communist Party of the Soviet Union* (Moscow, 1960), pp. 163–64, 169–70, 173, 175–76, 182–83.

the blind suicidal course pursued by the government and its handful of supporters, the Octobrist Party had split at the seams. . . .

Indeed, many signs of economic and social progress could be found in the Russian provinces of the year 1914—the introduction of new crops, new techniques and forms of organization in agriculture, and the industrialization of the countryside; growing literacy among the lower strata and invigorated cultural life among the upper strata of provincial society. But no more than in the major cities were these signs of progress and changes in the localities to be viewed as evidence of the achievement or indeed the promise of greater social stability. . . ."Official" and "unofficial" Russia had now turned into two worlds completely sealed off one from the other.[11]

The Optimists' View

Leonard Schapiro, a British historian, stresses the weakness and disorganization of the Bolsheviks on the eve of World War I, providing a sharp contrast to Soviet accounts:

The Bolsheviks, or those of them who supported Lenin, could now [1914] no longer persist in their policy of maintaining the split [with the Mensheviks] at all costs. . . . There was also more unity now on the non-Bolshevik side than ever before. . . . If Lenin were isolated in his intransigence, there was every chance that many of his "conciliator" followers, who had rejoined him in 1912, would break away again. The Bolshevik organization was, moreover, in a poor state in 1914, as compared with 1912. The underground committees were disrupted. There were no funds, and the circulation of *Pravda* had fallen drastically under the impact of the split in the Duma "fraction."

Intensive propaganda for unity now began inside Russia. The Mensheviks and organizations supporting them drew up an appeal to the Russian workers, blaming the Bolsheviks for the split, and

urging support for the efforts of the International to reunite the whole party. But it was too late. War broke out . . . and before long, the Russian social democrats were rent asunder by new and even less reconcilable dissensions.[12]

Alexander Gerschenkron, an American economic historian, argues that Russia was following the path that western Europe had taken earlier and suggests that without war it would have avoided revolution:

Russia before the First World War was still a relatively backward country by any quantitative criterion. . . . Nevertheless . . . Russia seemed to duplicate what had happened in Germany in the last decades of the 19th century [in industrial development]. One might surmise that in the absence of the war Russia would have continued on the road of progressive westernization. . . . The likelihood that the transformation in agriculture would have gone on at an accelerated speed is very great. . . .

As one compares the situation in the years before 1914 with that of the [18]90s, striking differences are obvious. In the earlier period, the very process of industrialization with its powerful confiscatory pressures upon the peasantry kept adding . . . to the feeling of resentment and discontent until the outbreak of large-scale disorders became almost inevitable. The industrial prosperity of the following period [1906–1914] had no comparable effects, however. Modest as the improvements in the situation of peasants were, they were undeniable and widely diffused. Those improvements followed rather than preceded a revolution, and accordingly tended to contribute to a relaxation of tension. . . .

Similarly, the economic position of labor was clearly improving. . . . There is little doubt that the Russian labor movement of those years was slowly turning toward revision and trade-unionist lines. As was true in the West, the struggles for general and equal franchise to the Duma and for a cabinet responsible to the Duma, which probably would have occurred sooner or later, may well have further accentuated this development. . . .

[11] Leopold Haimson, "The Problem of Social Stability in Urban Russia, 1905–1917: II," *SR* 24, no. 1 (March 1965): 1–3, 8–10.

[12] Leonard Schapiro, *The Communist Party of the Soviet Union* (New York, 1959), pp. 139–140.

. . . It seems plausible to say that Russia on the eve of the war was well on the way toward a westernization or, perhaps more precisely, a Germanization of its industrial growth.[13]

An English View

In a recent study of the Russian Revolution and how it affected the Russian people, the English scholar Christopher Read writes:

We need to look at the immediate causes of the collapse of tsarism, the particular conjuncture that brought about the emergence of the Provisional Government and the abdication of Nicholas II. There can be no doubt that, in the short term, it was Russia's disastrous performance in the First World War that brought about the final destruction of tsarism.

The initial impact of the war was favourable to the regime. Internal conflicts were put to one side as the whole country took up the national cause of fighting the enemy. Militarily, too, the tsarist army scored some limited successes that may even have been decisive in preventing a rapid German victory (in France). . . . The moment of success was brief. The new German reinforcements soon pushed the Russians back and even started to advance into Russian Poland.

Worse quickly followed. The 1915 campaigning season was a series of unmitigated catastrophes from which the autocracy never recovered. The Russian army was soon in headlong retreat as the Central Powers marched forward into the Carpathians and through Poland. . . . Warsaw was evacuated in early and mid-August. . . . Reinforcements going to the front were met by a constant stream of civilian refugees and bedraggled, broken units heading into the interior to regroup.

. . . From 1915 on, the regime was caught in a trap. It could only save itself by undermining its erstwhile closest supporters and abandoning all it held dear. Essentially, this was only an acute form of the problem it had faced since the mid-19th cen-

tury, but in the turmoil of total war the old tactics of evading the real issues and diverting or repressing opposition were even more ineffective than usual.

The final scene of the autocracy's long-drawn-out demise was played out within the limits of the situation that emerged in the high summer of 1915. The crisis of August 1915 brought all the conflicting pressures into focus. The military commanders thought the only solution was that they should have more power. The civilian government were afraid that, given the military's incompetence, such a development would hasten disaster. . . . The more competent members of the administration were horrified by the continuing encroachment of the military on their preserve. As the front fell back, the army chiefs demanded that more and more of the rear territory should be put under military rule. The government was determined to resist this process, not only because of its natural inclination to preserve its own power, but also because of the total incompetence of some of the army commanders when it came to politics and the administration of civilians.

. . . Thus, by 1916 the basic elements of tsarism's final crisis were in place. . . . Had the autocracy been prepared to make a major gesture of reconciliation with the Duma a new start might still have been possible, but nothing illustrates the entrenched obtuseness of Nicholas II and those around him better than the events of the last months of the dynasty.[14]

Conclusion

Neither "optimists" nor "pessimists" have proved their case fully, yet both present valid arguments. Unquestionably, there was serious social tension and a major worker upsurge early in 1914, yet to call this a "revolutionary situation" appears to be as misleading as to claim that one existed in 1861. The workers remained largely isolated from the rest of Russian society; their movement was confined mainly to the larger cities. To be sure, the alienation of educated society from a narrow-minded regime was evi-

[13] "Patterns of Economic Development," in C. Black, *The Transformation of Russian Society* (Cambridge, MA, 1960), pp. 57–61.

[14] Christopher Read, *From Tsar to Soviets: The Russian People and Their Revolution* (New York and Oxford, 1996), pp. 35–38.

Problem 2 continued

dent and growing, as was fragmentation of the political parties (notably Kadets and Octobrists).

On the other hand, Russia for the first time was experiencing self-sustaining industrial and agricultural growth, as well as an unparalleled degree of prosperity. ■

InfoTrac® College Edition Search Terms

Enter the search term *Nicholas II* in Keywords.
Enter the search term *Rasputin* in Keywords.
Enter the search term *World War I* in the Subject Guide.
Enter the search term *Russia* in the Subject Guide, and then go to subdivision *history.*

Suggested Additional Reading

ACTON, E., et al., eds. *Critical Companion to the Russian Revolution, 1914–1921* (Bloomington, IN, 1997).

BERNSTEIN, H. *The Willy-Nicky Correspondence, 1914–17* (New York, 1918).

BRUSSILOV, A. A. *A Soldier's Notebook, 1914–18* (Westport, CT, 1971).

BUCHANAN, G. W. *My Mission to Russia,* 2 vols. (New York and London, 1923).

BURDZHALOV, E. *Russia's Second Revolution: The February 1917 Uprising in Petrograd,* trans. and ed. Don Raleigh (Bloomington, IN, 1987).

COCKFIELD, J. H. *With Snow on Their Boots: The Tragic Odessey of the Russian Expeditionary Force in France during World War I* (New York, 1998).

DE JONG, A. *The Life and Times of Grigorii Rasputin* (New York, 1982).

EDELMAN, R. *Gentry Politics on the Eve of the Russian Revolution* (New Brunswick, NJ, 1980).

FRAME, M. *The St. Petersburg Imperial Theaters: Stage and State in Revolutionary Russia* (Jefferson, NC, 2000).

FRANCIS, S. R. *Russia from the American Embassy* (New York, 1971).

GEIFMAN, A. *Entangled in Terror: The Azef Affair and the Russian Revolution* (Wilmington, DE, 2000).

GEYER, D. *The Russian Revolution: Historical Problems and Perspectives* (New York, 1987).

GOLOVIN, N. N. *The Russian Army in the World War* (New Haven, CT, 1931).

GRAYSON, B. L. *Russian-American Relations in World War I* (New York, 1979).

GRONSKY, P. P., and N. I. ASTROV. *The War and the Russian Government* (New Haven, CT, 1929).

HASEGAWA, T. *The February Revolution: Petrograd 1917* (Seattle, 1981).

KATKOV, G. *Russia 1917: The February Revolution* (New York, 1967).

KNOX, A. *With the Russian Army: 1914–1917* (New York, 1921).

LIH, L. *Bread and Authority in Russia, 1914–1921* (Berkeley, 1990).

MANDEL, D. *The Petrograd Workers and the Fall of the Old Regime* (New York, 1984).

MASSIE, R. *Nicholas and Alexandra* (New York, 1967).

MCKEAN, R. *St. Petersburg Between Revolutions . . . June 1907–February 1917* (New Haven, CT, 1990).

MICHELSON, A. M., et al. *Russian Finance During the War* (New Haven, CT, 1928).

ODINETS, D. M., and P. J. NOVGORODTSEV. *Russian Schools and Universities in the World War* (New Haven, CT, 1929).

PALÉOLOGUE, M., *An Ambassador's Memoirs,* 3 vols. (New York, 1972).

PARES, B. *The Fall of the Russian Monarchy . . .* (New York, 1939; reprint, New York, 1961).

———, ed. *The Letters of the Tsar to the Tsaritsa, 1914–1917* (London, 1929).

———. *The Letters of the Tsaritsa to the Tsar . . .* (London, 1923).

PAVLOVSKY, G. *Agricultural Russia on the Eve of Revolution* (London, 1930).

PEARSON, R. *The Russian Moderates and the Crisis of Tsarism, 1914–1917* (New York, 1977).

PERRY, J. C., and C. PLESHAKOV. *The Flight of the Romanovs: A Family Saga* (New York, 1999).

POLNER, T. I., et al. *Russian Local Government During the War and the Union of Zemstvos* (New Haven, CT, 1930).

PORTER, C. *Women in Revolutionary Russia* (New York, 1988).

PRICE, M. P. *Dispatches from the Revolution: Russia 1916–1918*, ed. Tania Rose (Durham, NC, 1997).

PURISHKEVICH, V. M. *The Murder of Rasputin*, ed. M. Shaw (Ann Arbor, MI, 1985).

RADZINSKY, E. *The Rasputin File* (New York, 2000).

READ, C. *From Tsar to Soviets: The Russian People and Their Revolution* (New York and Oxford, 1996).

RODZIANKO, M. V. *The Reign of Rasputin* (London, 1927).

RUTHERFORD, W. *The Russian Army in World War I* (London, 1975).

SENN, A. E. *The Russian Revolution in Switzerland* (Madison, WI, 1971).

SIEGELBAUM, L. H. *The Politics of Industrial Mobilization in Russia, 1914–1917* (New York, 1983).

SMITH, C. J. *The Russian Struggle for Power, 1914–17* (New York, 1956).

SOLZHENITSYN, A. *August 1914* (New York, 1972). (Historical novel.)

STONE, N. *The Eastern Front* (New York, 1975).

THATCHER, I. D. *Leon Trotsky and World War I: August 1914–February 1917* (New York, 2000).

THURSTON, R. *Liberal City, Conservative State: Moscow and Russia's Urban Crisis, 1906–1914* (New York, 1987).

WILDMAN, A. K. *The End of the Russian Imperial Army . . .* (Princeton, 1979).

ZAGORSKY, S. O. *State Control of Industry in Russia During the War* (New Haven, CT, 1928).

7

From March to November 1917

The politically freest, most exciting year in Russian history was 1917, and it has generated more controversy than any other. Bolshevik victory in November brought to power an intransigent, antiliberal element. Ever since 1917, Soviet and Western historians have debated why the Bolsheviks won and what it signified for humankind. The Soviet view presented Bolshevik victory as the inevitable result of historical development. The Bolsheviks, it noted, assumed power for the proletariat under Lenin, their revered leader. A few Western historians, such as E. H. Carr, agree that the Bolsheviks were bound to triumph because of their clear purpose and determination. Some Western accounts, especially Robert Daniels's *Red October,* stress spontaneity and the role of chance in 1917. Others cite conspiracy as the decisive factor, but most Western histories reject an explanation of the outcome on the basis of a single factor.

How do the Revolutions of March and November 1917 compare with one another? Were the events and outcome in 1917 predetermined? Did the Provisional Government's liberal democratic experiment founder because of Russia's weak constitutional tradition, because it failed to keep its promises, or because it kept Russia in World War I? What produced Bolshevik victory: Lenin's and Trotskii's leadership, superior organization, an attractive program, mass action, or a combination of these elements? Did the Bolsheviks win because of their strengths or their opponents' weaknesses and blunders?

The "Dual Power"

In March 1917, a "Dual Power," to use Trotskii's phrase, succeeded tsarism. Dual power, he noted, does not necessarily imply equal division of authority or a formal equilibrium, and it arises from class conflict in a revolutionary period when hostile classes rely upon incompatible ruling institutions—one outlived, the other developing. The Provisional Government, argued Trotskii, represented a Russian bourgeoisie too weak to govern long; the Petrograd Soviet was a proletarian organ, which surrendered power initially to the bourgeoisie. Both convened, at first, in the Tauride Palace, where they competed for loyalty and popular support.

The Provisional Government represented landed and industrial wealth, privilege, and educated society. Its premier and interior minister, Prince G. E. Lvov, a distinguished aristocrat and wealthy landowner, had been a prominent *zemstvo* leader and member of the right wing of the Kadet party. "I believe in the great heart of the Russian people filled with love for their fellow men. I believe in this fountain of truth, verity, and freedom," declared this idealistic Slavophile liberal. "An illustrious but notoriously empty spot," commented Trotskii.[1] Lvov's government, despite good intentions, was poorly equipped to maintain order or to govern Russia. Its dominant figure and real brains was Foreign Minister Paul Miliukov, the erudite but unrealistic history professor who had led the Kadet party since 1905. War Minister Alexander I. Guchkov, a big Moscow industrialist, strove to preserve army discipline and create reliable military support for the regime. Finance Minister M. I. Tereshchenko owned property worth some 80 million rubles, spoke excellent French, and was a ballet connoisseur. Only A. F. Kerenskii, Minister of Justice and leader of the leftist Labor Group, represented even vaguely those who had unseated the tsar. A young lawyer of rare oratorical power and febrile energy, he believed fully in the revolution and his own destiny, but Kerenskii, noted Trotskii, "merely hung around the revolution." The Petrograd Soviet had barred its members from the Government, but Kerenskii, a vice-chairman of the Soviet, after a dramatic speech, secured permission to enter the cabinet.

This liberal Provisional Government was to exercise authority only until a democratically elected constituent assembly could establish a permanent regime. "Its orders," noted War Minister Guchkov, are "executed only insofar as this is permitted by the Soviet . . . which holds in its hand the most important elements of actual power such as troops, railroads, the postal and telegraph service." The Provisional Government pledged to

Library of Congress

Alexander Fedorovich Kerensky, 1881–1970. Photograph taken at the time of his graduation from St. Petersburg University in 1904.

prepare national elections with all possible speed, and the constituent assembly became an article of faith—the holy grail of Russian democracy—for moderates and revolutionaries, including Bolsheviks. Meanwhile the Government took what steps it could toward democracy by granting full freedom of speech, press, assembly, and religion, and equality to all citizens. An amnesty released political prisoners and allowed exiles to return. Provincial governors were abolished, and local governmental officials were to be elected. Unprecedented freedom and euphoria prevailed in Russia. All restrictive legislation imposed on national and religious minorities under tsarism was abolished, and the administration of the borderlands was placed mostly in local hands.

---

[1] M. T. Florinsky, *Russia: A History and an Interpretation* (New York, 1953), vol. 2, p. 1384.

The Petrograd Soviet, hastily formed and ill-defined in membership, powers, and procedure, promptly took political control in the capital and coordinated other soviets that sprang up throughout Russia, elected by workers in their factories and in army units by ordinary soldiers by direct democracy. On March 15 the Petrograd Soviet had 1,300 members; a week later soldier delegates swelled the number to more than 3,000. Even when reduced to its former size, it was too large and noisy to do much real business. A small Executive Committee, chaired by the Menshevik N. S. Chkheidze, was chosen to reach and implement important decisions. Moderate socialists dominated it and the Soviet, with Bolsheviks in opposition. At first, party affiliations were unimportant in the Soviet.

The drama of Russia in 1917 was captured wonderfully by this eyewitness, the radical American journalist John Reed:

> Lectures, debates, speeches—in theatres, circuses, schoolhouses, clubs, Soviet meeting-rooms, Union headquarters, barracks. . . . Meetings in the trenches at the front, in village squares, factories. . . . What a marvelous sight to see the Putilov factory pour out its 40,000 to listen to Social Democrats, Socialist Revolutionaries, Anarchists, anybody, whatever they had to say, as long as they would talk! For months in Petrograd, and all over Russia, every street-corner was a public tribune.[2]

The Soviet approved the Government's initial program and measures, but their relations soon grew strained over control of the army and foreign policy. On March 14 the Soviet's army section issued Order No. 1, which authorized all army units to elect soldier committees and send representatives to the Soviet. Enlisted men were to obey their officers and the Government only if their orders did not conflict with the Soviet. This Order, confirmed most reluctantly by War Minister Guchkov, prevented the Government from con-trolling the army and further undermined army discipline. Meanwhile, Foreign Minister Miliukov insisted that the March Revolution had not changed Russian foreign policy: Russia would fulfill its commitments to the Allies and fight for "lasting peace through victory." Allied governments and the United States, which had entered the war in April, quickly recognized the Provisional Government and supplied it generously with war credits. Russia, insisted Miliukov, must obtain Constantinople and the Straits and "merge the Ukrainian provinces of Austria-Hungary with Russia." This expansionist program based on secret inter-Allied treaties provoked a Soviet appeal, on March 27, to European peoples to overthrow their imperialist governments and achieve a just and democratic peace "without annexations and indemnities." Meanwhile, until peace came, the Russian Revolution must defend itself. Within the Government, Miliukov and Guchkov contended with ministers who repudiated an imperialist peace, though for the time being an atmosphere of democratic unity muted these differences.

The Bolsheviks Gain Leaders and a Program

Moderates controlled the Government and Soviet, but the Bolsheviks grew into a formidable opposition. Late in March, L. B. Kamenev and Joseph Stalin (I. V. Djugashvili) returned to Petrograd from Siberian exile. Briefly turning the Bolsheviks to the right, they pledged to support the Provisional Government in a defensive struggle against Germany. (Later Stalin blamed Kamenev for this rightist orientation, claiming that he had always opposed the Provisional Government and the war.) Though described by N. N. Sukhanov in 1917 as "a grey blur," Stalin was an able organizer and contributed from behind the scenes to Bolshevik victory, but neither he nor Kamenev supplied dynamic leadership.

Lenin's return to Russia in mid-April proved vital to Bolshevik success. In Switzerland, directing

---

[2] John Reed, *Ten Days That Shook the World* (New York, 1987), p. 11.

a small group of socialist émigrés, he had feared that he would not live to see the revolution. Though taken unaware by the March Revolution, he grasped its significance immediately and telegraphed his party comrades: "Our tactic: absolute lack of confidence, no support to the new Government."[3] His "Letters from Afar" to *Pravda*, the Bolshevik newspaper, envisioned an armed seizure of power by the proletariat fused with an armed populace. To arrange his return home, Lenin negotiated through Swiss socialists with the German government, which readily consented to send home socialists dedicated to overthrowing a pro-Allied government and ending Russia's participation in the war. Temporary identity of interests and even Lenin's receipt of "German gold," though, does not prove his opponents' assertion that he was a German agent. Lenin was prepared to accept help from whatever source (only the Germans provided it) without compromising his principles or altering his goals. He and other Russian socialist exiles passed through Germany on a sealed train.

At Petrograd's Finland Station on April 16, the Bolsheviks gave Lenin a triumphal welcome, although he had been in neither the Soviet nor the Duma. The Soviet's chairman, Chkheidze, greeted him: "We think that the principal task of the revolutionary democracy is now the defense of the revolution from any encroachment, either from within or without . . . , the closing of democratic ranks. We hope that you will pursue these goals together with us." Lenin, disregarding Chkheidze, turned to the entire Soviet delegation:

> Dear Comrades, Soldiers, Sailors and Workers! I am happy to greet in your persons the victorious Russian revolution, and greet you as the vanguard of the worldwide proletarian army. . . . The piratical imperialist war is the beginning of civil war throughout Europe. . . . The worldwide socialist revolution has already dawned. . . . Germany is seething. . . . Any day now the whole of European capitalism may

crash. The Russian revolution accomplished by you has prepared the way and opened a new epoch. Long live the worldwide socialist revolution.[4]

Lenin's exhortation caused dismay and incredulity among most Bolshevik leaders, who were moving toward accommodation with the Provisional Government.

The following day—April 17—Lenin presented a series of proposals, known as his "April Theses," to the Petrograd Bolshevik Committee. "The basic question," explained Lenin, "is our attitude toward the war." Because the new Provisional Government favored continuing in World War I, he condemned it as "imperialistic through and through." There must be "no support for the Provisional Government; exposure of the utter falsity of all its promises." He added, "Not the slightest concession must be made to 'revolutionary defensism'! . . . since the war on Russia's part remains a predatory imperialist war. . . . Russians must transform this 'imperialist war' into a civil war against capitalism." According to Lenin, Russia was moving from the first, bourgeois, stage of the revolution to its second stage, "which is to place power in the hands of the proletariat and the poorest strata of the peasantry." The Bolsheviks must tell the masses that the Soviet of Workers' Deputies was "the only possible form of revolutionary government."[5] Spurning Western parliamentary democracy, Lenin advocated a republic of soviets of worker and peasant deputies. The police, army, and bureaucracy were to be abolished. Private lands must be confiscated and all land in Russia nationalized. All banks should be merged into one general national bank under the Soviet. Bolsheviks should seize the initiative to form a revolutionary international. However, the Petrograd Committee rejected Lenin's "April Theses" 13 to 2, *Pravda*

---

[3] V. I. Lenin, *Collected Works*, vol. 23, pp. 297*ff.*

[4] N. Sukhanov, *The Russian Revolution* (New York, 1962), vol. 1, pp. 272–73.
[5] V. I. Lenin in "The Tasks of the Proletariat in the Present Revolution," *Pravda*, April 17, 1917, reprinted in *The Lenin Anthology* (New York, 1975), pp. 295–301.

dubbed them "unacceptable," and Plekhanov, the father of Russian Marxism, declared: "A man who talks such nonsense is not dangerous." Lenin argued, cajoled, and persuaded until three weeks later an all-Russian Bolshevik conference approved his program by a wide margin. The Bolsheviks took over the initial Soviet program: bread, land, and peace.

In May, Leon Trotskii returned from exile in New York and, in July, joined the Bolsheviks with his followers. Lenin had adopted (or stolen) Trotskii's idea of permanent revolution: Instead of awaiting full development of capitalism, Russia could move directly to socialism by revolution. When Trotskii, the most effective orator of the Revolution, joined Lenin, its ablest strategist and organizer, the Bolsheviks gained a great advantage in leadership.

The Revolution Moves Left (May–July)

As Lenin won control of the Bolsheviks, a severe crisis shook the Provisional Government. It was touched off by Foreign Minister Miliukov's May 1st Note, which rejected a separate peace and pledged that Russia would fight to the end to secure "sanctions and guarantees." The profoundly patriotic Kadet party, led by Miliukov, wished almost unanimously to fight to final victory. This stance alienated the Kadets from war-weary soldiers and workers. The Soviet viewed Miliukov's Note as a thin disguise for an imperialist peace, notably seizure of the Turkish Straits, which he had advocated repeatedly. Massive, spontaneous demonstrations of workers and soldiers erupted in Petrograd and Moscow with the slogans "Down with Miliukov!" and "Down with the Provisional Government!" The demonstrators could have overturned the Government, but when the latter disavowed the Note, the Soviet prohibited further demonstrations. Nonetheless, Miliukov, disliked for his cool arrogance, and Guchkov, the conservative war minister, were forced to resign.

Since the Soviet's Executive Committee now permitted member parties to join the Provisional Government, the cabinet was reorganized as a coalition of nine nonsocialist (mainly Kadet) and six socialist ministers. Its dominant figure was Alexander Kerenskii, a right-wing SR, as war and navy minister. Victor Chernov, the SRs' chief ideologist, became minister of agriculture. Supported by most peasants and many soldiers, the SRs retained, by far, the largest popular following, but they were starting to disintegrate. During 1917 they achieved none of their social program, especially drastic land reform. Their mass support became dissatisfied with the leadership. By entering the Government, moderate socialists became vulnerable to Bolshevik criticism of their inaction, mistakes, and continuation of the war. The extremist Bolsheviks, like the Jacobins (radicals in the French Revolution), profited from the moderates' passivity and incompetence as rulers and war leaders.

The coalition ministry's policies differed little from its predecessor's. Caught between Allied insistence upon a total military effort and Soviet pressure for a democratic peace, the Government issued vague statements to mask internal divisions. War Minister Kerenskii, Foreign Minister Tereshchenko, and Premier Lvov advocated an active war role. Responding to French pleas to tie down German troops in the east, Kerenskii prepared a great offensive in Galicia, hoping thereby to revive army morale, provide the regime with reliable troops, and secure Allied financial and political support. A patriot and a democrat, he believed that a free Russia was linked indissolubly with the Allied cause. Conservatives of the Kadet party expected an offensive to restore order in Russia and perhaps bring military victory. Kerenskii toured the front to whip up patriotic enthusiasm. Special volunteer "shock battalions" were recruited to lead the way. Kerenskii's oratory was applauded warmly, but it had few lasting effects on the war-weary Russian troops.

In June 1917 moderate socialists seemed securely in control of the Government and the

Soviet. When the first all-Russian Congress of Soviets opened on June 16, the Bolsheviks and their allies had only 137 out of 1,000 delegates. The Menshevik Tsereteli told the delegates that the Government was safe; no party in Russia would say "Give us power!" To his surprise, Lenin shouted "Yes, there is one!" and attacked the bourgeoisie, demanding that the war be ended and capitalist aid repudiated. The moderate majority disregarded Lenin, but in the factories Bolshevik strength and worker radicalism were rising. On June 23 the Bolsheviks, pressed by workers and soldiers, agreed to lead a demonstration against the Government, but the next day the Congress of Soviets called it off. A week later, however, a demonstration organized by the Congress to display revolutionary unity was dominated by such Bolshevik slogans as "End the war!" The Bolsheviks, not the Soviet, now clearly led the Petrograd workers.

On July 1 Kerenskii's much heralded offensive began in Galicia with a great artillery barrage. After initial gains against the Austrians, it was halted after 12 days, and on July 19 German and Austrian forces counterattacked and easily broke through Russian lines. Demoralized Russian troops threw down their weapons and fled. Their panicky retreat ended only after all Galicia had been lost and enemy attacks ceased. On July 25 the Government restored the death penalty for desertion, but this action failed to revive the army's will to fight.

As the Russian offensive faltered, disorders broke out in Petrograd (July 16–18) following the resignation from the Provisional Government of four Kadet ministers who opposed the cabinet's decision to grant demands for autonomy by the Ukrainian Rada (Assembly). Troops of the garrison, sailors from the Kronstadt naval base, and factory workers clashed with Government supporters. The Bolshevik-dominated First Machine Gun Regiment, after refusing to leave for the front, began the demonstrations. Some 500,000 soldiers and workers marched on the Tauride Palace to force the Soviet to assume power. Radical Bolsheviks from the Military Organization and

Petersburg Committee supported this movement, but more cautious Central Committee leaders considered it premature. The Bolshevik party finally decided, reluctantly, to lead the demonstration. The Soviet's Executive Committee, though frightened, refused to take power or implement Bolshevik demands. Without clear purpose, the demonstrators, after roughing up some ministers, gradually dispersed, and the July Days petered out. Later Stalin explained the curious Bolshevik tactics: "We could have seized power [in Petrograd] . . . , but against us would have risen the fronts, the provinces, the soviets. Without support in the provinces, our government would have been without hands and feet." Lenin, too, believed that national support for the Bolsheviks was still inadequate. Their unwillingness to lead damaged the Bolsheviks temporarily among militant soldiers and workers.

Kornilov and the Rightward Shift (July–September)

As the July Days ended, the Provisional Government and Petrograd Soviet regained control. Guard regiments in Petrograd, hearing that Lenin was a German agent, rallied to the Government, and a reaction set in against the Bolsheviks as newspapers published documents accusing their leaders of treason. The Government disarmed the First Machine Gun Regiment and occupied Bolshevik headquarters. The next day, troops searched *Pravda*'s editorial office, wrecked its press, and closed down Bolshevik newspapers. The Bolshevik Military Organization wished to resist, but the workers were cowed. Realizing that the party had suffered a severe setback, Lenin convinced the Central Committee of the need to retreat. He considered standing trial to refute the Government charges, but fearing that he might be murdered in prison, Lenin took refuge in Finland. Trotskii and some other Bolshevik leaders were arrested.

Kerenskii, reshuffling the coalition cabinet on July 25, replaced Prince Lvov as premier. Mensheviks and SRs held most ministerial posts, but the moderate Government failed to implement the measures that the impatient masses demanded. Kerenskii, the democrat, began his rule with half-hearted repression. Insurgent troops and civilians mostly retained their arms, and though the central Bolshevik apparatus was shaken, Bolshevik support in Petrograd's factories continued to grow. By mid-August the Bolshevik party numbered about 200,000 members, compared with 80,000 in April, and had outstripped the Mensheviks, whose support declined partly because of the inactivity of the Provisional Government.

Early in August Kerenskii again reshuffled his cabinet and moved into the Winter Palace, seat of the tsars. To build support for his shaky regime before the elections to the Constituent Assembly, he convened the Moscow State Conference drawn from Russia's elite: members of the four Dumas, the soviets, the professions, and army leaders. The Bolsheviks boycotted the Conference (August 26–28) and sought to embarrass it with a general strike in Moscow. Instead of strengthening Kerenskii's government, the Conference exposed the chasm between conservatives and moderate socialists.

As the Moscow State Conference met, General Lavr Kornilov emerged as leader of the conservatives. The son of a Siberian Cossack with a reputation for bravery and rigid discipline, he had been appointed commander in chief of the army by Kerenskii on July 31. Though Kornilov lacked political acumen (General Alekseev described him as "a man with the heart of a lion and the brains of a sheep"), he headed a movement of bourgeoisie, landowners, and the military organized by Rodzianko and Miliukov. About August 20 he ordered his Cossacks and Caucasian Wild Division to take up positions within striking distance of Moscow and Petrograd. After talking with Kerenskii, Kornilov told his chief of staff: "It is time to hang the German supporters and spies with Lenin at their head and to disperse the Soviet . . . once and for all." When Kornilov entered the chamber of the Moscow State Conference, the Right cheered wildly; the Left applauded Kerenskii with equal warmth. The Conference

convinced Kornilov that Kerenskii was too weak to restore order in Russia. Supported by conservative Duma leaders, financiers, and the Allied powers, Kornilov pushed plans to march on Petrograd and crush the revolution. Learning of the conspiracy, Kerenskii secured authorization from socialist members of his cabinet to take emergency measures, but the Kadet ministers resigned. Kerenskii's dismissal of Kornilov as commander in chief, on September 9, forced the general's hand.

The threat of a military coup united Petrograd socialists, who mobilized workers and soldiers to defend the revolution. While Kerenskii postured equivocally, hoping that Kornilov would crush the Bolsheviks and leave him in command, the Soviet's Executive Committee set up a "Committee for Struggle against Counterrevolution" to coordinate resistance. Bolshevik leaders were released and directed the Committee's work, and arms were gathered everywhere to equip the Red Guard, a workers' militia. Kronstadt sailors, pouring in to defend Petrograd, swiftly rounded up Kornilovites. The Executive Committee instructed army committees and railroad and telegraph workers to obstruct Kornilov's advance; his small forces were enveloped and never reached Petrograd. His troop trains were delayed or derailed while Bolshevik agitators turned his soldiers against their officers. The Wild Division, won over by a Muslim delegation, elected a committee that apologized to the Petrograd Soviet for participating in a counterrevolutionary plot. Kornilov and his supporters were arrested, and the only serious Rightist attempt in 1917 to seize power fizzled out ingloriously.

The Rising Tide (September–November)

After Kornilov's defeat, the Bolsheviks rode a wave of mass discontent that finally overwhelmed the weak Provisional Government. In the Kornilov affair, the party had displayed leadership and control of the workers, who were becoming increasingly radical. On September 13 the Petrograd Soviet approved a Bolshevik resolution for the first time; five days later this action was repeated in Moscow. On September 22, when the Petrograd Soviet again voted Bolshevik, the moderate Executive Committee, interpreting this as a vote of no confidence, resigned, and soon thereafter Trotskii was elected chairman. Control of the principal soviets gave the Bolshevik party a strategic base as important as radical Paris was for the French Jacobins in 1792.

Kerenskii's moderate regime might still have survived had it acted swiftly to begin land reform, end the war, and convene the Constituent Assembly, but it did none of these. Alexander Verkhovskii, the new war minister, urged Russia and the Allies to conclude a just peace and carry out immediate social reforms, but the Provisional Government, ignoring his suggestions, soon removed him. Instead, Kerenskii made more cabinet changes and proclaimed Russia a republic. On September 27 he convened a 1,200-man Democratic Conference in Petrograd, drawn from soviets, trade unions, *zemstva*, and cooperatives. Representing mostly the Russian educated classes, whose influence and popular support were dwindling, this Conference voted to establish the Council of the Republic, or Preparliament, dominated by moderate socialists but including nonsocialists and some Bolsheviks. At the Council's first meeting, on October 20, Trotskii denounced it and the Bolsheviks walked out; the other deputies took no action.

Extreme elements were growing at the expense of the moderates. Between July and October, while the Bolshevik vote in Moscow city elections rose from 11 to 51 percent, and the Kadets (now the conservatives) from 17 to 26 percent, the moderate SRs dropped from 58 to 14 percent. Chernov, the only SR leader of real stature, was a theoretician, not a practical politician. Its other leaders (Kerenskii and Savinkov) grew more conservative while the militant rank and file drew closer to the Bolsheviks. As the SRs neared an open split, the Mensheviks were losing worker support to the Bolsheviks. The radical masses were rejecting moderate leaders and parties and moving the revolution to the left.

The breakdown of the army, which had been developing since March, contributed greatly to extremism. Kornilov's fiasco hastened the collapse of discipline among the exhausted troops; the men regarded officers as enemies of the revolution. For months thousands of peasant soldiers had been deserting their units and filtering back to their villages, ragged, hungry, and disgruntled. Soldier soviets in most army units swung toward the Bolsheviks, who accelerated the trend with leaflets and agitation. National groups demanding independence also helped dissolve the army, until by November few reliable units remained.

The peasantry moved spontaneously during 1917 to seize and divide up landowners' estates, though at first they had waited and listened to Government promises. In May the first National Peasant Congress in Petrograd, wholly SR-dominated, outlined a program: All property in land was to be abolished, even for smallholders, and land was to belong to the entire people. Anyone might use land if he tilled it himself; hired labor was to be prohibited. Final solution of the land question was to be left to the Constituent Assembly. By midsummer, angered by official grain requisitioning, shortages of manufactured goods, and postponement of land reform, the peasants began to act. Violent land seizures and murders of landowners grew in number week by week, reaching a peak in October and November. The Bolsheviks did not lead the peasants, but exploited their discontent. The Government, helpless to protect landlord property, reluctantly recognized local peasant committees and soviets, which controlled much of the countryside. By November most peasants backed leftist SRs who were cooperating with the Bolsheviks.

The workers grew more discontented as they were squeezed by galloping inflation, dwindling food supplies, and shrinking real wages. Food riots and long lines of hungry workers became common in the cities. Disorder mounted in factories as strikes intensified and industrial sabotage and murders of hated foremen by workers increased. The owners, lacking essential raw materials and fuel, shut down many factories, but the workers believed that such closures were meant to prevent strikes for higher wages. The Government could neither mediate between workers and employers nor coerce the workers. By November the rapidly growing trade union movement had more than 2 million members. Moderate socialists retained influence in central trade union conferences, but by June more radical local factory committees were endorsing Bolshevik proposals for worker control of the factories, and by November factory committees and district soviets in Petrograd were firmly Bolshevik. The largely spontaneous and militant worker movement converged with the Bolshevik drive for political power and supplied the mass base for the Bolshevik Revolution. By November peasants were seizing the land and workers the factories, soldiers were deserting and making peace, and soviets were taking power. All this coincided with the Bolshevik short-term program.

With increasing urgency national minorities— almost half the population of the Russian Empire —demanded autonomy or independence. In March 1917 the Provisional Government, while promising the Poles independence and making concessions to the Finns, refused to recognize Ukraine as a separate administrative entity. Ukrainian moderates established a Central Council (Rada) in Kiev that favored autonomy, but Ukrainian radicals soon dominated the Rada and pushed it toward independence. In June the Rada demanded that Petrograd recognize Ukrainian territorial and administrative autonomy and permit separate Ukrainian army units. Though sympathetic, the Provisional Government avoided specific promises and admonished: "Wait until the Constituent Assembly." By July the Rada was virtually an independent government, but the Ukrainian national movement remained fragmented. Ukrainian quarrels with Petrograd over the extent of autonomy merely weakened liberal and moderate socialist elements in Russia. Native nationalist movements also developed rapidly in the Baltic provinces, soon to become independent as Latvia, Lithuania, and Estonia. In Central Asia the Russians had crushed a Kazakh revolt in 1916, but during 1917 Kazakh congresses in Orenburg

demanded a "Greater Kirghizia." Almost everywhere the Provisional Government's control over the borderlands was slight, moderate socialists leading the Petrograd government temporized, and the Bolsheviks exploited the resulting confusion.

Kornilov's defeat signaled a sharp upturn in Bolshevik popularity. To Lenin, still hiding in Finland, the achievement of Bolshevik majorities in leading soviets proved that it was time to strike. The soviets could become the foundation for a revolutionary regime. "They represent a new *type* of state apparatus which is incomparably higher, incomparably more democratic," he wrote. Crucial for Lenin were majorities in the chief soviets, not victories in parliamentary elections. The Bolsheviks were now strong in the capitals, Volga cities, the Urals, Donets Basin, and Ukrainian industrial centers, while their allies, the Left SRs, had widespread support among peasants and soldiers. No longer could an isolated Red Petrograd be crushed by the rest of Russia.

Lenin and Trotskii, certain that it was time to seize power, had to convince the Central Committee in Petrograd. Lenin wrote the Central Committee in late September, "The Bolsheviks can and must take power into their own hands."[6] To await the Constituent Assembly, warned Lenin, would merely enable Kerenskii to surrender Petrograd to the Germans. "The main thing is to place on the order of the day *the armed uprising in Petrograd and Moscow. . . .* We will win *absolutely* and *unquestionably.*"[7] Insurrectionary detachments should be formed and placed in position immediately. Shocked by Lenin's urgent messages, the Central Committee burned one of his letters and disregarded the other.

Early in October Lenin moved to Vyborg, closer to the capital. Bolshevik leaders in Petrograd were calling for the Second Congress of Soviets, set for early November, to assume power peacefully. In the pamphlet *Will the Bolsheviks Retain State Power?* Lenin insisted that the masses would

[6] Lenin, *Collected Works,* vol. 26, pp. 19–21.
[7] Lenin, *Collected Works,* vol. 26, pp. 83–84.

© Mary Evans Picture Library/Photo Researchers, Inc.

Red Guards (armed factory workers) on patrol in defense of the revolution in Petrograd, 1917.

support a purely Bolshevik government. Nothing except indecision could prevent the Bolsheviks from seizing and keeping power until the world socialist revolution triumphed. As the Central Committee stalled, Lenin wrote in *The Crisis Has Matured* (October 12): "We are on the threshold of a world proletarian revolution" that the Bolsheviks must lead. If the Central Committee showed misguided faith in the Congress of Soviets or Constituent Assembly, its members would be "miserable traitors to the proletarian cause." When this, too, was disregarded, Lenin threatened to resign and campaign in the lower ranks of the party.

On October 20 Lenin came to Petrograd in disguise to convert the Central Committee to armed insurrection. He and 11 Committee members argued through the night of October 23–24 in the apartment of the unsuspecting Sukhanov. They approved a Political Bureau (subsequently Politburo) of seven: Lenin, Zinoviev, Kamenev, Trotskii, Stalin, Sokolnikov, and Bubnov. After long debate, the idea of armed uprising was approved in principle, though Zinoviev and Kamenev, arguing that armed insurrection would be contrary to

Marx's teachings, remained opposed and kept the party leadership in turmoil until the November Revolution. Trotskii urged that the insurrection be coordinated with the imminent Second Congress of Soviets, thus giving it a measure of legitimacy, and he stuck to this position despite Lenin's demand for immediate action. Without Lenin's and Trotskii's leadership, it seems unlikely that the Bolsheviks would have taken power.

The November Revolution

Unlike the spontaneous overthrow of tsarism, the November Revolution was an armed seizure of power by one party under cover of the Second Congress of Soviets. Had the Bolsheviks not acted in November, Trotskii concludes, their opportunity would have passed.

Preparations for an armed showdown were haphazard on both sides. Trotskii, chairman of the Petrograd Soviet and its Military Revolutionary Committee (MRC), directed the insurrection and was the most active Bolshevik leader at large in Petrograd. The MRC and the Bolshevik Military Organization won over or neutralized the

UPI/Corbis-Bettmann

Lev (Leon) Davidovich Trotskii (Bronstein), 1879–
1940. Photograph taken when Trotskii was in exile.

150,000-man Petrograd garrison. Composed
mostly of overage, sick, or green troops, the garrison leaned politically toward the SRs, but was
loyal to the Soviet and to whoever kept it away
from the front. The MRC sent revolutionary commissars to all its regiments, ousted Government
commissars, and won control. When the garrison
recognized MRC and Soviet authority on November 5, the Government was virtually powerless,
but the uprising was "postponed" until the meeting of the Second Congress of Soviets on November 7.

The Provisional Government remained outwardly confident. Colonel G. P. Polkovnikov,
commander of the Petrograd Military District,
announced he was ready for trouble. Premier
Kerenskii hoped the Bolsheviks would act so that
the Government could crush them. The Government had a thorough defense plan that anticipated most Bolshevik moves and concentrated on
holding the city center and Neva bridges (see Map

7.1). Kerenskii had some 1,000 military cadets,
officers, and Cossacks—sufficient, he believed, to
paralyze Bolshevik centers if used boldly.

As both sides waited, Government strength
ebbed. On November 5 Trotskii and Lashevich
literally harangued the garrison at Peter and Paul
Fortress into surrendering and procured weapons
there for 20,000 Red Guards. Next morning the
Government sent military cadets to close down
Bolshevik newspapers and moved to the Winter
Palace the Women's Battalion of Death, recruited
by Kerenskii in June to shame Russian males into
fighting. Accusing Lenin of treason and ordering
MRC leaders arrested, Kerenskii sought plenary
powers from the Preparliament to crush the
Bolsheviks.

Government moves and Lenin's exhortations
prodded the MRC into counteraction. Early on
November 7 Red Guards and sailors occupied
railroad stations, the State Bank, and the central
telephone exchange without resistance. Kerenskii
lacked troops that would defend his regime and
left Petrograd to locate loyal units outside. The
capture of the Winter Palace that evening was
anticlimactic and virtually bloodless. About 10
P.M., when the Women's Battalion tried a sortie,
the besiegers rounded it up, raped a few, and dispersed the rest. The ministers surrendered meekly
to invading Red Guards and were placed under
house arrest. In this "assault," unduly glorified in
Soviet accounts, only six attackers and no defenders were killed. The Provisional Government had
fallen almost without resistance.

Bolshevik Petrograd withstood Kerenskii's
counterattack combined with an internal revolt. At
Pskov, Kerenskii had persuaded General N. N.
Krasnov to move on Petrograd with about 700
Cossacks, and on November 12 they occupied
Tsarskoe Selo, just to the south. The previous day,
however, an uprising in Petrograd by military
cadets organized by moderate socialists had been
crushed. Red Guards and sailors repelled Krasnov's feeble attack on Petrograd, and his force,
neutralized by Red propaganda, melted away.
Kerenskii escaped in disguise and eventually
reached England.

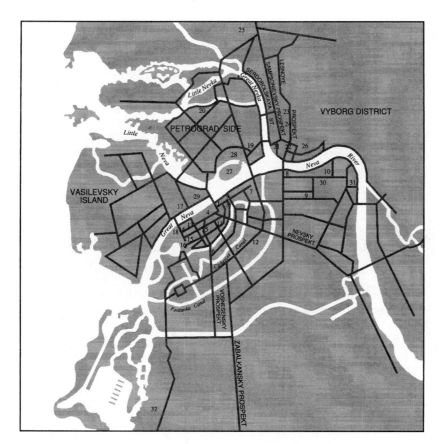

1.	Winter Palace	17.	Menshikov Palace (First Congress of Soviets)
2.	Palace Square and Alexander Column	18.	Location of Aurora, Oct. 25
3.	General Staff	19.	Ksheshinskaya Mansion
4.	Admiralty	20.	Sukhanov's Apartment (Bolshevik Central Committee, Oct. 10)
5.	Ministry of War	21.	Bolshevik Editorial Office
6.	Marinsky Palace	22.	Mikhailovsky Artillery School
7.	Pavlov Barracks	23.	Site of Sixth Party Congress
8.	Bolshevik Military Organization	24.	Vyborg District Bolshevik Headquarters
9.	Bolshevik Secretariat, Fall 1917	25.	Fofanova's Apartment (Lenin's Hideout)
10.	Bolshevik Printing Plant	26.	Arsenal
11.	Telephone Exhange	27.	Peter–Paul Fortress
12.	State Bank	28.	Finland Station
13.	Central Post Office	29.	University
14.	Central Telegraph Office	30.	Tauride Palace
15.	Kexholm Barracks	31.	Smolny Institute
16.	Baltic Crew Barracks	32.	Putilov Factory

Map 7.1 Petrograd, 1917

In most of Russia the Bolsheviks established control in a few weeks. In Moscow there were several days of severe fighting before the Red Guards[8] overcame military cadets and stormed the Kremlin on November 15, but there was no active defense of the Provisional Government elsewhere. Georgian Mensheviks set up a nationalist regime, and in Kiev the Ukrainian Rada took over, but these actions did not then threaten Bolshevik rule. The Bolsheviks generally favored nationalist movements against the old Russian Empire.

Screened by the Second Congress of Soviets, the Bolsheviks created a new regime even before the Government yielded. Lenin emerged from hiding the afternoon of November 7 to tell the Petrograd Soviet: "The oppressed masses themselves will form a government. The old state appa-

ratus will be destroyed root and branch. Now begins a new era in the history of Russia."[9] That evening the Second Congress of Soviets convened with Bolsheviks predominating (390 out of 650 delegates). After verbal fireworks, the moderate socialists denounced the Bolshevik coup as illegal, walked out, and went into opposition. The remainder (Bolsheviks and Left SRs) set up an all-Bolshevik regime: Lenin became president of the Council of People's Commissars, Trotskii foreign commissar, and Stalin commissar of nationalities. Lenin read his Decree on Peace, which urged immediate peace without annexations and indemnities, the end of secret diplomacy, and publication of all secret treaties. To win peasant support, he issued the Decree on Land, which confiscated state and church lands without compensation. Lenin was acting swiftly to implement his promises.

---

[8] The Red Guards numbered about 20,000 in Petrograd and between 70,000 and 100,000 in all Russia. D. N. Collins, "A Note on the Numerical Strength of the Russian Red Guard in October 1917," *Soviet Studies* 24, no. 2 (October 1972): 270–80.

[9] Lenin *Collected Works*, vol. 26, pp. 247–48.

Problem 3

Why Did the Bolsheviks Win?

The seizure of power by the Bolshevik Party of Lenin and Trotskii in November 1917 (October by the Old Style calendar), was a crucial turning point in Russia's political history, and one of the most momentous events in modern world history. This and the subsequent bitter civil war placed Russia squarely on a path leading toward Stalin's totalitarianism and the epic transformations of agriculture and industry in the 1930s. The Russian Revolutions of 1917, unlike the French, American, or Chinese conquest of power, occurred in wartime amid military defeat, economic collapse, and governmental disintegration. How did the Bolshevik party—with scarcely

250,000 members and apparently weaker than its socialist rivals, the Mensheviks and SRs—achieve power in a vast peasant country whose people had just discarded the 300-year authoritarian regime of the Romanovs and made Russia briefly into "the freest country in the world"? Was this Bolshevik takeover, condemned by many contemporary Russian socialists as Blanquism, or insurrection for its own sake, consistent with Marxism? In the 1840s Marx had predicted that socialism would inevitably replace capitalism through a violent revolution, but initially in fully developed capitalist countries. Was Bolshevik victory the inevitable outcome of Russia's historical and economic development, or an accidental by-product of Russia's defeat and breakdown in 1917?

Problem 3 continued

The Soviet View

Soviet and many Western scholars have ascribed Bolshevik success primarily to the Bolsheviks' strengths. Official Soviet accounts, holding to the orthodox Marxist view, emphasized that the November Revolution was the inevitable outcome of Russian historical development, but also ascribed great importance to the decisive role of the Bolshevik party and Lenin's individual qualities of leadership. Declared *The History of the USSR* in 1967:

> The October armed insurrection in Petrograd was the first victorious proletarian uprising. The insurrection triumphed because the Bolshevik Party was armed with the Leninist theory of socialist revolution and utilized the experience of past uprisings of the workers. The Party, guided by the teachings of Marxism, treated insurrection as an art, insured its organization and decisiveness. The Central Committee of the party correctly utilized revolutionary forces . . . V. I. Lenin worked out the plan of insurrection and conscientiously executed it. . . .
>
> The success of the October insurrection was the result of the vast organizational activity of the Bolshevik Party and its Central Committee. The Bolsheviks were at the head of the insurgents. By their bravery and courage, their unexampled devotion to the revolution, they raised the masses to this heroic feat. The soul and brain of the insurrection was the great Lenin. Wherever he was in the hours of insurrection . . . , he was in the center of events. . . . The October armed uprising in Petrograd . . . showed what heroic deeds the people can accomplish when led by the Marxist-Leninist party.[10]

The 27th Party Congress in 1986 adopted a revised "Program of the Communist Party of the Soviet Union," which reiterated these themes, attributing Bolshevik victory to the well-organized, revolutionary Russian working class led by the Bolsheviks under Lenin. The March

Revolution, argued that document, had failed to deliver the Russian masses "from social and political yokes" or from the burden of the "imperialist war," and it had not resolved social contradictions. "Thus a socialist revolution became an undeniable demand."

> The working class of Russia was distinguished by great revolutionary qualities and organization. At its head stood the Bolshevik Party, hardened in political struggles and possessing an advanced revolutionary theory. V. I. Lenin armed it with a clear plan of struggle after formulating theses on the possibility of the victory of a proletarian revolution under conditions of imperialism originally in one of a few separate countries.
>
> At the summons of the Bolshevik Party and under its leadership the working class undertook a decisive struggle against the power of capital. The party united in one powerful stream the proletarian struggle for socialism, peasant struggle for the land, the national-liberation struggle of the oppressed peoples of Russia, into a general [*obshchenarodnoe*] movement against the imperialist war and for peace, and directed it with the overthrow of the bourgeois order.[11]

Western Views

Many Western accounts also consider the Bolshevik victory as the inevitable outcome of the momentum of an invincible party, or the product of clever, even diabolical, plotting by Lenin. On the surface, in November 1917 the Bolsheviks possessed many strengths: a highly centralized, disciplined organization, leadership, and mass support. Although indecisive, unsure, and weak back in March, the party allegedly had become a potent instrument under Lenin and Trotskii, who combined organizational skill, intellectual and oratorical power, and ruthless purpose to exploit opportunities that arose late in 1917. The Bolsheviks' mass following—the industrial workers of Petrograd and Moscow—was militant, impa-

---

[10] *Istoriia SSSR s drevneishikh vremen do nashikh dnei* (Moscow, 1967), vol. 7, pp. 145–46.

[11] *Programma Kommunisticheskoi Partii Sovetskogo Soiuza* (Moscow, 1986), pp. 6–7.

tient, and readily mobilized, living mostly in well-defined workers' quarters. Lenin's short-term program, outlined in his "April Theses," of bread, land, peace, and all power to the soviets coincided largely with the workers' aspirations at that moment.

However, one can also view the reasons for Bolshevik success in more negative terms: the product of fortunate accidents, circumstances, and divisions, weaknesses, and mistakes of their opponents. The Bolsheviks' chief socialist rivals —the SRs and Mensheviks—were badly split internally. Indeed the SRs by November were becoming two parties: a right wing favoring peaceful methods and moving toward democratic socialism, and a radical, terrorist Left that would ally with the Bolsheviks. Both of these rivals lacked cohesion and discipline, failed to put forward practical programs, and proved unable to mobilize mass support. The thesis of Professor Crane Brinton about the weaknesses of moderates in periods of revolution seems pertinent: "The moderates in control of the formal machinery of government are confronted by . . . radical and determined opponents. . . . This stage [dual sovereignty] ends with the triumph of the extremists." Continues Brinton:

> Little by little the moderates find themselves losing the credit they had gained as opponents of the old regime, and taking on more and more of the discredit [as] . . . heir to the old regime. Forced on the defensive, they make mistake after mistake.[12]

Thus the Right SRs, Mensheviks, and Kadets were all moderate parties caught between an intransigent leftist opposition (Bolsheviks) and a weak and incompetent Provisional Government, which they had joined and whose blunders and foot-dragging exacerbated their internal weak-

nesses. The Provisional Government's ineffectiveness provided the Bolsheviks with the opportunity to take power. Establishing in March 1917 broad personal and political freedom in Russia, that government failed to implement promptly its most important pledge: to hold elections for a Constituent Assembly. Had that Assembly been convened in late summer or early fall 1917, as was wholly feasible, Bolshevik opportunities might have disappeared with the creation of a legitimate and permanent Russian government. Instead, Premier Kerenskii resorted to legalistic devices, harangues, and exhortations and kept Russia locked in a disastrous and unpopular war. Given the deepening mood of popular extremism in the fall of 1917, his democratic regime was virtually foredoomed to failure.

In sharp contrast to the Soviet thesis that the Bolsheviks succeeded because of their correct theory, careful plans, and decisive action with mass support, the American scholar Robert Daniels argues that the Soviets fostered a myth with little basis in reality and that the Bolshevik Revolution succeeded because of an incredible series of accidents and miscalculations by its opponents.

> One thing that both victors and vanquished were agreed on . . . was the myth that the insurrection was timed and executed according to a deliberate Bolshevik plan. . . . The stark truth about the Bolshevik Revolution is that it succeeded against incredible odds in defiance of any rational calculation that could have been made in the fall of 1917. . . . While the Bolsheviks were an undeniable force in Petrograd and Moscow, they had against them the overwhelming majority of the peasants, the army in the field, and the trained personnel without which no government could function. . . . Lenin's revolution . . . was a wild gamble with little chance that the Bolsheviks' ill-prepared followers could prevail against all the military force that the government seemed to have, and even less chance that they could keep power even if they managed to seize it temporarily. To Lenin, however, it was a gamble that entailed little risk, because he sensed that in no other way and at no other time would he have any chance at all of coming to power.

---

[12] Crane Brinton, *The Anatomy of Revolution*, rev. ed. (New York, 1965), p. 137. In his classic study, Brinton compares the English, American, French, and Russian revolutions.

Nor was the subsequent exaltation of Lenin's leadership really accurate.

> There is some truth in the contentions, both Soviet and non-Soviet, that Lenin's leadership was decisive. By psychological pressure on his Bolshevik lieutenants and his manipulation of the fear of counterrevolution, he set the stage for the one-party seizure of power. But . . . in the crucial days before October 24 [November 6], Lenin was not making his leadership effective. The party, unable to face up directly to his brow-beating, was tacitly violating his instructions and waiting for a multi-party and semi-constitutional revolution by the Congress of Soviets. Lenin had failed to seize the moment, failed to nail down the base for his personal dictatorship—until the government struck on the morning of the 24th of October. Kerenskii's ill-conceived countermove was the decisive accident.[13]

An American View

Professor Richard Pipes, a conservative American scholar, in a recent full-length treatment of the Russian Revolution, stresses errors of the moderates and conservatives, as well as the leadership qualities of Lenin and Trotskii, as fostering Bolshevik victory in 1917. Pipes ascribes great importance to the "Kornilov Affair" as undermining the authority of Kerenskii's Provisional Government:

> The clash fatally compromised his [Kerenskii's] relations with conservative and liberal circles without solidifying his socialist base. The main beneficiaries of the Kornilov Affair were the Bolsheviks: after August 27 the SR and Menshevik following on which Kerensky depended melted away. The Provisional Government now ceased to function even in that limited sense in which it may

be said to have done so until then. In September and October, Russia drifted rudderless. The stage was set for a counterrevolution from the left. Thus when Kerensky later wrote that "it was only the 27th of August that made [the Bolshevik coup of] the 27th of October [November 7 New Style] possible," he was correct, but not in the sense in which he intended.

During August 1917, continues Pipes, the Bolsheviks "were reasserting themselves as a political force."

> They benefited from the political polarization which occurred during the summer when the liberals and conservatives gravitated toward Kornilov, and the radicals shifted toward the extreme left. Workers, soldiers, and sailors, disgusted with the vacillations of the Mensheviks and SRs, abandoned them in droves in favor of the only alternative, the Bolsheviks.
>
> The Kornilov Affair raised Bolshevik fortunes to unprecedented heights. To neutralize Kornilov's phantom putsch . . . , Kerensky asked for help from the Ispolkom. . . . But since the Bolshevik Military Organization was the only force which the Ispolkom could invoke, this action had the effect of placing the Bolsheviks in charge of the Soviet's military contingent. . . . A no less important consequence of the Kornilov Affair was a break between Kerensky and the military. . . . The officer corps . . . despised Kerensky for his treatment of their commander [Kornilov], the arrest of many prominent generals, and his pandering to the left. When, in late October, Kerensky would call on the military to help save his government from the Bolsheviks, his pleas would fall on deaf ears. . . . It was only a question of time before Kerensky would be overthrown by someone able to provide firm leadership. Such a person had to come from the left. . . .
>
> The growing disenchantment with the soviets and the absenteeism of their socialist rivals enabled the Bolsheviks to gain in them an influence out of proportion to their national following. . . . As their role in the soviets grew, they reverted to the old slogan: "All Power to the Soviets." . . . In the more favorable political environment created by the Kornilov Affair and their successes in the soviets, the Bolsheviks revived the question of a coup d'état. . . . The Kornilov incident convinced

[13] Robert Daniels, excerpted from *Red October: The Bolshevik Revolution of 1917.* Copyright © 1967 Robert V. Daniels. Reprinted with the permission of Prentice-Hall, Inc., Upper Saddle River, NJ.

Problem 3 continued

him (Lenin) that the chances of a successful coup were better than ever and perhaps unrepeatable.[14]

Despite such revisionist Western views, in the USSR the concept of a carefully conceived Marx-

---

[14] Richard Pipes, *The Russian Revolution* (New York, 1990), pp. 464–67, 471–72.

ist revolution with wide popular support was cultivated assiduously and on the whole successfully. This was accompanied by the rather incongruous assertion that the success of the revolution depended heavily on the individual leadership and driving energy of its guiding genius, Lenin. This evident contradiction reflects the persistent dichotomy in Marxism between determinism (inexorable laws) and voluntarism (dynamic leadership). ■

InfoTrac® College Edition Search Terms

Enter the search term *Vladimir Lenin* in the Subject Guide.

Enter the search term *Russian Revolution* in the Subject Guide.

Enter the search term *Bolshevik* in Keywords.

Enter the search term *Trotsky* in Keywords.

Suggested Additional Reading

ABRAHAM, R. *Alexander Kerensky* (New York, 1987).

ADAMS, A., ed. *The Russian Revolution and Bolshevik Victory* (Boston, 1972).

AVRICH, P. *The Russian Anarchists* (Princeton, 1967).

BOLL, N. M. *The Petrograd Armed Workers Movement in the February Revolution (February–July 1917)* (Washington, 1979).

BRINTON, C. *The Anatomy of Revolution* (New York, 1965).

BROWDER, R., and A. KERENSKY, eds. *The Russian Provisional Government, 1917,* 3 vols. (Stanford, 1961).

BROWER, D. R., ed. *The Russian Revolution: Disorder or New Order?* (Arlington Heights, IL, 1986).

BUNYAN, J., and H. H. FISHER, eds. *The Bolshevik Revolution, 1917–1918: Documents and Materials* (Stanford, 1934).

CARR, E. H. *The October Revolution: Before and After* (New York, 1971).

CHAMBERLIN, W. H. *The Russian Revolution, 1917–1921,* 2 vols. (New York, 1935).

CHERNOV, V. *The Great Russian Revolution* (New Haven, CT, 1936).

CLARK, K. *Petersburg, Crucible of Revolution* (Cambridge, MA, 1995).

DANIELS, R. *Red October: The Bolshevik Revolution of 1917* (New York, 1967).

———. *The Russian Revolution* (Englewood Cliffs, NJ, 1972).

DUNE, E. *Notes of a Red Guard,* ed. and trans. D. Koenker and S. Smith (Urbana, IL, 1993).

ELWOOD, R. C., ed. *Reconsiderations on the Russian Revolution* (Cambridge, MA, 1976).

FERRO, M. *October 1917: A Social History of the Russian Revolution,* trans. N. Stone (Boston, 1980).

———. *The Russian Revolution of February 1917 . . . ,* trans. J. Richards (Englewood Cliffs, NJ, 1972).

FIGES, O. *A People's Tragedy* (New York, 1988).

———. *Interpreting the Russian Revolution* (New Haven, CT, 1999).

FRANKEL, E., et al. *Revolution in Russia: Reassessments of 1917* (Cambridge and New York, 1992).

GALILI, Z. *The Menshevik Leaders in the Russian Revolution* (Princeton, 1989).

GILL, G. J. *Peasants and Government in the Russian Revolution* (New York, 1979).

HARTLEY, L. *The Russian Revolution* (New York, 1980).

HEALD, E. *Witness to Revolution: Letters from Russia, 1916–1919,* ed. James Gidney (Kent, OH, 1972).

HILL, C. *Lenin and the Russian Revolution* (New York, 1978).

HORSBRUGH-PORTER, A., ed. *Memories of Revolution: Russian Women Remember* (New York, 1993).

KAISER, D. H., ed. *The Workers' Revolution in Russia, 1917: The View from Below* (Cambridge, 1987).

KATKOV, G. *The Kornilov Affair . . .* (London, 1980).

KERENSKII, A. F. *The Catastrophe . . .* (New York, 1927).

———. *The Crucifixion of Liberty* (New York, 1934).

———. *Russia and History's Turning Point* (London, 1965).

KOENKER, D. *Moscow Workers and the 1917 Revolution* (Princeton, 1981).

KOENKER, D., and W. G. ROSENBERG. *Strikes and Revolution in Russia, 1917* (Princeton, 1990).

LOCKHART, R. H. B. *The Two Revolutions: An Eyewitness Study of Russia, 1917* (London, 1957).

MAWDSLEY, E. *The Russian Revolution and the Baltic Fleet* (London, 1978).

MELGUNOV, S. P. *The Bolshevik Seizure of Power* (Santa Barbara, CA, 1972).

MILIUKOV, P. N. *The Russian Revolution: Vol. I. The Revolution Divided: Spring 1917*, trans. T. and R. Stites (Gulf Breeze, FL, 1978).

MOHRENSCHILDT, D. VON, ed. *The Russian Revolution of 1917: Contemporary Accounts* (New York, 1971).

PALÉOLOGUE, M. *An Ambassador's Memoirs*, 3 vols. (New York, 1972).

PERRY, J. C., and C. PLESHAKOV. *The Flight of the Romanovs: A Family Saga* (New York, 1999).

PETHYBRIDGE, R. *The Spread of the Russian Revolution: Essays on 1917* (London, 1972).

———, ed. *Witnesses to the Russian Revolution* (London, 1964).

PIPES, R. *The Russian Revolution* (New York, 1990).

———, ed. *Revolutionary Russia: A Symposium* (New York, 1969).

RABINOWITCH, A. *The Bolsheviks Come to Power* (New York, 1976).

———. *Prelude to Revolution: . . . the July Uprising* (Bloomington, IN, 1969).

RADKEY, O. H. *The Agrarian Foes of Bolshevism: . . . Russian Socialist Revolutionaries . . .* (New York, 1958).

READ, C. *From Tsar to Soviets: The Russian People and Their Revolution* (New York and Oxford, 1996).

REED, J. *Ten Days That Shook the World* (New York, 1919, and reprints).

REES, et. al. *In Defense of October: A Debate on the Russian Revolution* (London, 1997).

ROSENBERG, W. *Liberals in the Russian Revolution: The Constitutional Democratic Party, 1917–1921* (Princeton, 1974).

SAUL, N. E. *Sailors in Revolt: The Russian Baltic Fleet in 1917* (Lawrence, KS, 1978).

SCHAPIRO, L. *The Russian Revolution of 1917: The Origins of Modern Communism* (New York, 1984).

SERGE, V. *Year One of the Russian Revolution* (New York, 1972).

SERVICE, R. *Lenin: A Biography* (Cambridge, MA, 2000).

———. *The Russian Revolution, 1900–1917* (New York, 1999).

SLUSSER, R. *Stalin in October: The Man Who Missed the Revolution* (Baltimore, 1987).

SOBOLEV, P. N., ed. *The Great October Socialist Revolution*, trans. D. Skvirskii (Moscow, 1977).

SUKHANOV, N. N. *The Russian Revolution of 1917*, 2 vols., ed. J. Carmichael (New York, 1962).

SUNY, R. G. *The Baku Commune 1917–1918 . . .* (Princeton, 1972).

SUNY, R. G., and A. ADAMS, eds. *The Russian Revolution and Bolshevik Victory: Problems in European Civilization*, 3d ed. (Lexington, MA, 1990). (Includes and discusses various viewpoints.)

THOMPSON, J. M. *Revolutionary Russia, 1917* (New York, 1981).

TROTSKY, L. *The History of the Russian Revolution*, 3 vols. (New York, 1932).

WADE, R. A. *The Russian Revolution, 1917* (Cambridge, England, and New York, 2000).

———. *The Russian Search for Peace: February–October 1917* (Stanford, 1969).

WILDMAN, A. *The End of the Russian Imperial Army . . .* (Princeton, 1980).

WILLIAMS, A. R. *Through the Russian Revolution* (New York, 1978).

8

Civil War and War Communism, 1917–1921

After the November Revolution it took the Bolsheviks, governing a divided, war-torn country, a decade to achieve full military and political control and begin to build a new autocracy. After making peace with the Central Powers with the Treaty of Brest-Litovsk, they murdered the Tsar and his family and defeated their domestic counterrevolutionary opponents in a bitter civil war (1918–1921) complicated by foreign intervention. They moved simultaneously to destroy the old state, political parties, society, and economic order and erect new socialist ones. By 1927 they had succeeded in their destructive mission, but had taken only initial and tentative steps in socialist construction. One can divide this first decade of Bolshevism in power into the hectic initial months, a period of extremism and revolutionary fervor (1918–1921), and one of recovery, compromise, and power struggle (1921–1927). In 1918–1919 it seemed dubious that the Soviet regime could retain power in semibackward Russia without revolutions abroad. Provided they succeeded, could the Bolsheviks build socialism in isolated Soviet Russia? Why and how did they win

the Civil War? Why did the Allies intervene, and how did this affect the outcome? Was "War Communism" an unplanned response to the war crisis or a conscious effort to build socialism?

First Steps, 1917–1918

After the Bolshevik coup in Petrograd, many Russian and foreign leaders believed that Bolshevik rule would be but a brief interlude and that Lenin could not implement his program of bread, land, and peace. Predicting that 240,000 Bolsheviks, running Russia for the poor, could "draw the working people . . . into the daily work of state administration," Lenin counted on imminent European revolutions to preserve his infant regime; otherwise, its prospects appeared dim. Bolshevik leaders recalled the Paris Commune of 1871, in which radical Paris was crushed by conservative France, and their initial measures seemed designed to make a good case for posterity in case world capitalism overwhelmed them.

Bolshevik power spread swiftly from Petrograd over central Russia, but it met strong opposition in borderlands and villages, from other socialist parties, and even from some Bolsheviks. Lenin, however, acted decisively to crush other socialist parties, dissident Bolsheviks, and workers' groups in Russia proper. Mensheviks and Right SRs were demanding a regime of all socialist parties without Lenin and Trotskii, who had led the "un-Marxian" November coup. Right Bolsheviks under Gregory Zinoviev and Lev Kamenev temporarily left the Central Committee and proclaimed: "Long live the government of Soviet parties!" Retorting that the Congress of Soviets had approved his all-Bolshevik regime, Lenin called the Rightists deserters and until they submitted, threatened to expel them from the party. Bringing a few Left SRs into his government, Lenin hailed it as the dictatorship of the proletariat (Bolsheviks) and poor peasantry (Left SRs). This action completed the split of the SRs.

The Constituent Assembly represented a severe political challenge because during 1917 the Bolsheviks had pledged to convene it. Even after November *Pravda* proclaimed: "Comrades, by shedding your blood, you have assured the convocation of the Constituent Assembly." Lenin knew his Bolshevik party could not win a majority, but he found it too risky to cancel the scheduled and promised elections. Held only three weeks after the Bolshevik coup, the elections to the Constituent Assembly were the only fundamentally free elections contested by organized and divergent political parties under universal suffrage ever held in Russia until 1991, when Boris Yeltsin was elected Russian president. Despite continuing political turmoil, more than 40 million votes were cast using secret, direct, and equal suffrage. Despite some intimidation and restrictions imposed on the Kadets and the Right, the elections were remarkably fair and orderly. The SRs obtained about 58 percent of the vote, the Bolsheviks 25, other socialists 4, and the Kadets and the Right 13 percent. Soviet accounts stress that major cities returned Bolshevik majorities and that many SR votes were cast for pro-Bolshevik Left SRs. Nonetheless, non-Bolshevik parties had won the elections.

Lenin swiftly neutralized, then dissolved the Constituent Assembly. In December the Kadets were banned as counterrevolutionary, and their leaders and many right-wing socialists were arrested. The Constituent Assembly, warned Lenin, must accept the Soviet regime and its measures or be dissolved. When the Assembly convened in Petrograd January 18, 1918, it was surrounded by sharpshooters, and armed Red[1] soldiers and sailors packed its galleries. After Bolshevik resolutions were defeated and Chernov, a moderate SR, was elected president, the Bolsheviks walked out. Early next day, on Bolshevik orders, a sailor told Chernov to suspend the session because "the guards are tired." Red troops then closed down the Assembly and dispersed street demonstrations in its behalf. Moderate socialists during the Civil War tried to use the Assembly as a rallying point, only to find that most peasants knew nothing about it. The Constituent Assembly's dissolution marked the demise of parliamentary democracy in Russia.

Old political agencies, principles, and parties were crushed ruthlessly. Decrees abolished the Senate, *zemstva*, and other organs of local self-government. Even before counterrevolutionary threats materialized, the sinister Cheka (Extraordinary Commission), an incipient Soviet secret police, began Red terror under the dedicated Polish revolutionary Felix Dzerzhinsky. The imperial family, transported to Ekaterinburg (Sverdlovsk) in the Urals, was murdered at Lenin's orders in a cellar in July 1918.[2] The Left SRs, who left the cabinet after Brest-Litovsk and sought to overthrow the regime, were expelled from the soviets and proscribed. At the December 1920 Congress

---

[1] The Bolsheviks were known as the Reds; their nonsocialist opponents, from monarchists to Kadets (KD), were known as the Whites.

[2] Unsubstantiated reports abound that the tsar's daughter Anastasia—or even the entire family—escaped execution and went abroad. The remains of nine bodies, but not that of the heir, Aleksei, were discovered in 1991; subsequent DNA testing proved that Anastasia did not survive the massacre. See Robert K. Massie, *The Romanovs: The Last Chapter* (New York, 1995).

Smolny Institute, Bolshevik headquarters in Petrograd, where Lenin declared the triumph of the Bolshevik revolution, November, 1917.

Michael Curran

of Soviets, individual Mensheviks and SRs appeared legally for the last time.

At first Lenin sought to achieve his short-term economic program without antagonizing mass elements. The peasantry were allowed to seize landowners' estates and divide them up into small holdings. Worker committees were authorized to take over factories. "Workers' control" undermined private capitalism, dislocated production, and fed economic chaos. All banks, railroads, foreign trade, and a few factories were nationalized, but a mixed economy functioned for the time being. The Supreme Council of National Economy (*Vesenkha*) was created to coordinate economic affairs and supervise regional economic councils (*sovnarkhozy*), which ran local activities. These initial efforts at economic planning proved rather ineffective.

The Bolsheviks acted promptly to destroy the traditional patriarchal family, army, and church associated with the tsarist regime and clear the way for a new socialist society. Early in 1918 they adopted the Western calendar. Marriage and divorce were removed from church control, and only civil marriage was recognized. One spouse could cancel a marriage before a civil board without citing reasons, then notify the absent partner of the "divorce" by postcard. Incest, bigamy, and adultery were no longer prosecuted. In the army, ranks and saluting were abolished, and officers were to be elected. A major campaign against the Orthodox church began because Lenin considered religion as part of the Marxist superstructure that must reflect economic conditions. Declared Lenin, "God is before all a complex of ideas produced by the stupefying oppression of man"; he predicted a struggle between religion and the socialist state until the former disappeared. Orthodoxy's link with tsarism, the Bolsheviks believed, made it counterrevolutionary and an obstacle to building socialism. Lenin warned, however, that attacking religious "superstitions" directly might alienate the masses from the Soviet state. Instead, a multi-faceted campaign began to pen the church in a corner until it withered and died. A decree of February 1918 separated church and state and deprived churches of property and rights of ownership. The church hierarchy was destroyed and its lands, buildings, utensils, and vestments nationalized. Believers had to apply to a local soviet to secure a place of worship and religious articles, and parish churches could operate only with irregular donations of believers. Twenty years of intensive Soviet persecution of all religions had begun.

Lenin had promised peace, and the Russian army had disintegrated to the point where it could no longer fight. When the Allies failed to respond to his Decree on Peace, Lenin urged a separate peace, but only German advances on Petrograd, in February 1918, overcame Central Committee opposition to such a peace. Lenin considered the Treaty of Brest-Litovsk (Soviet Russia's separate peace with the Central Powers), despite its severity, essential for his regime's survival. The Baltic provinces and the entire Ukraine were surrendered to German occupation. As he predicted, it provided a breathing space, allowed demobilization of the army, and perhaps saved the Soviet regime.

Civil War, 1918–1920

The Russian Civil War between the Bolsheviks (Reds) and their political opponents (Whites) did as much to create the USSR as the Revolutions of 1917, argues one American scholar.[3] Bolshevik objectives in November 1917 were unclear, but the merciless civil strife between Reds and Whites laid the foundations of the autocratic Soviet system. The Bolshevik party was hardened and militarized, systematic terror began, extreme economic policies were adopted, and implacable hostility developed toward the West. The Civil War, though not wholly responsible for these developments, made Bolshevik policies much more draconian.

---

[3] Peter Kenez, *Civil War in South Russia: The First Year of the Volunteer Army* (Berkeley, 1971).

After moving to Moscow early in 1918, Lenin's regime came under intense military and political pressure. As White forces approached, Lenin set up a ruthless emergency government, which sought to mobilize central Russia's total resources. "The republic is an armed camp," Nicholas Bukharin declared. "One must rule with iron when one cannot rule with law." Relatively democratic norms of party life in 1917 yielded to dictatorship, and local popular bodies were suppressed. Lenin made major political and economic decisions and reconciled jealous subordinates. Wisely, he let Trotskii handle military affairs, confirmed his decisions, and defended the able war commissar against intrigues by Stalin and others. Jakob Sverdlov ran the party organization until his death in 1919; Stalin then assumed that role. The Eighth Party Congress in 1919 created the first operating Politburo with five full members (Lenin, Trotskii, Stalin, Kamenev, and N. M. Krestinskii) and three candidates (Bukharin, Zinoviev, and M. Kalinin), constituting Bolshevism's general staff.

In January 1918 Lenin, proclaiming the Third Congress of Soviets the supreme power in Russia, had it draft a constitution. At the Congress some delegates advocated genuine separation of powers and autonomy for local soviets, but the successful Stalin-Sverdlov draft instead outlined a highly centralized political system that concentrated all power in top government and party bodies. The Constitution of 1918, disfranchising former "exploiters" (capitalists, priests, and nobles) and depriving them of civil rights, supposedly guaranteed all democratic freedoms to the working class. Urban workers received weighted votes to counteract the peasantry's huge numerical superiority. Between congresses of soviets, a 200-member Central Executive Committee was to exercise supreme power and appoint the executive, the Council of People's Commissars. A hierarchy of national, regional, provincial, district, and local soviets was to govern Soviet Russia. The Constitution, however, omitted mention of the Bolshevik party, possessor of all real political power!

As the Soviet regime consolidated political control over central Russia, long repressed national aspirations for independence disintegrated the former tsarist empire until Russia was reduced virtually to the boundaries of 1600. The Civil War, like the Time of Troubles, brought political conflict, social turmoil, foreign intervention, and ultimate national Russian resurgence and reunification. Soviet accounts stressed heroic Russian resistance in both instances to foreign aggression. The southern frontier—the "Wild Field"—again became a refuge for rebels against a shaky regime in Moscow, and western borderlands broke away to secure independence. Anti-Communist Finns defeated Bolshevik-supported Red Finns to create an independent Finland, and the Baltic states of Latvia, Lithuania, and Estonia, assisted by German occupiers, declared independence and retained it until 1940. In Ukraine a moderate General Secretariat signed a treaty with the Germans who occupied that region and set up a puppet regime under *Hetman* Skoropadski, opposed by Bolsheviks and many Ukrainian nationalists. In Byelorussia an anti-Communist group, the Hromada, declared independence, but the national movement there was less developed and lacked a broad popular following. In the Caucasus a Transcaucasian Federative Republic existed briefly in 1918 before yielding to separate regimes in Georgia, Armenia, and Azerbaijan under British protection. In Central Asia Tashkent was an isolated Bolshevik fortress in a sea of disunited Muslims. The SRs created regimes in western Siberia and at Samara on the Volga, while Cossack areas of the Urals and the North Caucasus formed a Southeastern Union. Russia had almost dissolved.

To undermine the tsarist empire and the Provisional Government, the Bolsheviks had used the slogan of national self-determination. However, as early as 1903 most Russian Social Democrats, preferring, like Marx, large, centralized states, had rejected federalism. Viewing nationalism as a capitalist by-product that would disappear under socialism, the Bolsheviks underestimated its power and attractiveness, though Lenin exploited

national movements to bring his party into power. He advocated political self-determination in 1917 for every nation in the Russian Empire, but aimed to reunite them subsequently with a Russian socialist state. Grigorii Piatakov, a Bolshevik leader in Ukraine, expressed the party's view bluntly:

> On the whole we must not support the Ukrainians, because their movement is not convenient for the proletariat. Russia cannot exist without the Ukrainian sugar industry, and the same can be said in regard to coal (Donbass), cereals (the black earth belt), etc.[4]

Realizing that without the resources of the western borderlands Soviet Russia would not be a major power, Lenin strove to reconcile advocacy of national self-determination with Soviet Russian unity. At his instruction Joseph Stalin formulated a Bolshevik doctrine of "proletarian self-determination" limited to "toilers," denying it to the bourgeoisie and intelligentsia. National independence would be recognized only "upon the demand of the working population"—meaning, in fact, local Bolsheviks subject to control by Moscow.

Civil War and Allied Intervention, 1918–1920

Opposition to Lenin's government began in November 1917 but at first was disorganized and ineffective. Many Russians believed that the Soviet regime would soon collapse, and an ideological gulf divided conservative military elements from moderates and socialists. In August 1918 Fania Kaplan, a terrorist, attempted to kill Lenin and wounded him severely. In the Don region General M. V. Alekseev, former imperial chief of staff, began organizing anti-Bolshevik elements soon after November into the Volunteer Army, which became the finest White fighting force. Before the Bolsheviks seized Russian military headquarters at

---

[4] Quoted in R. Pipes, *The Formation of the Soviet Union* (Cambridge, MA, 1954), p. 68.

Library of Congress

Vladimir Lenin and his sister Maria in Moscow, 1918. Lenin is still in good health, moving vigorously on his way to the Fifth Congress of Soviets, his sister trying to keep up with him.

Mogilev, some leading tsarist generals (Kornilov, A. I. Denikin, and others) escaped and joined Alekseev. The anti-Bolshevik White movement included socially and ideologically disparate elements lacking in unity and coordination. Former tsarist officers exercised military and often political leadership and played a disproportionate role. Though some were of humble origin, their education and status separated them from a largely illiterate peasantry. White soldiers were mostly Cossacks, set apart from ordinary peasants by independent landholdings and proud traditions. Officers and Cossacks had little in common ideologically with Kadet and SR intellectuals except antipathy for Bolshevism.

Facing this motley opposition was a Red Army, created in January 1918. At first an undisciplined volunteer force, by late 1918—after Trotskii had become war commissar—it became a regular army with conscription and severe discipline imposed by former imperial officers. Trotskii defended this risky and controversial policy as "building socialism with the bricks of capitalism." To get Red soldiers to obey their officers, officers' families

were often held hostage to ensure the officers' loyalty. Trotskii raised uncertain Red Army morale by appearing in his famous armored train at critical points. In August 1918, at Sviiazhsk near Kazan, he rallied dispirited Red troops and helped turn the tide against the SRs.

Full-scale civil war and Allied intervention followed an uprising in May 1918 of the Czechoslovak Brigade in Russia. The Czechs had joined the imperial Russian army during World War I and, surviving its collapse, remained perhaps the best organized military force in Russia. Wishing to go to the western front to fight for an independent Czechoslovakia, the Czechs quarreled with Soviet authorities. Then they seized the Trans-Siberian Railroad, cleared the Reds from most of Siberia, and aided their White opponents. The Allies, claim Soviet accounts, employed the Czechs to activate all enemies of Red power and intervened militarily to overthrow the Soviet regime. Western accounts claim that Allied intervention was designed to restore a Russian front against Germany. President Wilson allowed United States participation in the Allied expeditions to north Russian ports in the summer of 1918 only after the Allied command insisted it was the sole way to win World War I.[5] Such individual Allied leaders as Winston Churchill and Marshal Foch, however, did aim to destroy Bolshevism through intervention but lacked the power to do so. The Soviet-Western controversy over its nature and purpose still rages.

The Civil War, fought initially with small Russian forces of uncertain morale, grew in scope and bitterness. Villages and entire regions changed hands repeatedly in a fratricidal conflict in which both sides committed numerous atrocities. At first the main threat to the Soviet regime came from the east. In August 1918, SR troops, encouraged by the Czechs' revolt, captured Kazan and the tsarist gold reserve and formed SR regimes in Samara and in Omsk in western Siberia. After the Red Army regained Kazan, the SRs in Omsk were

---

[5] George Kennan, *Russia and the West Under Lenin and Stalin* (Boston, 1960), p. 64.

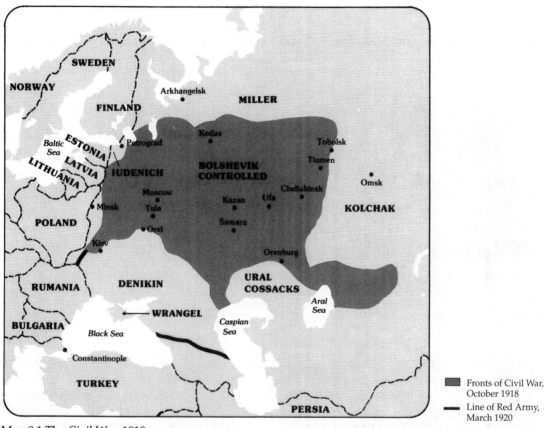

Map 8.1 The Civil War, 1919

Source: Treadgold, Donald W., *Twentieth Century Russia.* Fourth Edition, © 1976, 1972, 1959, by Rand McNally College Publishing Company, Chicago. Map, page 114.

ousted by Admiral A. Kolchak, who won Czech and later Allied support for his conservative Siberian regime. Early in 1919, pledging to reconvene the Constituent Assembly, Kolchak moved westward toward Archangel and Murmansk, controlled by the Allies and the White Russian army of General Evgenii Miller. By late summer, however, the Red Army had forced him back across the Urals (see Map 8.1). White and Allied armies hemmed in the Bolsheviks on every side. In the west General Iudenich, commanding a British-equipped White army in Estonia, advanced close to Petrograd in October 1919, but Trotskii rallied its defenders and Iudenich's army dissolved. The

chief military threat came from the south. Early in the fall of 1919 General Denikin, commanding Don Cossacks and the elite Volunteer Army equipped with British tanks, reached Orel, 250 miles south of Moscow. Then numerically superior Red forces counterattacked and drove him back, and in March 1920 the British evacuated the remnants of his army from Novorossiisk.

The Bolsheviks gradually reasserted military and political control over the tsarist borderlands, except for Poland, Finland, and the Baltic states. In the west, they dissolved the Byelorussian *Rada* and incorporated Byelorussia. After the Central Powers withdrew from Ukraine at the end of 1918, the

Michael Curran

The monument to the Legendary Machine Gun Cart at Kakhovka, site of an important battle of the Civil War fought in Ukraine. Horse-drawn machine gun carts of this type were instrumental in the Bolsheviks' victory in the Civil War.

Ukrainian nationalist Directory ousted their puppet, Hetman Skoropadski. Conservative and liberal nationalist elements competed with the Red Army for control of Ukraine, which experienced anarchy and turmoil. Early in 1919 the Red Army removed the Directory, but much of Ukraine was conquered by Denikin's Whites. In 1920 Red forces restored the rule of Ukrainian communists, now wholly subservient to Moscow, virtually ending the abortive Ukrainian struggle for independence. Though the Allied powers recognized de facto independence of the three Caucasian republics early in 1920, Moscow's rapprochement with Turkish nationalists paved the way for Soviet incorporation of the Transcaucasus. That spring the Red Army occupied Azerbaijan; in December unfortunate Armenia succumbed; and in March 1921 Red forces conquered Menshevik-controlled Georgia against strong resistance. In Central Asia the Bolsheviks conquered the khanates of Khiva and Bukhara and set up several artificial client national states. Bands of mounted Basmachi guerrillas resisted Red rule in Turkestan until the mid-1920s. With most of the former Russian Empire reunited

forcibly with its Great Russian core, the way was prepared for creation of the Soviet Union.

By then the Allies, except for the Japanese in Vladivostok, had departed and White resistance had weakened, but a Soviet-Polish war prolonged Russia's agony. To reconstitute a Greater Poland, the forces of Marshal Joseph Pilsudski invaded western Ukraine and captured Kiev in May 1920. A Soviet counteroffensive carried General M. N. Tukhachevskii's Red Army to Warsaw's outskirts, and Lenin sought to communize Poland. The Poles, however, with some French support, rallied, drove out the Red Army, and forced Soviet Russia to accept an armistice and later the unfavorable Treaty of Riga (March 1921). Soviet preoccupation with Poland enabled Baron Peter Wrangel, Denikin's successor and the ablest White general, to consolidate control of the Crimea. Wrangel employed capable Kadet leaders to carry through land reform, won peasant support, and occupied considerable areas to the north. After the Soviet-Polish armistice in October 1920, the Red Army smashed Wrangel's resistance and forced the evacuation of some 150,000 Whites to Constantinople.

The Whites lacked coordination and were plagued by personal rivalries among their leaders. They denounced Bolshevism, but affirmed nothing. Denikin and Kolchak were moderates who lacked effective political or economic programs. Their slogan—"A united and indivisible Russia"—alienated national minorities and played into Bolshevik hands. White generals made military blunders, but their political mistakes and disunity proved decisive. Allied intervention was of dubious value: Foreign arms and supplies aided the Whites, but were insufficient to ensure victory and let the Reds pose as defenders of Mother Russia. Bolshevik propaganda portrayed White generals (wrongly) as reactionary tools of Western imperialism and (more correctly) as aiming to restore the landlords. Conversely, the Reds possessed able leadership, a disciplined party, clever propaganda, and a flexible policy of national self-determination. The Red Army had central positions, better discipline, and numerical superiority. Retaining worker support in the central industrial region and controlling its railways, the Bolsheviks won the Civil War as they had won power in 1917, with superior leadership, unity, and purpose.

Russian women, theoretically granted full civil, legal, and electoral equality in January 1918 by the new Bolshevik regime, played significant roles, some quite novel, during the Civil War. Their participation in medical services and combat was far broader than in World War I. In the Civil War, Russian women fought on every front and with every weapon; the female machine-gunner made frequent appearances in early Soviet literature. From October 1919 women's activities were coordinated by Zhenotdel, the Women's Department of the Party's Central Committee, and by 1920 women were being conscripted for noncombatant service and held important positions in the Red Army's political departments. Inessa Armand, a close friend of Lenin, was Zhenotdel's first director. She, along with Alexandra Kollontai and Nadezhda Krupskaia, Lenin's wife, were leaders of women's rights in early Soviet Russia. An esti-

Nadezhda K. Krupskaia (1869–1939), Lenin's wife, women's activist, who unsuccessfully opposed Stalin's drive for power.

mated 74,000 women participated in the Russian Civil War, suffering casualties of about 1,800.

"War Communism": An Economic Disaster

During the Civil War the government adopted War Communism, an emergency program of nationalization, grain requisitioning, and labor mobilization. With the Whites holding the richest food-producing regions, in Lenin's words, "Hunger and unemployment are knocking at the doors of an ever greater number of workers . . . , there is no bread." In May 1918 he launched a "crusade for bread," and in June all large-scale industry was nationalized and labor conscripted. This development marked the true beginning of War Communism. State administration of industry by the Supreme Council of National Economy (*Vesenkha*) and its numerous boards proved to be inefficient. Almost one-fourth of Petrograd's adult population became officials, perhaps outnumbering actual factory workers. According to Maurice Dobb, an English economist, representatives of some 50 boards surrounded a dead mare in the streets of Petrograd and disputed responsibility for disposing of its carcass! In a speech in Moscow in 1922, Lenin admitted:

> Carried away by a wave of enthusiasm . . . , we thought that by direct orders of the proletarian state, we could organize state production and distribution of products communistically in a land of petty peasants. Life showed us our mistake.

By 1920 industrial production—a victim of inefficiency and civil war—had fallen to one-fifth of the 1913 level.

In the countryside, as the Bolsheviks denounced "rich" peasants (kulaks), Sverdlov warned that the Soviet regime would survive "only if we can split the village into two irreconcilably hostile camps, if we succeed in rousing the village poor against the village bourgeoisie." Red Army detachments aided "committees of the poor" (kombedy) to seize "surplus" grain—everything above a bare minimum for subsistence—from kulaks and middle peasants. Compulsory grain deliveries, though later regularized, amounted to virtual confiscation because peasants were paid in almost worthless paper currency. When farmers hid their grain, sold it on the black market, or brewed vodka, the government responded with forcible seizures. Lacking incentives, the peasantry reduced sowings, and agricultural output under War Communism fell to about one-half of what it had been. Government attempts to organize collective farms and cooperatives failed because few peasants would enter them voluntarily, and only fear that the Whites would restore landlordism kept some peasants loyal to the Bolshevik regime.

With most state expenditures financed by the printing of money as needed, the ruble was undermined and paper currency became almost worthless. Worker rations were free, and wages were paid mostly in kind. As doctrinaire Bolsheviks rejoiced at an increasingly moneyless economy, production plummeted. With the government unable to obtain enough food for the cities, illegal bagmen brought foodstuffs to city dwellers in return for consumer goods. A black market thrived.

Once the Civil War ended, the population found War Communism unbearable. In the winter of 1920–1921, in the Don and Volga regions, Ukraine and north Caucasus peasant uprisings broke out. Soviet sources blame SR-led kulaks, but most middle peasants joined the revolts as the worker-peasant alliance, the cornerstone of Soviet power, tottered. Grain requisition detachments were attacked everywhere, and in February 1921 the Cheka reported 118 separate peasant uprisings. In Tambov province Alexander Antonov, a former SR, led almost 50,000 insurgent peasants demanding "Down with Communists and Jews!" and "Down with requisitioning!" From all over Russia peasant petitions demanded a fixed tax on agricultural produce instead of grain seizures. In the towns the situation was equally dismal: Industry and transport lay idle, workers starved, and city life was falling apart. Despite the Reds' military victory, Soviet Russia seemed about to collapse.

The Kronstadt Revolt of 1921

In March 1921 a major revolt by sailors of the Kronstadt naval base on Kotlin Island near Petrograd confirmed Lenin's decision to yield to peasant demands to scrap War Communism. Ironically, Red sailors, the most revolutionary, pro-Bolshevik element during 1917, led an insurrection against the Bolshevik regime only four years later. As in March 1917, hunger was again a factor. A one-third reduction in the bread ration triggered worker strikes and demonstrations in Petrograd in February. These encouraged the crews of two warships of the disaffected Baltic Fleet to draw up a list of demands. Their Petropavlovsk Resolution condemned War Communism and demanded elections to the soviets by secret ballot, the abolition of grain requisitioning and state farms, and full freedom for peasants on their land. Advocating anarcho-syndicalism, the sailors sought land, liberty, and a federation of autonomous communes. The Resolution appealed to the Soviet regime to live up to its Constitution of 1918 and grant rights and freedoms that Lenin had proposed during 1917. A Provisional Revolutionary Committee led by S. M. Petrichenko, a sailor of Ukrainian peasant background, seized control of Kronstadt, whose Communist party virtually dissolved. During their two-week regime the Kronstadt rebels recaptured briefly the enthusiastic idealism and freedom of the March Revolution.

Fearing for their power, the Bolshevik authorities, realizing the Kronstadt uprising might ignite a massive rebellion in Russia, sought from the start to discredit it as a White émigré plot manipulated from abroad. They depicted the Kronstadt sailors of 1921—whom Trotskii in 1917 had called "the pride and glory of the Russian Revolution"— as demoralized, drunken roughnecks. Actually, the revolt was native and spontaneous. Declared Petrichenko, "Our revolt was an elemental movement to get rid of Bolshevik oppression . . . [so] the will of the people will manifest itself." Spurning conciliation or concessions that might have averted bloodshed, Bolshevik leaders headed by Trotskii demanded that the "counterrevolutionary mutineers" immediately lay down their arms. When the rebels rejected his ultimatum, the Red Army launched an infantry assault across the ice from Petrograd, only to be repulsed. In the final attack of March 16, some 50,000 Red troops finally conquered defiant Kronstadt. The bloody suppression of the revolt revealed the Bolshevik regime as a repressive tyranny relying on naked force. Kronstadt, admitted Lenin, "lit up reality better than anything else." Revealing the need for new economic policies and a relaxation of state pressure, the revolt marked the end of the Russian revolutionary movement.[6]

---

[6] Paul Avrich, *Kronstadt 1921* (Princeton, 1970).

InfoTrac® College Edition Search Terms

Enter the search term *Soviet Union* in the Subject Guide, and then go to subdivision *history*.
Enter the search term *Vladimir Lenin* in the Subject Guide.
Enter the search term *Russian Revolution* in the Subject Guide.
Enter the search term *Bolshevik* in Keywords.

Suggested Additional Reading

ADAMS, A. *The Second Ukrainian Campaign of the Bolsheviks* (New Haven, CT, 1963).

AVRICH, P. *Kronstadt 1921* (Princeton, 1970).

BASIL, J. D. *The Mensheviks in the Revolution of 1917* (Columbus, OH, 1984).

BRADLEY, J. F. *Civil War in Russia, 1917–1920* (New York, 1975).

BRINKLEY, G. *The Volunteer Army and the Allied Intervention in South Russia, 1917–1921* (Notre Dame, IN, 1966).

BROVKIN, V. N. *The Mensheviks After October . . .* (Ithaca, NY, 1988).

———, ed. and trans. *Dear Comrades: Menshevik Reports on the Bolshevik Revolution and Civil War* (Stanford, 1991).

———, ed. *The Bolsheviks in Russian Society: The Revolution and the Civil Wars* (New Haven, CT, 1997).

BUNYAN, J., and H. H. FISHER, eds. *Intervention, Civil War and Communism in Russia, April–December 1918: Documents and Materials* (Baltimore, 1936).

BURBANK, J. *Intelligentsia and Revolution: Russian Views of Bolshevism, 1917–1922* (Oxford, 1989).

BUTT, V. P., et al. *The Russian Civil War: Documents from the Soviet Archives* (New York, 1996).

CLEMENTS, B. E. *Bolshevik Women* (Cambridge, England, 1997).

D'ENCAUSSE, H. C. *The Great Challenge: Nationalities and the Bolshevik State, 1917–1930* (New York, 1992).

DENIKIN, A. *The Russian Turmoil* (London, 1922).

ENGEL, B. A., and A. POSADSKAYA-VANDERBECK. *A Revolution of Their Own: Voices of Women in Soviet History* (Boulder, CO, 1998).

FIGES, O. *Peasant Russia, Civil War, and the Volga Countryside in Revolution, 1917–1921* (New York, 1989).

———, ed. *People's Tragedy: The Russian Revolution, 1891–1924* (New York, 1997).

FISCHER, L. *The Life of Lenin* (New York, 1964).

FOOTMAN, D. *Civil War in Russia* (New York, 1962).

GELDERN, J. VON. *Bolshevik Festivals, 1917–1920* (Berkeley, 1993).

GETZLER, I. *Kronstadt, 1917–1921: The Fate of a Soviet Democracy* (Cambridge, 1983).

HEYWOOD, A. *Modernizing Lenin's Russia* (Cambridge, England, 1999).

HUSBAND, W. *"Godless Communists": Atheism and Society in Soviet Russia, 1917–1932* (DeKalb, IL, 2000).

KAZEMZADEH, F. *The Struggle for Transcaucasia, 1917–1921* (New York, 1951).

KENEZ, P. *Civil War in South Russia: The First Year of the Volunteer Army* (Berkeley, 1971).

KENNAN, G. F. *Soviet-American Relations, 1917–1920,* 2 vols. (New York, 1967).

KENNEDY-PIPES, C. *Russia and the World, 1917–1991* (Oxford, England, 1998).

KINGSTON-MANN, E. *Lenin and the Problem of Marxist Peasant Revolution* (Oxford, 1983).

KOZLOV, V.A., and V.M. KHRUSTALEV, eds. *The Last Diary of Tsaritsa Alexandra* (New Haven, CT, 1997).

LEHOVICH, D. *White Against Red: The Life of General Denikin* (New York, 1974).

LINCOLN, W. B. *Red Victory: A History of the Russian Civil War* (New York, 1989).

LUCKETT, R. *The White Generals . . .* (London, 1987).

MORLEY, J. W. *The Japanese Thrust into Siberia, 1918–1920* (New York, 1957).

NOVE, A. *An Economic History of the USSR, 1917–1991* (London and New York, 1992).

PERRY, J. E., and C. PLESHAKOV. *The Flight of the Romanovs: A Family Saga* (Boulder, CO, 1999).

RADKEY, O. *The Election to the Russian Constituent Assembly of 1917* (Cambridge, MA, 1950).

———. *The Unknown Civil War in Russia* (Stanford, 1976).

RESHETAR, J. S., Jr. *The Ukrainian Revolution, 1917–1920* (Princeton, 1952).

SERVICE, R. *Lenin: A Political Life: Vol. 3. The Iron Ring* (Bloomington, IN, 1995).

SHOLOKHOV, M. *The Quiet Don* (New York, 1966). (Historical novel of the Civil War.)

SMELE, J. D., *Civil War in Siberia: The Anti-Bolshevik Government of Admiral Kolchak, 1918–1920* (Cambridge, England, 1996).

SWAIN, G. *The Origins of the Russian Civil War* (London and New York, 1996).

ULLMAN, R. H. *Intervention and the War: Anglo-Soviet Relations, 1917–1920,* 2 vols. (Princeton, 1961, 1968).

UNTERBERGER, B. *America's Siberian Expedition, 1918–1920* (Durham, NC, 1956).

VERNECK, E. *The Testimony of Kolchak and Other Siberian Material* (Stanford, 1935).

VOLKOGONOV, D. A. *Lenin: A New Biography,* trans. and ed. Harold Shukman (New York, 1994).

WHITE, J. A. *The Siberian Intervention* (Princeton, 1950).

WOOD, E. A. *The Baba and the Comrade: Gender and Politics in Revolutionary Russia* (Bloomington, IN, 2000).

WRANGEL, P. N. *The Memoirs of General Wrangel* (London, 1929).

9

The New Economic Policy and Power Struggle, 1921–1927

In March 1921, in the face of a rising tide of peasant uprisings and the Kronstadt Revolt, the 10th Congress of the Soviet Communist Party under Lenin's leadership scrapped the disastrous economic policies of War Communism. In their place were instituted the basic elements of a New Economic Policy (NEP), described by Lenin as a step backward toward capitalism in order to prepare the way for a subsequent surge forward toward the promised land of socialism. NEP promoted the recovery of the Soviet economy devastated by seven years of war and doctrinaire Bolshevik economic experimentation. NEP also relaxed somewhat the economic and political pressures exerted by the state and allowed more scope to individual enterprise and creativity. Did NEP represent a genuine retreat toward capitalism or the initial stage of socialist construction? Did it signify Lenin's abandonment of the more extreme features of the Bolshevik dictatorship in favor of moderate policies and the slower advance toward socialism advocated by N. I. Bukharin?

Lenin suffered his first cerebral stroke in May 1922, which triggered a major struggle over the succession among the principal Soviet leaders. Stalin and Trotskii soon became the chief contenders for power, but neither was given Lenin's full blessing. How did Stalin, a "grey blur" in 1917, eventually defeat his rivals and achieve absolute power in the Soviet Union? Did Stalin's triumph signify a logical continuation of Leninist rule and principles or a dastardly betrayal of the ideology of Marxism-Leninism?

Economic and Political Controls of NEP

Lenin had written that tactical retreats would sometimes be necessary. To save the regime, the peasantry had to be wooed and the worker-peasant alliance restored. Toward this end, Lenin, overcoming objections to "compromise with capitalism," persuaded the 10th Party Congress to end grain requisitioning and approve a fixed tax in kind per acre. Initially, the New Economic Policy was a limited move to stimulate peasant production for the urban market, but by late 1921 private buying and selling had swept the country. Private

The Red Army passing in review before Trotskii (first from left, marked with an X at his feet) in Red Square, Moscow, ca. 1918 as the Civil War begins.

ownership was restored in consumer sectors, while the state retained control over the "commanding heights"—large industry, transport, and foreign trade.

Postponing socialist agriculture indefinitely, NEP stimulated small private farming. Class war in the village was abandoned, and richer peasants were allowed to prosper. Once they had paid their tax in kind, farmers were free to dispose of their surplus and were guaranteed secure tenure. Within limits, they could lease additional land and hire labor. With these stimuli, agriculture recovered rapidly until threatened by the "scissors crisis" of 1922–1923, involving rising industrial prices while prices of farm products remained low. Marketing their grain in order to buy consumer goods, farmers found that industrial prices, kept up by inefficient state trusts, were three times higher relative to agricultural prices than before World War I. Farmers again curtailed their marketings of grain and purchases of manufactures. When this reaction threatened economic recovery by reducing urban food supplies and causing consumer goods to pile up, the government forced state industry to lower prices and to prune excess staff. These measures overcame the worst effects of the scissors.

Scrapping War Communism also fostered industrial recovery. Denationalization began in May 1921, and soon about 4,000 small firms controlled three-fourths of retail and 20 percent of wholesale trade. Inefficient state enterprises were forced to close, and free contracts among remaining state firms gradually replaced centralized allocation of raw materials and equipment. State-owned big industry employed more than 80 percent of all workers, but handicrafts and small firms with up to 20 employees were private. Real wages recovered roughly to prewar levels, but unemployment became an increasing problem. By 1923 the USSR possessed the first modern mixed economy, with both state and private sectors. A degree of economic planning was achieved by Gosplan (State Planning Commission).

In 1924–1925 the mixed NEP economy, overcoming currency difficulties and the price scissors, reached its peak. As state-controlled big industry coexisted with individual and family enterprises, production in industry and agriculture neared prewar levels. In 1927 about 25 million farms, held through communal arrangements, composed 98.3 percent of all agricultural units, while state and collective farms included only a tiny minority of peasants and land. Some 350,000 peasant communes with their village assemblies, not local soviets, dominated rural life. More than 90 percent of the peasantry belonged to *mirs* and had reverted to traditional strip farming and periodic land redistribution. Millions of households still used wooden plows, and half the 1928 grain harvest was reaped by scythe or sickle! Whereas Soviet sources divide the peasantry neatly into kulaks, middle peasants, and poor peasants, actually each group shaded into the next. Middle peasants, poor by European standards, often lacked horses. Redefined to suit political convenience, kulaks were estimated at 5 to 7 percent of the total, yet only 1 percent of households employed more than one laborer. Nonetheless, the resurgence of the kulaks suggested peasant differentiation and capitalist revival. Individual farmers sought to consolidate their land and increase production for the market, but success meant being labeled "kulak exploiters." In 1925 the sown area was about that of 1913, but the grain harvest was some 10 percent smaller. Whereas Stalin claimed that only half as much grain was mar-

keted in 1927 as in 1913, recent studies report that marketings in 1927 almost equaled the 1909–1913 average. Urban demand for grain was rising while peasants, discouraged by low prices, ate better and sold less. Grain exports, which reached 12 million tons in 1913, were only 300,000 tons in 1927–1928.

Party moderates, led by Bukharin, advocated continuing NEP indefinitely in order to reach socialism. Peasant prosperity, they argued, would stimulate rural demand for industrial goods and increase marketable agricultural surpluses. In 1925 Bukharin declared, "Peasants, enrich yourselves!" but soon had to repudiate that slogan. The party's goal, he stated, was "pulling the lower strata up to a high level," because "poor peasant socialism is wretched socialism." Lower industrial prices would spur peasant demand and achieve socialism without coercion "at a snail's pace."

Serious economic problems still faced Russia in 1927. A primitive peasant agriculture barely surpassed prewar levels of productivity. An overpopulated countryside inundated towns with unskilled workers, threatening Bolshevik industrial goals and urban-rural market relationships. As industrial growth leveled off, the economy, unable to draw from capital accumulated under tsarism, faced hard decisions on how to generate more investment and savings. Grain marketings were insufficient to support industrial progress, yet short of coercion, the only ways to increase them were to provide cheaper consumer goods or to raise farm prices significantly.

The experience and results of NEP were debated and reassessed in the USSR under Gorbachev after 1985. At the 27th Party Congress of February 1986, Gorbachev himself advocated "something like a Leninist food tax (*prodnalog*) in the new conditions of today" to stimulate lagging agricultural production. The numerous Soviet articles in 1987–1989 that referred to NEP were overwhelmingly favorable and often exaggerated its beneficial economic results. Soviet specialists attributed NEP's successes primarily to the economic freedom it gave the peasant. Some stressed the efficiency of individual peasants producing for the marketplace, whereas others, apparently with official approval, argued that voluntary peasant cooperatives were needed for any long-term solution of agrarian problems. Many Soviet intellectuals praised the NEP years as an era of political, legal, and cultural freedom.[1]

How much did Soviet women benefit from this increased freedom? Proclaiming a women's emancipation and equality that they failed to implement fully in practice, the Bolsheviks had created Zhenotdel, directed after Inessa Armand's death by Alexandra Kollontai (1920–1921). She emphasized the liberation of "women of the East," notably Muslim women of Central Asia, from their traditional subservience. Opposing the increasing centralism and bureaucracy overtaking the Bolshevik party, Kollontai advocated creative efforts by the workers themselves; in 1921 she drafted and distributed the program for the Workers' Opposition faction, advocating syndicalism. Lenin and his colleagues, denouncing the Workers' Opposition as a threat to party unity and discipline, removed Kollontai from Zhenotdel and packed her off to Norway on a minor diplomatic mission. Her political career was over, but later she became the first Soviet ambassador to Sweden. Lenin's regime, while providing educational and economic equality for women, granted them little political power. Before November 1917 only three women had served in the party leadership; few thereafter even reached the Central Committee, and no woman served on the Politburo until Ekaterina Furtseva achieved full membership, 1957–1961. Observed Kollontai correctly in 1922: "The Soviet state is run by men." Soviet women enjoyed broad civil rights but little political power.

Under NEP, though a degree of freedom persisted, political controls were tightened. Remaining Menshevik and SR leaders were exiled, and late in 1921 a party purge excluded about one-fourth of the Bolshevik membership. Within the party, factions were banned and political dissent

became more dangerous. Punitive powers of the expanding central party apparatus over the members increased, and decision making by top leaders grew more arbitrary. Party decrees, however, failed to end debate or factions during NEP, even though the defeated might be expelled or lose their posts.

The Constitution of 1918 had proclaimed federalism, but relations among Soviet republics remained undefined until December 1922, when a unified, centralized Union of Soviet Socialist Republics replaced the several independent republics. Within the huge Russian Republic (RSFSR) were 17 autonomous republics and regions for national minorities, all ruled from Moscow. Other republics, such as Ukraine and Byelorussia, had to accept the RSFSR's constitution verbatim. Because the soviets were subordinate to party direction and other Communist parties were Russian led, the Russian party's Central Committee exercised full de facto power everywhere. The RSFSR government became the highest state authority in all areas occupied by the Red Army. Soviet histories under Gorbachev, minimizing national resistance to integration in Soviet Russia, attributed the USSR's formation partly to "imperialist" pressure and foreign plots to overthrow Soviet power. Actually, it resulted mainly from the Red Army's subjugation of tsarist borderlands, such as Transcaucasia. When Red troops entered Vladivostok in 1922, following Japanese withdrawal, the Far Eastern Republic dissolved instantly and merged with the RSFSR. The nominally independent republics of Khiva and Bukhara in Central Asia were abolished in 1924 and their territory distributed arbitrarily among five new Soviet republics: Uzbek, Turkmen, Tajik, Kazakh, and Kirghiz.

The new USSR was an apparent compromise between Bolshevik desires for centralization and autonomist aims of nationalists and federalists in the borderlands. The Bolsheviks viewed the USSR as a stage in the advance toward an ultimate worldwide Soviet state. Within it, national minorities often enjoyed less autonomy than under

---

[1] R. W. Davies, ed., *Soviet History in the Gorbachev Revolution* (Bloomington, IN, 1989), pp. 28*ff.*

tsarism. Gone were their political parties and separate religious and cultural institutions, though they received linguistic autonomy, distinct national territories, and political representation—a fake federalism, concealing complete Russian and Bolshevik predominance that failed to win the support of the nationalities.

Once Lenin achieved power, his doctrines changed considerably. Before the November coup he had declared in *State and Revolution:*

> To destroy officialdom immediately, everywhere, completely—this cannot be thought of. ... But to *break up* at once the old bureaucratic machine and to start immediately the construction of a new one which will enable us gradually to reduce all officialdom to naught, this is *no* Utopia, it is the experience of the [Paris] Commune, the ... direct and urgent task of the revolutionary proletariat.[2]

Capitalism had so simplified governmental functions, Lenin believed, that ordinary workers could perform such "registration, filing and checking." He had conceived of a "state apparatus of about 10, if not 20 million" class-conscious workers as part-time civil servants. (How poorly he understood the problems of running an industrial society!) Once in power, the flexible Lenin discarded former views that proved inapplicable. The transition to socialism, he admitted in 1918, would require bourgeois experts, and in 1920 he conceded sadly: "We have to administer [the proletarian state] with the help of people belonging to the class we have overthrown" and pay them well. In his final years Lenin, in his writings, grew cautious and reformist. Criticizing War Communism's "furious assaults," he described "exaggerated revolutionism" as dangerous in domestic policy and advocated "conquering peacefully" by careful economic construction.[3] The contrast between his

militant views in 1917–1920 and the reformist, evolutionary emphasis of 1921–1923 makes one wonder which was the "real" Lenin.

Nonetheless, Lenin bequeathed an elitist doctrine and party as one foundation of a new autocracy (others were provided by tsarism, the Civil War, and War Communism). His central doctrine —the dictatorship of the proletariat—he had defined as "power won and maintained by the proletariat against the bourgeoisie, power unrestricted by any laws."[4] Having designed a theoretically centralized party able to strike ruthlessly and outlawing factions within it (which failed to end factionalism), he hoped that "democratic centralism" would encourage free intraparty debate, then unanimous action. Discussion was to be free until a decision was reached, then all party members were expected to execute it loyally. Although Lenin prevailed within the party not by force or because of any position he held, but by persuasion, charisma, and moral stature, nevertheless he left to Stalin certain tools which Stalin used to build his brutal dictatorship: a centralized party, predominant central organs, subservient soviets, and police terror. It was Lenin who authorized creation of a secret police and who banned factionalism within the party. By applying these elements ruthlessly and vindictively, Stalin altered the Soviet system fundamentally.

The Struggle over Succession

In May 1922 Lenin suffered his first stroke. Through his writings, pragmatic leadership, and ability to handle people, he had dominated Bolshevism since its inception, and his semiretirement sparked a struggle for succession within the party. Lenin named no successor, and his "Testament," or "Letter to the Congress" of December 1922, found fault with all the leading contenders. Increasingly dismayed by Stalin's Great Russian chauvinism and brutal domination of the party apparatus, Lenin wrote, "Comrade Stalin, having

---

[2] Lenin, *Polnoe Sobranie Sochineniia,* 5th ed. (Moscow, 1962), vol. 33, pp. 48–49.
[3] "The Immediate Tasks of the Soviet Government, April 1918," in R. Tucker, ed., *The Lenin Anthology* (New York, 1975), pp. 441–44.

[4] Ibid., p. 464.

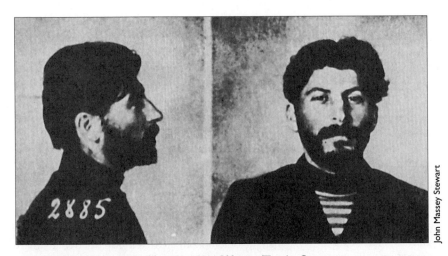

John Massey Stewart

Joseph Stalin (Dzhugashvili), 1879–1953, *Okhrana* (Tsarist Secret Police) mug shots of Stalin from about 1909 or 1910.

become *gensek* [General Secretary] has concentrated boundless power in his hands, and I am not sure that he will always manage to use this power with sufficient caution." He had a second stroke in December 1922. In January 1923 he added, "Stalin is too rude. . . . I propose to the comrades that they devise a way of shifting Stalin from this position." Apparently, only a third stroke in March 1923 prevented Lenin from removing Stalin. Concern for the party and their own positions induced other contenders at first to form a collective leadership and present a united front. Behind the scenes the struggle for succession went through several phases until Stalin triumphed. These issues were debated fiercely: Where was the Revolution heading? Would NEP lead to capitalism or socialism? How should Russia be industrialized? Factions, though illegal, were too ingrained in party traditions to be easily eradicated, though politics grew ever more dangerous and secretive. By Lenin's death in 1924, four major groups had formed: a Stalin faction, the Trotskii Left, Bukharin's moderates, and a Zinoviev-Kamenev group based in Leningrad.

Joseph Stalin, the eventual winner, was born in 1879 as Iosif Vissarionovich Djugashvili of semiliterate Georgian parents descended from serfs. As a boy, Soso was devoted to his mother and rebelled against a drunken father and all authority. An excellent student who expected to excel in everything, he idealized Koba, a fearless 19th-century Caucasian mountain chieftain, and adopted his view of vindictive triumph as a worthy goal in life. He resented the strict discipline in his five years at the Tiflis Orthodox seminary and was expelled as a socialist in 1899. Between 1902 and 1917 he was arrested and exiled repeatedly for underground revolutionary activity. He became a Bolshevik soon after the faction's formation; as Lenin's admiring disciple, he modeled himself after his hero and adopted the name Stalin partly because it resembled Lenin. Stalin adopted a Great Russian outlook and dedicated his life to revolution. His *Marxism and the National Question* (1913) established him as a major leader and a mature Marxist. In 1917, as a party organizer and close colleague of Lenin, he belonged to the Bolshevik general staff. During the Civil War he gained military experience and political influence but was intensely jealous of Trotskii, who overshadowed him. The traditional Western view of Stalin as a nonintellectual "organization man," building the party state, however, actually fitted Sverdlov better. Stalin handled crises well, but he was too impatient, hot tem-

Michael Curran

Stalin's birthplace, surrounded by the Stalin museum, in Gori, Georgia. The museum remains a source of pride and respect among many Georgians for whom Stalin is a local hero.

pered, and uncooperative to be a gifted organizer or administrator. In 1923 he confided to Kamenev: "The greatest delight is to mark one's enemy, prepare everything, avenge oneself thoroughly, and then go to sleep."

Aiming to control the Bolshevik movement, Stalin achieved his commanding position through the politics of power and influence and by cultivating a political following built up over the years. In exile, using Machiavelli's *The Prince* as a primer, he studied the strategy and tactics of politics. He had an intuitive eye for men's strengths and weaknesses and how to exploit them. After Sverdlov's death in 1919, Stalin acquired key posts in the Orgburo (concerned with organizational matters), Politburo, and Secretariat; election as general secretary consolidated his organizational position. Stalin dominated the party apparatus that Sverdlov had built, forged his personal machine, and obtained a controlling voice on party bodies that selected and placed personnel.

Stalin exploited cleverly the cult of Lenin, which developed during the leader's final illness,

when Stalin may have poisoned him. Lenin had prohibited public adulation of himself and detested ceremony, but after his death his teachings—Leninism—became sacred doctrine. Official decrees ordered monuments to Lenin erected all over the USSR, renamed Petrograd as Leningrad, and authorized a huge edition of his writings. Stalin urged that Lenin's body be embalmed and placed on public display in a tomb on Red Square, although his widow, Trotskii, and Bukharin all protested that this was un-Marxian. As Lenin's devoted disciple, Stalin gathered the reins of power and won public acclaim.

Before achieving full power, Stalin survived some tense moments. In May 1924 a Central Committee plenum heard Lenin's "Testament," which urged Stalin's removal as general secretary. But Zinoviev and Kamenev, who had formed a triumvirate with Stalin in 1922, supported him out of fear of Trotskii. Stalin used the triumvirate to undermine Trotskii, whose inept tactics and arrogance antagonized many party members, and who spurned overtures from Kamenev and Zinoviev when Stalin's rise might still have been prevented. Only after his rivals had voted him into all positions of power did Stalin begin an open struggle with them. His repetitious, catechistic style won support from younger, semieducated Bolsheviks, who sought a single authoritative chief to lead their party forward.

In 1925 the triumvirate broke up: Zinoviev and Kamenev drifted belatedly toward Trotskii, while Stalin joined Bukharin's moderates. At the 14th Congress, Kamenev, too late, challenged Stalin's credentials as the new party chief, but Stalin's machine defeated him and broke up Zinoviev's Leningrad organization. Because Stalin still lacked enough prestige to seize sole power, his alliance with Bukharin proved most advantageous. As chief theorist and spokesman for NEP, Bukharin shielded Stalin from accusations that he was usurping Lenin's place and compensated for his lack of ideological clout. Through 1927 Stalin supported NEP, Bukharin's gradualist economics, and his ideological warfare against Trotskii.

During the growing debate over socialist construction, Stalin developed his major theory: socialism in one country. He had declared at a Bolshevik conference in April 1917, "The possibility is not excluded that Russia will . . . blaze the trail to socialism." In 1925 Bukharin affirmed that the USSR could build its own socialism gradually but added, "Final practical victory of socialism in our country is not possible without the help of other countries and of world revolution." Posing as a moderate and Lenin's true interpreter, Stalin restated the Leninist view in *Foundations of Leninism* (1924):

> To overthrow the bourgeoisie the efforts of one country are sufficient; for the final victory of socialism, for the organization of socialist production the efforts of one country, particularly of a peasant country like Russia, are insufficient; for that the efforts of the proletariats of several advanced countries are required.[5]

To prove that Trotskii and his theory of world revolution were anti-Leninist, however, Stalin later that year suddenly asserted that Russia alone could organize a completely socialist economy with advanced industry and high living standards. He developed the nationalistic view that Russia alone might blaze the trail of socialist construction. Soviet Russia, the pioneer of proletarian revolution, could construct a fully socialist society by its own exertions with or without revolutions abroad. To ensure that the old order would not be restored, however, the proletariat must win power in "at least several other countries." Carefully selecting his quotations, Stalin insisted that this was Lenin's theory, too. Stalin's program of Russian self-sufficiency in building socialism proved highly effective, especially among new, young party members and a burgeoning Soviet officialdom, composed largely of semieducated worker and peasant elements. These greedy and often incompetent officials welcomed Stalin's nationalism and growing "personality cult." The new bureaucracy, manipulated by Stalin, replaced the proletariat as the bearer of socialism.[6] The doctrine of socialism in one country made Stalin an authoritative ideological leader who could shrug off his opponents' belated criticisms.

In 1926–1927 Stalin defeated and silenced the Left with support from the Bukharinists. Trotskii and Zinoviev were removed from the Politburo and the latter ousted as Comintern chief. Trotskii's denunciations of the Stalin-dominated Politburo as "Thermidorean," his critique of its blunders in foreign policy, and his street demonstration of November 1927 hastened his expulsion from the party and exile. As Zinoviev and Kamenev recanted their views to save their party membership, only the Bukharinists stood between Stalin and complete power.

Soviet Russia under NEP was a one-party dictatorship modified by social pluralism—an economic compromise between socialism and

---

[5] Quoted in R. Tucker, *Stalin as Revolutionary, 1879–1929* (New York, 1973), p. 371.

[6] See Moshe Lewin, "The Social Background of Stalinism," in R. Tucker, ed., *Stalinism* (New York, 1977), pp. 111*ff*.

capitalism. Though the state sector predominated in industry and was growing, the private sector remained vital and dominant in agriculture. Most Soviet citizens, especially peasants, worked and lived far from party or state control, which did not extend far outside the urban centers. NEP was an era of rival theories, contention, and exciting experiments. Tolerance of political, economic, and social diversity marked it as a period of liberal Communism, recovery, and civil peace. As Stalin built his party autocracy, however, these compromises could not long endure.

Problem 4

From Lenin to Stalin: Continuity or Betrayal?

Who, if anyone, was responsible for putting Soviet Russia on a course leading to renewed autocracy, repression, and massive purges? Was this the work of Lenin or Stalin, or was it inherent in Bolshevism or in the previous development of Russian history? Were there fundamental differences in approach, policy, and personality between Lenin and Stalin? Was Stalin's regime the logical culmination of Leninism, or did his one-man rule and personality cult represent a breach with and repudiation of Bolshevik ideals and practice? Did Stalin's dictatorship constitute an aberration, a temporary interruption of a Bolshevik tradition of "collective leadership," as N. S. Khrushchev would later intimate?

Until 1960 most Western scholars stressed elements of continuity between early Bolshevism and the Stalin era. This theory of the "straight line" was later reinforced by Alexander Solzhenitsyn's *Gulag Archipelago*, which traced the roots of mass terror and the system of forced labor camps to the first days of Lenin's regime. Western scholars tended to view Stalin's "great transformation" of 1929–1933 as perfecting an inherent, inevitable totalitarianism.

Recently some Western historians, using newly accessible Soviet materials, have challenged this continuity thesis. These revisionists argue that Stalinism differed fundamentally from earlier Bolshevism—that Stalin's policies were so violent and extreme that they changed the very nature of the Soviet state and Bolshevik party. By emphasizing statism, Great Russian nationalism, and anti-Semitism and by encouraging his own deification, Stalin repudiated the beliefs of Lenin and his "Old Bolshevik" colleagues, such as Trotskii, Zinoviev, and Bukharin. To view Stalinism as merely the outgrowth of the militant Lenin of *What Is to Be Done?* (1902), argues Stephen Cohen, is a grievous oversimplification. Instead, Bolshevism evolved over the years from an unruly, loosely organized group of independent-minded revolutionaries into the centralized, bureaucratic organization of the 1920s; under Stalin the Communist Party was terrorized and its influence sharply reduced. In actuality, the Bolshevik party had never been quite the disciplined vanguard of professionals advocated in *What Is to Be Done?* Even official party historians complained repeatedly that its history was one of "factional struggle." Despite the ban on factions engineered by Lenin in 1921, the party remained oligarchical or, as Bukharin put it, "a negotiated federation between groups, groupings, factions, and tendencies." Thus, Cohen concludes, the party's "organizational principles" did not produce Stalinist dictatorship and conformity.[7]

Indicative of the widely disparate views on the relationship between the regimes of Lenin

---

[7] S. Cohen, "Bolshevism and Stalinism," in R. Tucker, ed., *Stalinism: Essays in Historical Interpretation* (New York, 1977), pp. 19–29. See also Tucker, *The Soviet Political Mind* (New York, 1963).

Problem 4 continued

(1917–1923) and Stalin (1928–1953) are the following excerpts: two from official Soviet publications, one by a Soviet dissident scholar, one from a recent Russian biography of Stalin, two from statements by Soviet émigrés, and two from Western accounts.

Official Soviet Interpretations

History of the Communist Party of the Soviet Union (Bolsheviks): Short Course (New York, 1939) is the official party history prepared ostensibly by the Central Committee following the Great Purge (discussed in Chapter 34). It was edited and perhaps partly written by Joseph Stalin and reflects the "classical" Stalinist interpretation of the purges. The "dregs of humanity" referred to in the text included the leading "Old Bolsheviks," the closest colleagues of Lenin—the original leaders of Soviet Russia, the Bolshevik party, and the Third International (Comintern)!

> In 1937, new facts came to light regarding the fiendish crimes of the Bukharin-Trotsky gang. The trial[s] . . . all showed that the Bukharinites and Trotskyists had long ago joined to form a common band of enemies of the people, operating as the "Bloc of Rights and Trotskyites." The trials showed that these dregs of humanity, in conjunction with the enemies of the people, Trotsky, Zinoviev, and Kamenev, had been in conspiracy against Lenin, the Party, and the Soviet state ever since the early days of the October Socialist Revolution. The insidious attempts to thwart the Peace of Brest-Litovsk at the beginning of 1918, . . . the deliberate aggravation of differences in the party in 1921 . . . , the attempts to overthrow the Party leadership during Lenin's illness and after his death, . . . the vile assassination of Kirov . . . —all these and similar villainies over a period of 20 years were committed, it transpired, with the participation or under the direction of Trotsky, Zinoviev, Kamenev, Bukharin, Rykov and their henchmen, at the behest of espionage services of bourgeois states.

> . . . These Whiteguard pygmies, whose strength was no more than that of a gnat, apparently flattered themselves that they were the masters of the country, and imagined that it was really in their power to sell or give away the Ukraine, Byelorussia, and the Maritime Region. . . . These contemptible lackeys of the fascists forgot that the Soviet people had only to move a finger, and not a trace of them would be left. The Soviet court sentenced the Bukharin-Trotsky fiends to be shot. . . . The Soviet people approved the annihilation of the Bukharin-Trotsky gang and passed on to the next business.[8]

A Dissident Marxist Historian

Roy Medvedev is a Russian Marxist scholar who became absorbed in study of the Stalin era after Khrushchev's revelations at the 20th and 22nd Party Congresses. However, by the time he had completed his book *Let History Judge: The Origins and Consequences of Stalinism* in 1968, the Brezhnev regime was moving toward a partial rehabilitation of Stalin and it had to be published in the United States. Medvedev was subsequently expelled from the party but remains a Marxist living in Russia. This book represented an "insider's" view of the Stalin phenomenon. Medvedev accepted Khrushchev's view that Stalinist terror and the personality cult were temporary departures from an essentially sound Soviet system, but he was much more vigorous in denouncing that terror.

> To many people in the Soviet Union the mass repression of 1937–38 was an incomprehensible calamity that suddenly broke upon the country and seemed to have no end. Explanations abounded, some of them representing a search for the truth, but more attempting to escape the cruel truth, to find some formula that would preserve faith in the Party and Stalin. . . . One widespread story was that Stalin did not know about the terror, that all those crimes were committed behind his back. Of course it was ridiculous to suppose that Stalin,

[8] *History of the Communist Party of the Soviet Union (Bolsheviks): Short Course* (New York, 1939), pp. 346–48.

master of everyone and everything, did not know about the arrest and shooting of members of the Politburo and the Central Committee, . . . about the arrest of the military high command and the Comintern leaders. . . . But that is a peculiarity of the mind blinded by faith in a higher being. This naive conviction of Stalin's ignorance was reflected in the word, *yezhovshchina,* "the Yezhov thing," the popular name for the tragedy of the thirties . . . , a new version of the common people's faith in a good tsar surrounded by lying and wicked ministers. But it must be acknowledged that this story had some basis in Stalin's behavior. Secretive and self-contained, Stalin avoided the public eye; . . . he acted through unseen channels. He tried to direct events from behind the scenes, making basic decisions by himself or with a few aides . . . preferring to put the spotlight on other perpetrators of these crimes, thereby retaining his own freedom of movement.

Some confusion about the nature of Stalin's power must be cleared away. By the end of the twenties and the early thirties he was already called a dictator, a one-man ruler . . . , but the unlimited dictatorship that he established after 1936–38 was without historical precedent. For the last fifteen years of his bloody career Stalin wielded such power as no Russian tsar ever possessed. . . . In the years of the cult, Stalin held not only all political power; he was master of the economy, the military, foreign policy; even in literature, the arts, and science he was the supreme arbiter. . . .

It was an historical accident that Stalin, the embodiment of all the worst elements in the Russian revolutionary movement, came to power after Lenin, the embodiment of all that was best. . . . The Party must not only condemn Stalin's crimes; it must also eliminate the conditions that facilitated them. . . . Stalin never relied on force alone. Throughout the period of his one-man rule he was popular. The longer this tyrant ruled the USSR, coldbloodedly destroying millions of people, the greater seems to have been the dedication to him, even the love, of the majority of people. . . .

One condition that made it easy for Stalin to bend the Party to his will was the hugely inflated

cult of his personality. . . . The deification of Stalin justified in advance everything he did. . . . All the achievements and virtues of socialism were embodied in him. . . . Not conscious faith, but blind faith in Stalin was required. Like every cult, this one tended to transform the Communist Party into an ecclesiastical organization with a sharp distinction between ordinary people and leader-priests headed by their infallible pope. The gulf between the people and Stalin was not only deepened but idealized. The business of state in the Kremlin became as remote and incomprehensible for the unconsecrated as the affairs of the gods on Olympus. . . . Just as believers attribute everything good to God and everything bad to the devil, so everything good was attributed to Stalin and everything bad to evil forces that Stalin himself was fighting. "Long live Stalin!" some officials shouted as they were taken to be shot.[9]

A Contemporary Russian Historian

D. A. Volkogonov, a prominent military historian, wrote *Triumph and Tragedy,* the first complete biography of Stalin published in the USSR. "I want to show that the triumph of one person can turn into a tragedy for the whole people," Volkogonov explained. As director of the Institute of Military History, Volkogonov used many reminiscences and documents from the hitherto secret archives of the Defense Ministry, stressing how Stalin's psychotic personality resulted in tragedies for the Soviet people. "I am profoundly convinced that the socialist development of society could have avoided those dark stains . . . if a deficit of popular authority had not developed after the death of Lenin." But none of the other available leaders, Volkogonov concluded, would have been preferable to Stalin:

If Trotskii had been in charge of the Party, even more burdensome experiences would have awaited it, involving loss of our socialist achievements—all

---

[9] Roy A. Medvedev, *Let History Judge: The Origins and Consequences of Stalinism* (New York, 1968), pp. 289–90, 355, 362–63.

the more because Trotskii did not have a scientific and clear programme for the construction of socialism in the USSR. Bukharin had such a programme . . . , but in spite of his great attractiveness as a person . . . and his humanity Bukharin for a long time did not understand the necessity of a sharp leap by the country in the growth of its economic power.[10]

Soviet Émigrés

Born in Brussels, Belgium, in 1890 of Russian émigré parents, Victor Serge (Viktor L. Kibalchich) became a radical socialist and after the Russian Revolution returned to Soviet Russia. He joined the Bolshevik party and became prominent in the Comintern, barely escaping to the West before the Great Purge. Like his "Old Bolshevik" contemporaries, Serge greatly admired and idealized Lenin, but was profoundly disillusioned by Stalinist tyranny.

> Everything has changed. The aims: from international social revolution to socialism in one country. The political system: from the workers' democracy of the soviets, the goal of the revolution, to the dictatorship of the general secretariat, the functionaries, and the GPU [secret police]. The party: from the organization, free in its life and thought and freely submitting to discipline, of revolutionary Marxists to the hierarchy of bureaus, to the passive obedience of careerists. The Third International: from a mighty organization of propaganda and struggle to the opportunist servility of Central Committees appointed for the purpose of approving everything, without shame or nausea. . . . The leaders: the greatest militants of October are in exile or prison. . . . The condition of the workers: the equalitarianism of Soviet society is transformed to permit the formation of a privileged minority,

more and more privileged in comparison with the disinherited masses who are deprived of all rights. Morality: from the austere, sometimes implacable honesty of heroic Bolshevism, we gradually advance to unspeakable deviousness and deceit. Everything has changed, everything is changing, but it will require the perspective of time before we can precisely understand the realities.[11]

In his massive, three-volume work, *The Gulag Archipelago, 1918–1956,* Alexander Solzhenitsyn, a great contemporary Russian writer forcibly exiled from the USSR in 1974, describes the labor camp system in the USSR and its history, based on personal experience and the testimony of 227 witnesses. Begun in 1958, *Gulag* was first published abroad in 1973. Arbitrary arrest and detention, argues Solzhenitsyn, originated with Lenin in 1918 and was merely extended and intensified under Stalin. He sees repression as an inalienable part of an evil Soviet totalitarianism. Note how Solzhenitsyn's interpretation of Lenin differs from that of Roy Medvedev, who considers him a true Marxist, invariably adhering to norms of socialist legality.

> When people today decry the *abuses of the cult* [of Stalin's personality], they keep getting hung up on those years which are stuck in our throats, '37 and '38. And memory begins to make it seem as though arrests were never made *before* or *after,* but only in those two years. . . . The *wave* of 1937 and 1938 was neither the only one nor even the main one, but only one, perhaps, of the three biggest waves which strained the murky, stinking pipes of our prison sewers to bursting. *Before* it came the wave of 1929 and 1930 . . . which drove a mere 15 million peasants, maybe even more, out into the taiga and the tundra. . . . And *after* it was the wave of 1944 to 1946 . . . when they dumped whole *nations* down the sewer pipes, not to mention millions and millions of others who . . . had been prisoners of war, or carried off to Germany and subsequently repatriated. . . .
>
> It is well known that any *organ* withers away if it is not used. Therefore, if we know that the Soviet

---

[10] D. A. Volkogonov, "Fenomen Stalina," *Literaturnaia gazeta,* December 9, 1987; *Trud,* June 19, 1988; and *Pravda,* June 20, 1988. These excerpts are from Volkogonov's book, translated as *Stalin: Triumph and Tragedy,* trans. Harold Shukman (New York, 1991).

[11] Victor Serge, *From Lenin to Stalin* (New York, 1973), pp. 57–58.

Security organs or *Organs* (and they christened themselves with this vile word), praised and exalted above all living things, have not died off even to the extent of one single tentacle, but instead, have grown new ones and strengthened their muscles—it is easy to deduce that they have had *constant* exercise. . . .

But even before there was any Civil War, it could be seen that Russia . . . was obviously not suited for any sort of socialism whatsoever. . . . One of the first blows of the dictatorship was directed against the Cadets—the members of the *Constitutional Democratic Party.* At the end of November 1917 . . . the Cadet Party was outlawed and arrests of its members began. . . . One of the first circulars of the NKVD [initially the Cheka, renamed NKVD in 1934], in December 1917, stated: "In view of sabotage by officials . . . use maximum initiative in localities, *not excluding* confiscations, compulsion, and arrests." . . . V. I. Lenin proclaimed the common, united purpose [in January 1918] of "purging the Russian land of all kinds of harmful insects." And under the term *insects* he included not only all class enemies but also "workers malingering at their work. . . ." It would have been impossible to carry out this hygienic purging . . . if they had had to follow outdated legal processes and normal judicial procedures. And so an entirely new form was adopted: *extrajudicial reprisal,* and this thankless job was self-sacrificingly assumed by the Cheka . . . , the only punitive organ in human history which combined in one set of hands investigation, arrest, interrogation, prosecution, trial and execution of the *verdict.*[12]

Western Views

An American specialist in Russian affairs, George F. Kennan served in the U.S. Foreign Service from 1926 to 1953, including a stint as ambassador in Moscow. Following his retirement he became a professor at the Institute for Advanced Studies in Princeton, New Jersey,

where he wrote *Soviet-American Relations, 1917–1920. Russia and the West Under Lenin and Stalin,* from which the following passage is excerpted, was based on lectures delivered at Oxford and Harvard universities, 1957–1960. After World War II Kennan won renown as the author of the "containment theory" that advocated preventing Soviet expansion by means of non-Communist alliances and bases.

It remains only to mention the contrast between Stalin, as a statesman and [Lenin]. . . . The differences are not easy ones to identify, for in many instances they were only ones of degree and of motive. Lenin, too, was a master of internal Party intrigue. He, too, was capable of ruthless cruelty. He, too, could be unpitying in the elimination of people who seriously disagreed with him. . . . No less than Stalin, Lenin adopted an attitude of implacable hostility toward the Western world.

But behind all this there were very significant differences. Lenin was a man with no sense of inferiority. Well-born, well-educated, endowed with a mind of formidable power and brilliance, he was devoid of the angularities of the social parvenu, and he felt himself a match for any man intellectually. He was spared that whole great burden of personal insecurity which rested so heavily on Stalin. He never had to doubt his hold on the respect and admiration of his colleagues. He could rule them through the love they bore him, whereas Stalin was obliged to rule them through their fears. This enabled Lenin to run the movement squarely on the basis of what he conceived to be its needs, without bothering about his own. And since the intellectual inventory of the Party was largely of his own creation, he was relieved of that ignominious need which Stalin constantly experienced for buttressing his political views by references to someone else's gospel. Having fashioned Leninism to his own heart's desire out of the raw materials of Marx's legacy, Lenin had no fear of adapting it and adjusting it as the situation required. For this reason his mind remained open throughout his life—open, at least, to argument and suggestions from those who shared his belief in the basic justification of the second Russian Revolution of 1917. These people could come to him and talk to him, and could find their thoughts not only accepted in the spirit they

---

[12] Alexander Solzhenitsyn, *The Gulag Archipelago, 1918–1956* (New York, 1973), vol. 1, pp. 24–25.

were offered but responded to by a critical intelligence second to none in the history of the socialist movement. They did not have to feel, as they later did under Stalin, that deep, dangerous, ulterior meanings might be read into anything they said, and that an innocent suggestion might prove their personal undoing.

   This had, of course, a profound effect on the human climate that prevailed throughout the Soviet regime in Lenin's time. Endowed with this temperament, Lenin was able to communicate to his associates an atmosphere of militant optimism, of good cheer and steadfastness and comradely loyalty, which made him the object of their deepest admiration and affection and permitted them to apply their entire energy to the work at hand. . . . While Lenin's ultimate authority remained unquestioned, it was possible to spread initiative and responsibility much further than was ever the case in the heyday of Stalin's power. This explains why Soviet diplomacy was so much more variegated and colorful in Lenin's time than in the subsequent Stalin era. In the change from Lenin to Stalin, the foreign policy of a movement became the foreign policy of a single man.[13]

Stephen Cohen, professor of politics at Princeton University, has specialized in the Soviet period and written an outstanding biography of Nikolai Bukharin, a leading theoretician and close colleague of Lenin.

   While the internal party battles of 1923–9 constituted prolonged attempts to reconstruct the power and authority previously exercised by Lenin, the idea that there could be a successor—a "Lenin of today"—was impermissible. Lenin's authority within the leadership and in the party generally had been unique. Among other things, it had derived from the fact that he was the party's creator and moving spirit, from his political judgment which had been proved correct so often and against so much opposition, and from the force of his personality, which united and persuaded his fractious

colleagues. In no way did it derive from an official post. As Sokolnikov pointed out: "Lenin was neither chairman of the Politburo nor general secretary; but nonetheless, Comrade Lenin . . . had the decisive political word in the party." It was . . . a kind of charismatic authority, inseparable from Lenin as a person and independent of constitutional or institutional procedures.

   Some of his heirs intuitively understood this and commented on it in different ways. "Lenin was a dictator in the best sense of the word," said Bukharin in 1924. Five years later, describing Lenin as the singular "leader, organizer, captain, and stern iron authority," and contrasting his preeminence with Stalin's brute machine power, Bukharin tried to explain further. "But he was for us all *Ilich*, a close, beloved, person, a wonderful comrade and friend, the bond with whom was indissoluble. He was not only 'Comrade Lenin,' but something immeasurably more."[14]

Conclusion

A wide divergence of views persists among scholars about the relationship between Lenin's rule and that of Stalin. Among Russian scholars, Lenin remains a generally respected figure, but viewpoints about Stalin range from hero worship by Russian and Georgian neo-Stalinists, to the relatively balanced verdicts of the Khrushchev years, to bitter denunciation by Roy Medvedev and most writers and historians under Gorbachev and after. Many Soviet citizens, notably workers, appeared to believe that Stalin's positive contributions to the USSR outweighed his monstrous crimes. Those crimes were downplayed under Brezhnev when the emphasis once again was placed on Stalin's achievements as collectivizer, industrializer, and war-time leader. Even under Gorbachev many military memoirs continued to praise Stalin's leadership during World War II. Solzhenitsyn's view, on the other hand, repudiates Soviet totalitarianism in toto, Lenin included, in favor of Russian nationalism and neo-Orthodoxy.

---

[13] George F. Kennan, *Russia and the West Under Lenin and Stalin* (Boston, 1960), pp. 256–58.

[14] Stephen Cohen, *Bukharin and the Bolshevik Revolution* (New York, 1971), pp. 223–24.

Problem 4 continued

Whether Stalin's regime represented a continuation of Lenin's principles and rules or their antithesis remains debated. Among those Russian citizens who harbor feelings of nostalgia for the past, Stalin's strength, authority, and achievements contrast sharply with the pain and suffering of post-Communist Russia. ∎

InfoTrac® College Edition Search Terms

Enter the search term *Trotsky* in Keywords.
Enter the search term *Vladimir Lenin* in the Subject Guide.
Enter the search term *Stalin* in the Subject Guide.
Enter the search term *Bolshevik* in Keywords.

Suggested Additional Reading

BALL, A. M. *Russia's Last Capitalists: The NEPMEN 1921–1929* (Berkeley, 1987).

BROVKIN, V. *Russia after Lenin: Politics, Culture, and Society, 1921–1929* (London, 1998).

CARR, E. H. *A History of Soviet Russia,* 10 vols. (New York, 1951–1972).

CHASE, W. *Workers, Society, and the Soviet State: Labor and Life in Moscow, 1918–1929* (Champaign, IL, 1990).

CLARK, C. E. *Uprooting Otherness: The Literacy Campaign in NEP-Era Russia* (Cranbury, NJ, 2000).

COHEN, S. *Bukharin: A Political Biography* (New York, 1974).

D'AGOSTINO, A. *Soviet Succession Struggles . . . from Lenin to Gorbachev* (Winchester, MA, 1987).

DANIELS, R. *The Conscience of the Revolution: Communist Opposition in Soviet Russia* (Cambridge, MA, 1960).

DAVIES, R. W. *Soviet Economic Development from Lenin to Khrushchev* (Cambridge, England, 1998).

DESAI, M., ed. *Lenin's Economic Writings* (Atlantic Highlands, NJ, 1989).

DEUTSCHER, I. *The Prophet Unarmed: Trotsky, 1921–1929* (Oxford, 1951).

FISHER, H. *The Famine in Soviet Russia, 1919–1923 . . .* (Stanford, 1927).

FITZPATRICK, S., ed. *Russia in the Age of N.E.P.* (Bloomington, IN, 1991).

HEYWOOD, A. *Modernising Lenin's Russia: Economic Reconstruction, Foreign Trade, and the Railways* (Cambridge, England, 1999).

JAKOBSON, M. *Origins of the GULAG: The Soviet Prison Camp System, 1917–1934* (Lexington, KY, 1993).

KOLLONTAI, A. *The Workers' Opposition in Russia* (Chicago, 1921).

KRUPSKAIA, N. *Memories of Lenin* (London, 1942).

LEWIN, M. *Lenin's Last Struggle* (New York, 1968).

MEYER, A. *Leninism* (Cambridge, MA, 1957).

PAGE, S. *Lenin and World Revolution* (New York, 1959).

PIPES, R. *The Formation of the Soviet Union* (Cambridge, MA, 1954).

———. ed. *The Unknown Lenin* (New Haven, CT, 1996).

READ, C. *Culture and Power in Revolutionary Russia . . .* (New York, 1990).

REIMAN, M. *The Birth of Stalinism: The USSR on the Eve of the "Second Revolution,"* trans. G. Saunders (Bloomington, IN, 1987).

SERGE, V. *From Lenin to Stalin* (New York, 1973).

SIEGELBAUM, L. *Soviet State and Society Between Revolutions, 1918–1929* (Cambridge, 1992).

TARBUCK, K. *Bukharin's Theory of Equilibrium* (Winchester, MA, 1989).

TROTSKY, L. *The Revolution Betrayed* (Garden City, NY, 1937).

TUCKER, R. *Political Culture and Leadership in Soviet Russia from Lenin to Gorbachev* (New York, 1987).

———. *Stalin as Revolutionary, 1879–1929* (New York, 1973).

———, ed. *Stalinism: Essays in Historical Interpretation* (New York, 1977).

ULAM, A. *The Bolsheviks* (New York, 1965).

VOLKOGONOV, D. *Lenin: A New Biography,* trans. H. Shukman (New York, 1994).

———. *Stalin: Triumph and Tragedy,* trans. H. Shukman (New York, 1991).

VON LAUE, T. *Why Lenin? Why Stalin?* 2d ed. (Philadelphia, 1971).

ZALESKI, E. *Planning for Economic Growth in the Soviet Union, 1918–1932* (Chapel Hill, NC, 1971).

10

The Politics of Stalinism, 1928–1941

By 1928 Stalin had ousted Trotskii and the Left opposition and taken major steps away from Lenin's collective leadership and freer intraparty debate. Moving toward personal rule, Stalin acted to secure predominant power over party and state by crushing the Right opposition and purging other colleagues of Lenin who retained influential positions. He manipulated the Lenin cult and created the monstrous myth of his own omniscience. To secure awesome power, the Stalin regime crushed passive opposition from the peasantry and secured control over the countryside by forcibly collectivizing agriculture. With the rapid industrialization of the Five Year Plans, it won support from a growing working class. (These economic policies will be discussed in Chapter 11.) A seemingly monolithic state swallowed society as most Soviet citizens became state employees, subject to increasing party supervision and controls. After all significant opposition had seemingly been overcome, Stalin launched the Great Purge of 1936–1938, which eliminated the Old Bolsheviks and left his minions apparently triumphant over a purged party, army, and state, and over a supine and frightened populace.

Recently, however, the monolithic, apparently unified nature of the Stalin regime depicted in most Western and dissident Soviet accounts has been sharply disputed. Recent specialized studies, notes J. Arch Getty, have revealed that policymaking in the early Stalin years was often uncertain and tentative. Like Hitler, Stalin employed an indirect, sometimes erratic "formula of rule" in the 1930s. Differences of opinion persisted within the party, and Soviet administration was chaotic, irregular, and confused. Getty concludes: "Although the Soviet government was certainly dictatorial, . . . it was not totalitarian."[1]

In the Stalinist political system, theory and practice were often totally at odds. The federal system and Constitution of 1936 gave national minorities and the Soviet people the appearance of self-government and civil rights; actually power, although inefficient, resided primarily in a self-perpetuating party leadership in Moscow. Did Stalin's aims and methods derive from Ivan the Terrible? Was he a loyal Marxist and true heir of Lenin, or an Oriental

[1] J. Arch Getty, *Origins of the Great Purges* (Cambridge, 1985), p. 198.

despot paying mere lip service to Marxism-Leninism? Did he truly initiate all decisions, as was claimed officially, and did contending factions remain concealed within the party? How did Stalin's political system actually function? And why was the Great Purge undertaken?

Intraparty Struggles and Crises, 1929–1934

A growing personality cult aided Stalin's drive to dominate the party and rule the USSR. Launched cautiously at the 14th Congress in 1925, it developed notably after Stalin's 50th birthday (December 21, 1929), celebrated as a great historic event. In contrast with Lenin's modest, unassuming pose, the Stalin cult by the mid-1930s took on grandiose, even ludicrous forms. At a rally during the Purges in 1937, N. S. Khrushchev, Stalin's eventual successor, declared slavishly:

> These miserable nonentities wanted to destroy the unity of the party and the Soviet state. They raised their treacherous hands against Comrade Stalin . . . , our hope; Stalin, our desire; Stalin, the light of advanced and progressive humanity; Stalin, our will; Stalin, our victory.[2]

Within the party, the area of dissent narrowed, then disappeared. As Stalin crushed the Left in 1926–1927, it became clear that he would exclude factions or individuals who opposed his personal authority. But though Trotskii and the rest were stripped of influential positions, they still underestimated Stalin. Trotskii's expulsion from the USSR in 1929 brought predictions that power would pass to a triumvirate of Bukharin, Alexis Rykov, and M. P. Tomskii, who appeared (mistakenly) to dominate the Politburo selected after the 15th Congress.

Once the Left had been broken, Stalin adopted a moderate stance, and split with the Right led by

Joseph Stalin, 1879–1953, wearing his generalissimo's uniform during World War II. Stalin received great adulation as the "victor" over Nazi Germany. This portrait depicts a masterful military leader.

UPI/Corbis-Bettmann

Bukharin. The Stalin-Bukharin struggle developed behind the scenes during a growing economic crisis: Better-off peasants (kulaks), taxed heavily by the regime, withheld their grain from the market. Whereas Bukharin favored further concessions to the peasantry, including raising state grain prices, Stalin began urging strong action against the kulaks and officials who sympathized with them. Denouncing the still unnamed opposition for blocking industrialization, Stalin used his control of the Secretariat and Orgburo to remove Bukharin's supporters from key party and government posts. Belatedly contacting Kamenev from the broken Left, Bukharin warned "*He* [Stalin] will strangle us." He added:

> Stalin . . . is an unprincipled intriguer who subordinates everything to the preservation of his power. He changes his theories according to whom he needs to get rid of at any given

---

[2] Quoted in E. Crankshaw, *Khrushchev's Russia* (Harmondsworth, England, 1959), p. 53.

moment. . . . He maneuvers in such a way as to make us stand as the schismatics.[3]

By early 1929 Stalin attacked the Right openly and told a Politburo meeting, "Comrades, sad though it may be, we must face facts: a factional group has been established within our party composed of Bukharin, Tomskii, and Rykov" that was blocking industrialization and collectivization. Though the Right controlled the Moscow party organization, Stalin won majority support in the Politburo, bypassed the Moscow leaders, and broke their resistance. In April 1929 the Central Committee condemned the Right and removed its leaders from their posts; in November they surrendered, recanted their views, and bought themselves a few years of grace.

Open political opposition in the party ended, but during 1932–1933 Stalin faced a grave economic and political crisis. Forced collectivization had brought on famine and hunger in the cities and provoked widespread nationalist opposition, especially among Ukrainian peasants. As Stalin's popularity fell to its nadir, Trotskii's *Bulletin of the Opposition* declared abroad: "In view of the incapacity of the present leadership to get out of the economic and political deadlock, the conviction about the need to change the leadership of the party is growing." Trotskii reminded his readers of Lenin's "Testament," which had urged Stalin's removal as general secretary. In November 1932, after Nadezhda Allilueva, Stalin's second wife, spoke out about famine and discontent, the overwrought Stalin silenced her roughly, and she apparently committed suicide. Victor Serge notes that Stalin submitted his resignation, but none of the Politburo's obedient Stalinist members dared accept it. Finally V. M. Molotov said, "Stop it, stop it. You have got the party's confidence," and the matter was dropped.

Stalin surmounted this personal danger and the economic and political crisis in the country. Opposition remained unfocused, confused, and leaderless. In 1932 Stalin had Kamenev and

[3] Quoted in I. Deutscher, *Stalin* (London, 1949), p. 314.

Zinoviev expelled from the party and exiled to Siberia, but after more abject recantations, they were allowed to return. After similar admissions of guilt, other Old Bolsheviks received responsible posts. They might have tried to kill Stalin, but who would rule in his place? Even Trotskii declared, "We are concerned not with the expulsion of individuals but the change of the system." Stalin temporarily adopted a moderate, conciliatory course. His speech of January 1934 called for consolidating earlier gains and inaugurated a brief period of relative liberalism. Within the Politburo the youthful and popular Leningrad party chief, S. M. Kirov, backed by Voroshilov and Kalinin, supported concessions to the peasantry and an end to terror; hard-liners such as Molotov and Kaganovich opposed them. During 1934 Stalin apparently wavered indecisively between these groups.

The Great Purge

This interlude ended with Kirov's murder in December 1934. The accused assassin, Nikolaev, and his accomplices were promptly apprehended, tried secretly, and shot. They were described officially as Trotskyites working for the clandestine, foreign-directed United Center, which had allegedly plotted to kill Stalin and other top leaders. Zinoviev and Kamenev, supposedly implicated in the plot, were sentenced to penal servitude.

Ominous changes proceeded in the political police. Early in 1934 the secret police (GPU), which had gained a sinister reputation, was dissolved. Its tasks were assumed by the People's Commissariat of Internal Affairs (NKVD), which combined control over political, regular, and criminal police. Henrikh Iagoda, its first chief, perhaps fearing that Kirov's liberal line threatened his power, may have engineered the assassination at Stalin's order. NKVD employees were highly paid and obtained the best apartments and other privileges. This "state within a state" maintained a huge network of informers, kept dossiers on millions of persons, and spied on all party agencies. Special sections watched the NKVD's own regular personnel, whose members were expected to show loyalty first to the NKVD and only secondarily to the party. Special NKVD courts, exempt from control by government or judicial agencies, were set up to conduct secret trials.

While surface calm prevailed, Andrei Zhdanov, Kirov's successor as Leningrad party chief, conducted a ruthless purge there, deporting tens of thousands of persons to Siberia, and the NKVD prepared the greatest mass purge in history. In May 1935 a Special Security Commission was created to investigate all party members, "liquidate enemies of the people," and encourage citizens to denounce suspected counterrevolutionaries and slackers. Its members included Stalin, N. I. Yezhov (later head of the NKVD), Zhdanov, and Andrei Vyshinskii, subsequently chief prosecutor at the public trials. That spring 40 members of Stalin's personal bodyguard were tried secretly for conspiracy, and "terrorists" were hunted in every party and Komsomol (Young Communist League) agency. As the rapidly growing NKVD justified its existence by uncovering conspiracies everywhere, Stalin ordered careful surveillance even of Politburo members.

A reign of terror was unleashed, dwarfing that of the French Revolution. Perhaps that precedent had previously deterred Stalin, who once remarked, "You chop off one head today, another one tomorrow. . . . What in the end will be left of the party?" Unlike the French case, terror in Russia reached its murderous peak two decades after the Revolution. The French terror claimed about 40,000 victims; Stalin's from 1935 to 1938 killed hundreds of thousands and sent millions into exile.[4] Stalin, not the NKVD, initiated the Great Purge and approved executions of prominent figures. A Stalinist account explained:

> The Trotsky-Bukharin fiends, in obedience to the wishes of their masters—the espionage services of foreign states—had set out to destroy the party and the Soviet state, to undermine the defensive power of the country,

to assist foreign military intervention . . . [and] to bring about the dismemberment of the USSR . . . , to destroy the gains of the workers and collective farmers, and to restore capitalist slavery in the USSR.[5]

The party had to become an impregnable fortress to safeguard the country and the gains of socialism from foreign and domestic enemies. Stalin added: "As long as capitalist encirclement exists, there will be wreckers, spies, diversionists, and murderers in our country, sent behind our lines by the agents of foreign states." The Soviet public found this distorted view credible.

Three great public trials of party leaders accused of treason were held in Moscow. At the Trial of the Sixteen (August 1936), Prosecutor Vyshinskii accused Kamenev, Zinoviev, and others of conspiring to overthrow the regime and to remove Stalin and other Politburo leaders. After confessing and incriminating the Right opposition, the defendants were convicted and shot. When this severe treatment of Lenin's old colleagues provoked opposition in the Central Committee, Stalin removed Iagoda and appointed as NKVD chief Yezhov, under whom the purge reached its bloody climax. Each group of defendants incriminated the next in a chain reaction of denunciations. At the Trial of the Seventeen (January 1937), featuring Piatakov, Muralov, and Radek (all Old Bolshevik leaders), the accused confessed to treasonable dealings with Germany and Japan. The greatest public spectacle of them all, the Trial of the Twenty-One (March 1938) included Bukharin, Rykov, and Iagoda. Foreign espionage agencies, claimed the prosecutor, had set up a "bloc of Rightists and Trotskyists" on Soviet soil to bring a bourgeois-capitalist regime to power and detach non-Russian regions from the USSR. Allegedly Bukharin had been a traitor since 1918. Vyshinskii concluded his prosecution with the invariable appeal, "Shoot the mad dogs!" and the leading defendants would be executed.

---

[4] In 1989 demographer Paul Robeson, Jr., estimated that the USSR during the Stalin era had about 29.3 million "excess deaths" from terror and famine.

[5] *Short History of the Communist Party* (New York, 1939), p. 347.

Why did the accused, many of them prominent, courageous revolutionaries, publicly admit crimes they could not have committed, when their confessions constituted the only legal basis for conviction? Most had recanted several times already, each time admitting greater guilt, and hoped to save their lives, positions, and families. Some believed that the party, to which they had dedicated their lives, must be right. The defendants, mostly middle-aged, were broken down by lengthy NKVD interrogations and sleeplessness, or were hypnotized by the terror. Doubtless they hoped to save something from blasted careers by bowing to Stalin's tyranny.

Those who were tried and executed, or died by other means, included all surviving members of Lenin's Politburo except Stalin and Trotskii, the defendant in chief tried in absentia. A former premier, two former chiefs of the Comintern, the trade union head, and two chiefs of the political police were executed. Survivors must have wondered how the great Lenin could have surrounded himself with so many traitors and scoundrels. In 1914, to be sure, Roman Malinovskii, Lenin's close colleague, had been exposed as a police agent. The legacy of police infiltration of revolutionary organizations under tsarism provided some basis for believing the revelations of the 1930s.

The Great Purge decimated the leadership corps of the Soviet armed forces. The military chiefs, especially Marshal Tukhachevskii, who had made the Red Army an effective fighting force, apparently had been highly critical of the early trials. In May 1937 he and other prominent generals were arrested, accused of treasonable collaboration with Germany and Japan, and shot. None of them resisted or attempted a military coup. Purged later were most members of the Supreme War Council, three of five marshals, 14 of 16 army generals, and all full admirals. About half the entire officer corps was shot or imprisoned, a terrible insult to Red Army patriotism and a grave weakening of the armed forces. (After Stalin's death, all leading military figures who were purged were rehabilitated, many posthumously, and declared innocent of all charges brought against them.)

In addition to Old Bolsheviks, many Stalinist party leaders were eliminated. Purged were 70 percent of the Central Committee members and candidates chosen in 1934. At the 18th Party Congress in 1939, only 35 of 1,827 rank-and-file delegates from the previous congress were present! From the party and army the purge reached downward into the general populace as friends and relatives of those purged were arrested. Thousands of ordinary citizens were denounced orally or by poison-pen letters, often out of jealousy and meanness, of crimes they had not and could not have committed. For two years (1937–1938), most of a helpless population lived in abject terror of sudden arrest and deportation. Special targets for arbitrary arrest included former members of other political parties and former White soldiers, priests, intellectuals (especially writers), Jews and other national minorities in Russian towns, and professionals who had been abroad. Many ordinary workers and peasants were also denounced and forced to confess to imaginary crimes against the state. Stalin even issued orders to arrest a percentage of the population. His bloodthirstiness grew as members of all social groups were rounded up.

Why this terrible bloodbath? wondered the survivors. Some victims were scapegoats for economic failures of the early 1930s. Stalin's chief motive, suggests the British scholar Isaac Deutscher, was to destroy those who might lead an alternate regime or criticize his policies. This strategy required killing or exiling party and military men trained by purged leaders, then rebuilding the chief levers of Soviet power: the party, the army, and the security forces. The general public may have been involved deliberately to create the climate of fear essential to Stalin's total control. The need for millions of forced laborers in the Arctic and Siberia supplied a reason for mass deportation of workers and peasants. Perhaps Stalin became utterly mad, making pointless the search for rational explanations. Certainly casualties were too great to be justified by ordinary political or social aims. Robert Conquest's estimate of about 8 million purge victims in camps by 1938, plus another million in prisons, seems reasonable. During the 1930s a huge NKVD empire of forced labor camps and prisons, begun in the White Sea area under Lenin and described graphically in Alexander Solzhenitsyn's *Gulag Archipelago,* mushroomed in European Russia and Siberia. Major projects included constructing the White Sea and Moscow-Volga canals, double-tracking the Trans-Siberian Railway, and gold mining in the frigid Kolyma region. Usually fed below the subsistence level and working under extremely arduous conditions, the inmates died off rapidly only to be replaced by new millions.

In December 1938, with the arrest of master purger Yezhov, blamed for excesses ordered by Stalin, the purge's intensive phase ended. By then half the urban population of the USSR was on police lists, and 5 percent had actually been arrested.[6] Large-scale terror remained endemic to the Soviet system until Stalin's death. The epilogue to the Great Purge was the brutal murder of Trotskii in Mexico (August 1940) by an NKVD agent, the son of a Spanish Communist. Besides terrorizing the USSR, the purge opened up numerous vacancies in civil and military posts, filled by obedient but often inexperienced men who ensured Stalin's omnipotence. The Politburo lost most of its power and became Stalin's rubber stamp, while his private Secretariat became a modern Oprichnina. Otherwise the purge altered the Soviet political system remarkably little.

The Great Purge necessitated the rewriting of Communist Party history. Directed by Zhdanov and Stalin's secretaries, historians prepared the *History of the All-Union Communist Party (Bolshevik): Short Course* (1938). Apparently Stalin corrected the manuscript and wrote the section on philosophy. Portraying Stalin as Lenin's only true disciple, the *History* claimed that other Old Bol-

sheviks had conspired against Lenin and the party since 1917. Thus the all-powerful dictator had altered history to serve his present purposes. After 1938 Stalin worked intensively to foster patriotism, restore unity, and rebuild the army leadership and the armed forces as the Nazi threat to the USSR grew.

Government and Party Organization

The Stalin regime combined systematic terror and massive use of force with a democratically phrased constitution, apparent federalism, and representative institutions. Operating ostensibly through a hierarchy of soviets, the political system was run actually by the party leadership and NKVD. Often theory and practice were wholly at odds, and in many ways Stalinism marked a return to tsarist autocracy. Stalin himself, no longer the apparently patient, humble, and accessible party functionary of the early 1920s, retreated into the Kremlin's recesses or to his country villa at nearby Kuntsevo. Rarely appearing in public, he clothed himself in mystery, and many in the younger generation regarded him and his oracular pronouncements with awe and reverence. Once his rivals had been eliminated, he grew more dictatorial and, after 1938, became an all-powerful father figure. His Politburo contained bureaucrats and party officials, not active revolutionaries or creative ideologists as in Lenin's time. Men such as Molotov, Kaganovich, and Kuibyshev, though able administrators, were narrow and ignorant of foreign lands. In the Politburo, Stalin listened impatiently to their arguments, then often decided an issue with a sarcastic remark or vulgar joke. All important matters were decided there, under the dictator's jealous eye.

The legal basis of this Soviet political system was the Constitution of 1936. Constitutions under Marxism were supposed to reflect existing socio-economic conditions and had to be altered as these conditions changed. Earlier Soviet constitutions (1918 and 1924), with a franchise heavily

---

[6] See R. Conquest, *The Great Terror* (New York, 1968).

weighted to favor urban elements and excluding "exploiters," represented the proletarian dictatorship's first phase. In November 1936 Stalin explained to the Eighth Congress of Soviets that because rapid industrialization and collectivization had eliminated landlords, capitalists, and kulaks, "There are no longer any antagonistic classes in [Soviet] society . . . [which] consists of two friendly classes, workers and peasants." Restrictions and inequalities in voting could be abolished, and a democratic suffrage instituted. The Stalin Constitution, he claimed, would be "the only thoroughly democratic constitution in the world." It was designed to win approval abroad.

The promises of the Stalin Constitution (finally superseded by a new one in 1977) often meant little in practice. "The USSR," it proclaimed, "is a federal state formed on the basis of a voluntary union of equal Soviet socialist republics." Most republics, however, had been conquered or incorporated forcibly, and the predominance of the Russian Republic, with about half the population and three-fourths the area of the Union, negated equality. Theoretically, a republic, as formerly, could secede, but to advocate secession was a crime and a "bourgeois nationalist deviation." Only the working class, through its vanguard, the Soviet Communist Party, could approve secession or create and abolish republics. In 1936 Transcaucasia split into Azerbaijan, Armenia, and Georgia, which were admitted as separate republics; then the Kazakh and Kirghiz republics in Central Asia were added. A Karelo-Finnish Republic was created partly out of territory taken from Finland in 1940, but it was abolished equally arbitrarily in 1956. The Moldavian Republic was established also in 1940, mostly from territory acquired by treaty with Hitler, and the formerly independent Baltic countries of Estonia, Latvia, and Lithuania were occupied and became Soviet republics. An amendment of 1944 permitted republics to establish relations with foreign countries (none ever did so), and Ukraine and Byelorussia obtained separate United Nations representation in 1945.

Smaller national groups (more than 100 in the Russian Republic alone) obtained autonomous republics and national areas, plus legislative representation.

Soviet federalism provided an illusion of autonomy and self-government, but the central government, retaining full power, repressed any group or individuals who advocated genuine autonomy or independence, especially in Ukraine, populous and agriculturally valuable. Each nationality received its own territory, language, press, and schools, but the Russian-dominated all-Union Communist Party supervised and controlled them. This federal system, in Stalin's words "national in form, socialist in content," though preferable to tsarism's open Russification and assimilation, perpetuated Russian rule over most areas of the old empire. National feeling persisted nonetheless among many minority peoples of the USSR.

Under the Stalin Constitution a bicameral Supreme Soviet became the national legislature, supposedly the highest organ of state authority. The Council of the Union was directly elected from equal election districts, one deputy per 300,000 population. The Council of Nationalities represented the various administrative units: 25 deputies from each union republic, 11 from autonomous republics, and so on. Delegates, elected for four-year terms by universal suffrage, received good pay during brief sessions but, unlike members of the U.S. Congress, retained their regular jobs and had no offices or staffs. A Presidium, elected by both houses, could issue decrees when the Soviet was not meeting, and its chairman was titular president of the USSR. Bills became law when passed by both houses. Under Stalin, however, the Supreme Soviet never recorded a negative vote. It was a decorative, rubber-stamp body without real discussion or power of decision. Below it lay a network of soviets on republic, regional, provincial, district, and village or city levels—more than 60,000 soviets in all—with some 1,500,000 deputies elected for two-year terms. Sovereign in theory, soviets were controlled in fact at every level by their party members and parallel party organizations. Elections were uncontested with only one candidate, selected by the party, in each election district.

The Constitution entrusted executive and administrative authority to the Council of People's Commissars (called the Council of Ministers after 1946). Some ministries operated only on the all-union level, others there and in the republics, and still others in the republics only. Theoretically, but not in practice, these ministries were responsible to the soviets. Coordinating the administrative and economic system, the Council of People's Commissars possessed more power than the Constitution suggested. The Supreme Court of the USSR headed a judicial system including supreme courts in the republics, regional courts, and people's courts. Lower courts were elected and higher ones chosen by the corresponding soviet. Judges, supposedly independent, were subject to party policies, and many important cases were tried in secret by the NKVD.

Article 125 of the Constitution promised Soviet citizens freedom of speech, conscience, press, assembly, and demonstrations "in conformity with the interests of the working people and in order to strengthen the socialist system." Citizens were guaranteed the right to work, education, rest, and maintenance in sickness and old age. Article 127 pledged freedom from arrest except by court decision. In fact, the Soviet people never enjoyed most of these rights. As the new constitution was printed, the NKVD was conducting mass arrests and deportations without trial. The state assigned workers to jobs arbitrarily and prohibited strikes and independent trade unions. Constitutional rights could be used only to support the regime, not to criticize it.

The Stalin Constitution, unlike its predecessors, at least suggested in Article 126 the true role of the Communist Party:

> The most active and politically conscious citizens in the ranks of the working class, working peasants, and working intelligentsia voluntarily unite in the Communist Party of the Soviet Union, which is the vanguard of the working people in their struggle to build communist society and is *the leading core of all organizations of the working people, both public and state.* [Italics added for emphasis.][7]

Still organized on Leninist principles, the party remained an elite force of about 4 percent of the population in which intellectuals and bureaucrats outnumbered ordinary workers. Operating supposedly by democratic centralism, it exercised decisive authority over domestic and foreign affairs. Under Stalin all power passed to higher party organs co-opted by the leaders, not elected democratically as the party rules stipulated. The rank and file could merely criticize minor shortcomings and lost all influence over the self-perpetuating leadership. The party became Stalin's monolithic, disciplined, and increasingly bureaucratic instrument. Intraparty debate avoided major issues and was limited to *how* to implement decisions, with no discussion of alternative policies or leaders.

The all-union congress, a periodic gathering of leaders from the entire USSR, theoretically exercised supreme authority within the party. Once factions were banned (1921) and the Right was defeated (1929), however, congresses lost power to initiate policies. Important decisions were made in advance by the Politburo and approved unanimously by the congress, which merely ratified policies of the leadership pro forma. In Lenin's time, the Central Committee, supposedly elected by the congress to direct party work between congresses, was an important decision-making body; under Stalin it grew in size (to 125 full members and 125 candidates in 1952) but declined in power. It comprised mostly regional party secretaries and ministers from the all-union and republic governments.

The Central Committee, stated the party rules, elected three subcommittees—the Politburo, Orgburo, and Secretariat; in fact, they determined the

---

[7] *Constitution (Fundamental Law) of the Union of Soviet Socialist Republics* (Moscow, 1957), p. 103.

Committee's membership and policies. With about a dozen full members and a few candidates, the Politburo ostensibly "directs the work of the Central Committee between plenary sessions." It always included the most powerful party and state officials and decided the chief domestic and foreign policy issues; after 1920 it was the main power center in the USSR. Its meetings were secret and its debates presumably free. Stalin purged the Politburo, refilled it with his own men, and made it an instrument of his personal power. During the 1930s it experienced great insecurity and high turnover; after that its members enjoyed much stability of tenure. The Orgburo, Stalin's original power base, directed the party's organizational work until its merger with the Politburo in 1952. The Secretariat directed the party's permanent apparatus. Stalin, as general secretary with four assistants, managed its professional staff and controlled all party personnel and appointments.

With five levels the party, like the soviets, was directed centrally by its all-union organs (see Figure 10.1). Thus the Ukrainian party, run generally by Great Russians, was controlled from Moscow, which decided its policies and personnel. Lower party officials were often sacrificed as scapegoats for unpopular or mistaken national policies. Some regional party secretaries became miniature Stalins, dictating to frightened subordinates. At the bottom of the party hierarchy stood some 350,000 primary organizations, or cells, composed of at least three members, in villages, collective farms, factories, offices, and military units. Acting like nerves of the human body, they permeated and controlled all organizations and agencies.

Party membership was open, in theory, to all persons over 21 years of age (over 18 for Komsomol members). Applicants filled out a detailed questionnaire, submitted recommendations from three members in good standing to a primary party organization, and served at least a year's candidacy. Applications had to be approved by the primary organizations and ratified by the district party unit. Rank-and-file members performed party work besides their regular jobs. They had to pay dues, work actively in agitation and propa-

ganda among their fellows, explain Marxian theory and the party line, and set examples of leadership and clean living. Their rewards included power and influence because the party was the only road to political success, plus material benefits. Disobedient or undisciplined members were reprimanded, censured, or in graver cases, expelled. Periodic purges were designed to cleanse the party of opportunists, slackers, and the disloyal. Under Stalin, Communists occupied the key positions in most walks of life; factory managers, collective farm chairmen, school superintendents, and army officers were generally party members. Within the party, urban elements predominated over rural ones and Great Russians over national minorities.

The highly centralized Stalinist political system was based on interlocking presidia of the party and the state. The main decisions, made by Stalin personally and approved by the Politburo, were transmitted by lower party organs, soviets, trade unions, and media of mass communication to the people. The party manipulated the soviets skillfully to maintain links with the population and provide a semblance of legitimate rule. The main weaknesses were lack of local initiative and the absence of any legal means to transmit power from one leader or group of leaders to another. This intensified intrigue, suspicion, and power struggles behind the scenes at the top.

Stalinism

Stalin had risen in the party as an organizer and administrator, not an ideologist. Marx had been a theorist, not an active revolutionary; in Lenin, the two aspects were in rare balance. At first Stalin marched carefully in Lenin's footsteps (his chief theoretical work was *Problems of Leninism*), but once in power he altered and gravely distorted the doctrines of Marx and Lenin. Stalin's major doctrinal innovation—socialism in one country—developed accidentally and pragmatically during his struggle with Trotskii (see Chapter 9). Trotskii's apparently contrasting theory of "permanent revolution" stressed using the Comintern (Communist International, organization of Communist

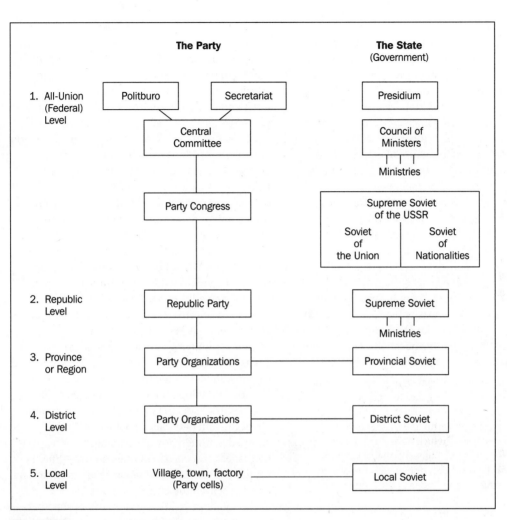

Figure 10.1
Soviet power centers under Stalin

Both the Communist Party of the Soviet Union and the Soviet government were organized on five levels, from the all-union hierarchy at the top to the local bodies at the bottom. At each level, the party organization controlled the corresponding governmental (soviet) bodies. Of the 15 Soviet socialist republics, the Russian Republic was by far the largest. Among the others were Ukraine, Byelorussia, Georgia, and Armenia. Each republic possessed its own supreme soviet and ministries. Autonomous republics (for smaller nationalities) also had their own supreme soviets and councils of ministers. The Communist Party of each republic was subordinated to the All-Union party organs.

parties) to foment revolutions abroad; Stalin emphasized building socialism in Russia first. They differed somewhat over means and tactics, but shared the goal of an eventual global triumph of communism. But could socialism be *completely* built in a single country? Stalin claimed in 1936 that it had already been *essentially* constructed in Russia, although final victory must await worldwide revolution. Stalin's national emphasis won him continuing support from industrial workers, the intelligentsia, and military men, as well as from a party anxious to believe that Russians could build socialism themselves. Socialism in one country provided the ideological basis and social support for forced collectivization and the Five Year Plans.

Since Stalin claimed that socialism had triumphed in the USSR and that class enemies had been broken, why was proletarian dictatorship not withering away, as Marx had predicted? Stalin had already answered this question in rather cynical fashion at the 16th Party Congress in 1930:

> We are in favor of the state dying out, and at the same time we stand for the strengthening of the dictatorship of the proletariat, which represents the most powerful and mighty authority of all forms of state which have existed up to the present day. The highest possible development of the power of the state with the object of preparing the conditions of the dying out of the state? Is this contradictory? Yes, it is contradictory. But this contradiction is a living thing and completely reflects Marxist dialectics.[8]

Apparently Stalin derived this view from Lenin's statement that state machinery must be perfected in the lower phase of socialism before withering. To justify strengthening the proletarian state, Stalin argued that hostile capitalist powers, surrounding the USSR, threatened armed intervention. Until "capitalist encirclement" was replaced by socialist encirclement of capitalism, the proletarian state must remain strong and alert, eliminate "bourgeois survivals," and hasten the transition to the final goal—communism.

---

[8] *Problems of Leninism* (Moscow, 1933), vol. 2, p. 402.

Stalin was reacting instinctively against a Marxian internationalism that had already been undermined by the apparent failure of world revolution. For Stalin the interests of the Soviet fatherland clearly preceded those of the international proletariat and foreign Communist parties. Thus in the years before World War II, Soviet nationalism and patriotism were developed partly as an affirmation of what the working class had built in the USSR and partly to counter separatism in the borderlands. The regime fostered pride in Soviet industrial and technological achievements, with considerable success among workers and the younger generation. The shift away from internationalism was reflected in repudiation of the works of the Marxist historian M. N. Pokrovskii, who had condemned Russian tsars and imperialism unreservedly. From the mid-1930s there occurred a selective rehabilitation and even praise of such rulers as Peter the Great and Ivan the Terrible for unifying and strengthening Russia. Tsarist generals such as Suvorov and Kutuzov, and certain admirals in the Crimean War, were glorified for defending their country heroically. New Soviet patriotism contained elements of traditional Great Russian nationalism, which Stalin had adopted. Through Soviet nationalism—one positive aspect of socialism in one country—Stalin sought to overcome and replace narrower national loyalties within the USSR.

The Stalinist political system established patterns of authority, many of which—unlike Stalin's cult of personality—persisted until the end of the USSR in 1991. With maximum use of force and terror, Stalin crushed all political opposition, as Ivan the Terrible had sought but failed to do. Stalin created perhaps the most powerful centralized state in history, with a developed industry and a vast bureaucracy. In so doing, he perverted Marxist ideology almost beyond recognition by accumulating personal power analogous to that of Oriental despotism. The Communist Party, though supreme over obedient soviets, was itself eventually transformed into a bureaucracy of frightened automatons by the Great Purge. Stalin's successors would repudiate mass terror and the cult of individual dictatorship, but not a centralized regime.

Problem 5

The Great Terror: Old and New Approaches

One of the most difficult periods of Soviet history to comprehend, and one of the most complex and controversial, is the period of the mid-1930s, when the Stalinist regime subjected the Soviet population, and especially the Communist party, to unprecedented levels of violence. The horrifying events of 1935–1938 led to the total destruction of the Leninist Party. Why did Stalin elect to pursue such a policy against the party over which he enjoyed almost total control? Why did he resort to such brutal and merciless cruelty?

A common explanation is that Stalin suffered from a debilitating mental disorder, that he was deranged. The traditional view has been to hold Stalin solely responsible for the terror, whether sane or insane. The recent opening of Soviet archives has, however, provided the basis for new and sometimes controversial interpretations of that dark period.

Who Was Responsible?

Martin McCauley, a British historian, identifies two schools of thought that characterize the study of Stalinism as a whole and the period of the Great Terror in particular. He labels the two schools the "totalitarian and the pluralist, or the intentional and the structural."[9] The totalitarian school emerged during the Cold War, and focused attention on the Soviet state and primarily on the personality and mind-set of Stalin himself. In this view, he alone bears responsibility for the deaths of millions and the imprisonment of millions more. This school argues that Stalin was a ruthless leader who imposed his will on the party and on society, destroying millions of people in the

process. The pluralist approach, on the other hand, argues in favor of multiple causes for the terror, and suggests that the state served as a kind of mediator among competing interests in society. Those competing groups, in an atmosphere of siege, created conditions in which violence was inevitable. Pluralists argue that Stalin was not a ruthless dictator, but merely a leader who shifted support, often abruptly, among various conflicting groups within society, playing one faction or group against another.

The standard "totalitarian" treatment of Stalinist terror is Robert Conquest's *The Great Terror,* published originally in 1968 and revised in 1990. It originally relied on unofficial sources, but with the release during Gorbachev's *glasnost* of long-secret archival material, the author rewrote his study. He added many new details but retained his original conclusion that the terror was largely the product of Stalin's personal ambition, his vindictiveness, and his thirst for glory, adulation, and unrestricted power.[10] Conquest repeatedly argues that Stalin's was the crucial role in the great terror:

> Over this major sector of the Purge [of the central Party hierarchy], Stalin and Yezhov themselves presided. They received valuable help from Molotov and Voroshilov when required, but on the whole Stalin kept an extremely tight personal grip on proceedings, working through Yezhov alone.
>
> In 1937 and 1938, Yezhov sent to Stalin 383 lists, containing thousands of names of figures important enough to require his personal approval for their execution. As Yezhov was only in power for just over two years . . . this means that Stalin got such a list rather more often than every other day of "persons whose cases were under the jurisdiction of the Military Collegium." A *samizdat* historian of the 1970s indicated that the lists included 40,000 names. However, a Soviet periodical now tells us

---

[9] M. McCauley, *Stalin and Stalinism,* 2nd ed. (London, 1995), p. 78.

[10] R. Conquest, *The Great Terror: A Reassessment* (New York, 1990).

Problem 5 continued

that at a recent plenum of the Central Committee, the total number shot, whose names appeared on lists signed by Stalin, Molotov, Kaganovich, and Malenkov, though perhaps over a longer period, was given as 230,000. At any rate, we can envisage Stalin, on arrival in his office, as often as not finding in his in-tray, a list of a few hundred names for death, looking through, and approving them, as part of the ordinary routine of a Kremlin day. We are told in recent Soviet articles that on 12 December 1937 alone, Stalin and Molotov sanctioned 3,167 death sentences, and then went to the cinema.[11]

Conquest concluded that *The Great Terror* left the country ". . . broken, and henceforward a limited number of arrests of men who had given some sort of cause for suspicion of disloyalty was sufficient to maintain the habit of submission and silence."[12]

Roy Medvedev, a former Soviet dissident and now a Russian liberal historian, agrees in large part with Conquest's view of Stalin's ultimate responsibility for the Great Terror.

His [Stalin's] main motive [for the terror] was lust for power, boundless ambition. This all-consuming lust appeared in Stalin much earlier than 1936. Even though he had great power, it was not enough—he wanted absolute power and unlimited submission to his will. He understood at the same time that the generation of party and government leaders formed in the years of underground work, revolution, and civil war would never become totally submissive. They too had taken part in the creation of the party and the state and demanded a share of the leadership. But Stalin did not want to share power.[13]

Edvard Radzinsky, a well-known Russian playwright and biographer of Nicholas II and, most recently, of Stalin,[14] agrees that the Gensec bears full responsibility for the bloodletting unleashed in the mid-1930s.

The Seventeenth Congress [1934, "Congress of Victors"] had finally convinced Stalin that they [the old Bolsheviks] would never let him create the country of his dreams—a military camp where unanimity and subservience to the Leader reigned. Only with such a country could the Great Dream be realized.[15]

A tremendous task confronted him. The creation of a Party united in obedience to himself, Ilyich [Lenin] had seen the need for it, but experience showed that he had left the task unfinished. Now Stalin resolved to complete it.[16]

Among the "pluralists" are J. Arch Getty and Robert W. Thurston. They have written studies that challenge Conquest's, Medvedev's, and Radzinsky's general accounts and conclusions.

Getty suggests, in his study *The Origins of the Great Purges*, that the Bolshevik Party was far from being a totalitarian monolith, and while Stalin was a dominant figure he was not omnipotent, and the terror was not the product of his careful personal planning. He argues that the Great Terror was a bloody and ad hoc result of Moscow's efforts to centralize power in the country.

It is not necessary for us to put Stalin in day-to-day control of events to judge him. A chaotic local bureaucracy, a quasi-feudal network of politicians accustomed to arresting people and a set of perhaps insoluble political and social problems created an atmosphere conducive to violence. All it took from Stalin were catalytic and probably ad hoc interventions at three pivotal points—early 1936 (to reopen the Kirov investigation), November 1936 (to condemn Piatakov), and June 1937 (to unleash Ezhov)—to spark an uncontrolled explosion. That he did so intervene speaks for itself.[17]

---

[11] Conquest, (1990), pp. 234–35.

[12] Conquest, pp. 434–35.

[13] R. Medvedev, *Let History Judge: The Origins and Consequences of Stalinism* (New York, 1989), p. 585.

[14] Edvard Radzinsky, *Stalin*, trans. H.T. Willetts (New York, 1996).

[15] Ibid., p. 320.

[16] Ibid.

[17] J. Arch Getty, *Origins of the Great Purges: The Soviet Communist Party Reconsidered, 1933–1938* (New York, 1985), p. 206.

Getty argues that the conditions within the party and the country were ripe for an "explosion" of terror. He concludes his study of the Party and the terror as follows:

> The evidence suggests that the Ezhovshchina—which is what most people really mean by the "Great Purges"—should be redefined. It was not the result of a petrified bureaucracy's stamping out dissent and annihilating old radical revolutionaries. In fact, it may have been just the opposite. It is not inconsistent with the evidence to argue that the Ezhovshchina was rather a radical, even hysterical, *reaction* to bureaucracy. The entrenched officeholders were destroyed from above and below in a chaotic wave of voluntarism and revolutionary puritanism.[18]

Robert W. Thurston also represents the "pluralist" approach. His *Life and Terror in Stalin's Russia, 1934–1941,* which appeared in 1996, largely rejects the "totalitarian" interpretation of the Great Terror.

> Stalinism in the second half of the 1930s was characterized not by reliance on any one practice [terror] but by a series of rapid, profound shifts. The pattern reflects the great ability of the country's leader to set policies in motion, if not to control their outcome. The Stalin of these pages was an evil man, but a man nonetheless. He did not emerge from childhood vindictive, opportunistic, and power hungry—in short, as the master plotter. Instead, he could and did change his behavior and political stance. The evidence is now strong that he did *not* plan the Terror. By 1935–36, the country had relaxed substantially in political terms. Coercion was steadily declining. Then came a huge new internal crisis and bloodletting. It too passed, although it left a gruesome trail. By late 1938, the regime admitted that many mistakes had occurred. Once more the leadership reduced tension and curtailed the political use of law. Without the sharpening international situation of the years

immediately preceding the war, more liberalization would have taken place.[19]

Thurston also rejects Conquest's view that Stalin's Great Terror cowed and broke the spirit of the population:

> . . . Terror affected many citizens and caused great tragedy. But when it struck people down, it did not necessarily shake their relatives' and acquaintances' faith in the regime. In any case, terror touched a minority of the citizens, albeit a substantial one, and the violence was concentrated among the country's elite. Many citizens, however, did not experience or even notice the Terror except in newspapers and speeches.[20]

Thurston concludes:

> It is doubtful that any state could administer its people by imposing terror on them; assuming that a regime might try, severe contradictions and widespread avoidance behavior would quickly arise. Only an invading army might rule by terror, and then perhaps only for a limited time. Countries that become enemies of the West may be labeled systems of terror, but this judgment is of little help in understanding their internal workings or longevity.[21]

In 1999, J. Arch Getty and Oleg V. Naumov published a collection of top-secret KGB and party documents relating to the Great Terror, which they culled from recently opened Soviet archives.[22]

> When we reflect on the terror of the 1930s and ask, "What made it possible?" we must look beyond Stalin's personality for answers. It is possible, after all, to analyze and even on some level to understand a homicidal maniac or serial murderer. Accounts of the deeds of such sociopaths are depressingly common in today's newspapers, and

---

[18] Ibid.

[19] Robert W. Thurston, *Life and Terror in Stalin's Russia: 1934–1941,* (New Haven, CT, 1996), p. 233, emphasis added.

[20] Thurston, p. 232.

[21] Ibid., p. 233.

[22] J. Arch Getty and Oleg V. Naumov, eds., *The Road to Terror: Stalin and the Self-Destruction of the Bolsheviks, 1932–1939* (New Haven, CT, 1999). Used by permission.

Problem 5 continued

the tools of modern psychoanalysis give us quite a few clues to the motivations of these criminals. In the case of Stalin, a good bit has been written on his presumed personality. Yet to understand how a generalized terror erupted in the USSR in the 1930s we must look farther afield. Why were his orders carried out? Why was there fertile soil for terror to grow? Even if we decide that Stalin was always the main actor, unless we study society and the political system, the scale and spread of the terror must remain incomprehensible.[23]

Further:

Historians have often posed another question: How did one man manage to inflict such wholesale terror on an experienced political elite? The literature treats of Stalin's careful plans, his cunning, deception, threats, and blackmail. In some views, Stalin simply decided to kill a lot of people and then tricked or intimidated large numbers of otherwise intelligent people into helping him do it. . . . The only factors worth mentioning are the plans of the ruler; everyone else was a passive recipient. Many basic accounts of the terror operate at this interpretive level: once one decides who is guilty, there are no more questions to ask, and research becomes the farther enumeration of foul deeds by the evil prince.[24]

The editors of this collection of documents try to look beyond Stalin's role in order to understand the Terror. They try to analyze the social, political, and economic system in which people lived and worked in the 1930s, and they seek to assess the actions of individuals as they interacted with their environments. The authors attempt to allow the available archival evidence to speak for itself, to demonstrate the complexity of the process.

In our study we have not asked the question: What caused the terror? Questions like What caused the Thirty Years' War? Or What caused the Great Depression? similarly invite easy answers to complex problems. To identify a single main "cause" would also introduce notions of inevitability or determinism: the existence of the causal factor appears to make the result seem preordained.

The main causal element in the literature has always been Stalin's personality and culpability. In most accounts there were no other authoritative actors, no limits on his power, no politics, no discussion of society or social climate, no confusion or indecision. Stalin gave and everyone else received. The actions of others, or the environment within which he worked, were largely irrelevant or impotent. As a result, these accounts came perilously close to falling into the literary genre of fairy tales, complete with an evil all-powerful sorcerer working against powerless victims.

. . . Even with Stalin in the role of master conductor, orchestrating from a prepared score, a more complete explanation of the terror must include other factors in the equation—to acknowledge that other powerful persons and groups had an interest in repression, that the social and political climate may have facilitated terror, that the road to terror may have been crooked and roundabout. . . . even a terrorist Stalin would have needed fertile soil to spread violence, and it is our contention that the environment was as important as the agent in explaining the phenomenon as a whole.

Other factors included:

. . . The tradition of party discipline, corporate mentality and self-interest of the nomenklatura elite, political relations and struggles among numerous groups within the party, elite anxiety and perceptions of state-society relations, and, last but not least, the "Stalin factor." It is our view that each of these elements, and others as well—foreign relations, social identities, and Russian cultural perceptions, for example—was necessary but insufficient to explain the terror. For the terror was more than a top down police operation; it involved people denouncing their bosses, their underlings, their comrades. Stalin played a major role in starting the violence, but we can begin to understand it as a historical phenomenon only by considering him among many factors.[25]

---

[23] Ibid., Introduction, p. 8. Used by permission.

[24] Ibid., pp. 9–10. Used by permission.

[25] Ibid., pp. 570–71. Used by permission.

Problem 5 continued

Numbers of Victims?

In the 1968 edition of his study, Robert Conquest attempted to assess the breadth and depth of the terror by giving estimates of the approximate number of casualty figures based largely on indirect sources. His *Reassessment* of 1990 cites his 1968 figures and argues that they were too conservative. The 1968 figures:

Arrests, 1937–1938	about 7 million
Executed	about 1 million
Died in camps	about 2 million
In prison, late 1938	about 1 million
In camps, late 1938	about 8 million (assuming 5 million in camp at end of 1936)

His *Reassessment* raises the figure for arrests to 8 million, reaffirms the number of executions at about 1 million, deaths in the camps is increased by 600,000 to 700,000, and the number in prison at 1 million, although he reduces the number of prisoners in the camps in late 1938 to 7 million.

> . . . *The Great Terror* was only peripherally concerned with the total casualties of the Stalin epoch. But it reckoned the dead as no fewer than 20 million. . . . And the general total of "repressed" is now stated as around 40 million, about half of them in the peasant terror [collectivization] of 1929 and the other half from 1937 to 1953.[26]

Thurston's figures for numbers arrested and executed in 1937–1938 are considerably lower than Conquest's:

Arrests	1,575,259
Executed	681,692[27]

---

[26] Conquest, (1990), pp. 485–86, figures cited from the 1968 edition.

[27] Thurston, p. 63. He cites from the archives a report prepared in 1953 for Stalin's successors.

Getty and Naumov cite the same sources as Thurston. They add the following by way of a conclusion:

> Finally, in 1962–63 and 1988 secret high-level government investigations produced results very similar to ours. On both occasions, the Politburo sought the most damning figures possible for use as political capital and commissioned blue-ribbon Politburo commissions to comb KGB files for data. In 1963, Khrushchev sought data condemning his current rivals Molotov and Kaganovich. In 1988, Gorbachev wanted to discredit Stalinism as part of a *perestroika* policy. In both cases, the results . . . published are analogous to those presented here.[28]

Robert Conquest has suggested, however, that full and complete accuracy on casualty figures for the Great Terror is unattainable. He cites Soviet analyses for this, which suggest that some records have been lost, and some never existed.[29]

Conclusion

In the end, it is clear that the Great Terror consumed frighteningly large numbers of Soviet citizens. We may never know the precise number. It is also clear that Stalin played a major role in unleashing the Great Terror, but the "pluralist" historians have forced us to look beyond Stalin's personal role to examine the complex historical environment of the party and society during the 1930s. We have much more information at our disposal now, and their work has brought us closer to the truth, although there remain many unanswered questions, contributing to a continuing controversy about this horrifying period of Soviet history. ■

---

[28] Getty and Naumov, p. 594. Used by permission.

[29] Conquest, (1990), p. 487.

InfoTrac® College Edition Search Terms

Enter the search term *Soviet Union* in the Subject Guide, and then go to subdivision *history*.
Enter the search term *Stalin* in the Subject Guide.
Enter the search term *Trotsky* in Keywords.
Enter the search term *NKVD* in Keywords.

Suggested Additional Reading

ADAMS, A. *Stalin and His Times* (New York, 1972).

ANDREEV-KHOMIAKOV, G. *Bitter Waters: Life and Work in Stalin's Russia,* trans. Ann Healy (Boulder, CO, 1997).

ANDREW, C. and V. MITROKHIN. *The Sword and the Shield: The Mitrokhin Archive and the Secret History of the KGB* (Boulder, CO 1999).

BAUER, R., A. INKELES, and C. KLUCKHOHN. *How the Soviet System Works* (Cambridge, MA, 1956).

BERMAN, H. J. *Justice in the USSR* (New York, 1963).

CARMICHAEL, J. *Stalin's Masterpiece: The Show Trials and Purges of the Thirties* (New York, 1976).

CARR, E. H. *The Bolshevik Revolution: Socialism in One Country, 1924–1926,* 3 vols. (London, 1958–1964).

CONQUEST, R. *The Great Terror* (New York, 1968).

———. *Inside Stalin's Secret Police: NKVD Politics, 1936–1939* (Stanford, 1985).

———. *Stalin and the Kirov Murder* (Oxford and New York, 1990).

DANIELS, R., ed. *The Stalin Revolution* (Lexington, MA, 1990).

DAY, R. B. *Leon Trotsky and the Politics of Economic Isolation* (New York, 1973).

DE JONG, A. *Stalin and the Shaping of the Soviet Union* (New York, 1986).

DEUTSCHER, I. *Stalin: A Political Biography,* 2d ed. (New York, 1967).

DJILAS, M. *The New Class* (New York, 1957).

ERICKSON, J. *The Soviet High Command . . . 1918–1941* (New York, 1962).

FAINSOD, M. *How Russia Is Ruled,* 2d ed. (Cambridge, MA, 1963).

———. *Smolensk Under Soviet Rule* (Cambridge, MA, 1958).

FITZPATRICK, S. *Everyday Stalinism: Ordinary Life in Extraordinary Times: Soviet Russia in the 1930s* (New York and Oxford, 1999).

———. ed. *Stalinism: New Directions* (New York, 1999).

FRIEDRICH, C. J., and Z. K. BRZEZINSKI. *Totalitarian Dictatorship and Autocracy,* 2d ed. (New York, 1966).

GETTY, J. A. *Origins of the Great Purges . . . 1933–1938* (Cambridge, 1985).

GETTY, J. A. and O. V. NAUMOV. *The Road to Terror: Stalin and the Self-Destruction of the Bolsheviks, 1932–1939* (New Haven, CT, 1999).

GILL, G. *Stalinism,* 2nd ed. (London, 1998).

GITELMAN, Z., ed. *Bitter Legacy: Confronting the Holocaust in the USSR* (Bloomington, IN, 1997).

GLUCKSTEIN, D. *The Tragedy of Bukharin* (London, 1994).

HAZARD, J. N. *The Soviet System of Government,* 5th ed. (Chicago, 1980).

HOCHSCHILD, A. *The Unquiet Ghost: Russians Remember Stalin* (New York and London, 1994).

HYDE, A. M. *Stalin, the History of a Dictator* (New York, 1982).

KATKOV, G. *The Trial of Bukharin* (New York, 1969).

KNIGHT, A. *Beria: Stalin's First Lieutenant* (Princeton, NJ, 1996).

———. *Who Killed Kirov?* (New York, 1999).

KOESTLER, A. *Darkness at Noon* (New York, 1951). (Novel relating to the Great Purge.)

KOTKIN, S. *Magnetic Mountain: Stalinism as a Civilization* (Berkeley, CA, 1995).

LEVYTSKY, B., comp. *The Stalinist Terror in the Thirties: Documentation from the Soviet Press* (Stanford, 1974).

LEWIS, J. *Stalin: A Time for Judgment* (New York, 1990).

MARPLES, D. R. *Stalinism in Ukraine in the 1940s* (New York, 1992).

MARRIN, A. *Stalin* (New York, 1988).

MAWDSLEY, E. *The Stalin Years: The Soviet Union, 1929–1953* (Manchester, UK, 1998).

MCCAULEY, M. *Stalin and Stalinism,* 2nd ed. (London, 1995).

MEDVEDEV, R. A. *Let History Judge: The Origins and Consequences of Stalinism* (New York, 1971, 1973).

NOVE, A. *Stalinism and After,* 3d ed. (London, 1989).

———, ed. *The Stalin Phenomenon* (New York, 1993).

ORWELL, G. *1984* (New York, 1949). (Novel on totalitarianism.)

RESIS, A., ed. *Molotov Remembers: Inside Kremlin Politics* (Chicago, 1993).

ROGOVIN, V. Z. *1937: Stalin's Year of Terror,* trans. F. S. Choate (Oak Park, MI, 1998).

SCHAPIRO, L. *The Communist Party of the Soviet Union,* rev. ed. (New York, 1970).

SHEARER, D. R. *Industry, State and Society in Stalin's Russia, 1926–1934* (Ithaca, NY, 1996).

SERGE, V. *Memoirs of a Revolutionary, 1901–1941* (New York, 1963).

SOLOMON, P. H. *Soviet Criminal Justice under Stalin* (Cambridge, UK, 1996).

SOLZHENITSYN, A. *The Gulag Archipelago, 1918–1956,* 3 vols. (New York, 1974–1975).

———. *One Day in the Life of Ivan Denisovich* (New York, 1963). (Novel about labor camps under Stalin.)

STOECKER, S. W. *Forging Stalin's Army: Marshal Tukhachevskii and the Politics of Military Innovation* (Boulder, CO, 1999).

THORNILEY, D. *The Rise and Fall of the Rural Communist Party, 1927–39* (New York, 1988).

THURSTON, R. W. *Life and Terror In Stalin's Russia, 1934–1941* (New Haven, CT, 1996).

TROTSKY, L. D. *The Revolution Betrayed* (Garden City, NY, 1937).

———. *Stalin: An Appraisal of the Man and His Influence* (New York, 1941).

———. *Trotsky's Notebooks, 1933–1935,* trans. and ed. P. Pomper (New York, 1986).

TUCKER, R. *Stalin in Power: The Revolution from Above, 1928–1941* (New York, 1990).

———, ed. *Stalinism: Essays in Historical Interpretation* (New York, 1977).

TUMARKIN, N. *Lenin Lives! The Lenin Cult in Soviet Russia.* (Cambridge, MA, 1983).

ULAM, A. *Stalin: The Man and His Era* (New York, 1973).

URBAN, G. R., ed. *Stalinism: Its Impact on Russia and the World* (New York, 1982).

VOLKOGONOV, D. *Stalin: Triumph and Tragedy,* trans. and ed. H. Shukman (New York, 1991).

VYSHINSKY, A. *The Law of the Soviet State* (New York, 1948).

WARD, C., ed. *The Stalinist Dictatorship* (New York, Oxford, 1998).

———, ed. *Stalinism: A Reader* (London, 2000).

11

The Great Transformation

Once the economy had recovered to prewar levels and Stalin had consolidated his power, he launched the "Second Socialist Offensive" of rapid industrialization and forced collectivization of agriculture. This policy followed a bitter debate within the party over how to modernize the Soviet economy. In the decade after 1928, the USSR became a major industrial country, collectivized its agriculture, and acquired the basic economic and social forms that characterize it today. The price paid for these advances by the Soviet people, however, was very high. Did Stalin's "revolution from above" reflect Marxist-Leninist principles or betray the ideals of 1917? Were rapid industrialization and forced collectivization necessary and worth their terrible cost, or was Bukharin's alternative of gradual evolution toward socialism preferable? Should Stalin be called "the great" for overcoming Russia's backwardness and weakness? If so, then 1929 marks a greater turning point in Russian history than 1917. After continuing to smash or remodel traditional social pillars—family, school, and church—why did Stalin retreat toward tsarist patterns in the later 1930s and make concessions to the church?

The Great Industrialization Debate, 1924–1928

During the mid-1920s, leading Soviet politicians and economists debated Russia's economic future. They agreed on goals of socialism and industrialization, but disagreed on how they could best be achieved. The success of the New Economic Policy (NEP) meant that survival was not at issue, but in a largely hostile world the USSR, unlike tsarist Russia, had to rely on its own resources to industrialize.

The party Left, led by Trotskii but with Evgeni Preobrazhenskii as chief economic spokesman, advocated rapid industrial growth at home while promoting revolutions abroad. The key to industrialization and socialism, Preobrazhenskii argued, was "primitive socialist accumulation": Lacking colonies to exploit, the USSR must obtain necessary investment capital by keeping farm prices low and taxing private farmers heavily. NEP, he believed, could restore the economy, but it could not produce the vast capital required for industrialization and the development of transportation and housing. Central state planning would permit immediate major investment in heavy industry.

The Left accused the Stalin-Bukharin leadership of favoring kulaks, "surrendering" to NEP men, and isolating the USSR. It stressed the intimate connection between developing Soviet socialism and ending "our socialist isolation." Opposing forcible expropriation of kulaks, Trotskii believed that revolutions in advanced countries would promote Soviet industrialization.

Bukharin, chief official spokesman and later leader of the Right, urged the continuation of NEP until the USSR gradually "grew into" socialism. Leftist "superindustrializers and adventurers" would alienate better-off peasants, undermine the worker-peasant alliance, and threaten the regime. Taxing peasants heavily would price industrial goods beyond their reach and induce them to market less grain. Instead, industrial prices should be cut and peasants encouraged to produce and save freely. Agricultural surplus would provide investment capital, expand the internal market, and stimulate industrial production. Citing Lenin's last writings, Bukharin advocated gradual "agrarian cooperative socialism." He overestimated peasant economic power and considered the peasant-worker alliance inviolable. Unless Soviet industrialization were more humane than under capitalism, he warned, it might not produce socialism. "We do not want to drive the middle peasant into communism with an iron broom." Bukharin spoke of "moving ahead slowly . . . dragging behind us the cumbersome peasant cart," and of creeping "at a snail's pace."

All leading Bolsheviks viewed industrialization as a vital goal and realized that it must rely mainly on internal resources. Agreeing that investment capital must be shifted from agriculture into industry, they differed over how much to take and how to take it. Bukharin emphasized development of the internal market, imposition of progressive income taxes, and voluntary savings. Such methods, retorted the Left, would produce too little capital because peasants would consume most of the surplus. Bolsheviks agreed that central planning was needed, but what did this involve? The Left advocated a single, state-imposed plan stressing rapid growth of heavy industry. Bukharin

called that "a remnant of War Communist illusions" that disregarded market forces of supply and demand; instead, he would stress consumer industry.

The factions also argued about capitalist elements in the countryside. Official figures of 1925 stated that poor peasants composed 45, middle peasants 51, and kulaks 4 percent of the peasantry. Asserting that more than 7 percent were kulaks, who were exploiting and dominating the village, the Left argued that continuing NEP would restore capitalism. Peasant differentiation had increased, replied Bukharin, but kulaks were still less than 4 percent, and state control of large-scale industry prevented any serious capitalist danger. Class conflict in the countryside, he predicted, would subside as the economy approached socialism.

As the debate continued, these differences lessened. Bukharin began to admit the need for rapid growth; Preobrazhenskii warned of its considerable risks. The chief beneficiary of this apparent synthesis was Stalin. Supporting Bukharin during the debate, he expelled the Left and stole its plank of rapid industrialization. To break peasant resistance, he combined it later with forced collectivization and demanded industrial goals far higher than those of the Left.

Bukharin's gradualist solution was doomed as the private sector lost its ability to compete with the state sector. Taxing heavily the profits of private producers, imposing surcharges for transportation and exorbitant levies on kulaks, the state squeezed private producers severely. By cutting industrial prices despite severe shortages of industrial goods, the state undermined the basis of NEP, which was based upon a free market and incentives. To the party, the perceived stagnation of the restored Russian economy by 1926 was intolerable because without rapid growth the party's élan and morale would deteriorate.

Some later Soviet accounts claimed that the demise of the NEP was natural and inevitable. Unlike capitalist countries, the USSR could not exploit colonies, conduct aggressive wars, or obtain foreign credits. To achieve socialism the state had to industrialize quickly by concentrating resources in its hands and tapping all sources of internal capital, especially agriculture. Accepting most of Preobrazhenskii's theory of primitive socialist accumulation, some Soviet historians concluded that the populace, especially the peasantry, had to make major sacrifices in order to achieve industrialization. Recent Western studies, however, conclude that NEP agriculture could have satisfied immediate urban needs; they question the necessity and value of collectivization, either to solve the grain problem or to increase capital formation.[1]

Forced Collectivization

Stalin's adoption in 1929 of a policy of forced collectivization of agriculture, after inciting a "war scare" on alleged Western plans to renew intervention, provoked a grim struggle between the regime and the peasantry. One factor in his decision was an apparent grain crisis in 1927–1928. Farm output had reached prewar levels, but grain marketings remained somewhat lower (though higher than Stalin claimed), largely because of government price policies. Better-off peasants, awaiting higher prices, withheld their grain, and the state could not obtain enough to feed the cities or finance new industrial projects. Peasants, roughly 80 percent of the Soviet population, operated about 25 million small private farms; collective and state farms were few and unimportant.[2] Most peasants still carried on traditional strip farming and remained suspicious of the Soviet regime. Kulaks tended to be literate, enterprising, and hardworking, envied by other peasants for their relative prosperity but respected for their industry. Employing a hired worker or two and perhaps renting out small machines to poorer

neighbors, kulaks performed most of their own labor and scarcely qualified as "Lists" or semi-capitalists, as Soviet historians described them.

Marx and Lenin—and even Stalin before 1928 —had never suggested *forced* collectivization. Marx intimated that large industrial farms would evolve gradually. Lenin considered collective, mechanized agriculture essential to socialism but warned that amalgamating millions of small farmers "in any rapid way" would be "absolutely absurd." Collective farming must develop "with extreme caution and only very gradually, by the force of example without any coercion of the middle peasant."[3] Following this advice closely, Stalin told the 15th Party Congress in 1927:

> What is the way out? The way out is to turn the small and scattered peasant farms into large united farms based on cultivation of the land in common, go over to collective cultivation of the land on the basis of a new higher technique. The way out is to unite the small and dwarf peasant farms *gradually but surely, not by pressure but by example and persuasion,* into large farms based on common, cooperative collective cultivation of the land. . . . There is no other way out.[4] [Italics added for emphasis.]

Perhaps from ignorance or misinformation, Stalin disregarded Lenin's warnings and his own statements. Touring the Urals and Siberia in January 1928, he arbitrarily closed free markets, denounced hesitant officials, and had grain seized from the peasants. His "Urals-Siberian method" marked a return to War Communism's forced requisitioning. Faced with strong Rightist protests, Stalin retreated temporarily, but during 1928–1929 this brutal method was used repeatedly in scattered areas. Bukharin objected to it as "military-feudal exploitation" of the peasantry and referred to Stalin as Chingis-khan. Until he had destroyed the Right, Stalin refrained from a general assault on private agriculture, and the First Five Year Plan, approved in 1929, proposed that state and collec-

---

[1] J. Karcz, "From Stalin to Brezhnev . . . ," in J. Millar, ed., *The Soviet Rural Community* (Urbana, IL, 1971), pp. 36*ff.* See also R. W. Davies, *Soviet History in the Gorbachev Revolution* (Bloomington, IN, 1989), especially pp. 40–46.
[2] In 1928 individual farmers tilled 97.3 percent of the sown area, collectives 1.2 percent (of which 0.7 percent were of the loose *toz* type), and state farms 1.5 percent.

[3] Lenin, *Collected Works* (New York, 1927–1942), vol. 30, p. 196.
[4] Stalin, *Works* (Moscow, 1953–1955), vol. 10, p. 196.

tive farms provide only 15 percent of agricultural output. The predominance of private farming seemed assured indefinitely.

Late in 1929, after crushing the Right, Stalin moved abruptly to break peasant resistance and secure resources required for industrialization. Voluntary collectivization had clearly failed, and most Soviet economists doubted that the First Plan could be implemented. Recalled N. Valentinov, a Menshevik: "The financial base of the First Five Year Plan was extremely precarious *until Stalin solidified it by levying tribute on the peasants in primitive accumulation by the methods of Tamerlane.*"[5] Stalin may have viewed collectivization also as a means to win support from younger party leaders opposed to kulaks, NEP men, and the free market. Privately, he advocated "industrializing the country with the help of *internal* accumulation," à la Preobrazhenskii. Once the peasantry had been split and rural opposition smashed, Stalin believed that rural proletarians would spearhead collectivization under state direction. The grain shortage induced the Politburo to support Stalin's sudden decision for immediate, massive collectivization.

A great turn was underway, Stalin asserted in November. The Central Committee affirmed obediently that poor and middle peasants were moving "spontaneously" into collectives. In secret, Stalin and his colleagues had ordered local officials to try out massive collectivization in selected areas. When results seemed positive (the number of collective farmers had allegedly doubled between June and October), Stalin ordered general collectivization, led by many urban party activists. Entire villages had to deliver their grain to the state at low prices. Kulaks were deliberately overassessed for grain deliveries, then expropriated for failure to obey. The party had not discussed how to implement collectivization, and so initial measures were sudden, confused, and ill prepared. Many officials interpreted them to mean incorporating all peas-

ants in *kolkhozy* (collective farms). Stalin and Molotov pressed for speed, overruled all objections, and rejected proposals for private peasant plots and ownership of small tools and livestock. Local officials took Stalin at his word.

The initial collectivization drive provoked massive peasant resistance and terrible suffering. Isaac Deutscher notes that rebellious villages, surrounded by Red Army detachments, were bombarded and forced to surrender. So much for voluntary, spontaneous collectivization! Within seven weeks about half the peasantry had been herded into collectives, but bringing in as little as possible, the peasants slaughtered more than half the horses, about 45 percent of the large cattle, and almost two-thirds of the sheep and goats in Russia. In December 1929 Stalin authorized liquidation of the kulaks:

> Now we are able to carry on a determined offensive against the kulaks, eliminate them as a class. . . . Now dekulakization is being carried out by the masses of poor and middle peasants themselves. . . . Should kulaks be permitted to join collective farms? Of course not, for they are sworn enemies of the collective farm movement.[6]

Poor neighbors often stole kulaks' clothing and drank up their vodka, but Stalin prohibited their dividing kulak land because he thought if they did so they would be reluctant to enter collectives. By a decree of February 1930, "actively hostile" kulaks were to be sent to forced labor camps; "economically potent" ones were to be relocated and their property confiscated. The "least noxious" kulaks were admitted to collectives. A party history claimed that only 240,757 kulak families were deported, but eventually deportation overtook nearly all so-called kulaks, up to 5 million persons counting family members. Few ever returned, thousands of families were broken up, and millions of peasants were embittered. Soviet sources claim that such excesses reflected peasant hatred of kulaks, but there is little evidence to

---

[5] Ruthless Central Asian conqueror of the early 15th century.

[6] Quoted in *Istoriia KPSS* (Moscow, 1959), p. 441.

Table 11.1 Agricultural output during collectivization

Category	1928	1929	1930	1931	1933	1935
Grain (million tons)	73.7	71.7	83.5	69.5	68.4	75.0
Cattle (million)	70.5	67.1	52.5	47.9	38.4	49.3
Pigs (million)	26.0	20.4	13.6	14.4	12.1	22.6
Sheep and goats (million)	146.7	147.0	108.0	77.7	50.2	61.1

SOURCE: Adapted from A. Nove, *The Soviet Economy*, 2d ed. (New York, 1967), p. 186.

support this claim. In March 1930, with the spring sowing threatened by lack of seed grain, Stalin in an article "Dizzy with Success" called a temporary halt and blamed overly zealous local officials for excesses he had authorized. Interpreting this retrenchment as a repudiation of compulsory collectivization, the majority of peasants hastily left the *kolkhozy*.

After a brief pause, peasants were lured into collectives by persuasion and discriminatory taxation. By 1937 nearly all land and peasants were in *kolkhozy*; remaining individual peasants worked inferior land and paid exorbitant taxes. But *kolkhoz* peasants were demoralized: Crops lay unharvested, tractors were few, and farm animals died of neglect. Large grain exports to western Europe in 1930–1931 exhausted reserves, and city requirements increased. In 1932, amid widespread stealing and concealment of grain, collectivization hung by a thread and was maintained by force. In Ukraine and north Caucasus, the state seized nearly all the grain, causing a terrible famine, which the Soviet press failed to report. (Table 11.1 reveals the impact of collectivization.) Between 1928 and 1933, forced collectivization cost the Soviet Union roughly 27 percent of its livestock and contributed to the death of some 5 million persons, mostly peasants, in the famine of 1932–1934, notes J. Karcz. Damage to agriculture during this period was so severe that it could contribute little to the initial Five Year Plans. Collectivization was supposed to ensure more agricultural products for towns and industry, but though state grain procurements increased dramatically from 1928 to 1931, procurement of other products, notably meat and industrial products, declined sharply.

At first collective farm organization and management were confused. The city activists sent to supervise collectivization and manage the farms misunderstood the peasantry and made many blunders. Peasant rights in *kolkhozy* were few and vague, and pay was low. The regime initially favored state farms (*sovkhozy*) as being fully socialist, but their inefficiency and costliness provoked second thoughts, and after 1935 they received less emphasis.

The Model Statute of 1935 described the *kolkhoz* as supposedly a voluntary cooperative whose members pooled their means of production, ran their own affairs, and elected their officials in a general meeting. Actually local party organizations nominated farm chairmen and issued orders to farms, while state procurement agencies and Machine Tractor Stations (MTS) assured party control. The state-controlled MTS received all available machines and tractors and rented them to *kolkhozy*. Only after fixed requirements were met (taxes, insurance, capital fund, administration, and production costs) were *kolkhoz* members paid from what remained according to their work. Wages varied sharply according to skill and the farm's success, but as late as 1937, 15,000 *kolkhozy* paid their members nothing at all. The statute recognized the peasant's right to a private plot of up to one acre per household and some livestock. This grant created the chief private sector in the economy. After 1937 *kolkhozy* produced mainly grain and industrial crops (cotton, sugar beets, flax); private peasant plots provided most meat, milk, eggs, potatoes, fruits, and many vegetables. Peasants sold these products after paying taxes. Low state prices, however, discouraged agricultural output. Industrial prices in 1937 were far higher than in 1928–1929, a recurrence of the price "scissors" against the peasant. On *kolkhozy* there was much coercion and unhappiness, but as the output of private plots increased, living conditions gradually improved.

During the last prewar years arbitrary state decisions, ignoring local conditions, caused agriculture to stagnate or decline. In 1939 the party reduced the allowable size of private plots and transferred millions of acres to collective control. Stricter discipline and compulsory minimums of labor days were instituted for collective farmers, and fodder shortages brought a decline in already low *kolkhoz* livestock production. Crop yields and private livestock ownership declined substantially, but state procurements for urban consumption and for exports rose. Providing few incentives, collective farming remained very unpopular with Soviet peasants. Even by Soviet official figures, agricultural output increased very little during the 1930s. To achieve rapid industrialization and socialism, Stalin had uselessly sacrificed Russia's best, most enterprising farmers. Less compulsory methods, such as those of NEP, might well have proved less costly and more effective.

Industry: The Five Year Plans

One rationale for collectivization was to ensure food supplies adequate to support the rapid industrialization of the First Five Year Plan, which aimed immediately to provide a powerful heavy industry and only later an abundant life. The plan's psychological purpose was to induce workers and young people to make sacrifices, by holding before them a vision of the promised land of socialism in their own lifetimes. The state would benefit because the economy would become fully socialist, production and labor would be wholly state controlled, and security against capitalist powers would be strengthened. Stalin stated in February 1931: "We are 50 to 100 years behind the advanced countries. We must cover this distance in 10 years. Either we do this or they will crush

us." Ten years and four months later, Hitler invaded the USSR!

The First Five Year Plan did not inaugurate Soviet economic planning. Gosplan (State Planning Commission) had operated under NEP, and there had been annual control figures (see Chapter 9). As private market forces declined, central economic control increased. The goods famine of 1926–1927 promoted state distribution of key commodities, especially metals, and regulation of production. Soviet economists had long discussed a Five Year Plan, but serious work on one began only in 1927.

Realistic early drafts of the First Plan in 1928 yielded to optimistic (and fantastic) variants in 1929. In 1927 Gosplan's mostly nonparty professional staff outlined a plan for relatively balanced growth, with industry to expand 80 percent in five years; it recognized probable obstacles. Party pressure, however, soon forced estimates upward, and resulting variants represented overly optimistic predictions made largely for psychological purposes. The version of S. G. Strumilin, a leading party planner, allowed for possible crop failures, little foreign trade or credits, and potentially heavier defense spending, but it set goals far exceeding those of the Left, which Stalin had denounced as superindustrialist. Stalin boasted in 1929:

> We are going full steam ahead toward socialism through industrialization, leaving behind the age-long "Russian" backwardness. We are becoming a land of metals . . . , automobiles . . . , tractors, and when we have put the USSR on an automobile and the muzhik on a tractor, let the noble capitalists . . . attempt to catch up. We shall see then which countries can be labeled backward and which advanced.[7]

Because 1928 was a successful year, goals were boosted higher. In April 1929 the 16th Congress approved an optimal draft of the plan, which assumed that no misfortunes would occur. Gross industrial output was to increase 235.9 percent and labor productivity 110 percent; production

---

[7] Quoted in Maurice Dobb, *Soviet Economic Development Since 1917* (New York, 1948), p. 245.

costs were to fall 35 percent and prices 24 percent. To fulfill such goals would require a miracle (in which Stalin presumably did not believe!). In December 1929 a congress of "shock brigades" urged the plan's fulfillment in four years; soon this became official policy. Constantly sounding notes of urgency, Stalin forced the tempo and brought former party oppositionists into line. Riding a wave of overoptimism, party leaders chanted: "There is no fortress that the Bolsheviks cannot storm." Perhaps Stalin knowingly adopted impossible targets largely for political reasons. Those urging caution were denounced as "bourgeois" wreckers working for foreign powers.

During the First Plan some wholly unanticipated obstacles appeared. The Great Depression in the United States and Europe made Soviet growth look more impressive, but it dislocated world trade and made imported foreign machinery more expensive relative to Soviet grain exports. Defense expenditures, instead of declining, were increased in response to Japanese expansion in East Asia. Ignorance and inexperience of workers and managers caused destruction or poor use of expensive foreign equipment, blamed on deliberate wrecking and sabotage. Resources were used inefficiently: Industrial plants often lacked equipment or skilled workers. The inexorable drive for quantity brought a deplorable decline in quality as strains and shortages multiplied.

The First Plan had mixed results. Vast projects were undertaken, but many remained unfinished. Some, such as the Volga–White Sea Canal, were built by forced labor; others reflected genuine enthusiasm and self-sacrifice. At Magnitogorsk in the Urals, previously only a village, a great metallurgical center arose as workers and technicians labored under primitive conditions to build a bright socialist future. As industrial output rose sharply, the regime announced late in 1932 that the plan had been basically fulfilled in four years and three months; in fact, goals were surpassed only in machinery and metalworking, partly by

statistical manipulation.[8] Nonetheless, the new powerful engineering industry reduced Soviet dependence on foreign machinery. Fuel output rose considerably, but iron and steel fell far short because necessary plants took longer to complete than anticipated. Supposed increases in consumer production concealed sharp declines in handicrafts. To the party, the First Plan was a success (though goals for steel were fulfilled only in 1940, for electric power in 1951, and for oil in 1955) because industrial expansion and defense output could now be sustained from domestic resources. Lifting itself by its own bootstraps, the USSR was vindicating Stalin's idea of socialism in one country. Consumer production, agriculture, and temporarily military strength, however, were sacrificed to a rapid growth of heavy industry. (See Map 11.1.)

Labor was mobilized and lost much freedom. Once the state controlled all industry, Stalin declared trade union opposition anti-Marxist: How could the proletariat strike against its own dictatorship? Early in 1929 Tomskii and other trade union leaders were removed and replaced by Stalinists. Henceforth trade unions were to help build socialist industry by raising labor productivity and discipline. Unions exhorted workers to raise production and organize "shock brigades." Factory directors took control of wages, food supplies, housing, and other worker necessities. Russian workers, losing the right to strike or protest against their employer, reverted to their status of 75 years earlier, and Stalin's attitude toward labor resembled that of early Russian capitalists. By 1932 unemployment disappeared in towns and a seven-hour day was introduced, but real wages fell sharply. As millions of untrained peasants, escaping collectivization, sought industrial jobs, labor discipline deteriorated. Machinery was ruined, and workers hunted for better conditions. (In 1930, the

---

[8] Overfulfillment in machinery resulted chiefly from assigning high prices in 1926–1927 rubles to many new machines, thus increasing the "value" of total output. See A. Nove, *The Soviet Economy* (New York, 1967), p. 192.

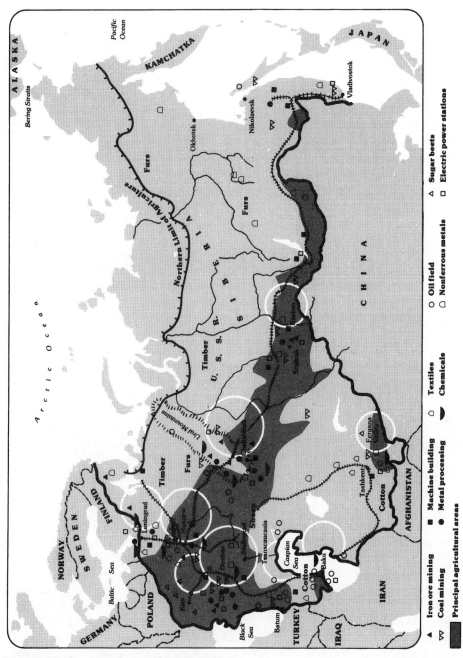

Map 11.1 Industry and agriculture to 1939

SOURCE: Adapted from *A History of Russia, Second Edition* by Nicholas V. Riasanovsky. Copyright 1969 by Oxford University Press, Inc. Used by permission.

average worker in the coal industry shifted jobs three times!) Cities grew rapidly, housing construction lagged, and urban services were grievously overtaxed.

Burgeoning industrial employment and rising incomes without a comparable rise in consumer goods or services spurred inflation. Seeking to achieve impossible goals, managers hired more and more labor, sending wage bills skyrocketing. Rationed goods remained cheap, leaving people much money but little to buy. By 1929 a wide gap opened between official and private prices. To absorb excess purchasing power, the government in 1930 instituted the turnover tax in place of many excise levies. Generally imposed at the wholesale level, it amounted to the difference between the cost of production and the retail selling price. In 1934, for instance, the retail price of rye was 84 rubles per centner (100 kilograms), of which 66 rubles was turnover tax. Its burden fell mainly on the peasantry because the state paid them so little for their grain; in this way, agriculture indirectly financed the Five Year Plan.

By 1932 the Soviet economy was badly overstrained; 1933 brought shortages and privation. The Second Five Year Plan, redrafted during its first year, was adopted in February 1934 by the 17th Congress. More realistic than the First Plan, its execution was aided by more experienced planners and managers. Unlike its predecessor, final goals were lower than preliminary ones. Heavy industrial targets were mostly met, and machinery and electric power output rose dramatically. Labor productivity surpassed expectations, and technical sophistication improved as the First Plan's investments bore fruit. The Second Plan stressed consolidation, mastering techniques, and improving living standards. Initially a greater increase was planned for consumer goods than for heavy industry, but then came a shift toward heavy industry and defense. Consumer goals were underfulfilled, and per capita consumption fell below the 1928 level. Completed metallurgical works in Magnitogorsk, Kuznetsk, and Zaporozhye further reduced Soviet dependence on foreign capital

goods, relieved the strain on the balance of payments, and permitted repayment of earlier debts. By 1937 the basic tools of industry and defense were being made in the USSR. Growth followed an uneven pattern: After a bad year, 1933, came three very good ones in industry and construction, and then relative stagnation began in 1937 (between 1937 and 1939 steel production actually declined). Table 11.2 shows some results of the two plans.

During the Second Plan labor productivity rose substantially and industrial employment fell below estimates as training programs gradually created a more skilled labor force. Pay differentials widened, rationing was gradually abolished, and more consumer goods were made available. After 1934 high prices of necessities stimulated harder work under the prevailing piecework system. Labor productivity was improved by Stakhanovism, a by-product of "socialist competition." In September 1935 Alexis Stakhanov, a Donets coal miner, by hard work and intelligent use of unskilled helpers, produced 14 times his norm. Fostered by the party, Stakhanovism spread to other industries, and low labor norms were raised. Harsh penalties for absenteeism and labor turnover reduced these problems and improved labor discipline. However, the Great Purge, Soviet historians later admitted, swept away managers, technicians, statisticians, and even foremen. The shaken survivors often rejected responsibility. This reaction, and the growing shift of resources into arms production, created an industrial slowdown after 1937.

The diversion of resources into defense plagued the Third Five Year Plan (1938–1941), which the Nazi invasion interrupted. Industrial output increased an average of less than 2 percent annually, compared with 10 percent under the first two plans. Progress remained uneven, with much growth in production of machinery, but little in steel and oil. New western frontier territories such as the Baltic states considerably increased productive capacity. Labor was severely restricted in mobility and choice of occupation, the work week rose to 48 hours, and workers required permission

Table 11.2 First and Second Plan results

Category	1927–1928	1932 (target)	1932–1933 (actual)	1937 (target)	1937 (actual)
National income in 1926–1927 rubles (billions)	24.5	49.7	45.5	100.2	96.3
Gross industrial output (billions of rubles)	18.3	43.2	43.3	92.7	95.5
Producer goods	6.0	18.1	23.1	45.5	55.2
Consumer goods	12.3	25.1	20.2	47.1	40.3
Gross agricultural production (billions of 1926–1927 rubles)	13.1	25.8	16.6	—	—
Electricity (100 million Kwhs.)	5.05	22.0	13.4	38.0	36.2
Hard coal (millions of tons)	35.4	75.0	64.3	152.5	128.0
Oil (millions of tons)	11.7	22.0	21.4	46.8	28.5
Steel (millions of tons)	5.9	19.0	12.1	17.0	17.7
Machinery (millions of 1926–1927 rubles)	1,822.0	4,688.0	7,362.0	—	—

SOURCE: Adapted from T. Nove, *The Soviet Economy*, 2d ed. (New York, 1967), pp. 191, 225.

from their enterprise to change jobs. A million high school students were conscripted for combined vocational training and industrial work.

In summary, rapid industrialization (1928–1941) brought increases in heavy industrial production unprecedented in history for a period of that length, as shown in Table 11.3. The USSR became a leading industrial power, but living standards, real wages, and housing conditions declined. Dire predictions made during the industrialization debate came true: Bukharin foresaw the human sacrifices and inflation, and Preobrazhenskii's concept of primitive socialist accumulation was implemented by methods that appalled him. (He was executed for protesting the excesses of collectivization.)

Shifts in Social Policies

A continued assault on social institutions associated with the old regime accompanied the Second Socialist Offensive. After 1933 or 1934 policy shifted to consolidation of Soviet institutions that often resembled their tsarist models, and emphasis on discipline and social stability was renewed to overcome unfavorable effects of the preceding offensive. Social policies of 1934–1941 represented "a great retreat,"[9] or Soviet Thermidor, except that they coincided with the bloody terror of the purges.

Efforts to undermine the traditional family in order to strengthen the socialist state continued during the First Five Year Plan. Husbands and wives were often assigned to different cities, yet any available job had to be accepted. When a teacher complained of being separated from her husband, the Labor Board advised her to find a husband at her new job. In Stalingrad, "socialist suburbs" featuring single rooms were built, but only bachelors would live in them. Such policies did weaken family ties, but the by-products were grim. Free divorce and abortion caused a serious decline in birthrates, which threatened the supply

[9] See Nicholas Timasheff, *The Great Retreat* (New York, 1946).

Table 11.3
Selected statistical indicators, 1928–1940
(1928 = 100)

Category	1940 Output (in percent of 1928)
Industrial production	263
Industrial materials	343
Ferrous metals	433
Electric power	964
Chemicals	819
Machinery	486
Consumer goods	181
Agricultural production	105
Crops	123
Animal products	88
Individual consumption (per capita)	93
Real wages	54
Capital stock	286
Urban housing space (per capita)	78

SOURCE: Stanley H. Cohen, *Economic Development in the Soviet Union* (Lexington, MA, 1970), p. 39.

of labor and army recruits. Moscow medical institutions in 1934 recorded only 57,000 live births and 154,000 abortions. Early in 1935 divorces numbered more than 38 per 100 marriages. Communities were confronted with spiraling juvenile delinquency and hooliganism. Children were beating up their schoolteachers!

In 1934–1935 the regime—largely for economic reasons—shifted course abruptly. "The family," it was now stated officially, "is an especially important phase of social relations in socialist society" and must be strengthened. Marriage is "the most serious affair in life" and should be regarded as a lifelong union; men who changed their wives like shirts were threatened with prosecution for rape. In 1939 the journal of the Commissariat of Justice proclaimed:

> The State cannot exist without the family. Marriage is a positive value for the Socialist State only if the partners see in it a lifelong union. So-called free love is a bourgeois inven-

tion and has nothing in common with the principles of conduct of a Soviet citizen.[10]

Marriage was now dignified with well-staged ceremonies in comfortable registration centers. Soon wedding rings were being sold again, and non-Communists frequently reinforced the civil ceremony with a church wedding. Strict regulations, replacing the quickie divorce of earlier days, greatly curtailed divorces and raised fees sharply. Divorce became more difficult and expensive to obtain in the USSR than in many of the United States, and unregistered marriage, instituted in 1926, was abolished. After June 1936 abortion was permitted only if the mother's life was endangered or to prevent transmission of serious illness. Parental authority was reinforced, and young people were urged to respect and obey parents and elders. Motherhood was glorified (Stalin made a pilgrimage to Tiflis to show how much he loved his old mother), and mothers of large families were compensated. After destroying the old extensive patriarchal family, the authorities reinforced the new Soviet nuclear family.

Joseph Stalin, the self-styled "man of steel," emphasized women's economic and personal dependence, reflecting the attitude of male superiority prevalent in the Caucasus and Central Asia. To Stalin women epitomized ignorance and conservatism, threatening social progress: "The woman worker . . . can help the common cause if she is politically conscious and politically educated. But she can ruin the common cause if she is downtrodden and backward." Under Stalin's rule there was strong emphasis on women's duties and responsibilities at home and at work, while less and less was heard of their former oppression. In the Stalin era the role of women was transformed primarily by industrialization, collectivization, and urbanization. Their massive influx into the Soviet work force after 1929 coincided with greatly expanded educational opportunities, growth of

---

[10] Quoted in Timasheff, *The Great Retreat*, p. 198.

child-care institutions, and protective legislation for all workers, but not equal pay. However, unlike early Bolshevik libertarian concern with female emancipation, the Soviet aim was no longer to enhance women's independence but to improvise a response to urgent needs created by rapid urbanization and burgeoning female employment. Development of social services, such as child-care centers, because of the low priority assigned to them by the Stalin regime, failed conspicuously to keep pace with demands.

Experimentalism in education yielded during the First Plan to a structured, disciplined school program. Not Leninist theory, but industry's insistent demands for trained specialists triggered the shift. Applicants to higher educational institutions were found to be woefully deficient in reading skills and parroted vague generalizations. In 1929 A. Lunacharskii, chief exponent of experimentalism, was removed, and a shift to serious study began under the slogan "Mastery of knowledge." In 1931–1932 came partial curricular reforms: Teaching of Marxism was reduced, history revived, and "progressive education" was largely abandoned. Book learning, academic degrees, systematic textbooks, and traditional grading practices were reemphasized. Examinations were reinstituted after a 15-year lapse. Noisy, undisciplined classrooms disrupted by hooligans yielded to quiet, disciplined ones as the authority of teachers and professors was restored. Decrees from above specified every detail of instruction and school administration as a new Soviet school emerged, patterned after the conservative tsarist school of the 1880s. Curricula resembled tsarist and European ones, and pupils were dressed in uniforms like those of the 1880s. For pragmatic reasons, a retreat to traditional models began earlier in education than in other fields. The authoritarian school reflected the Stalinist autocracy.

Soviet religious policies fluctuated. During the First Plan there was a widespread campaign to close churches. In 1930 the Soviet press reported the burning of icons and religious books by the carload, and restrictions, disfranchisement, and discriminatory taxation plagued the clergy. The atheist League of Militant Godless, featuring the young and growing to almost 6 million members, induced many collective farms to declare themselves "godless." Then between 1933 and 1936, partly to allay peasant discontent, came some relaxation of persecution. The Stalin Constitution of 1936 restored the franchise to clergymen and gave them full civil rights. The Purge of 1937–1938 brought another wave of persecution, but few priests were executed. After 1938 a more tolerant religious policy developed to win popular support and counter the rising threat of Nazi Germany. Christianity was now declared to have played a progressive, patriotic role in Russian history. Violence against churches and believers was forbidden, and the closing of churches and political trials of clergymen were halted. The regime adopted a subtler approach of emphasizing that scientific advances had made religion outmoded. Soviet leaders, recognizing the persistence of religious belief, sought to use it to consolidate their power. The Soviet census of 1937 revealed that more than half the adult population still classified themselves as believers. (The census takers were sent to Siberia!) Meanwhile, the Orthodox church recognized the regime and wished to cooperate with it to achieve greater social discipline, a strong family, and restriction of sexual activity. Twenty years of official persecution had greatly weakened the church as an organization and reduced markedly the numbers of the faithful, but had strengthened their faith. Marxism-Leninism had proved an inadequate substitute for religion.

During the 1930s the Stalin regime, abandoning experimentalism and radical policies, retreated toward tradition and national and authoritarian tsarist patterns. There emerged an increasingly disciplined, status-conscious society headed by a new elite of party bureaucrats, economic managers, engineers, and army officers, which differed sharply in attitudes and habits from the revolutionary generation.

Problem 6

Forced Collectivization: Why and How?

The transformation of Russian agriculture under Stalin from 25 million individual farms into several hundred thousand collective and state farms was one of the 20th century's most dramatic and important events. It involved a massive conflict between the Soviet regime and the peasantry, the destruction of many of the best Soviet farmers and much of the livestock, and produced a terrible famine in 1933. Soviet collectivized agriculture, plagued by low productivity, lack of incentives for farmers, and incompetent organization, sought without conspicuous success to satisfy domestic needs. Was forced collectivization necessary or wise? Why was it undertaken? Who was responsible for the accompanying mass suffering? Here these issues are explored from various viewpoints, including Stalin's contemporary speeches, a Soviet account from 1967, and the work of a Soviet historian published in the West.

Stalin's View

Stalin and his Politburo colleagues claimed in 1929 that it was necessary to collectivize agriculture to achieve economic progress and socialism. They affirmed that the decision to collectivize was imposed upon them by kulak treachery and the insistent demands of an expanding industry. Poor and middle peasants, Stalin claimed, were entering collective farms voluntarily and en masse. Declared Stalin as forced collectivization began:

> The characteristic feature of the present collective farm movement is that not only are the collective farms being joined by individual groups of poor peasants . . . but . . . by the mass of middle peasants as well. This means that the collective farm movement has been transformed from a movement of individual groups and sections of the laboring peasants into a movement of millions and millions of the main mass of the peasantry. . . . The collective farm movement . . . has assumed the character of a mighty and growing *antikulak* avalanche . . . paving the way for extensive socialist construction in the countryside [speech of December 27, 1929].

At the beginning of forced collectivization Stalin, summarizing the party's problems and achievements in agriculture, stressed the rapid development of a new socialist agriculture against desperate resistance from "retrograde" elements:

> The party's third achievement during the past year . . . [is] the *radical change* in the development of our agriculture from small, backward *individual* farming to large-scale advanced *collective* agriculture, to joint cultivation of the land . . . , based on modern techniques and finally to giant state farms, equipped with hundreds of tractors and harvester combines.
>
> . . . In a whole number of areas we have succeeded in *turning* the main mass of the peasantry away from the old, *capitalist* path . . . to the new *socialist* path of development, which ousts the rich and the capitalists and reequips the middle and poor peasants . . . with modern implements . . . so as to enable them to climb out of poverty and enslavement to the kulaks onto the high road of cooperative, collective cultivation of the land. . . . We have succeeded in bringing about this *radical change* deep down in the peasantry itself and in securing the following of the broad masses of the poor and middle peasants in spite of incredible difficulties, in spite of the desperate resistance of retrograde forces of every kind, from kulaks and priests to philistines and Right Opportunists.
>
> . . . Such an impetuous speed of development is *unequaled* even by our socialized large-scale industry. . . . All the objections raised by "science" against the possibility and expediency of organizing large grain factories of 40,000 to 50,000 hectares each have collapsed. . . .
>
> What is the new feature of the present collective-farm movement? . . . The peasants are

joining the collective farms not in separate groups, as formerly, but as whole villages, *volosts,* districts, and even *okrugs.* And what does that mean? It means that *the middle peasant is joining the collective farm* [November 1929].

Only a month later, however, Stalin hinted that forcible means were having to be employed after all:

It is necessary . . . *to implant* in the village large socialist farms, collective and state farms, as bases of socialism which, with the socialist city in the vanguard, can drag along the masses of peasants.

In March 1930, at his colleagues' insistence, Stalin temporarily halted forced collectivization. His article "Dizzy with Success" blamed local party workers and extremists for errors and perversions of official policy:

People not infrequently become intoxicated by such successes, . . . overrate their own strength. The successes of our collective-farm policy are due . . . to the fact that it rests on the *voluntary character* of the collective-farm movement and *on taking into account the diversity of conditions* in various regions of the USSR. Collective farms must not be established by force. That would be foolish and reactionary. The collective-farm movement must rest on the active support of the main mass of the peasantry. . . . In a number of the northern regions of the consuming zone . . . , attempts are not infrequently made to *replace* preparatory work for the organization of collective farms by bureaucratic decreeing . . . , the organization of collective farms on paper.
. . . Who benefits from these distortions, . . . these unworthy threats against the peasants? Nobody, except our enemies! In a number of areas of the USSR . . . attempts are being made . . . to leap straight away into the agricultural commune. . . . They are already "socializing" dwelling houses, small livestock, and poultry. . . .
How could there have arisen in our midst such blockhead excesses in "socialization," such ludicrous attempts to overleap oneself? . . . They could have arisen only in the atmosphere of our "easy"

and "unexpected" successes on the front of collective farm development . . . as a result of the blockheaded belief of a section of our Party: "We can achieve anything!" [March 2, 1930].

In his report to the 17th Congress in January 1934, Stalin hailed the results of rapid collectivization in the USSR:

From a country of small individual agriculture it has become a country of collective, large-scale mechanized agriculture. . . . Progress in the main branches of agriculture proceeded many times more slowly than in industry, but nevertheless more rapidly than in the period when individual farming predominated. . . . Our Soviet peasantry has completely and irrevocably taken its stand under the Red banner of socialism. . . . Our Soviet peasantry has quit the shores of capitalism for good and is going forward in alliance with the working class to socialism.[11]

The Official Position, 1967

The *History of the USSR* (Moscow, 1967), issued early in the Brezhnev era, while defending the necessity and correctness of collectivization and stressing the voluntary entry of many peasants into *kolkhozy,* admitted the widespread use of force and "administrative methods" (secret police). It credited the party (not Stalin) with successfully implementing collectivization, but criticized the extremism of some party leaders. Stalin was reprimanded mildly, and his role in deciding upon and implementing collectivization was deemphasized.

Under conditions of worsening international relations, increasing economic difficulties, and the growth of class struggle within the USSR, the Communist Party had to achieve simultaneously industrialization and the socialist reconstruction of agriculture. Life demanded a colossal application of energy by party and Soviet people and sacrifices. . . .
In the course of fulfilling the First Five Year Plan, the Communist Party came out decisively for

---

[11] J. Stalin, *Works* (Moscow, 1955), vol. 12, pp. 131–38, 147, 155, 198–206; vol. 13, pp. 243–61.

speeding the tempo of constructing socialism. Collectivization was part of that construction. The decision that it was necessary to reduce the period of implementing it ripened gradually. . . . In the spring of 1929 were heard the words "full collectivization" for the first time as a practical task. . . . In the second half of 1929 the village seethed as in the days of the revolution [of 1917]. At meetings of the poor peasants, at general village assemblies only one question was raised: organizing *kolkhozy*. From July through September 1929 were attracted into *kolkhozy* as many peasants as during the whole 12 years of Soviet power. And during the last three months of 1929 the numerical growth of *kolkhozy* was twice as fast again. This was, as the party emphasized, "an unprecedented tempo of collectivization, *exceeding the most optimistic projections.*" . . .

The choice of the moment for a transition to massive collectivization was determined by various reasons. Among them the most important was the spurt in the country's economy. Socialist construction was advancing at an accelerating pace. The industrial population was growing considerably faster than had been assumed. The demand for commercial grain and raw materials rose sharply. The inability of small peasant production to supply a growing industry with food . . . became unbearable. It became clear that the economy of the country could not be based on two different social foundations: big socialist industry and small individual peasant farming. . . .

One of the new methods of struggle of the kulaks against the policy of the Soviet state in 1928–29 was so-called kulak self-liquidation. The kulaks themselves reduced their sowings, sold their stock and tools. "Kulak self-liquidation" thus began before the state shifted to a policy of consistent liquidations of the kulaks as a class. . . .

Along with the achievements in socialist reconstruction of the village, inadequacies were revealed. . . . Such a leap was to a significant degree caused by serious extremes, by the broad use of administrative measures. . . . In a majority of cases local leaders themselves forced by every means the process of collectivization. . . . Leaders of one region issued at the beginning of 1930 the follow-

ing slogans: "Collectivize the entire population at any cost! Dekulakize no less than seven percent of all peasant farms! Achieve all this by February 15 [1930] without delaying a moment!" . . . Administrative methods, violation of the voluntary principle in *kolkhoz* construction, contradicting the Leninist cooperative plan caused sharp dissatisfaction among the peasantry. . . . All that represented a serious danger for the country, for the alliance of the working class with the peasantry. In the struggle against these extremes rose all the healthy forces of the party. The Central Committee was inundated by letters of local Communists, workers, and peasants. . . . Numerous signals of the dissatisfaction of the peasantry with administrative methods of *kolkhoz* construction caused serious concern in the Central Committee. Thus the party and government in February and March 1930 took a series of emergency measures to correct the situation in the countryside. . . . On March 2, 1930, was published the article of I. V. Stalin, "Dizzy with Success" . . . against leftist extremes. . . . Many people noted, to be sure, that it had come too late when extremes had taken on a massive character. . . . One must note that in describing the causes of the extremes, I. V. Stalin was one-sided and not self-critical. He placed the entire blame for mistakes and extremes on local cadres, accused them of dizziness and demanded harsh measures against them. This caused a certain confusion among party workers, which hampered the task of eliminating excesses.[12]

A Dissident Marxist Historian

Roy Medvedev, a Marxist historian, in *Let History Judge* (New York, 1973), published in the USSR under Gorbachev about 1990, castigates forced collectivization and Stalin's role in it. Unlike the previous selection, which ascribed "mistakes" mainly to a few "leftists," Medvedev points directly at Stalin and the Politburo and suggests that forced collectivization was unwise and unnecessary. He ascribes Stalin's decision to

---

[12] *Istoriia SSSR* (Moscow, 1967), vol. 8, pp. 443, 541–43, 553–57.

pursue forced collectivization and elimination of the kulaks mainly to economic conditions for which Stalin and his colleagues were responsible.

> The economic miscalculations of Stalin, Bukharin, and Rykov and the kulaks' sabotage of grain procurement brought the USSR at the end of 1927 to the verge of a grain crisis. . . . Mistakes . . . in the previous years did not leave much room for political and economic maneuvering, [but] there were still some possibilities for the use of economic rather than administrative measures, that is for the methods of NEP rather than War Communism.

Medvedev attributed the traumatic implementation of collectivization to Stalin's incompetent and disastrous leadership:

> His inclination toward administrative fiat, toward coercion, instead of convincing, his oversimplified and mechanistic approach to complex political problems, his crude pragmatism and inability to foresee the consequences of alternative actions, his vicious nature and unparalleled ambition—all these qualities of Stalin seriously complicated the solution of problems that were overwhelming to begin with.
> . . . Stalin could not appraise correctly the situation taking shape in the countryside. At the first signs of progress [of collectivization] he embarked on a characteristically adventurous course. Apparently, he wanted to compensate for years of failures and miscalculations in agricultural policy and to astonish the world with a picture of great success in the socialist transformation of agriculture. So at the end of 1929, he sharply turned the bulky ship of agriculture without checking for reefs and shoals. Stalin, Molotov, Kaganovich, and several other leaders pushed for excessively high rates of collectivization, driving the local organizations in every possible way, ignoring . . . difficulties. . . .
> Although at the beginning of the 30s, grain production decreased, bread was in short supply, and millions of peasants were starving, Stalin insisted on exporting great quantities of grain. . . . Moreover, Soviet grain was sold for next to nothing. . . . The most galling aspect of the sacrifices that the people suffered—the peasants most of all—is that they

were unnecessary. . . . The scale of capital investment in industry, which Stalin forced in the early 1930s, was too much for the economy to bear.

Stalin was likewise responsible, claims Medvedev, for the extreme tempo and excessive socialization of the initial collectivization drive.

Soviet Views under Gorbachev

Under the Gorbachev regime, Soviet writings about Stalin's policy of forced collectivization exhibited much continuity with critiques from the Khrushchev period. However, there was far more outright condemnation of forced collectivization as a whole as well as of Khrushchev's agricultural policies. Thus academician V. A. Tikhonov claimed that the kulaks had virtually disappeared during the Civil War period (1918–1920), so that those "dekulakized" by Stalin from 1929 to 1933 were peasants who produced somewhat more than the average—that is, the ablest and thriftiest Soviet farmers; Tikhonov described forced collectivization as an unmitigated disaster. Sociologist V. Shumkin stated bluntly:

> Stalin decided to eliminate NEP prematurely, using purely administrative measures and direct compulsion; this led, speaking mildly, to pitiable results. Agricultural production was disrupted; in a number of districts of the country famine began. In towns measures against artisans and small producers in practice destroyed a whole sphere of services. The lives of tens of millions of people . . . were filled with incredible deprivations and difficulties, often at the limit of purely biological existence.

And the economist V. Seliunin castigated Stalin's "Year of the Great Break" (1929) instituting forced collectivization as the "year of the breaking of the backbone of the people."[13]

---

[13] R. W. Davies, *Soviet History in the Gorbachev Revolution* (Bloomington, IN, 1989), pp. 49–50. The three Soviet articles cited by Davies—by Tikhonov, Shumkin, and Seliunin—were all published in 1987 or 1988.

Problem 6 continued

A Western View

Recent Russian critiques of forced collectivization tend to confirm the findings of an outstanding Western study by Moshe Lewin,[14] who generally endorsed Medvedev's conclusions. Lewin affirms that Stalin, in asserting that the middle peasant was entering the *kolkhoz* voluntarily, was arguing from false premises:

> There were no grounds for suggesting that there had been a change of attitude among the mass of the peasantry with regard to the *kolkhozes*. The supposed change was a product of Stalin's peculiar form of reasoning which consisted of taking the wish for the deed. It followed that the peasants were being won over because this spring *there would be* 60,000 tractors in the fields, and in a year's time there would be over a hundred thousand.

---

[14] Moshe Lewin, *Russian Peasants and Soviet Power: A Study of Collectivization* (New York, 1975).

As to the results of forced collectivization, Lewin concludes:

> The rash undertaking of the winter 1929–30 cost the country very dearly. . . . Indeed, it is true to say that to this day Soviet agriculture has still not fully recovered from the damaging effects of that winter.

The cost of collectivization was enormous: "Seldom was any government to wreak such havoc in its own country."[15] Economically, forced collectivization was counterproductive even in the short run, concludes James Millar; in the long run it had no economic rationale at all.[16] It is revealing that forced collectivization à la Stalin was not tried elsewhere in eastern Europe. Instead, wealthier farmers were squeezed out, as Lenin had suggested, by economic measures and their managerial talents used in the collective farms. ∎

---

[15] Lewin, *Russian Peasants and Soviet Power*, pp. 457, 515.

[16] James Millar, "Mass Collectivization . . . ," *Slavic Review*, December 1974, p. 766.

☞ InfoTrac® College Edition Search Terms

Enter the search term *Soviet Union* in the Subject Guide, and then go to subdivision *history*.
Enter the search term *Soviet Union* in the Subject Guide, and then go to subdivision *economic policy*.
Enter the search term *Stalin* in the Subject Guide.

Suggested Additional Reading

BALL, A. M. *And Now My Soul Is Hardened: Abandoned Children in Soviet Russia, 1918–1930* (Berkeley, CA, 1994).

BELOV, F. *A History of a Soviet Collective Farm* (New York, 1955).

BERGSON, A. *The Real National Income of Soviet Russia Since 1928* (Cambridge, MA, 1961).

BERLINER, J. S. *Factory and Manager in the USSR* (Cambridge, MA, 1957).

BLACKWELL, W. *The Industrialization of Russia . . .* (New York, 1982).

BROWN, E. *The Soviet Trade Unions and Labor Relations* (Cambridge, MA, 1966).

CARR, E. H. *Foundations of a Planned Economy, 1926–1929* (New York, 1972).

CONQUEST, R. *The Harvest of Sorrow: Soviet Collectivization and the Terror-Famine* (New York, 1986).

CURTISS, J. S. *The Russian Church and the Soviet State* (Boston, 1953).

DANIELS, R. V., ed. *The Stalin Revolution* (Lexington, MA, 1972).

DAVIES, R. W. *Crisis and Progress in the Soviet Economy, 1931–1933* (New York, 1996).

———. *The Industrialization of Soviet Russia: Vol. 3: The Soviet Economy in Turmoil 1929–1930* (Cambridge, MA, 1989).

———. *The Soviet Collective Farm, 1929–1930* (Cambridge, MA, 1980).

——— et al. *The Economic Transformation of the Soviet Union, 1913–1945* (Cambridge, 1993).

DAVIES, S. *Popular Opinion in Stalin's Russia: Terror, Propaganda, and Dissent, 1934–1941* (New York, 1997).

DEUTSCHER, I. *The Prophet Outcast: Trotsky, 1929–1940* (Oxford, 1963).

DUNMORE, T. *The Stalinist Command Economy* (New York, 1980).

EDMONDSON, L., ed. *Women and Society in Russia and the Soviet Union* (Cambridge, 1992).

ERLICH, A. *The Soviet Industrialization Debate* . . . (Cambridge, MA, 1960).

FARNSWORTH, B., and L. VIOLA, eds. *Russian Peasant Women* (Oxford, 1992).

FITZPATRICK, S. *Stalin's Peasants: Resistance and Survival in the Russian Village After Collectivization* (New York, 1994).

GERSCHENKRON, A. *Economic Backwardness in Historical Perspective* (Cambridge, MA, 1962).

GOLDMAN, W. *Women, the State and Revolution: Soviet Family Policy and Social Life, 1917–1936* (Cambridge, 1993).

HODGEMAN, D. R. *Soviet Industrial Production, 1928–1951* (Cambridge, MA, 1954).

HOFFMAN, D. L. *Peasant Metropolis: Social Identities in Moscow, 1929–1941* (Ithaca, NY, 1994).

HOLMES, L. E. *Stalin's School* . . . *1931–1937* (Pittsburgh, PA, 1999).

HOLZMAN, F. D. *Soviet Taxation* (Cambridge, MA, 1955).

HUNTER, H., and J. SZYMER. *Faulty Foundations: Soviet Economic Policies, 1928–1940* (Princeton, 1992).

IVANOVA, G. M. *Labor Camp Socialism: The Gulag in the Soviet Totalitarian System,* ed. Donald J. Raleigh, trans. Carol Faith (Armonk, NY, 2000).

JASNY, N. *Soviet Industrialization, 1928–1952* (Chicago, 1961).

KOTKIN, S. *Magnetic Mountain: Stalinism as a Civilization* (Berkeley, CA, 1995).

KRAVCHENKO, V. *I Chose Freedom* (New York, 1946).

LAIRD, R. D., ed. *Soviet Agriculture and Peasant Affairs* (Lawrence, KS, 1963).

LEWIN, M. *Russian Peasants and Soviet Power* . . . (New York, 1975).

MALE, D. J. *Russian Peasant Organization Before Collectivization* . . . (Cambridge, 1971).

MCCANNON, J. *Red Arctic: Polar Exploration and Myths of the North in the Soviet Union, 1932–1939* (Oxford, England, 1998).

MORRIS, M. W. *Stalin's Famine and Roosevelt's Recognition of Russia* (Lanham, MD, 1994).

NOVE, A. *Was Stalin Really Necessary?* (London, 1964).

POSADSKAYA, A. *Women in Russia: A New Era in Russian Feminism,* ed. and trans. K. Clark (New York, 1994).

PREOBRAZHENSKY, E. A. *The Crisis of Soviet Industrialization,* ed. D. Filtzer (White Plains, NY, 1979).

RADZINSKY, E. *Stalin* (New York, 1996).

REES, E. A., ed. *Decision-Making in the Stalinist Command Economy, 1932–1937* (New York, 1997).

ROSENBERG, W. G., and L. H. SIEGELBAUM, eds. *Social Dimensions of Soviet Industrialization* (Bloomington, IN, 1993).

SAMUELSON, L. *Plans for Stalin's War Machine: Tukhachevskii and Military-Economic Planning, 1925–1941* (New York, 2000).

SHEARER, D. R. *Industry, State, and Society in Stalin's Russia, 1926–1934* (Ithaca, NY, 1996).

SHOLOKHOV, M. *Virgin Soil Upturned* (New York, 1959). (Novel.)

SIEGELBAUM, L. H. *Strakhanovism and the Politics of Productivity in the USSR, 1935–1941* (New York, 1988).

SIEGELBAUM, L. H., and A. SOKOLOV, eds. *Stalinism as a Way of Life* (New Haven, CT, 2000).

SMITH, K., ed. *Soviet Industrialization and Soviet Maturity: Economy and Society* (London, 1986).

STALIN, J. *Problems of Leninism* (Moscow, 1940).

STONE, D. *Hammer and Rifle: The Militarization of the Soviet Union, 1926–1933* (Lawrence, KS, 2000).

SWIANIEWICZ, S. *Forced Labor and Economic Development* . . . (London, 1965).

TIMASHEFF, N. *The Great Retreat* (New York, 1946).

VIOLA, L. *The Best Sons of the Fatherland: Workers in the Vanguard of Soviet Collectivization* (New York, 1989).

WEINER, D. R. *Models of Nature: Ecology Conservation and Cultural Revolution in Soviet Russia* (Bloomington, IN, 2000).

WHEATCROFT, S. G., and R. W. DAVIES, eds. *Materials for a Balance of the Soviet National Economy, 1928–1930* (Cambridge, 1985).

ZALESKI, E. *Stalinist Planning for Economic Growth,* trans. and ed. M. C. MacAndrew and J. Moore (Chapel Hill, NC, 1979).

12

Soviet Culture under Lenin and Stalin, 1917–1953

From the very outset of the Soviet regime, culture became the handmaiden of politics and could not be viewed in isolation from it. However, profound differences in cultural policy developed in the era of Lenin and Stalin. Under so-called War Communism (1917–1921) there was no real official policy on cultural affairs because Bolshevik leaders were beset on all sides by foreign and domestic enemies and were therefore too preoccupied to formulate one. Many outstanding Russian writers, artists, and musicians sought refuge abroad, and some remained there. During the New Economic Policy (1921–1928) liberal and permissive policies toward the arts generally prevailed. Experimentation and debate were largely accepted as essential for a healthy cultural life, and some émigré intellectuals returned to Soviet Russia. Then, in 1929, Stalin's "revolution from above" altered irrevocably the nature of Soviet society and restructured the country. Cultural and scientific life could not escape the momentous transformations fostered by forced collectivization and rapid industrialization and urbanization. As Stalin loomed ever larger in all spheres of life, the freewheeling culture of NEP, with its lively debates and numerous controversies, ended abruptly. No longer could one remain neutral or aloof; independent views were no longer tolerated. Party-mindedness (*partiinost*) became paramount. Following considerable relaxation of party pressures and controls during World War II, the screws of conformity tightened once again over Soviet cultural life in Stalin's final years.

Initial Policies

The November Revolution caused no abrupt break with established cultural patterns and traditions. Indeed, during the first years of the Soviet regime Russian culture underwent little apparent change. Having seized power, the Bolsheviks strove desperately to retain it, leaving them little time or energy to devote to the arts. They realized that they could not introduce pervasive cultural controls with their limited trained personnel. But the disruptions of revolution and civil war meant that little of enduring cultural value was produced. Scarce paper was quickly consumed to print Bolshevik propaganda leaflets and revolutionary tracts. Artists who managed to continue working found little demand for their works, and basic materials were in short supply and poor in quality; musicians faced similar problems. Concert halls were often filled with raucous political debates and revolutionary agitation. Deaths from hunger, disease, war, and execution had severely thinned the ranks of the intelligentsia. Emigration was an escape from what seemed to many to be the onset of the apocalypse. Many prominent artists chose to live in foreign exile rather than face an uncertain life in Soviet Russia. Émigrés included such leading artists as Maxim Gorkii, Alexis Tolstoy (a distant relative of Leo Tolstoy), Igor Stravinskii, Sergei Prokofiev, and Marc Chagall. Some returned later to the Soviet Union; others resided abroad permanently.

The chaotic uncertainty of the early years of Soviet rule constituted only one obstacle to elaborating a coherent cultural policy. From an ideological or theoretical vantage point there was equal confusion and uncertainty. In Marxism, culture was part of the superstructure. Only changes in the substructure (methods of production) would bring changes in the arts. A new socialist culture would emerge only gradually after a new economic order and a genuine proletarian society had taken shape.

Lenin outlined this moderate view of culture as a basis for a Soviet policy toward the arts:

> Art belongs to the people. It must have its deepest roots in the broad masses of the workers. It must be understood and loved by them. It must be rooted in, and grow with their feelings, thoughts, and desires. It must arouse and develop the artist in them. Are we to give cake and sugar to a minority while the mass of workers and peasants still eat black bread? So that art may come to the people, and people to art, we must first of all raise the general level of education and culture.[1]

This was neither very new nor even particularly Marxist, but it echoed what V. V. Stasov had

espoused in the 19th century in defending the art of the Itinerants and the music of The Five. Art had to be rooted in the life of the people, be clear and understandable, and serve a useful purpose: to educate the people. This became the essence of the Soviet concept of art.

Lunacharskii: The Politics of Culture

Anatolii Lunacharskii (1875–1933) was responsible for making Lenin's views on culture and art a reality. The son of a successful tsarist civil servant, Lunacharskii studied philosophy and literature and developed sophisticated, cosmopolitan tastes. Joining the Bolshevik party in 1904, he described himself as "an intellectual among Bolsheviks, and a Bolshevik among the intelligentsia." As the party's leading cultural authority, Lunacharskii was the natural choice to be the first People's Commissar of Education. From 1917 to 1929 he guided the Soviet regime's efforts to improve education and develop a socialist culture. He proved a skillful, imaginative administrator, exercising considerable authority flexibly and tolerantly. He sought to initiate and oversee a program of basic education to teach the illiterate masses— 60 to 70 percent of the population—to read and write. He aimed to secure the allegiance of the artistic intelligentsia and emphasize their social obligations to the state. He had to persuade party leaders of the importance of the arts in order to conduct an effective cultural program. Recognizing the need for a delicate balance between conservative social elements, on the one hand, and fanatical enthusiasm for new directions and radical demands for a complete break with the past, on the other, he worked frantically to prevent wanton destruction of churches and sculptures associated with the old regime by those aiming to obliterate "bourgeois culture." Seeking to preserve the best of Russia's heritage, Lunacharskii refused to be limited by it.

Lunacharskii strove to restrain enthusiasm by proletarian supporters of the new regime and to persuade anti-Communists to shift to neutrality or

---

[1] Quoted in Sheila Fitzpatrick, *The Commissariat of Enlightenment* (New York, 1971), p. 24.

Anatolii Vasilievich Lunacharskii, 1875–1933.
A writer and literary critic, Lunacharskii
served as the first Commissar of Education in
the Soviet Union.

support the Soviet order. He preferred persuasion
and patience to pressure and coercion. His was a
reasonable voice in an era of impatience and intolerance. His actions were generally sensible and
humane in an inhumane, irrational age. As commissar of education he encouraged give-and-take,
in clear contrast to the rigid authoritarianism of
the Stalin era. The 1920s represented a type of
"Golden Era" of Soviet culture, an age of experimentation and innovation.

The "ideological reorientation" implied by the
revolution soon affected social life and schools.
Radicals predicted that the traditional family
would wither away and urged a sharp breach with
bourgeois social patterns. In education the curriculum was transformed to stress practical learning, promote economic specialization and material
production, and develop socially responsible individuals. Schools were to be nondiscriminatory,
free, and compulsory until age 17. Schooling and

work experience were to be integrated; ideological
loyalty and Soviet patriotism were incorporated
into the curriculum. Schools were to become
political and economic instruments to overcome
Russia's backwardness. Lunacharskii's commissariat made significant educational progress
despite shortages of buildings, teachers, and
books. By 1926 literacy had risen to about 51 percent of those over age nine.

Soviet Culture in the Making: *Proletkult* and Other Vanguard Groups

To implement a wide-ranging educational program, Lunacharskii had to recruit "bourgeois
specialists" needed to train future "socialist specialists." Wishing to alienate no one, Lunacharskii
helped finance numerous literary, artistic, and
educational groups that retained much freedom
and autonomy. Among the groups his commissariat sponsored was the Association of Proletarian Cultural and Educational Organizations
(*Proletkult*). Founded in 1917 (before November)
by A. A. Bogdanov as an outlet for working-class
cultural activity and to promote a broad educational program, Proletkult created workers' cultural clubs, toilers' universities, and palaces of
culture. In August 1918 Proletkult sponsored a
conference of proletarian writers that urged setting up an All-Russian Union of Writers of "working-class origin and viewpoint." That first effort
failed, but the idea was not forgotten. However,
Proletkult's aggressiveness caused friction with
Lunacharskii's commissariat. Their competition
finally induced Lenin to intervene. In 1920 he
ordered Proletkult merged with the commissariat;
he would not allow Proletkult to undermine
Lunacharskii's more traditional approach.

In opposition to Proletkult's aim to reorient
culture radically, there emerged a group of writers
that Trotskii dubbed the Fellow Travelers. These
"bourgeois specialists" were mostly established
prerevolutionary writers who remained in Soviet
Russia. They analyzed problems of adjustment in a

new and alien world and wrote of the Revolution, the Civil War, and their effects on individuals. Less interested in cosmic historical forces than the proletarian writers, they wrote about romantic love, violence, and passion. In 1921 some Fellow Travelers formed a loosely organized fraternity known as the Serapion Brotherhood (from a hermitlike character of the early-19th-century German Romantic writer E. T. A. Hoffmann). Lacking clear aesthetic doctrines, the Brotherhood sought to preserve artistic freedom. "Most of all," wrote one, "we were afraid of losing our independence." By 1924, however, the Brotherhood's unity began to crumble.

Another literary group of this period was associated with *Pereval* (The Mountain Pass), the first important Soviet "thick" journal—that is, one with serious intellectual content, with essays on politics, economics, literature, and the arts. The *Pereval* group consisted largely of young writers dedicated to the Revolution; more than half were party members. Regarding emerging Soviet society as transitional, they criticized as well as praised it. Favoring artistic freedom, they advocated literary "sincerity" and artistic "realism" and stressed each writer's unique personality as critical in developing talent. Their humanistic outlook was uncomplicated by ideology. Individualism and humanism brought *Pereval* into conflict with militant proletarian writers, who accused it of a lack of revolutionary enthusiasm. Lunacharskii monitored such disputes to prevent them from becoming disruptive.

Larger, more influential organizations of proletarian writers grew from the Proletkult movement.[2] They claimed to be the only true literary spokespersons for the working class. In their journal, *On Literary Guard,* they attacked the Fellow Travelers and *Pereval* writers aggressively. In 1925 these proletarian groups convened the first All-Union Conference of Proletarian Writers

as a forum to attack "bourgeois" writers for opposing the revolution and espousing bourgeois values such as individualism. Their accusations against the Fellow Travelers were mostly groundless, but there was open debate, not intimidation. The Fellow Travelers vigorously defended their literary freedom and intellectual integrity.

These intense debates provoked the party to issue a formal statement on culture, "The Policy of the Party in the Field of Artistic Literature." It revealed that many leading Bolsheviks were sophisticated culturally and understood that artistic creativity could not be dictated. The party accepted a variety of literary trends reflecting the diversity of NEP. Remaining aloof from partisan debate, the party advocated fair competition among the groups, guaranteeing that cultural ferment would persist and that proletarian writers would not devour the Fellow Travelers.

Painting and music of the 1920s revealed similar patterns of struggle between "left" and "right" factions. The Soviet musical world was split by intense debates between warring factions. The Association for Contemporary Music (ASM) maintained close ties with western European musical circles, thus assuring Soviet composers contact with advanced and progressive Western ideas. ASM in turn acquainted the West with the best music of Soviet composers. Such Western contacts proved especially stimulating to young composers like Dmitri Shostakovich (1906–1975). Members of ASM rejected completely the idea that music was a political tool.

Opposing the ASM were proletarian musicians, many of whom had participated in the short-lived Proletkult, which collapsed in 1920. The Russian Association of Proletarian Musicians (RAPM), founded in 1923, sought to embody proletarian ideology in music. Its members rejected most past composers and adopted a negative attitude toward the classical heritage. Scorning ASM's more traditional composers, they announced a life-and-death struggle with "decadent formalism" of "bourgeois" composers. Seeking to mediate, Lunacharskii cautioned the proletarian musicians not to forcibly "revolutionize" Russian music.

---

[2] The Moscow Association of Proletarian Writers (MAPP) was founded in 1923; the Russian Association of Proletarian Writers (RAPP) and the All-Union Combined Association of Proletarian Writers (VOAPP) were founded in 1928.

Uneasy coexistence prevailed in music until the end of the 1920s.

Literature

Two Poets of the Revolution

Uncertainty and ambiguity pervaded Russian literature of the early Soviet period. This was reflected clearly in the last works of the brilliant Symbolist poet Alexander Blok (1880–1921). Well established in 1917, Blok welcomed the Revolution as the painful birth of a new world order, yet its violence frightened him. He stood precariously over a widening gulf between old and new, uncertain where to leap. Two famous poems written in 1918 amid revolution and civil war revealed his— and the intelligentsia's—ambiguous reactions. *The Scythians* celebrated the Revolution as an elemental expression of the Russian national spirit: "Yea, we are Scythians, / Yea, Asians, a slant-eyed, greedy brood." Russia, proclaimed Blok, had long shielded a haughty and ungrateful Europe from the Mongol hordes. Now, to collect that debt, it beckoned to Europe to join it in promoting peace and cooperation for the welfare of humanity: "Come unto us from the black ways of war, / Come to our peaceful arms and rest. / Comrades, before it is too late, / Sheathe the old sword; may brotherhood be blest." If Europe spurned this call to peace, a Scythian and Asiatic horde would descend and destroy corrupt, dying Western civilization.

Even more somber and controversial was Blok's foreboding poem *The Twelve,* which elicited enormous interest and impassioned debate. Did Blok intend *The Twelve* to affirm the Revolution, or to predict destruction of a refined and ancient culture? Was it a hymn of praise or a deceitful blasphemy? The "twelve" are Red Army soldiers tramping through Petrograd in a blizzard, intent on murder and pillage against the bourgeois enemy. The poem begins forebodingly: "Black night, / White snow, / The wind, the wind! / It all but lays you low, / The wind, the wind, / Across God's world it blows!" The Revolution, like the

Alexander Alexandrovich Blok, 1880–1921, the most important Russian Symbolist poet, close friend of Akhmatova.

wind, sweeps all before it. After recording the soldiers' bloody acts, the poem ends cryptically: "Forward as a haughty host they tread. / A starved mongrel shambles in the rear. / Bearing high the banner, bloody red, / . . . With mist-white roses garlanded! / Jesus Christ is marching at their head."[3] Thus 12 terrorists become the 12 apostles, vanguard of a new era, following Christ and leading humanity into a new millennium, justifying a destructive revolution. Is that what Blok meant?

These were Blok's last two poems. His final diary entries, written as he was dying in 1921, confirm his despair and personal incompatibility with the Soviet era: "At this moment, I have neither soul nor body. . . . Vile rotten Mother Russia has devoured me . . . as a sow gobbles one of its

---

[3] A. Yarmolinsky, ed., *An Anthology of Russian Verse, 1812–1960,* trans. Babette Deutsch (New York, 1962), pp. 109, 120.

suckling pigs."[4] Trying to leap to the new, he had slid into the abyss.

Another major poet devoured by Mother Russia and the Revolution was Vladimir Mayakovskii (1893–1930). No other writer identified so closely with the Revolution received such adulation. A prominent Futurist poet before 1917, Mayakovskii hailed the November Revolution, joined the Bolshevik party, and confidently set out to create a new "proletarian art" appealing to the masses. A "cultural radical" who rejected all bourgeois art as obsolete, he argued, "The White Guard is turned over to a firing squad: Why not Pushkin?" Art now must celebrate the Revolution, the proletariat, the machine—all modern life. Futurists regarded themselves as the vanguard of proletarian culture, and Mayakovskii was out in front. To achieve these grandiose aims, he and his friends organized LEF (Left Front in Art), whose members proclaimed art that was utilitarian to the state. "Art for art's sake" repelled him. To engage in idle dilettantism during historic change was to betray art. Commenting on current issues, he even put his poetry to work selling products in the service of the people and the Revolution.

Typical of his approach was the poem *150,000,000* (the 1919 population of Soviet Russia), published in 1920: "Its rhythms—bullets, / its rhymes—fires from building to building, / 150,000,000 speak with my lips . . . / Who can tell the name / of the earth's creator—surely a genius? / And so / of this / my / poem / no one is the author."[5] It depicts the struggle between good and evil, socialism and capitalism, Moscow and Chicago, and 150 million Russians and the rest of the world. This blatantly propagandist work was a failure. Lenin chastised Mayakovskii for printing *150,000,000* in 5,000 copies; 1,500 "for libraries and cranks" would have been enough, he claimed.

Among Mayakovskii's most popular works were two plays, *The Bedbug* (1929) and *The Bath-*

house (1930), revealing his growing disillusionment with a Soviet regime that to him was increasingly remote from the heroic dreams of the Revolution. In *The Bedbug* a worker, Prisypkin, becomes a self-important bureaucrat indulging his bourgeois tastes and values. A fire set by his drunken guests disrupts his wedding day. Everyone except Prisypkin and one bedbug are incinerated. Fifty years later, Prisypkin and the bedbug are found perfectly preserved in a block of ice. Prisypkin recovers fully after thawing out, but his miraculous resurrection is a mixed blessing for the purified future Communist society he now enters. His bourgeois habits—drinking, smoking, and swearing—and especially the "ancient disease" of love all prove contagious and potentially disruptive. Thus the authorities display him and the bedbug in a cage as curiosities. Prisypkin symbolized everything Mayakovskii hated in himself and in Soviet citizens of the late 1920s. Revolutionary fervor and self-sacrifice had begun to fade, replaced by "bourgeois" values: self-satisfaction, complacency, and pursuit of the material. Soviet society, he feared, was fostering a generation of Prisypkins.

The Bathhouse more directly indicted Soviet life, notably the Stalinist bureaucracy, which radiated vulgarity characteristic of Stalinism at its worst, with its anti-intellectualism, crudeness, and sterility. Mayakovskii was continuing a literary tradition, dating back at least to Gogol, in which literature was used to expose bureaucratic humbug, abuse of power, and corruption. Dreams given substance by the Revolution had begun to dissipate, Mayakovskii felt, like bubbles in the air. The spontaneity and freedom of NEP were yielding to a soulless bureaucratic state supported by a vast police apparatus resembling that of tsarism. His efforts to publicize and ridicule shortcomings of Soviet society were attacked viciously by petty, narrow-minded bureaucrats who felt the sting of his critiques. Their attacks only convinced him that his assessment was accurate.

Harassed by enemies, adrift in a society that spurned his high standards, beset with personal problems, and suffering from boredom and

---

[4] Quoted in Marc Slonim, *Modern Russian Literature* (New York, 1953), p. 206.

[5] Quoted in Edward J. Brown, *Russian Literature Since the Revolution* (New York, 1969), p. 54.

isolation, Mayakovskii shot himself in April 1930. His suicide note avoided self-pity: "Don't blame anyone for my death, and please don't gossip about it." His tragic death shocked the entire intelligentsia. He had been *the* poet of the Revolution, spokesman of the working class, and the advocate of socially useful literature, yet his suicide seemed to many a slap in the face of the Revolution. But even in death he served it. His legacy as a poet and a symbol has been enormous, and his genius unchallenged.

Two Novelists of Dissent

Mayakovskii's prose counterpart was Evgenii Zamiatin (1884–1937), author of the influential anti-utopian novel *We.* Joining the Bolshevik party as a youth, he soon found the atmosphere sectarian and petty and left it before the Revolution. Zamiatin began publishing stories in 1911 and was well known by 1914. During World War I he spent much time in England supervising ship construction for the Russian navy. After the Revolution he found it difficult to fit into Soviet society, finally finding employment only with the help of his friend, Maxim Gorkii, as a lecturer on literature. Zamiatin became the spiritual godfather of the Serapion Brotherhood but not a formal member. *We* (1920), circulated but not published in the USSR until 1989, appeared in English translation in 1924, the first of many Soviet writings to enjoy great success in the West.

In *We* Zamiatin reveals a frightening vision of the society he saw emerging in the Soviet Union. He foresaw both a degeneration of communism and the destruction of freedom and individuality by the monolithic state. *We* satirizes a future utopian city where science provides every convenience (including a glass cover to protect it from the elements), but its people have been reduced to ciphers. "Wise authorities" control every facet of human activity—work, thought, leisure, and sex. Transparent living quarters and constantly monitored activity eliminate privacy. Every thought and

utterance is recorded; every deviation from the norm is ruthlessly suppressed. The novel's hero is D-503, a rebel against sterile conformity who dares to engage in free thought, to love, and to show interest in nature; he is a more sophisticated Prisypkin. D-503 eventually is "reprogrammed" (destroyed) and his "irrationality" ended by the "wise authorities."

Zamiatin's novel warned of future dangers to freedom and individuality stemming from the regime's manipulation of science, thus anticipating Aldous Huxley's *Brave New World* and George Orwell's *1984. We,* of course, could not then be published in the Soviet Union. Zamiatin's other writings, too, alienated the Soviet authorities, who in 1929 launched a vicious campaign of vilification (a familiar practice later) against him. Prevented from publishing, he was forced to resign his teaching position and was ostracized by all. Finally, in 1931, Gorkii personally delivered Zamiatin's letter of appeal to Stalin:

> For me as a writer to be deprived of the opportunity to write is a sentence of death. Matters have reached a point where I am unable to exercise my profession because creative writing is unthinkable if one is obliged to work in an atmosphere of systematic persecution that grows worse every year.[6]

Owing to Gorkii's intercession, Zamiatin and his wife were allowed to leave the USSR in 1932.

Zamiatin's contemporary, Boris Pilniak (pen name of Boris Vogau, 1894–1937), was an influential and popular Fellow Traveler with great impact on Soviet literature of the 1920s. His first and most important work, a novel, *The Naked Year* (1922), was a series of vignettes of the Revolution that recount the cruelty and hatreds it unleashed and portray with compelling pathos the suffering and optimism of this age. Pilniak sympathized not with the Bolsheviks but with all those seeking freedom, whether anarchists, SRs, or disillusioned

---

[6] Quoted by Michael Glenny in his introduction to E. Zamiatin's *We* (New York, 1972), p. 12.

Bolsheviks. He shared Zamiatin's concern about the dangers to human freedom and individuality from efforts to organize all life by a preconceived plan. Pilniak's "The Tale of the Unextinguished Moon" resembled closely the actual death of Red Army commander in chief Mikhail Frunze. A Red Army Civil War hero falls ill; the party orders him to undergo surgery, which he knows instinctively will kill him. The party leader—"Number One"—insists that the hero be repaired so as to remain useful, like a piece of machinery. Pilniak castigates this callous attitude, and in his story the Red Army commander dies on the operating table as if cut down on the battlefield. This story provoked a storm of criticism, and Pilniak and the editors of the journal in which it appeared had to denounce it publicly as "a gross error."

Pilniak was thus already suspect when his short novel *Mahogany* appeared in Germany in 1929. Pilniak had sent it there for publication simultaneously with the Soviet edition to gain international copyright protection because the USSR then did not subscribe to the International Copyright Convention. The novel was issued in the USSR in 1930 only after complete rewriting, under the title *The Volga Falls to the Caspian Sea.* It describes construction of a dam and a hydroelectric plant that will destroy a historic town. The theme is the struggle between history and technological progress; Pilniak clearly sympathizes with history. His heroes are not construction workers but mahogany collectors who cherish true craftsmanship and preserve the old in the face of the advance of the new.

The Cinema

"The cinema is for us the most important of all the arts," declared Lenin. As a means of mass communication in an era of mass culture, the cinema is unsurpassed. Sophisticated messages can be filmed, duplicated, distributed, and projected on screens for millions of people, with little technical equipment and personnel. Thus conditions were right to develop Soviet cinema. Most prerevolu-

tionary Russian film directors, actors, and technical personnel left Russia after the Revolution. Thus, unlike literature, music, and painting, the Soviet cinema had no "bourgeois specialists" to worry about and was free to develop on its own. The first Soviet film directors were young enthusiasts whose spontaneity, ingenuity, and artistry deeply influenced Soviet filmmaking.

Two important early Soviet directors were Lev Kuleshov, who directed his first film at age 17, and Dziga Vertov, who filmed the Civil War at age 20. Vertov's Civil War documentaries helped shape future Soviet films. He developed the "camera-eye" (*kino-glaz*) concept, which records what is occurring live. The director gives meaning to the raw experience recorded by the camera by cutting and arranging—editing—the film. Thus the film becomes an instrument that interprets and educates. Later Vertov perfected his techniques, recording scenes from Soviet life, editing them, and arranging them into virtual filmed newspapers, calling them "film truth" (*kino-pravda*) after the newspaper *Pravda.*

Lev Kuleshov applied Vertov's techniques to feature films, utilizing Vertov's documentary realism to stimulate the viewer's imagination and anticipation and making film both an intellectual and a visual experience. He used his simple equipment creatively and intelligently. He combined documentary footage with pure fiction to create an artistic montage, and he paved the way for Sergei Eisenstein, the greatest Soviet film director.

Trained as an architect, Eisenstein (1898–1948) worked as a poster artist during the Civil War. As a set designer he joined the Proletkult theater, where he was influenced by the director, V. E. Meierhold. Later, after staging his own theatrical productions, he moved exclusively to cinema in 1924. He combined Meierhold's theatrical techniques—stressing the visual, caricature, and contrast—with Kuleshov's documentary montage to develop his own imaginative style. Eisenstein's first film, *Strike* (1924), which began as a documentary, became a powerful portrait of the inequities of capitalist Russia. Eisenstein's use of visual symbolism enhanced the film's psychological impact. He jolted audiences with powerful scenes and shocked them with startling visual effects, creating a "film-fist" (*kino-kulak*) to pummel the viewer. *The Battleship Potemkin* (1926), Eisenstein's greatest cinematic triumph, depicted the mutiny of the crew of the *Potemkin* in Odessa in the 1905 Revolution. The hero is the battleship, which sustains the crew's revolutionary enthusiasm. The film indicted tsarist callousness, represented by the mechanical march down the steps of Odessa harbor by a phalanx of tsarist troops and by the repulsive image of maggot-infested meat fed to the battleship crew by inhumane officers. *The Battleship Potemkin* demonstrated how significant a political instrument the cinema could be. Still, in the 1920s Eisenstein's films were not great popular successes. Audiences preferred lighter foreign imports, and party censors suspected Eisenstein's unorthodox methods. By the late 1920s he began having trouble with the authorities.

Vsevolod Pudovkin, another major Soviet director of the 1920s, was less original than Eisenstein but more popular with audiences. Relying on professional actors and a clear story line, which gave his works smoothness and continuity, Pudovkin drew his subject matter from works of fiction. He involved the viewer in development of individual characters rather than in great historic events. His often sentimental and unsophisticated films were very influential in a developing Soviet cinema. His most critically acclaimed film was *Mother* (1926).

By the late 1920s party authorities, becoming more interested in the cinema, moved to control it as they did other arts. The party supported Vertov's "film-eye" documentary techniques, harnessed to the industrialization drive of the 1930s. Some imaginative directors and prominent film actors emigrated in protest.

Education

From the inception of the Bolshevik regime, the party placed high priority on eliminating illiteracy, which was especially widespread in rural areas but also affected many urban workers. As early as 1919 a campaign was inaugurated to eradicate illiteracy: The *likbez* (liquidation of illiteracy) aimed at expanding the educational system, emphasizing practical education and hands-on experience. In 1921 so-called *rabfaki* (workers' schools) were established in factories to offer instruction in basic reading, writing, and arithmetic. Evening classes were held in factories; their success may be measured by the millions who learned the rudiments of literacy in their crash courses.

The effort to create a "workers' culture" resulted from a desire to develop a new cultural and educational level worthy of the new era. However, the result was often a lowering of the overall cultural level, as many intellectuals, officials, and white-collar workers sought to identify completely with the new "leading class" and began to dress and speak like workers, carefully disguising their more refined tastes and attitudes.

Despite the assault on illiteracy and creation of a new workers' culture, the party did not neglect higher education. Intent on training a new generation of scientists with the proper political and intellectual outlook, the party established a Communist Academy rivaling the old Imperial Academy of Sciences and staffed largely by members of the old guard. A number of Communist universities were also established. A limited coexistence between these institutions prevailed until the late 1920s. In general, Bolshevik attitudes prevailed in the social sciences (economics, history, politics), whereas prerevolutionary views predominated in the natural sciences and humanities.

Education at all levels had two fundamental purposes: (1) to train a new generation in socialist thinking and counteract lingering bourgeois influences and (2) to establish a solid foundation for a new socialist culture expressed in all the arts and sciences. A correct socialist world outlook among the students was emphasized. If that could be established early and then continuously reinforced, the subjects studied would assume an appropriate "socialist character" no matter what they were—literature, chemistry, economics, or astronomy. Intensive efforts were made to open up educational opportunities for the former lower classes, notably workers.

Science

As the 1920s progressed—a period of relative freedom and peaceful coexistence between the Marxist and non-Marxist camps—tensions grew and a showdown was clearly inevitable, the outcome of which was never really in doubt. Scientists experienced a growing intolerance at the hands of the party on issues of central scientific and philosophical importance, such as Freudian psychology, Einstein's theory of relativity, quantum mechanics, and modern genetic theory. Intellectual debates over interpretation of these theories, crucial to the development of 20th-century science, acquired political overtones. Serious scientists found it increasingly difficult to reconcile dialectical materialism, as interpreted by the party, with basic principles of quantum mechanics or Einstein's relativity theory. Many scientists chose to retreat from public debate about scientific theory and pursue their own research unobtrusively. Thus many gifted scientists shunned controversial theoretical work, which was viewed as politically dangerous if one ended up on the losing side of a theoretical debate.

Nowhere were these dangers more apparent than in genetics. The controversies that plagued Soviet genetics for more than a generation were typical of those affecting many aspects of Soviet intellectual life. Traditional geneticists agreed that a gene reproduces itself essentially unchanged from generation to generation, with very infrequent instances of mutation. Soviet scientists tended to reject that view as not squaring with Marxism's dialectical materialism. Some Soviet geneticists now suggested that evolution involved a series of adaptations to environmental conditions capable of transmission to subsequent generations—that is, the inheritance of acquired characteristics. Such a view was consistent with the Soviet view that the USSR had created an entirely new and superior social environment from which triumphant Soviet men and women would emerge. The debate between traditionalists and Soviet Lamarckians moved back and forth during the 1920s. (Lamarck, a pre-Darwinian philosopher, had formulated the idea that acquired characteristics could be transmitted to successive generations.) Only with the emergence under Stalin of a young pseudoagronomist, Trofim D. Lysenko, would the genetics debate take on real and dire political dimensions. During the New Economic Policy politics did not impinge seriously on scientific work, but the specter of dialectical materialism hung malevolently over an infant Soviet science like the sword of Damocles. The agony of Soviet genetics would begin with the emergent Stalinist dictatorship of the 1930s.

Toward the end of the 1920s, tension and unease developed in scientific circles and in all realms of Soviet culture, as the party manifested impatience at the slow pace of development. In 1928 a mere 6 percent of all scientific workers were members of the Communist Union of Scientific Workers (*Varnitso*). Among scientists the party was winning few adherents, and the Academy of Sciences remained impervious to party influence. The frightening possibility arose that the party might be excluded from the country's intellectual life. Advocacy of peaceful coexistence between party and nonparty scientists was deleted abruptly from official pronouncements as the party began with increasing regularity to assert its authority in scientific matters. With the consolidation of Stalin's position and the rise of the cult of personality, Stalin began to intervene in scientific debates. Soon his arbitrary view became official and exclusive in all branches of learning.

Stalinist Culture, 1929–1953

Tightened controls on Soviet intellectual life began soon after Stalin's consolidation of power with an attack on the Academy of Sciences, which had sought to remain aloof from political involvement. Using a method typical of his drive for power, Stalin insisted that Academy membership be expanded and proceeded to nominate carefully selected candidates. By 1929 older academicians had been mostly replaced by aggressive party-minded members who transformed the Academy into a tool of Stalinist cultural policy. After a pliable majority had been seated, some distinguished older members were arrested beginning in 1930, including Sergei Platonov and Evgenii Tarle, highly respected nonparty historians. This campaign brought the prestigious Academy into line in support of the Five Year Plan. Those who resisted or evaded the party's demands paid dearly for it in the Great Purge of 1936–1938.

The party now intervened in such fields as linguistics. Nicholas Marr, a distinguished linguist, had applied Marxist theory to linguistics. Language, Marr argued, was an aspect of social life that reflected productive relations. As part of the superstructure, language would reflect fundamental changes in the socioeconomic base. A new socialist language would emerge as socialist productive relations developed, he predicted. Marr discerned an embryonic socialist language in Russian and non-Russian languages of the USSR. After Marr's death in 1934, Stalin distorted his views to claim that Russian was socialism's international language to which non-Russian languages must yield. This became a theoretical basis for a new Russification of Soviet national minorities.

A flagrant example of party interference in Soviet intellectual life was in genetics. Collectivization enabled unscrupulous individuals to win party support for preposterous theories. Lysenko argued that classical genetics, disregarding dialectical change, had misinterpreted the genetic process. Lysenko claimed that hereditary characteristics resulted from an organism's dialectical interaction with its environment. He argued that altering the environment would change organisms' natural properties; these changes could then be transmitted to succeeding generations. This amazing theory was supplemented by the belief that organisms could somehow select which acquired characteristics could be passed on. This belief coincided with and reinforced the conviction that the November Revolution had begun a new era in which a new, superior Soviet individual would emerge. Change the environment and change humankind! With conditions ripe for a new genetic theory, Lysenko became Stalin's scientific hero.

With such support, Lysenko asserted first that he could turn winter wheat into spring wheat merely by treating the seeds, then that he could transform one species into another (for example, wheat into rye). His experiments, though never duplicated outside his laboratory, were officially hailed as epitomizing socialist science. Lysenko convinced few scientists, but the omnipotent Stalin accepted his assertions fully. Thus Lysenko acquired enormous power, destroyed his enemies, and made his views into "scientific law." Even Nicholas Vavilov, the USSR's most distinguished geneticist, who was elected president of the International Congress of Genetics in 1939, succumbed to Lysenko's intrigues, perishing in prison after valiant efforts to maintain his scholarly integrity. Lysenko's impact on Soviet biology and agriculture was disastrous. His harebrained schemes inflicted untold damage on crops and livestock, but he was so formidable that agronomists falsified tests of his theories, fearing they might be "planted" for opposing them. Promoted by Stalinist terror, Lysenkoism destroyed most Soviet genetics research for a generation.

Scientists, like artists, were expected to serve the party and Stalin unequivocally. The spirit of inquiry, long characteristic of Russian and Soviet science, died, and many branches of science suffered irreparable harm. Science, art, and literature all became the party's humble servants. Many talented people retreated into abstract, theoretical studies, hoping to avoid the risks of applied science that might endanger their positions and even their lives. Writers composed for their desk drawers; scientists left their laboratories for their private offices. Zhores Medvedev, distinguished scientist and chronicler of the Lysenko affair, described the general atmosphere:

> An unprecedented number of discussions took place in 1935–37 in all fields of science, the arts and literature. As a rule, because of the historical conditions, they were all harsh. Differences of opinion, approach, method, and evaluation of goals are completely natural occurrences in science. Truth is born from argument. But in the environment of the massive repressions of the thirties, the spy hunts and centralized inflaming of passions, and under the conditions of a feverish search after the "enemies of the people" in all spheres of human activity, any scientific discussion tended to become a struggle with political undertones. Nearly every discussion ended tragically for the side represented by the more noble, intellectual, honest, and calm men, who based their arguments on scientific facts.[7]

Only the strength and courage of many men and women dedicated to the pursuit of truth allowed Soviet science and culture to survive at all in this hostile environment.

The political ambiguity of many works of the Fellow Travelers in literature and the lack of conformity in other cultural fields could no longer be tolerated in Stalinist Russia. By 1929 Stalin's personal dictatorship began to impinge directly on the lives of Soviet citizens as industrialization and collectivization moved forward. Stalinist controls were now extended over every aspect of culture. One sign of the shift away from the tolerance of NEP days was Lunacharskii's removal as commissar of education early in 1929. Shortly after came the first signs of tightening party control over literature.

---

[7] Zhores Medvedev, *The Rise and Fall of T. D. Lysenko,* trans. I. M. Lerner (New York, 1971), pp. 5–6.

Partiinost in Literature

The Stalinist technique of extending party controls to literature, repeatedly used and continually refined, was to settle on scapegoats and thus terrorize an entire group into obedience. Scapegoats in literature were Pilniak, heading the All-Russian Union of Writers, and Zamiatin, leading the Leningrad Union of Writers. The attack on them and, by implication, on all Fellow Travelers, signaled a sharp change in literary policy. The prosecution totally bungled charges brought against Pilniak and Zamiatin of arranging publication of their works abroad to avoid Soviet censorship. Both writers presented solid evidence that they had not authorized such foreign publications. Their embarrassed accusers then asserted that these works (and those of other Fellow Travelers) were "anti-Soviet"—defined as any hostile or neutral position. Either one favored socialist construction in the USSR, or one became an "enemy of the people." The message was clear: Fellow Travelers must cease writing unless they wrote politically "correct" literature.

Zamiatin, Pilniak, and their supporters were removed as leaders of the All-Russian Union of Writers, more than half of whose members were purged; it became the All-Russian Union of Soviet Writers, stressing "Soviet." NEP tolerance ended, yielding to an era of "party-oriented" literature. Fellow Travelers now had to prove their "solidarity" with the proletariat, serve the party, and help construct socialism. The Russian Association of Proletarian Writers (RAPP) now dominated the literary scene. Pilniak recanted, but Zamiatin stood his ground and later appealed successfully to Stalin. RAPP, led by Leopold Averbakh and Alexander Fadeev, strongly pressured the Fellow Travelers and attacked "neobourgeois elements" in literature.

RAPP proved ineffective in controlling literature because its members rejected the party view that writings could be produced by directive. Trumpeted a 1930 *Pravda* editorial: "Literature, the cinema, and the arts were levers in the proletariat's hands which must be used to show the masses positive models of initiative and heroic labor." This "positive" emphasis proved too simple and one-sided even for the sincere proletarian writers Averbakh and Fadeev. To them literature had to depict life honestly, both the negative and the positive. Despite their enthusiastic pro-regime stance, proletarian writers of RAPP were out of step with party authorities, who wanted literature and art to portray the heroic struggle to achieve socialism only positively and optimistically and viewed culture as a party weapon to propagandize and mobilize the masses. RAPP writers were still too wedded to "objective art" and individualism, so RAPP was dissolved in 1932. Diverse literary groups were abolished, and henceforth all writers had to belong to a monolithic Union of Soviet Writers, which was wholly party-dominated.

A New Aesthetic: Socialist Realism

More than two years passed before the full impact of the 1932 decisions was felt. Much opposition to party control of literature had to be overcome before the authorities could convene an open writers' congress to formalize the situation. The First All-Union Congress of Soviet Writers met in August 1934. Of the 590 Soviet delegates, more than 60 percent were party members; many prestigious foreign guests were also present. At the congress Andrei Zhdanov (1896–1948) emerged as the party's new authority on cultural affairs and presented the main address, which outlined Soviet literature's future form and content:

> Our Soviet literature is not afraid of being called tendentious, because it *is* tendentious. In the age of the class struggle a non-class, non-tendentious, apolitical literature does not and cannot exist. In our country the outstanding heroes of literary works are the active builders of a new life. . . . Our literature is permeated with enthusiasm and heroism. It is optimistic, but not from any biological instinct. It is optimistic because it is the literature of the class

which is rising, the proletariat, the most advanced and most prospering class.[8]

This was the genesis of "socialist realism," the aesthetic that until the mid-1980s dominated every facet of Soviet culture. Zhdanov defined it as the portrayal of "real" life in all its revolutionary development, the aim of which was to promote the masses' ideological reeducation in socialism. Endorsement of the new doctrine by Gorkii, who presided over the congress and lent his enormous prestige to the new policy, made the doctrine respectable. Delegate after delegate rose mechanically to reiterate Zhdanov's remarks and to endorse "socialist realism." So carefully orchestrated was the congress that even the most prominent writers dared not protest openly against literature's complete identification with party goals. How far would Stalin go to ensure conformity to his "literary" views? In 1934, to be a practicing writer one had to join the Writers' Union and accept its statutes embodying Zhdanov's concepts. Compare this with the tolerant attitude of the 1925 party resolution on literature!

The enormous significance of the First Congress and of "socialist realism" was not recognized immediately. Literary contacts with Western writers increased, and many translations of "progressive" Western authors appeared in the USSR, including works by Hemingway, Dreiser, and Dos Passos. Despite the imposition of narrow-minded socialist realism and the terror of the Great Purge, some decent literature was still being produced as authors skirted ingeniously around socialist realism's dogmas. An example was Iuri Krymov's *Tanker Derbent* (1938), which focused on the personal problems of men engaged in intense competition in the oil shipping business on the Caspian Sea.

Nazism's triumph in Germany and gathering war clouds in the 1930s stimulated Russian nationalism. In 1934 a new orientation in histori-

---

[8] A. Zhdanov et al., *Problems of Soviet Literature* (New York, n.d.), p. 21.

cal writing was decreed. M. N. Pokrovskii (1868–1932), a friend of Lunacharskii, had promoted a Marxist orientation among Soviet professional historians and had virtually eliminated national history from school curricula. History was reduced to vague sociological categories involving class struggle. National heroes were deleted from history texts, and a generation of Soviet schoolchildren grew up largely ignorant of their past. In 1934 Pokrovskii and his followers were denounced as anti-Marxists who had denied Russian history's progressive development. National history and a cult of national heroes were revived. Many authors sounded patriotic themes in their plays and novels. Many works dealt with wars by the Russian people against foreigners. The leading historical novel of the period was Alexis Tolstoy's unfinished three-volume *Peter I* (1929–1944), which became a great popular success considered comparable to Leo Tolstoy's *War and Peace.* Based on extensive research, *Peter I* depicted the "Great Transformer" of Russia very positively.

Appearing simultaneously was Mikhail Sholokhov's four-volume *The Quiet Don* (1928–1940), which masterfully portrays the lives of peasants and Cossacks during World War I, the Revolution, and the Civil War. Sholokhov focused on the moral and psychological problems of individuals struggling to understand events that were engulfing them. Soviet critics claimed that *The Quiet Don* embodied concepts of socialist realism, but it resembles very little the precepts of Zhdanov and the hack writers of the 1930s. Conceived on a scale comparable to *War and Peace, The Quiet Don* traces life in a quiet Cossack village before World War I. As war's outbreak disrupts the village, Sholokhov measures its impact on individuals and families. The second volume probes the difficulties of war, growing discontent, and the Revolution's impact on villagers' lives. The last two volumes record the bitter fighting of the Civil War. The novel touched a responsive chord in Soviet readers, who discovered in it more substance, originality, and power than in all the proletarian writers'

Five Year Plan novels. The first parts of the novel were so moving that many grew skeptical about its authorship. Some claimed Sholokhov had obtained the manuscript of a White Army officer killed during the Civil War and passed it off as his own work. Such charges were denied officially, but rumors persisted (repeated later by Solzhenitsyn) that Sholokhov did not write *The Quiet Don.* Without concrete evidence to the contrary, we must assume that Sholokhov was the author and that his study of human resiliency and fortitude represented a rare bright spot in Soviet literature of the Stalin era.

Literary Victims of Stalinism

The Great Purges (1936–1938) constituted a frightening, sterile period in Soviet history when virtually no one felt safe. The purge cut deeply into intelligentsia ranks. (In the 1970s Solzhenitsyn claimed that more than 600 writers disappeared.) Many established writers were publicly branded "enemies of the people" and disappeared without trace until hastily "rehabilitated" after Stalin's death. The literary intelligentsia was ordered to devour itself, and the Soviet cultural world was terrorized. Those terrible years revealed awesome contrasts—heroism, cowardice, hypocrisy, and shrewd maneuvering. Some hastily denounced friends as traitors, spies, and Trotskyites. Others tried to remain unnoticed or waited in meek resignation. The result was devastation of Soviet culture. The untalented and unscrupulous emerged as Soviet spokespersons. The list of great talents lost in the purge reads like a Who's Who of Soviet literature.

Prominent among the distinguished literary victims of Stalinism was Osip Mandelshtam (1892–1938), a highly educated Jewish poet and one of the 20th century's most talented writers. His elaborate poetry was replete with magnificent archaisms revealing strong Greek Orthodox influence. In 1933 his work was criticized for not reflecting Soviet life and for "distorting reality." Unusual outspokenness doomed Mandelshtam.

Recalled the writer V. Kataev, "He was a real opponent of Stalin. . . . [In 1936 or 1937] he was shouting against Stalin; what a terrible man Stalin was." For writing an acid poem about the dictator, he was arrested during the Great Purge and died in a labor camp.[9]

The Nazi invasion of June 1941 offered a respite from the terror and the inanities of socialist realism. The struggle for national survival against the Germans required unity and cooperation, possible only in a more tolerant, flexible atmosphere. Culture was enlisted in the war effort; party controls, including censorship, were relaxed; and writers and artists were freer to express their talents. Many writers became war correspondents, went to the front, and reported about personal heroism, great battles, and partisan warfare. Some of this writing was sheer propaganda to bolster morale; some was first-rate eyewitness reporting; a few pieces qualified as literature. Ilia Ehrenburg (1891–1967) wrote a memorable two-volume collection, *War* (1941–1942), an extremely moving portrait of a nation resisting the Nazi onslaught. The sieges of Leningrad and Stalingrad (especially K. Simonov's *Days and Nights* about Stalingrad) and cases of personal sacrifice and heroism provided material for hundreds of literary works that inspired and informed the people. This literary outpouring reflected greater party tolerance and flexibility early in the war, reminiscent of NEP. Writers and artists who contributed to the war effort were allowed greater latitude than at any time since the 1920s.

As victory approached, the war-weary Soviet people anticipated being allowed to pursue their interests without interference. Terrible sacrifices had brought triumph and unprecedented prestige to the USSR. Was it not time to loosen the heavy-handed Communist dictatorship and create better lives for all? During the war hints of change were evident everywhere. Strident party ideology was toned down during wartime cooperation with the Western democracies. The Soviet people expected this more open atmosphere to continue, only to be disillusioned cruelly by an abrupt return to prewar harshness.

As early as 1943, when the Red Army began a sustained counteroffensive, the party deplored erosion of ideological orthodoxy. Renewed party ideological vigilance was shown in an attack in late 1943 on the popular satirist Mikhail Zoshchenko (1895–1958), whose humorous collection of autobiographical sketches, *Before Sunrise,* was being successfully serialized in a Soviet journal. Party publications denounced them as unpatriotic "vulgar philistinism" (a favorite term of opprobrium in the postwar era). The series was halted abruptly. Several other prominent writers were criticized for disregarding party guidelines, which reminded them that there were limits to the party's tolerance. Cultural controls remained, but many hoped for liberal changes in postwar party policies toward culture. Some delegates to the first postwar Soviet writers' conference (May 1945) openly opposed renewed party interference in cultural matters.

The party quickly made it clear that such "harmful attitudes" and wartime lapses of discipline would no longer be tolerated. On August 14, 1946, a Central Committee resolution condemned two prominent Leningrad journals, *The Star* and *Leningrad,* for publishing ideologically harmful apolitical works, kowtowing to bourgeois culture, and disparaging Soviet values. This party resolution contained in germ the *Zhdanovshchina,* or era of Andrei Zhdanov's ideological dominance. *Leningrad* was closed down, and a party bureaucrat who became editor of *The Star* obediently banished from its pages "debased" works of Zoshchenko, the poet Anna Akhmatova (1888–1966), and others holding their "antiparty" views. The party again chose scapegoats to initiate a new crackdown, focusing on Leningrad's journals and authors. The party—actually Stalin—feared the city's traditional Western orientation and peculiar sense of independence after heroically surviving a three-year wartime siege. Nor

---

[9] Under the aegis of *glasnost* Mandelshtam was "rehabilitated," and his poetry is again in fashion.

Library of Congress

Anna Andreyevna Akhmatova, 1888–1966. Among the most gifted poets of the 20th century, Akhmatova was a bastion of intellectual integrity during the Stalinist and post-Stalinist periods. Drawing by A. G. Tyshler, from 1965, a year before her death.

the right to evaluate the conduct of human beings. The picture of Soviet life is deliberately and vilely distorted, and caricatured so that Zoshchenko can put into the mouth of his monkey the vile, poisonous anti-Soviet sentiment to the effect that life is better in the zoo than at liberty, and that one breathes more easily in a cage than among Soviet people. Is it possible to sink to a lower political and moral level? And how could the Leningraders endure to publish in their journals such filth and nonsense?[10]

Zoshchenko's work, concluded Zhdanov, was "a vile obscenity." Unless he changed his ways, he could not remain a Soviet writer.

Zhdanov devoted even greater vituperation to Akhmatova, a most distinguished Russian poet. Her poetry's main themes were love and religion, which required her to remain mostly silent in the 1930s. She resumed publishing her lyric poems during and after the war in Leningrad journals. Declared Zhdanov brutally:

> [Her] subject matter is throughout individualist. The range of her poetry is pathetically limited. It is the poetry of a half-crazy gentlelady, who tosses back and forth between the bedroom and the chapel. . . . Half-nun and half-harlot, or rather both nun and harlot, her harlotry is mingled with prayer.[11]

This was no idle criticism, but rather a lethal vendetta.

These official denunciations were quickly translated into action. Both writers were expelled summarily from the All-Russian Union of Writers. Zoshchenko, a broken man, lived in poverty and loneliness until his death in 1958. Akhmatova, too, was forced to remain silent, living isolated and poor, sustained only by her great moral courage until she could publish again after Stalin's death.

was the choice of Zoshchenko and Akhmatova accidental. Influenced by prerevolutionary models, both had won recognition before 1917 and neither had praised the Soviet regime.

Elaborating on the Central Committee resolution at a meeting of Leningrad writers, Zhdanov bitterly denounced Zoshchenko's story "The Adventures of a Monkey" (1945), which had appeared in *The Star.* Zhdanov saw something sinister in this apparently harmless satire about a monkey who escapes from a zoo:

> If you will read that story carefully and think it over, you will see that Zoshchenko casts the monkey in the role of supreme judge of our social order, and has him read a kind of moral lesson to the Soviet people. The monkey is presented as a kind of rational principle having

---

[10] Quoted in Brown, *Russian Literature,* pp. 226–27.
[11] Quoted in Brown, p. 227.

Anticosmopolitanism and the Arts

The campaign against nonconformity, not limited to literature, also engulfed cinema and the arts. Numerous films and artistic works were pilloried as insufficiently ideological or too Western. To ensure clarity about the party's new policies, the Central Committee began issuing a weekly, *Culture and Life*. Its first issue announced:

> All forms and means of ideological and cultural activity of the party and the state—whether the press, propaganda and agitation, science, literature, art, the cinema, radio, museums, or any cultural and educational establishment—must be placed in the service of the Communist education of the masses.

Culture and Life castigated the "degenerate bourgeois culture of the West" and its followers in the USSR. A grave accusation against nonconformists was "cosmopolitanism," defined as servility to Western bourgeois culture. Part of this campaign was to glorify everything Soviet and emphasize Stalin's universal genius. *Culture and Life*, Zhdanov's speeches, and the growing Stalin cult spelled out in narrow limits what cultural workers must do. The results were disastrous. Soviet culture was reduced to a parody of itself. With everything in Soviet life idealized, the Soviet people were touted as the world's most advanced and progressive people with the most creative, original culture. The harsh facts of life in the postwar USSR were ignored. Any attempt to describe Soviet life realistically was branded a slander.

The anticosmopolitan campaign peaked after Zhdanov's mysterious death in 1948, but its roots lay in the immediate postwar period and were first elaborated in Zhdanov's 1946 speeches. "Cosmopolitan" became a synonym for unpatriotic and anti-Soviet. Everything in the West was condemned, and imitating Western models was considered toadyism, or servility before Western bourgeois culture. Any deviation from approved party policies could be labeled cosmopolitanism, the equivalent of treason. Writers ceased to write, wrote for the desk drawer, or produced party-approved drivel and then had to face themselves.

Music

The only branch of cultural activity to survive the deadly party directives was music, perhaps because the USSR boasted some of the world's most talented and famous composers: Prokofiev, Shostakovich, Aram Khachaturian, and N. Ia. Miaskovskii. Idolized by party and public alike as exemplars of Soviet creativity, they were awarded year after year every honor and prize the Soviet Union could bestow. There was also a group of remarkable performers: the violinist David Oistrakh, the pianist Sviatoslav Rikhter, and the cellist Mstislav Rostropovich.

Direct and oppressive political intervention by the party began in 1936 against Shostakovich's opera, *Lady Macbeth of Mtsensk,* based on Nicholas Leskov's novella of 1865. An innovative and controversial work, Shostakovich's opera enjoyed a triumphal premiere in Leningrad in January 1934. During the next two years *Lady Macbeth* achieved unparalleled success for a new Soviet work, with more than 170 performances in Moscow and Leningrad. Soviet critics, while criticizing the opera's more lurid aspects, hailed it as reflecting "the general success of socialist construction, of the correct policy of the party." Such an opera, they gushed, "could have been written only by a Soviet composer brought up in the best traditions of Soviet culture." The youthful Shostakovich had "torn off the masks and exposed the false and lying methods of the composers of bourgeois society." So poorly were the implications of socialist realism then understood, noted a Western critic, that *Lady Macbeth* was then accepted as its epitome.[12]

All went well for *Lady* and its composer until Stalin saw the opera. Having just heard and

---

[12] Boris Schwarz, *Music and Musical Life in Soviet Russia* (Bloomington, IN, 1983) pp. 119*ff.*

praised a patriotic piece for its realism and positive hero, Stalin, whose musical tastes were very conservative, found *Lady Macbeth* repulsive, raucous, and obscene. An unsigned and therefore authoritative article in *Pravda* on January 28, 1936, titled "Confusion Instead of Music," denounced the work as formalist and vulgar, a repudiation of operatic form:

> The listener is flabbergasted from the first moment of the opera by an intentionally ungainly, muddled flood of sounds. Snatches of melody, embryos of musical phrases, drown, escape and drown once more in crashing, gnashing, and screeching. Following this "music" is difficult, remembering it is impossible.[13]

A week later another *Pravda* article denounced Shostakovich's ballet on Soviet themes, *A Limpid Stream,* destroying his career as a ballet composer. With the Great Purge underway, the composer's friends climbed swiftly aboard the bandwagon of criticism. This was a clear warning to composers and other creative artists to conform to the dictates of socialist realism as interpreted by the party and by Stalin personally.

Then the storm subsided, allowing the chastened Shostakovich and other composers to resume writing, but they were more careful to avoid experimental forms of musical expression. During World War II Shostakovich and Prokofiev in particular were once more in vogue, rewarded generously for compositions such as the former's Symphony no. 7 (1942), the *Leningrad* Symphony, and the latter's opera *War and Peace,* based on patriotic themes. Until the beginning of 1948 the Soviet musical world enjoyed a degree of artistic freedom and creative independence out of reach of the literary and artistic intelligentsia. Suddenly, in January 1948, Zhdanov announced that this adulation had been a terrible mistake, that these "great" composers were anti-Soviet hacks, unworthy to use the title "Soviet composer." How did this abrupt about-face occur?

A curious silence descended over the Soviet musical world beginning in December 1947, when some long-awaited premiere performances went practically unnoticed in the press and a number of secondary musical figures simply disappeared without mention. Then, in January 1948, Zhdanov presided over a turbulent meeting of composers and musicians. On February 10th the party Central Committee issued a resolution on music comparable to that on literature of 1946. This resolution on music viciously attacked long-honored and respected artists. The resolution announced:

> The state of affairs is particularly bad in the case of symphonic and operatic music. The Central Committee has here in mind those composers who persistently adhere to the formalist and anti-people school—a school which has found its fullest expression in the works of composers like Comrades Shostakovich, Prokofiev, Khachaturian, Shebalin, Popov, Miaskovskii, and others. Their works are marked by formalist perversions, anti-democratic tendencies which are alien to the Soviet people and their artistic tastes.[14]

The composers were further accused of creating music incomprehensible to the masses. "Disregarding the great social role of music, [these composers] are content to cater to the degenerate tastes of a handful of estheticizing individualists." The intent of the resolution was to drag serious music down to the level of "pop music."

> The divorce between some Soviet composers and the people is so serious that these composers have been indulging in the rotten "theory" that the people are not sufficiently "grown up" to appreciate their music. They think it is no use worrying if people won't listen to their complicated orchestral works, for in a few hundred years they will. This is a

---

[13] D. MacKenzie, "D. D. Shostakovich," in *MERSH* 35 (1983), pp. 33–34.

[14] N. Slominsky, *Music since 1900,* 4th ed. (New York, 1971), pp. 684–88.

thoroughly individualist and anti-people theory, and it has encouraged some of our composers to retire into their own shells.[15]

Thus music was not serving as a vehicle to reeducate the masses in the spirit of socialism! Give the people what they want, Zhdanov told the composers—simple ditties they could sing and hum while they merrily filled, or overfilled, their production quotas.

The impact of the decree on Soviet music was as disastrous as that of the 1946 decree on literature. Khachaturian and Prokofiev adapted themselves as best they could to the new party demands. Shostakovich publicly repented for past "errors," then went right on composing as he always had, making an occasional obeisance to the party authorities. Miaskovskii, already an elderly man whose career stretched back into prerevolutionary times, was destroyed by the resolution and died embittered and defeated in 1951. Prokofiev's work deteriorated in his last years, a change for which the resolution on music of 1948 was at least in part responsible.

These decrees on music and literature must be viewed as part of a general anti-intellectual policy designed to drag culture down to the level of the masses rather than lift the masses up to the level of a sophisticated, creative culture. The Zhdanovshchina represented the triumph of the Stalinist bureaucratic mentality, which enjoyed kicking around those with genuine talent and ability. Zhdanov died in August 1948, but unfortunately his policies did not die with him. One of the supreme ironies of the postwar era was the renaming of the famous University of Leningrad (in 1991 renamed St. Petersburg University) to honor this man who had done so much to poison the intellectual climate of the Soviet Union. It took the death of Stalin to unleash winds of change and usher in a more tolerant and creative atmosphere.

---

[15] Quoted in A. Werth, *Russia: The Postwar Years* (New York, 1971), pp. 356, 358.

Popular Culture

The 1930s witnessed a sea change in Soviet popular culture. The proponents of a new cultural direction assaulted forms they associated with "bourgeois culture," which they had reluctantly tolerated since the revolution. A new "proletarian" culture was needed to replace the mindless entertainment of science fiction, detective stories, romances, fairy tales, folk tales, folk songs, and escape films. Cultural policy in the 1920s had recognized the need to accommodate bourgeois specialists who embodied the traditions of Russian culture and the technical skills that produced it. The new cultural elite, however, sought to fill traditional forms of expression with new Soviet content. What was needed were detective stories that focused on the search for saboteurs and enemies of the people, romances about triumphant Soviet values—hard work, loyalty, responsibility, social consciousness—as opposed to the individualism and self-indulgence of "bourgeois" romances. Fairy tales and folk tales were to be built around confident, optimistic Soviet heroes struggling against the enemies of socialism or against nature itself. Folk traditions were revived, but deprived of all-important religious elements.

Jazz (*dzhaz*) was an enormously popular musical form during the late twenties and early thirties, not only in America and Europe but also in the Soviet Union. This was a form of expression, wildly popular, that Soviet authorities could not effectively control, reshape, or obliterate. Jazz would remain a Russian passion throughout much of the Soviet period. The most popular and successful jazz artists of the Stalin era were Alexander Tsfasman and Leonid Utesov. They were heard everywhere in recordings, on the radio, in concerts, and in films. They were among the most recognizable faces in the Soviet Union, and they were certainly the richest Russians. Tsfasman was a champion of American jazz. He assembled a number of notable jazz groups ranging from a handful to large ensembles of a Glenn Miller type, playing swing music. His heroes were Jimmy

Dorsey and Benny Goodman. He was a master at improvisation and set a generation's toes tapping to American jazz tunes translated into a Russian idiom. Tsfasman's contemporary, Leonid Utesov, was a singer and bandleader who achieved a level of popularity equal to Tsfasman's. Utesov organized his Theatrical Jazz Ensemble in 1929 and quickly made a name for himself touring factories to play during lunch breaks.[16] His hugely successful theatrical jazz was a combination of classic jazz tunes and adaptations of traditional Russian folk songs. Even Stalin enjoyed Utesov's band and brand of music, something that did not endear him to his fellow bandleaders.

Despite that, jazz did not escape the mid-1930s purges unscathed. Many jazz musicians were swept up in the purges, and some of the leading figures in the show trials were jazz fans. Tsfasman and Utesov survived, due in part to protectors in high places. S. Frederick Starr, author of a fine book on Soviet jazz, pointed out, "Soviet jazz endured the Great Terror the way a bear survives winter: by entering a changeless state of hibernation. . . . The survival of jazz was bought at the price of its vitality."[17] The Communist Party elected to co-opt the jazz idiom rather than destroy it. The State Jazz Orchestra of the USSR was established in 1938, and because Tsfasman's ensemble was known to have the best jazz musicians in the country, eleven of its fourteen members were conscripted into the new orchestra.[18] Tsfasman himself declined to participate. The group eventually numbered forty-three, an unwieldy number for a jazz orchestra, which required far greater spontaneity than such size would permit. What the authorities hoped to do was to create a peculiar Soviet brand of jazz with no resemblance to Western, especially American, jazz. Similar state-supported "big bands" spread throughout the Soviet Union, playing music called

dzhaz but bearing little relationship to classical jazz forms.

Dzhaz, like all cultural forms, was called upon to serve the nation in the Great Patriotic War against fascism. As a result of the wartime alliance with the West, Soviet jazz was granted greater freedom and given an opportunity to return to its Western roots. If anything, jazz became more popular during the suffering of wartime and, after a brief backlash in the postwar period, a new generation was prepared to embrace jazz. Jazz bands proliferated throughout the Soviet Union following Stalin's death in 1953.

InfoTrac® College Edition Search Terms

Enter the search term *socialist realism* in the Subject Guide.
Enter the search term *Lysenko* in Keywords.
Enter the search term *Akhmatova* in Keywords.

Suggested Additional Reading

LENINIST CULTURE, 1917–1929

ALEXANDROVNA, V. (pseud.). *A History of Soviet Literature,* trans. M. Ginsburg (Garden City, NY, 1963).

BARNES, A. *Boris Pasternak . . . ,* vol. 1 (New York, 1989).

BAROOSHIAN, V. D. *Russian Cubo-Futurism, 1910–1930* (The Hague, 1974).

BEREDAY, G. F., et al., eds. *The Changing Soviet School* (Boston, 1960).

BLOK, A. *The Twelve,* ed. A. Pyman (Durham, England, 1989).

BROWN, E. J. *Major Soviet Writers: Essays in Criticism* (London, 1973).

———. *Russian Literature Since the Revolution* (Cambridge, MA, 1982).

CHAPPLE, R. L. *Soviet Satire of the Twenties* (Gainesville, FL, 1980).

COMPTON, S. *Russian Avant-Garde Books, 1917–34* (Cambridge, MA, 1993).

CORLEY, F., ed. and trans. *Religion in the Soviet Union: An Archival Reader* (New York, 1996).

[16] S. Frederick Starr, *Red & Hot: The Fate of Jazz in the Soviet Union,* 1983, p. 144.
[17] Ibid., p. 172.
[18] Ibid., p. 176.

CROSS, J. *The Stravinsky Legacy* (Cambridge, England, 1998).

DAVID-FOX, M. *Revolution of the Mind: Higher Learning among the Bolsheviks, 1918–1929* (Ithaca, NY, 1997).

ENTEEN, G. M. *The Soviet Scholar-Bureaucrat: M. N. Pokrovskii and the Society of Marxist Historians* (University Park, PA, 1978).

ERMOLAEV, H. *Soviet Literary Theories, 1917–1934* (New York, 1963, 1977).

FAUCHEREAU, S. *Moscow, 1900–1930* (New York, 1988).

FITZPATRICK, S. *The Commissariat of Enlightenment . . . 1917–1921* (Cambridge, 1970).

———. *The Cultural Front: Power and Culture in Revolutionary Russia* (Ithaca, NY, 1993).

GELDERN, J. VON. *Bolshevik Festivals, 1917–1920* (Berkeley, 1993).

GORKII, M. *On Literature* (Seattle, 1973).

GUERMAN, M. *Art of the October Revolution* (New York, 1979).

HINGLEY, R. *Nightingale Fever: Russian Poets in Revolution* (New York, 1981).

JANECEK, G. *The Look of Russian Literary Avant-Garde Visual Experiments, 1900–1930* (Princeton, 1984).

JOSEPHSON, P. R. *Physics and Politics in Revolutionary Russia.* (Berkeley, 1991).

KENEZ, P. *Cinema and Soviety Society, 1917–1953* (Cambridge, 1992).

KOPP, A. *Soviet Architecture and City Planning, 1917–1953* (New York, 1970).

LEACH, R. *Vsevolod Meyerhold* (Cambridge, 1989).

MAGUIRE, R. *Red Virgin Soil: Soviet Literature in the 1920s* (Evanston, IL, 2000).

MOLLY, L. *Culture in the Future: The Proletkult Movement . . .* (Berkeley, 1990).

NAIMAN, E. *Sex in Public: The Incarnation of Early Soviet Ideology* (Princeton, NJ, 1997).

PHILLIPS, L. L. *Bolsheviks and the Bottle: Drink and Worker Culture in St. Petersburg, 1900–1929* (Dekalb, IL, 2000).

PLATT, K. *History in a Grotesque Key: Russian Literature and the Idea of Revolution* (Stanford, CA, 1997).

POGGOLI, R. *The Poets of Russia, 1890–1930* (Cambridge, MA, 1930).

ROMAN, G. H., and V. H. MARQUARDT. *The Avant-Garde Frontier: Russia Meets the West, 1910–1930* (Gainesville, FL, 1995).

RUSSIAN MUSEUM. *Soviet Art: 1920s–1930s* (Leningrad, 1988).

SIEGELBAUM, L. H. *Soviet State and Society Between Revolutions* (New York, 1992).

STANISLAVSKY, C. *My Life in Art,* trans. J. J. Robbins (London, 1967).

STARR, S. F. *Red and Hot: The Fate of Jazz in the Soviet Union* (New York, 1983).

STRUVE, G. *Russian Literature Under Lenin and Stalin* (Norman, OK, 1971).

TROTSKY, L. *Literature and Revolution* (Ann Arbor, MI, 1960).

TSIVIAN, Y. *Early Cinema and Its Cultural Reception,* trans. A. Bodger (New York, 1994).

YEDLIN, T. *Maxim Gorkey: A Political Biography* (Westport, CT, 1999).

YOUNGBLOOD, D. J. *Movies for the Masses: Popular Cinema and Soviet Society in the 1920s* (New York, 1992).

STALINIST CULTURE, 1929–1953

AKHMATOVA, A. *The Complete Poems,* 2 vols., trans. J. Hemschemey (Somerville, MA, 1990).

ATWOOD, L. *Creating the New Soviet Woman: Women's Magazines as Engineers of Female Identity, 1922–1953* (New York, 1999).

BARTLETT, R. ed., *Shostakovich in Context* (New York, 2000).

BOFFA, G. *The Stalin Phenomenon,* trans. Nicholas Fersen (Ithaca, NY, 1992).

BONNELL, V. *Iconography of Power: Soviet Political Posters under Lenin and Stalin* (Berkeley, CA, 1999).

BORDWELL, D. *The Cinema of Eisenstein* (Cambridge, MA, 1993).

BOWLT, J. E., ed. and trans. *Russian Art of the Avant-Garde . . . , 1902–1934* (New York, 1976).

BOWRA, C. M. *Poetry and Politics, 1900–1960* (Cambridge, 1966).

BRINTLINGER, A. *Writing a Usable Past: Russian Literary Culture, 1917–1937* (Evanston, IL, 2000).

BROOKS, J. *Thank you, Comrade Stalin! Soviet Public Culture from Revolution to Cold War* (Princeton, NJ, 2000).

BROWN, E. J. *The Proletarian Episode in Russian Literature, 1928–1932* (New York, 1953, 1971).

DUNHAM, V. *In Stalin's Time: Middle-Class Values in Soviet Fiction* (New York, 1976).

EHRLICH, V. *Modernism and Revolution: Russian Literature in Transition* (Cambridge, MA, 1994).

ERMOLAEV, H. *Mikhail Sholokhov and His Art* (Princeton, 1982).

FAY, L. E. *Shostakovich: A Life* (New York and Oxford, 1999).

FITZPATRICK, S. *Education and Social Mobility in the Soviet Union, 1921–1934* (New York, 1979).

FITZPATRICK, S., A. RABINOWITCH, and R. STITES, eds. *Russia in the Era of NEP: Explorations in Soviet Society and Culture* (Bloomington, IN, 1991).

GARRARD, J., and C. GARRARD. *Inside the Soviet Writers' Union* (New York, 1990).

GLEASON, A., et al., eds. *Bolshevik Culture: Experiment and Order in the Russian Revolution* (Bloomington, IN, 1985).

GRAHAM, L. *Science and Philosophy in the Soviet Union* (New York, 1970).

GÜNTHER, H., ed. *The Culture of the Stalin Period* (New York, 1990).

HAYWARD, M. *Writers in Russia: 1917–1978,* ed. Patricia Blake (San Diego, 1983).

HAYWARD, M., and L. LABEDZ, eds. *Literature and Revolution in Soviet Russia, 1917–1962* (New York, 1963).

HOLMGREN, B. *Women's Works in Stalin's Time: On Lidia Chukovskaia and Nadezhda Mandelstam* (Bloomington, IN, 1993).

HUSBAND, W. B. *"Godless Communists": Atheism and Society in Soviet Russia 1917–1932* (Dekalb, IL, 1999).

JORAVSKY, D. *The Lysenko Affair* (Cambridge, MA, 1970).

KENEZ, P. *Cinema and Soviet Society, 1917–1953* (New York, 1992).

KREBS, S. D. *Soviet Composers and the Development of Soviet Music* (New York, 1970).

MARGOLIN, V. *The Struggle for Utopia: Rodchenko, Lissitsky, Moholy-Nagy, 1917–1946* (Chicago, 1997).

MARSH, R. *Images of Dictatorship: Portraits of Stalin in Literature* (London, 1989).

MATHEWSON, R. W. *The Positive Hero in Russian Literature* (Stanford, 1978).

MCDONALD, I. *The New Shostakovich* (Boston, 1990).

MEDVEDEV, Z. A. *The Rise and Fall of T. D. Lysenko,* trans. I. M. Lerner (Garden City, NY, 1971).

MILLER, F. J. *Folklore for Stalin: Russian Folklore and Pseudo-folklore of the Stalin Era* (Armonk, NY, 1990).

ROBIN, R. *Socialist Realism: The Impossible Aesthetic,* trans. Catherine Porter (Stanford, 1992).

ROSENBERG, W. G., ed. *Bolshevik Visions: First Phase of the Cultural Revolution in Soviet Russia,* 2 vols. (Ann Arbor, MI, 1989).

RUBENSTEIN, J. *Tangled Loyalties: The Life and Times of Ilya Ehrenburg* (New York, 1996).

SCHWARZ, B. *Music and Musical Life in Soviet Russia, 1917–1981* (Bloomington, IN, 1983).

SCHWEITZER, V. *Tsvetaeva.* trans. R. Chandler and H. T. Willetts (New York, 1992).

SICHER, E. *Jews in Russian Literature After the October Revolution* (Cambridge, 1995).

SLONIM, M. *Soviet Russian Literature . . . , 1917–1967* (New York, 1967).

STEWART, B. H. *Mikhail Sholokhov: A Critical Introduction* (Ann Arbor, MI, 1967).

STITES, R. *Russian Popular Culture: Entertainment and Society Since 1900* (New York, 1995).

———, ed. *Culture and Entertainment in Wartime Russia* (Bloomington, IN, 1995).

STRUVE, G. *Russian Literature Under Lenin and Stalin, 1917–1953* (Norman, OK, 1971).

TARKHANOV, A. and S. KAVTARADZE. *Architecture of the Stalin Era* (New York, 1992).

TAYLOR, R., and I. CHRISTIE, eds. *Inside the Film Factory: New Approaches to Russian and Soviet Cinema* (New York, 1991).

TAYLOR, R., and D. SPRING, eds. *Stalinism and Soviet Cinema.* (New York, 1993).

VARSHAVSKY, S., and B. REST. *The Ordeal of the Hermitage: The Siege of Leningrad, 1941–1944* (Leningrad and New York, 1985).

VELINSKY, S. ed. *Till My Tale Is Told: Women's Memoirs of the Gulag* (Bloomington, IN, 1999).

WALSH, S. *The Music of Stravinsky* (New York, 1988).

WELLS, D. *Anna Akhmatova: Her Poetry* (Oxford, UK, 1996).

YARMOLINSKY, A., ed. *A Treasury of Russian Verse* (New York, 1949).

13

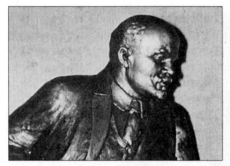

Soviet Foreign Relations to 1941

After the Bolshevik Revolution, Soviet foreign policy comprised an intricate combination of national and ideological elements. Some Western historians, stressing the elements of continuity between tsarist Russian and Soviet policies, have argued that geography and historical experience determine a country's basic interests, regardless of political regime. Emphasizing such persistent aims as the desire for security, urge for access to the sea, manifest destiny in Asia, and leadership of the Slav peoples, they contend that Soviet policy was pragmatic and power oriented. Other foreign scholars (notably Western ex-Communists), at least until the 1960s, considered Marxism-Leninism paramount and a blueprint for world domination. Soviet leaders, they argued, sought by every means to create a world Communist system run from Moscow and regarded relations with the capitalist world as a protracted conflict that would last until one side triumphed. Believing that all Soviet moves aimed to promote world revolution, this group concluded it was fruitless, even harmful, for the West to make agreements with the USSR. A middle view inter-

preted Soviet foreign policy as combining traditional and ideological elements: Revolutionary beliefs and ideology predominated at first, then pragmatic nationalism increased as Soviet leaders gradually reverted to more conservative policies based on power, geography, and history.

An important ideological foundation for Soviet foreign policy was provided by Lenin's pamphlet *Imperialism, the Highest Stage of Capitalism* (1916), which long remained established doctrine in Soviet Russia. Written in Swiss exile in the midst of World War I, it updated and globalized Marxism despite being singularly unoriginal. (It was based chiefly on works of two European socialists, J. A. Hobson and Rudolf Hilferding.) The pamphlet revealed Lenin's thinking about the capitalist world, positing an inevitable and protracted conflict between it and Soviet socialism. Lenin defined imperialism as finance or monopoly capitalism, controlled by bankers, that had developed from the earlier industrial capitalism of Marx's time:

> Imperialism is capitalism in that stage of development in which the domination of

monopoly and finance capital has taken shape; in which the export of capital has acquired pronounced importance; in which the division of the world by international trusts has begun, and in which the partition of all the territory of the earth by the greatest capitalist countries has been completed.

A relentless search for raw materials, markets, and investment opportunities had provoked quarrels among leading capitalist countries, ending in World War I. That war, Lenin predicted, would bring capitalism crashing down, breaking first like a chain at its weakest link, perhaps in Russia. Eventually imperialism would succumb to its internal contradictions—among imperialist powers and power blocs, and between individual imperialist countries and their rebellious overseas colonies. The final outcome, gloated Lenin, could only be worldwide socialist revolution and the demise of capitalism.

What were the major aims of Soviet foreign policy until 1941? At first Lenin and Trotskii strove to foment revolution abroad because they believed that otherwise world capitalism would crush Soviet Russia. War-weary Europe, especially Germany, seemed ripe for revolution, and Comintern leaders long remained confident that one would occur. A second, apparently conflicting aim soon emerged and became paramount: to preserve the Soviet regime and power base, if need be at the expense of foreign Communists. Moscow, therefore, sought to divide capitalist powers, prevent anti-Soviet coalitions, and woo colonial peoples. As long as their military weakness persisted, Soviet leaders aimed to avoid war with major capitalist powers.

To achieve these goals Soviet leaders forged a variety of instruments. The Comintern and Soviet party coordinated the Communist parties that developed in most foreign countries. Because until 1945 the USSR was the only Communist power, most foreign Communists looked to Moscow for inspiration and direction. Especially under Stalin, Communist parties abroad became subservient to Soviet policy. Each had a legal organization, which propagated Soviet views in democratic countries, was represented in legislatures, led labor unions, and criticized anti-Soviet cabinets. Illegal underground bodies, operating if the open ones were suppressed, conducted subversion and sabotage. Soviet commercial missions and skillful radio and newspaper propaganda supplemented the work of these parties.

The Soviet regime instituted a new diplomacy. As commissar of foreign affairs, Trotskii believed initially that diplomacy would soon disappear because world revolution was supposedly imminent. He declared confidently: "We'll issue a few decrees, then shut up shop." At Brest-Litovsk he had repudiated the norms and even the dress of old, secret European diplomacy, but once the revolutionary wave subsided, Soviet diplomacy became important and its diplomats donned traditional formal dress. Moscow, however, scorned permanent accommodation with other nations, and Soviet diplomacy prepared the way for future expansion by lulling capitalist countries into false security, winning temporary concessions, and splitting the capitalist camp. Whereas under Lenin and Chicherin diplomacy remained innovative and flexible, Stalin bound his diplomats with rigid, detailed instructions.

The Soviets before 1941 made little use of force—the ultimate sanction in foreign policy—because of military weakness. During the Polish-Soviet War of 1919–1920, they attempted unsuccessfully to spread revolution on Red Army bayonets, but only in 1939–1940 was force used effectively against weaker Finland and the Baltic states.

In matters of foreign policy, Lenin's voice proved decisive. In the first months of the regime, policies were debated freely in the Central Committee and Politburo, and sometimes he was outvoted. Then the Politburo, under Lenin's direction, became the chief policymaking body in foreign affairs, and its decisions were transmitted to the People's Commissariat of Foreign Affairs (Narkomindel) for implementation. Lenin formulated foreign policy and built up the Soviet diplomatic service. Noted Foreign Commissar Georgi Chicherin right after Lenin's death:

> In the first years of the existence of our republic, I spoke with him by telephone several times a day, often at length, and had frequent, personal interviews with him. Often I discussed with him all the details of current diplomatic affairs of any importance. Instantly grasping the substance of each issue . . . , Vladimir Ilich [Lenin] always provided in his conversations the most brilliant analysis of our diplomatic situation and his counsels . . . were models of diplomatic art and flexibility.[1]

Tsarist traditions in foreign affairs were restored fully by Stalin. Let us now examine Soviet policies chronologically. Each of the five periods between 1917 and 1941 reflected a different approach toward the antagonist—the capitalist world.

First Revolutionary Era, 1917–1921

For the new Soviet government, a first priority was to redeem Bolshevik pledges to take Russia out of World War I. That war, which Lenin had long proclaimed to be an imperialist struggle, had undermined both the tsarist regime and its successor, the Provisional Government. Lenin's "Decree on Peace," approved on November 7, 1917, by the Second All-Russian Congress of Soviets, had been foreshadowed by his fourth "Letter from Afar" in March, in which he had stated that the Petrograd Soviet should repudiate treaties concluded by previous Russian governments. The Decree on Peace proposed to all warring peoples and their governments "to begin immediately negotiations for a just and lasting peace . . . without annexations . . . and indemnities." It continued: "The [Soviet] government abolishes secret diplomacy and . . . expresses the firm intention to carry on all negotiations absolutely openly before all the people and immediately begins to publish in full the secret treaties concluded or confirmed

by [previous Russian governments]."[2] Following this declaration was President Wilson's "Fourteen Points" (January 1918), which resembled it closely in phraseology. Lenin urged all belligerents to conclude an immediate armistice, during which their representatives could negotiate a permanent and nonimperialistic peace settlement. One purpose of his Decree was to provoke general peace negotiations so that a weak Soviet Russia need not face the Central Powers alone. Bolshevik leaders may have believed also that the appeal would touch off revolutions throughout Europe.

The allied powers ignored Lenin's appeal and his Soviet regime, but the German imperial government responded eagerly to his call for an armistice. Disregarding Lenin's demagogic appeal to German workers, the Berlin government and high command saw great potential strategic and psychological advantages from concluding a separate peace with Soviet Russia. By liquidating the eastern front, Germany could shift millions of troops westward and perhaps deliver a knockout blow in France to Allied armies before American troops could arrive in great force.

Leon Trotskii, after firing diplomats of the Provisional Government, had taken charge of the new People's Commissariat of Foreign Affairs (Narkomindel). Believing world revolution to be imminent, and traditional European secret diplomacy outmoded, Trotskii directed the new agency haphazardly with inexperienced personnel until replaced in March 1918 by Georgii Chicherin, who restored order and improved efficiency.

Peace negotiations between Soviet Russia and the Central Powers dragged on with interruptions from late December 1917 until March 1918 at Brest-Litovsk, German headquarters for the eastern front. The Soviet delegation, soon headed by Trotskii himself, proposed a peace without annexations and delivered inflammatory revolutionary appeals over the heads of the German delegates to the war-weary peoples of Europe. General Max

---

[1] *Izvestiia*, January 30, 1924, p. 2.

[2] A. Rubinstein, *The Foreign Policy of the Soviet Union* (New York, 1972), pp. 51–52.

von Hoffman of Germany, however, aiming to erect satellite states in western Russia, insisted that all German-occupied areas be separated from Russia. To obtain Ukrainian resources, the Germans reached agreement with the anti-Bolshevik Rada (February 9th) and detached all of Ukraine from Russia. These stiff German territorial demands caused Trotskii to suspend negotiations in January and return to Petrograd.

The Bolshevik Central Committee now held its first great debate over foreign policy. Left Bolsheviks and Left SRs urged a revolutionary war to promote the triumph of world revolution. Lenin argued that preservation of revolution in Russia must take precedence over the uncertain prospects of world revolution and over the interests of the international proletariat. He demanded an immediate end to the war: "For the success of socialism in Russia, . . . not less than several months will be necessary . . . to vanquish the bourgeoisie in our own country." The Central Committee approved Trotskii's compromise formula of "no war, no peace"; that is, Russia would neither fight nor sign a treaty with Imperial Germany.

The Germans responded with a swift offensive toward Petrograd. As they advanced, the alarmed Bolshevik leaders, including Lenin, favored seeking aid from the Allies. Despite efforts in this direction by unofficial Allied agents in Russia, Allied governments ignored these overtures. With the Germans approaching Petrograd, Lenin finally convinced the majority of the Central Committee to accept new, harsher German peace terms.

In the summer of 1918 the Allies intervened militarily in Russia's civil war (see Chapter 32). According to Soviet historians, they sought to overthrow Bolshevism, set up spheres of interest, and exploit Russia's resources. But George Kennan, a leading American diplomat, asserted that the Allies had aimed to restore an eastern front, win the war, and keep their supplies out of German hands. British and French military leaders pushed for intervention, but President Wilson sent token U.S. forces most reluctantly. Allied troops did little fighting in Russia, but the Allies equipped and supplied Russian White forces long after World War I ended. Proponents (Churchill) argued that Allied intervention prolonged White resistance and stalled world revolution; recent opponents (Kennan) claim that it helped alienate Soviet Russia from the West. Allied intervention produced international stalemate because neither Soviet Russia nor the West could destroy the other; this situation suggested that outside powers cannot decide a civil war in a major country.

Allied hostility fed the extreme Soviet policies of those years. As German revolutionary socialists (Spartacists) fought for power in Berlin, Lenin, in January 1919, invited leftist European socialists to the First Comintern Congress. Of 35 delegates who attended, only 5 came from abroad, and even they did not truly represent their parties. Russian-dominated from the start, the Comintern, or Third International, gave Lenin a nucleus for a world Communist movement, though it was too feeble then to organize revolutions abroad. During the Second Comintern Congress of August 1920, as the Red Army advanced in Poland, delegates from 41 countries waxed optimistic over prospects for world revolution, until Soviet defeat before Warsaw dashed their hopes. Twenty-one conditions for admission, which sought to impose the Russian party's tight discipline, were approved, but for some years the Comintern remained a loose collection of parties with factions and heated debates. By 1924, when it became a disciplined tool of Soviet policy, revolutionary opportunities abroad had dwindled.

The Allies excluded war-torn Soviet Russia from the Paris Peace Conference of 1919. Soviet-Western ideological and military antagonisms were at their peak, and in the West people were searching for Communists under every bed. Before the Conference, Prime Minister David Lloyd George of Great Britain wrote:

> Personally, I would have dealt with the Soviets as the de facto government of Russia. So would President Wilson. But we both agreed that we could not carry to that extent our colleagues at the Congress nor the public

opinion of our countries which was frightened by Bolshevik violence and feared its spread.[3]

Preoccupied with Germany, the Allies neglected Soviet Russia and its relationship with Europe. (See Map 13.1.) This rebuff fed Bolshevik hostility to the peace settlement and the League of Nations, which the Soviets regarded as a potential capitalist coalition against them, and drew the two outcasts—Weimar Germany and Soviet Russia—together.

In 1919 halfhearted private Allied overtures to Soviet Russia failed, but during 1920 relations began to improve. Once the Allies withdrew from Russia and the White armies were defeated, the Bolsheviks sought Western aid to restore Russia's wrecked economy. Lloyd George, favoring recognition of Soviet Russia and restoration of normal economic ties, helped end the Allied blockade. "We have failed to restore Russia to sanity by force. I believe we can save her by trade," he told Parliament. The Polish-Soviet War delayed normal relations, but by early 1921 Red Army defeats in Poland and Western desires to win Russian markets laid a basis for accommodation.

Accommodation, 1921–1927

Lenin warned Moscow leftists late in 1920 that an era of coexistence with capitalism was dawning. European capitalist economies were reviving, and even the intransigent Trotskii admitted, "History has given the bourgeoisie a fairly long breathing spell. . . . The revolution is not so obedient, so tame that it can be led on a leash as we imagined."[4] The Polish conflict, ended by the Treaty of Riga (March 1921), left Soviet Russia weakened. Ukraine proper became a Soviet republic, but Poland acquired parts of Belorussia and western Ukraine. After seven years of strife, Russia's economy faced collapse. Lenin, confronting peasant uprisings and the Kronstadt revolt, launched the

New Economic Policy at home and a conciliatory policy toward the West.

To strengthen itself for subsequent conflict, Soviet Russia now sought diplomatic recognition, trade, and credits from the West. Recognition would provide some security against attack and aid Soviet efforts to divide capitalist countries and win trade concessions. The West reacted favorably because European industries needed export markets and their governments, never truly committed to overthrowing the Soviet regime, longed for normal relations. Obstacles to settlement included Comintern propaganda in the West and its colonies and, in particular, Russian debts. Western claims, totaling about 14 billion rubles (roughly 7 billion dollars), included pre–World War I tsarist debts, wartime borrowing, and compensation for nationalized European property; the Soviets made huge counterclaims for damage done by Allied intervention. The West agreed that wartime debts and Allied damage to Russia nearly canceled each other out, but the French especially sought repayment of the prewar debt, most of which they held, and reimbursement for confiscated property. When Russia demurred, debt negotiations broke down; but the Soviets, making token concessions on propaganda, obtained some short-term credits, trade agreements, and diplomatic recognition from all major powers except the United States. Even this refusal of recognition did not prevent extensive U.S. technological assistance and some Soviet-American trade during the 1920s.

The shift to accommodation enhanced the role of Soviet diplomacy directed by an able professional, Georgii Chicherin (foreign commissar, 1918–1930). An ex-Menshevik of noble birth who had once worked for the tsarist foreign ministry, Chicherin was an idealistic socialist, dedicated, scholarly, and hardworking. However, with his dubious past (from a Bolshevik standpoint), he never achieved high rank or influence in the Soviet Communist Party. Abroad, he had to contend with the Comintern, Profintern (international trade union organization), secret police, and foreign trade and tourist agencies. Furthermore, the Narkomindel lacked even the degree of authority

---

[3] Quoted in George Kennan, *Russia and the West Under Lenin and Stalin* (Boston, 1960), p. 124.
[4] Quoted in Kennan, *Russia and the West*, p. 179.

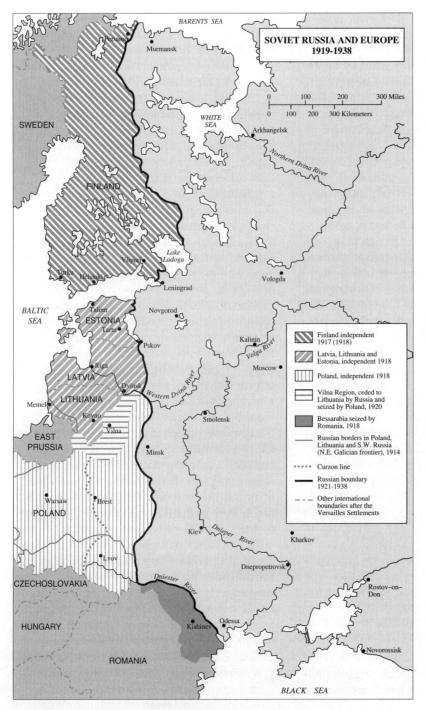

Map 13.1 Soviet Russia and Europe, 1919–1938

enjoyed by the tsarist foreign office. After 1919 formulation and decision making in both foreign and domestic affairs were concentrated in the Politburo of the Russian Communist Party, rather than the Party Congress or Central Committee. During Lenin's illnesses of 1922–1923, the Politburo decided foreign policy issues collectively, then transmitted its decisions to Chicherin for implementation. However, when healthy, Lenin formulated basic theoretical and practical concepts of foreign policy himself and devoted much attention to organizing the new Soviet diplomatic service. His fertile political imagination and tactical skill made him preeminent in determining the general outlines of early Soviet foreign policy. With Lenin acting basically as his own foreign minister, Chicherin's position resembled that of Foreign Minister Gorchakov in the 1860s—executing policies already determined by the head of state. The Politburo frequently bypassed the Narkomindel, the rival Comintern did not keep it informed, and the government, affirming that the Comintern was an independent agency, disclaimed responsibility for its moves. Nonetheless, Chicherin achieved real gains by persistent diplomacy.

The Genoa Conference (April 1922) marked his, and Soviet Russia's, diplomatic debut. In western Europe, Genoa was conceived as an international effort to restore Europe's depressed economy by drawing in both of its pariahs— Weimar Germany and Soviet Russia. At the opening session of the Conference, Chicherin declared:

> While maintaining . . . their communist principles . . . , the Russian delegation recognize that in the present period of history, which permits the parallel existence of the old social order and of the new [socialist] order now being born, economic collaboration between the states representing these two systems of property is imperatively necessary for the general economic reconstruction.[5]

To the West, Chicherin held out alluring prospects of extensive trade with Soviet Russia and lucrative investment in nascent Siberian industries, coupling this with a proposal for general disarmament. However, his main objective remained to separate Weimar Germany from the victor powers and reach a diplomatic accord with it.

Chicherin achieved this objective brilliantly at Rapallo, Italy. Exploiting Western coolness and snubs toward the Germans at Genoa, he induced Weimar delegates to meet with him at nearby Rapallo. To the consternation of the British and French, Germany and Soviet Russia promptly concluded the Treaty of Rapallo involving mutual diplomatic recognition, cancellation of debts and claims, and agreements to expand and normalize trade. Although Western liberals viewed Rapallo as a sinister Soviet-German conspiracy, the Germans regarded it as inaugurating for them an independent foreign policy and escape from the consequences of defeat in World War I. The Soviets considered Rapallo a model agreement with a bourgeois state, leaving them full freedom of action. They interpreted it as splitting European capitalism and enabling them to reach useful accords with the weaker segment. Rapallo, Moscow concluded, scotched dangers of European economic action against Soviet Russia and brought it out of diplomatic and economic isolation. Simultaneously, clandestine military cooperation was taking shape: The Germans were constructing arms factories in Soviet Russia and trying out new weapons, including tanks, prohibited to them by the Treaty of Versailles. (The Soviets had a share of the weapon production.) During the severe crisis that confronted Weimar Germany during 1923, policy differences surfaced between Narkomindel and the Comintern. While Chicherin supported the Weimar government and Soviet Russia shipped grain to Germany, the Comintern backed efforts by the German Communist Party to overthrow it. The Comintern suffered a grave reversal as evidence mounted that prospects for a Communist revolution in Germany were all but dead. Continuing rivalry between Narkomindel and Comintern, however, reflected merely differing tactics, not a conflict of basic aims.

[5] Jane Degras, ed., *Soviet Documents on Foreign Policy* (New York, 1951–1953, 1983), vol. 1, p. 298.

Chicherin's policy of normalizing relations with the rest of Europe, though generally successful, also suffered setbacks. During Anglo-Soviet negotiations for trade and credits erupted the "Zinoviev Letter" (October 1924), whose authenticity remains disputed. Supposedly containing instructions from the Comintern president to British Communists to subvert the armed forces, the letter caused a furor, provoking a "Red scare" in Great Britain, contributing to the downfall of the Labor government, and severely straining Anglo-Soviet relations. Another diplomatic reverse followed: The Locarno Agreements of 1925 between Germany and the former Allied powers excluded the USSR completely and achieved a brief era of apparent European unity and harmony. Despite such reverses, Chicherin's diplomacy, by ending Soviet isolation and reaching accord with Weimar Germany, enhanced Soviet security and contributed to its economic recovery. Only a year after Locarno the Soviet-German Treaty of Berlin (April 1926), reaffirming the provisions of Rapallo, stipulated neutrality if either country were attacked by a third power.

However, Soviet hostility toward the League of Nations persisted. From its inception the League had been viewed in Moscow as a concealed capitalist coalition against Soviet Russia. Soviet hostility resulted partly from the latter's exclusion from the Paris Peace Conference of 1919 and partly because the League was dominated in the interwar period by leading capitalist powers, Great Britain and France. Furthermore, international stability and prosperity, fostered by the League, would reduce Communist prospects for world revolution. A Soviet press statement on the League of Nations declared in November 1925:

> We regard the League of Nations . . . not as a friendly association of peoples working for the general good, but as a masked league of the so-called Great Powers, who have appropriated to themselves the right of disposing of the fate of weaker nations. . . . Certain Powers are counting on using Germany to assist in carrying out . . . their hostile designs against the USSR. . . . The League is a cover for the prepa-

ration of military action for the suppression of small and weak nationalities.[6]

Not until 1934 would the Soviets alter their hostility toward the League.

Asia had remained secondary in Soviet policy. Lenin recognized the revolutionary potential of colonial peoples in undermining Western imperialism, but Soviet Russia was too weak to exploit it. Soviet Russia promptly repudiated tsarist imperial privileges and spheres of interest, most of which it could not retain anyway. To weaken Franco-British influence in the Near East and enhance Soviet security, Lenin supported such nationalists as Kemal Pasha of Turkey. The Soviets appealed to colonial peoples, notably at the Comintern-sponsored Baku Congress of September 1920. Zinoviev told delegates from 37 nationalities: "The Communist International turns today to the peoples of the East and says to them: 'Brothers, we summon you to a Holy War first of all against British Imperialism.'"[7] This was purely a propaganda campaign, but later many Asian revolutionaries were trained in the USSR, with profound consequences for the West.

Justifiably, Soviet leaders regarded China as the key to Asia. They promptly condemned European imperialism there and renounced most special Russian privileges, though in 1921 the Red Army entered Outer Mongolia, ostensibly pursuing White generals, and established a Communist puppet government. Mongolia served until 1991 as a buffer and Russian base on China's frontier. During the early 1920s Moscow maintained formal relations with the weak Beijing government while Soviet agents, led by Mikhail Borodin, penetrated the Canton regime. Its leader, Sun Yat-sen, who had led the Chinese Revolution of 1912, aimed to expel foreign imperialism and to achieve national unity and social reform. With Borodin's aid, he built the Kuomintang (Nationalist Party) on the model of the Soviet Communist Party.

---

[6] Degras, *Soviet Documents,* vol. 2, pp. 65–66.
[7] Quoted in Louis Fischer, *The Soviets in World Affairs, 1917–1929* (Princeton, 1951), vol. 1, p. 283.

Sun's death in 1925 left a vacuum in Canton soon filled by Chiang Kai-shek, a young Moscow-trained nationalist officer. The Stalin-Trotskii struggle affected Soviet policy: Convinced that China was entering its bourgeois-democratic revolution, Stalin favored proletarian participation in a national bloc including peasants and bourgeoisie and urged the Communists to enter the Kuomintang. Trotskii, however, advocated an armed Communist uprising and a direct transition to socialism in China. Stalin's policy prevailed, but during his northward expedition in 1926, Chiang slaughtered Communists in Shanghai, expelled Soviet advisers, and soon ruled much of China. Stalin's policies there, based on inadequate knowledge of the situation, had plainly failed.

Neoisolationism, 1928–1933

Stalin's ascendancy brought a return to autocracy in Soviet domestic and foreign policies and produced a docile and subservient Comintern. Removing potential and actual rivals from positions of power and influence at home and launching forced collectivization and massive industrialization, Stalin abroad raised as a smokescreen the danger of imminent attacks on the USSR by powerful capitalist states. Envious and distrustful of cosmopolitan, intellectual Old Bolsheviks such as Zinoviev and Bukharin, he acted to undermine their influence and sever ties with European socialism. In these years occurred a marked growth of deliberate isolation from European affairs.

In his report to the 15th Party Congress (December 1927), Stalin intimated that a major shift in Soviet foreign policy was imminent and raised the specter of renewed capitalist assaults against the USSR:

> Whereas a year or two ago it was possible and necessary to speak of . . . "peaceful coexistence" between the USSR and the capitalist countries, today . . . *the period of "peaceful coexistence" is receding into the past,* giving place to a

period of imperialist assaults and preparation for intervention against the USSR.[8]

Soon afterward Stalin accused France, which he considered the dominant European power, of making preparations to attack the Soviet Union, which he surely did not believe and for which there was not a shred of evidence. The Sixth Comintern Congress of September 1928, an obedient Stalinist body, proclaimed the USSR to be the sole bastion of world revolution and stressed that all Communist parties owed exclusive allegiance to Moscow; their local interests must be subordinated to preserving the USSR.

While accusing Western capitalist nations of plotting war, Stalin emphasized that Soviet foreign policy sought consistently to preserve peace. At the 16th Congress of June 1930 he affirmed:

> As a result of this policy of negotiating trade and non-aggression pacts . . . we have succeeded in maintaining peace . . . in spite of a number of provocative acts . . . of the warmongers. We will continue to pursue this policy of peace with all our might. . . . We do not want a single foot of foreign territory, but we will not surrender a single inch of our territory to anyone.[9]

Indeed, despite Stalin's intransigent and frequently alarmist tone, Soviet foreign policy in these years remained cautious and pacific, avoiding confrontations with capitalist powers. Stalin appears to have counted on the preservation of world peace during the First Five Year Plan and continued to sound this theme until 1939.

The Great Depression (1929–1933) convinced Moscow of the correctness of its policy line against Western democratic socialists. Predicting the imminent demise of world capitalism, Soviet leaders concluded that this would leave Social Democrats as the only important remaining barrier throughout the world to the conquest of power by the working class led by the Communists. Declared Politburo member V. M. Molotov: "Social

---

[8] Joseph Stalin, *Works* (Moscow, 1955), vol. 10, pp. 282*ff.*
[9] Stalin, *Works,* vol. 12, pp. 268–69.

fascism with its 'left' wing is the last resource of the bourgeoisie among the workers."

Stalin's theory of "social fascism," which claimed that Western socialists had adopted fascist policies, helped undermine democracy in Weimar Germany and bring Adolf Hitler to power. Stalin detested the democratic, pro-Western policies of the German Social Democrats (SPD), but he also distrusted the large and volatile German Communist Party (KPD) and doubted he could control it if it achieved power. Thus, Stalin, playing Communists against Social Democrats, ordered the KPD to collaborate with the Nazis against a Weimar Republic undermined by the Depression. Believing that the capitalists were already in power in Germany and that the Nazis were likewise bourgeois, Stalin concluded that Hitler in power, rather than launch a revolution against capitalism, would crush moderate socialism and cause Germany's defection from the Western camp and its dependence on the USSR. To desperate pleas by German Social Democrats for Communist aid against the Nazis, the reply of the Soviet embassy was: The road to a Soviet Germany lies through Hitler. Thus Stalin bears considerable responsibility for the triumph of Nazism in Germany, which later would prove so costly to the USSR. Even after Hitler assumed power (January 1933), Stalin persisted in regarding France as the chief Soviet foe, apparently out of ignorance about German conditions.

In the Far East, Stalin pursued a cautious, defensive course. In 1928 he severed relations with Chiang's nationalist regime, and the next year, after local authorities seized the Chinese Eastern Railway, the Red Army restored it to Soviet control. Once Japan seized Manchuria in 1931 and turned it into the puppet state of Manchukuo, Stalin became gravely concerned about Japanese militarism. Reinforcing the Red Army in the Far East, he sought agreement with Japan, even offering to sell it the Chinese Eastern Railway. He restored relations with Chiang, tried to prevent Sino-Japanese cooperation against the USSR, and sought rapprochement with the United States.

Meanwhile the USSR was advocating peace and disarmament for Europe. Maxim Litvinov,

Chicherin's longtime assistant who succeeded him as foreign commissar in 1930, proposed total disarmament at the Geneva Disarmament Conference of 1932 but found little response. In January 1933 Hitler assumed power in Germany and influenced Stalin to alter his foreign policy. Deep in the Depression, the West no longer threatened the USSR, but the chief beneficiaries were not Communism but aggressive German Nazism and Japanese militarism.

Collective Security, 1934–1937

Worried by the rising Nazi threat, Stalin gradually abandoned isolationism and opposition to the Versailles system to seek reconciliation with the West. During 1932 the Soviets had normalized relations with such neighbors as Finland, Estonia, and Poland, then with France. In 1934 Soviet diplomacy tried to erect an east European alliance to protect its western borders, but Poland demurred. Meanwhile, diplomatic relations were established with the United States. Soviet leaders, admiring American enterprise and efficiency, had long desired recognition from the United States, but conservative Republican presidents, Communist propaganda, and unpaid Russian debts had blocked it. Invited to Washington by President Franklin Roosevelt, Litvinov provided assurances on propaganda and legal protection for Americans in the USSR. In November 1933 the United States recognized the USSR, and William Bullitt, who had led an unofficial mission to Russia in 1919, became the first American ambassador there. Receiving him warmly and ignoring strong American isolationism, Stalin mistakenly expected the United States to block Japanese penetration of China.

By 1934, after the Polish-German pact, Stalin realized that Nazism represented a real danger to the USSR. Though holding out an olive branch to Hitler, he noted that "revanchist and imperialist sentiments in Germany" were growing. Hitler's nonaggression pact with Poland roused Soviet fears that he might encourage the Poles to seize Ukraine.

SOVFOTO

Maxim M. Litvinov (1876–1951) as Soviet ambassador to the United States (1941–1943) in his Washington, D.C., office with Lenin looking over his shoulder. As commissar of foreign affairs (1930–1939), Litvinov became associated with a policy of collective security against Hitler.

Growing concern over Germany accelerated a Soviet shift toward the Western democracies.

In September 1934 the USSR finally joined the League of Nations and abandoned its hostility to the Paris peace settlement. Litvinov, a Jew, an anti-Nazi, and a pro-Westerner, became a convincing spokesman for Soviet cooperation with the West. He used the League of Nations to proclaim a Soviet policy of peace, disarmament, and collective security against aggression. Contrary to assumptions in the West, Litvinov never made policy but merely executed Stalin's orders. His sincere belief in the new line won the confidence of Western liberals and socialists, but the League's failure to halt Italy in Ethiopia in 1935 revealed once again its weakness as a peacekeeping instrument.

Stalin also sought security through mutual defense pacts. In May 1935 France and the USSR,

driven together again by fear of Germany, concluded a mutual assistance pact, but it lacked the military teeth of the old Franco-Russian alliance; politically divided France took almost a year to ratify even a watered-down version. The USSR pledged to aid Czechoslovakia militarily against a German attack if the French did so first, as Stalin insured cautiously against being drawn into war with Germany while the West watched.

The Comintern obediently adopted a new Popular Front policy. Its Seventh (and last) Congress of July–August 1935 announced that all "progressive forces" (workers, peasants, petty bourgeoisie, and intelligentsia) should cooperate against fascism, the most dangerous form of capitalist imperialism. Communists were instructed to work with socialists and liberals while retaining their identity within the Popular Front.

Failures of collective security in 1936 caused growing Soviet disillusionment. In March Nazi troops marched into the Rhineland in clear violation of the Versailles and Locarno treaties, using French ratification of the pact with the USSR as justification. Disregarding feeble French and British protests, the Germans refortified the Rhineland. This action shattered the collective security approach and, by weakening the French position, undermined the Franco-Soviet pact, shifting the balance of power to Germany. Stalin realized that he could not count on the West to resist Nazi aggression, which was now likely to turn eastward. Soon Stalin began the Great Purge, eliminating rivals in case he later had to deal with Hitler. The West's apathy toward the Spanish Civil War, beginning in July, reinforced Stalin's suspicions. While Germany and Italy supported General Francisco Franco's fascist revolt against the Spanish Republic, the West proclaimed nonintervention. The USSR, explaining that it was aiding the Popular Front against fascism, provided important military aid to the Republic, saved Madrid from early capture, and greatly prolonged the conflict. Stalin may have hoped to draw the West into the war or thought that lengthy fascist involvement in Spain would delay a move against the USSR. However, during 1937 he withdrew most military aid from Spain and purged Russian Communists associated with it as Trotskyites. Soviet efforts to cooperate with the West against Hitler before World War II virtually ended.

The Nazi-Soviet Pact, 1939–1941

The formation of the Axis (Germany and Italy) in October 1936 and its conclusion of the Anti-Comintern Pact with Japan in November apparently deepened antagonism between communism and fascism, but Stalin was already abandoning collective security. For him 1937 was a year of watchful waiting abroad and relentless purging at home. Litvinov covered his retreat by continuing to advocate collective resistance to fascism.

Nazi gains during 1938 demolished the remnants of collective security and alienated the USSR from the appeasement-minded West. Hitler's annexation of Austria drew only ineffectual Western protests, and Stalin doubtless concluded that the West would not fight Hitler to save eastern Europe. Litvinov warned repeatedly that time was running out if the West wanted Soviet cooperation against fascism. Collective security's last gasp was the May Crisis between Germany and Czechoslovakia: The Czechs mobilized, the West and the USSR pledged aid if Czechoslovakia were attacked, and Hitler backed down. But at the Munich Conference in October, with the USSR excluded, France and Great Britain surrendered the Czech Sudetenland to Hitler and made Czechoslovakia indefensible. Western appeasement and Stalin's purge of the Red Army, which weakened the USSR, had destroyed collective security.

Tension with Japan stimulated Stalin's desire to settle with Hitler. He had tried to appease Japan by selling it the Chinese Eastern Railway in 1935. The outbreak of the Sino-Japanese War in 1937 temporarily relaxed pressure on the USSR. Stalin signed a friendship treaty with China and supplied Chiang with arms and credits. When the Japanese army probed the Soviet border in major attacks at Changkufeng (July 1938) and Nomonhan (May 1939), it was repulsed with heavy losses, apparently convincing Tokyo that expansion into Siberia would be too costly.

By 1938 Stalin had eliminated all opposition and could dictate to the Politburo. "Stalin thought that now he could decide all things alone and that all he needed were statisticians," recalled N. S. Khrushchev. "He treated all others in such a way that they could only listen to and praise him."[10] In May 1939 V. M. Molotov, Stalin's loyal secretary, replaced Litvinov as foreign commissar, suggesting that Stalin was preparing a major move in foreign policy. Molotov imposed rigid conformity upon the hitherto flexible and cosmopolitan Narkomindel, as Stalin sought to obtain a recognized sphere of influence in eastern Europe.

During early 1939 the West and the Nazis vied for Soviet support. In March Hitler's occupation of the rest of Czechoslovakia finally ended Western appeasement. France and Great Britain belatedly guaranteed the integrity of Poland and Romania but failed to convince Stalin that they would really fight Hitler. In a speech to the 18th Party Congress in March Stalin, accusing the West of trying to provoke a Soviet-German conflict, warned that the USSR would not be drawn into a war "to pull somebody else's chestnuts out of the fire." In August the West finally sent a military mission to Russia, but it had moved too slowly and indecisively. Hitler, having decided to attack Poland, had already begun intensive negotiations with the USSR.

On August 23, 1939, the Nazi-Soviet Pact, concluded in Moscow between former ideological archenemies, shocked the world. (See Problem 13 at the end of this chapter.) That fateful agreement included a public nonaggression pact pledging absolute neutrality if either partner were attacked by a third power. Securing Hitler's eastern flank, the pact encouraged him to invade Poland on September 1. A secret territorial protocol partitioned Poland, with the USSR to receive roughly

---

[10] *Khrushchev Remembers* (Boston, 1970), pp. 297, 299.

Foreign Commissar Viacheslav M. Molotov
(1890–1986) signing Nazi-Soviet Pact in August
1939. He served as foreign commissar and foreign
minister 1939–1949 and 1953–1957. Standing left to
right: German Foreign Minister Joachim von
Ribbentrop, Stalin, and V. Pavlov.

the eastern third. Latvia, Estonia, Finland, and
Bessarabia were assigned to the Soviet sphere, and
Lithuania was added to it later. (See Map 13.2.)
Reflecting the worst traditions of the old secret
diplomacy, the two dictators' cynical bargain
resembled the alliance of 1807 between Napoleon
and Alexander I. Once again Russia, bribed with
temporary peace and eastern European territory,
gave a Western tyrant a free hand to deal with
Europe and England. Stalin apparently interpreted
the pact as a diplomatic masterstroke, securing the
USSR from invasion, giving it a buffer zone, splitting the capitalist world, and encouraging its parts
to fight, all of which might enable Russia to
become the arbiter of Europe.

If so, Stalin's hopes were soon shattered. He
was appalled at the awesome Nazi blitzkrieg that
rolled over Poland, the Low Countries, and France;
he watched helplessly as the Soviet Union, having

agreed to supply Germany with raw materials,
became economically dependent on Germany. At
Hitler's insistence the Soviet-controlled Comintern abandoned its hostility to Nazism. Seeking
compensation, Stalin occupied the Baltic states
militarily, deported many of its citizens to Siberia,
then engineered a sham plebiscite that, Moscow
claimed, overwhelmingly (more than 99 percent)
approved their annexation to the USSR. The
Soviets also demanded Finnish territory near
Leningrad in exchange for part of Soviet Karelia.
When the Finns refused, the Red Army attacked
but met heroic resistance, suffered huge casualties,
and displayed embarrassing weakness in the aftermath of the military purge. This unprovoked
Soviet aggression, which the Soviets justified as an
essential defensive measure, brought sharp West-
ern condemnation and expulsion from the League
of Nations, and almost provoked war with the
West. Once Finnish defenses had been broken,
Stalin hastily concluded peace, taking much of the
Karelian Isthmus and many of the Finnish bases.
Later in 1940 he seized Bessarabia and northern
Bukovina from Romania to protect vulnerable
Ukraine.

Despite their large and mutually profitable
trade, friction increased between Germany and
the USSR. As early as July 1940 Hitler apparently
decided to invade Russia, and Soviet stubbornness
during the Molotov-Ribbentrop talks in November merely confirmed his decision. The German
foreign minister tried in vain to turn Soviet aspirations southward to the Persian Gulf against Great
Britain. Abandoning any pretense of Marxist internationalism, Molotov stated Soviet demands in
pragmatic, power-political terms. The Soviet
Union, he declared, would accept Ribbentrop's
proposals on politicoeconomic cooperation only
on the following terms:

1. Provided that the German troops are immediately withdrawn from Finland, which
   under the compact of 1939, belongs to the
   Soviet Union's sphere of influence. . . .

2. Provided that within the next few months
   the security of the Soviet Union in the

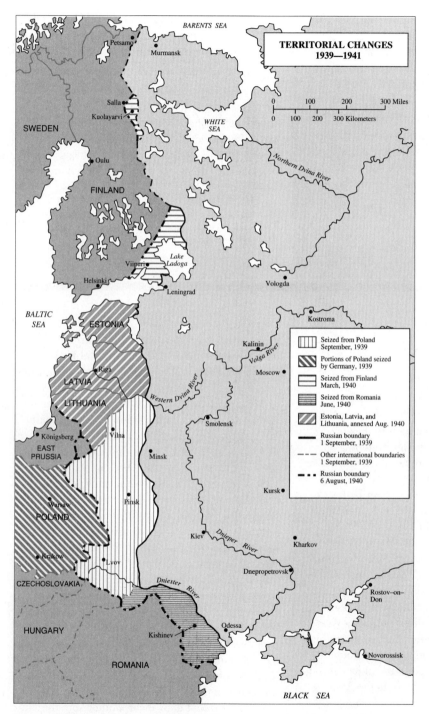

**TERRITORIAL CHANGES
1939—1941**

0   100   200   300 Miles
0   100   200   300 Kilometers

Seized from Poland
September, 1939

Portions of Poland seized
by Germany, 1939

Seized from Finland
March, 1940

Seized from Romania
June, 1940

Estonia, Latvia, and
Lithuania, annexed Aug. 1940

Russian boundary
1 September, 1939

Other international boundaries
1 September, 1939

Russian boundary
6 August, 1940

Map 13.2 Territorial changes, 1939–1941

[Turkish] Straits is assured by the conclusion of a mutual assistance pact between the Soviet Union and Bulgaria, which geographically is situated inside [its] security zone . . . and by the establishment of a base for land and naval forces of the USSR within range of the Bosphorus and Dardanelles by means of a long-term lease.

3. Provided that the area south of Batum and Baku in the general direction of the Persian Gulf is recognized as the center of the aspirations of the Soviet Union.

4. Provided that Japan [renounces] her rights to concessions for coal and oil in northern Sakhalin.[11]

Molotov's statement marked an evident return to traditional 19th-century tsarist objectives, secret diplomacy, and even language—"spheres of influence," military bases, and long-term leases. Nazi-Soviet friction over Finland and the Turkish Straits resembled that between tsarist Russia and Napoleonic France preceding the French invasion of Russia in 1812.

---

[11] R. J. Sontag and J. Beddie, eds., *Nazi-Soviet Relations, 1939–1941* (Washington, 1948), pp. 258–59.

Problem 7

The Nazi-Soviet Pact: Then and Now

Prevalent historical opinion remains that the conclusion of the Nazi-Soviet Pact on August 23, 1939, gave Hitler the green light to invade Poland just eight days later, thus touching off World War II. Still disputed, however, is whether Stalin, the realistic statesman, had a genuine alternative in 1939 to an accord with Hitler. Could the Red Army, shattered by the terrible purge of its officer corps in 1937–1938, have resisted a Nazi invasion then? Would Hitler indeed have invaded the Soviet Union had Stalin aligned the USSR with the Western powers, Great Britain and France? Would Hitler have attacked Poland, already backed by the Western powers, without guaranteed neutrality from the Soviet Union? Was there a realistic chance for a military alliance between the xenophobic Stalin and the Western powers in 1939, given the abject surrender by France and Great Britain to the Axis powers in September 1938 at the Munich Conference, which had excluded the USSR? How much

responsibility for the outbreak of World War II actually rests on the shoulders of Stalin's USSR?

Another series of questions relates to Stalin's motives and objectives, which have recently been scrutinized by Russian historians and commentators. This debate centers around the secret additional protocol of August 23 on territorial divisions in eastern Europe and the subsequent protocol of September 28, 1939, under which the USSR secured Lithuania while surrendering Warsaw and portions of central Poland to Germany. Can Stalin's actions be defended on the grounds of security—a defensive move to create a buffer zone to protect the USSR against a possible subsequent Nazi attack? Or was Stalin's objective primarily expansionist—an aggressive move to secure control of the Baltic states and eastern Poland while agreeing with Hitler to destroy an independent Slav Poland? Probably it represented a combination of the two aims. Some Soviet commentators condemned the pact and protocols as violations of Leninist principles in foreign affairs. Leaders in the Baltic republics have argued that their incorporation into the USSR in 1939–1940 took place forcibly against the background of secret agreements that were illegal both under international law and in light of Leninist principles. If their incorporation was indeed involuntary, were the Baltic republics not therefore justified in demanding secession from the USSR?

Some basis for answering these questions can be provided by examining the relevant documents from 1939: the Soviet-German Nonaggression Pact, the secret territorial protocol of August 23, and the additional secret protocol of September 28. Foreign Minister Molotov provided the official Soviet explanation of reasons for the Nazi-Soviet Pact. Half a century later, in 1989, the debate over the pact intensified, and excerpts from that Soviet debate, both Russian and Baltic, have also been included.

The Treaty of August 23, 1939

ARTICLE 1: Both High Contracting Parties obligate themselves to desist from any act of violence, any aggressive action, and any attack on each other, either individually or jointly with other powers.

ARTICLE 2: Should one of the High Contracting Parties become the object of belligerent action by a third power, the other High Contracting Party shall in no manner lend its support to this third power. . . .

ARTICLE 4: Neither of the two High Contracting Parties shall participate in any grouping of powers whatsoever that is directly or indirectly aimed at the other party.

Disputes between the two nations were to be settled through "friendly exchange of opinion" or through arbitration (Article 5). The treaty was to run for 10 years; if neither party denounced it a year before its scheduled expiration, the treaty would be extended automatically for five more years.

ARTICLE 7: The present treaty shall be ratified within the shortest possible time. . . . The agreement shall enter into force as soon as it is signed.

For the government of the German Reich	With the full power of the Soviet government
J. von Ribbentrop	V. M. Molotov[12]

The Secret Additional Protocol of August 23, 1939

The undersigned plenipotentiaries of each of the two parties discussed in strictly confidential conversation the question of the boundary of their respective spheres of influence in eastern Europe. These conversations led to the following conclusions:

1. In the event of a territorial and political rearrangement in the areas belonging to the Baltic States (Finland, Estonia, Latvia, Lithuania), the northern boundary of Lithuania shall represent the boundary of the spheres of Germany and the USSR. In this connection the interest of Lithuania in the Vilna area is recognized by each party.

2. In the event of a territorial and political arrangement of the areas belonging to the Polish state the spheres of influence of Germany and the USSR shall be bounded approximately by the line of the rivers Narew, Vistula and San. The question of whether the interests of both parties make desirable the maintenance of an independent Polish state and how such a state should be bounded can only be definitely determined in the course of further political developments. . . .

4. This protocol shall be treated by both parties as strictly secret.

v. Ribbentrop   V. Molotov[13]

The Secret Supplementary Protocol of September 28, 1939

When German armies marched into Poland on September 1, 1939, the Soviet Union remained neutral according to the terms of the Nonaggression Pact. On September 17 Soviet armies

---

[12] Sontag and Beddie, *Nazi-Soviet Relations*, pp. 76–77.

[13] Sontag and Beddie, p. 78.

invaded eastern Poland and occupied the region assigned to it by the Secret Additional Protocol. At Soviet request, on September 28 in Moscow von Ribbentrop and Molotov signed a Secret Supplementary Protocol. This document amended the Secret Protocol of August 23 under Article 1

> to the effect that the territory of the Lithuanian state falls to the sphere of influence of the USSR, while, on the other hand, the province of Lublin and parts of the province of Warsaw fall to the sphere of influence of Germany. As soon as the Government of the USSR shall take special measures on Lithuanian territory to protect its interests, the present German-Lithuanian border . . . shall be rectified in such a way that the Lithuanian territory situated to the southwest of the line marked on the attached map should fall to Germany.[14]

This protocol confirmed that Nazi Germany had assigned all the Baltic states to the Soviet sphere.

The Official Soviet Explanation: 1939

On August 31, 1939, Foreign Minister Molotov provided this interpretation of the preceding Nazi-Soviet agreements in a speech to the Supreme Soviet of the USSR. Emphasizing the tense international situation that then prevailed in Europe and Asia, Molotov declared:

> In view of this state of affairs, the conclusion of a nonaggression pact between the USSR and Germany is of tremendous positive value, eliminating the danger of war between Germany and the Soviet Union. In order more fully to define the significance of this pact, I must first dwell on the negotiations which have taken place in recent months in Moscow with representatives of Great Britain and France . . . for conclusion of a pact of mutual assistance against aggression in Europe. . . . The initial proposals of the British Government were, as you

> know, entirely unacceptable . . . ; they ignored the principle of reciprocity and equality of obligations. . . . These negotiations encountered insuperable obstacles. . . . Poland, which was to be jointly guaranteed by Great Britain, France and the USSR, rejected military assistance on the part of the Soviet Union. . . . After this it became clear to us that the Anglo-French-Soviet negotiations were doomed to failure. . . . The British and French military missions came to Moscow without any definite powers and without the right to conclude any military convention. . . .

> The decision to conclude a nonaggression pact between the USSR and Germany was adopted after military negotiations with France and Britain had reached an impasse. . . . It is our duty to think of the interests of the Soviet people, the interests of the USSR. . . . In our foreign policy towards non-Soviet countries, we have always been guided by Lenin's well-known principle of peaceful coexistence of the Soviet state and capitalist countries. . . . The Non-Aggression Pact . . . marks a turning point in the history of Europe, and not only of Europe. Only yesterday, the German fascists were pursuing a foreign policy hostile to us. . . . Today, however, the situation has changed and we are enemies no longer. The art of politics in the sphere of foreign relations . . . is to reduce the number of enemies and to make the enemies of yesterday good neighbors. . . . The two largest states of Europe have agreed to put an end to the enmity between them, to eliminate the menace of war and live in peace with the other. . . . Is it really difficult to understand that the USSR is pursuing and will continue to pursue its own independent policy, based on the interests of the peoples of the USSR and only their interests?[15]

Thus Molotov justified the agreements with Germany on the basis of Soviet national interests and the "insuperable obstacles" to an accord with the Western powers. He made no allusion whatsoever to the establishment of Soviet-German spheres of interest.

[14] Sontag and Beddie, p. 107.

[15] V. M. Molotov, "The Meaning of the Soviet-German Non-Aggression Pact," Speech to the Supreme Soviet, August 31, 1939. In Alvin Rubinstein, *The Foreign Policy of the Soviet Union* (New York, 1960), pp. 145–51.

Soviet Views of the Agreements: 1989

A. N. Iakovlev, a member of the Soviet Politburo, in a *Pravda* interview published on August 18, 1989, declared that "serious researchers" agreed that when Stalin authorized Ribbentrop's visit to Moscow on August 22, 1939, the Soviet Union no longer had any choice of partners. Unable to prevent war by itself and having failed to enlist England and France as allies, "the only thing left for it to do was to think about how to avoid falling into the maelstrom of war for which the USSR was even less prepared in 1939 than in 1941." As to the Secret Additional Protocol of September 28, 1939, Iakovlev stated:

> From a political standpoint . . . , it represented a deviation from Leninist norms of Soviet foreign policy and from Lenin's break with secret diplomacy. . . . [The protocol] conflicted with the sovereignty and independence of a whole series of countries [including the Baltic states] . . . and with the treaties which the USSR had previously concluded with those countries, with our commitments to respect their sovereignty, territorial integrity and inviolability. In my opinion, Stalin took an unjustified risk in giving his blessing to Molotov's signature to the "territorial-political rearrangement" of Poland. . . . The venture could have ended with the USSR's being drawn into the war rather than being given a breathing spell. . . . This way of acting by the Soviet leaders then in no way reflected the will of the Soviet people and was not in tune with their mood. I think we will be acting responsibly . . . by unequivocally condemning the prewar Soviet leadership's departure from Leninist principles of foreign policy.

Asked to compare the Nonaggression Pact of August 23, 1939, with the Secret Supplementary Protocol of September 28, Iakovlev found them to be qualitatively different:

> The first was a treaty made in peacetime; the second was concluded with a country [Nazi Germany] which had committed an overt act of aggression.

The first was basically in keeping with the international practices of the time; the second essentially cast doubt on the USSR's status as a neutral—if it did not undermine that status—and pushed our country toward unprincipled cooperation with Nazi Germany. There was no direct need at all for the September 28 treaty. . . . For opportunistic motives, however, in late September Stalin made a move that entailed major political and moral costs in order, as he supposed, to fix Hitler firmly in a position of mutual understanding—not with the USSR, but with Stalin himself.[16]

On August 23, 1989—the 50th anniversary of the Nonaggression Pact—an interview with F. N. Kovalev, director of the Foreign Ministry's Diplomatic Historical Administration, appeared in the Soviet newspaper *Izvestiia*. Discussing the forced incorporation of the Baltic republics of Latvia, Lithuania, and Estonia into the USSR, Kovalev said:

> When the agreements were signed in August 1939, what was primarily intended was to establish a definite boundary to German fascist expansion. And only that. It was certainly not intended, say, that the Baltic republics would eventually be incorporated into the USSR. The purport of Moscow's instructions to our representatives in the Baltic republics . . . was that Soviet garrisons stationed in the Baltic republics on the basis of treaties . . . concluded with them in late September and October 1939 should in no way interfere in those countries' internal affairs. There could be no question of any Sovietization of the three Baltic republics . . . but the presence of Soviet garrisons created an atmosphere in which leftist forces and democratic circles in the three republics began to step up efforts which ultimately led to the events that occurred in 1940 [incorporation]. From my viewpoint . . . , the Baltic republics then faced a very clear alternative; either side with Hitler or the USSR.[17]

On August 28, 1989, *Izvestiia* reported from the Lithuanian capital of Vilnius that the

---

[16] Interview with A. N. Iakovlev, *Pravda*, August 18, 1989.

[17] Interview with F. N. Kovalev, *Izvestiia*, August 23, 1989.

Problem 7 continued

presidium of the Lithuanian Supreme Soviet had examined the conclusions reached by its commission studying the Soviet-German treaties of 1939. The assertion that Lithuania's incorporation into the Soviet Union in 1940 had been illegal, affirmed that Moscow newspaper, "is leading the republic of Lithuania into a political impasse and will be of little help during the transition to economic independence."[18]

---

[18] "Search for the Road Together," *Izvestiia*, August 28, 1989.

Conclusion

Soviet and Russian views on the Nazi-Soviet agreements of 1939 have changed significantly over the years. Under Gorbachev the Nonaggression Pact of August 23 was disavowed as mistaken and "anti-Leninist," as were Soviet-German accords over spheres of influence. The Soviet incorporation of the Baltic states in 1940, facilitated by the Nazi-Soviet Pact, was finally reversed in 1991 when Latvia, Lithuania, and Estonia became independent countries, and Russian troops were later withdrawn. ■

InfoTrac® College Edition Search Terms

Enter the search term *Stalin's foreign policy* in Keywords.
Enter the search term *Comintern* in Keywords.
Enter the search term *popular front* in Keywords.
Enter the search term *Molotov* in Keywords.

Suggested Additional Reading

ANGRESS, W. T. *Stillborn Revolution: The Communist Bid for Power in Germany, 1921–1923* (Princeton, 1963).

BELOFF, M. *The Foreign Policy of Soviet Russia, 1929–1941*, 2 vols. (London, 1947–1949).

BORKENAU, F. *World Communism: A History of the Communist International* (Ann Arbor, MI, 1962).

BRANDT, C. *Stalin's Failure in China, 1924–1927* (Cambridge, MA, 1958).

BROWDER, R. P. *The Origins of Soviet-American Diplomacy* (Princeton, 1953).

BUDUROWYCZ, B. *Polish-Soviet Relations, 1932–1933* (New York, 1963).

CARR, E. H. *German-Soviet Relations Between the Two World Wars, 1919–1929* (Baltimore, 1951).

———. *Twilight of the Comintern, 1930–1935* (New York, 1983).

CRAIG, G., and FELIX G., eds. *The Diplomats, 1919–1939* (Princeton, 1953). (See chapters on Chicherin and Litvinov.)

CROWE, D. M. *The Baltic States and the Great Powers: Foreign Relations, 1938–1940* (Boulder, CO, 1993).

DANIELS, R. *Russia: The Roots of Confrontation* (Cambridge, MA, and London, 1985).

DEGRAS, J. *Calendar of Soviet Documents on Foreign Policy, 1917–1941* (New York, 1948).

———, ed. *The Communist International, 1919–1943* (New York, 1956).

———, ed. *Soviet Documents on Foreign Policy, 1917–1941*, 3 vols. (New York, 1951–1953, 1983).

DMYTRYSHYN, B., and F. COX. *The Soviet Union and the Middle East: A Documentary Record of Afghanistan, Iran and Turkey, 1917–1985* (Princeton, 1985).

DUNN, D. J. *Caught between Roosevelt and Stalin: America's Ambassadors to Moscow* (Lexington, KY, 1998).

ELLEMAN, B. A. *Diplomacy and Deception: The Secret History of Sino-Soviet Diplomatic Relations, 1917–1927* (Armonk, NY, 1997).

EUDIN, X., and H. FISHER, eds. *Soviet Russia and the West, 1920–1927* (Stanford, 1957).

———, and R. NORTH, eds. *Soviet Russia and the East, 1920–1927* (Stanford, 1957).

———, and R. SLUSSER, eds. *Soviet Foreign Policy, 1928–1934*, 2 vols. (University Park, PA, 1966–1967).

FILENE, P. G. *Americans and the Soviet Experiment, 1917–1933* (Cambridge, MA, 1967).

FISCHER, L. *Russia's Road from War to Peace . . .* (New York, 1969).

———. *The Soviets in World Affairs . . . 1917–1929*, 2d ed. (New York, 1960).

FREUND, G. *Unholy Alliance: Russo-German Relations from the Treaty of Brest-Litovsk to the Treaty of Berlin* (New York, 1957).

GARRISON, M., and A. GLEASON, eds. *Shared Destiny: Fifty Years of Soviet-American Relations* (Boston, 1985).

GOLDBERG, H. J., ed. *Documents of Soviet-American Relations: Vol. I. Intervention, Famine Relief, International Affairs, 1917–1933.* (Gulf Breeze, FL, 1993).

GROMYKO, A. A., and B. N. PONOMAREV. *Soviet Foreign Policy 1917–1980,* 2 vols. (Moscow, 1981).

HASLAM, J. *Soviet Foreign Policy, 1930–1933: The Impact of the Depression* (New York, 1983).

HILGER, G., and A. G. MEYER. *The Incompatible Allies: A Memoir History of German-Soviet Relations 1918–1941* (New York, 1953).

HULSE, J. W. *The Forming of the Communist International* (Stanford, 1964).

KENNAN, G. F. *Russia and the West Under Lenin and Stalin* (Boston, 1960).

KOCHAN, L. *Russia and the Weimar Republic* (Cambridge, 1978).

MACKENZIE, D. *From Messianism to Collapse: Soviet Foreign Policy, 1917–1991* (Fort Worth, TX, 1994).

MCKENZIE, K. E. *Comintern and the World Revolution, 1928–1943 . . .* (New York, 1964).

MCLANE, C. B. *Soviet Policy and the Chinese Communists, 1931–1946* (New York, 1958).

MOSELY, P. E. *The Kremlin and World Politics* (New York, 1961).

NEKRICH, A., ed. and trans. Gregory L. Freeze. *Pariahs, Partners, Predators: German-Soviet Relations, 1922–1941* (New York, 1997).

NELSON, D. N., and ROGER ANDERSON, eds. *Soviet-American Relations: Understanding Differences, Avoiding Conflicts* (Wilmington, DE, 1987).

ROBERTS, G. *The Unholy Alliance: Stalin's Pact with Hitler* (Bloomington, IN, 1989).

RUBINSTEIN, A. Z., ed. *The Foreign Policy of the Soviet Union* (New York, 1972).

SONTAG, R. J., and J. BEDDIE, eds. *Nazi-Soviet Relations* (Washington, 1948).

SUVOROV, V. *Icebreaker: Who Started the Second World War?* (London, 1990).

SWORD, K., ed. *The Soviet Takeover of the Polish Eastern Provinces, 1939–1941* (New York, 1991).

TROTTER, W. *The Russo-Finnish Winter War of 1939–1940* (Chapel Hill, NC, 1990).

ULAM, A. *Expansion and Coexistence . . . 1917–1973,* 2d ed. (New York, 1974).

ULDRICKS, T. J. *Diplomacy and Ideology: The Origins of Soviet Foreign Relations, 1917–1930* (London, 1980).

VAN DYKE, C. *The Soviet Invasion of Finland, 1939–1940* (Portland, OR, 1997).

WEINBERG, G. *Germany and the Soviet Union, 1939–1941* (New York, 1972).

WHITE, S. *The Origins of Detente: The Genoa Conference and Soviet-Western Relations, 1921–1922* (London and New York, 1985).

ZENKOVSKY, S. A. *Pan-Turkism and Islam in Russia* (Cambridge, MA, 1960).

14

War and Reconstruction, 1941–1953

Between 1941 and 1945, the USSR fought the greatest war in Russian history. Despite poor military preparation and massive popular hostility to the Stalin regime, Soviet Russia eventually defeated the Nazi invasion, and the Red Army advanced triumphantly into central Europe. The USSR was joined by Britain and the United States, but Soviet relations with the West were complicated by suspicion and differences over strategy and war aims. The Soviet role in World War II and Stalin as wartime leader remain controversial: Did Stalin plan to invade Germany in 1941? or Was Soviet Russia caught by surprise in 1941 and, if so, why? Why did the Red Army suffer terrible early defeats, then recover and defeat Germany? How important was Allied aid in the Soviet victory, and how great were the respective Soviet and Western roles in defeating Germany and Japan?

When the war ended, Stalin reimposed tight controls over a Soviet people yearning for liberalization and relaxation. Reindoctrinating or imprisoning millions exposed to Western influences

during the war, he again isolated the USSR and blamed the West for domestic hardships. Heavy industry was stressed again at the consumer's expense, but reconstruction was rapid, and the USSR soon produced atomic and hydrogen weapons. Soviet Russia achieved dominance over eastern Europe, except for Yugoslavia, which escaped Stalin's grasp in 1948. Soviet expansion and Western resistance produced the Cold War between the two superpowers, and in Asia Communist China emerged as a huge Soviet ally. How did postwar Stalinism compare with the prewar regime? How and why did the Soviet Union win control of eastern Europe? Was Stalin mainly responsible for the Cold War?

Invasion

At dawn on June 22, 1941, more than 3 million German and auxiliary troops from Nazi-controlled Europe crossed the Soviet frontier on a 2,000-mile front. Their unprovoked attack inaugurated what the Soviets called "the great fatherland war," the greatest land conflict in world history, and a struggle that tested the Soviet regime and people to the limit. Despite accurate warnings from Soviet spies (such as Richard Sorge in Tokyo) and foreign intelligence of impending German attack, the Nazis achieved complete tactical surprise. At first, uncertain whether it was invasion or a provocation, Moscow ordered Soviet troops to remain passive. Apparently Stalin believed that Hitler would not attack if the USSR fulfilled its commitments under the Nazi-Soviet Pact. Finally, at noon on June 22, eight hours after the Nazis attacked, Deputy Premier Molotov informed the Soviet people of the German assault. Stalin, in a state of shock, remained in seclusion for almost two weeks at his dacha outside Moscow. When Ambassador Schulenburg delivered the German declaration of war, Foreign Minister Molotov queried: "Do you believe that we deserved this?"

Hitler's aim in Operation Barbarossa was to crush the "barbarian" USSR by crippling the Red Army in encirclements near the frontier, then to advance to the Archangel-Astrakhan line. Moscow, Leningrad, and most of European Russia would be occupied, and Russian remnants expelled into Asia. Nazi Germany would obtain sufficient oil, grain, and manpower to dominate Europe and defeat England. Hitler and his commanders were confident that these objectives could be achieved before winter.

At first Nazi victories exceeded even Hitler's expectations. Soviet frontier forces were overwhelmed and hundreds of planes destroyed on the ground as Soviet soldiers and civilians were stunned by the suddenness and power of the German onslaught. In four weeks General Heinz Guderian's tank forces pierced to Smolensk, only 225 miles from Moscow, while the northern armies sliced through the Baltic states toward Leningrad. Hundreds of thousands of demoralized Soviet troops surrendered; border populations in eastern Poland, the Baltic states, and Ukraine welcomed the Germans with bread and salt as liberators from Stalinist tyranny.

Overconfidence and fanaticism caused Hitler and his associates to overlook or fumble golden military and political opportunities. On July 19 Hitler rejected Guderian's plea for an immediate strike against Moscow, ordering him instead against Kiev. That operation netted more than 600,000 Soviet prisoners, but produced fatal delay in assaulting Moscow, the key to Soviet power, which was very vulnerable in the fall of 1941. By October the Germans had occupied most of Ukraine and surrounded Leningrad, but Red Army resistance was stiffening. Guderian was now unleashed, and by early December reached Moscow's outskirts, but an early winter, lack of warm clothing and tracked vehicles, and major Siberian reinforcements stalled his advance. The year 1941 ended with a Soviet counteroffensive that drove the Nazis back from Moscow, opened a relief route into Leningrad, and recaptured Rostov in the south. (See Map 14.1.) Hitler's attempt to achieve quick victory in Russia had failed.

The Germans wasted unique chances to overturn Stalin's regime. Nazi agencies in Russia pursued conflicting policies. Many German army leaders and foreign officials sought Russian popular support, but Nazi party and SS elements treated the people as subhumans, exterminating or exploiting even those ready to cooperate with Germany. Alfred Rosenberg's Ministry for the East favored autonomous German-controlled satellite states in non-Russian borderlands, but Goering's economic agencies grabbed their resources for Germany. No single course was implemented consistently, but German eastern policy (*Ostpolitik*) was brutal and inefficient. The Nazis aimed to colonize choice areas with Germans and exploit Soviet resources, but they achieved remarkably little. Occupying some 400,000 square miles of Soviet territory with 65 million people and rich grain areas, the Germans obtained only a fraction of what they secured from France or from Nazi-Soviet trade agreements. Incompetent and corrupt German officials, who flooded the USSR like carpetbaggers, contributed to this economic failure as they disregarded popular aspirations for religious freedom, self-government, and decollectivization. Himmler's extermination detachments liquidated

Map 14.1 USSR in World War II

SOURCE: Adapted from *A History of Russia*, Second Edition by Nicholas V. Riasanovsky.
Copyright © 1969 by Oxford University Press, Inc. Used by permission.

not just Bolsheviks but also thousands of innocent men, women, and children.

Why the initial Soviet collapse followed by recovery? Stalinists blamed setbacks on the Nazi surprise attack and credited recovery to a loyal populace that rallied to the motherland. Later Khrushchev blamed early defeats mainly on Stalin's deafness to warnings of attack and inefficiency in using the breathing spell of the Nazi-Soviet Pact. In the West many attributed Soviet collapse to a revolt of the borderlands and Soviet recovery mainly to Nazi brutality. The American political scientist George Fischer suggested that Stalin's initial paralysis of will had left an army and population used to dictation without instructions; once he reasserted leadership, the Soviet people again obeyed the regime.

By the end of 1941 the Soviet leadership had regained widespread public support. After two weeks of silence and seclusion (some reports claim he suffered a near nervous breakdown), Stalin appealed to the Soviet people by radio for national resistance to an invader seeking to turn them into "the slaves of German princes and barons" and to restore the tsar and the landlords. A scorched earth policy must deny the Germans factories, food, and matériel. Stalin's call for guerrilla warfare behind German lines was reinforced by skillful patriotic propaganda. Soon forests in the German rear were infested with partisans who tied down many German troops and disrupted communications. A State Committee for Defense, headed by Stalin and including Molotov, Voroshilov, Beria, and Malenkov, became a war cabinet. As de facto commander in chief, Stalin concentrated military and political leadership in his own hands. In that capacity he made many arbitrary and harmful military decisions, often interfering in tactical matters, about which he knew little. Stalin's mistakes apparently contributed to major Red Army defeats, especially in the initial Nazi advance in 1941, but his decision to remain in threatened Moscow in October 1941 halted panic provoked by the movement of diplomats and government offices to Kuibyshev on the Volga. If Stalin is partially to blame for early Soviet defeats,

he deserves some credit for the Red Army's outstanding victories during 1944–1945.[1] His wartime leadership remains controversial.

The Grand Alliance—Britain, the USSR, the United States, and later France—formed against the Nazis and their allies in 1941 sent significant aid to the USSR. The day after the invasion Prime Minister Churchill of England offered the USSR friendship and military aid, while refusing to recant his earlier attacks on Bolshevism. After President Roosevelt's adviser Harry Hopkins went to Moscow in July, the United States began Lend-Lease assistance to Russia, which totaled some 15 million tons of supplies worth more than $11 billion. Anglo-American aid contributed to the Soviet repulse of German attacks in 1942 and proved indispensable in subsequent Soviet counteroffensives. Japan's attack on Pearl Harbor in December 1941 brought the United States into the European war as well.

The 1942 Campaign: The Turning Point

In 1941 German losses were so heavy that in 1942 Hitler's offensive had to be more limited. The Nazis still retained the potential to reach the Archangel-Astrakhan line and knock out the USSR, but Hitler removed most of his high command and interfered frequently in military decisions, with disastrous results. Instead of trying to envelop and capture Moscow, he sought economic and psychological objectives: seizing the Caucasus oil fields and Stalingrad on the Volga.

In June the Germans broke through the Don front, but Soviet resistance at Voronezh prevented an advance to the mid-Volga. Nazi armies rolled east, then southward into the Caucasus, but were halted short of the main oil fields. Stalingrad became the focus and symbol of the entire Soviet-German war. In bitter street fighting during August and September, Stalingrad was virtually

---

[1] A. Seaton, *Stalin as Military Commander* (New York, 1976), p. 271.

reduced to rubble. Despite brave Soviet resistance, General von Paulus's Sixth Army captured most of the city, but his army was bled white in frontal assaults instead of crossing the Volga and encircling the city. Heroic Soviet defense, Siberian reinforcements, and U.S. equipment turned the tide. In November a massive Soviet counteroffensive broke through Romanian and Italian lines on the exposed northern German flank and cut off the entire Sixth Army. After relief efforts failed, von Paulus and the hungry remnants of his army surrendered. Here was the psychological and perhaps military turning point of the Soviet-German war. After Stalingrad the Nazis were mostly on the defensive, and ultimate Allied victory in World War II became a matter of time and blood.

In 1942 the Nazis again neglected a major political weapon. In July Lieutenant General Andrei Vlasov, an able Soviet commander, surrendered with his men and agreed to help Germany achieve a free, non-Bolshevik Russia. He denounced the Soviet regime, collective farms, and Stalin's mass murders. Some on the German General Staff wished to use him and several million Soviet war prisoners against Stalin. Named head of a Russian National Committee, Vlasov sought to form an army of liberation (ROA), but Hitler blocked its use until German defeat was inevitable. The Germans employed more than a million Soviet volunteers as cooks, drivers, and orderlies, but not in combat.

To counter an appalling desertion rate, Stalin appealed to Russian traditions and completed a reconciliation with the Orthodox Church. Soviet soldiers were told to serve the fatherland without socialist obligations. The army restored ranks, saluting, insignia, and officer privileges reminiscent of tsarist times, and the regime's tone became strongly nationalist. At the 25th anniversary of the Bolshevik Revolution (November 1942), Soviet leaders, instead of calling for world revolution, stressed Slav solidarity. To convince the West that the USSR had abandoned world revolution, Stalin abolished the Comintern in 1943 and rewarded the loyal Orthodox hierarchy by restoring the patriarchate under state supervision. A church synod unanimously elected Metropolitan Sergei patriarch in September 1943; Sergei then proclaimed Stalin "the divinely anointed." These moves promoted unity and countered German efforts to foment disloyalty, but did not signify changes in Stalin's domestic or foreign aims.

Inter-Allied relations remained good in 1942, primarily because the USSR badly needed Lend-Lease supplies. Even then, friction developed over a second front and over Poland. Throughout 1942 Stalin pressed for a cross-Channel invasion; he was only partially mollified by the Allied invasion of North Africa in November. Stalin sought Western recognition of the USSR's June 1941 frontiers, but England and the United States, though making concessions, refused to sanction Soviet annexation of eastern Poland and the Baltic states.

Soviet Offensives and Allied Victory, 1943–1945

After Stalingrad, with brief exceptions, Soviet armies were on the offensive everywhere and bore the heaviest military burden until victory was achieved. After the defeat of a German offensive at Kursk in July 1943, producing the greatest tank battle in history, the Red Army attacked, jabbing ceaselessly at various points. U.S. tanks, trucks, and planes ensured the success of the Soviet drive westward by making the Red Army highly mobile. The Red Army's numerical superiority grew steadily. By the summer of 1944 the Germans were outnumbered about three to one, and the Soviets commanded the skies and used their artillery effectively. Named chief of the Soviet General Staff in 1941, Marshal Georgii Zhukov led the defense of Moscow later that year and also directed the great Soviet counteroffensive of 1943–1945. His U.S. counterpart was General Dwight Eisenhower. The Germans could merely delay the Soviet advance and hope to exploit Allied divergences.

Once the Allies were advancing everywhere, their relations cooled. Both the Soviets and the West feared that the other might make a separate peace, though there is little evidence that either planned to do so. As Soviet armies advanced, Stalin's attitude hardened as he sought to dominate eastern Europe and Germany. The Western allies, still sensitive in 1943 over the absence of a true second front, proved vulnerable to Stalin's diplomacy. Hitherto Soviet war aims had been defensive: to preserve Soviet frontiers, the Communist system, and Stalin's total control. Now Stalin sought also Carpatho-Ukraine from Czechoslovakia to forestall Ukrainian disaffection. The USSR joined in the formation of the United Nations in 1942 and approved its high-sounding declarations, but Stalin never accepted Western democratic aims. He refused to alter his views or make major concessions to his partners. Stalin realized that the surest way to achieve his aims was to advance westward as far as possible, then secure what he wanted from the West. Stalin and Molotov, notes George Kennan, played their cards skillfully and carefully while the Western allies, holding a stronger hand, remained confused, divided, and unrealistic and let the Soviets score large gains.

Poland was the stickiest issue in inter-Allied relations. Early in 1943 the Germans discovered the corpses of thousands of Polish officers in the Katyn Forest near Smolensk. The Soviets accused the Nazis of the murders, but evidence was strong that Soviet security forces had killed the Poles in 1940.[2] Assertions of Soviet responsibility by the Polish government in exile in London induced Stalin to sever relations with them. At Teheran in November 1943 Churchill proposed the Curzon Line of 1920 as Poland's eastern frontier, with Poland to be compensated in the west at German expense. Stalin promptly agreed and suggested the Oder-Neisse Line as the western boundary. Poland's drastic shift westward would make it dependent on Soviet favor. Churchill finally persuaded the London Poles to accept this bargain; but when their new leader, Stanislas Mikolajczyk, went to Moscow in July, the USSR had already

recognized the Communist-dominated Lublin Committee political group in Poland and turned over to it liberated Polish territory. Because the Western allies took no firm stand, Mikolajczyk was powerless. In August 1944, with the Red Army in Praga, across the Vistula River from Warsaw, Poles aligned with the London exiles rose against the Nazis: General Bor's men fought heroically, but the Soviet army did not aid them. Once the Germans had destroyed this core of potential opposition to a Soviet-dominated Poland, the Red Army drove the Nazis from Warsaw.

The second-front issue caused serious inter-Allied friction until the Normandy invasion of June 1944. At the Moscow foreign ministers' conference (October 1943), the Soviets sought a definite Western pledge to invade France by the next spring. At the Teheran Conference in November, Churchill's idea of invading the Balkans, partly to prevent Soviet control there, was blocked by Stalin, whose support of Overlord, the American plan to invade France, ensured its adoption. The Normandy invasion relieved Soviet fears of a Nazi-Western separate peace and speeded the end of the war. Later Soviet historians claimed that Normandy was invaded to prevent a Soviet sweep to the Atlantic but contributed little to Germany's defeat.

As Soviet forces advanced through Poland and the Balkans, Churchill sought to delimit postwar spheres of influence, a proposal Roosevelt repudiated as immoral. In October 1944 Churchill proposed a numerical formula for influence in eastern Europe: 90-percent Soviet influence in Romania and Bulgaria and similar British control in Greece; Yugoslavia and Hungary would be split 50–50. Such formulas, however, meant little: The USSR could gain total control in its sphere by military occupation.

In February 1945, with Allied armies at the border of or inside Germany, the Big Three met at Yalta in the Crimea to outline a postwar settlement. Because the Red Army controlled most of Poland, only united and determined Western action might have salvaged some Polish independence. The West (especially Roosevelt), however,

---

[2] In 1990 the Soviet Union admitted responsibility for the Katyn Forest Massacre.

UPI/Corbis-Bettmann

Churchill, Roosevelt, and Stalin at Yalta, February 1945. The Big Three laid plans for the post-war era at Yalta. Roosevelt was already ill and would be dead within two months.

wished to continue cooperation with the USSR after the war. In regard to Polish frontiers, Stalin insisted on the Curzon Line, overcoming half-hearted Western efforts to obtain Lvov and the Galician oil fields for Poland. In the west, Poland was to administer the region to the Oder-Neisse Line until the peace conference, and more than 7 million German residents were expelled. Stalin insisted that the West repudiate the London Poles and recognize the Soviet-controlled Lublin Committee as the core of a new Polish government; the West proposed a wholly new regime formed from all political parties. Finally the Allies agreed to broaden the Soviet-dominated Polish provisional government and hold "free and unfettered elections" as soon as possible, but Stalin secured his basic aim: a Soviet-dominated Poland. Germany was to be de-Nazified, demilitarized, and occupied, and France was to receive an occupation zone from the Western share. The USSR would

receive half of a suggested total of $20 billion in German reparations. The Allies also agreed on voting in the United Nations and, by secret protocols, to Soviet entry into the Far Eastern war. Soviet gains at Yalta resulted from a strong military position, shrewd bargaining, and Western uncertainty.

After Yalta, Allied armies advanced swiftly. The Red Army overran Hungary, much of Austria, and crossed the Oder River. The Americans surged across the Rhine, and as Nazi resistance collapsed, the British urged them to occupy Berlin. General Eisenhower, however, halted at the Elbe River, then turned south to destroy the reputed German fortress in Bavaria. On April 17 Marshal Zhukov began his final offensive against Berlin, and on the 25th Soviet and American forces joined on the Elbe. While the Red Army was storming Berlin, Hitler committed suicide, and on May 8, 1945, his successors surrendered unconditionally.

The USSR and the Far Eastern War

The United States had long sought Soviet participation in the war against Japan, but until victory in Europe was in sight, Stalin avoided the issue. Japanese neutrality in the German-Soviet war had permitted him to bring in Siberian troops to stop the Germans at Moscow and Stalingrad. Late in 1943 Stalin hinted to the United States that the USSR would enter the Pacific conflict soon after Germany's defeat and did so. At Teheran Roosevelt assured Stalin that Russia could recover territories lost in the Russo-Japanese War. U.S. military chiefs estimated before Yalta that without Soviet participation it would take the United States 18 months and cost up to a million casualties to subdue Japan after Germany's surrender. Consequently, to ensure Soviet entry into the war against Japan, at Yalta Roosevelt accepted Stalin's demands for territory and spheres of interest in China and agreed to secure Chiang Kai-shek's consent to them. Stalin agreed to US requests for aid against Japan.

On August 8, 1945, two days after the American atomic attack on Hiroshima, the USSR declared war on Japan. Justifying his action, Stalin cited somewhat lamely the "treacherous Japanese attack" in 1904 and the "blemish on the tradition of our country" left by Russia's defeat. "For 40 years we, the men of the older generation, have waited for this day." Stalin omitted to mention that in 1904 Russian Social Democrats had encouraged the Japanese to beat Russia quickly and later had celebrated Russia's defeat! Large Soviet forces overwhelmed the Japanese in Manchuria, continuing operations even after Japan's surrender on August 14. Soviet accounts claimed that the Red Army's invasion of Manchuria, not the atomic bomb, caused Japan's surrender and brought the subsequent victory to the Chinese Communists. For one week's participation in the fighting, the USSR was rewarded generously: It recovered southern Sakhalin, Port Arthur, Dairen, and the Manchurian railways, secured all the Kuril Islands, and occupied North Korea. General MacArthur, however, rejected Soviet demands for an occupation zone in Japan.

The USSR's balance sheet in World War II revealed some gains in territory and population at enormous human and material cost. About 265,000 square miles of territory with some 23.5 million people were annexed forcibly to the Soviet Union of 1939: the Baltic states, eastern Poland, Bessarabia, northern Bukovina, eastern Karelia, Carpatho-Ukraine, northern East Prussia, and the Kuril Islands. Estimates of Soviet war deaths range from 20 to 27 million, about half civilians.[3] By contrast, German casualties were about one-third as great; U.S. losses of 295,000 were 72 times less! The Soviets suffered about 38 percent of all fatalities caused by World War II, partly because the massive conflict was fought over their territory for three and one-half years, during which the invading Nazis sought deliberately to annihilate Jews and enslave other nationalities. The criminal negligence of its political and military leaders increased Soviet losses. At Stalin's orders Soviet commanders often sought to win battles at any cost, sending many soldiers to needless slaughter. Mass civilian starvation, notably in besieged Leningrad, where an estimated 1 million died and Stalin's deportation of more than a million people from the Crimea and Caucasus led to additional deaths.[4] The Nazi invaders caused colossal material damage: They destroyed 1,710 towns and working settlements and more than 70,000 villages, leaving 25 million Soviet citizens homeless; they wrecked some 32,000 industrial plants and tore up more than

---

[3] According to N. S. Khrushchev in 1961, Soviet deaths equaled 10 million soldiers and 10 million civilians. Soviet figures from 1973 (*Istoriia SSSR*, Moscow, 1973, vol. 10, p. 390) for the European republics listed as "killed and tortured to death" 6,844,551 civilians and 3,932,256 war prisoners. Western historians have come up with a total of 21.3 million—13.6 million soldiers and 7.7 million civilians killed, or 11 percent of the Soviet population in 1941.

[4] Mikhail Heller and Alexander Nekrich, *Utopia in Power: The History of the Soviet Union from 1917 to the Present* (New York, 1982), pp. 443–44.

40,000 miles of railway.[5] At war's end, western European Russia was devastated. The country emerged from the conflict depleted in manpower and its economy a shambles.

Postwar Stalinism

Domestic Affairs

As World War II ended, the exhausted Soviet people hoped for liberal change, freedom, and well-being. Instead Stalin restored total control, resumed rapid industrialization, and isolated the USSR from the West. After the brief euphoria of victory celebrations, Stalin reimposed terror and party dominance, concealing rather successfully from the West signs of mass discontent revealed early in the war.

At war's end, some 5 million Soviet citizens were outside Soviet borders. At Yalta the Allies agreed to help one another bring home those of their citizens living abroad. About 3 million Soviet war prisoners, forced laborers, and defectors resided in areas under Western control, mostly Germany, and about 2 million in Soviet-occupied regions. Until 1947 Western authorities cooperated by urging or forcing (as with General Vlasov) Soviet citizens to return home. In displaced persons camps, U.S. troops forced many to leave with Soviet officials. Western leaders believed naively that with the war over, all but traitors and criminals would happily return home. About half a million "nonreturnables" stayed in the West by claiming they were Baltic or Polish nationals or by melting into the populace of disorganized Germany. The formerly pro-Soviet American journalist Louis Fischer noted that when Soviet Russians had a choice, they "voted against the Bolshevik dictatorship with their feet." Others committed suicide or redefected on the way to the USSR. Between 1945 and 1948 some 20,000 Soviet soldiers and officers defected from occupation forces, though until 1947 they were usually turned over to the Soviets for execution by their units. By 1948

Western cooperation ceased, but so did most opportunities to defect.

Returning Soviet soldiers and civilians, having seen Europe at first hand, confronted Stalin with a massive "debriefing" problem comparable with that of the tsarist regime after the Napoleonic Wars. Both governments solved it by repression and cutting ties with Europe, not with needed reforms. Isolation was essential for Stalin because Soviet living standards had fallen sharply while Russia's productive capacity had grown. His regime could not admit failure to produce abundance. Refusing economic dependence upon the West, Stalin found an alternative in quarantining his people. Thus Stalin exiled many returning POWs to Siberia and other distant regions.

Even before the war ended, a campaign began against the supposedly decaying "bourgeois" West. Closed party meetings learned: "The war on fascism ends, the war on capitalism begins" anew. Stalin's victory toast to the Russian people began the glorification of everything Russian while minimizing or ignoring debts to the West. In a February 1946 speech, Stalin reaffirmed that while capitalism survived, war was inevitable; he revived the bogey of capitalist encirclement to justify internal repression and economic sacrifice. In 1946 began the Zhdanovshchina—an ideological campaign associated with Andrei Zhdanov, Leningrad party chief, who emerged during the war as heir apparent to Stalin. (See Chapter 12.) Zhdanov, who had proclaimed socialist realism *the* acceptable art form in 1934, urged a struggle against foreign influences in Soviet life that amounted to ideological war with the West in order to demonstrate socialism's cultural superiority. "Our role . . . is to attack bourgeois culture, which is in a state of miasma and corruption." Soviet intellectuals were denounced for subservience to Western influence or using Western themes or sources. The economist Eugene Varga was castigated for doubting there would be a postwar depression in the United States. Zhdanov's campaign, demanding absolute conformity to party dictates, stifled Soviet intellectual development.

---

[5] *Istoriia SSSR* (Moscow, 1973), vol. 10, p. 390.

Stalin's assertions of Russian achievement reached absurd extremes. Russian or Soviet scientists were credited with almost every major scientific discovery of modern times. The desire to prove Russian self-reliance reflected a persistent Russian inferiority complex toward the West. In 1950 Stalin, attacking the late N. Marr's linguistic theories, suggested that in the socialist future a single superior language, presumably Russian, would prevail. As in the 1930s, T. D. Lysenko, an obscure plant breeder, was encouraged to denounce Western genetic theories and Soviet scientists who accepted them. (See Chapter 12.) Stalin combined xenophobic Russian nationalism and anti-Semitism: Jews were "homeless bourgeois cosmopolitans." Connected with Israel's emergence as a state and the desire of Soviet Jews to emigrate there, this campaign featured ugly anti-Semitic cartoons and severe persecution, though certain prominent Jews such as Lazar Kaganovich and the writer Ilia Ehrenburg were spared to "prove" that the regime was not anti-Semitic.

Soviet economic problems in 1945 were staggering. About one-fourth of the nation's capital resources had been destroyed, including some two-thirds in Nazi-occupied regions. Industrial and agricultural outputs were far below prewar levels; railroads were damaged or disrupted. United Nations relief and British and Swedish credits aided reconstruction, as did reparations from Germany and former Axis satellites such as Finland. Newly sovietized eastern Europe had to supply minerals, foodstuffs, and machinery, and German war prisoners helped rebuild devastated cities. Without major U.S. credits, which Stalin had hoped for, however, the reconstruction burden fell largely on the Soviet people. The Fourth Five Year Plan, stressing heavy industry and mineral production, aimed at complete rebuilding and at exceeding prewar levels in industry and agriculture. Prewar "storming" and rigid labor discipline were revived; slave labor controlled by the NKVD was used extensively. Heavy investment in construction sought to overcome a catastrophic urban housing shortage. In heavy industry the plan was largely fulfilled, although spectacular industrial growth rates partly reflected restoration of existing capacity in western Russia. More than half the 2,500 industrial plants shifted eastward during the war remained there, heightening the importance of new Siberian industrial areas. Consumer production and agriculture, however, lagged seriously, and during Stalin's lifetime Soviet living standards remained among the lowest in Europe.

With drought and severe shortages of livestock plaguing agricultural recovery, food rationing continued until December 1947. Wartime peasant encroachments on collective farms were ended, and Khrushchev, who was a close colleague of Stalin and who was placed in charge of Ukraine, vigorously recollectivized the western Ukraine. By 1950 the 250,000 prewar collectives had been amalgamated into about 125,000, but Khrushchev's ambitious scheme to build agricultural cities (*agrogoroda*) with peasants living in massive housing projects foundered on peasant opposition and lack of funds. In 1948 in the eastern Ukraine Stalin inaugurated a giant afforestation program, called modestly his "plan to transform nature," to stop drought and sandstorms, but it achieved little. Stalin continued to neglect agriculture as, ensconced in the Kremlin, he apparently believed stories of agricultural prosperity related by fearful subordinates. Meanwhile collective farmers remained miserably poor and lacked incentives to produce.

Nonetheless, Stalin's draconian policies brought major heavy industrial growth and some agricultural recovery. By 1953 the USSR, the world's second greatest industrial power, was moving toward Stalin's seemingly fantastic 1960 goals of 60 million tons of steel, 500 million metric tons of coal, and 60 million metric tons of oil.

Foreign Affairs

In the first postwar years the USSR greatly expanded its influence in Europe and Asia. Stalin, despite a U.S. atomic monopoly until 1949, built a bloc of satellite states in eastern Europe and promoted Communist victories in China, North Korea, and North Vietnam. His blustering tone and actions, however, then caused the West to rearm and ended opportunities for advances. Soviet expansion clashed with U.S. containment to produce the Cold War.

Between 1945 and 1948 the Soviet Union established complete control over eastern Europe. According to Soviet accounts, Communist states there emerged from native revolutions against exploitative landlords and capitalists. To construct a security shield against a German resurgence or possible Western action, Stalin ensured control in eastern European countries by "progressive elements"—that is, pro-Soviet regimes. Stalin wished to use these countries' resources to rebuild the Soviet economy and their territory to influence events in central Europe.

Soviet methods of achieving control varied, but the general pattern was similar, except in Yugoslavia where Marshal Tito won power independently. Red Army occupation was the first step, except in Czechoslovakia and Yugoslavia. National Communist parties, decimated during the war, were rebuilt and staffed mainly with Soviet-trained leaders subservient to Moscow. Usually the Soviets secured key levers of power for Communists—the army, police, and information media. Then coalition governments were formed from all "democratic, antifascist" parties. With NKVD aid, political opposition was intimidated, disorganized, and fragmented. Conservative parties, accused (often falsely) of collaborating with the Nazis, were banned while socialist parties were split, then merged forcibly with the Communists. Resulting socialist unity parties allowed Communists to control the working-class movement. Elections were often delayed until the Communists and their allies were assured of victory.

Poland, whose control was vital for Soviet domination of eastern Europe and influence in Germany, reflects these techniques clearly. Despite Yalta guarantees, Poland succumbed to Soviet domination after mild Western protests. During the war the Nazis and Soviets had decimated its intelligentsia and officer class. Then the Red Army occupied Poland, and the Communist-dominated Lublin Committee formed the nucleus of a coali-

tion government. Mikolajczyk and three other London Poles were included, but they were powerless against the Communists, who controlled the chief ministries and forced the socialists into a coalition. Mikolajczyk, very popular with peasants, democrats, and conservatives, probably would have won a free election, but the police intimidated members of his Peasant party. In the manipulated elections of 1947 the leftist bloc won, and Mikolajczyk escaped into exile.

In Czechoslovakia the script was different but the results similar. It was the only eastern European country with an advanced industry and strong democratic traditions. A genuine democrat, Eduard Beneš, returned as president. At first the Communists (and the USSR) were popular, won 38 percent of the vote in the 1946 elections, and took over several key ministries. Under Beneš Czechoslovakia was friendly toward the USSR and sought to be a bridge between East and West, but Stalin could not tolerate a Western-type democracy on his borders. In February 1948, when democratic elements tried to force the Communist interior minister to resign, the Communists, supported by armed workers and a Red Army demonstration on the frontier, seized power and forced Beneš to resign. Klement Gottwald established a Communist regime subservient to Moscow.

Soviet expansion in eastern Europe and tension over Germany helped produce the Cold War. In March 1945 Stalin and Roosevelt exchanged heated notes over Poland; the Potsdam Conference in July revealed widening Soviet-Western differences. President Truman (who succeeded to the presidency after Roosevelt's death) and Foreign Minister Ernest Bevin of Britain (who replaced Churchill during the conference) criticized Soviet policies in eastern Europe that violated the Yalta accords. Rapid deterioration of Soviet-Western relations stemmed partly from suspicion left after Western intervention in Russia in 1918–1919 and partly from deepened differences between Soviet and Western ideologies and political systems. With the common enemy defeated, there was little to hold the USSR and the Western powers together. Stalin's xenophobia and paranoia were contributory: He considered the cessation of Lend-Lease in May 1945 and refusal of postwar American credits unfriendly acts, which they do not seem to have been. In a speech in February 1946, Stalin blamed the West for World War II and was pessimistic about prospects of future Soviet-Western friendship. Churchill's "Iron Curtain" speech at Fulton, Missouri, on March 5, 1946, cited by Western revisionist historians as having launched the Cold War, came a month later. Churchill described prophetically the Soviet domination of eastern Europe:

> From Stettin on the Baltic to Trieste on the Adriatic an iron curtain has descended across the Continent. All these famous cities and the populations around them lie in the Soviet sphere and are subject, in one form or another, not only to Soviet influence, but to a very high and increasing degree of control from Moscow.[6]

The Iranian crisis was the first skirmish in the Cold War. During World War II Allied troops had occupied Iran to guard supply routes to the USSR, but they were supposed to withdraw afterward. Soviet troops, however, remained in Iran, ostensibly to protect the Baku oil fields, while in the north the Soviets, barring Iranian troops, fostered a Communist-led movement for autonomy. Accusing the USSR of interfering in its domestic affairs, Iran appealed to the United Nations, where it received strong support from the United States and Britain. In April 1946 the Soviets, after signing an agreement with Iran for joint exploitation of its oil resources, reluctantly pledged to withdraw. Once the Red Army had left, Iran suppressed the northern separatists, and its parliament rejected the Soviet-Iranian treaty.

In the eastern Mediterranean, Soviet pressure and British weakness produced another crisis. Demanding the return of Kars and Ardahan (Russian from 1878 to 1918) and bases in the Turkish Straits, Stalin massed Soviet troops on Turkey's borders and conducted a war of nerves, but Turkey

refused concessions. In neighboring Greece, the Soviets, Yugoslavia, and Bulgaria supported a Communist-led guerilla movement against the conservative British-backed government. Because Roosevelt had hinted at Yalta that U.S. forces would withdraw from Europe within two years, Stalin hoped to dominate the region once Britain pulled out of Greece. To his surprise, President Truman in March 1947 pledged economic and military support to Greece and Turkey, describing the issue as a struggle between democracy and Communism. Reversing traditional U.S. isolationism, this "Truman Doctrine" began a permanent U.S. commitment to Europe. The USSR denounced it as subversive of the United Nations and a "smokescreen for expansion."

In June 1947 the U.S.-sponsored Marshall Plan for European recovery confronted Stalin with a difficult decision because all European states were invited to participate. Molotov attended preliminary meetings, and Poland and Czechoslovakia showed deep interest, until Stalin abruptly recalled Molotov, forbade east European participation, and denounced the Marshall Plan as concealed American imperialism. Doing so was a serious blunder: Soviet acceptance probably would have doomed the plan in the U.S. Congress, thus enhancing Soviet prospects of dominating western Europe. Instead Stalin set up the Council of Mutual Economic Assistance (Comecon) as an eastern European equivalent. But until 1953 Comecon served largely as a device to extract resources from the satellites for the USSR.

George Kennan, a leading U.S. expert on the USSR, in July advocated long-term containment of the Soviet Union by strengthening neighboring countries until Soviet leaders abandoned designs of world domination. "For no mystical Messianic movement—and particularly not that of the Kremlin—can face frustration indefinitely, without eventually adjusting itself in one way or another to the logic of that state of affairs."[7] Kennan urged

[6] *New York Times,* March 6, 1946, p. 4.

[7] "The Sources of Soviet Conduct," *Foreign Affairs* (July 1947), pp. 581–82.

the West to adopt a patient policy of strength and await changes in Soviet conduct.

Creation of the Soviet-dominated Cominform (Communist Information Bureau) in Belgrade in September 1947, ostensibly to coordinate the Communist parties of France, Italy, and eastern Europe, deepened ideological rifts with the West. At its founding congress Zhdanov, confirming the end of Soviet-Western cooperation, described the division of international political forces into two major camps: imperialist (Western) and demo-cratic (Soviet). Zhdanov, stating that coexistence between them was possible, warned that the United States had aggressive designs and was building military bases around the Soviet Union.

Soon the breach widened further. The Czech coup of February 1948 ended any Western illu-sions about Soviet policy in eastern Europe. Early that year the British and U.S. zones in Germany merged and a currency reform was implemented. Stalin responded in June by cutting off rail and road traffic to Berlin—despite a 1945 four-power agreement that guaranteed access—in order to expel the West from that city. Some U.S. generals, such as Lucius Clay, favored forcing the blockade, but instead the United States flew in necessary supplies until Stalin lifted the siege in May 1949. Separate German regimes were soon formed: the Federal Republic in the west and the German Democratic Republic, a Soviet satellite, in the east. Alarmed and united by the Berlin crisis, the coun-tries of western Europe and North America formed the North Atlantic Treaty Organization, a collective security system to counter huge Soviet conventional forces with European and American armies and atomic weapons.

In June 1948 Stalin's expulsion of the Yugoslav Communist Party from the Cominform opened a breach in eastern European communism. Previ-ously Tito had been a loyal Stalinist, but for Stalin his independent policies and tight control over his party and state proved intolerable. The Soviets accused the Yugoslavs of slandering the Red Army and the USSR and deviating from Marxism-Leninism. Behind the verbiage lay more funda-mental conflicts: Tito, already dominant in

Albania, aspired to lead a Balkan federation that would break Soviet domination. Stalin overrated Soviet power ("I will shake my little finger and there will be no more Tito. He will fall."), tried to remove Tito, and ordered his satellites to blockade Yugoslavia. But the Yugoslavs rallied behind Tito, who turned to the West for support, and danger of general war probably restrained Stalin from invad-ing Yugoslavia. Tito developed a national commu-nism that diverged markedly from that of the USSR in ideology, economy, and politics.

Stalin promptly purged other potential eastern European Titos. In Poland Wladyslaw Gomulka was removed in 1949 as the party's general secre-tary; in other satellites there were show trials and forced confessions resembling the Soviet purges of 1937. Soviet control was ensured by an elaborate network that included Soviet troops, diplomats, secret police agents, and "joint companies" under Soviet control. Bilateral treaties enabled the USSR to exploit the satellites economically while Stalin's towering figure dominated a monolithic eastern European bloc.

In October 1949 the Chinese Communist vic-tory over the Nationalists created a huge Eurasian Communist bloc of more than 1 billion people. Moscow, while aiding the Communists secretly, maintained formal ties with Chiang Kai-shek to the end. Mao Tse-tung, like Tito, had controlled a party and territory before achieving power, and China was too vast to become a satellite. In Febru-ary 1950, after two months of tough bargaining in Moscow, Stalin and Mao concluded a mutual defense treaty against Japan and the United States. The USSR retained its privileges, treaty ports, and control of Outer Mongolia in return for modest amounts of economic aid, but a united Communist China would clearly be harder to control than a weak Nationalist China.

In his last years Stalin continued a forward policy while carefully avoiding war. Soviet support for national liberation movements tied down large British and French forces in Malaya and Indo-china. In June 1950, after Secretary of State Dean Acheson hinted that the United States would not defend South Korea, Stalin encouraged the

Soviet-equipped North Koreans to invade it, but a prompt military response by the United States and other United Nations members prevented a Communist victory. Subsequent Chinese intervention in Korea, probably arranged by Stalin, produced a stalemate but enhanced China's independence of Moscow. The United States in 1951 concluded a separate peace with Japan, which emerged as its partner in the Pacific. Stalin's miscalculations in Asia revealed the limitations of Soviet power and the fact that opportunities for expansion had vanished.

The 19th Party Congress and Stalin's Death

In October 1952 Stalin convened the 19th Congress, the first party congress in 13 years. It approved the Fifth Five Year Plan, which featured the development of power resources, irrigation, and atomic weapons. The party now numbered more than 6 million members, but its top organs had become self-perpetuating and it had lost its proletarian character. Stalin instructed Khrushchev, former party boss of Ukraine, to revise party statutes and carry through reform. Top party bodies were recast: A larger Presidium replaced the Politburo, and the Orgburo and Secretariat were merged. Georgii Malenkov had been Stalin's heir apparent since Zhdanov's sudden and mysterious death in 1948. Malenkov's 50th birthday in January 1952 was celebrated with much fanfare, and he delivered the chief report at the Congress. But his position was under challenge, and before Stalin's death there was much jockeying for position within the party hierarchy.

Stalin had drawn the party line for the Congress in *Economic Problems of Socialism in the USSR*. Often considered his political testament, it dis-

cussed the transition from socialism to communism in the USSR without setting a timetable and emphasized the deepening crisis of capitalism. Stalin predicted that wars among capitalist states had become more likely than an anti-Soviet coalition. Stressing this theme at the Congress, Malenkov hinted that Soviet expansion would end temporarily while the USSR overtook the United States in military technology.

In January 1953 *Pravda* claimed that nine Kremlin doctors, six of them Jews, had hastened the deaths of high Soviet officials, including Zhdanov. This "Doctors' Plot," part of Stalin's crude anti-Semitic campaign, may have been engineered partly by Alexander Poskrebyshev, sinister head of Stalin's personal secretariat. Seemingly it was one event in a power struggle between the nationalist former adherents of Zhdanov and the more internationally oriented faction of Malenkov and Beria, the secret police chief. The atmosphere of suspicion and fear in Moscow suggested strongly that Stalin was planning a new purge. On March 4, however, Stalin, who long had suffered from heart trouble and high blood pressure, had a massive stroke and died the next day. The Malenkov-Beria group, facing demotion or destruction at his hands, may have speeded his demise, ending a quarter century of personal dictatorship and bloody brutality unmatched in world history. But unlike Hitler, who left only ruins, Stalin bequeathed to his successors a powerful industrial state that owed much to his determination and satanic energy. Because Stalin failed to designate a successor, and the Soviet system provided no legal means to select one, a ruthless power struggle was inevitable.

Problem 8

Did Stalin Plan to Attack Nazi Germany in July 1941?

Was Hitler or Stalin responsible for the outbreak of the bloody and destructive Nazi-Soviet War? The traditional Western and Soviet view was that Nazi Germany launched a sudden and unprovoked attack—Operation Barbarossa—on an innocent USSR on June 22, 1941. That interpretation views the Nazi- Soviet War as the result of unprovoked but planned Nazi aggression against a Stalin anxious to avoid a conflict. In sharp contrast stands Viktor Suvorov's (pseudonym for Viktor Rezun) article of 1985, and 1988 book *Icebreaker*,[8] asserting that Stalin was preparing to attack Nazi Germany on July 6, 1941, invade Western Europe and communize it. In his *Day-M* book of 1994, Suvorov claimed that Stalin had decided in August 1939 on such a Soviet war of conquest as an "icebreaker" to arouse European workers to initiate a socialist revolution.

Suvorov's "icebreaker" thesis was promptly criticized by Western scholars as bad journalism based on inadequate and false documentation. A devastating critique came from the Russian scholar Gabriel Gorodetsky in *The Icebreaker Myth* (1995), then in *Grand Delusion* (1999),[9] based on exceptional access to Russian archives. Some German scholars, anxious to exonerate Hitler and blacken Stalin and Soviet Russia, accepted much of Suvorov's thesis. They claimed Hitler only turned against the USSR after learning of the planned Soviet invasion of Germany. Some Russian scholars in the post-Soviet era have partially supported Suvorov's claims.

Here we will present the pros and cons of this still hotly disputed controversy for student evalu-

ation. First, comes a summary of the Suvorov thesis followed by critiques of one Russian and one American scholar. Then we will summarize recent German and Russian partial support for Suvorov and a brief conclusion.

The Suvorov Thesis

Viktor Rezun, who defected to the West from Russian Military Intelligence, adopted the pseudonym *Suvorov*, the name of Catherine the Great's brilliant general. Beginning in 1985 he affirmed that Stalin had been seeking a war between Germany and the West since the rise of Hitler, which he had promoted—viewing a Nazi attack against western European countries as an "icebreaker" that could reopen the possibility of a Communist revolution in Europe. The European working class would acquire a powerful ally in the form of the Red Army, which Stalin would insert after the competing "imperialist powers" had exhausted one another in war. Suvorov asserted that Stalin planned to attack Nazi German forces on July 6, 1941, reach Western Europe and communize it. Suvorov envisioned thousands of Soviet wheeled tanks speeding along Germany's *Autobahnen*. Stalin's plan was frustrated, noted Suvorov, when the Nazis, discovering Soviet preparations, launched "Operation Barbarossa," a preemptive strike that was amazingly successful because it caught Soviet forces in forward deployment preparing to strike west and thus unprepared for defensive operations. Claimed Suvorov:

> I would like to suggest that, from the beginning of the war, the Soviet communists made accusations against every country in the world with the deliberate intention of concealing their own role as instigators (of World War II) (xv).
>
> From the 1920s on . . . Stalin revived the strike power of German militarism. Certainly not against himself . . . [but] so that war could be declared on the rest of Europe. Stalin understood that a powerful, aggressive army does not start a war by itself.

---

[8] Viktor Suvorov, *Icebreaker: Who Started the Second World War?* trans. T. R. Beattie (London, 1990).

[9] Gabriel Gorodetsky, *Grand Delusion: Stalin and the German Invasion of Russia* (New Haven, CT, 1999).

A mad, fanatical leader is also needed. Stalin did a great deal to see that just such a leader [Hitler] should appear at the head of the German nation. Once the fascists had come to power, Stalin persistently and doggedly pushed towards war . . . In the Molotov-Ribbentrop pact (Nazi-Soviet Pact of August 1939), Stalin guaranteed Hitler freedom of action in Europe and, in effect, opened the floodgates of the Second World War (xvi).

Even before the Nazis came to power, the Soviet leaders had given Hitler the unofficial name of "Icebreaker for the Revolution." . . . The communists understood that Europe would be vulnerable only in the event of war and that the Icebreaker for the Revolution could make it vulnerable. Unaware of this, Adolf Hitler cleared the way for world communism by his actions. . . . The Icebreaker committed the greatest crimes against the world and humanity, and in so doing, placed in Stalin's hands the moral right to declare himself the liberator of Europe at any time he chose. . . . Stalin understood better than Hitler that a war is won by that side which enters it last and not by the one which goes into it first. Stalin granted Hitler the doubtful honor of being the first, while he himself prepared for his unavoidable entry into the war "after all the capitalists (will) have fought amongst themselves." (*Stalin*, VI, 158) (xvi–xvii).

In a chapter towards the end of Icebreaker entitled "The War Which Never Was," Suvorov affirmed:

Hitler considered that a Soviet invasion was inevitable, but he did not expect it to happen in the very near future. German troops were diverted to activities of secondary importance, and the beginning of Operation Barbarossa was postponed. The operation finally began on 22 June 1941. Hitler himself clearly did not realize what a tremendous stroke of luck he had had. If Operation Barbarossa had been put off again . . . to July 22, Hitler would have had to do away with himself considerably earlier than in 1945.

Suvorov was referring to Stalin's alleged plan to attack Nazi Germany on 6 July 1941:

There are quite a few indications that the date for the beginning of the Soviet Operation Groza ("Thunderstorm") was fixed for 6 July 1941. . . . Zhukov and Stalin liked to deliver their surprise strikes on Sunday mornings, and 6 July 1941 was the last Sunday before the concentration of Soviet troops was complete (pp. 344–45).

Then Suvorov described the scenario for "Operation Groza":

At 3:30 A.M. Moscow time on 6 July 1941, tens of thousands of Soviet guns shatter the silence, announcing to the world that the great "liberation" campaign of the Red Army has begun. The Red Army's artillery is superior both in quality and quantity to any in the world. There are vast reserves of ammunition stockpiled on the Soviet frontiers (p. 345).

Suvorov asserted that Stalin had decided on a war of conquest at a meeting of the Politburo of August 19, 1939 (p. 345).

Refutations of the "Icebreaker" Thesis

Gabriel Gorodetsky, a contemporary Russian scholar, had crossed literary swords with Viktor Rezun, better known as Suvorov, ever since the latter had presented his "icebreaker" thesis, stating:

Suvorov depicted Soviet Russia as the aggressor, rather than the victim, in June 1941. He advanced the preposterous and unsubstantiated claim that throughout 1930–41 Stalin had been meticulously preparing a revolutionary war against Germany. Operation "Groza" was planned for 6 July 1941 but was preempted by Hitler's own invasion of Russia. The implication is breathtaking: in executing his foreign policy, Stalin, like Hitler, was pursuing a master plan which sought world domination by transforming the Second World War into a revolutionary war.

The acclaim that *Icebreaker* of Suvorov received in Russia and Germany, and the failure of Russian military and diplomatic historians to condemn it, induced Gorodetsky, after careful

Problem 8 continued

examination of numerous archival materials, to denounce it in his *Grand Delusion:*

> As a former master of disinformation in the GRU (Russian Military Intelligence), Suvorov exploited the fact that the period in question was rife with myth and conspiracy, most of it deliberately propagated. . . . The popularity of Suvorov's flimsy and fraudulent work in Russia and in many quarters in the West proves that the oldest, stalest conspiracies survive longest. His books engender myths and consistently and deliberately obstruct the search for truth by simplifying a complex situation (x).

Suvorov's views, continued Goredetsky, coincided with a bitter debate in Germany about the nature and course of its history, known as *Historikerstreit.* Thus some German and Austrian scholars adopted Suvorov's views in order to support their defense of the policies of Nazi Germany. "If Stalin had indeed been intent on 'liberating' Central Europe, then Hitler's decision to fight Russia could no longer be viewed . . . as a strategic folly or crude aggressive act" (x).

The American military historian, David B. Glantz,[10] who has devoted much writing to the history of the Red Army, rejected Suvorov's conclusions about Stalin's offensive military plans and the Red Army's ability to launch a massive invasion of central Europe in July 1941:

> Thus Rezun (Suvorov) resurrected the hitherto muffled and generally discounted argument. . . . that Stalin and his cronies were directly responsible for fostering the outbreak of the war. . . . In *Icebreaker* Rezun documented his contentions with personal recollections and material culled from a host of Soviet open sources with questionable regard to context. While claiming to have had access to classified archival materials while serving as a captain and major in the Soviet Army over twenty years ago, he undercut the possible argu-

ments of those who might use such materials in the future to refute his claims by asserting that the most controversial information in the archives has been suppressed or removed. At the least one can validly question how an officer of his lowly rank could have had access to such material in the first place and, if he had access, how could he recall the minute details of such an extensive collection after so long a period.

> In his expose, Rezun wove a complex mass of credible facts taken from Soviet memoirs and postwar studies into a less credible web of intrigue surrounding the circumstances associated with the outbreak of war. . . . He presented considerably less evidence to support his more radical contentions concerning Stalin's war plans for 1941. . . . He contended that Stalin planned offensive action in the summer of 1941 (specifically, on 6 July), that he deliberately mobilized and deployed a massive strategic second echelon to achieve victory . . . consisting of imposing "black-shirted" NKVD formations and crack shock armies . . . , that Stalin deliberately dismantled existing defensive fortifications to facilitate his impending offensive, and that General A.M. Vasilevsky. . . . was the architect and designated implementer of Stalin's cunning plan (pp. 4–5).

Thus Glantz found Suvorov's whole case regarding Soviet intentions in 1941 incredible because of his misuse and distortion of often-questionable source materials. Four years of catastrophic purges, affirmed Glantz, and in the midst of a badly handled force expansion and rearmament program, "the Red Army was clearly not suited to the conduct of large-scale offensive operations in summer 1941" (pp. 6–7).

Recent Russian Evaluation of the "Icebreaker" Thesis

Since the collapse of the USSR, Russian scholars have been free to reach their own conclusions about controversial questions relating to Soviet history. On the back cover of *Stalin's Lost*

---

[10] David M. Glantz, *Stumbling Colossus: The Red Army on the Eve of World War* (Lawrence, KS, 1998).

Chance, by Mikhail Mel'tiukov,[11] contemporary Russian historian, appears:

> Political conditions for a blow at Germany on the part of the USSR were sufficiently favorable. Unfortunately, Stalin, fearing an Anglo-German compromise, as a minimum delayed for a month the attack on Germany which was the only chance to defeat a German invasion. Probably, this decision is one of the basic historic miscalculations of Stalin, losing a favorable opportunity to destroy the most powerful European state and by going to the shores of the Atlantic Ocean, to eliminate a longstanding Western threat to our country. As a result the German leadership could begin on June 22, 1941 the realization of the plan, "Barbarossa," which under the conditions of unpreparedness of the Red Army for defense, led to the tragedy of the year 1941 (for Russia).

Since 1993, noted Mel'tiukov, the military and political problems of the USSR on the eve of the Great Fatherland War (Nazi-Soviet War) were at the center of a discussion sparked by the publication in Russia of Suvorov's books. "Although written in a genre of historical journalism and representing a type of 'puff-pastry,' in which truth is mixed with half-truths and lies, they rather clearly outlined the circle of problems . . . insufficiently developed in (Soviet) historiography." New materials and investigations, argued Mel'tiukov, showed that the traditional official Soviet version about the exclusively defensive intentions of the USSR was invalid (p. 8).

An Austrian Reinforcement of "Icebreaker"

In 1985, before Suvorov's book on the "icebreaker" theory, the Austrian scholar and former *Wehrmacht* soldier Ernst Topitsch,[12]

reached some similar conclusions regarding Stalin's plans to attack Hitler and move westward in 1941 or 1942. In his preface to *Stalin's War,* Topitsch argues:

> Hitler and Nazi Germany forfeit their position at the centre of the stage and make only episodic appearances—chess pieces rather than players— forming part of a long-term strategy already conceived by Lenin which aimed at the subjugation of the "capitalist world." . . .

Topitsch went on to emphasize the key role and outstanding ability of Stalin revealed during World War II and to deprecate Hitler's role and prescience: "It became more and more apparent that Stalin was not only the real victor, but also the key figure in the war; he was, indeed, the only statesman who had at the time a clear, broadly-based idea of his objectives." Topitsch stressed that his purpose in composing "a radical new theory" of the origins of World War II was not to exonerate Adolf Hitler but "rather to *reduce* the German dictator to his real political and intellectual stature and to correct the widely accepted overestimation of his ability." Stalin, affirmed the Austrian, had utilized and exploited Hitler's weaknesses to spark the outbreak of World War II:

> What we know of the development of the Red Army in the spring and early summer of 1941 . . . speaks much more for than against the aggressive intentions of the Kremlin. . . . By late summer the preparations for a mass offensive against Germany would have been concluded and such an attack was planned for 1942. The latter date was named by Stalin himself on 5 May 1941 in a private speech to officer cadets. . . . Stalin had excellent information about German plans and preparations for (Operation) Barbarossa, but in spite of this, he did nothing to guard his forces against the tactical surprise of the invasion. . . . There is a red thread woven into the fabric of these events, a thread which represents a well-conceived policy, positioned with astonishing finesse and carried into practice in accordance with clear and logical principles. This proves Stalin to be a statesman of genius . . . , far superior to Hitler and those guiding the destiny of

[11] Mikhail Mel'tiukov, *Upushchennyi shans Stalina* (Moscow, 2000).

[12] Ernst Topitsch. *Stalin's War: A Radical New Theory of the Origins of the Second World War* (London, 1987).

Problem 8 continued

the western powers. . . . It was Stalin who emerged the real victor of the Second World War.

After the conclusion of the Nazi-Soviet Pact of August 1939, affirmed Topitsch, Hitler became the dupe of Stalin, who utilized him to defeat France in 1940 and drive the British from the European continent. That Nazi victory "would naturally shake the capitalist world to its foundations and open up the possibility of revolutionary subversion in the centres of 'imperialism.'" The German conquest of France, asserted Topitsch, finally created the situation Stalin had hoped for. "The 'imperialist' war had now broken out in all its violence." He continued:

> Without knowing it or wanting to, the Germans had performed a surprising and very important service for Moscow: they had eliminated the military capacity of Russia's most important opponent, the Western powers, from the continent. . . . Only the Wehrmacht stood between the Red Army and the Atlantic. If the German army were defeated, the Soviets would be masters of the European continent.

Up to then, affirmed Topitsch, Hitler had unwittingly aided Stalin, but after summer 1940 he became a hindrance "whose removal . . . wouldn't seem to be too great a task." The author then cited clues to suggest Stalin's resolve to exploit a unique opportunity. On June 30, 1940, Foreign Minister Molotov told the Lithuanian foreign minister: "We are more than ever convinced that our brilliant comrade Lenin made no mistake when he asserted that the Second World War would enable us to seize power in Europe. . . ." Thus Hitler was to be utilized as "a battering ram against the allegedly strongest bastion of capitalism, Great Britain." Topitsch intimated that the Kremlin decided to embark on

an offensive strategy right after the Nazi victory over France.

Topitsch concluded from a Molotov speech in August 1940 that Stalin aimed to provoke Nazi Germany to attack the USSR "in order then to inflict a defeat by counterattack, and so gain mastery over the continent of Europe. The USSR, asserted the author, "felt itself more and more in the position . . . in case of war (in) . . . completely wiping out the enemy aggressor on his own territory." Regarding this as his "new theory," Stalin ordered it tried out in war games and exercises during the winter of 1940–41. However, his plans were preempted by the Nazi invasion of June 1941. "Yet Operation Barbarossa not only covered up Stalin's plans (for an attack) to perfection, but ensured the complete success of his intention to thrust onto Hitler the odium of the aggressor" (pp. 4, 8–9, 40–41, 54, 66, 69, 119).

Conclusions

What, then, is our verdict on the "Icebreaker" theory? Despite its considerable support by some Russian and German scholars, most historians reject it for (1) lack of adequate documentary proof of a Soviet assault plan for July 1941; (2) evident weaknesses and shortcomings in the Red Army in 1941 that would have made its implementation virtually impossible; (3) Stalin's basic caution and reluctance to place the USSR at risk, as shown by his appeasement of Hitler in 1940–41; (4) the absence, as Stalin surely realized, of any significant revolutionary sentiment or agitation among European workers; and (5) most scholars who support "Icebreaker" or a variant thereof appear personally motivated—Russians in order to vilify Stalin and the USSR, Germans to exonerate Hitler of responsibility for provoking World War II. Most scholars thus still accept the view that Hitler was the aggressor in June 1941 against Soviet Russia in Operation Barbarossa. ■

InfoTrac® College Edition Search Terms

Enter the search term *Stalin* in the Subject Guide.
Enter the search term *Stalingrad* in Keywords.
Enter the search term *Cold War* in the Subject Guide.
Enter the search term *George Kennan* in Keywords.

Suggested Additional Reading

ANDREYEV, C. *Vlasov and the Russian Liberation Movement* . . . (Cambridge, 1987).

ARMSTRONG, J. A. *Soviet Partisans in World War II* (Madison, WI, 1964).

ARONSEN, L., and M. KITCHEN. *The Origins of the Cold War in Comparative Perspective . . . 1941–48* (New York, 1988).

BACON, E. *The Gulag at War: Stalin's Forced Labour System in the Light of the Archives* (New York, 1994).

BEEVOR, A. *Stalingrad: The Fateful Siege: 1942–1943* (New York, 1998).

BIALER, S. *Stalin and His Generals* . . . (New York, 1969).

BOTERBLOEM, K. *Life and Death under Stalin: Kalinin Province, 1945–1953* (Montreal, 1999).

BREINDEL, E. *The Verona Secrets: The Soviet Union's World War II Espionage Campaign against the United States* (Boulder, CO, 2000).

BRZEZINSKI, Z. *The Soviet Bloc: Unity and Conflict,* 2d ed. (Cambridge, MA, 1961).

BUHITE, R. D. *Soviet-American Relations in Asia 1945–1954* (Norman, OK, 1981).

CARRELL, P. *Scorched Earth: The Russian-German War, 1943–44* (Boston, 1970).

CHUIKOV, V. I. *The Battle for Stalingrad* (New York, 1964).

CLARK, A. *Barbarossa: The Russian-German Conflict, 1941–1945* (New York, 1965).

CLEMENS, D. S. *Yalta* (New York, 1970).

CONQUEST, R. *The Nation Killers: Soviet Deportation of Nationalities* (New York, 1970).

COOPER, M. *The Nazi War Against Soviet Partisans, 1941–1944* (New York, 1979).

COUNTS, G. S. *The Country of the Blind: The Soviet System of Mind Control* (Westport, CT, 1959).

CRAIG, W. *Enemy at the Gates: . . . Stalingrad* (New York, 1973).

DALLIN, A. *German Rule in Russia, 1941–45* (New York, 1957, 1980).

DOUGLAS, R. *From War to Cold War 1942–48* (New York, 1981).

DMYTRYSHYN, B. *Moscow and the Ukraine, 1918–1953* (New York, 1956).

DUNN, W. S., JR. *The Soviet Economy and the Red Army, 1930–1945* (Westport, CT, 1995).

ERICKSON, J. *The Road to Stalingrad: Stalin's War with Germany* (New Haven, CT, 1999).

———. *The Road to Berlin: Continuing the History of Stalin's War with Germany* (Boulder, CO, 1983).

FEIS, H. *Churchill–Roosevelt–Stalin* (Princeton, 1957).

FISCHER, G. *Soviet Opposition to Stalin* (Cambridge, MA, 1952).

FUGATE, B. *Operation Barbarossa* (Novato, CA, 1984).

GORODETSKY, G. *Grand Delusion: Stalin and the German Invasion of Russia* (New Haven, CT, 1999).

GLANTZ, D. M. *Zhukov's Greatest Defeat: The Red Army's Epic Disaster in Operation Mars, 1942* (Lawrence, KS, 2000).

———. *Stumbling Colossus: The Red Army on the Eve of World War* (Lawrence, KS, 1998).

GLANTZ, DAVID M., and J. M. HOUSE. *The Battle of Kursk* (Lawrence, KS, 1999).

HAHN, W. G. *Postwar Soviet Politics . . . 1946–53* (Ithaca, NY, 1982).

HARBUTT, F. *The Iron Curtain: Churchill, America, and the Origins of the Cold War* (New York and Oxford, 1986).

HARRISON, M. *Accounting for War: Soviet Production, Employment, and the Defence Burden, 1940–1945* (Cambridge, Eng., 1996).

HAYWARD, J. S. *Stopped at Stalingrad: The Luftwaffe and Hitler's Defeat in the East* (Lawrence, KS, 1998).

HERRING, G. *Aid to Russia, 1941–46* . . . (New York, 1973).

HOLLOWAY, D. *Stalin and the Bomb: The Soviet Union and Atomic Energy, 1939–1956* (New Haven, CT, 1994).

KORIAKOV, M. *I'll Never Go Back: A Red Army Officer Talks,* trans. N. Wreden (New York, 1948).

KUZNETSOV, A. *Babi Yar,* trans. D. Floyd (New York, 1970).

LIDDELL-HART, B. H. *The Red Army* . . . (Gloucester, MA, 1956).

LIGHTBODY, B. *The Cold War* (New York, NY, 1999).

LOTH, W. *Stalin's Unwanted Child: the Soviet Union, the German Question and the Founding of the GDR,* trans. Robert Hogg. (New York, 1998).

LUCAS, J. S. *War on the Eastern Front 1941–45* (New York, 1982).

LYONS, G., ed. *The Russian Version of the Second World War* (New York, 1983).

MASTNY, V. *Russia's Road to the Cold War* . . . (New York, 1979).

MCCAGG, W. O. *Stalin Embattled, 1943–1948* (Detroit, 1978).

NAIMARK, N. and L. GIBIANSKI, eds. *The Establishment of Communist Regimes in Eastern Europe, 1944–1949* (Boulder, CO, 1998).

NEKRICH, A. M. *The Punished Peoples* . . . , trans. G. Saunders (New York, 1978).

PATERSON, T. G., and R. J. MCMAHON, eds. *The Origins of the Cold War* (Lexington, MA, 1991).

PETROV, V., comp. *June 22, 1941* (Columbia, SC, 1968).

PURDUE, A. W. *The Second World War* (New York, 1999).

REDLICH, S. *War, Holocaust and Stalinism* (Toronto, 1995).

REESE, R. R. *The Soviet Military Experience: A History of the Soviet Army, 1917–1991* (London and New York, 2000).

REINHARDT, K. *The Turning Point: The Failure of Hitler's Strategy in the Winter of 1941–42,* trans. Karl B. Keenan (Oxford and New York, 1992).

RZHESHEVSKY, O. *War and Diplomacy: The Making of a Grand Alliance* (Toronto, 1996).

SALISBURY, H. *The 900 Days: The Siege of Leningrad* (New York, 1969).

SEATON, A. *Stalin as Military Commander* (New York, 1976).

SHULMAN, M. *Stalin's Foreign Policy Reappraised* (Cambridge, MA, 1963).

SIMONOV, K. *Days and Nights* (New York, 1945). (Novel on Stalingrad.)

SNELL, J., ed. *The Meaning of Yalta* (Baton Rouge, 1956).

STEENBERG, S. *Vlasov* (New York, 1970).

TARRANT, V. E. *Stalingrad: Anatomy of an Agony* (New York, 1992).

VITUKHIN, I., ed. *Soviet Generals Recall World War II* (New York, 1981).

WERTH, A. *Russia at War, 1941–45* (New York, 1964, 1984).

WOHLFORTH, W. C. *The Elusive Balance: Power and Perceptions during the Cold War* (Ithaca, NY, 1993).

ZAWODNY, J. K. *Death in the Forest: . . . the Katyn Forest Massacre* (Notre Dame, 1980).

———. *Nothing But Honour: The Story of the Warsaw Uprising, 1944* (Stanford, 1978).

ZHUKOV, G. E. *Marshal Zhukov's Greatest Battles* (New York, 1969).

ZINNER, P. *Communist Strategy and Tactics in Czechoslovakia, 1918–1948* (New York, 1963).

ZUBOK, V., and C. PLESHAKOV. *Inside the Kremlin's Cold War: From Stalin to Khrushchev* (Cambridge, MA, 1996).

"ICEBREAKER" THEORY: BOOKS

BEEVOR, A. *Stalingrad: The Fateful Siege: 1942–1943* (New York, 1998).

DUNN, W. S. Jr. *Hitler's Nemesis: The Red Army, 1930–1945* (New York, 1994).

GLANTZ, D. M. *Stumbling Colossus: The Red Army on the Eve of World War* (Lawrence, KS, 1998).

GLANTZ, D. M. and J. HOUSE. *When Titans Clash: How the Red Army Stopped Hitler* (Lawrence, KS, 1995).

GORKOV, I. *Kremi, Stavka, Genshtab* (Tver, 1995).

GORODETSKY, G. *Grand Delusion: Stalin and the German Invasion of Russia* (New Haven, CT, 1999).

MELTIUKHOV, M. *Upushchennyi shans Stalina* (Moscow, 2000).

NEVEZHIN, V. *Sindrom nastupatel'noi voiny* (Moscow, 1997).

RAACK, R. *Stalin's Drive to the West, 1939–1945* (Stanford, CA, 1995).

SEVOSTYANOV, P. *Before the Nazi Invasion: Soviet Diplomacy in September 1939–June 1941* (Moscow, 1984 [a Soviet view]).

STOLFI, R.H.S. *Hitler's Panzers East* (Norman, OK, 1991).

SUVOROV, V. (Viktor Rezun). *Den' M. 6 iuliia 1941* (Moscow, 1994).

——— *Posledniai'a respublika* (Moscow, 1996).

———. *Icebreaker: Who Started the Second World War?* trans. T. R. Beattie (London, 1990).

TOPITSCH, E. *Stalin's War: A Radical New Theory of the Origins of the Second World War* (London, 1987).

WEINBERG, G. *A World at Arms: A Global History of World War II* (Cambridge, England, 1994).

ARTICLES

DALLIN, A. "Stalin and the German Invasion," *Soviet Union,* XVIII, nos. 1–3 (1991): pp 19–37.

KIPP, J. W. "Barbarossa, Soviet Covering Forces and the Initial Period of War. . . ." *The Journal of Slavic Military Studies* 1, 2 (June 1988): 188–212.

NEVEZHIN, V. A. "The Pact with Germany and the Idea of an 'Offensive War', 1939–1941)," *JSMS* 8, 4 (December 1995), pp. 809–843.

ULDRICKS, T. "The Icebreaker Controversy: Did Stalin Plan to Attack Hitler?" *Slavic Review* (Fall 1999).

15

The Khrushchev Era, 1953–1964

Stalin's death in March 1953 touched off a power struggle involving the major forces in the Soviet system: the party, the state, the army, and the police. As Stalin's successors tried new methods of rule and sought public support, controls over the USSR and eastern Europe were relaxed considerably. Nikita S. Khrushchev (1894–1971), the eventual winner, lacked Stalin's absolute authority and wooed the public by denouncing Stalin's crimes, improving living standards, and barnstorming around the country. Khrushchev retained the chief features of the Soviet system, but he instituted important changes. Abroad, revolts in Poland and Hungary loosened Soviet control over the satellites. Between the USSR and Communist China ideological and political conflict erupted, which produced a Communist world with several power centers and varying approaches. How and why did Khrushchev win the power struggle in the USSR? How great was his authority afterward? Why did he institute de-Stalinization, and what were its effects? How fundamental were the differences between Khrushchev's Russia and Stalin's? How did the Soviet position in world affairs change

under Khrushchev? How was he viewed by his successors?

Politics: Repudiating Stalinism

After Stalin's death, the principle of collective leadership revived and individual dictatorship was repudiated. As Stalin was placed in the Lenin-Stalin Mausoleum, his chief pallbearers—Georgii Malenkov, Lavrenti Beria, and V. M. Molotov—appealed to the populace for unity and to avoid "confusion and panic." Briefly Malenkov held the two chief power positions of premier and first party secretary, but within two weeks he resigned as first secretary, and in September Khrushchev assumed that post. Marshal Zhukov, the World War II hero, became deputy defense minister as genuine collective rule and surface harmony prevailed.

In April 1953 *Pravda* announced that the "Doctors' Plot" had been a hoax. There was a shake-up in the secret police, and its chief, Beria, suddenly posed as a defender of "socialist legality" and urged liberal revisions of the criminal code. In June his security forces apparently tried a coup, but

SOVFOTO

Stalin's coffin being carried out of the House of Trade Unions
in March 1953. Right to left: L. Beria, G. Malenkov, Vassily Stalin
(J. Stalin's son), V. Molotov, Marshal Bulganin, L. Kaganovich, and N.
Shvernik.

party, state, and army leaders combined against
him. Beria was arrested. In December his "execution" was announced, and he became an "unperson." Subscribers to the *Great Soviet Encyclopedia*
were instructed to remove his biography and paste
in an enclosed article on the Bering Sea! The
secret police came under closer party control.

For the rest of 1953 the Soviet press featured a
jovial-looking Malenkov as the principal leader,
who stressed consumer goods production and
pledged that Soviet living standards would soon
rise markedly. *Izvestiia,* the government news-

paper, pushed this proconsumer line until December 1954, but *Pravda,* the party organ controlled by
Khrushchev, denounced it as "a belching of the
Right deviation . . . , views which Rykov, Bukharin,
and their ilk once preached." (And they had been
executed!) In February 1955 Malenkov resigned as
premier, citing "inexperience" and accepting
blame for agricultural failures. Marshal N. A. Bulganin, a political general and Khrushchev
appointee, replaced him as premier.

Khrushchev, like Stalin, consolidated his power
behind the scenes. A genuine man of the people,

he epitomized the revolutionary principle: careers open to talent. Khrushchev was born in Kalinovka, a village in Kursk province near the Ukrainian border; his ancestors were serfs, his father a peasant, then a coal miner, and his own childhood full of hardships. His image while Soviet leader reflected his peasant heritage. Attending the parish school, Khrushchev was the first member of his family to become literate. He joined the Bolshevik party in 1918, worked by day and attended school at night, fought in the Civil War, and revealed leadership and strong ambition. In 1929, still rough and uncouth, he was sent to the Moscow Industrial Academy to complete his education. By sheer ability and drive he came to lead its party organization. Three years later he became a member of the Central Committee and in 1935 headed the key Moscow party organization and guided it through the Great Purge. Invaluable to Stalin, he kept making speeches while others fell silent. In 1938 he was assigned to Ukraine, completed ruthless purges there, and the next year entered the Politburo as a full member. During and after World War II he served as boss of Ukraine. Throughout his career Khrushchev displayed toughness, resourcefulness, practicality, and a frank independence uncharacteristic of Stalin's henchmen. In 1950, surviving the failure of his untimely agricultural cities scheme, he stormed again into the inner circle of power.

After Malenkov's fall, Khrushchev was the most powerful member of the collective, sharing power with Premier Bulganin and Defense Minister Zhukov. During 1955–1956, he and Bulganin traveled to eastern Europe and Asia and undermined the power position of Foreign Minister Molotov. Meanwhile Khrushchev was replacing his rivals' supporters in the Secretariat with his own men.

Khrushchev dominated the 20th Party Congress of February 1956. In a dramatic secret speech, he denounced the crimes of the Stalin era and began building up his own image as Lenin's loyal follower as steps toward full power. (See Problem 9 at the end of this chapter.) He over-

came strong conservative opposition to the proposed speech by threatening to denounce Stalin publicly. In the speech, he accused Stalin of fostering a personality cult, claiming infallibility, and liquidating thousands of honest Communists and military leaders out of paranoidal suspicion. Stalin, he claimed, had gravely weakened the Red Army by executing its top leaders, and his inaction in June 1941 had brought the USSR to the brink of defeat. Khrushchev's speech established him as a reform leader campaigning for basic political changes and won him wide support from younger provincial party leaders. He sought to break the hold that Stalin retained over the party even from the grave, absolve himself of responsibility for Stalin's crimes, and dissociate himself from the dictator's closest lieutenants, Molotov and Malenkov. Khrushchev depicted Stalinism as an aberration and urged a return to Leninism and collective leadership. Molotov's resignation as foreign minister in June 1956 confirmed the power of Khrushchev's forces.

Opposition to Khrushchev was weakened, not broken. The upheavals in Poland and Hungary in late 1956 (discussed later in this chapter) temporarily lowered his prestige. By creating regional economic councils (sovnarkhozy), Khrushchev aimed to break the technocrats' hold over the central economic ministries, but this action stimulated his opponents to desperate countermeasures. In June 1957, while Khrushchev and Bulganin visited Finland, his rivals united, secured a Presidium majority, and voted him out of office. Returning hastily, Khrushchev proved his mastery over the party apparatus. He weaned waverers (Voroshilov, Bulganin, Saburov, and Pervukhin) from his chief opponents (Malenkov, Molotov, Kaganovich, and Shepilov) and insisted that the Central Committee vote on his removal. With Marshal Zhukov's support, Khrushchev's provincial supporters were flown to Moscow. The Central Committee then reversed the Presidium's action and expelled his chief rivals, henceforth dubbed the "antiparty group." Through maneuver and compromise, Khrushchev had won a decisive though limited victory.

Khrushchev moved swiftly to consolidate his power. Marshal Zhukov, accused of building a personality cult in the Red Army, was removed from the Presidium and as defense minister and replaced by Marshal Rodion Malinovskii. In March 1958 Bulganin resigned and Khrushchev became premier, confirming his predominant role in party and state. He became an undisputed and very popular leader, with enthusiastic support from the Soviet people who enjoyed his informality, his appearances around the country, and his well-publicized trips abroad. However, even during his six years of personal rule, Khrushchev never possessed Stalin's authority. He could not dictate to the Presidium, and he needed almost four years to remove his opponents from their posts. The "antiparty" leaders were exiled but not imprisoned, and even then Khrushchev's reform program was opposed strongly by a conservative group led by Mikhail Suslov.

Nikita Khrushchev represented something new and exciting for the Soviet public: an ordinary-looking Russian, open and garrulous, who had a real flair for public relations. Unlike Stalin, a suspicious paranoid ensconced within the Kremlin, Khrushchev plunged boldly into crowds and expressed his opinions flamboyantly. He was a risk taker and innovator who promised to improve living conditions for average people. He contrasted with Stalin in character and approach as dramatically as Gorbachev would later differ from his elderly predecessors. However, city intellectuals scorned Khrushchev for his ungrammatical Russian and boorish, often reckless behavior.

Once in power, Khrushchev reduced the apparatus of terror and rebuilt the party as his chosen instrument of power. Malenkov had released some political prisoners, but Khrushchev released millions, especially in 1956. Victims of Stalin's terror were rehabilitated, often posthumously, notably Marshal Tukhachevskii and other Red Army leaders purged by Stalin. Police influence declined, and a more relaxed and hopeful political climate devel-

UPI/Corbis-Bettmann

Nikita Sergeevich Khrushchev, 1894–1971. An official photograph of Khrushchev as First Secretary of the Communist Party.

oped. Khrushchev sought popularity by mixing with the people, traveling around the USSR, and delivering homey speeches to workers and peasants. Unlike Stalin, the Kremlin recluse, Khrushchev remained informal, jovial, and talkative, bringing new and able people from industry to revive the party, which Stalin had demoralized by terror. Promoting his youthful provincial supporters, he increased party authority over the technocrats. Like Lenin, Khrushchev stressed persuasion, not coercion, and party congresses, rare under Stalin, now met regularly.

In January 1959 Khrushchev convened a special 21st Congress to approve a Seven Year Plan to begin building communism. Khrushchev launched a miniature personality cult, which described him as "Lenin's comrade-in-arms" and architect of the transition to communism. Urging preparation of a new party program, he stressed that the state's coercive aspects were "withering away" and that some administrative and police functions could be transferred to "public" organizations such as the Komsomol. Opponents, however, objected to any premature dissolution of the state, and after the congress Khrushchev's erratic behavior and policy shifts revealed his continuing problems with the opposition.

The 22nd Congress of October 1961 convened mainly to adopt a new party program, which proclaimed: "The present generation of Soviet people shall live under communism." But at the congress Khrushchev renewed his anti-Stalin campaign and depicted Stalin's atrocities publicly in greater depth and detail. He accused Stalin of authorizing Kirov's assassination in 1934, which led to the Great Purge, and linked Molotov and Voroshilov with him in that affair. "Antiparty" elements, he claimed, had executed Stalin's repressive policies, whereas his own regime had broken cleanly with the past. In response to demands of some delegates, Stalin's body was removed from the mausoleum and reburied in the Kremlin wall. Moderates in the Presidium (Aleksei Kosygin and Anastas Mikoian), however, blocked Khrushchev's efforts to expel "antiparty" leaders from the party. Then the Cuban missile crisis shattered his prestige, and only at the Central Committee's June 1963 plenum, which named Leonid Brezhnev and Nicholas Podgorny (his allies in the Presidium) as party secretaries, did Khrushchev seem to recover his authority. The "antiparty" leaders were expelled from the party but not tried. Khrushchev's 70th birthday in April 1964 was appropriately celebrated by the Soviet press, but he was not portrayed as absolute or indispensable. His struggle with the opposition remained inconclusive and his victory incomplete. Khrushchev's personal rule lasted only six years, 1958–1964.

After 1953 the relaxation of some totalitarian controls enhanced the Soviet regime's legitimacy for most of the population. With the overpowering authoritarian image of Stalin gone and brutal police repression ended, a political reform movement developed among younger intellectuals and those released from Stalin's camps. This movement aimed at democratization, civil liberties, and preventing a reversion to Stalinism. Marxist-Leninist ideology became less effective and credible. The critical reaction of youthful dissidents ("sons") to the values of Stalinist "fathers" was reflected in the reactions of Vladimir Osipov, later editor of the underground journal *Veche*, to Khrushchev's secret speech:

> Overthrown was the man who had personified the existing system and ideology to such an extent that the very words "the Soviet power" and "Stalin" seemed to have been synonymous. We all, the future rebels, at the dawn of our youth, had been fanatical Stalinists [and] had believed with a truly religious fervor. . . . Khrushchev's speech and the 20th Congress destroyed our faith, having extracted from it its very core . . . , Joseph Stalin.[1]

The ensuing Hungarian Revolution profoundly affected Soviet university students. In Leningrad alone, some 2,000 were disciplined or expelled for condemning Soviet armed intervention in Hungary. They formed a number of political and literary groups that produced self-published (*samizdat*) underground journals.

Toward the non-Russian nationalities of the USSR Khrushchev pursued generally conciliatory policies while pushing efforts at linguistic and cultural Russification. Some of the peoples Stalin had deported during World War II were allowed to return home, but the Crimean Tatars and Volga Germans remained conspicuous exceptions. Finally, in 1964, Khrushchev rehabilitated the Volga Germans by decree in an effort to improve relations with West Germany, but he did not restore their autonomous republic. Crimean Tatar petitions to the government to permit their return to their ancestral homeland were pointedly ignored.

---

[1] Quoted in H. Morton and R. Tökes, *Soviet Politics and Society in the 1970s* (New York, 1974), p. 10.

Economy: Focus on Agriculture

After 1953, despite some major policy changes, the Soviet economy retained the chief strengths and weaknesses of the Stalin period and was run by men trained under Stalin. It remained a centrally planned economy in which heavy industry and defense were emphasized, though the consumer sector now received more resources. Under Malenkov the collective leadership, to win public support, pledged that for the first time since 1928 consumer industry would grow faster than heavy industry. In April 1953 food prices were considerably reduced, but since key items such as meat were in short supply, the result was long lines and shortages. Compulsory bond purchases were reduced and the worker's take-home pay increased, but not the supply of available goods.

Khrushchev emphasized agriculture and began with a frank statement on its sad condition. Soviet collective farming in 1953 was unproductive and unworthy of a great power: Half the population barely fed the other half. Soviet livestock herds, noted Khrushchev, were smaller than in 1928 or even 1916. Heavy taxes on private peasant plots discouraged production of desperately needed meat, milk, and vegetables. These shortcomings must be overcome in two to three years, warned Khrushchev, always in a hurry. During the next five years many steps were taken to foster agricultural growth. State prices for farmers' compulsory deliveries and over-quota shipments were raised sharply, especially for grains. In 1954 the average price paid for all agricultural products was more than double the 1952 level; in 1956 it was two and one-half times higher. The state assumed most collective farm transportation costs, wrote off their old debts, and reduced taxes on private plots and limitations on private livestock holdings. Tractor and fertilizer production were expanded. Greater incentives to farmers and increased state investment in agriculture stimulated a 50-percent rise in output between 1953 and 1958.

Khrushchev's most controversial gamble was plowing up millions of acres of semiarid soil in the virgin lands of northern Kazakhstan. Reviving a plan of 1940 that had never been implemented, he sought to solve the grain shortage by greatly increasing the cultivated area of the USSR. By the end of 1956, 88.6 million additional acres had been placed under cultivation, an area equal to the total cultivated land of Canada. Hundreds of new state farms were created, some 300,000 persons permanently relocated in Kazakhstan, and additional hundreds of thousands helped bring in the harvest. Leonid I. Brezhnev, then second party secretary of Kazakhstan, directed this campaign. In 1955 drought brought a poor crop and threatened Khrushchev's position, but an excellent harvest in 1956 apparently vindicated his risky experiment: Kazakhstan alone provided 16 million tons of grain.

The Sixth Five Year Plan, approved in 1956 by the 20th Congress, set ambitious goals for agriculture, including a grain output of 180 million tons. In 1957 began a hectic campaign to overtake the United States in per capita production of meat, milk, and butter. Khrushchev toured the country, made many speeches, and dismissed numerous officials. He pushed the development of state farms at the expense of collectives (*kolkhozy*) and amalgamated the latter into larger units. (*Kolkhozy* decreased from 125,000 in 1950 to 69,100 in 1958.) In 1958 Machine Tractor Stations were abolished and *kolkhozy* were forced to purchase their machines.

Industrial growth in the 1950s continued to be rapid despite management problems. The Fifth Plan's goals were mostly fulfilled, and the Sixth Plan prescribed creation of a third major metallurgical base in Kazakhstan and western Siberia. Industrial management, however, became entangled with Khrushchev's drive for political supremacy. In February 1957 Khrushchev's scheme to scrap central industrial ministries in Moscow and replace them with regional economic councils (*sovnarkhozy*), eventually 107 in number, under Gosplan was approved. Causing a massive exodus of ministry personnel to the provinces, it made regional party secretaries virtual economic dictators. Khrushchev achieved his political aim of weakening the ministerial hierarchy but not the economic goal of greater industrial efficiency. The *sovnarkhozy* were supposed to overcome supply problems, avoid duplication, and improve regional planning, but they catered to selfish local interests, and individual enterprises often received no clear directives or got conflicting orders from various agencies. In the partial recentralization of 1963, *sovnarkhozy* were reduced in number and 17 larger economic planning regions were created. Khrushchev's insistence in 1962 on splitting party organizations into industrial and agricultural hierarchies caused much confusion and uncertainty, especially because *sovnarkhozy* rarely corresponded with the new party units. By 1963 industrial and agricultural management were chaotic.

Meanwhile, in 1959, the Sixth Five Year Plan had been scrapped in midcourse in favor of Khrushchev's grandiose Seven Year Plan "to construct the bases of communism."[2] It featured heavy investment in the chemical industry, non-solid fuels, and development of Asiatic Russia. In 1961 Khrushchev raised some of the plan's goals, including steel output. During its first years industrial progress remained impressive, but thereafter declining growth rates in industry and agriculture made a mockery of Khrushchev's 1961 party program, which foresaw the attainment by 1980 of industrial output and living standards far exceeding those of capitalist countries. In 1963 the Seven Year Plan was abandoned as impossible of achievement, a tacit admission that the party program likewise was unrealizable.

Agricultural stagnation and lagging labor productivity slowed overall Soviet economic growth after 1958. Agricultural output, supposed to rise 70 percent during the Seven Year Plan, increased only 14 percent (crops only 7 percent). Bad weather

was a factor, especially in 1963, but other reasons were more important. Suddenly dissolving most Machine Tractor Stations and compelling the collective farms to purchase their machinery virtually bankrupted poorer farms. Dispersed among *kolkhozy*, the machines could not be properly maintained or repaired. Because *kolkhozy* lacked the capital to purchase new machinery, the agricultural equipment industry was brought to the verge of ruin. This poorly thought out and irresponsibly executed reform had a depressing effect on collective farm production.

Equally harmful was Khrushchev's optimistic but ill-conceived campaign, announced in May 1957, to overtake the United States in production of meat, milk, and butter within three to four years. This campaign provoked what the Medvedevs call "the Riazan fiasco." Responding to Khrushchev's appeal, A. N. Larionov, ambitious party secretary of Riazan province, pledged to more than double meat deliveries to the state in 1959. This goal was achieved by slaughtering beef and milk cows and buying animals and meat from other provinces; Larionov became a Hero of Socialist Labor. However, by 1960 Riazan's agriculture was ruined, its herds decimated, and its *kolkhozy* in debt. With Riazan unable to deliver even half its normal quota of meat and grain, the "heroic" Larionov shot himself. National production of meat fell sharply, and Khrushchev's boast to overtake America in meat production became a bad joke.[3] Thus Khrushchev's personal campaigns, interference, and hasty reorganizations did considerable harm. He did not create the nation's agricultural problems, but his policies often made them worse. In March 1962 he told the Central Committee:

> Communism cannot be conceived of as a table with empty places at which sit highly conscious and fully equal people. . . . It is necessary to double and triple the output of major farm products in a short period. . . . The develop-

---

[2] Khrushchev's Plan called for an increase of 62 to 65 percent in national income (58 percent was achieved); 80 percent in gross industrial output (84 percent achieved); grain, 164 to 180 million tons (121 million achieved); and meat, 6.13 million tons (5.25 million achieved). See Alec Nove, *An Economic History of the USSR, 1917–1991* (New York, 1992), p. 363.

[3] Roy Medvedev and Zhores Medvedev, *Khrushchev: The Years in Power,* trans. A. Durkin (New York, 1978), pp. 80–100.

ment of agriculture is an integral part of the creation of the material and technical bases of communism.

Instead Soviet grain production in 1963 fell 27 million tons below the high point reached in 1958, and millions of tons had to be imported from the United States and Canada. Poor economic performance after 1958 made Khrushchev increasingly vulnerable politically.

Beginning in 1958 the Soviet wage system was reformed with a trend away from the piece rates that had been prevalent under Stalin. New minimum wages in town and country gave the lowest paid workers substantial increases. To cut pay differentials, some higher salaries (for example, those of professors) were reduced. The workweek was gradually shortened, maternity leaves were lengthened, and industrial pensions and disability benefits were much improved. The currency reform of 1961 exchanged 1 new ruble for 10 old ones; the rate of 4 rubles to the dollar was altered arbitrarily to 0.90 rubles per dollar. As direct taxes were further reduced, the turnover tax remained the chief source of state revenue.

In foreign trade, important changes occurred under Khrushchev. The USSR abandoned Stalin's policy of exploiting the European satellites economically, scrapped the joint companies that had done so, and paid fairer prices for eastern European goods. In 1954 the multilateral Council for Mutual Economic Assistance (Comecon) was revived, though most Soviet trade with eastern Europe remained bilateral. The USSR moved into the foreign aid field and, in 1953 China received a long-term Soviet credit of 520 million rubles. (The Soviets had removed equipment worth more than three times that much from Manchuria in 1945!) After Khrushchev visited India in 1955, a major program of foreign economic aid to that country began, partly to compete with the United States in the Third World. The Soviets supplied goods on credit, especially to India and Egypt, for later repayment in goods. Soviet imports and exports increased sharply. Using 1955 as the base year (100), imports in 1950 had been 54.6 and

exports 56.7. By 1958 they were 148.4 and 130, respectively.[4]

Living standards of most Soviet citizens improved considerably under Khrushchev, but this rise whetted their appetites for more. Beginning in 1956, housing construction spurted and private home building received more state support. Even millions of new apartments, mostly in massive, ugly blocks derisively dubbed "Khrushchev slums," could not satisfy demand. Between 1953 and 1964 the Soviet population rose from 188 to 228 million, mostly in cities. Just before his fall, Khrushchev declared that the chief task of the near future was "a further rise in the living standard of the people. . . . Now when we have a mighty [heavy] industry, the party is setting the task of the more rapid development of the branches that produce consumer goods." Performance did not match these promises.

Foreign Affairs: Crises in the Communist Bloc Countries

Soviet foreign policy quickly discarded its rigid Stalinist mold to adopt flexible, varied tactics. Malenkov began the shift and Khrushchev, stressing peaceful coexistence with the West from February 1956, continued and extended this new approach. It had to overcome a conservative hardline opposition, led first by Molotov and later apparently by Suslov, which favored a more aggressive anti-Western course. Stalin's successors found it increasingly difficult to maintain leadership of the Communist bloc and world Communist movement in the face of Chinese and Yugoslav challenges.

After Stalin's death, the collective leadership promoted détente with the West and China, as Premier Malenkov warned that nuclear war might destroy all humankind, not just capitalism. In July 1953 an armistice ended the Korean War, and at

[4] A. Nove, *An Economic History of the USSR* (London, 1969), p. 352.

the Geneva Conference of 1954 the USSR supported settlement of the Indochina conflict, although no settlement was forthcoming. The tone and manners of Soviet diplomacy began to mellow. Unable to coerce China, Soviet leaders courted it, promising technical aid, loans, and experts to assist Chinese industrialization, and agreed to end special privileges, abolish joint companies, and return Port Arthur to China.

Soviet leaders wished to prevent West Germany from rearming and entering NATO, but they refused to sacrifice their East German satellite. Early in 1954 a four-power conference called to reach a general German settlement ended in stalemate. After West Germany joined NATO, the Soviets in May 1955 set up the Warsaw Pact, a defensive alliance of the satellites and the USSR, with the latter commanding all the military forces, thus legalizing the presence of Soviet troops in eastern Europe.

Foreign trips by top Soviet leaders, beginning in 1955, fostered a new image of Soviet foreign policy. Khrushchev made a pilgrimage to Belgrade, blamed the Soviet-Yugoslav breach of 1948 on Beria, and over Molotov's strong objections achieved reconciliation with Marshal Tito. The expanding Soviet foreign aid program and the wooing of such neutral countries as India signified the replacement of Zhdanov's two-camp thesis (socialism versus capitalism) with a more flexible three-camp concept to include neutral countries. In May 1955 the USSR signed an Austrian peace treaty, which ended four-power occupation and made Austria a neutral country. (See Map 15.1.) Apparently Moscow hoped that West Germany would leave NATO in order to achieve German reunification on a similar basis. This policy culminated in the Geneva Summit Conference (July 1955) between President Eisenhower and a smiling Khrushchev and Bulganin. The amiable "Geneva spirit" produced no substantive agreements, but reduced Cold War tensions and enhanced Khrushchev's prestige abroad.

A crisis confronted the USSR in eastern Europe in 1956. Without Stalin's awesome image, the unpopular satellite regimes proved vulnerable to public agitation for change. As Soviet controls relaxed and a degree of diversity appeared, a workers' uprising in East Germany (June 1953) had to be crushed by Soviet tanks. Khrushchev's secret speech further undermined the satellite regimes. In June 1956 riots in the Polish industrial city of Poznan swelled into a national movement of liberalization and brought the hasty restoration of Wladyslaw Gomulka, purged by Stalin, as first secretary of the Polish Communist Party. When top Soviet leaders stormed into Warsaw on October 19, the new Polish leadership presented a united front. In a compromise solution, Poland won domestic autonomy while remaining in the Warsaw Pact and pledging loyalty to the USSR in foreign affairs. Such "domesticism" became a model for other eastern European countries. Preserving Soviet domination of the region, it freed the USSR from detailed supervision of domestic affairs in the satellites.

Meanwhile in Hungary a broad popular movement led by students and intellectuals demanded drastic political reforms. Premier Imre Nagy failed to halt Stalinist Hungary's rapid disintegration. After a revolt in Budapest (October 23), Nagy announced that Hungary would leave the Warsaw Pact, become a neutral country, and restore a multiparty system. Much of the Hungarian army joined the insurgents, who appealed to the West for aid. Janos Kadar, hastily named the new first secretary of the Hungarian Communist Party, "invited" in Soviet troops, which soon crushed the rebels as thousands of Hungarians fled into exile. The Soviet response in Hungary showed that the USSR would act militarily within its sphere of interest whenever Communist rule was threatened, demonstrating anew that Communist control in eastern Europe was based not on consent but on Soviet bayonets and the unreliability of satellite armies.

Toward the West, Khrushchev combined "peaceful coexistence" with bluster and threats. To him coexistence meant avoiding war and preventing nuclear rearmament of West Germany. The USSR sponsored the Rapacki Plan (October 1957), named after the Polish foreign minister, for a

Russian occupied zones in Austria (evacuated in 1955) and Germany

British, French, and American occupied zones

The "Iron Curtain" in 1948

Former German and Czechoslovak territory annexed by Russia in 1945

Principal areas of anti-Soviet protest and revolt 1953–1968 crushed by Soviet military intervention (East Germany, Hungary, Czechoslovakia) and by strong political pressure (Poland)

Map 15.1 USSR and Eastern Europe, 1945–1989

SOURCE: Adapted with permission of Macmillan Publishing Co., Inc. from *Russian History Atlas* by Martin Gilbert. Cartography by Martin Gilbert. Copyright © by Martin Gilbert.

nuclear-free zone in central Europe. Khrushchev's caution in 1958 during crises over Taiwan and Lebanon involving the United States distressed hard-liners in Moscow and Beijing. The growing Chinese challenge helped provoke Khrushchev to deliver an ultimatum to the West over Berlin in November 1958, hoping to force Western powers out of that city. When his ultimatum instead stimulated Western unity and determination, Khrushchev backed down. His erratic policies toward the West reflected his weakness at home and vulnerability to conservative critics.

At a meeting in November 1957 to celebrate the 40th anniversary of the Bolshevik Revolution, the 12 ruling Communist parties issued the Moscow Declaration, which stressed the unity of the socialist camp headed by the USSR. The Yugoslavs, affirming that every country should determine its own road to socialism, refused to sign and accused the USSR of bureaucracy and departures from true Marxism-Leninism; Moscow retorted that Tito was a revisionist kowtowing to U.S. imperialism. Although the second Soviet-Yugoslav dispute (1958–1961) avoided an open breach, Yugoslav independence and the potential threat of national communism to Soviet leadership were reaffirmed.

After 1957 Soviet foreign policy was influenced strongly by the triangular Soviet-U.S.-Chinese relationship. Khrushchev was caught between his desire for détente with the West and the maintenance of Soviet leadership of the Communist Bloc against more militant China. Seeking to score points against "American imperialism" in the Middle East, he backed Arab states against pro-Western Israel and Turkey and rattled his rockets. The growing Soviet commitment to the Arabs proved expensive, especially the construction for Egypt of the Aswan Dam, which the United States had refused to finance.

Renewed Soviet overtures to the United States ended in failure. After his Berlin ultimatum had failed to budge the West, Khrushchev at the 21st Congress (January 1959) made warm references to the United States, and in September he became the first Russian ruler to visit the United States. This trip was a personal triumph for Khrushchev and cemented his relationship with a flexible President Eisenhower; they agreed to hold a summit conference in Moscow in 1960. When a U.S. U-2 reconnaissance plane spying over Soviet territory was shot down and its pilot captured, Eisenhower took responsibility for the flight but refused to apologize officially. An angry Khrushchev then sabotaged the summit and withdrew his invitation to Eisenhower to visit the USSR.

More serious was a growing rift between the USSR and China, which now became public and disrupted Bloc unity. Between 1957 and 1960, though their relations seemed harmonious, mounting Soviet criticism of China's industrial "Great Leap Forward" suggested that China might reach communism before the USSR. Khrushchev's party program of 1961 was in direct response to this Chinese challenge. The Chinese also condemned Soviet détente with the West. In 1960 began thinly concealed mutual vilification: The Chinese attacked Yugoslav "revisionism," and the Soviets denounced the Stalinist Albanian regime, which sought Chinese support, as "dogmatic," but clearly they were striking at each other. Sino-Soviet tension was only partly ideological. Mao was now the senior leader of world communism, and in intra-Bloc disputes the Chinese adopted an orthodox, Stalinist line, which was supported by some of the Soviet "antiparty group." Militance in promoting revolution and national liberation won the Chinese widespread support in Asia and Africa. A unified Communist China challenged the Soviet position in Asia and posed a potential threat to underpopulated Siberia. Noting niggardly Soviet economic aid to them, the Chinese complained that Khrushchev was more generous to nonaligned India and Egypt. Asserting that tsarist Russia in the 1850s had acquired the Maritime Province unfairly, Chinese maps showed portions of the Soviet Far East as Chinese territory. Khrushchev withdrew some Soviet technicians from China and sought to dissuade the Chinese from developing nuclear weapons, but in 1959 Beijing decided to manufacture its own. In April 1960 *Red Flag,* a Beijing journal, denouncing Khrushchev's policy of coexistence with capitalism, affirmed that nuclear war would destroy imperialism but not the socialist camp. At the Romanian Party Congress in June, Khrushchev, quarreling violently with the Chinese delegates, castigated their leaders as nationalists, adventurists, and "madmen" seeking to unleash nuclear war.

Attempts to resolve the Sino-Soviet dispute failed. In the summer of 1960 a world Communist

Congress in Moscow, representing 81 parties, sought to restore unity. Khrushchev, however, clashed with the Chinese over power-political issues. Soon afterward Albania, smallest and most backward of European Communist states, defied Khrushchev openly, praised Stalin, relied upon Chinese support, and boycotted the Soviet 22nd Congress. Chou En-lai, after defending Albania at the congress, left suddenly and was greeted vociferously in Beijing. Romania also began to assert independence of the USSR, especially in economic matters, and established good relations with China. In 1963 Romania proclaimed virtual neutrality in the Sino-Soviet dispute and even voted occasionally against the Soviet Union in the United Nations. The Sino-Soviet quarrel promoted polycentrism in the Communist world and disintegration of the Bloc.

After President John Kennedy's inauguration in 1961, Khrushchev sought concessions from the youthful American leader as compensation for his troubles in the Bloc. Cuba and Berlin were the key issues. In January 1959 Fidel Castro, heading a radical insurgent movement, took power in Cuba with Communist support and soon aligned himself with the Soviet Union. In April 1961 Cuban exiles supported by the United States sought unsuccessfully to overthrow the Castro regime in the inept Bay of Pigs invasion, whose failure revived Khrushchev's self-assurance. Meeting Kennedy in Vienna that June, Khrushchev threatened to sign a separate peace with East Germany unless an overall German settlement was reached soon. The ensuing Berlin crisis, however, revealed Kennedy's coolness and determination. To halt a westward surge of refugees, the East German regime built the Berlin Wall, which stood until late 1989. Finally Khrushchev removed his time limit on a German settlement and advocated nuclear-free zones in Europe and the Far East.

In the fall of 1962 the Cuban missile crisis threatened to provoke nuclear war between the USSR and the United States. Khrushchev had been seeking to conclude a German peace treaty and prevent China and West Germany from acquiring nuclear weapons. His decision to install medium-range missiles in Cuba was apparently a gamble to solve mounting domestic and foreign problems with one bold stroke: Once his missiles were installed, he might bargain with the West over Berlin and nuclear-free zones. U.S. aircraft detected the Soviet installations, however, and President Kennedy ordered a sea blockade of Cuba (October 22). Khrushchev had the choice of withdrawing the missiles or fighting a United States far superior in long-range missiles and local naval power. Khrushchev prudently chose withdrawal, only to be taunted by the Chinese for "adventurism" in placing the missiles in Cuba and cowardice in removing them!

Peaceful resolution of the missile crisis improved Soviet-American relations. In 1963 the United States, the USSR, and Britain agreed to ban the testing of nuclear weapons in the atmosphere. A "hot line" was set up between Washington and Moscow to reduce the danger of accidental nuclear war. Khrushchev's freedom of maneuver was sharply restricted by the Sino-Soviet quarrel. During 1963–1964 he tried but failed to round up support for a world Communist conference to expel the Chinese and reassert Soviet hegemony over world communism.

Khrushchev's Fall

In October 1964 Khrushchev was suddenly removed from power. The official statement of October 16 in *Pravda* declared:

> The plenum of the Central Committee satisfied the request of N. S. Khrushchev to relieve him of the duties of first secretary of the Central Committee, member of the Presidium of the Central Committee and chairman of the Council of Ministers of the USSR in connection with advanced age and poor health.

Actually his health was good, and many statesmen older than he were directing their countries' destinies. Subsequently his successors accused Khrushchev of "harebrained schemes," recklessness at home and abroad, fostering a new personality cult, undignified behavior, and dangerous experimentation. His prestige had suffered severely from the Cuban crisis, and between 1960 and 1963 he had almost been toppled on several occasions, but in 1964 his power still far exceeded that of other Presidium members. Apparently a powerful coalition of interest groups organized against him. While Khrushchev was on vacation in the Crimea, after he had refused to depart gracefully, the Presidium voted him out of office and disregarded his demand to submit the issue to the Central Committee. Having antagonized the military leaders by reducing the size of the ground forces, Khrushchev this time lacked the army support to reverse the verdict. Overnight Khrushchev became emeritus—an unperson rarely mentioned and relegated to obscurity but granted a fine apartment and limousine. The transfer of power, smooth and orderly, to Brezhnev and Kosygin marked a peaceful evolution of the Soviet political system away from Stalinist terror. The Presidium had become a society of relative equals, whose collective weight exceeded that of an individual leader.

A combination of foreign and domestic failures caused Khrushchev's unexpected downfall. His Presidium colleagues blamed him for the Cuban fiasco and setbacks in Berlin. The intensifying conflict with China had split the world Communist movement and encouraged Albania and Romania to assert full or partial independence. The Soviet position in eastern Europe, and with it Soviet security, were imperiled. At home the Soviet economy was stumbling. Industrial growth rates were falling, agriculture had stagnated, and Khrushchev's boasts of soon overtaking the United States sounded hollow. His decision in 1962 to split the party into industrial and agricultural segments had created confusion and antagonized party traditionalists and technocrats. Reduction of Soviet ground forces and efforts to promote détente with the West had alienated influential military men. Khrushchev's hasty reforms and mistakes welded together a potent conservative coalition. However, his basic policies —de-Stalinization, reducing terror, aiding agriculture and the consumer, and increasing contacts with the West—were apparently sound. Khrushchev had led the Soviet Union through the difficult post-Stalin transition, ensured the party's predominance, and maintained the Soviet Empire without resort to mass terror.

Problem 9

De-Stalinization: Stalin's Role in the Purges and in World War II

Was Joseph Stalin a "great revolutionary despot" (Deutscher) or a monster worse than Caligula, as his successor, Khrushchev, suggested in 1956? Did Stalin exemplify Soviet communism or represent an aberration from it because of his "cult of personality" after 1934? Why was the Great Purge launched, and what were its results? Did Stalin or his generals deserve blame for Soviet defeats early in World War II or the credit for eventual victory? Should Stalin be praised for his wartime leadership, or should he have been shot for failing to prepare or lead the country adequately? These and similar issues were debated inside and outside the Soviet Union after Khrushchev's "secret speech" in February 1956 at the 20th Party Congress lifted part of the veil that had shrouded Stalin's actions.

Stalinist Defense

The following sources glorify Stalin's leadership, contending that he was a genius and that what he did was necessary and correct. The first is an excerpt from the *History of the All-Union Com-*

munist Party (Bolshevik): Short Course, published originally in 1938. Approved by Stalin and sometimes attributed at least partly to him personally, this official party history seeks to explain and justify the Great Purge, then underway.

> The successes of socialism in our country gladdened . . . all honorable citizens of the USSR . . . , but infuriated more and more the . . . yesmen of the defeated classes—the miserable remnants of the Bukharinites and Trotskyites. These gentlemen . . . sought revenge upon the party and people for their failures. . . . On December 1, 1934 in Leningrad at Smolny, S. M. Kirov was most foully murdered with a shot from a revolver. The murderer, arrested at the scene of the crime, turned out to be a member of an underground counterrevolutionary group which was organized from members of the anti-Soviet Zinovievite group in Leningrad. . . . This group set itself the aim of murdering the leaders of the [Soviet] Communist Party. . . . From the depositions of the participants . . . it became evident that they were connected with representatives of foreign capitalist states and received money from them. The participants in this organization who were uncovered were sentenced by the Military Tribunal of the Supreme Court of the USSR to the extreme punishment—shooting.
>
> Soon thereafter the existence of an underground counterrevolutionary "Moscow center" was established. Investigation and trial clarified the vile role of Zinoviev, Kamenev, Evdokimov, and other leaders of this organization in arousing among their followers terrorist inclinations and to prepare the murder of members of the Central Committee and the Soviet government. . . . Already then in 1935 it became clear that the Zinovievite group was a hidden White Guardist organization which fully deserved to be dealt with like the White Guardists. . . .
>
> The chief inspirer and organizer of this whole band of murderers and spies was the Judas, Trotskii. Aiding Trotskii and executing his counterrevolutionary instructions were Zinoviev, Kamenev, and their Trotskyist yesmen. They prepared the defeat of the USSR in case of an attack on it by the imperialists, they became defeatists toward the worker-peasant state, they became the despicable servants and agents of the German and Japanese fascists.[5]

The following excerpts from a speech by Khrushchev in 1939 show him as a loyal follower of Stalin, praising the dictator and his work slavishly; they are included in a volume of similar speeches dedicated to Stalin.

> Today, on the 60th anniversary of Comrade Stalin's birth, all eyes will be turned on our great leader of nations, on our dear friend and father. Working people all over the world will write and speak words of love and gratitude about him. Their enemies will foam at the mouth with rage when . . . speaking on this theme. The working men of the world see in Comrade Stalin their leader, their liberator from the yoke of capitalism. . . . The imperialists of all countries know full well that every word uttered by Comrade Stalin is backed by a people of 183,000,000 strong, that every idea advanced by Comrade Stalin is endorsed by the great and mighty multinational Soviet people. . . .
>
> The biography of Comrade Stalin is the glorious epic of our Bolshevik party. . . . Lenin together with Stalin created the great Bolshevik party. . . . In Comrade Stalin the working class and all toilers possess the greatest man of the present era, a theoretician, leader, and organizer of the struggle and victory of the working class. . . . All nations of the Soviet Union see in Stalin their friend, their father, their leader. . . . Stalin is the father of his people by virtue of the love he bears them. Stalin is the leader of nations for the wisdom with which he guides their struggle. . . . The army and the navy are the creation of our great Stalin, who increases their might with every day.[6]

Khrushchev's Critique

In his "secret speech" of February 24–25, 1956, Khrushchev detailed Stalin's crimes and blunders while concealing that as Stalin's loyal follower he had participated in them. Khrushchev did not condemn Stalin unconditionally because

---

[5] *Istoriia VKP(b), Kratkii kurs* (Moscow, 1946), pp. 309–12.

[6] Quoted in Marin Pundeff, ed., *History in the U.S.S.R.* (San Francisco, 1967), pp. 135–39.

that would have meant repudiating industrialization, collectivization, and social benefits. While affirming Stalin's contributions in the Revolution and Civil War and in building socialism until 1934, Khrushchev focused on an aberration: the cult of the individual leader and its destructive results. World War II generals led by Marshal Zhukov had pressed Khrushchev to rehabilitate purged military leaders and the Red Army's reputation, partly by discrediting Stalin's wartime leadership. Engaged in a bitter power struggle, Khrushchev may have believed he could undermine conservative opponents such as Molotov by destroying the image of Stalin as an all-wise, all-powerful leader. He glorified Lenin as embodying socialist modesty, comradely behavior, and socialist legality and posed as his true follower. Declared Khrushchev:

> At present we are concerned . . . with how the cult of the person of Stalin gradually grew . . . , the source of a whole series of exceedingly grave perversions of party principles, party democracy, of revolutionary legality. . . . The great harm caused by the violation of collective direction of the party and . . . accumulation of immense and limitless power in the hands of one person, the party Central Committee considers it absolutely necessary to make the material pertaining to this matter available to the 20th Congress.

Marx and Lenin, Khrushchev reminded the delegates, had denounced any cult of an individual leader. Lenin had invariably displayed great modesty while emphasizing the role of the people and party in making history. Instead of dictating to his colleagues, "Lenin never imposed by force his views upon his co-workers. He tried to convince; he patiently explained his opinions to others." Lenin had realized Stalin's grave character defects, but premature death had prevented him from removing Stalin from office. After Stalin assumed power:

> Grave abuse of power by Stalin caused untold harm to our party. . . . Stalin . . . absolutely did not toler-
> ate collegiality in leadership and work, and practiced brutal violence. . . . Stalin acted . . . by imposing his concepts and demanding absolute submission to his opinion. Whoever opposed this concept . . . , was doomed to removal from the leading collective and to subsequent moral and physical annihilation. . . . Stalin originated the concept "enemy of the people" . . . which made possible the use of the most cruel repression, violating all norms of revolutionary legality against anyone who in any way disagreed with Stalin.

During the Great Purge, continued Khrushchev:

> Stalin . . . used extreme methods and mass repressions at a time when the Revolution was already victorious, . . . when the exploiting classes were already liquidated, . . . when our party was politically consolidated. . . . Stalin showed in a whole series of cases his intolerance, his brutality and his abuse of power. . . . He often chose the path of repression and physical annihilation, not only against actual enemies, but also against individuals who had committed no crimes against the party and the Soviet government.

Generally the only proof of guilt was a "confession" exorted by force and torture. Such incongruous methods, noted Khrushchev, were employed when the Revolution had already triumphed, the exploiters had been wiped out, and socialism had been firmly established. "In the situation of socialist victory there was no basis for mass terror in the country." This terror had been blamed on N. I. Yezhov, chief of the security police, but clearly Stalin had made the decisions and issued the arrest orders.

Khrushchev, seeking to discredit Stalin's role as the chief Soviet leader in World War II, accused Stalin of failing to prepare the USSR for war, of disregarding numerous clear warnings of impending German attack, and of gross incompetence and negligence in directing military operations. Moreover, after victory Stalin denied the crucial role of his generals and people in achieving victory, taking all the credit for himself. Khrushchev noted the improbable role that many Soviet war novels and films attributed to Stalin. Supposedly harkening to Stalin's "genius," the

Problem 9 continued

Red Army had retreated deliberately, then counterattacked and smashed the Nazi invaders. Such works ascribed the glorious victory achieved by the heroic Soviet people solely to Stalin's brilliant strategy. Stalin blamed early severe Soviet defeats on the German surprise attack, though Hitler had announced his intent to destroy communism back in 1933. In the months before the attack, numerous warnings came from the West, Soviet diplomats, and military men that a Nazi invasion was imminent, but Stalin disregarded them. "Despite these particularly grave warnings, the necessary steps were not taken to prepare the country properly for defense and to prevent it from being caught unaware," said Khrushchev.

Khrushchev was equally critical of Stalin's performance as wartime commander in chief. When the Nazis invaded, Soviet troops had orders not to return fire because Stalin just could not believe that war had really begun. In border areas much of the Soviet air force and artillery were lost needlessly, and the Germans broke through. Believing that the end was near, Stalin declared in panic, "All that Lenin created we have lost forever." For a long time Stalin neither directed operations nor exercised real leadership. He was ignorant of the true situation at the front, which he never visited except for one brief look at a stabilized sector, yet his constant interference with military operations caused huge manpower losses. Exclaimed Khrushchev derisively, "Stalin planned operations on a globe . . . and traced the front line on it!" As a result, early in 1942 the Germans surrounded large Red Army units in the Kharkov area, and hundreds of thousands of soldiers were lost. Yet Stalin believed that he was always right and never made mistakes. "This is Stalin's military genius; this is what it cost us," declared Khrushchev.

Right after Soviet victory, Stalin began unfairly to denigrate the contributions to victory of many top Red Army commanders. "Stalin excluded every possibility that services rendered at the front should be credited to anyone but himself." All Soviet victories, Stalin claimed, had been due solely to his courage and genius. In the postwar Soviet film *The Fall of Berlin* (1949), only Stalin issued orders; there was no mention of the military commanders, the Politburo, or the government. "Stalin acts for everybody . . . in order to surround Stalin with glory, contrary to the facts and to historical truth."[7]

Post-Khrushchev Debate on Stalin

On February 16, 1966, at the Institute of Marxism-Leninism in Moscow, a discussion was held on a book by Soviet historian A. M. Nekrich, *June 22, 1941*, which used the "secret speech" to blame Stalin for Soviet unpreparedness. This debate reflected a major issue disputed in the USSR throughout the more open Khrushchev era. It related not only to Stalin's alleged mistakes and crimes, but also to the role of Khrushchev in implementing de-Stalinization. The debate was wide open by Soviet standards then, though most participants and the audience believed that Nekrich had not gone far enough in criticizing Stalin. In the extracts that follow, note the critical attitude of Professor G. A. Deborin of the Institute of Marxism-Leninism in Moscow toward the fallen Khrushchev and his partial defense of Stalin.

> **Deborin** Nekrich adopts an erroneous position; he explains everything by the obstinate stupidity of Stalin himself. That is a superficial analysis. . . . Stalin was not the only person involved. . . . It is unnecessary to refer to Khrushchev's declarations which are not objective. . . . Insofar as [Stalin] received false information, Stalin reached false conclusions. He placed too much hope in the German-Soviet pact, . . . but Stalin's estimate of German intentions was endorsed by all those around him. So Stalin cannot be considered solely responsible for his mistakes.

---

[7] N. S. Khrushchev, "The Crimes of the Stalin Era," *The New Leader*, 1956.

Problem 9 continued

Anfilov (General Staff) And now let us come to the beginning of the war. If all our forces had been completely ready for action, which was entirely Stalin's responsibility, we should not have begun the war with such disasters! And in general the war would not have been so long, so bloody, and so exhausting. . . . Stalin remains the chief culprit.

Dashichev (General Staff) [Nekrich] should have gone deeper. . . . It was [Stalin] who made the situation in which the country then found itself [in 1941]. Stalin's greatest crime was to have eliminated the best cadres of our army and our party. All our leaders understood the international situation, but not one of them was courageous enough to fight to get the necessary measures taken for the defense of the country. . . . The driver of the bus is responsible for every accident that happens through his fault. Stalin assumed the responsibility for every accident that happens through his fault. Stalin assumed the responsibility of sole driver. His guilt is immense.

Slezkin (Institute of History of the Academy of Sciences) I was at the front and took part, at the age of 19, in the June 1941 fighting. There can be no hesitation in saying that Stalin's behavior was criminal. There was a vicious circle of personality cult, provocation and repression. Everyone tried to please his superior by supplying only the information that might gratify him. . . . All this was the cause of immeasurable damage to the country and everyone is guilty in his own way. . . . And the responsibility is heavier in proportion to one's place in the hierarchy. . . . Stalin is the chief culprit.

Peter Yakir (Institute of History of the Academy of Sciences) Some of the speakers . . . have referred to "Comrade Stalin." . . . Stalin was nobody's comrade and above all, not ours. Stalin impeded the development of our armaments by eliminating many eminent technicians, and among them the creators of our artillery. . . . In the concentration camps there were millions of able-bodied men, specialists in every department of the country's economic and military life. And the task of guarding them absorbed considerable forces.

Snegov [who had been imprisoned in one of Stalin's labor camps] Nekrich's book is honest and useful. If a unit is disorganized on the eve of combat, . . . then that unit suffers a defeat. The head of such a unit is generally shot by order of the high command. . . . Stalin was both the supreme commander, and the head of the unit and that unit, in a state of disorganization, was our whole country. Stalin ought to have been shot. Instead of which, people are now trying to whitewash him. . . . How can one be a Communist and speak smoothly about Stalin who betrayed . . . Communists, who eliminated nearly all the delegates of the Eighteenth Congress . . . , and who betrayed the Spanish Republic, Poland, and all Communists in all countries?

Deborin It has not been my task to defend or justify Stalin. What is needed is to examine the personality cult more deeply in all its aspects. . . . It is strange that Snegov should hold the same view [as West German Professor Jacobson]. Comrade Snegov, you ought to tell us which camp you belong to!

Snegov The Kolyma [concentration] camp.

Nekrich It is Stalin who bears the chief responsibility for the heavy defeat and all the tragedy of the first part of the war. All the same, nobody ought to provide his superiors with inexact information because it will give them pleasure. Stalinism began because of us, the small people. Stalin wanted to trick Hitler; but instead of that he got himself into a maze which led to disaster. He knew better than anyone about elimination of the leading cadres and the weaknesses of the army.[8]

Gorbachev's Position

President M. S. Gorbachev continued and in some ways deepened the critique of Stalin that General Secretary Khrushchev began in 1956. Public pressure virtually compelled Gorbachev to

[8] Selected excerpts reprinted from *June 22, 1941: Soviet Historians and the German Invasion* by Vladimir Petrov, pp. 250–61, by permission of The University of South Carolina Press. Copyright © 1968 by The University of South Carolina Press in cooperation with the Institute for Sino-Soviet Studies, The George Washington University, Washington, D.C.

Problem 9 continued

address the Stalin issue in his speech of November 2, 1987, but he failed to face it squarely.

> To remain faithful to historical truth we have to see both Stalin's indisputable contribution to the struggle for socialism, to the defense of its gains, as well as the gross political mistakes and the abuses committed by him and his circle, for which our people paid a heavy price and which had grave consequences for society. Sometimes it is said that Stalin did not know about many incidents of lawlessness. The documents at our disposal show that this is not so. The guilt of Stalin and his immediate entourage before the party and the people for wholesale repressive measures and acts of lawlessness is enormous and unforgivable. This is a lesson for all generations.[9]

In his speech of November 25, 1989, Gorbachev returned to this theme, arguing that Stalin's unfortunate legacy—a centralist bureaucratic system—had to be replaced if the USSR was to progress.

> Why did Stalin succeed in imposing on the Party and on all of society his program and his methods? . . . Stalin played cleverly upon the revolutionary impatience of the masses, on the utopian and egalitarian tendencies of any mass movement, on the vanguard's aspiration for the quickest possible achievement of the desired goal. . . . The idea of socialism became equated more and more with an authoritarian command and bureaucratic administrative system.
>
>   . . . An ever greater rift [opened] between the theory of Marxism and reality, between the humane ideals and practice. A bureaucratic, extremely centralized economic and political system acted by its own laws. And theory had . . . to create the illusion of the "correctness" of these actions. . . . In the name of the achievement of "the great idea" of socialism were justified the most inhumane means. . . . The 20th Congress, rejecting and condemning the dark sides of the Stalin regime and its ex-

tremes, generally left unchanged the bureaucratic system itself. It managed to survive, aided by a new illusion that it was enough to eliminate the extremes of the Stalinist regime—and the liberated energy of socialism in the near future could bring our society to the higher phase of communism. Stalinist distortions led to the loss of the main content of the Marxist and Leninist concept of socialism: an understanding of the individual as the goal, not the means.[10]

Two Western Evaluations

The U.S. scholar Severyn Bialer, in his introduction to Soviet wartime memoirs, seeks to strike a balance between exaggerated praise of Stalin and Khrushchev's one-sided and partisan denunciation. Up to 1953, he points out, Soviet war history had glorified Stalin as an infallible and omnipotent genius. Soon after Stalin's death "war history came to serve the cult of the party," whose infallibility replaced Stalin's. Khrushchev's attack in 1956 had aimed to use Stalin's crimes as a lever to achieve power:

> The singlemindedness with which Khrushchev concentrated on his goal . . . led him to seek not comprehension, not rectification, but destruction of Stalin's role as war leader. . . . Soviet war memoirs testify to Stalin's complete control over the political, industrial, and military aspects of the Soviet war effort. . . . The Soviet dictator personally made every wartime decision of any importance. He alone seems to have possessed the power to impose his will on both civilian and military associates alike. . . .
>
>   . . . It appeared to [Western observers] that Stalin had an extraordinary grasp of war goals and major long-range plans for conducting the war and a talent for adjusting the conduct of military operations to political realities. . . . On the second level, that of tactical and technical expertise, Western observers were struck by Stalin's mastery of detail. . . . Their descriptions are corroborated in the memoirs of Soviet commanders and industrial managers. . . .
>
>   The task of military leadership is located to an overwhelming extent, however . . . in the area of

---

[9] M. Gorbachev, *October and Perestroika: The Revolution Continues, 1917–1987* (Moscow, 1987), p. 21.

[10] *Pravda*, November 26, 1989, pp. 1–3.

Problem 9 continued

operational leadership which involves planning and control of large-scale military operations—battles and campaigns. In this middle area . . . , Stalin made no real contribution. . . . Stalin's crucial contribution to victory . . . [derived] from his ability to organize and administer the mobilization of manpower and material resources. . . . Stalin . . . regarded his role as that of arbiter and ultimate judge of his generals' strategic plans and operational designs. His major asset as a military leader was the ability to select talented commanders and to permit them to plan operations, while reserving for himself the ultimate power of decision. . . .

Thus what was crucial to Soviet survival and eventual victory was Stalin's ability to mobilize Soviet manpower and economic resources over a sustained period, his ability to assure the political stability of his armed forces and the population at large despite disastrous initial defeats, and his ability to recognize and reward superior military talent at all levels under his command. . . . It was in just the area of Russia's greatest need that Stalin showed his greatest strength. . . . He was above all an administrator better suited to directing the gigantic military and civilian bureaucracy than to initiating and formulating military plans.[11]

The historian Robert Conquest, who has written authoritatively on the Stalin terror, provides this largely negative evaluation of Stalin in a recent book:

The long-term effects of the life which ended in Kuntsevo on that night in March [1953] . . . were dreadful and enduring. . . . Meanwhile, the politico-economic system Stalin had created remained in being. It was only in the late 1980s that the Soviet leadership saw that the Stalin-style "command economy" had ruined the country. . . . [In the late 1980s] there came a campaign of continuous, wholesale and devastating revelation of the truth about Stalinism and about Stalin personally—including . . . the digging up of mass graves. . . .

Stalin was in almost every way an outsider. He had no natural allegiance to his family, his home, his nation, his schoolmates. He was neither a Georgian nor a Russian. He was neither a worker nor an intellectual. . . . His marital life was an empty front. His social life was an imperfectly maintained pretence, which eventually degenerated into forced jollity with coarse and terrified toadies. . . . As so often with Stalin, we seem to find normal human faculties either lacking or withered to vestigial form. One of his outstanding characteristics was, in many respects, a profound mediocrity melded with a superhuman willpower. It is as though he had a very ordinary brain, but with some lobes extravagantly overdeveloped. . . . It is clear that a profound feeling of insecurity was thickly woven into his personality. This manifested itself in the continuous falsification of his part in events. . . .

The question of whether Stalin was, or became, insane is now being publicly argued. . . . That he was psychologically abnormal is clear enough. . . . Above all, he was by nature cruel. . . . For Stalin's personal inclination to terror and death, it is indeed hardly necessary to do more than look at the record. . . . Impersonally ordering and signing scores of thousands of death sentences, as often as not of men who had supported him in all his earlier acts of tyranny. . . . And he inflicted not only death, but also torture, giving personal instructions on the beating of innocent prisoners. Despots who revelled in killing and torture are to be found in various periods of history, and among them Stalin occupies a very high place. But . . . he ruled not only by terror but also by falsification. . . . The image of a tiger came to the minds of many: not merely the quintessential beast of prey, the most dangerous killer in the jungle, but also one that lies in wait for its victim with no more than an occasional sign of impatience.[12] ■

[11] *Stalin and His Generals: Soviet Military Memoirs of World War II*, ed. Severyn Bialer (New York, 1969), pp. 34–44.

[12] Robert Conquest, *Stalin: Breaker of Nations* (New York, 1991) pp. 314–19.

InfoTrac® College Edition Search Terms

Enter the search term *Khrushchev* in Keywords.
Enter the search term *Cold War* in the Subject Guide.
Enter the search term *Warsaw Pact* in Keywords.
Enter the search term *Hungary* in the Subject Guide, and then go to subdivision *Revolution, 1956.*

Suggested Additional Reading

BOFFA, G. *Inside the Khrushchev Era* (New York, 1963).

BRESLAUER, G. W. *Khrushchev and Brezhnev as Leaders* (London, 1982).

BURLACHUK, F. F. *Khrushchev and the First Russian Spring: The Era of Khrushchev Through the Eyes of His Advisor* (New York, 1991).

CHOTINER, B. A. *Khrushchev's Party Reform* (Westport, CT, 1984).

COHEN, S., ed. *The Soviet Union Since Stalin* (Bloomington, IN, 1980).

CRANKSHAW, E. *Khrushchev: A Career* (New York, 1966).

CRUMMEY, R. O., ed. *Reform in Russia and the USSR: Past and Prospects* (Urbana, IL, 1989).

DALLIN, A., ed. *The Khrushchev and Brezhnev Years* (New York, 1992).

DINERSTEIN, H. S. *The Making of a Missile Crisis: October 1962* (Baltimore, 1976).

FEIFER, G. *Justice in Moscow* (New York, 1964).

FILTZER, D. *Soviet Workers and De-Stalinization: The Case of the Modern System of Soviet Production Relations, 1953–1964* (New York, 1992).

FRANKLAND, M. *Khrushchev* (New York, 1967).

GITTINGS, J. *Survey of the Sino-Soviet Dispute, 1963–1967* (New York, 1968).

GRIFFITH, W. E. *Albania and the Sino-Soviet Rift* (Cambridge, MA, 1963).

HILSMAN, R. *The Cuban Missile Crisis: The Struggle over Policy* (Westport, CT, 1996).

HYLAND, W., and R. SHRYOCK. *The Fall of Khrushchev* (New York, 1969).

KHRUSHCHEV, N. S. *Khrushchev Remembers* (Boston, 1971).

———. *Khrushchev Remembers: The Last Testament* (Boston, 1974).

KHRUSHCHEV, S. N. *Nikita Khrushchev and the Creation of a Superpower,* trans. Shirley Benson (University Park, PA, 2000).

LARSON, D. W. *Anatomy of Mistrust: U.S.–Soviet Relations during the Cold War* (Ithaca, NY, 1997).

LEE, W., and R. STAAR. *Soviet Military Policy Since World War II* (Stanford, 1986).

LINDEN, C. A. *Khrushchev and the Soviet Leadership, 1957–1964* (London, 1967).

MASTNY, V. *The Cold War and Soviet Insecurity* (New York and Oxford, 1996).

MCCAULEY, M., ed. *Khrushchev and Khrushchevism* (Bloomington, IN, 1987).

MEDVEDEV, R., and Z. MEDVEDEV. *Khrushchev: The Years in Power* (New York, 1978).

MITROVICH, G. *Undermining the Kremlin: America's Strategy to Subvert the Soviet Block, 1947–1956* (Ithaca, NY, 2000).

NOGEE, J. L. and R. DONALDSON. *Soviet Foreign Policy Since World War II,* 4th ed. (New York, 1992).

PISTRAK, L. *The Grand Tactician: Khrushchev's Rise to Power* (New York, 1961).

PLOSS, S. *Conflict and Decision-Making Process in Soviet Russia: A Case Study of Agricultural Policy, 1953–1963* (Princeton, 1965).

RICHTER, J. G. *Khrushchev's Double Bind: International Pressures and Domestic Coalition Politics* (Baltimore, 1994).

ROTHBERG, A. *The Heirs of Stalin: Dissidence and the Soviet Regime, 1953–1970* (Ithaca, NY, 1972).

ROTHSCHILD, J. *Return to Diversity: A Political History of East Central Europe Since World War II,* 2d ed. (New York and Oxford, 1993).

RUSH, M. *Political Succession in the USSR,* 2d ed. (New York, 1965).

SMOLANSKY, O. *The Soviet Union and the Arab East Under Khrushchev* (Lewisburg, PA, 1974).

STOKES, G., ed. *From Stalinism to Pluralism: A Documentary History of Eastern Europe Since 1945* (New York and Oxford, 1991).

SYROP, K. *Spring in October: The Polish Revolution of 1956* (New York, 1958).

TATU, M. *Power in the Kremlin: From Khrushchev to Kosygin* (New York, 1969).

TAUBMAN, W., S. KHRUSHCHEV, and A. GLEASON, eds. *Nikita Khrushchev* (New Haven and London, 2000).

THOMPSON, W. J. *Khrushchev: A Political Life* (New York, 1995).

ULAM, A. *New Face of Soviet Totalitarianism* (New York, 1965).

WESTAD, O. A., ed. *Brothers in Arms: The Rise and Fall of the Sino-Soviet Alliance, 1945–1963* (Stanford, CA, 1998).

WOLFE, B. *Khrushchev and Stalin's Ghost* (New York, 1957). (On the secret speech.)

ZAGORIA, D. *The Sino-Soviet Conflict, 1955–1961* (Princeton, 1962).

———. *Vietnam Triangle: Moscow, Peking, Hanoi* (New York, 1967).

ZINNER, P. *Revolution in Hungary* (Cambridge, MA, 1961).

ZUBOK, V., and C. PLESHAKOV. *Inside the Kremlin's Cold War: From Stalin to Khrushchev* (Cambridge, MA, 1996).

ZUBKOVA, E. *Russia after the War: Hopes, Illusions, and Disappointments, 1945–1957*, trans. and ed. Hugh Ragsdale (Armonk, NY, 1998).

16

The Brezhnev Era, 1964–1982

After the Politburo removed Khrushchev from power abruptly in October 1964, a collective leadership assumed control, led by Leonid I. Brezhnev (1906–1982) and Alexei N. Kosygin (1904–1980), both engineers. Following a concealed power struggle with Kosygin and other rivals, Brezhnev gradually accumulated power and by 1971 had established modified one-man rule over the USSR. Despite declining health and vigor after 1975, he dominated the Soviet scene until early 1982. The new leaders, repudiating Khrushchev's risky economic and political experiments at home and his flamboyant foreign policy, acted cautiously, stressing efficiency, order, and stability. Abandoning Khrushchev's de-Stalinization campaign, they returned partially to Stalinism. The new oligarchs tightened controls over intellectuals and dissidents and at first combined industrial and agricultural growth with an impressive military buildup. Abroad, the USSR tightened its control of eastern Europe after invading Czechoslovakia in 1968 while pursuing détente and arms control agreements with the West. China confronted it with ideological and geopolitical challenges that threatened to provoke a Sino-Soviet war. Was the Brezhnev period an "era of stagnation," as M. S. Gorbachev later characterized it, or did it pursue reform? Were genuine stability and consensus achieved, or did resurgent minority peoples, especially Muslims, begin to undermine an apparently solid Soviet Empire? Why did economic growth slow dramatically after 1970? What were the implications of Soviet invasions of Czechoslovakia in 1968 and Afghanistan in 1979 and severe tensions with a liberalizing Poland in 1980–1981?

Politics: Brezhnev's Rise

After Khrushnev's sudden ouster, an oligarchy in the Presidium (renamed the Politburo in 1966) and Secretariat of the party's Central Committee, headed by Brezhnev, Kosygin, N. V. Podgorny, and Mikhail Suslov, assumed power. Right after Khrushchev's removal, *Pravda* castigated his methods rather than his specific policies:

> The Leninist Party is an enemy of subjectivism and drift in communist construction. Wild

schemes, half-baked conclusions and hasty decisions and actions divorced from reality; bragging and bluster; attraction to rule by fiat; unwillingness to take into account what science and practical experience have already worked out—these are alien to the Party. The construction of Communism is a living, creative undertaking. It does not tolerate armchair methods, one-man decisions, or disregard for the practical experience of the masses.[1]

Subsequently Khrushchev was not criticized by name and under Brezhnev was hardly ever mentioned by the press, almost as if he had never ruled the USSR. Consigned to the oblivion of retirement, he was supplied with an apartment and limousine and retained his country dacha. Khrushchev appeared in public only at election times to cast his ballot. As a pensioner, he wrote two volumes of fascinating memoirs and died of heart disease in 1971.[2]

The new leaders, at first insecure, were absorbed in a protracted power struggle that raged beneath a placid surface from the day of Khrushchev's removal. A veil of anonymity, sobriety, and secrecy enveloped them as they jockeyed for position. Group and individual photographs were avoided so as not to reveal the leaders' order of prominence. In the Presidium, which soon reasserted primacy over the Secretariat, former Khrushchev supporters at first retained their posts. Some Western observers did not expect this collective leadership to last, but it proved surprisingly durable and effective. Powerful interest groups competed behind the scenes: the party apparatus, high state administrators, "steeleaters" (heavy industry), and less influential army and police elements. None of these lobbies could dictate to or ignore the interests of the others; clashes among them generally ended in compromise. Whereas the successors of Lenin and Stalin soon had achieved complete or modified one-man rule,

this time the top posts of secretary general (Brezhnev) and premier (Kosygin, later N. A. Tikhonov) remained in different hands.

The coup of October 1964 was apparently planned by Mikhail Suslov, chief party ideologist, and executed by opponents of Khrushchev who considered Brezhnev the most acceptable moderate replacement. At the outset Brezhnev's position was highly vulnerable and insecure. The new party first secretary began by wooing elements alienated by Khrushchev's reforms: the party, industrial managers, bureaucrats, and the military. Promptly rescinding Khrushchev's most unpopular policies, the new regime ended his short-lived division of the party and insistence on rotating its leaders. Brezhnev sought to replace conflict and suspicion among powerful interest groups with cooperation and consensus, summed up in the slogan "Trust in cadres." In official life a more relaxed atmosphere prevailed as disagreements were limited to ascertaining the best means to achieve agreed goals. The frenetic administrative reorganizations of the Khrushchev era virtually ceased.

Confounding the skeptics, Brezhnev emerged as a clever and adroit politician and a master of compromise. Within 18 months, after achieving working control of the Secretariat, he had begun to emerge from a pack of contenders as first among equals. A Presidium consensus enabled him to replace followers of Khrushchev with his own adherents. The 23rd Party Congress (March–April 1966), named Brezhnev secretary general of the party. A Western diplomat admitted having underestimated Brezhnev's acumen: "We just didn't give him enough credit. . . . Everybody wrote him off as a party hack, as a colorless *apparatchik*, as a compromise candidate."

Leonid Brezhnev had risen from lowly origins by hard, persistent work, mainly in the party apparatus. Born in 1906 in Ukraine of Russian worker parents, he was graduated from a classical gymnasium and later obtained a degree as a metallurgical engineer. From 1938 on, his career was linked closely with Khrushchev's. Serving as a political commissar in World War II, Brezhnev became a major general, and once in power his military

---

[1] *Pravda*, October 17, 1964, quoted in J. Dornberg, *Brezhnev: The Masks of Power* (New York, 1974), p. 184.
[2] *Khrushchev Remembers* (Boston, 1971); and *Khrushchev Remembers: The Last Testament* (New York, 1974).

career was inflated beyond measure. Leaving the military service in 1946, Brezhnev, as a chosen member of Khrushchev's entourage, became party chief in Zaporozhe and a member of the Ukrainian Politburo. In the early 1950s he served as party chief in Moldavia, then in Kazakhstan. Under Khrushchev he became a secretary of the Central Committee and a member of the Politburo. Kicked upstairs in 1960 as titular president of the USSR, he returned from that political graveyard to true power. After Kozlov's stroke in April 1963 (a stroke of fortune for Brezhnev!), he was restored to the Secretariat and became Khrushchev's heir apparent. In the brutal world of Soviet politics, Brezhnev succeeded through patronage, manipulation, and maneuver. He built a strong political machine—the so-called Dnieper Mafia—of officials from his home region. Brezhnev won the reputation of being efficient, quiet, sensible, and of keeping a low profile—a man of experience and moderation.

Soviet leaders under Brezhnev operated as an exclusive, self-renewing elite, or *nomenklatura*, living in a very private world. The roughly 25 members of the Politburo and Secretariat, stressing stability and order, had defined rules of conduct that none could disregard with impunity. They acted purposefully to prevent Politburo disputes' being aired in the much larger Central Committee by manipulating its semiannual plenums. If agreement could not be achieved, the plenum would be delayed. Politburo members who violated these procedures would be punished, often by losing their posts. If a non-Politburo member criticized the leaders' policies at a plenum, he would normally be dismissed. The oligarchs jealously guarded special decision-making powers that separated them from lower party bodies, which merely executed Politburo decisions. Even junior members of the Secretariat or candidate members of the Politburo belonged to this privileged elite. Under Brezhnev, four or five top men were included: the premier, titular president, and the top three party secretaries. The Secretariat, normally chaired by Brezhnev, managed the party machine and appointed candidates to all senior posts. Moscow-based Politburo members possessed advantages over party leaders of Leningrad, Ukraine, or Kazakhstan, who normally could not attend weekly Politburo meetings.[3]

Powerful Politburo members representing major interest groups blocked Brezhnev's initial efforts at supremacy. However, between 1966 and 1971 Brezhnev removed or isolated leading rivals and accumulated power without dictating to the Politburo. His authority spread outward from the party base to include foreign policy, state affairs, and agriculture. In 1967 he ousted his main rivals from the Secretariat, and the 24th Party Congress in 1971 confirmed his personal ascendancy as he enlarged the Politburo to include his cronies. Brezhnev's summit diplomacy with Western leaders reaffirmed his authority. During 1973 leading representatives of important interest groups entered the Politburo: Marshal Andrei Grechko (defense minister), Iuri Andropov (KGB chief), and Andrei Gromyko (foreign minister). In May 1975 Alexander Shelepin, his only remaining major rival, was removed from the Politburo; and the July 1975 Helsinki Security Conference vindicated his policy of détente. By the time of the 25th Party Congress of 1976, 10 of 16 full Politburo members were Brezhnev's appointees, and his rivals had been weakened and isolated. In 1977, asserting that the USSR had entered the phase of "developed socialism," Brezhnev assumed the title President of the Soviet Union. Despite repeated bouts of illness beginning in 1975, which sharply reduced his capacity to work, Brezhnev remained in command, repeatedly removing younger men who might aspire to replace him. In October 1980 Premier Kosygin retired and died two months later. He was replaced as premier by Nikolai A. Tikhonov, an elderly Brezhnev crony. Careful not to groom a dynamic successor, Brezhnev placed his stamp firmly on an entire era of Soviet history and retained preeminent authority until 1982, his final year of life. His legacy was stability, orderly procedure, and stagnation.

[3] Gelman, *The Brezhnev Politburo,* pp. 51–58.

Under Brezhnev the role of the party was further enhanced, and tenure at all levels became more secure. After 1964 there were some abrupt removals from the Politburo, but few changes in the Central Committee or lower. In 1977 only 2 percent of party members failed to retain membership. Party congresses after 1971 were to convene every five years to coincide with Five Year Plans. Losing some of its power, the Central Committee was expanded to 241 full members and 155 nonvoting candidates, 90 percent of whom were reelected in 1976. The party continued to grow, reaching 17.4 million members in 1983. Now almost 10 percent of the adult population, it had lost its Leninist vanguard character; its apparatus of full-time paid workers exceeded 250,000. Meanwhile the educational level and technical expertise of party members had risen sharply. About 25 percent of them were women, but few held important positions and none were in top party agencies. Under "developed socialism" the party was to initiate major reforms, coordinate a complex socioeconomic system, and push forward a cautious bureaucracy. The theme of party control over the ministries was emphasized. Party spirit (partiinost), declared Brezhnev, must be combined with expertise.

Western scholars wondered whether the Brezhnev regime represented a stable oligarchy or a modified one-man rule. Was it reverting to Stalinist autocracy or permitting freer debate? Concealing its rivalries from the public, the Brezhnev leadership projected an image of harmony and unity. One Western scholar, Zbigniew Brzezinski, called the Brezhnev regime a "government of clerks" that, seeking to preserve its power and privileges, had repudiated social change. With a decaying ideology, its leaders presided over a petrifying political order. However, Robert Daniels stressed institutional pluralism in which the chief agencies—party, state, army, and police—shared power. Brezhnev adopted no major policies that would endanger the influence of any of them. Stalin's "permanent purge" of top officials had yielded to a remarkably stable leadership. With

wider-ranging debate in the Soviet press, important decisions were reached after extensive discussion and compromise. The party became a "political broker," reconciling and mediating differences among several bureaucracies.

Khrushchev's removal by a large Politburo majority served as a deterrent to a potential dictator. Totalitarian discipline, pointed out French Sovietologist Michel Tatu, could be reimposed only by a massive purge, which party leaders scrupulously avoided. In some ways Brezhnev had fewer prerogatives than democratic chief executives. Lacking sole decision-making authority, he could have policies imposed on him by a Politburo majority that could dismiss or retire him at any time. He required his colleagues' consent to alter the composition of the Politburo or Secretariat.

After a brief, relatively liberal interlude, the Brezhnev regime cracked down on political dissent, with enforcement by the KGB under the able direction of Iurii V. Andropov, Brezhnev's eventual successor. De-Stalinization ended abruptly. Beginning in 1965, memoirs by leading Soviet generals of World War II praised Stalin's wartime leadership, which Khrushchev had castigated. Stalin and the party, went the new line, fully aware of the Nazi danger in 1941, had taken essential precautions, then guided the heroic Soviet people to victory. A prominent neo-Stalinist intimate of Brezhnev, S. Trapeznikov, described the Stalin era in *Pravda* in October 1965 as "one of the most brilliant in the history of the party and the Soviet state." Brezhnev agreed with powerful party conservatives that discussion of Stalin's crimes and forced labor camps must cease. Official treatment of Stalin grew increasingly positive, with only perfunctory criticism of his cult of personality. In an abortive attempt to rehabilitate Stalin completely, Devi Sturua, ideological secretary of the Georgian Communist Party, declared in October 1966:

> I am a Stalinist because the name of Stalin is linked with the victories of our people in the years of collectivization and industrialization. I am a Stalinist because the name of Stalin is linked with the victories of our people in the

Table 16.1 Ethnic groups as a percentage of total population

Ethnic groups	1897	1926	1959	1970	1989
Russians	44.4	47.5	54.6	53.4	50.8
Ukrainians	19.4	21.4	17.8	16.9	15.4
Byelorussians	4.5	3.6	3.8	3.7	3.5
Tatars	1.9	1.7	2.4	2.5	—
Turko-Moslems	12.1	10.1	10.3	12.9	15.4
Jews	3.5	2.4	1.1	0.9	0.7
Europeans (Georgians, Armenians, Latvians, Estonians)	3.9	3.6	3.8	3.8	3.8
Lithuanians	1.3	1.2	1.1	1.1	1.1
Finns	2.3	2.2	1.5	1.4	1.4
Moldavians (Romanians)	1.0	1.2	1.1	1.2	1.2

Great Patriotic War [World War II]. I am a Stalinist because the name of Stalin is linked with the victories of our people in the postwar reconstruction of our economy.[4]

A closed nationwide "seminar" of party ideological officials applauded.

Nationalism and Dissent

During the Brezhnev era, nationalism revived in various parts of the USSR. "Of all the problems facing Moscow the most urgent and the most stubborn is the one raised by the national minorities," wrote Hélène d'Encausse prophetically.[5] Brezhnev's official goal of a "fusion of the nations" was resisted by non-Slavic elements seeking genuine Soviet federalism and autonomy. Efforts at Great Russian linguistic and educational assimilation, effective with smaller ethnic groups, failed in the Caucasus, Lithuania, and Central Asia, where religion (Catholicism or Islam) reinforced a local sense of historic and national identity. The Soviet regime provided few mosques for its large Muslim

minority, but many worshiped unofficially. Muslim leaders, affirmed d'Encausse, were making communism a by-product of Islam. (For statistics on the relative size of ethnic groups, see Table 16.1.)

The Brezhnev regime persecuted "bourgeois nationalism," especially in the Ukraine. In April 1966 two Ukrainian literary critics were accused of smuggling "nationalist" verses to the West. V. Chornovil, who reported their trial to the world and denounced KGB tactics, was sentenced to forced labor. That fall Articles 190/1 and 190/3, making it a crime to spread "slanderous inventions about the Soviet state and social system" or to "disturb public order," were added to the Soviet criminal code and were used frequently against nationalists and other dissidents. In 1972 Peter Shelest, the Ukraine's political boss, was removed partly for glorifying Ukrainian history and culture and seeking to re-Ukrainize its political apparatus. The Brezhnev regime reacted harshly to efforts by national minorities to assert their rights or to complaints of Russian domination. (See Map 16.1.) While declining as a percentage of the total Soviet population, Great Russians remained dominant and privileged, holding with other Slavic elements most top political positions. In the socioeconomic realm, most non-Russians lost ground relative to Great Russians. Industrial development and urbanization centered in Slavic

[4] Stephen F. Cohen, ed., *An End to Silence* (New York, 1982), p. 158.
[5] Hélène Carrère d'Encausse, *Decline of an Empire: The Soviet Socialist Republics in Revolt* (New York, 1979), pp. 231, 274.

Map 16.1 The Soviet political units in 1970

republics with a low rate of population increase and growing labor shortages. In contrast, Turkic-Muslim areas suffered from economic under-development, growing labor surpluses, and rapid population increases. In Muslim urban centers non-Muslims, only 21 percent of the total Muslim-area population in 1970, frequently took the best jobs. A 44-percent increase in the Turkic-Muslim population from 1959 to 1970 created powerful demographic pressures in Central Asia, with a large rural population surplus and intensified pressures on agriculture.[6]

Frequently the Brezhnev regime imprisoned dissidents in psychiatric hospitals. In 1966 the writer Valeri Tarsis, in exile in England, published *Ward Seven,* which described compulsory treatment in a Moscow psychiatric hospital. "I believe in God and I cannot live in a country where one cannot be an honest man," wrote Tarsis. The USSR "is not a democratic country; this is fascism."[7] The Politburo declared Tarsis insane and a traitor and deprived him of Soviet citizenship! In 1967 former major general Peter Grigorenko, campaigning for the right of Crimean Tatars to

---

[6] Robert Lewis et al., *Nationality and Population Change in Russia and the USSR* (New York, 1976), pp. 350ff.

[7] Quoted in A. Rothberg, *The Heirs of Stalin* (Ithaca, NY, 1972), p. 170.

return home from exile, was arrested, committed to a hospital for the criminally insane, and beaten by the KGB. Explained another dissident, Vladimir Bukovskii:

> The inmates are prisoners, people who committed actions considered crimes from the point of view of the authorities . . . but not . . . of the law. And in order to isolate them and punish them somehow, these people are declared insane and kept in the ward of the psychiatric hospital.[8]

Andrei Amalrik, a young historian, compared dissident trials under Brezhnev with medieval heresy trials. "Recognizing their ideological hopelessness, they [the leaders] cling in fear to criminal codes, to prison camps, and psychiatric hospitals."[9] Losing his job, Amalrik was convicted of "parasitism" and served 16 months in Siberia at hard labor.

Many scientists and intellectuals joined the dissident Human Rights Movement. Its leading statement was the *Sakharov Memorandum*, published abroad in 1968 by the outstanding scientist Andrei Sakharov. His protest reflected growing support by Soviet scientists for civil liberties and democratization. Citing the deadly danger to humankind of nuclear war, overpopulation, bureaucracy, and environmental pollution, Sakharov urged Soviet-American cooperation to save civilization. The Soviet and American systems, borrowing from each other, were converging toward democratic socialism, he argued. Castigating Stalinism and its vestiges, Sakharov urged democratic freedoms for the USSR and denounced collectivization as an "almost serflike enslavement of the peasantry." He demanded rehabilitation of all Stalin's victims: "Only the most meticulous analysis of the [Stalinist] past and its consequences will now enable us to wash off the blood and dirt that befouled our banner."[10] In May 1970 Sakharov warned Brezhnev that

unless secrecy was removed from science, culture, and technology, the USSR would soon become a second-rate provincial country.

Despite a severe crackdown by the Brezhnev regime, Soviet dissent during the 1970s expanded as one component of an emerging "contrasystem" with a flourishing illegal "second economy" and a major system of underground religious belief and *samizdat* publications.[11] Under Brezhnev, Soviet dissent acquired a history, heroes, and martyrs. According to Amnesty International, more than 400 Soviet dissidents were imprisoned or restricted in their movements after 1975, notably before important events such as the Moscow Olympics of 1980. A steadily growing volume of dissident information kept Soviet repression in the world spotlight and gave visibility to dissatisfied national and religious groups. From late 1976 the regime reacted vigorously, often applying Article 190/1. Particular targets were dissidents monitoring Soviet violations of the Helsinki Accords; several political trials of these leaders were staged in 1977–1978. Another police offensive of 1979–1980 brought arrests of nine Helsinki monitors and the internal exile of Andrei Sakharov to Gorkii. KGB tactics included trumped-up criminal charges against dissidents, increased use of psychiatric terror, and the employment of official hooligans to beat up dissidents or burglarize their homes. There was a major increase in forced deportations of prominent opponents of the regime. Nonetheless, the strength of the Soviet counterculture and information about its activities in the West increased.

Economy and Society

After a decade of moderate growth and relative prosperity, the Brezhnev regime faced declining economic growth rates and increasing demands on limited Soviet resources. Weather conditions

---

[8] Quoted in Rothberg, *Heirs of Stalin,* p. 301.
[9] Quoted in Rothberg, p. 304.
[10] Quoted in Rothberg, pp. 332, 338.

[11] Robert Sharlet, "Growing Soviet Dissidence," *Current History* 79 (October 1980), pp. 96–100.

caused fluctuations in agricultural production, but the general trend was slower growth. Some Soviet economists affirmed that the Stalinist model was holding back economic development. Reformers urged drastic changes: eliminating much central planning of prices and introducing competitive bidding between the State Planning Commission (Gosplan) and individual plants. However, the party apparatus and the bureaucracy refused to dismantle the central planning empire, relax controls, or move toward market socialism. Conservative ideologists opposed any concessions to capitalism.

Premier Kosygin, supporting reform, backed many suggestions of Professor Evsei Liberman of Kharkov University, who advocated that state enterprises sell their goods and be expected to show a profit. Liberman also rejected Stalinist economics based on commands from above and absolute obedience from below and the stress on quantity regardless of cost or quality. He wished to free the individual enterprise from outside controls, except for overall production and delivery goals. Wage increases and bonuses for managers and workers would depend on profitability—that is, on the sale of products—not on fulfilling centrally decided production norms. Using supply and demand, suppliers and manufacturers would deal directly with one another rather than going through central economic ministries. In July 1964 Khrushchev authorized an experiment with aspects of Libermanism in two clothing combines. Profits and sales increased sufficiently to encourage the new leadership to try Liberman's theories on a modified basis in some 400 consumer enterprises. Greater ability to adjust to consumer demand and more emphasis on quality resulted.

This experiment was underway when Kosygin's proposals for general economic reform, heralded as "a new system of planning and incentives," were approved in September 1965. That April Kosygin had challenged the party's role in planning:

We have to free ourselves completely . . . from everything that used to tie down the planning

officials and obliged them to draft plans otherwise than in accordance with the interests of the economy. . . . We often find ourselves prisoners of laws we ourselves have made.[12]

The September 1965 reforms included Liberman's managerial economics and profit ideas, but Kosygin also restored the central economic ministries, often under their Stalinist bosses. Khrushchev's *sovnarkhozy*, defended chiefly by local party officials anxious to retain control of regional industry, were scrapped. The Moscow technocrats regained all of their pre-1957 powers: The new head of Gosplan, N. K. Baibakov, had been removed from that post by Khrushchev in 1957!

Opposition from conservative party elements and Stalinist managers first watered down the Kosygin reforms, then halted their implementation. By January 1967 some 2,500 enterprises had adopted the new incentive system; by 1970 the reforms supposedly applied to all firms, but plant managers' authority was reduced as the ministers determined daily operations more and more. Gross value of output, not profit, remained the key index. Conservatives realized that to free managers from central tutelage would reduce bureaucratic power over industry. To orthodox party members, Libermanism was "goulash communism"; to allow market forces to prevail over central planning would be "unscientific." Many managers, fearing responsibility, acted in the old Stalinist manner. Thus the 1965 reforms eventually failed; rather than implementing Libermanism, they temporarily took up slack in the old system. A Soviet economist lamented: "I thought they [the leaders] understood from their experience that repressive measures would never achieve results and that they were therefore ready to employ purely economic tools. Now I see there was nothing to it."[13]

As industrial growth rates under Brezhnev declined, Soviet planners were faced with a clear

[12] Quoted in Michel Tatu, *Power in the Kremlin* (New York, 1968), p. 447.
[13] Quoted in R. Conquest, "A New Russia? A New World?" *Foreign Affairs* 54 (April 1975), p. 487.

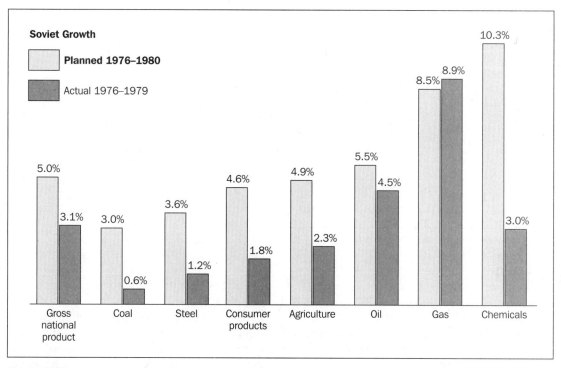

Figure 16.1
Soviet economic growth under Brezhnev: Planned versus actual

need to improve productivity and quality. (See Figure 16.1.) The traditional Soviet economic policy of concentrating on heavy and defense-related industries and on quantity produced great imbalances and backward light industry and service sectors. Huge investments were required to maintain even lower levels of growth; bottlenecks were promoted by overexpansion of key industries. The centralized Soviet system's economic inefficiencies included a waste of capital on ill-conceived, protracted construction projects, underutilized capacity, mismanagement of human resources, overcentralization, inertia, lack of initiative, and excessive bureaucracy.[14] Key goals of the

Ninth (1971–1975) and Tenth (1976–1980) Five Year Plans were not fulfilled, even though scaled well below levels of previous plans and consumption was slated to grow about as fast as accumulation. Complicating the picture in the 1980s were high labor turnover, labor shortages, and rising consumer demand. At the 25th Party Congress of 1976, Brezhnev urged a rapid increase in productivity, a sharp cutback in manual labor, increased automation, and improved quantity and quality of consumer goods. However, such exhortations had little effect.

Although output rose during Brezhnev's early years, agriculture remained a weak link in the Soviet economy. Unfavorable weather and inefficient, oversized farms caused the USSR to suffer seven bad grain harvests in a row beginning in 1979. Soviet grain exports shrank; by the 1980s the

---

[14] George Feiwel, "Economic Performance and Reforms in the Soviet Union," in D. R. Kelley, ed., *Soviet Politics in the Brezhnev Era* (New York, 1980), pp. 70–101.

Table 16.2 Collective and state farms

	1940	1960	1976
Kolkhozy			
Total number	235,000	44,900	27,300
Workers per farm	110	445	542
Sown area per farm	500 hectares	2,746	3,597
Livestock	297 head	3,031	4,509
Tractors	4.4	14.4	39
Sovkhozy			
Total number	4,200	7,400	19,617
Workers per farm	381	783	559
Sown area per farm	2,750	9,081	5,680
Tractors	20	54	57

SOURCE: D. R. Kelley, ed., *Soviet Politics in the Brezhnev Era* (New York, 1980), p. 57.

USSR imported more grain than any other country. In *Letter to the Soviet Leaders* (1973), Solzhenitsyn urged scrapping the entire collective farming system. Soviet agriculture remained subservient to ideology and under tight central bureaucratic control. Despite higher investments, agricultural growth slowed: a roughly 26-percent increase during Brezhnev's first decade compared with a 41-percent increase under Khrushchev. Fluctuating grain yields—for example, a record 237.2 million metric tons in 1978 falling to 179 million in 1979—prompted Brezhnev to conclude long-term import agreements with the United States and Argentina. Although costs were high, in 1975 Soviet storage capacity was increased to 40 million metric tons. Brezhnev emphasized extension of irrigated lands and undertook a vast land-improvement program for the northwest. With agricultural production roughly 80–85 percent of U.S. output, the Soviet population received enough total calories and proteins, but lacked variety and quality.

Under Brezhnev the trend away from collective farms (*kolkhozy*) to state farms (*sovkhozy*) continued. (See Table 16.2.) Soviet farms became huge, impersonal rural factories whose farmers were controlled as strictly as by the estate manager under serfdom. Soviet farmers tilled about 70 percent more land area than did farmers in the United States, with more than seven times the manpower, but with only about one-third the tractors and trucks and 60 percent of the grain combines. The Brezhnev regime did establish a minimum wage for collective farmers and raised the income of all farmworkers. In 1980 the average collective farmer received 116 rubles per month, compared to 170 rubles for an urban worker; state farmers' income fell in between. Despite these improvements, in 1977 about 15 million private plots, averaging about one acre, produced 27 percent of all Soviet agricultural products, including 34 percent of livestock products and almost half of its vegetables and potatoes.[15] Private crop yields per acre and livestock output per animal exceeded substantially those on collective and state farms. These superior results reveal the stronger incentives to produce on private farms than on collective and state farms. More than 50 million people worked on private plots at least part-time. Whereas Khrushchev had taken steps to curtail and restrict private plots, Brezhnev promised to foster them. Small garden machines began to be manufactured for sale to private farmers.

[15] Karl-Eugene Wädekin, *The Private Sector in Soviet Agriculture* (Berkeley, 1973); Roy Laird, "The Political Economy of Soviet Agriculture Under Brezhnev," in Kelley, *Soviet Politics*, pp. 55*ff.*

Table 16.3 Selected consumer goods per thousand

Item	1965	1970	1975	1977
Watches, clocks	885	1,193	1,319	1,408
TV sets	68	143	215	229
Refrigerators	29	89	178	210
Washing machines	59	141	189	200

SOURCE: D Kelley, ed., *Soviet Politics in the Brezhnev Era* (New York, 1980), p. 116

Soviet foreign trade in the 1970s rose sharply, spurred by imports of Western technology and grain and exports of oil and natural gas. In a marked departure from traditional Soviet policies of autarky, the USSR was opened more to foreign technology, especially to increase its output of energy. Besides military equipment and gold, about 85 percent of all Soviet hard-currency exports were raw materials; more than half of these earnings came from petroleum. Soviet oil exports rose from 96 million tons in 1970 to about 125 million in 1975, mostly to Europe and Cuba. However, Soviet oil output then peaked at 12–13 million barrels per day. Output in older Soviet oil fields in the Caucasus fell rapidly, partly because of technological bottlenecks, while exploitation of newer Siberian fields required advanced and expensive foreign technology.

Soviet living standards, having risen markedly during the early Brezhnev years, leveled off during the 1970s and remained the lowest of the major industrial countries. (See Table 16.3.) The average citizen obtained an adequate but uninspiring diet featuring potatoes and cabbage, suffered chronic meat and milk shortages, and lived in shabby, overcrowded housing. Consumption in 1970 amounted to about 57 percent of total output (GNP), considerably less than in the United States and other industrial countries. Strong consumer pressure spurred the Brezhnev regime, anxious to avoid strikes like those in neighboring Poland, to provide more and improved consumer goods and services. A more selective urban populace demanded quality products, especially automobiles, motorcycles, and carpets. But for such

"high demand" goods no credit was available: The purchase price had to be paid in cash before delivery. Considerable resources were devoted to producing private cars, providing repair facilities, and building decent roads. Five Year Plans under Brezhnev channeled much more state investment into consumer products than ever before. Brezhnev's speech to the 26th Party Congress in 1981 stressed the political significance of improving consumption:

> The problem is to create a really modern sector producing consumer goods and services for the population, which meets their demands. . . . The store, the cafeteria, the laundry, the dry cleaners are places people visit every day. What can they buy? How are they treated? . . . The people will judge our work in large measure by how these questions are solved.[16]

Nonetheless, compared with earnings, the prices of Soviet consumer goods remained very high.

Under Brezhnev there was growing official concern over crime and corruption, symptoms of social malaise. A new gun-control law of February 1974 prescribed up to five years' imprisonment for unauthorized possession of firearms. As crimes of violence increased, notably in southern areas, severe penalties were imposed for drug abuse, especially involving hashish and marijuana. Juvenile delinquency increased sharply. As the food situation outside of major cities deteriorated, parts of the USSR instituted rationing and even Muscovites searched for food and other consumer goods. As items of real commercial value disappeared from state stores into illegal or semilegal channels, the black and gray markets became crucial for most Russians. Old values and restraints broke down, as cheating and stealing from the state increased. As Russians lost faith that things would improve and regarded the promise of communism as a cynical joke, public morale plummeted. Many Russians told George

---

[16] Quoted in Robert F. Byrnes, ed., *After Brezhnev: Sources of Soviet Conduct in the 1980s* (Bloomington, IN, 1983), p. 74.

Feifer, an American journalist: The whole country is sick and getting sicker.[17]

That seemed to be literally true. Whereas earlier the USSR was in the forefront of improving public health, raising life expectancy, and reducing infant mortality, after 1960 an astounding reversal occurred, marked by rampant alcoholism, burgeoning infant mortality, and declining life expectancy. Measured by its public health, noted Nick Eberstadt in 1980, the USSR was no longer a developed nation.[18] In no other European country, not even primitive Albania, were lives so short or the infant death rate so high. Western accounts emphasized the devastating effects of alcoholism, especially on Russian men, but also on women and even children. In the early 1970s the Soviet per capita consumption of hard liquor was more than twice the American or Swedish level. Despite sharp increases in state vodka prices, consumption rose, and almost as much moonshine (*samogon*) was consumed as legally purchased liquor. Alcohol purchases accounted, noted Feifer, for almost one-third of consumer spending in food stores. Christopher Davis and Murray Feshbach, leading Western experts on Soviet society, attributed the Soviet health crisis to a number of factors, including poor-quality baby foods and nursing formulas, rising illegitimacy and abortion (averaging six to eight per woman during childbearing years), alcoholism, high accident rates, pollution of the air and soil, and a breakdown in the health-care system. The Brezhnev regime, busily building up its military forces, economized at the expense of public health: The Soviet Union devoted a declining percentage of total output to combating illness.[19] Another Western scholar suggested that the Soviet system itself was wearing down from a combination of inefficiency, corruption, and rampant cynicism.[20]

Nor, despite official claims, did women's equality exist in the USSR. The Soviet leadership pursued the goal of sexual equality until it conflicted with economic or military priorities. Under Brezhnev males continued to dominate the higher ranks of all scientific disciplines and most other branches of the economy. However, Soviet women finally had achieved equal pay for equal work and equal entry into most professions.[21] In 1970 women represented 53.9 percent of the Soviet population and 51 percent of the workforce. However, women comprised only 22.6 percent of party members, and just 14 of some 300 full or candidate members of the Central Committee were women. The USSR had a higher percentage of women doctors, lawyers, and machine operators than any Western country, but women had only token representation in top economic, cultural, and political bodies. That situation partly reflected traditional Russian male predominance. Women were channeled mainly into low-skilled, low-income, physical-labor job categories. Lingering traditional concepts of women's role in the home and at work promoted their dual exploitation. The Brezhnev regime, while admitting problems, promoted legal equality of women but permitted economic, cultural, and political inequality to persist.

Soviet society under Brezhnev, despite reduced wage differentials, remained one of concealed privilege and inequality. The "new class"—an elite of party, police, state, and military leaders—had established itself as an hereditary aristocracy. This Communist aristocracy, without manners, taste, or real competence, passed position and wealth on to its offspring and seemed mainly concerned with its creature comforts. It possessed limousines, special luxury apartment blocks, country estates

---

[17] George Feifer, "Russian Disorders," *Harper's*, February 1981, pp. 41–55.

[18] Nick Eberstadt, "The Health Crisis in the USSR," *New York Review of Books*, February 19, 1981.

[19] The USSR spent about 9.8 percent of GNP on health care in 1955 but only 7.5 percent in 1977; in the United States, largely due to Medicare and Medicaid, the percentage rose from 8 to 11. Eberstadt, "The Health Crisis," p. 25.

[20] Robert Wesson, *The Aging of Communism* (New York, 1980).

[21] D. Atkinson et al., eds., *Women in Russia* (Stanford, 1977), pp. 219, 224, 355.

(dachas), and sanatoria closed to ordinary citizens. It utilized special shops with quantities of otherwise unobtainable goods at heavily subsidized prices. The elevated status of this privileged minority, as in tsarist Russia, separated it from a resentful mass of ordinary workers and peasants. Industrial workers still enjoyed high status in Soviet media, but their wages and pensions remained low. Collective farmers, their position improved by wage and pension increases under Brezhnev, remained at the bottom of the social ladder. "Developed socialism" in Brezhnev's USSR seemed a far cry from the Marxist ideal.

Popular Culture

The Brezhnev era was one in which Soviet citizens found themselves enjoying a higher standard of living than at any time since World War II. Urbanization increased at a rapid pace (about 70 percent by 1985) and housing improved, along with the availability of consumer goods—cars, refrigerators, TVs. Educational levels were rising rapidly, as were cultural expectations. A dissident intellectual movement developed, along with clandestine countercultures that attracted many of the young. On the surface things seemed to be improving but beneath growing stagnation, apathy and corruption sapped energies and interests, resulting in a retreat into religion, nationalism, cultural preservation, and a cult of an idealized past.

People found solace in television and in the traditional Russian passion for reading. Detective stories and historical novels, along with the traditional classics of Russian and Soviet literature, were published in huge editions. The reading audience was eager for novels, and interest in historical accounts of the victorious drama of World War II was paralleled by a new attention to pre-revolutionary history. Valentin Pikul (1928–1990) became one of the most popular and widely read authors in the Soviet Union, writing books that brought to life the past of tsarist Russia, which had been *terra incognita* for Soviet readers. Detective stories were hugely popular, both in

print and on TV. Science fiction, stimulated by the triumph of Soviet space exploration, became equally popular, especially with a new generation of highly educated science and technology workers and students. Sci-fi novels provided a way of stimulating broad popular interest in the success of Soviet science and outlined prospects for new worlds to conquer.

Although classical music always remained popular in the Soviet Union, young people were most interested in Soviet pop music, which was known as *estrada* music. The recording industry turned out millions of recordings annually in response to this demand.

The first true pop icon was Alla Pugacheva (born 1949), who became the most popular pop singer in the Soviet Union with her 1975 hit "Harlequin." Not only was her singing voice a hit, her lifestyle of frequent and flamboyant love affairs, scandalous behavior, and a consciously cultivated "un-soviet" style—mini-skirts and boots and flaming red hair—won her a mass following. She helped introduce an entire Soviet generation to the counterculture of pop music. Even in her 50s, Pugacheva's popularity continues among a new generation of Russians for whom the cultural controls of the former Soviet Union are totally alien.

Foreign Affairs and Armed Forces

Abroad, a generally prudent Brezhnev regime, carrying a bigger military stick, avoided Khrushchev's dramatic initiatives, threats, and violent reversals. Until 1968 Soviet foreign policy seemed to lack self-confidence. Successful military intervention in Czechoslovakia, halting the erosion of Soviet control over eastern Europe, reversed this picture. Brezhnev thereafter became more decisive and self-assured. As the Sino-Soviet quarrel continued to rage, détente with the West produced important agreements with West Germany and the United States.

Détente and Defense Spending

The new leaders' initial approach abroad was conciliatory, with this message: We are not angry with anyone. They sought to mend their fences with China, but from 1965 on Sino-Soviet competition sharpened over influence in Asia; the gap widened between the bellicose Chinese stance and the moderate Soviet position in the Vietnam War. Exploiting this quarrel to enhance its autonomy, Romania established warm relations with China and increased its trade with the West. In 1966, as the so-called Cultural Revolution began in China, the Chinese boycotted the Soviet 23rd Party Congress, and Russians in China were abused and beaten up. Chinese students left the USSR, and Sino-Soviet trade shrank almost to zero. In January 1969 *Pravda* called Maoism "a great power adventurist policy based on a petty bourgeois nationalistic ideology alien to Marxism-Leninism." As friction mounted along the 4,000-mile Sino-Soviet frontier, the Soviet writer Evgeni Yevtushenko compared the Chinese unflatteringly with the Mongols of Chingis-khan. War between the Communist giants seemed a real possibility, despite the contrary assertions of Marxist-Leninist doctrine. In March 1969 began six months of intermittent but bloody frontier skirmishes over their disputed Ussuri River frontier. According to the dissident historian Roy Medvedev, Brezhnev, who was rabidly anti-Chinese, personally ordered a massive artillery assault and a deep penetration into Chinese territory that killed several thousand Chinese soldiers and poisoned Sino-Soviet relations for years. Rumors circulated that the Soviet military was considering a preemptive nuclear strike against China. In any case, the Chinese were intimidated and agreed not to patrol in areas claimed by the USSR. Meanwhile the USSR began a major buildup of ground forces along the Chinese border.

Faced with this rising menace in the East, Soviet leaders scrupulously avoided trouble in the West while increasing the USSR's military strength. The Soviets stepped up trade with western Europe, and during Charles de Gaulle's presi-dency sought to exploit Franco-American coolness in order to split NATO. The similarly independent roles of Romania and France suggested the weakening hold by the two blocs over their members, as contacts increased between eastern and western European countries. The Cuban missile crisis of 1962 had altered Soviet-American relations considerably. Both sides, noted Hans Morgenthau, an American political scientist, renounced active use of nuclear weapons but retained them as deterrents; both sides aimed at a balance of power and realized that neither could achieve true predominance.[22] Their rivalry in the Third World began to cool as they discovered that neutral countries would not commit themselves totally to either side. In their relations, the United States and the USSR deemphasized ideology and stressed pragmatic power considerations. During the late 1960s, heavy American involvement in Vietnam and massive shipments of Soviet arms to North Vietnam damaged their relations. The subsequent declining conflict there fostered détente.

In the late 1960s and early 1970s, Soviet policy in the Third World produced both setbacks and successes. Several pro-Soviet regimes collapsed, notably those of Sukarno in Indonesia in 1965 and Nkrumah in Ghana in 1966, and were replaced by anti-Communist military governments. The Brezhnev regime shifted to practical economic assistance and military aid. Seeking to build up India as a bulwark against China, Moscow viewed the Indo-Pakistan War of 1965 with dismay. Premier Kosygin met with Pakistani and Indian heads of state in Tashkent early in 1966, and the resulting settlement enhanced the USSR's image as a peacemaker in Asia. India's dependence upon Soviet industrial, military, and diplomatic support increased, trade between the two nations expanded, and Soviet naval vessels in the Indian Ocean challenged the former Western monopoly. In the Middle East the USSR supplied major economic and military aid to Egypt and Syria to

---

[22] "Changes and Chances in American-Soviet Relations," *Foreign Affairs* 49, no. 3 (April 1971), pp. 429–41.

undermine the Western position and win political influence. Their defeat by Israel in the June 1967 war was a costly setback to Soviet policy, but it increased Arab distrust of the West and dependence on Moscow. After the war the Soviets rebuilt their clients' military forces, and thousands of Soviet advisers trained Egyptians to use more sophisticated equipment. Iraq, the Sudan, and Algeria also relied heavily on Soviet arms. Soviet influence in the Middle East reached unprecedented proportions, only to decline considerably during the early 1970s. President Anwar Sadat of Egypt in 1972 expelled all Soviet military advisers. Then in October 1973 Israel, with which the USSR had severed diplomatic ties, again defeated Egypt and Syria.

A crucial turning point in Brezhnev's foreign policy was the Soviet invasion of Czechoslovakia in August 1968. (See Problem 10 at the end of this chapter.) Earlier that year Czechoslovakia, under Premier Alexander Dubček, had moved rapidly toward democratic socialism, virtually ended domestic censorship, and increased ties with the West. Soviet intervention followed months of hesitation and an apparent agreement with the Czechoslovak Politburo at Čierna-nad-Tisou. Large Soviet forces and token contingents from several Warsaw Pact countries met only moral resistance, and Moscow disregarded Yugoslav and Romanian objections and Western denunciations. This move, successful from the Soviet viewpoint, revealed that the Brezhnev-Kosygin collective leadership could act decisively. Without hindrance from the United States, the USSR placed six Soviet divisions in Czechoslovakia, altering the strategic balance in central Europe. The Soviet press even echoed Bismarck's famous statement: "Whoever rules Bohemia holds the key to Europe." The subsequent so-called Brezhnev Doctrine warned that the USSR would tolerate neither internal nor external challenges to its hegemony in eastern Europe and that it would use force if necessary to prevent the overthrow of a fellow Communist regime. The Yugoslavs and Romanians wondered whether Brezhnev might apply his "doctrine"

against them, but their clear determination to resist apparently dissuaded Moscow. Nonetheless, the Czech intervention reconsolidated the Soviet Bloc in eastern Europe and muted the Yugoslav and Romanian challenge of national communism.

After this major success, the USSR early in 1969 adopted a flexible foreign policy and tried to improve relations with the West. To accelerate Soviet economic growth, Brezhnev sought increased trade with the West and American technology. The replacement of Konrad Adenauer's hard-line rule in West Germany with that of Willy Brandt, a Social Democrat who favored reconciliation with the USSR, weakened NATO and helped Brezhnev heighten his influence in Europe. During 1970 landmark treaties were concluded among the USSR, Poland, and West Germany confirming their post–World War II boundaries and undercutting U.S. bridge-building with eastern European countries. Next the Soviets sought a general European security conference, again to weaken NATO and relax tensions on their western frontiers. But the Soviet hold over eastern Europe remained insecure because of persistent nationalism and the waning force of Marxist ideology. Riots in Poland in 1971 forced the conservative Gomulka to resign and brought the more flexible regime of Edward Gierek to power.

Major increases in military strength enhanced Soviet power and prestige under Brezhnev and created a new world balance of forces. Thus by 1979 the USSR spent an estimated $165 billion on defense, with armed forces totaling some 3.65 million men and women, nearly twice the personnel of the United States' forces. The Red Army, with about 160 divisions, had some 30 percent of its strength along the tense Sino-Soviet border. Possessing huge numbers of tanks and supporting aircraft, the Red Army proved its efficiency and power in the invasion of Czechoslovakia. Whereas during the Cuban missile crisis of 1962 the United States held at least a 3-to-1 advantage in strategic nuclear weapons, by 1969 the USSR had equaled the United States in intercontinental missiles and a decade later was well ahead in ICBMs and submarine-launched missiles.

The achievement of approximate nuclear parity and the growing expense of nuclear armament encouraged the two superpowers to reach significant agreements to limit nuclear weapons, including the first Strategic Arms Limitation Treaty (SALT I). Until April 1971 the Soviet commitment to SALT remained tentative, but then Brezhnev apparently accepted the concept of strategic parity and championed détente. To Brezhnev this meant developing a working relationship with the United States, although Soviet ideology required him to regard the leading capitalist power as an adversary. Explained a Soviet publication of 1972:

> Peaceful coexistence is a principle of relations between states which does not extend to relations between the exploited and the exploiters, the oppressed peoples and the colonialists. . . . Marxist-Leninists see in peaceful coexistence a special form of the class struggle between socialism and capitalism in the world, a principle whose implementation ensures the most favorable conditions for the world revolutionary process.[23]

At their Moscow summit meeting of 1972, President Nixon and General Secretary Brezhnev agreed to limit construction of antiballistic missile defense systems and reached an interim accord on offensive missiles. Additional modest steps toward limitation were taken at meetings in Moscow and Vladivostok in 1974, which set a ceiling on the number of offensive missiles for both sides. These agreements slowed the arms race and inaugurated better relations between the two superpowers. At the European Security Conference, which included all European countries except Albania, plus the United States and Canada, the Helsinki Declaration of August 1975 was signed. The nearest thing to a peace conference ending World War II, it announced: "The participating states regard as inviolable all one another's frontiers . . . and therefore they will refrain now and in the future from assaulting those frontiers." The signatories,

including the USSR, also pledged to respect human rights.[24]

During a Soviet-American détente lasting until 1980, the Brezhnev regime moderated Soviet policies to permit large-scale Jewish emigration, more contacts with the outside world, and limited diplomatic cooperation to end the Vietnam War. As Robert Kaiser pointed out, during eight years of détente the Soviet Union became a more open society than it had been since the 1920s, and the West learned much more about its internal workings—political, economic, and military—than before.[25] Tens of millions of Soviet citizens listened regularly to Western radio broadcasts, which undercut the official Soviet version of the truth. The Soviet economy, no longer seeking self-sufficiency as under Stalin, became inextricably linked with the world capitalist system and dependent on Western technology and credits; the eastern European states were increasingly dependent on Western markets and credits. Soviet political controls over the eastern European bloc relaxed somewhat, but its members relied more on Soviet energy sources.

Improving Soviet-American relations failed to halt an ominous Soviet military buildup. After the mid-1960s the Soviet navy was greatly strengthened, becoming second only to the American. The Soviets established a naval presence in all oceans, especially the Mediterranean Sea, to support their Middle East policies. *Red Star,* the Soviet army newspaper, declared in 1970: "The age-old dreams of our people have become reality. The pennants of Soviet ships now flutter in the most remote corners of the seas and oceans." Russia's voice must be heard the world over, declared Foreign Minister Gromyko. Russia's merchant fleet became one of the world's largest. A new, more technically trained generation of Soviet army and navy officers took command of these growing

---

[23] Shalva Sanakeev, *The World Socialist System* (Moscow, 1972), pp. 289–90.

[24] J. Nogee and R. Donaldson, eds., *Soviet Foreign Policy Since World War II* (Elmsford, NY, 1988), p. 263.

[25] Robert Kaiser, "U.S.-Soviet Relations: Goodbye to Détente," *Foreign Affairs* 59, no. 3 (1981), pp. 500–21.

forces from retiring World War II commanders. The armed forces' role in Soviet politics, however, remained stable. Military representation in the Politburo and Central Committee stayed small, and the military did not wish to disrupt a regime that supplied its forces so generously.

The War in Afghanistan

Détente ended in 1980 after growing disillusionment with its fruits on both sides. In December 1979 the USSR, partly to prevent collapse of a Communist regime, abruptly invaded neighboring Afghanistan, a primitive country of warring Muslim tribesmen, where British and Russian imperial interests had clashed in the 19th century. During 1977, under apparent Soviet pressure, the Afghan Communists, divided between a Khalq faction led by Nur Mohammed Taraki and the Parcham group under Babrak Karmal, reunited. In April 1978, in a bloody coup, army officers and Communists seized power from the unpopular republic led by elderly President Daoud. Taraki promptly set up a one-man dictatorship—"the People's Democratic Republic of Afghanistan"—and aligned it closely with the USSR. His regime carried out large-scale purges and executions of opponents and removed army leaders and members of the Parcham faction. Babrak Karmal, the Parcham leader, took refuge in Moscow. Khalq leaders, headed by H. Amin, sought to implement socialism overnight in a backward tribal society, violating every Afghan cultural and religious norm. The new regime's blatant brutality and its identification with atheism and the USSR alienated much of the Afghan population.

In August 1978 Afghans from every province rose in revolt against the Taraki-Amin regime under Muslim leaders who proclaimed a jihad (holy war) against godless communism; parts of the Afghan army defected to the rebels. Originally delighted by the Communist takeover, Moscow was now appalled at the new regime's unwise and hasty policies. "The revolutionary transformations [were] . . . accompanied by gross errors and extremist exaggerations on the left, which failed to give due consideration to religious and tribal trends," declared a Soviet spokesman. Initially Moscow supported Taraki, but in September 1979, after a shootout in the palace, Amin removed Taraki and ruled as dictator. As the popular revolt against him intensified, the Soviets escalated their role until by November there were some 4,500 Soviet "advisers" backing Amin in Afghanistan, and Soviet pilots were bombing rebel positions. (See Map 16.2.) Moscow was being sucked gradually into an Afghan civil war much as the United States had earlier been drawn into the Vietnam imbroglio.

Meanwhile, as he had done in Czechoslovakia in 1968, General I. G. Pavlovskii surveyed the situation in Kabul and concentrated Soviet troops and equipment. On December 24, 1979, regular Soviet units invaded Afghanistan; three days later a special Soviet assault force attacked the palace in Kabul and killed Amin and his family. As in Czechoslovakia, the Soviet incursion was massive and militarily efficient, but again the political and propaganda aspects were handled with incredible clumsiness. The Afghan "request" for military "assistance" arrived in Moscow three days *after* the invasion began! Only hours after a Soviet minister had called on President Amin, Moscow announced that Amin had been executed for crimes "against the noble people of Afghanistan." Babrak Karmal, installed as the new Afghan leader, arrived from Moscow four days later in the baggage train of the Soviet army. Then Moscow proclaimed that its army had intervened, overthrown the government, and killed the president in order to forestall "foreign intervention," adding the absurd charge that Amin had plotted with the CIA and Muslim fanatics to destroy Afghan socialism! Yet that September Brezhnev had congratulated Amin upon his becoming president.

The Soviet invasion produced counteraction by the United States. President Carter declared that this Soviet action "has made a more drastic change in my own opinion of what the Soviets' ultimate goals are than anything they've done in

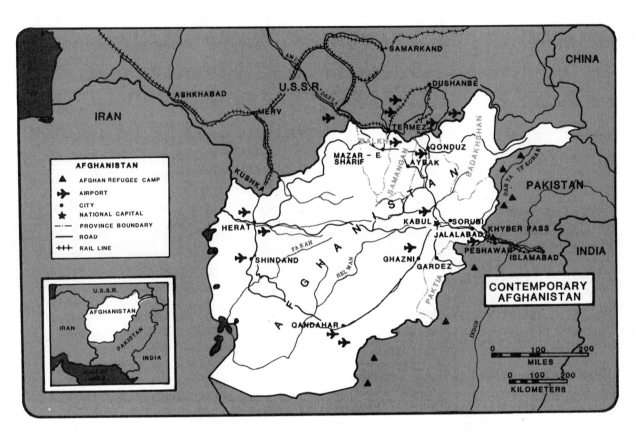

Map 16.2 Afghanistan at the time of the Soviet invasion

the previous time I've been in office." Washington proclaimed the Persian Gulf vital to American security, imposed partial embargoes for a while on shipments of grain and technology to the USSR, and organized a partially successful Western boycott of the 1980 Moscow Olympics. The United Nations urged the "immediate and unconditional withdrawal of foreign troops from Afghanistan," but Moscow paid no attention.[26]

Was the Soviet incursion part of an aggressive design to dominate the Persian Gulf region or a defensive move under the Brezhnev Doctrine to prevent the fall of a client Communist regime to Muslim fundamentalism? Was this action

unprecedented, as some Western observers believed, and thus a dangerous turning point in Soviet foreign policy, or merely the Asian counterpart of the Czech intervention? Even before the invasion, Afghanistan had been within the Soviet sphere of influence, affirmed Thomas Hammond, an American scholar.[27] Thus the Soviet move was really nothing new: Consistent with earlier actions by Moscow in the Third World, the invasion sought to secure Soviet frontiers by surrounding them with friendly and subservient clients and to prevent the fall of any Communist regime. Contributory causes included Soviet fears of Muslim

---

[26] Cited in *New York Times*, January 6, 1980.

[27] Thomas Hammond, *Red Flag over Afghanistan* (Boulder, CO, 1984).

fanaticism spreading into Soviet Central Asia and the Soviet desire to demonstrate effective support of its allies. The invasion of Afghanistan also continued traditional Russian imperialism in the area and aimed to create a more effective and obedient regime.

Babrak Karmal assumed the top posts in the new Soviet-installed government and named token non-Communists to his cabinet while protesting his patriotism and sincere support for Islam. He failed to win much public support because he was known to be an atheist, a Communist, and a Moscow puppet surrounded and controlled by Russian advisers who carried through progressive Sovietization of Afghanistan. Feuding Afghan tribal factions achieved unprecedented unity in a national liberation struggle and holy war against Russians whom they hated and despised. The rebels (*mujaheddin*) soon controlled most of the country despite the influx of some 115,000 Soviet troops. The strength of the unreliable Afghan army fell sharply. Soviet forces used massive firepower, indiscriminate bombing, and apparently chemical weapons in abortive efforts to root out the rebels. By 1984 some 3 million Afghans, or 20 percent of the total population, had fled their increasingly devastated and impoverished homeland; most went to neighboring Pakistan. The Soviet invasion and brutal conduct of the war undermined Soviet influence in Muslim lands of the Third World, hastened American rearmament, and severely drained Soviet resources.

Problems with Poland

During 1980 another and potentially even graver threat to the Soviet Bloc developed in Poland on the Soviet Union's western flank. Beginning in 1970 Edward Gierek, succeeding Gomulka as chief of the Polish Communist Party, had pushed a program of rapid industrialization, fueled by Western technology purchased on credit. After a boom period (1971–1975) and rising living standards, severe recession gripped Poland. Skyrocketing

energy costs, delays in completing large industrial projects, and rising consumer demand produced alarming deficits in Poland's balance of payments with the West. In the summer of 1980 a series of worker strikes triggered formation of an independent trade union movement, Solidarity, which soon obtained the support of most Polish workers. Gierek was forced from office, but his replacement, Stanislaw Kania, failed to stem the workers' campaign for benefits and freedom. As the Polish economy neared collapse and farmers and students also began to organize, party control was threatened. Reports multiplied of a massive Soviet military buildup on Poland's frontiers, and veiled threats of intervention from Moscow were designed to restore the Polish Workers' Party's monopoly of power.

The Soviets confronted an acute dilemma: Military intervention might provoke Polish armed resistance and complete Poland's economic ruin, but inaction would imperil fragile Communist regimes in East Germany and Czechoslovakia, and possibly foment discontent within the Soviet Union. Solidarity demanded the virtual replacement of communism with democracy; Polish farmers followed suit by organizing Rural Solidarity. The Poles sought not merely free trade unions but elimination of censorship, establishment of independent courts, removal of the police from party control, and institution of free elections. Wisely shunning any demand to withdraw Poland from the Warsaw Pact, the Poles urged reducing its military forces. Clearly the USSR could not tolerate such a program any more than it could approve the "Prague Spring." (See Problem 10.) But instead of resorting to direct military intervention, which could cause a bloodbath, Moscow encouraged the Polish army under a moderate, General Wojciech Jaruzelski, to take power and proclaim martial law (December 1981). Poland's military regime forced Solidarity underground and promised decentralizing economic reforms like those in Hungary. However, Jaruzelski failed to remedy a desperate economic situation.

The 26th Party Congress (February 23–March 3, 1981) in Moscow brought no real solutions to these difficult problems in Europe and Asia. Secretary Brezhnev, aged but still ascendant, sounded a conciliatory note by proposing a summit conference and renewed arms talks with President Ronald Reagan; otherwise there was complete reaffirmation of the status quo. Indeed, for the first time every full and alternate member of the Politburo and every member of the Secretariat was "reelected." The 5,002 delegates, including 12 cosmonauts, heard endless speeches praising the "titanic labors" and "colossal life experience" of Leonid Brezhnev. Premier Tikhonov appealed for greater efficiency and higher labor productivity; he promised more food and better consumer goods. The goals of the new Eleventh Five Year Plan (1981–1985) announced at the congress reflected continuing deceleration of Soviet economic growth.

Problem 10

Soviet Intervention in Czechoslovakia, 1968, and Its Repudiation, 1989

The armed invasion of Czechoslovakia on August 21, 1968, by the Red Army and smaller contingents from four Warsaw Pact allies shocked many in the Soviet Bloc as well as Communists and others in the West. Soviet intervention occurred only weeks after apparent agreement between Soviet and Czechoslovak leaders at Čierna-nad-Tisou just inside Czechoslovakia. Condemning the action, only Romania refused to participate in the massive Warsaw Pact invasion. The military operation was smooth, unopposed, and revealed Soviet military efficiency, but Czechoslovak passive resistance surprised Soviet leaders and military personnel. Why did the Soviet Politburo decide suddenly, even if reluctantly, to invade an ally still ruled by the Communist party? Was it Czechoslovak domestic liberalization under Alexander Dubček or the danger that the movement would spread to the rest of the Soviet Bloc that proved decisive? And why did the Soviet Union and its allies 21 years later repudiate their intervention as mistaken and unjustified?

Soviet invasion followed almost a year of liberalization in Czechoslovakia (the so-called Prague Spring), hitherto one of the most conservative Stalinist members of the Soviet Bloc. Profound change followed the downfall in January 1968 of the unpopular Stalinist leadership headed by Antonín Novotný despite Soviet objections and halfhearted support. Although before World War II Czechoslovakia had been the most democratic and economically advanced eastern European country, since 1963 it had suffered a grievous economic decline. Early in 1968 much of the rigid, overcentralized Stalinist economic system was dismantled. Under Dubček, the first Slovak to govern Czechoslovakia, liberal Communists instituted far-reaching economic and political reforms, wide freedom of the press, equality for the Slovaks, thorough party reform, and efforts to increase trade and improve relations with the West. Previous Soviet interference in Czechoslovak domestic affairs was denounced publicly by party members and intellectuals. This provoked alarm and fear in conservative Communist regimes in East Germany and Poland and among Soviet leaders that the Czech liberal fever might infect Ukraine and other Soviet republics. Initially Dubček apparently convinced Soviet leaders that he could control liberalization and restrict it to Czechoslovakia; he assured Moscow that his country would remain in the Warsaw Pact as a Soviet ally and that the Czechoslovak Communist Party (KSS or CCP) would retain its power monopoly.

Defiant Czech youth waves national flag before a Soviet tank after the Red Army's unpopular occupation of Prague, Czechoslovakia, in August 1968.

Problem 10 continued

The following excerpts depict the Soviet intervention from several contrasting viewpoints. Included are official Soviet explanations and justifications, Soviet dissident reactions, Czechoslovak protests and refutations of Soviet assertions, a Western view, and the 1989 Soviet repudiation.

Official Soviet Views

The following excerpts from the Soviet Communist Party newspaper, *Pravda*—one before the invasion and the other after—emphasize the deadly peril to socialism in Czechoslovakia and the Bloc posed by alleged Czech reactionaries aided by American and West German agents.

Pravda asserted that Soviet forces were invited into Czechoslovakia by elements loyal to socialism and that the Soviet Union and other Warsaw Pact countries had the right and duty to act forcefully in the face of such blatant threats to the entire socialist world.

A month before the August invasion, an open letter "To the Czechoslovak Communist Party Central Committee" appeared in *Pravda*, July 15, 1968.

> On behalf of the Central Committees of the Communist and Workers Parties of Bulgaria, Hungary, the G.D.R. [East Germany], Poland, and the Soviet Union we send you this letter, which is dictated by sincere friendship based on the principles of Marxism-Leninism and proletarian internationalism and by concern . . . for strengthening the positions of socialism and the . . . socialist commonwealth of the peoples.
>
> The developments in your country have aroused profound anxiety among us. The reactionaries' offensive, supported by imperialism, against your party and the foundations of the Czechoslovak Socialist Republic's social system . . . threatens to push your country off the path of socialism and, consequently, imperils the interests of the entire socialist system. . . . We have not had and do not have any intention of interfering in affairs that are purely the internal affairs of your party and your state or of violating the principles of respect, autonomy and equality in relations among Communist Parties and socialist countries. . . .
>
> . . . It is the common affair of our countries, which have united in the Warsaw Pact to safeguard their independence, peace and security in Europe and to place an insurmountable barrier in front of the schemes of imperialist forces, aggression and revanche. . . .
>
> The forces of reaction, taking advantage of the weakening of party leadership in Czechoslovakia and demagogically abusing the slogan of "democratization," unleashed a campaign against the C.C.P. . . . with the clear intention of liquidating the party's guiding role, undermining the socialist system and pitting Czechoslovakia against the other socialist countries. The political organizations and clubs that have cropped up lately outside the framework of the National Front have in

AP/Wide World Photos

---

essence become headquarters for the forces of reaction. The social democrats persistently seek to create their own party . . . and are attempting to split the workers' movement in Czechoslovakia and to secure leadership of the country so as to restore the bourgeois system. Antisocialist and revisionist forces have taken over the press, radio and television and have turned them into platforms for attacking the Communist party, for disorienting the working class . . . , for carrying out unchecked antisocialist demagoguery and for subverting the friendly relations between the Č. S. R. and the other socialist countries. . . . The reactionaries appeared publicly before the whole country and published their political platform, entitled "The 2,000 Words."

A month after the invasion, "Sovereignty and the International Duties of Socialist Countries" by Serge Kovalev was published in *Pravda*, September 26, 1968.

The question of the correlation and interdependence of the national interests of the socialist countries and their international duties has acquired particular topical and great importance in connection with the events in Czechoslovakia. The measures taken by the Soviet Union, jointly with other socialist countries, in defending the socialist gains of the Czechoslovak people, are of great importance for strengthening the socialist community. . . .

The peoples of the socialist countries and the Communist Parties certainly do have and should have freedom to determine the roads of advance for their respective countries. However, none of their decisions should do harm either to socialism in their own country or to the fundamental interests of other socialist countries. . . . This means that each Communist Party is responsible not only to its own people but also to all socialist countries and to the entire communist movement. . . .

. . . When a socialist country seeks to adopt a "non-affiliated" attitude, it . . . retains its national independence precisely thanks to the strength of the socialist community, and above all the Soviet Union as its central force, which also includes the

might of its armed forces. The weakening of any of the links in the world socialist system directly affects all the socialist countries, which cannot look on indifferently when this happens. Thus, with talk about the right of nations to self-determination the antisocialist elements in Czechoslovakia actually covered up a demand for so-called neutrality and Czechoslovakia's withdrawal from the socialist community. . . . In discharging their internationalist duty to the fraternal peoples of Czechoslovakia and defending their own socialist gains, the USSR and the other socialist states had to act decisively, and they did act, against the anti-socialist forces in Czechoslovakia. . . .

. . . The troops of the allied socialist countries who are now in Czechoslovakia . . . are not interfering in the country's internal affairs; they are fighting for the principles of the self-determination of the peoples of Czechoslovakia.[28]

This Soviet rationale for armed intervention in other Bloc countries became known as the Brezhnev Doctrine.

Protests by Soviet Intellectuals

The invasion of Czechoslovakia soon produced a protest movement by many Soviet intellectuals and the development of a dissident movement in the USSR. Among some courageous objections was one by a leading Soviet poet, Evgenii Yevtushenko, who telegraphed Chairman Brezhnev:

I cannot sleep. . . . I understand only one thing, that it is my moral duty to express my opinion to you. I am profoundly convinced that our action in Czechoslovakia is a tragic mistake. It is a cruel blow to Czechoslovak-Soviet friendship and to the world Communist movement. This action detracts from our prestige in the eyes of the world and in our own. For me this is also a personal tragedy because I have many friends in Czechoslovakia, and I do not know how I will be able to look them in the eye. . . . I tell myself that what has happened is a great gift to all the reactionary forces in the

---

[28] A. Rubinstein, *The Foreign Policy of the Soviet Union*, 3d ed. (New York, 1972), pp. 302–04.

world, that we cannot foresee the overall consequences of this act.[29]

Roy Medvedev, a dissident historian, asked, "Was the Invasion a Defense of Socialism?"

Pravda writes that thé Soviet Communist Party has had an "understanding attitude" toward the decisions made by the CPC at the January 1968 plenum of its Central Committee. But *Pravda* says nothing about the mistakes and crimes of the Novotny group, which brought Czechoslovakia to its present state of political crisis. *Pravda* asserts that the Soviet Communist Party leadership has no desire to impose its views on the CPC concerning forms and methods of social control or the road to socialism. But the facts testify to the opposite.

During the past six months we have tried to impose on the CPC our false understanding of events in that country, and when our point of view was rejected, we resorted to military action. *Pravda* admits that the Czechoslovak leaders insisted that they were in full control of the situation in their country. But the Soviet Party leadership [concluded] that "the course of events was such that it could lead to a counterrevolutionary coup." This was a totally wrong conclusion, based . . . on hysterical appeals by the Novotnýites . . . and by their obvious allies in the Soviet embassy in Czechoslovakia. There was no danger of a counterrevolutionary coup either in the spring of 1968 or later. . . .

. . . By violating Czechoslovak sovereignty, affronting the government of the CSSR and the leadership of the CPC, and offending the national sensibilities of the Czechs and Slovaks, we have weakened, not strengthened, the position of socialism in that country. Our action in Czechoslovakia was not the "defense of socialism" but a blow against socialism in Czechoslovakia and throughout the world.[30]

Aleksandr Ivanov, wrote of "Russia's Shame."

So here we see the Stalinists of our huge country, frightened to death, trying to drown out with the clatter of tank treads the voice of those Communists who in tiny Czechoslovakia were a bit too hasty in trying to cleanse the *human face* of socialism of the trappings of pseudo socialism. . . . With the blow of the iron fist they have, for the moment, saved themselves and the Czech Stalinists—ridiculously small in numbers!—from the irreversible forward march of socialism.

. . . August 1968 was a blow at the *practical reality* of socialism and at the Communist movement throughout the world. It was a blow against the ideas of socialism, against genuine Marxism, against the prestige of Communists in the eyes of all progressive humanity, because this blow was struck in the name of socialism and its ideas. . . . But it was our own "young and green" soldiers who carried out this reactionary deed. They did it without knowing or asking *who* they were going after, *who* they were crushing—whether it was a counterrevolution or a revolution. This blind and obedient willingness to follow any order, this unwillingness to consider the significance of one's own actions . . . —that is our national shame, the national disgrace of our times! . . . We are responsible for the enormous harm done to Czechoslovakia's development toward Communism, for all the consequences of our reactionary intervention.[31]

A Czech Reaction to the Invasion

In the first weeks after the Soviet invasion of August 21, the Czechoslovak people were mobilized in a movement of massive passive resistance by their press, radio, and television, freed from Stalinist controls earlier that year. The following extract is from "Commentary of the Day," *Reportér* no. 35 of August 26, 1968:

A country that does not need to be saved from anything or freed from anything, that is not asking for it and is actually rejecting it for weeks in advance as an absurdity—such a country cannot be "liberated." Such a country can only be occupied—unlawfully, brutally, recklessly. . . .

[29] Stephen F. Cohen, ed., *An End to Silence: Uncensored Opinion in the Soviet Union,* pp. 279–80. Copyright © 1982 by W. W. Norton.

[30] Cohen, *An End to Silence,* pp. 281–84.

[31] Cohen, pp. 293–95.

Problem 10 continued

These are unpleasant truths, and one cannot be surprised that the occupiers do not want to read them on the asphalt of the roads, on the walls of houses, . . . on millions of posters throughout the country. . . . But they cannot do away with these truths, least of all by driving the "natives" into the streets under their automatics and forcing them to tear down the posters. . . . Are they not acting "in the interests of socialism," have they not come as "class brethren" performing their "noble internationalist duty"? It is totally inconceivable to them that they should be compared with those who subjugated this country in an equally brutal manner three decades ago. . . . They did not come to liberate socialist Czechoslovakia on the 21st of August, but to trample it down; they did not come to save the Czechs and Slovaks, but to enslave them. . . .

. . . Stealthily, not like a government of a decent country, but like medieval conspirators, behind the backs of all the legal organs of this country, they joined in a compact with a handful of discredited political corpses and stool pigeons who feared punishment for their participation in the crimes of the 1950's and while still pretending to conduct a dialog in their formal contacts, they forcibly invaded the country. Like gangsters, they abducted the Premier of the legal government of a sovereign country, the Chairman of the legal parliament of that country, the First Secretary of the leading political party, and they restricted the movement and action of the head of state, the President of the Republic, a bearer of the highest medals of their own country.[32]

They trampled upon all agreements that had bound them with that country and yet they had enough arrogance to claim that they were doing so precisely on the basis of those agreements. They brutally surrounded the parliament of that country with their tanks and machine guns. . . . Within three days, they flooded that small country with 26 military divisions and 500,000 soldiers, with thousands of tanks and even rocket weapons, which they aimed against our capital city. They drove the voices of this country, its press, radio, and television, underground, and they tried to replace them with their disgusting prattle disseminated out of [East] Berlin in an insulting distortion of our language. . . .

Encountering the calm of the people, a country that fails to offer a single proof in support of their nonsensical pretext for aggression, they started a futile barrage from all their weapons in the middle of the night—perhaps to be able to pretend to themselves that there is, after all, a need to fight. . . .

Can all this be called a rescue, can all this be called a liberation? How does it actually differ from 15 March 1939?[33] Is this not a replica of all that we already went through once? Of *Wehrmacht* and Gestapo, of blood and iron? Of injustice and arrogance, cruelty and recklessness? Is anything changed by the fact that all this is being perpetrated not by enemies but by "friends," not by recognized aggressors but by allies, not by those of whom we might have expected it but by those whom we would never have thought capable of it?[34]

A Western Evaluation

In a scholarly study, Galia Golan, lecturer in political science at the Hebrew University of Jerusalem, ends with an examination of factors leading to the Soviet invasion of August 1968. She emphasizes the dangers to the Kremlin posed by the "Czechoslovak road to socialism."

While Czechoslovakia's reforms did not lead her to demand genuine independence from the Soviet Union, the growing pressures upon her did prompt more and more frequent references to sovereignty, equality, and a "Czechoslovak" road to socialism. The sources of these pressures, specifically Gomulka, Ulbricht, and the Kremlin, may well have believed that the reform movement would, eventually, lead Czechoslovakia out of the bloc. But subsequent actions—and revelations—suggested that what worried them most was this "Czechoslo-

---

[32] President Ludvik Svoboda was one of very few foreigners to receive the highest Soviet military decoration, Hero of the Soviet Union.

[33] On that date the Nazi armies of Hitler occupied Prague and the remainder of Czechoslovakia.

[34] Czechoslovak "Black Book," in R. Remington, ed., *Winter in Prague* (Cambridge, MA, 1969), pp. 407–09.

vak road to socialism," i.e., the threat it presented for socialism as the Soviets conceived it, both in Czechoslovakia and in the other countries of the Soviet bloc. . . . This issue was certainly used by both the East Germans and the Soviets in their accusations against Prague (*viz.* their efforts to link the reform movement with Bonn, revanchism, and the Sudeten Deutsche), but the Soviets never brought to bear all the means at their disposal to forestall such relations. Rather it would seem that something much more serious was deemed to warrant a full-scale invasion: . . . the threat to the continued rule of the party, the threat of pluralism, and the dangers of freedom of expression—all considered incompatible in Soviet eyes with the continuation or building of socialism. Thus Soviet and subsequent conservative Czechoslovak attacks focused on the abolition of censorship, the criticism of the militia (read security organs), and the tentatives towards pluralism, specifically the clubs, of the 1968 revival. . . .

The Soviets made every effort publicly to create the impression that their fear was that Czechoslovakia was falling into the hands of persons who wished to take her out of the socialist alliance, defy the Soviet Union and move towards the West. . . . Moscow's concerns focused on Czechoslovakia's traditional tendencies to democratic socialism, with all its implications for Eastern Europe and the Soviet Union. Like the Comintern and Cominform before them, Moscow, Warsaw, and Pankow were unwilling to accept or believe that this type of socialism could lead to and preserve communism. Specifically, the concept of the leading role of the party . . . had become so intricately connected with the concept of communist rule that Moscow could not conceive of a communist party's remaining in power if it were to abandon its leading role. . . . The implications of this danger were clear: pluralism in Prague . . . might well spread to other countries. . . . The fall of the communist regime in Prague would mean the loss of Czechoslovakia as a reliable ally or even friendly neighbor. . . . It was the democratic nature and content of the Czechoslovak experiment, rather than some fabricated "neutral-

ism" or pro-western tendency, which precipitated the invasion.[35]

The Repudiation of 1989

In November 1989, encouraged by dramatic political change in neighboring Poland, Hungary, and East Germany, the hard-line Communist regime of Czechoslovakia led by Miloš Jakeš fell before a massive but peaceful popular revolution. On December 2 the newly formed Czechoslovak government issued the following statement:

> The Government of the Czechoslovak Socialist Republic considers the entry into Czechoslovakia of the armies of the five states of the Warsaw Treaty in 1968 as an infringement to the norms of relations amongst sovereign states. The federal Government entrusts its chairman, Ladislav Adamec, to inform the Soviet Government of this position.
>
> The federal Government proposes, at the same time, to the Government of the Soviet Union to open negotiations on an inter-government agreement which concerns the temporary stay of the Soviet troops on the territory of the Czechoslovak Socialist Republic. It entrusts the Minister of Foreign Affairs, Jaromir Johanes, to conduct the negotiations. It premises that the question of the departure of the Soviet troops must be settled in conformity with the advance of the European disarmament process.
>
> The Government of the Czechoslovak Socialist Republic is prepared, together with the other countries involved, to create a group of historians who would consider, from all angles, the context of the events of August 1968.[36]

On December 4, 1989, in Moscow the USSR and the four Warsaw Pact allies that had joined in the 1968 intervention in Czechoslovakia jointly condemned that action. Furthermore, Soviet leaders agreed to discuss with the new Czechoslovak regime the withdrawal of Soviet troops that had been garrisoned in Czechoslovakia ever since August 1968. Here are the texts of

---

[35] Galia Golan, *The Czechoslovak Reform Movement: Communism in Crisis, 1962–1968* (Cambridge, 1971), pp. 316, 327–28.

[36] *New York Times,* December 3, 1989.

Problem 10 continued

the Soviet and Warsaw Pact repudiations of the intervention:

Soviet Statement

The Czechoslovak society is at the stage of a critical reassessment of the experience of its political and economic development.

This is a natural process. Many countries undergo it in one way or another.

Regrettably, the need for constant socialist self-renewal and realistic appraisal of the events has not always been taken for granted, particularly in situations when such events intertwined in a contradictory way and required bold answers to the challenges of the times.

In 1968, the Soviet leadership of that time supported the stand of one side in an internal dispute in Czechoslovakia regarding objective pressing tasks.

The justification for such an unbalanced, inadequate approach, an interference in the affairs of a friendly country, was then seen in an acute East-West confrontation.

We share the view of the Presidium of the Central Committee of the Communist Party of Czechoslovakia and the Czechoslovak Government that the bringing of armies of five socialist countries into Czechoslovak territory in 1968 was unfounded, and that that decision, in the light of all the presently known facts, was erroneous.

Warsaw Pact Statement

Leaders of Bulgaria, Hungary, the German Democratic Republic, Poland and the Soviet Union, who gathered for a meeting in Moscow on Dec. 4, stated that the bringing of troops of their countries into Czechoslovakia in 1968 was an interference in internal affairs of sovereign Czechoslovakia and should be condemned.

Disrupting the process of democratic renewal in Czechoslovakia, those illegal actions had long-term negative consequences.

History showed how important it is, even in the most complex international situation, to use political means for the solution of any problems, strictly to observe the principles of sovereignty, independence and noninterference in internal affairs in relations among states, which is in keeping with the provisions of the Warsaw Treaty.[37]

Conclusion

Explaining the Soviet invasion of Czechoslovakia in 1968, Soviet spokesmen emphasized that a powerful "reactionary movement" had sought to overturn socialism there, allied with West German militarists and revanchists. Moscow claimed the right to intervene anywhere in the "socialist world" to prevent the collapse of socialism and a consequent reversion to capitalism or feudalism. However, the Soviets failed to convince even their own intellectuals, to say nothing of foreign Communists, that such threats existed. Both groups deplored an invasion that tarnished Soviet prestige and undermined the world Communist movement. Faced with overwhelming Czechoslovak opposition to the invasion, the Soviets found few citizens who would welcome them into the country. By the intervention the Brezhnev regime regained its self-confidence and reconsolidated its hold over eastern Europe. However, the costs proved high: recementing the NATO alliance, alienating Eurocommunism, and exposing the USSR as a blatant violator of international law and national self-determination.

The eastern European revolutions of 1989 induced the Soviet regime to reassess drastically the 1968 invasion of Czechoslovakia. M. S. Gorbachev, the Soviet president, clearly encouraged the popular revolt in Prague, which was preceded by the appearance on Soviet television of Alexander Dubček, leader of the Prague Spring of 1968. Moscow hailed that movement as the harbinger of the Gorbachev reforms in the USSR. Soviet support for the removal of the Stalinist Czechoslovak regime confirmed Gorbachev's earlier repudiation of the interventionist Brezhnev Doctrine. ∎

---

[37]*New York Times*, December 5, 1989.

InfoTrac® College Edition Search Terms

Enter the search term *Brezhnev* in Keywords.
Enter the search term *Cold War* in the Subject Guide.
Enter the search term *Warsaw Pact* in Keywords. Enter the search term *Czechoslovakia* in the Subject Guide, and then go to subdivision *intervention, 1968*.

Suggested Additional Reading

THE BREZHNEV ERA

AMALRIK, A. *Will the Soviet Union Survive Until 1984?* (New York, 1970).

ANDERSON, R. D. *Public Politics in an Authoritarian State: Making Foreign Policy During the Brezhnev Years* (Ithaca, NY, and London, 1993).

BENNIGSEN, A. *The Islamic Threat to the Soviet State* (New York, 1983).

BERMAN, R. P. *Soviet Strategic Forces* (Washington, DC, 1982).

BIALER, S. *Stalin's Successors: Leadership, Stability and Change in the Soviet Union* (Cambridge, 1981).

————, ed. *The Domestic Context of Soviet Foreign Policy* (Boulder, CO, 1981).

BORNSTEIN, M., ed. *The Soviet Economy: Continuity and Change* (Boulder, CO, 1981).

BOUTENKO, I., and K. E. RAZLOGOV, eds. *Recent Social Trends in Russia, 1960–1995* (Montreal, 1997).

BRADSHER, H. S. *Afghanistan and the Soviet Union* (Durham, NC, 1983).

BREZHNEV, L. *Peace, Détente and Soviet-American Relations* (New York, 1979).

COLTON, T. J. *Commissars, Commanders, and Civilian Authority: The Structure of Soviet Military Politics* (Cambridge, MA, 1979).

DMITRIEVA, O. *Regional Development: The USSR and After* (New York, 1996).

DORNBERG, J. *Brezhnev: The Masks of Power* (New York, 1974).

EDMONDS, R. *Soviet Foreign Policy: The Brezhnev Years* (Oxford, 1983).

ELLISON, H., ed. *The Sino-Soviet Conflict: A Global Perspective* (Seattle, 1982).

ENCAUSSE, H. C. D'. *Decline of an Empire: The Soviet Socialist Republics in Revolt* (New York, 1979).

FRANCISCO, R., et al., eds. *Agricultural Policies in the USSR and Eastern Europe* (Boulder, CO, 1980).

FREEDMAN, R. U. *Soviet Jewry in the Decisive Decade 1971–1980* (Durham, NC, 1984).

FRIEDGUT, T. *Political Participation in the USSR* (Princeton, 1979).

GALEOTTI, M. *Afghanistan: The Soviet Union's Last War* (London, 1995).

GELMAN, H. *The Brezhnev Politburo . . .* (Ithaca, NY, 1984).

HAMMOND, T. *Red Flag over Afghanistan* (Boulder, CO, 1984).

HOUGH, J. *Soviet Leadership in Transition* (Washington, DC, 1980).

————, and M. FAINSOD. *How the Soviet Union Is Governed* (Cambridge, MA, 1979).

HUNTER, H. *The Future of the Soviet Economy, 1978–1985* (Boulder, CO, 1978).

HUTCHINGS, R. L. *Soviet–East European Relations: Consolidation and Conflict, 1968–1980* (Madison, WI, 1983).

KAKAR, M. H. *Afghanistan: The Soviet Invasion and the Afghan Response, 1979–1982* (Berkeley, 1995).

KELLEY, D. R. *The Solzhenitsyn-Sakharov Dialogue* (New York, 1982).

KUSHNIRSKY, F. I. *Soviet Economic Planning, 1965–1980* (Boulder, CO, 1982).

LIGHT, M. *Troubled Friendships: Moscow's Third World Ventures* (Royal Institute of International Affairs, New York, 1994).

LITVINOV, P., ed. *The Demonstration on Pushkin Square* (Boston, 1969).

LÖWENHARDT, J. *The Soviet Politburo* (New York, 1982).

MARCHENKO, A. *My Testimony* (New York, 1969).

MEDVEDEV, R. *A Question of Madness* (New York, 1971).

PIPES, R. *U.S.-Soviet Relations in the Era of Détente* (Boulder, CO, 1981).

ROTHBERG, A. *The Heirs of Stalin . . .* (Ithaca, NY, 1972).

RUTLAND, P. *The Politics of Economic Stagnation in the Soviet Union* (New York, 1992).

RYAVEC, K., ed. *Soviet Society and the Communist Party* (Amherst, MA, 1978).

RYWKIN, M. *Moscow's Muslim Challenge* (New York, 1982).

SAKHAROV, A. *Sakharov Speaks* (New York, 1974).

SMITH, H. *The Russians* (New York, 1975, 1984).

SMOLANSKY, O. M., and B. M. SMOLANSKY. *The USSR and Iraq: The Soviet Quest for Influence* (Durham, NC, 1991).

ULAM, A. B. *Dangerous Relations: The Soviet Union in World Politics, 1970–1982* (Oxford, 1984).

WEHLING, F. *Irresolute Princes: Kremlin Decision Making in Middle East Crises, 1967–1973* (New York, 1997).

WESSON, R. *The Aging of Communism* (New York, 1980).

YANOV, A. *Détente After Brezhnev: The Domestic Roots of Soviet Foreign Policy* (Berkeley, 1977).

CZECHOSLOVAKIA 1968

GOLAN, G. *The Czechoslovak Reform Movement: Communism in Crisis, 1962–1968* (Cambridge, 1971).

HOFFMANN, E. P., and F. J. FLERON, JR. *The Conduct of Soviet Foreign Policy,* 2d ed. (New York, 1980).

LITTELL, R., ed. *The Czech Black Book* (New York, 1969).

REMINGTON, R. A., ed. *Winter in Prague: Documents on Czechoslovak Communism in Crisis* (Cambridge, MA, 1969).

VALENTA, J. *Soviet Intervention on Czechoslovakia, 1968: Anatomy of a Decision,* 2d ed. (Baltimore and London, 1991).

ZARTMAN, I. W., ed. *Czechoslovakia: Intervention and Impact* (New York, 1970).

17

The Soviet Gerontocracy, 1982–1985

In a desperate holding action by the old men of the Politburo, for a decade beginning in 1975 the Soviet Union was ruled by the aged and the infirm. What a far cry from the revolutionary vigor and optimism of 1917, exemplified by Lenin and Trotskii! The Bolshevik Revolution of November 1917 had ushered in a Soviet regime led by dedicated, cosmopolitan revolutionaries with a vision of the socialist future and intellectually the equals of any leadership in the world. Only 60 years later Soviet rule had degenerated into a stagnant bureaucratic regime based on blatant privilege for an elite minority and endemic corruption. Deadly afraid of basic political, social, or economic reform, all long overdue, this conservative oligarchy proved unable or unwilling to tackle a formidable agenda of problems that Marx had never envisioned for a developed socialist state: a stagnating economy, dissatisfied and restive national minorities, and the embers of resurgent religion amid the ashes of Leninist ideology. The average age of Politburo leaders by 1982 was almost 70. With the general secretary often unable to mount unaided the steps of Lenin's Mausoleum, the Soviet Union at Brezhnev's death was drifting. The Stalinist economic system, consolidated under Brezhnev, once an attractive model for underdeveloped countries, was being repudiated even by some members of the Soviet Bloc as they sought to cast off the confining shackles of centralized planning and overemphasis on heavy industry. One of the elderly rulers, Iurii Andropov, inaugurated significant reforms but died before much progress could be made in implementing them.

Domestic Politics

Brezhnev: 1982, the Last Gasps

Evidence mounted during 1982 that Leonid Brezhnev, the consensus politician, was no longer in real command. The struggle for succession apparently began back in 1975, when Brezhnev suffered a stroke that removed him from political activity for several months. During that time Mikhail Suslov and Andrei Kirilenko shared leadership of the party. In 1978 Brezhnev's health weakened again, and from then on he relied

President Jimmy Carter and Leonid Brezhnev at 1979 signing of SALT II,
the second stage of the Strategic Arms Limitation Treaty.

increasingly upon Konstantin Chernenko, promoting this faithful follower by 1979 to party
secretary and full member of the Politburo. Chernenko became Brezhnev's clear choice to be his
successor. Economic failures and scandals involving Brezhnev's cronies and family damaged Chernenko's prospects, however, as Brezhnev's power
eroded. First breaking late in 1981, corruption
scandals compromised General Semen Tsvigun,
Brezhnev's main ally in the KGB. In January 1982
the KGB chief, Iurii Andropov, who had directed
the investigations, informed Suslov, the powerful
"kingmaker" and chief ideologist, of the general's
involvement. After a showdown between them,
Tsvigun apparently committed suicide, and Suslov
died of a stroke a few days later. Early in March
foreign correspondents in Moscow reported that
Brezhnev's daughter, Galina, had been involved in
a diamond smuggling ring through her intimate

friend, Boris Buriata, nicknamed "the Gypsy."
Apparently Andropov had leaked this information
in an effort to discredit Brezhnev and undermine
Chernenko.[1]

The death of Suslov in January 1982 paved the
way for the other political changes of that year,
destroying the stability and balance of the ruling
oligarchy and removing the guardian of proper
behavior in the Politburo. Indirect attacks on
Brezhnev by the Andropov group were directed
against his protection of corrupt cronies. On his
return flight from Tashkent in March Brezhnev
suffered another stroke and was taken near death
to the Kremlin hospital, where he remained
speechless for several weeks. During this illness

[1] Zhores Medvedev, *Andropov* (New York, 1983), pp. 93–96;
Harry Gelman, *The Brezhnev Politburo* . . . (Ithaca, NY, 1984),
pp. 183–86.

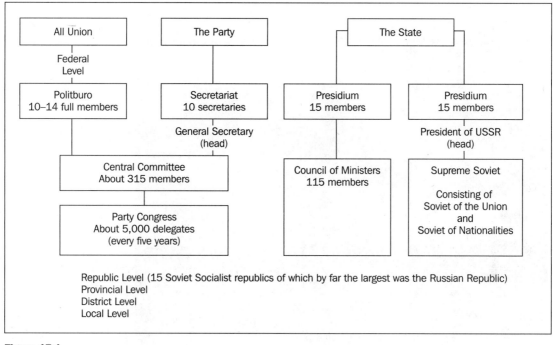

Figure 17.1
Top Soviet power centers, 1980s

Andropov consolidated control over Suslov's vacant ideological fief, delivered the main speech on Lenin's birthday (April 22), and spent most of his time in the Central Committee. (See Figure 17.1 for a chart showing the hierarchy of power.) In May, at a crucial Politburo meeting, Andropov was chosen to succeed Suslov as chief ideologist over the opposition of Brezhnev and Chernenko. In this dress rehearsal for the Brezhnev succession, Andropov moved back into the Secretariat as its second ranking secretary while his candidate, Vitaly Fedorchuk, replaced him as KGB chief. That summer, with the ailing Brezhnev on vacation in the Crimea, Andropov took charge of the Secretariat and arranged the dismissal of two corrupt Brezhnev stalwarts, who were regional party secretaries. Returning to Moscow that fall, Brezhnev, in an address to military leaders, sought to demonstrate that he was still in charge. However, Andropov's supporters then leaked rumors that Brezhnev would resign at the end of the year for

reasons of health. That might indeed have occurred had Brezhnev not died of natural causes in November, after clinging to power to the end.

Andropov: The Sick Reformer

In Moscow, the first hint that a top Soviet leader had died came on the evening of November 10, 1982. Instead of a scheduled pop concert, a film on Lenin was televised. At 9 P.M., the appearance of a newscaster in formal dress suggested that someone had died, but who? Next morning, more than a day after his actual demise, came simultaneous announcements by Soviet radio and television:

> The Central Committee of the Communist Party of the Soviet Union, the Presidium of the Supreme Soviet of the USSR and the Council of Ministers of the USSR inform with deep sorrow the party and the entire Soviet people that L. I. Brezhnev, General Secretary of the CPSU and President of the Supreme Soviet,

Iurii V. Andropov, general secretary of the CPSU 1982–1984 (right), conferring with Andrei A. Gromyko, Soviet foreign minister 1975–1985.

died a sudden death at 8:30 A.M. on November 10th.

Like all Soviet leaders except Khrushchev, Brezhnev had died in office. His death was probably hastened by an appearance three days earlier at the frigid celebration in Red Square of the anniversary of the November Revolution. Brezhnev had held the key post of general secretary of the CPSU for 18 years, longer than anyone but Joseph Stalin; he had dealt with five American presidents and four British prime ministers.

Thus the transfer of power to a new leader loomed as an apparent turning point in Soviet history. The swift and smooth transition that then elevated Iurii Andropov to the post of general secretary concealed the lengthy power struggle described previously. The 300-odd members of the Central Committee who filed solemnly into the Council of Ministers building November 12 knew they were merely to ratify the decision made on November 10 by an enlarged Politburo (including candidate members, marshals, and key Central Committee members). That Andropov would be selected had been foreshadowed by his appointment as chairman of Brezhnev's funeral committee. Andropov spoke briefly extolling Brezhnev's services, then Chernenko rose to nominate Andropov, who had outmaneuvered him in the competition for succession. After the Central Committee's unanimous approval was registered, the official power transfer was over. Commented a Soviet engineer: "We used to complain some . . . and tell jokes about the old man. But now that Brezhnev is dead, I feel sad because he conveyed a sense of security and stability."[2] Whereas after Stalin's death 30 years earlier there had been fear and near panic, now the Moscow public remained calm, hopeful of reform.

Iurii V. Andropov's rise through the party ranks had been speeded by Stalin's purges. Born in the village of Nagutskoe in the north Caucasus in June 1914, the son of a railway worker, Andropov left school at 16 to work as a Volga boatman and a telegraph operator. At age 22 he began his political career as an organizer for the Komsomol, the Communist youth organization. Later he resumed his education at a technical college, but he lacked a university degree. Andropov rose rapidly in Komsomol ranks in the short-lived Karelo-Finnish Republic, where he won the valuable support of Otto Kuusinen, later a Politburo member. During World War II, as a political commissar, he organized guerrilla forces behind German lines during their occupation of that region. Afterward he became a party official in Petrozavodsk near Leningrad, and in 1951 he was transferred to Moscow where he joined the staff of the Central Committee Secretariat. From 1954 to 1957 Andropov served as ambassador to Hungary, playing a significant role in the Soviet suppression of the Hungarian Revolution of 1956 and elevation of János Kádár to head the Hungarian Communist Party. During his stay in Hungary, Andropov grew more sophisticated about eastern European problems. In 1957 he returned to Moscow to direct the foreign affairs department of the Central Committee dealing with Bloc countries. At the 22nd Party Congress (1961), Andropov became a Central Committee secretary, serving under Khrushchev and Brezhnev and traveling to various eastern European countries. Then, in 1967, he became head of the KGB and a candidate member of the Politburo. Serving longer than any other KGB chief, Andropov proved very adept at suppressing

the dissident movement while giving that dread agency a better public image. Andropov was the only head of the KGB to survive that job while increasing his own power and influence. Eliminating remnants of arbitrary terror of the Stalin era, he combated corruption in the party and state apparatuses; he also inaugurated more flexible,sophisticated methods of control and more carefully prepared political cases. He acquired a reputation as a strong, just guardian of the Soviet system.

Andropov's return to the Secretariat in May 1982 proved crucial in his becoming general secretary of the CPSU six months later. He obtained the backing of the powerful Soviet military establishment, represented in the Politburo by Marshal Dmitrii Ustinov, and the influential elder statesman Foreign Minister Andrei Gromyko. Andropov, at 68 and in ill health—he suffered from diabetes and kidney disease—may have been the reason for his haste to implement changes and make a mark on the Soviet system. Contrary to some earlier predictions, Andropov swiftly consolidated his power. Within eight months he had become president of the Supreme Soviet and chairman of the Defense Council, posts that Brezhnev had acquired only after many years. Unlike previous Soviet successions, this time there was no prolonged power struggle as the new leader moved smoothly into a position of dominance.

However, Andropov found it harder to accumulate sufficient power to force political change than it was to acquire titular positions. Having achieved power without the support of the network of regional party secretaries who had backed Khrushchev and Brezhnev, he found it hard to move trusted supporters into key positions in the Politburo and Secretariat. Until the end of 1983 the only addition to full membership on the Politburo was the former Azerbaijan party secretary Geidar Aliyev, seemingly a consensus candidate. The coalition that had elevated Andropov to power proved reluctant to allow him to reshape and dominate the Politburo, and he was opposed there by a Brezhnevite "old guard" headed by his

---

[2] "Changing the Guard," *Time*, November 22, 1982, p. 14. See also Myron Rush, "Succeeding Brezhnev," *Problems of Communism* 32 (January–February 1983) and Medvedev, *Andropov.*

defeated rival, Chernenko, and including the elderly premier, Tikhonov. To be sure, Aliyev's designation as deputy premier made him the second most powerful figure in the state apparatus and put him in a position to inherit Tikhonov's position. Two other former subordinates of Andropov soon obtained key posts: Fedorchuk became interior minister, being replaced as KGB chief by his deputy, Viktor Chebrikov; and N. I. Ryzhkov was named a junior member of the Secretariat. Nonetheless, in his first year in office, wrote the American Sovietologist Harry Gelman late in 1983, Andropov failed to impart new dynamism or give new flexibility to Soviet policies. Instead the formidable weight of bureaucratic inertia impeded substantive changes. Only Andropov's political style was different: He needed fewer aides and advisers than the senile Brezhnev and made it clear that his speeches would be brief, frank, and infrequent. A key adviser was Georgii Arbatov, head of the Institute of the USA and Canada, a leading Soviet intellectual.

Between June and December 1983 Andropov, while losing a battle against kidney disease, managed to implement significant personnel and political changes. The Central Committee plenum in June confirmed the replacement of retiring A. Kirilenko with the former Leningrad party secretary Grigorii Romanov as a Central Committee secretary. The death of aged Arvid Pelshe enabled Andropov to replace him with Mikhail Solomentsev, who became a candidate member of the Politburo. Returning to Moscow from vacation in October, Andropov apparently realized he had only a few months to live and stepped up his campaign. Although too ill to attend the December plenum, Andropov nonetheless persuaded the Politburo to promote Solomentsev and Vitalii Vorotnikov to full Politburo membership and make Egor Ligachev, another KGB protégé, a Central Committee secretary.

He was greatly aided in these moves by a key ally in the Politburo, Mikhail S. Gorbachev, who was also in the Secretariat. Andropov rewarded Gorbachev, the youngest and best educated of the ruling oligarchy, with additional power over personnel changes in the Secretariat. Gorbachev, who shared Andropov's reformist sentiments and had become his choice as successor, was one of only two men who conferred regularly with the leader following his return to Moscow. They and Andropov's doctors perpetrated a deliberate deception by issuing reports of Andropov's imminent recovery and return to public view to enable him to retain full power until the end of his life. Acting through Gorbachev and Ligachev, Andropov, between November 1983 and January 1984, replaced almost one-fifth of all regional party secretaries, the greatest turnover in 20 years. Finally, claims Zhores Medvedev, Andropov enhanced and regularized the status of the second secretary of the Central Committee, who would chair Politburo meetings in the absence of the secretary general.[3] Chernenko, who held that post, favored this step, which received Politburo approval, but it would strengthen Gorbachev's position after Andropov's death. Also approved was Andropov's proposal to reduce administrative personnel in central and local organizations and the number of party and state officials in the Supreme Soviet while increasing the proportion of workers, farmers, and engineers. Having taken steps to undermine the power of the "old guard," Andropov died of kidney disease on February 9, 1984.

The Chernenko Succession: The "Old Guard" Hangs On

An emergency Politburo meeting convened the evening after Andropov's death failed to choose a successor. Indeed, not until Monday, February 13, was Chernenko selected. The delay suggests a power struggle between the Brezhnevite "old guard" favoring Chernenko, and the Andropov group, whose candidate was M. S. Gorbachev. Would an old, loyal party hack or a dynamic, sophisticated younger man be selected? If the Politburo were to remain deadlocked, the choice

---

[3] Medvedev, pp. 217ff.

under party rules would devolve upon the about 315-member Central Committee, which favored Chernenko. Thus Gorbachev's supporters in the Politburo, affirms Medvedev, agreed to support Chernenko's nomination as new party leader and keep the decision in the Politburo. In exchange, the Politburo would approve all of Andropov's recent suggestions on political reform. Gorbachev received the newly formalized post of second secretary, becoming the heir apparent behind the elderly Chernenko. This arrangement was apparently confirmed by the emergency Central Committee meeting of February 13 at which Premier Tikhonov nominated Chernenko as general secretary. Chernenko's previous appointment as chairman of Andropov's funeral commission suggested this outcome.

Andropov's funeral was smooth, efficiently organized, with a sense of continuity and propriety, and a total absence of grief. Recent party chiefs had been absent due to illness almost as much as they had been present and seemingly had become more a symbolic than an active force. About Andropov one Muscovite commented: "It is a pity. He was just, but he didn't have enough time." Those leaders closest to Andropov during his brief rule—Defense Minister Ustinov and Mikhail Gorbachev—lingered to pay their respects to his bereaved widow, Tatiana. E. M. Chazov, Andropov's chief physician, confirmed that the leader's kidneys had ceased functioning in February 1983, and that he had been on a dialysis machine after that.[4]

At age 72, Konstantin Ustinovich Chernenko succeeded Andropov as the oldest man ever chosen to lead the Soviet Union. Short and white-haired with slightly hunched shoulders, he delivered a lengthy, rambling, and stumbling acceptance speech, frequently mentioning Andropov and pledging to follow his reform initiatives. Significantly, there was no reference to his longtime mentor, Leonid Brezhnev. The old guard

Konstantin U. Chernenko, general secretary of the CPSU 1984–1985.

in party and state greeted Chernenko's accession jubilantly, believing that it would allow them to prolong their tenure of power. Chernenko's triumph represented a remarkable political comeback for this peasant's son from Siberia with little formal education. However one might assess his intelligence and ability—and there were numerous scornful comments from Russians and foreigners—this man from the people deserved respect for loyalty, toughness, and persistence. An ideologue who emphasized old-fashioned party slogans and virtues, his style was derived from many years of working in *agitprop* (agitation and propaganda) in Siberia and Moldavia and for the Central Committee. In the introduction to a collection of his speeches and articles, Chernenko wrote:

> I was born into a large and poor peasant family in the Krasnoiarsk region of Siberia in 1911. I left my mother when I was a young boy. At 12 I went to work for a wealthy master to earn my living. New Soviet life was just coming into its own and I felt its fresh winds when I joined the Young Communist League [Komsomol]. That was back in 1926. We studied and held down our jobs at the same time. We were underfed and poorly clothed, but the dreams

---

[4] John Burns, "Reporter's Notebook," *New York Times,* February 13, 1984.

of a radiant future for all fascinated us and made us happy.[5]

Chernenko stood forth proudly as a self-made Soviet man who, by dint of hard work, loyalty, and dedication to Leninist ideals, had climbed steadfastly to the top of the Soviet pyramid.[6] During a 50-year party career, Chernenko had never initiated projects nor enunciated original ideas. As an ideologist, carped Medvedev, he was even duller than his predecessor, Suslov. A pure product of the party apparatus, Chernenko remained an obscure provincial official until meeting Brezhnev in Moldavia in 1948. He followed his mentor upward through the party ranks, becoming a full member of the Central Committee in 1971. In 1976 Chernenko replaced Kirilenko as Brezhnev's closest colleague and heir apparent, being promoted with almost indecent haste as a party secretary in 1976 and full member of the Politburo in 1978. His philosophy was profoundly conservative: All problems could be solved with Leninist ideology, propaganda, and party discipline. Chernenko's short-lived regime, representing a holding action by the gerontocrats, was a throwback to Brezhnev's final years. Visibly feeble when he succeeded Andropov, Chernenko, like his two predecessors, was frequently out of public view, laid low by emphysema. As the torpor of the last Brezhnev years resumed, Andropov's 15 months in power stood out by contrast as an interlude of dynamism, initiative, and forward movement.

By early 1985 signs multiplied that the Chernenko era would be brief. Behind the scenes in the Kremlin, the dynamic Mikhail S. Gorbachev positioned himself for the succession. In December 1984 Marshal Dmitri Ustinov, defense minister and a powerful force in the Politburo, died and received a massive funeral. Chernenko appeared at the marshal's bier, pale and unsteady, but was absent from the burial ceremony conducted in

bitter cold. Instead Gorbachev led the way in escorting the burial urn, followed by his rival, Grigorii Romanov. The replacement of Ustinov by his deputy, Marshal Sergei Sokolov, suggested the aged leaders' reluctance to yield authority to the younger generation. During January 1985, as Chernenko failed to reappear, Soviet spokesmen admitted that he was gravely ill; rumors circulated that he would soon resign as general secretary. In late February he made two brief appearances on Soviet television, looking very feeble. However, contrary to initial fears, Chernenko, instead of undoing Andropov's reforms, continued them more gradually. One Moscow intellectual noted: "We have come to peace with Chernenko. He has contributed nothing new, the pace has slowed, the results are humble, but at least he has not turned back the clock."[7]

Economy and Society

"The Soviet Union simply does not have the resources to invest in all the necessary sectors. The leadership is going to have to make tough decisions on allocations of capital, raw materials, and labor," stated Robert Legvold of the Council on Foreign Relations. "The probable loser in the short term will be the Soviet consumer, accustomed since the 1950s to a steady, if unspectacular, rise in living standards. With Brezhnev's legacy of declining economic growth rates, Soviet citizens clearly would have to settle for minimal improvements during the 1980s," declared the American Sovietologist Walter Laqueur. Such statements reflected economic policies under Brezhnev's successors.

At Brezhnev's death, wrote Marshall Goldman, the USSR faced a severe economic crisis. The country had failed to adapt the rigid, highly centralized Stalinist planning model, which emphasized production of iron and steel, to meet radically new economic needs. Whereas

[5] Konstantin Chernenko, "Introduction," *Selected Speeches* (Philadelphia, 1984).
[6] Serge Schmemann, "A Bolshevik of Old Mold Rises to the Top," *New York Times,* February 14, 1984.

[7] "Chernenko's Status Shrouded in Rumor," *New York Times,* January 31, 1985.

Khrushchev had predicted confidently in 1958 that the USSR by 1980 would surpass levels of production of the United States and enjoy abundance, Soviet GNP (gross national product) during the early 1980s hovered between 55 and 60 percent of the American figure. The Stalinist system had developed a momentum of its own, continuing to churn out steel when food and consumer goods were required. As Khrushchev himself once stated:

> The production of steel is like a well-traveled road with deep ruts; here even blind horses will not turn off because the wheels will break. Similarly, some officials have put on steel blinkers; they do everything as they were taught in their day.[8]

With fulfillment of the central plan becoming an end in itself, with managers and planners rewarded for gross output and value of production, many resources were wasted by being diverted to needless increases in the capital intensity of industry producing large, expensive, and useless commodities. The Stalinist economic system neither rewarded intelligent decisions nor punished stupid ones. The obsolete could not readily be discarded, nor could innovation and technological change be readily fostered. Well-suited only to heavy industry and most difficult to restructure, the Stalinist model built up powerful political and economic vested interest groups resistant to basic changes. Reforms, when instituted, tended to get out of control, making the leadership loath to overhaul an outmoded system as long as it showed even minimal growth. Avoided far too long, economic change became more difficult with each passing year.

Yet by 1982 something clearly needed to be done. In 1981 Soviet steel production, previously a source of great pride for outpacing that of the United States, fell below the 1978 level; coal and oil output apparently had peaked, having become increasingly difficult and expensive to extract from remote regions. With almost a quarter of its own crop rotting in the fields or failing to be transported to markets, the USSR had become the world's largest importer of grain. The Soviet worker, with few incentives to produce or conserve and with few desirable consumer goods to buy, was suffering from falling morale and discipline. Beginning in 1980, strikes, demonstrations, and riots broke out in various cities; food rationing had to be reintroduced in major centers for the first time since the 1940s. Meanwhile Soviet leaders remained committed to a steadily rising military budget and an empire costing more than $20 billion per year in subsidies. How little the economy was serving consumer needs was revealed by a huge and growing volume of savings (from 91 billion rubles in 1975 to 156.6 billion in 1980), as consumers awaited desirable goods. This situation had stimulated development of a vast black market, estimated at almost 25 percent of GNP, but even that failed to close the gap between supply and demand.[9] Any sudden decontrol could trigger panic, huge inflationary pressure, and unemployment. Economic distortions had become too massive to be rectified quickly. A bold leader undertaking basic reform, predicted Goldman, must deal with prolonged inflation, severe unemployment, shortages of desirable capital, surpluses of outmoded capital, profiteering, and severe balance-of-payments deficits—evils from which only capitalist countries were supposed to suffer. Could the Soviet political system survive such severe strains? No aged or infirm interim leader would take such risks.

How then did Brezhnev's successors deal with these grave economic problems? Andropov began with harsh criticisms of the existing system's shortcomings, rather than with Brezhnev's ritualistic praise of past economic achievements; he bluntly distributed responsibility for current inadequate performance equally among government, workers, and farmers. His aim was not to introduce drastic reform of the economic system, which

---

[8] Marshall I. Goldman, *USSR in Crisis: The Failure of an Economic System* (New York, 1983), p. 36.

[9] Gregory Grossman, "The Second Economy of the USSR," *Problems of Communism* 26 (September–October 1977), p. 25.

he feared, but to improve management and worker efficiency, reduce waste, and ensure that everything produced or harvested would be made available. His priorities included raising productivity through harder work and better discipline, use of new planning methods, and accelerating introduction of new technology. Thus Andropov sought to make the old Stalinist system function more efficiently. In December 1982 he reorganized the Ministry of Railways and suggested improving coordination of all forms of transport. Lacking a new solution for agriculture, he echoed Brezhnev's expensive Food Program of May 1982 and campaigned for a reduction in food wastage and better storage facilities for farmers. Tougher policies were instituted to promote better work discipline. The police cracked down on loafing and absenteeism; they even corralled slackers in Moscow bathhouses! However, the regime's efforts to stifle the "second economy" by prohibiting unregistered freelance work proved premature and counterproductive and were soon abandoned.

Amid Western speculation that Andropov would institute economic reforms like those in Hungary (decentralization and more scope for market forces, for example), Soviet economic measures of early 1983, noted Medvedev, resembled those of General Wojciech Jaruzelski's martial law regime in Poland. The government raised food prices by rapidly expanding "commercial" trade by cooperatives, diverting more food into that system where prices and quality were far higher than in state shops. At a well-publicized meeting with workers and engineers at a Moscow machine tool plant that January, Andropov stressed better work discipline, stricter observance of the plan, and reduction of absenteeism and deliberately slow work if workers were to obtain more and better goods.[10]

Andropov also accelerated the anticorruption drive, which he had used earlier to undermine and discredit Brezhnev. Reports of high-level corruption and peculation appeared in the Soviet press.

Penalties against embezzlement and bribery were increased by a decree in January 1983. So readers would know the source of this campaign, Soviet newspapers published an unusual report entitled "In the Politburo of the CPSU," revealing that the Politburo had discussed numerous letters from workers and farmers complaining of shoddy work, false statistics, poor use of materials, and embezzlement of funds:

> The Politburo drew the attention of the Procurator General of the USSR and Ministry of Internal Affairs to the fact that it is necessary to take proper measures to improve socialist legality in towns and villages taking into consideration the fact that these problems are very frequently the cause of complaints in letters which are sent to the central Party organs.[11]

As Andropov intensified the anticorruption drive, millions of letters from citizens complaining about local abuses flooded into top agencies, which party leaders could not afford to ignore. Corruption at all levels had grown so widespread that the public believed that shortages of food and consumer goods resulted from officials' diverting better-quality goods into their closed shops and distribution centers.

British journalist Jonathan Steele and TV writer Eric Abraham claim Andropov supported the approach of Gorbachev, the Politburo's expert on agriculture, in encouraging decentralization and local initiative to stimulate the economy; both men favored fostering greater production on private peasant plots to supplement Brezhnev's Food Program.[12] An industrial reform program of July 1983 reduced the number of centrally imposed economic indicators and gave local managers more autonomy. Reintroducing some aspects of Premier Kosygin's 1965 reforms, it fell far short of the Hungarian economic reforms; there was no attempt to move away from the system of centrally administered prices. Andropov was merely willing to tolerate some experiments and limited decen-

---

[10] Medvedev, pp. 127–34.

[11] *Pravda*, December 11, 1982, quoted in Medvedev, p. 142.
[12] Jonathan Steele and Eric Abraham, *Andropov in Power*, Garden City, NY, 1984, pp. 162–65.

tralization to foster lower-level initiative, coupling these with greater social and industrial discipline. His economic reforms may have been limited by opposition within the Politburo, Gosplan, and the party bureaucracy. In his message to the December 1983 Central Committee plenum, Andropov warned: "The most important thing now is not to lose the tempo and the general positive mood for action." That became his legacy.[13]

Under Chernenko there was little apparent progress in remedying grave economic shortcomings. Observed one skeptical intellectual:

> The wheels are still turning from momentum. But they are beginning to slow down. And rot is setting in. But it will take a long time for anything conclusive to happen. It won't happen in my lifetime.

At least economic problems were being discussed more candidly in the Soviet press, noted Robert Kaiser, an American journalist.[14] Dr. Abel Aganbegyan of the Siberian department of the Academy of Sciences noted that too few people were entering the workforce. Raw materials and energy sources were disappearing from European Russia, where most industry still centered. Siberia and the Soviet Far East accounted for 88 percent of raw material and energy resources, which were becoming increasingly difficult and expensive to extract. Aganbegyan advocated radical reforms to prevent central industrial ministries from interfering with individual enterprises. He complained that Andropov's experimental reforms had been too tentative and limited.

A significant debate over economic policy proceeded under Chernenko between the Brezhnev "old guard" and reformers led by Gorbachev. While noting Andropov's "clear creative mind" and "keen sense for the new," Chernenko pleaded for caution and proven methods. Younger Polit-

buro members (Gorbachev, Vorotnikov) and Central Committee secretaries (Ligachev, Ryzhkov) promoted by Andropov, taking positions contrary to Chernenko in their election speeches, credited Andropov personally for successes in 1983 in raising output and urged continuing his policies and accelerating the tempo. Gorbachev became the chief advocate of innovation, presenting himself as Andropov's standard bearer and Chernenko's main challenger. Thus in Stavropol in February 1984, Gorbachev interpreted the party's task as to "consolidate and develop the positive trends, and bolster and augment *everything new and progressive that has become part of our social life recently.*" He advocated "the acceleration of the development of the national economy and the improvement of its efficiency, . . . a profound reorientation of social production toward increasing the people's well-being." In sharp contrast with Chernenko, Gorbachev called for training "cadres capable of thinking and acting in a modern way." Their divergent attitudes and proposals revealed major contradictions at the top level between "conservatives" and modernists, suggesting an ongoing power struggle between Brezhnev's "old guard" and Andropov's "Young Turks."[15]

Despite the absence of basic reforms, the Soviet economy showed signs of an upturn. In the wake of an encouraging trend during 1983, there was a 4.2-percent increase in industrial output and a 3.8-percent improvement in labor productivity in 1984. However, agriculture failed to advance, and there was a disquieting decrease in oil production.[16]

Foreign Policy

At Brezhnev's death the Soviet Union faced major and intractable problems abroad in a number of areas. A virtually bankrupt and resentful Poland drained Soviet resources and typified increasing

---

[13] Ernest Kux, "Contradictions in Soviet Socialism," *Problems of Communism* 33 (November–December 1984), pp. 1–4.

[14] Robert Kaiser in *Boston Sunday Globe,* September 30, 1984.

[15] Kux, "Contradictions in Soviet Socialism."

[16] Serge Schmemann, "Chernenko's Status . . . ," *New York Times,* January 31, 1985.

Soviet difficulties in eastern Europe. East Germany, Romania, and even Hungary were only slightly less in debt to Western banks than unfortunate Poland. A second set of problems related to Sino-Soviet relations, which had remained generally bad under Brezhnev. The Chinese had been alienated not only by the border conflict of 1969–1970 but also by the later Soviet invasion of Afghanistan and predominance in neighboring Vietnam. In addition, Beijing was still worried by large Soviet military forces stationed along China's frontiers. Third, the USSR appeared deeply mired in Afghanistan, seemingly committed to a military and political victory regardless of the cost in money, men, and prestige. Meanwhile, Soviet-American relations had plumbed depths of tension and acrimony not equaled since the worst period of the Cold War. Apparently despairing of reaching positive agreements with a fiercely conservative Republican administration whose chief, Reagan, had denounced the USSR as an "evil empire," Soviet leaders realized that American hostility might well deny them the high technology and equipment they needed to modernize their economy while driving up military expenditures as they strove to keep pace with a wealthier United States in a new arms race.

Changes in Soviet foreign policy under Andropov were limited primarily to style, greater flexibility, and personal command. Such new trends followed immediately after Brezhnev's death. His funeral brought an unprecedented number of high-level foreign delegations to Moscow; Andropov talked at length in friendly fashion with the Chinese foreign minister and President Zia of Pakistan. His meeting with Vice President Bush of the United States revealed an intelligence and flexibility in spontaneous exchanges on a variety of issues. Andropov made it clear to some 100 foreign delegations that he would direct Soviet foreign policy firmly and reasonably; the period of diplomatic stagnation was over.

A distinct improvement in Soviet relations with China occurred under Andropov and continued under Chernenko. Brezhnev's speeches during

1982 revealed that Moscow had decided to improve Sino-Soviet relations. Andropov promptly initiated a conciliatory policy toward China: Articles critical of China ceased to appear in the Soviet Union, and the Chinese found it much easier to deal with Andropov than they had with Brezhnev. Nonetheless, normalization of Sino-Soviet relations proceeded slowly, hampered by continuing friction over Afghanistan and Vietnam. Under Chernenko progress continued, marked by the visit of an important Soviet official, Ivan Arkhipov, to Beijing and agreements to expand trade and cultural relations.

No significant change in Soviet relations with eastern Europe was evident under Andropov and Chernenko, both of whom considered preservation of Soviet preeminence there of the highest importance. In his November 1982 speech, Andropov declared that the USSR should make better use of the experience of friendly socialist countries, perhaps an allusion to the successful Hungarian economic reforms. Meanwhile, both he and Chernenko welcomed General Jaruzelski's political success in controlling ferment in Poland by martial law and continued to supply some economic aid. Despite the lifting of martial law by 1984, the Polish economy continued to decline. The Polish economic plight adversely affected neighboring Communist countries as well as the USSR.

As to dealings with the West, Andropov from the outset possessed the distinct advantage of knowing more about the United States than Reagan did about the Soviet Union and employing more competent advisers on American affairs (notably Professor Iurii Arbatov, a close friend) than Reagan did on Soviet affairs. By late November 1982 the Western press was alluding to Andropov's "peace offensive," which began in earnest with a speech in December. By mid-January 1983 the West was considering some 20 new Soviet proposals in military fields. This offensive was provoked by the imminent installation in western Europe of 572 Cruise and Pershing II missiles and some divergence about them between western European NATO countries and the

United States. When the Reagan administration failed to respond very positively to this Soviet initiative, negotiations stalled.

Late in 1983 a tragic incident caused Soviet-American relations to deteriorate sharply. On September 1 a Korean commercial airliner, KAL-007, on a regular flight from the United States to Japan, flew far off course into Soviet airspace over Kamchatka Peninsula and was shot down by a Soviet missile off Sakhalin Island, killing all 269 passengers and crew. At first Moscow denied any responsibility for the plane's destruction, claiming that while Soviet pilots were tracking it the plane suddenly disappeared from their radar screens. Five days later, faced with aroused world opinion, Moscow admitted that one of its pilots had indeed destroyed the plane, but claimed that it had been performing a secret surveillance mission for U.S. intelligence. (See Figure 17.2.) In a dramatic nationwide address President Reagan asserted that the destruction of KAL-007 was a deliberate, brutal, and unjustifiable murder.[17]

The Soviet government responded that the Korean airliner had been mistaken for an RC-135 American spy plane that had been flying a parallel course. Soviet defense forces had merely exercised the right to protect Soviet airspace from unwarranted intrusion into a sensitive military area. American leaders, affirmed the Soviet statement, had staged this provocation precisely when ways of preventing a nuclear war were being discussed with the United States. Belatedly Moscow declared:

> The Soviet government expresses regret over the death of innocent people and shares the sorrow of their bereaved relatives and friends. The entire responsibility for this tragedy rests wholly and fully with the leaders of the USA.[18]

The KAL-007 incident of September 1, 1983, brought a measured response from the Reagan administration, which left his right-wing supporters dissatisfied. An order of 1981 denying Aeroflot, the Soviet airline, the right to land in the United States was reaffirmed. Reagan asked the U.S. Congress to pass a joint resolution denouncing the Soviet action. The United States suspended negotiations on several bilateral matters and demanded compensation to relatives of the victims; the Soviets refused. The affair effectively torpedoed nuclear arms negotiations on the basis proposed by Andropov and ended any plans for an Andropov-Reagan summit. The incident also raised disturbing questions about Soviet military confusion and bureaucratic rigidity. Secretary General Andropov apparently played no direct role in the Soviet decision to shoot down the plane.

In a thorough, balanced analysis of the KAL-007 affair, R. W. Johnson, a leading English scholar, discussed the four chief explanations for shooting down the plane: (1) the flight had strayed off course by accident, (2) the pilots had deliberately sought to shorten their route to save fuel, (3) the Soviets had attempted deliberately to lure the plane off course by electronic interference with its navigational equipment, and (4) the plane was involved in an American surveillance mission. Dismissing the first three as virtually impossible, Johnson concluded that the flight had been a risky attempt by the American military to obtain information about the newly discovered Krasnoiarsk radar installation in Siberia.[19] Interviewed July 19, 1984, Ernest Volkman, editor of *Defense Science,* stated:

> As a result of the KAL incident US intelligence received a bonanza the likes of which they have never received in their lives. . . . It managed to turn on just about every single Soviet electromagnetic transmission over a period of about four hours over about 7,000 square miles.[20]

Afghanistan remained a stumbling block in the path of improving Soviet relations with both China and the United States. Under Brezhnev the Soviet media remained overwhelmingly silent

---

[17] *New York Times,* September 6, 1983.
[18] *New York Times,* September 7, 1983, p. 16.

[19] R. W. Johnson, *Shootdown: Flight 007 and the American Connection* (New York, 1987), pp. 310*ff.*
[20] Johnson, *Shootdown,* p. 339.

1 An American RC-135 reconnaissance aircraft is spotted on radar at a Soviet air-defense station on Kamchatka Peninsula. It is a routine flight that provokes no Soviet reaction.

2 Another blip appears on the Soviet radar, and the Kamchatka command, suspecting it is a second spy plane, scrambles fighters to intercept the plane.

3 Flight 007 re-enters international airspace over the Sea of Okhotsk. The Kamchatka pilots observe it once again veering into Soviet airspace over Sakhalin. Low on fuel, they break off the chase and alert Sakhalin air defense of the incoming aircraft.

4 The American RC-135 lands at its base on Shemya Island.

5 Three Sakhalin Island interceptors, two Su-15s, and one MiG-23 catch up with the mystery plane. One Su-15 pilot makes visual contact with the plane from a distance of 1.2 miles.

6 Flight 007 has only seconds left inside Soviet airspace. The Su-15 pilot falls back behind the passenger plane and fires air-to-air missiles.

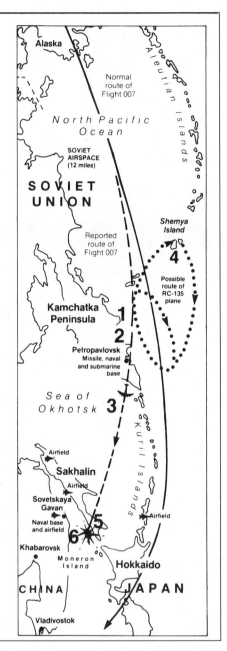

Figure 17.2
Confusion and mistakes doom KAL Flight 007

Soviet observers apparently mistook KAL Flight 007, an unarmed passenger plane, for an American RC-135 spy plane. The Soviets claimed they had tried to warn the KAL plane before they shot it down, but transcripts of the pursuit pilot's talk cast serious doubt on this claim. The incident imperiled Soviet-American relations.

(For more information, see *Newsweek*, "Death in the Sky," September 12, 1983)

about the war there except to make ritual accusations against both powers for "intervening" in Afghanistan's internal affairs. Under Andropov, who was inclined to greater frankness and realism, this attitude began to change. Finally, after almost five years of downplaying Russia's first war since World War II, the Soviet press discovered a war hero, a Byelorussian farm youth named Nikolai Chepik. In February 1984 Chepik reportedly sacrificed his own life to save his comrades while taking 30 of the enemy with him. Wrote *Literaturnaia Gazeta* in January 1985: "The last thing he could see was the peaks of the Hindu Kush, and above them the huge, bright sky, a sky stretching all the way to his motherland." The official creation of a Soviet war hero was part of increasing coverage of the Afghan conflict. Soon a song was composed about the exploits of Chepik, and many schools set up "Chepik corners" where the pupils could study his heroic deeds. Chepik was even awarded posthumously the coveted decoration Hero of the Soviet Union. Increasing parallels were drawn between the Soviet struggle in Afghanistan against the allegedly murderous and brutal rebels and the Nazi invasion of the USSR.[21] The Afghan war continued to drain the Soviet economy and to complicate Soviet foreign relations.

InfoTrac® College Edition Search Terms

Enter the search term *Brezhnev* in Keywords.
Enter the search term *Andropov* in Keywords.
Enter the search term *Cold War* in the Subject Guide.

Suggested Additional Reading

ARBATOV, G. A. *The Soviet Viewpoint* (New York, 1983).

BERGSON, A., and H. LEVINE, eds. *The Soviet Economy* (Winchester, MA, 1983).

BINYON, M. *Life in Russia* (New York, 1984).

BONNER, E. *Alone Together,* trans. A. Cook (New York, 1986). (By Andrei Sakharov's wife about their internal exile.)

BRUCAN, S. *The Post-Brezhnev Era: An Insider's View* (New York, 1983).

BYRNES, R. F., ed. *After Brezhnev: Sources of Soviet Conduct in the 1980s* (Bloomington, IN, 1983).

CHERNENKO, K. U. *Selected Speeches and Writings* (Elmsford, NY, 1982).

DUNLOP, J. B. *The Faces of Contemporary Russian Nationalism* (Princeton, 1983).

GOLDBERG, B. Z. *The Jewish Problem in the Soviet Union* (New York, 1982).

GOLDMAN, M. I. *USSR in Crisis* (New York, 1983).

GROMYKO, A. A. *Peace Now, Peace for the Future* (New York, 1984).

HAZAN, B. *From Brezhnev to Gorbachev: Infighting in the Kremlin* (Boulder, CO, 1987).

HOLLOWAY, D. *The Soviet Union and the Arms Race* (New Haven, CT, 1983).

HUTCHINGS, R. *Soviet Economic Development* (New York, 1982).

————. *Structural Origins of Soviet Industrial Expansion* (New York, 1984).

JOHNSON, D. G., and K. McBROOKS. *Prospects for Soviet Agriculture in the 1980s* (Bloomington, IN, 1983).

KEEBLE, C., ed. *The Soviet State: The Domestic Roots of Soviet Foreign Policy* (Aldershot, England, 1985).

KELLEY, D. R. *Soviet Politics from Brezhnev to Gorbachev* (New York, 1987).

LAIRD, R., and E. HOFFMAN, eds. *Soviet Policy in a Changing World* (New York, 1986).

MCCAULEY, M., et al., eds. *The Soviet Union After Brezhnev* (New York, 1983).

MEDVEDEV, Z. A. *Andropov* (New York, 1983).

MILLAR, J. R., ed. *Politics, Work, and Daily Life in the USSR: A Survey of Former Soviet Citizens* (Cambridge, 1987).

PARKS, J. D. *Culture, Conflict and Coexistence* (Jefferson, NC, 1983).

RUBINSTEIN, A. Z. *Soviet Policy Toward Turkey, Iran and Afghanistan* (New York, 1982).

[21] Seth Mydans, "An Afghan Footnote: Legend of a Soviet Farm Boy," *New York Times,* January 16, 1985, p. 2.

SHEVCHENKO, A. N. *Breaking with Moscow* (New York, 1985).

SHIPLER, D. K. *Russia: Broken Idols, Solemn Dreams* (New York, 1983).

TREML, V. G. *Alcohol in the USSR: A Statistical Study* (Durham, NC, 1982).

ZEMSTOV, I. *Andropov: Policy Dilemmas and the Struggle for Power* (Jerusalem, 1983).

18

The Gorbachev Revolution, 1985–1991

The succession of Mikhail Sergeevich Gorbachev as Soviet leader in March 1985 marked a major turning point in Soviet history both at home and abroad. Taking power after a decade of gerontocracy, stagnation, and growing demoralization of Soviet society and intelligentsia, Gorbachev faced daunting problems, resembling those facing the reforming emperor, Alexander II, and the reforming first secretary, Nikita Khrushchev. Succeeding Nicholas I and his undiluted autocracy under which the Russian Empire lagged further behind western Europe economically, technologically, and politically, Alexander II had instituted Great Reforms, which brought much change but remained incomplete. The heir of Stalin's brutal dictatorship, Khrushchev had attempted to liberalize the Soviet system and provide a better life for its people. All three reform leaders sought to improve the position of Russia or the USSR in the world by ending some of their predecessors' many restrictions or "iron curtain" on contacts with western Europe. Aiming to preserve basic institutions and ideologies, all three sought to rule over a sprawling empire by making it function more efficiently and humanely. The sad experience of his predecessors anticipated the ultimate fate of Gorbachev's reforms. Alexander II was assassinated by leftist extremists, and many of his reforms were halted; Khrushchev was removed by his Politburo colleagues and succeeded by Brezhnev's conservative regime; Gorbachev saw his country disintegrate.

The Leader and the Succession

At his accession to power Gorbachev seemingly possessed an intelligence and political skill greater than either Alexander II or Khrushchev. He was born March 2, 1931, of Russian peasant stock in a village in Stavropol province of the north Caucasus. Only 10 when Hitler invaded the Soviet Union, he was too young to fight in that conflict (though his father did), which left his native village devastated. Young Gorbachev worked summers on the local collective farm, driving a combine and assisting his father. Hard physical labor gave him both satisfaction and self-confidence. Interested in a wide variety of subjects, Gorbachev received a silver medal when he completed secondary school in 1950. At age 18, for excellence in political work in the Komsomol (Young Communist League) and physical labor on the *kolkhoz,* he was given the Order of the Red Banner of Labor.[1]

Those honors facilitated Gorbachev's acceptance by the law faculty of prestigious Moscow State University in 1951. There he met his future wife, Raisa Titorenko; they married in 1954 in a simple wedding. As a student he served as secretary of the law faculty's Komsomol organization and at age 21 joined the Communist Party. Graduated with honors in 1955, Gorbachev returned to Stavropol as a full-time Komsomol official. For his intelligence, dedication, and hard work, he was promoted rapidly, shifting to the party in 1962 and four years later becoming first secretary of the Stavropol party committee. In 1971 he was named to the Central Committee of the All-Union Communist Party, the youngest official to be so honored. He cultivated useful ties with several Politburo members and won their support. In September 1978 Gorbachev held crucial meetings with Brezhnev, Chernenko, and Andropov (his three predecessors as party chief) during their visits to Stavropol and the north Caucasus. Two months later he was called to Moscow as Central Committee secretary for agriculture, and in 1980, at 49, he became a full member of the Politburo.

Following Brezhnev's death in 1982, Gorbachev rose swiftly to the top of the Soviet power pyramid. With some younger Central Committee members, he backed Andropov's successful drive to succeed Brezhnev; he then served as his spokesman in the Politburo after the ill Andropov could no longer attend meetings. Checked temporarily when the old guard selected Chernenko as party leader in 1984, Gorbachev as de facto second party secretary controlled many power levers, including responsibility for ideology and personnel. His trip to Britain that summer and his

well-publicized meeting with British Prime Minister Thatcher enhanced his position as evident successor to the ill Chernenko.

On March 11, 1985, the Kremlin announced Chernenko's death after only 13 months as general secretary and Gorbachev's appointment as chairman of the funeral commission. Only hours later Moscow confirmed that the Central Committee had named Gorbachev first party secretary. *Pravda's* front page featured Gorbachev and his reform program; Chernenko's obituary was relegated to page two. Gorbachev's accession confirmed a decision evidently reached earlier. During Chernenko's illness he had apparently presided over Politburo meetings. As the eighth paramount Soviet political leader, Gorbachev at 54 was the youngest since Stalin to assume control, younger than anyone else in the Politburo or Secretariat. Foreign Minister Andrei Gromyko, the older generation's most respected leader, had nominated him warmly as first secretary. Mourning was minimal at Chernenko's funeral as a self-confident Gorbachev talked with the many world leaders who attended. Gorbachev's acceptance speech revealed his eager impatience to begin work: "We are to achieve a decisive turn in transferring the national economy to the tracks of intensive development." Later, he noted: "The very system was dying away; its sluggish senile blood no longer contained any vital juices."[2]

Gorbachev's succession of a pathetic and aged leader facilitated his swift consolidation of power. The Soviet public greeted its youthful, energetic new leader with unconcealed enthusiasm, hopeful that their manifold problems would now finally be tackled. "After ten years of gerontocracy," commented a young Soviet writer, "it is like spring." Since Khrushchev we have had nothing done for the people, only repression and rhetoric. Now that generation has come to an end." Leaving foreign policy initially in the capable although inflexible hands of Gromyko, Gorbachev focused on domestic problems.

---

[1] On Gorbachev's difficult and challenging youth, see Mikhail Gorbachev, *Memoirs,* trans. Georges Peronansky and Tatjana Varsavsky (New York, 1996), pp. 19–35.

[2] Gorbachev, *Memoirs,* p. 168.

At Gorbachev's accession four of ten full Politburo members clearly opposed him: Grishin, Kunaev, Romanov, and Tikhonov. Apparently it had been the Secretariat and perhaps the Central Committee rather than the Politburo that had elevated Gorbachev to power. In any case, he transformed these top party bodies with unprecedented speed. Two party secretaries allied with him soon received full Politburo membership. Egor K. Ligachev assumed control over personnel and ideology; Nikolai I. Ryzhkov was to plan economic reforms. KGB chief Viktor Chebrikov, another Gorbachev ally, became a full Politburo member. In July 1985 Gorbachev abruptly removed his leading rival, Grigori V. Romanov, from the Politburo and Secretariat for "reasons of health" and nudged his own elderly sponsor, Gromyko, "upstairs" into the titular post of Soviet president. Replacing him as foreign minister was a Gorbachev man with minimal experience in foreign affairs, Edvard A. Shevardnadze, former first secretary of the Georgian party. In September Nikolai Ryzhkov succeeded Tikhonov as premier, confirming the passage of leadership to a new generation.

Early in 1986 Gorbachev consolidated his hold. In March conservative Moscow party chief Viktor Grishin was replaced on the Politburo and in Moscow by Boris N. Yeltsin, a radical reformer. During Gorbachev's first year as party chief, five new full members entered the Politburo. The Secretariat too was transformed, with seven of its nine secretaries selected in that time span.[3] The 27th Party Congress of March 1986 brought 125 new members, mostly Gorbachev partisans, into the 307-member Central Committee. And in the executive branch, 38 of the 100 ministers were removed and 8 more received new posts.

Most of the leaders Gorbachev selected were recently arrived in Moscow and not identified with the Brezhnev regime. At Brezhnev's death most of these men had relatively low status and less seniority than Gorbachev, and they owed their

Mikhail Sergeevich Gorbachev, 1931– , General Secretary of the Communist party and chief Soviet leader from 1984 until 1991, when the Soviet Union dissolved.

subsequent promotions to him. A majority of those elevated into key power positions had worked with Gorbachev either in Stavropol or elsewhere in the Caucasus, had been Komsomol leaders, or were graduates of Moscow University in the 1950s. By August 1987 almost three-fourths of republic and regional first secretaries had been selected since Brezhnev's death while Gorbachev was either personnel chief or first party secretary, which gave him unprecedented control over the party apparatus. At the June 1987 Central Committee plenum, Gorbachev made three party secretaries who were his personal supporters full Politburo members: Viktor Nikonov, Nikolai Sliunkov, and Alexander Iakovlev.[4] (See Table 18.1.)

[4] Hough, *Russia and the West,* pp. 170–72.

[3] Jerry Hough, *Russia and the West: Gorbachev and the Politics of Reform* (New York, 1988), pp. 168–70.

Table 18.1 Membership in Politburo of the Party Central Committee, 1989

Full Members	Year of Birth	Year Elected Full Member	Position and Year Assumed
M. S. Gorbachev	1931	1980	General Secretary, Central Committee (1985)
V. M. Chebrikov	1923	1985	Chairman KGB (1983)
E. G. Ligachev	1921	1985	Agriculture Secretary of Central Committee
N. I. Ryzhkov	1929	1985	Premier (1985)
E. A. Shevardnadze	1928	1985	Foreign Minister USSR (1985)
V. I. Vorotnikov	1926	1983	Chairman Russian Republic Council of Ministers (1983)
A. N. Iakovlev	1923	1987	A Central Committee Secretary
V. A. Medvedev	1929	1989	A Central Committee Secretary
N. N. Sliunkov	1929	1987	A Central Committee Secretary
L. N. Zaikov	1923	1986	A Central Committee Secretary
V. V. Shcherbitskii*	1918	1971	First Secretary, Ukraine (1972)
V. P. Nikonov	1929	1987	

*Removed during 1989.

Glasnost and Political Reform

While consolidating control that first year, Gorbachev enjoyed a remarkable political honeymoon. Helpful to him were his youthfulness, vigor, openness, and skill at public relations revealed in a series of bold, frank speeches, radically different from previous stilted party pronouncements. Repeatedly Gorbachev waded into friendly crowds of ordinary Soviet citizens and workers to exchange banter as the populist Khrushchev had. Gorbachev, his highly educated and attractive wife, Raisa, and their children resembled the Kennedys and were featured at receptions, parades, and official gatherings in a drastic departure from Soviet traditions of secrecy. Gorbachev's restless activity, intellectual grasp, and directness contrasted completely with Chernenko's standpat and secretive regime. At first avoiding major controversial reforms that might alienate important groups, Gorbachev emphasized that the Soviet Union must emerge swiftly from political and economic stagnation or face inevitable decline. Enthralled with his style, the Soviet public and Western media overlooked the fact that Gorbachev had reached supreme power after a 30-year political apprenticeship in the Komsomol and party apparatus.

Before undertaking major economic reform, or *perestroika* (restructuring), Gorbachev sought to build support for essential changes among the Soviet intelligentsia with far greater openness—*glasnost*—in the public media. This *glasnost* would be a spotlight exposing problems. Soviet and Western reporters received freedom comparable to that in other world capitals to cover stories, interview Soviet officials, and reveal facts formerly shrouded in secrecy. The Soviet press began publishing sensitive statistics and reports of crimes and disasters previously only whispered about furtively by individuals. Growing Western fascination with Gorbachev and his policies soon made him and his Soviet Union a leading news story. *Glasnost* also involved efforts by the Gorbachev regime to educate Soviet citizens from above in new traditions of freedom and tolerance. Inevitably this provoked unsuccessful efforts by conservatives to block or curtail *glasnost*, especially in sensitive areas of culture and history. Party control over the media remained firm, but *glasnost* gathered force rapidly as a formerly dull press now captivated Soviet readers with amazing revelations. In the Baltic republics the official press became so outspoken that conservative Moscow newspapers accused it of being anti-Soviet.

Glasnost was severely tested and the Gorbachev regime embarrassed by technological and natural disasters. Late in April 1986 a near-total meltdown occurred at the Chernobyl nuclear energy station near Kiev, spewing radiation north and west into Byelorussia, Poland, and Scandinavia. Although Soviet authorities, including Gorbachev, were informed immediately and reacted swiftly, in an apparent repudiation of *glasnost* the outside world was not told that anything was wrong until three days later. Apparently Soviet authorities hoped to conceal the whole disaster as had been done in the past. Only 18 days later did Gorbachev speak publicly about Chernobyl, seeking to counter a public relations disaster. Chernobyl cast grave doubt on the future of nuclear power in the USSR and provided live ammunition to the growing environmental movement.[5] After this came a series of railroad accidents, coal-mine disasters, and ship and submarine mishaps that severely bruised Gorbachev's popularity. Then on December 7, 1988, while Gorbachev was visiting the United States, a massive earthquake in Soviet Armenia killed about 25,000 people and left more than half a million homeless. Costs of cleaning up and rebuilding the Chernobyl plant and devastated Armenia together kept on escalating. However, the unprecedented openness of Soviet authorities following the Armenian earthquake and massive American and worldwide aid to its victims confirmed the reality of *glasnost,* and enhanced Gorbachev's reputation and Soviet-Western relations.

As Gorbachev encouraged the press "to fill in the blank spots" in Soviet history, *glasnost* exposed the monstrous crimes of the Stalin era in an extension of Khrushchev's de-Stalinization.

While attacking Stalin and Stalinism, the media generally defended Lenin's policies and ideology. Novelists, playwrights, and journalists pioneered in historical reevaluation as professional historians hung back cautiously. Reexamining Soviet history, declared Iurii Afanasiev, new liberal rector of the Moscow State Historical-Archival Institute, resembled "awakening from a prolonged mythological dream." As Soviet citizens learned more about their past, "to many in the USSR it has become obvious that there is no people and no country with a history as falsified as Soviet history." In 1989 Afanasiev elaborated on that theme:

> To give a legal foundation to the Soviet regime in the USSR is, it seems to me, a hopeless task. To give a legal foundation to a regime which was brought into being through bloodshed with the aid of mass murders and crimes against humanity, is only possible by resorting to falsification and lies—as has been done up till now. It must be admitted that the whole of Soviet history is not fit to serve as a legal basis for the Soviet regime. By admitting this, we would be taking a step toward the creation of a democratic society.[6]

At a Central Committee plenum of January 1987, Gorbachev urged accelerating the application of *glasnost* to Soviet historical scholarship. After Stalin had been depicted very negatively in film and literature, Gorbachev's speech in November 1987 referred openly to Stalin's crimes. Abel Aganbegyan, Gorbachev's chief economic adviser, described "the misery and brutality of rural life" under forced collectivization. Lacking basic human rights, collective farmers had been paid less than subsistence wages.[7] The critique of forced collectivization under Gorbachev went far beyond anything revealed during Khrushchev's regime. Its beginning was described as a negative

---

[5] See Nigel Hawkes, ed., *Chernobyl: The End of the Nuclear Dream* (New York, 1986). In his *Memoirs,* Gorbachev affirmed that Chernobyl severely affected his regime's reforms "by throwing the country off its tracks." He added: "I absolutely reject the accusation that the Soviet leadership intentionally held back the truth about Chernobyl. We simply did not know the whole truth yet" (p. 189).

[6] Iurii Afanasiev at the Kennan Institute, Washington, DC, October 6, 1988; "Soviet Rule Questioned," *Radio Free Europe* 6, no. 30 (July 20, 1989).
[7] Abel Aganbegyan, *The Economic Challenge of Perestroika* (Bloomington, IN, 1988); Gorbachev, *Memoirs,* p. 113.

turning point in Soviet history, when Lenin's NEP was discarded in favor of Stalin's bureaucratic socialism.

Along with efforts to refurbish NEP as a truly Leninist model of reform came political rehabilitation of Stalin's opponents. In January 1988 Moscow's Central Lenin Museum displayed photographs of Bukharin, Zinoviev, Kamenev, and Trotskii—victims of Stalin's Great Purge. Bukharin's full civic rehabilitation in February 1988 contrasted his conciliatory, moderate rural program and political policies with Stalin's terror and "revolution from above." Khrushchev too was partially rehabilitated as Gorbachev described his beneficial reforms and praised his efforts to free the USSR from negative aspects of Stalinism, decentralize the economy, and democratize Soviet politics somewhat. However, Khrushchev was criticized for capricious behavior and unstable policies and for fostering his own personality cult.[8] Positive reassessment of Khrushchev's period coincided with a multifaceted critique of the Brezhnev era (1964–1982) as "the period of stagnation." Gorbachev blamed Brezhnev for failing to institute timely political and economic changes and for the USSR's loss of momentum and declining economic growth after 1975. He stressed Brezhnev's vindictiveness.[9] Brezhnev became a convenient scapegoat for most ills of Soviet society, politics, and foreign policy.

Historical *glasnost* even invaded the formerly sacrosanct preserves of Leninism and Soviet foreign policy. Stalin, affirmed one article, for personal political reasons had grossly exaggerated the danger of a capitalist-sponsored and French-led invasion of the USSR in 1928–1929.[10] Stalin's policy of "social fascism," alleged another, had split the German working class and contributed to Hitler's seizure of power and eventually to World War II. One scholar denounced the Nazi-Soviet

Pact of August 1939 as a cynical act.[11] In the Baltic republics that pact was denounced as the basis for their forced incorporation into the Soviet Union in 1940. Efforts to uncover the roots of Stalinism led to scattered criticisms of Leninism, chiefly in literature. Marxism-Leninism, suggested Vasili Seliunin, had played a destructive role by denigrating the principle of economic self-interest.[12] Unwittingly, Gorbachev had opened a Pandora's box of revelations that soon would undermine the entire Soviet system and its ideology.

Beginning in 1986, shocking revelations appeared in the Soviet press about a deteriorating Soviet social system. Statistics were published on infant mortality, incidence of disease, and numerous deaths from suicide and alcohol poisoning. Soviet commentators demanded open reporting of party affairs, even Politburo meetings; the 19th Party Conference in 1988 advocated more publicity in those areas. *Glasnost* did not imply an independent or free press, however, but rather instructions from above combined with frequent reminders by the leadership of limits and a continued need for controls. Inevitably *glasnost* provoked conservative efforts to curtail liberal probing of sensitive areas of culture, history, and foreign policy.

An offshoot of *glasnost* was the dramatic reappearance in the USSR, for the first time since the 1920s, of informal, voluntary organizations. Early "informals" were often devoted to the preservation of threatened historic monuments such as churches or to protection of the environment. *Pamiat* (Memory), a right-wing nationalist Russian organization with anti-Semitic overtones and an incipient political party, began as a preservationist group. By late 1985 informals had spread throughout the country, and in August 1987 their representatives meeting in Moscow's Hall of Columns called for creating a federation of informals and establishing a dialogue with the party. In 1988 the regime invited them to help defend *perestroika*.

---

[8] M. S. Gorbachev, *Perestroika* (New York, 1987), p. 43.
[9] Gorbachev speech of January 26, 1987; *Pravda,* March 1, 1987.
[10] *Komsomolskaia Pravda,* June 19, 1988.

[11] Dmitrii Volkogonov, *Pravda,* June 20, 1988.
[12] V. Seliunin, *Novyi mir,* no. 5 (1988).

Their number doubled from an estimated 30,000 such organizations in 1988 to 60,000 in 1989. During 1989 many of these groups put forward political goals and planned to operate as political parties and establish foundations for genuine political democracy in the USSR. Popular fronts, first set up in the Baltic republics during 1988, by 1989 were successfully challenging the leadership of the party and electing deputies to the Congress of People's Deputies. From the Baltic republics this popular front movement spread to other minority republics. One freelance Soviet journalist, Liudmila Alekseevna, concluded in October 1988 that informals had made Gorbachev's program of democratization irreversible. By then some 70 percent of Soviet youth aged 14 to 17 belonged to informals concerned with popular music.[13]

By 1990 Gorbachev's USSR had progressed much further toward political reform than toward economic transformation. At an early stage Gorbachev realized that implementation of essential economic change depended on political reforms. Expressing impatience at the slow pace of reform to the Central Committee in February 1988, Gorbachev attacked opponents of change and urged accelerating the "process of democratization" by restructuring the Soviet political system. He singled out the soviets as the place to start. In February 1987 a limited experiment of competitive elections to some local soviets was launched. In June 1987 elections, about 5 percent of deputies were so chosen in scattered districts, but the results were heartening. Deputies to local soviets were to be limited to two five-year terms. Elected representatives began to achieve some power over the bureaucrats. In June 1988 Gorbachev told the 19th Party Conference that prescribed quotas in the soviets of women, collective farmers, and workers were no longer necessary:

We should not be afraid of the disproportionate representation of various strata of the population. . . . All that needs to be done is to create a well-adjusted competitive mechanism ensuring that voters choose the best possible people out of this group. Then all the basic groups of the population and their interests will be reflected in the make-up of the soviets.[14]

At the 19th Conference significant political reforms were announced, including a new legislature—the Congress of People's Deputies—that was to be more freely elected and the new and powerful post of President of the Supreme Soviet for Gorbachev. (See Figure 18.1.) Gorbachev later called the conference "the real turning point when *perestroika* became irreversible."[15] (Party conferences were convened periodically, usually to deal with a specific issue, whereas Congresses after Stalin's death met every five years and were far longer.) Officeholders were to be limited to two five-year terms, and local elections were to be contested. Meanwhile, political debate intensified between conservative communists led by Egor Ligachev and radical reformers like Boris N. Yeltsin, destined to be Gorbachev's successor. Yeltsin, notes a sympathetic biographer,[16] was a fascinating, dynamic leader from Sverdlovsk in the Urals who was capable of influencing and leading millions. As a youth Boris habitually participated in dangerous adventures. In school Boris, an excellent but very undisciplined student, became a sports star excelling in skiing, gymnastics, track, and boxing; later, volleyball became his favorite sport. Young Yeltsin "wanted to embrace everything, to be able to do absolutely everything."[17] At his first job at a Sverdlovsk building trust, Yeltsin learned quickly to be a bricklayer, truck driver, carpenter, house painter, and crane operator.

[13] L. Alekseevna, "Informal Associations in the USSR," Kennan Institute, October 24, 1988; Fred Starr, "Informal Groups and Political Culture," at the Kennan Institute, December 9, 1988.

[14] Gorbachev to the 19th Party Conference, June 1988, p. 15.
[15] Gorbachev, *Memoirs*, p. 237.
[16] Leon Aron, *Yeltsin, A Revolutionary Life* (New York, 2000), xviii.
[17] Yeltsin, *Ispoved na zadannuiu temu* (Riga, 1990), p. 17.

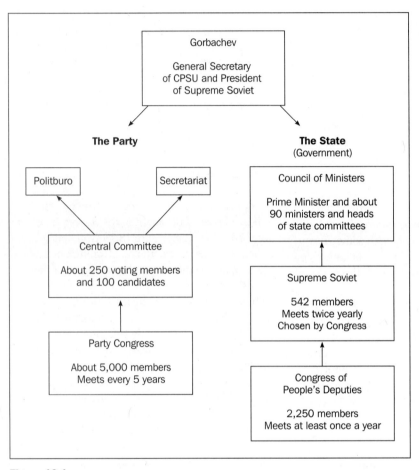

Figure 18.1
Soviet political structure, June 1990

Marrying Naina in Sverdlovsk, he entered the Communist Party, declaring "I want to be active in the building of communism." After serving as chief engineer of a Homebuilding Kombinat (a number of enterprises), Yeltsin entered Russia's power elite as first secretary of the Sverdlovsk Communist Party. His march to power came during the twilight of the Soviet regime. Named Moscow party chief in December 1985, Yeltsin's toughness and firm purpose were needed following Grishin's ineffectual and conservative tenure. Waging relentless war on bribery, Yeltsin sought to replace thieves with honest persons. At the 27th

Party Congress in February 1986, Yeltsin, as a candidate Politburo member, made a daring speech demanding radical change.[18]

In the political debate of the late 1980s, even more extreme was the neo-Stalinist letter of a Leningrad schoolteacher, Nina Andreeva.[19] Following animated Politburo discussion, on April 5, 1988, *Pravda* issued a sharp rebuttal, approved by Gorbachev, defending the reforms. The 19th

---

[18] Aron, Pp. 30–78.
[19] In *Sovetskaia Rossiia,* March 13, 1988.

Conference engineered a more reformist Central Committee than that elected in March 1986 without awaiting the 28th Party Congress scheduled for 1991.[20] However, in the United States former dissident Andrei Sakharov criticized Gorbachev's attempt to implement "democratic reform through undemocratic means." Elections to the new 2,250-member Congress, he predicted, would be controlled by the state administrative apparatus. By holding power as both party general secretary and Soviet president, Gorbachev or a successor might abuse it.[21]

Nonetheless, the March 1989 elections came as a welcome surprise to supporters of democratization. "For all their unfairness, fraud, undemocratic framework and stage-managing," wrote a Gorbachev critic, "the present elections will go down in history as the most democratic elections the Soviet people have seen in the whole period of Communist rule." After balloting for 1,500 territorial deputies was completed, one Muscovite exclaimed, "It was as exciting as . . . when we celebrated the defeat of Nazi Germany."[22] As party conservatives withdrew, stunned by their almost universal repudiation, 90 percent of Muscovites voted for Boris N. Yeltsin, a leading spokesman for radical political change. In one Moscow district Arkadi Murashov—a young engineer advocating a multiparty political system—triumphed. In Leningrad the five highest party officials met defeat when more than half the voters crossed out their names! However, more or less free elections were held in only 200 to 300 districts out of thousands; in most others, hand-picked party candidates ran unopposed. Despite their deficiencies, the March 1989 elections opened the way for a difficult evolution toward democracy.[23] Soon thereafter Gorbachev was elected president of the new Supreme Soviet,

which at its initial sessions in spring and fall 1989 subjected him and other leaders to unprecedentedly frank questioning. Containing a growing liberal opposition, that body was no rubber stamp.

The ouster and subsequent resurrection of Boris Yeltsin throws an interesting light on politics under Gorbachev. An ardent reformer, Yeltsin was named a Central Committee secretary in July 1985 and first secretary of the Moscow city committee in December, replacing Grishin. He issued emotional appeals for social justice and denounced privileges of the party elite (*nomenklatura*). But after a Central Committee plenum of October 1987 Yeltsin, denounced by conservatives and criticized by Gorbachev, was abruptly fired as Moscow party chief and removed from the Politburo soon thereafter. Receiving a modest post in the construction industry but soon named to the Council of Ministers, Yeltsin made a rapid comeback as spokesman for the Moscow intelligentsia and electoral reform.[24] Overwhelmingly elected to the Supreme Soviet over a conservative, Yeltsin took a leading role among its liberal opposition. During 1989 he emerged as Gorbachev's chief left-wing critic, protesting that Gorbachev's reforms were proceeding too slowly. On the right, Ligachev claimed that the pace of reform was too rapid. Gorbachev continued to hold the middle ground in Soviet politics.

The first lawyer to run the party since Lenin, Gorbachev fostered major improvements in human rights and advances toward a genuine rule of law. Nearly all political prisoners were freed and rehabilitated. Gorbachev's report to the 27th Congress in 1986 outlined desired legal changes, and the 19th Party Conference of June 1988 reiterated this theme. Henceforth laws were to be applied in

---

[20] Michel Tatu, "19th Party Conference," *Problems of Communism* 37 (May–August 1988), pp. 1–15.

[21] Sakharov at the Kennan Institute, November 14, 1988.

[22] Alexander Amerisov, *Soviet-American Review* 4, no. 2 (February 1989).

[23] Amerisov, *Soviet-American Review* 4, no. 3 (March 1989).

[24] Timothy Colton, "Moscow Politics and the Eltsin [Yeltsin] Affair," *The Harriman Institute Forum* 1, no. 6 (June 1988). Commented Gorbachev on Yeltsin's speech at the Central Committee plenum: "His remarks sounded like an ultimatum and caused a sharp reaction. Speakers mentioned his 'wounded pride' and 'excessive ambition.'" Added Gorbachev: "I never lowered myself to his level of kitchen squabbling." Gorbachev, *Memoirs*, pp. 243, 248.

Boris Yeltsin (1931–), maverick Soviet politician, meets the public in
Moscow. In 1991 Yeltsin was elected President of the Russian
Republic.

a democratic, evenhanded manner. Moves were
made to abolish or dramatically curtail capital
punishment, involuntary exile, and forced incar-
ceration in mental institutions. The Conference
recommended that "presumption of innocence"
be incorporated in a new Soviet law code. The
Central Committee decreed in November 1986
that defense counsel be admitted to preliminary
investigations in all criminal cases. Endorsing
many proposed legal reforms, the 19th Party
Conference gave this laudable campaign new
momentum.[25]

The dramatic and sudden eastern European
democratic revolutions of 1989–1990, encouraged
by Gorbachev's evident unwillingness to repress
them forcibly, accelerated Soviet political democ-

ratization. In the spring of 1989 Gorbachev told
Hungarian party leaders that he sought "pluralism
within a single party system" for the USSR. He
told Soviet workers in February that a multiparty
system in the Soviet Union was "rubbish." In
November, reassuring worried Moscow conservatives, Gorbachev insisted that Marxism would be
revived by the party and that the party would
continue to lead Soviet society. He defended Article 6 of the Soviet Constitution, which prescribed
a leading political role for the party, and headed
off efforts by reformers to debate that issue in the
Supreme Soviet.

However, in the face of an eastern European
democratic tide and the fading popularity of the
Soviet Communist Party, President Gorbachev had
to reverse his position. In December 1989 the
Lithuanian parliament voted overwhelmingly to
abolish the party's power monopoly. In January

---

[25] William Butler, "Legal Reform in the Soviet Union," *The
Harriman Institute Forum* 1, no. 9 (September 1988).

1990, confronted in Vilnius, Lithuania, by huge crowds chanting for democracy, Gorbachev declared that he saw "no tragedy" in a multiparty system for the USSR. At a dramatic party plenum in February, he advocated revoking Article 6, which was then implemented in a vote by the Congress of Peoples' Deputies. In republic elections from December 1989 to June 1990, the public repudiated many party-sponsored candidates. The opposition took over the governments of the USSR's three largest cities—Moscow, Leningrad, and Kiev. Power was shifting from a largely discredited Communist Party to the soviets. Gorbachev was losing control of the political system; his prestige was declining while that of Yeltsin and other radical reformers increased. In June 1990 a separate party organization dominated by conservatives was formed for the Russian Republic.

In early July 1990 the 28th—and last—Party Congress convened in Moscow in an effort to reorganize the CPSU and arrest its precipitous decline. "It was a battle between the reformist and orthodox-conservative currents in the Party," recalled Gorbachev. With some exaggeration, Gorbachev concluded: "The Party at this Congress condemned totalitarianism and swore allegiance to democracy, freedom and humanism." However, he admitted the congress widened the gulf between reformist and conservative forces in the CPSU.[26]

Nationalities and Nationalism

Under Gorbachev the Soviet nationalities emerged swiftly from apparent obedience to assert long-repressed aspirations to autonomy and even independence. This movement was spearheaded by the three Baltic republics, the most Westernized portion of the USSR. (See Map 18.1.) In some areas, notably the Caucasus and Central Asia, ethnic unrest led to widespread violence that threatened the entire fabric of Soviet federalism. Meanwhile Russian predominance declined fur-

ther. According to the 1989 Soviet census, Russians comprised barely over 50 percent of the Soviet population. The USSR's 53 million Muslims, the second largest group, were increasing four times as fast as the overall Soviet population.

In July 1988 a large crowd gathered in a soccer stadium in Vilnius to celebrate a reborn Lithuanian national identity repressed since 1940, when Lithuania, Latvia, and Estonia were annexed forcibly to the Soviet Union. Participants bore pre-Soviet Lithuanian flags, demanded self-rule, and sang their long-banned national anthem. Algirdas Brazauskas, Lithuania's first party secretary, endorsed "economic sovereignty" for Lithuania. Moscow permitted this, and a popular front dominated Lithuania's March 1989 elections. Such leniency stemmed partly from Baltic leadership in implementing *perestroika*, which lagged elsewhere.[27] However, Lithuania's declaration of independence in March 1990 provoked Moscow to cut off industrial and fuel supplies to the republic. In July that conflict was settled temporarily when the Lithuanians agreed to postpone independence and Moscow lifted its sanctions. However, all three Baltic republics remained committed to eventual independence.

Beginning in 1988, Gorbachev faced an explosive and bloody ethnic and religious dispute between Armenians (Christians) and Azeris (Muslims) over the Armenian enclave of Nagorno-Karabakh inside the republic of Azerbaijan. (See Map 18.2.) In February 1988 hundreds of thousands of Armenians went on strike, demonstrated, and demanded control over Nagorno-Karabakh. In ethnically mixed Sumgait, Azeris reacted by killing more than 30 Armenians. Moscow responded mildly at first, then used troops to suppress rioting in Sumgait. Armenians and Azeris emigrated en masse from areas where they comprised minorities. While rejecting Armenian demands to annex Nagorno-Karabakh, Moscow made some minor concessions. In November 1988

---

[26] Gorbachev, *Memoirs*, pp. 361, 372.

[27] Robert Cullen, "Human Rights: A Millenial Year," *The Harriman Institute Forum* 1, no. 12 (December 1988).

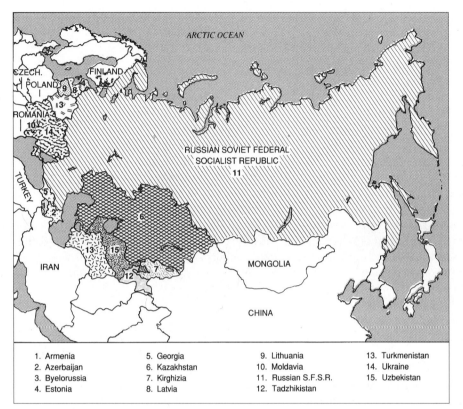

1. Armenia	5. Georgia	9. Lithuania	13. Turkmenistan
2. Azerbaijan	6. Kazakhstan	10. Moldavia	14. Ukraine
3. Byelorussia	7. Kirghizia	11. Russian S.F.S.R.	15. Uzbekistan
4. Estonia	8. Latvia	12. Tadzhikistan	

Map 18.1 Soviet Union Republics, June 1990

SOURCE: *Forbes*, February 19, 1990, p. 107. Map by Robert Mansfield.

Gorbachev expressed deep concern over ethnic unrest:

> We live in a multi-ethnic state, the Soviet Union is our common home. When drawing up and implementing plans of revolutionary perestroika . . . , we cannot count on success if the work for the transformation of society does not take into account the interests of all the nations inhabiting our vast country. . . . Our future is not in weakening ties among the republics but in strengthening them.[28]

Such soothing statements were combined with some repression, including arrests of some

Armenian nationalist leaders. In January 1989 Moscow imposed "special situation status" in Nagorno-Karabakh, resembling actions taken by the government of India in handling ethnic conflict. For the first time Soviet leaders recognized that the USSR shared common ethnic problems with various foreign countries and could learn from them. Further decentralization, warned Gorbachev, might lead to disastrous results in the USSR as in Yugoslavia.[29]

As feuding continued, Moscow issued a decree in mid-January 1990 declaring a state of emergency in Nagorno-Karabakh and surrounding areas. Later that month, as the Azerbaijan Popular

[28] Philip Taubman, "Gorbachev Says Ethnic Unrest Could Destroy Restructuring Effort," *New York Times,* November 28, 1988.

[29] Paul Goble at the Kennan Institute, January 23, 1989.

Lithuanians demonstrate in their capital, Vilnius, for independence, January 1990. Signs read "Independence for Lithuania" and "Freedom for Lithuania."

Front sought to assume power from a weakening Azerbaijani party, Gorbachev ordered Soviet troops into Baku, the Azerbaijani capital, where a general strike had brought industry to a halt. Armed Azeri resistance was broken, but no solution emerged to the Armenian-Azeri quarrel. However, Latvia invited Armenian and Azeri leaders to Riga to work out a compromise, bypassing the federal government in Moscow—another dramatic demonstration of the growing power of popular front movements.

During 1989 ethnic violence erupted also in Central Asia between Uzbeks and Meshketians, a small population in the Caucasus deported to Uzbekistan by Stalin, inducing Soviet authorities to remove many of the latter to European Russia. Commented Soviet émigré Valeri Chalidze:

> Separatism . . . is far from being the main problem of nationality relations in the USSR. The majority of people of non-Russian nationality has not even considered the possibility of separation from the Soviet Union. I believe these people do want free development of

their national culture and protection of their national uniqueness from unification . . . and a voice in solutions to their own problems.[30]

Chalidze cited past denial of political autonomy and massive persecutions of most Soviet nationalities, falsifying their histories to claim that they had joined the USSR voluntarily, massive corruption (especially in Central Asia), and ecological problems as causes of friction. There was an increasing tendency in virtually all Soviet republics to assert their rights—political, cultural, and linguistic—against the Russian center.

During the first half of 1990 the disintegration of the Soviet Union accelerated dangerously, and the country was spinning out of control. Following Lithuania's lead, other Baltic and Caucasian republics asserted their sovereignty. Potentially most serious was a decision by the legislature of

---

[30] Valeri Chalidze, "Nationalities in the USSR," *Commission on Security and Cooperation in Europe Digest* (October–November 1988).

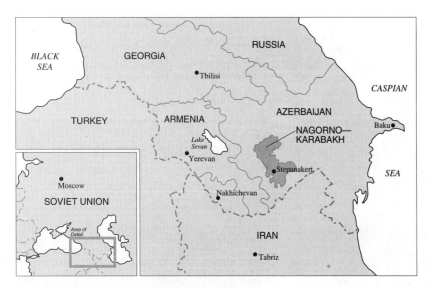

Map 18.2 The Southern Caucasus Region

After the Soviet assault in Baku, Nakhichevan proclaimed
independence. Nagorno-Karabakh, an Armenian-inhabited
region inside Azerbaijan, remains a focus of conflict between
Armenians and Azerbaijanis.
SOURCE: *New York Times*, January 21, 1990. Copyright © 1990 by The New York
Times Company. Reprinted by permission.

the Russian Republic (RSFSR) under its new president, Boris Yeltsin, that its laws would take precedence over those of the USSR. A nationalist tide
was rising throughout the Soviet empire, threatening its continued existence. In June President
Gorbachev promised that the Soviet Union would
be reformed to accord broad sovereignty to the
individual republics, but some of them continued
to press for full independence. As public order
began to break down, numerous Russian refugees
poured into Moscow seeking to escape ethnic
violence in the Caucasus and Central Asia.

Under Gorbachev, emigration from the USSR
of Germans, Jews, and Armenians was liberalized,
partly because of *glasnost* and partly to win foreign
approval and induce the United States to lift
trade restrictions. Relaxing restrictions on emigration reflected a trend toward loosening central
controls, recognizing more human rights, and
promoting the rule of law. Starting in 1986, considerable numbers of Jews, especially "refuseniks,"

emigrated, and even more Soviet Germans departed. However, there was little emigration of
Russians or other nationalities.

Russian nationalism was rekindled under Gorbachev as a backlash against Russophobic agitation outside the Russian Republic and as an
outgrowth of an intraparty struggle between radical reformers and conservatives. Initially, Russian
nationalism aimed to protect historic monuments
and the environment. Nationalists successfully
opposed a vast project designed to shift the course
of Russian rivers to irrigate arid areas of Central
Asia; it was abandoned in August 1986.[31] As Gorbachev's reform plans matured during 1987, neo-
Stalinists and conservative Russian nationalists
allied against *perestroika;* they objected especially
to official encouragement of Western "mass cul-

---

[31] Nicolae Petro, "The Project of the Century," *Studies in
Comparative Communism* (Fall 1987), pp. 235–52.

ture," which appealed to Soviet youth. However, many Russian nationalists hailed Gorbachev's initiative to celebrate in June 1988 the millenium of the Christianization of Rus, including his well-publicized meeting with Patriarch Pimen. *Pamiat,* the leading Russian nationalist group, whose members wore black military shirts or army great-coats, advocated "a great undivided Russia" free of Jews. By 1990 this Russian nationalism represented a significant, potentially dangerous force, but its fragmentation into several subgroups reduced its political strength.[32]

Perestroika's Impact on the Economy and Society

Political democratization and opening of the public media were designed to buttress Gorbachev's radical overhaul of the Soviet economy, or *perestroika*. The chief problem—a monumental one—was to shift a huge economy from a state-owned and -managed system, highly centralized and bureaucratized, to a semimarket economy in which some degree of individual initiative and local decision making would prevail. Another formidable problem was to transform a totally unrealistic price structure into one in which prices and costs would reflect market forces. In short, Gorbachev aimed to move from state to market socialism by using capitalist techniques without restoring a capitalist system.

Under Gorbachev, economic reform in 1985–1986 featured traditional approaches such as tightening work discipline and shifting investment. A second stage, beginning early in 1987, aimed to overhaul the state economic sector and create a socialist market economy. Richard Ericson dubbed a third phase, beginning in 1988, "the privatization of Soviet socialism" in a desperate effort to overcome stagnation; its reforms included a law on individual labor activity and a law on

cooperatives, granting long-term leases to private producers, especially in agriculture. The purpose was "to rescue *perestroika* for the Soviet consumer" by creating institutions promoting genuine competition and removing excessive central coordination and planning. But without steps to legalize essential middlemen, these changes remained ineffective. Legal, bureaucratic, and even public opposition and foot-dragging crippled the new private sector.[33]

Attempts at Agricultural Reform

Nowhere was reform more urgently required than in agriculture, which remained in the paralyzing grip of roughly 50,000 huge state farms (*sovkhozy*) and somewhat smaller but still large collectives (*kolkhozy*). On these grossly inefficient units that absorbed vast state subsidies, farmers still had few inducements to work hard or produce much. Meanwhile small individual garden plots, strictly limited in size by law, produced roughly one-third of Soviet vegetables, fruits, and other consumer staples. Gorbachev's initial response to this dilemma was to create Gosagroprom, an agricultural superagency, in November 1985, while continuing to provide huge state subsidies, especially for meat and milk production.

When this traditional approach failed to overcome the agricultural crisis, Gorbachev in October 1988 proposed leasing substantial amounts of land for up to 50 years to small groups of farmers with the state retaining overall land ownership. Teams of farmers were to purchase agricultural machinery, feed, seed grain, and fertilizers. After fulfilling annual delivery quotas to the state, they could dispose at will of any remaining surplus. Urging adoption of this leasing system throughout Soviet agriculture, Gorbachev by implication condemned Soviet forced collectivization: "What has happened is that people have been alienated from the soil. . . . Comrades, the most important thing today is to make people full-fledged masters of the land

[32] John Dunlop, "The Contemporary Russian Nationalist Spectrum," *Radio Liberty Research Bulletin,* December 19, 1988.

[33] Richard Ericson, "The Privatization of Soviet Socialism," *The Harriman Institute Forum* 2, no. 9 (September 1989).

again."[34] At a Central Committee plenum early in 1989, Gorbachev urged a radical reversal of 60 years of centralized farming. The superagency Gosagroprom was to be dismantled and free markets introduced gradually. After a transition period, farmers should receive "complete freedom" to market their products. Previous efforts at agricultural reform, such as Premier Kosygin's program of 1965, had failed, noted Gorbachev, because they had not been radical enough: "The essence of economic change in the countryside should be to grant farmers broad opportunities for displaying independence, enterprise, and initiative." At that March 1989 plenum, Gorbachev spoke more frankly than any previous Soviet leader had about the shortcomings of collectivized agriculture. The most inefficient farms, he urged, should be allowed to go bankrupt, then broken up and leased out to farmers or merged with more successful neighboring collectives. Egor Ligachev, leading the party conservatives, advocated supplying even larger state subsidies to bolster state farms. That policy, retorted Gorbachev, had proven its utter failure under Brezhnev.[35]

During a month-long tour of Soviet collectives in 1989, Mark Kramer, an American journalist, was told by a Soviet agronomist: "Our farms are disaster areas." Locally, the old failed system remained deeply entrenched. "Even if a collective farm earns money with honest labor," lamented a leading agrarian reformer, "in order to spend the rubles, to build a barn, you still need 1,000 signatures." Lack of incentives and a stifling bureaucracy meant that most collectives lost money. "There are still 200,000 orders, decrees, official instructions, and ministerial instructions. Our economy is tied by all these like a bound child."[36] Even if freed from controls imposed by a million bureaucrats, were

there enough genuine Soviet farmers left to rescue the country from agricultural disaster?

Fiscal Crisis Hampers Industrial Production

Gorbachev inherited an economy in the midst of a grave financial crisis. For years the USSR had been running up huge, carefully concealed budget deficits, amounting in 1985 to almost 20 percent of GNP, roughly twice the U.S. figure. Defense expenditures in the 1980s had continued to increase roughly 3 percent annually to pay for strategic weapons, missiles, and submarines. Soviet state banks had automatically loaned vast sums to inefficient state enterprises. These deficit rubles paid workers but produced no goods for them to buy. Thus from 1970 to 1986 personal deposits in Soviet savings banks rose fivefold because of endemic shortages and low-quality consumer goods. Meanwhile the ruble remained unconvertible inside the Soviet Union and worthless outside; currency black markets flourished. The USSR owed huge financial obligations to its citizens that it could not meet.[37]

Revamping Soviet finances and the economy proved far more difficult for Gorbachev to achieve than political reform. More radical economic reformers, for a time converting Gorbachev, urged abandoning centralized state planning and artificial prices set by the state for a system in which market forces would allocate most goods, services, and prices. They redefined socialism to embrace rules of the marketplace and private ownership of land. For a time Gorbachev envisioned speedy price reform by 1990–1991 to establish a realistic system; he backed away from such reform when faced with negative reactions from Soviet consumers and workers accustomed to state subsidies to keep prices low. Creating a market economy, realized Gorbachev, would be very difficult technically and dangerous politically.

---

[34] Gorbachev's Proposal to Lease Farms . . . ," *Radio Free Europe* 6, no. 4 (November 1, 1988).

[35] Bill Keller, "Gorbachev Urges New Farm Policy," *New York Times*, March 16, 1989.

[36] Mark Kramer, "Can Gorbachev Feed Russia?" *New York Times Magazine*, April 9, 1989.

[37] Judy Shelton, *Gorbachev's Desperate Pursuit of Credit in Western Financial Markets* (New York, 1989).

ITAR-TASS/SOVFOTO

Pizza prepared by cooks from Trenton, New Jersey, being served to Muscovites at the start of a joint Soviet-American enterprise in 1988.

Abel Aganbegyan, an advocate of such radical reformist views and a chief Gorbachev economic adviser, favored rapid and drastic price reform with sharp price increases. Confirming what Western economists had long affirmed, Aganbegyan admitted that in 1981–1985 there had been virtually no Soviet economic growth. Centrally dictated prices, he argued, should be retained "only for the most essential products in order to control their rate of growth and stave off inflation."[38] Soviet economic reformers, noted Ed Hewitt, created difficulties for themselves by allocating broad decision-making powers to individual enterprises before instituting price reforms. That allowed them to operate for several years "with distorted prices arbitrarily giving profits to new enterprises and losses to others." For the Soviet economy to become competitive and market oriented, argued Hewitt, it would have to integrate more fully into the world economy.[39] Gorbachev attempted this by abolishing the Ministry of Foreign Trade's monopoly and encouraging joint ventures with Bloc countries and capitalist companies, reflecting a dramatic change in Soviet attitudes.

Early efforts by the Gorbachev regime to reform Soviet industry mostly failed. A party plenum in June 1987 approved the complex law on state enterprise (LSE), which aimed to discard Stalinist economic practices and make Soviet enterprises into autonomous, democratic, financially independent producers. Individual firms were to exercise initiative, be fully accountable financially, and receive no guaranteed state financial support. Such a change would require

[38] Abel Aganbegyan, *The Challenge: Economics of Perestroika,* ed. N. Browne (Bridgeport, CT, 1988).

[39] Ed Hewitt, *Reforming the Soviet Economy* . . . (Washington, 1988).

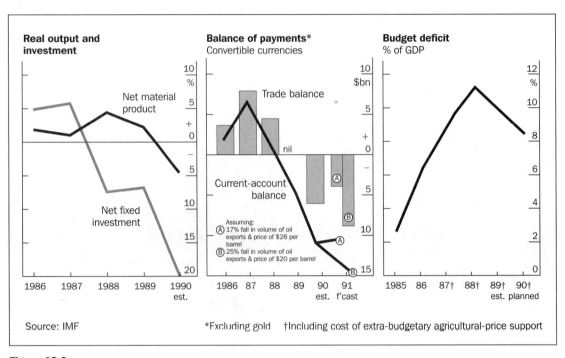

Figure 18.2
The Gorbachev Economic Balance Sheet, 1985–1990

SOURCE: *The Economist,* January 19, 1990, p. 40. © The Economist Newspaper Group, Inc. Reprinted with permission.

overhauling the banking and credit systems and implementing a price reform at the start of the 13th Five Year Plan in 1991. (Later those measures were deferred.) Indirect economic levers were to replace the former central command mechanism.[40] In January 1988 implementation of this radical industrial reform began, but soon it grew evident that the scheme was simply not working. "*Perestroika* has lost its first decisive battle," lamented a Soviet legal specialist. A major purpose of the LSE was to restrict the power of the ministerial bureaucracy by letting enterprises set their own annual and five-year plans partly through contracts freely negotiated with customers and suppliers. However, enterprise directors, used to receiving orders from above,

ensured that state orders would still represent 80 to 90 percent of their output, rather than the intended maximum of 50 to 70 percent. Factory managers remained bound to the ministries, obeying their orders as before and regularly ignoring decisions reached by workers and their elected councils. This situation resulted partly from the vaguely phrased LSE. The centralized Stalinist industrial system and its vast bureaucracy revealed an amazing capacity to survive.[41]

Despite Gorbachev's exhortations for drastic economic changes, during his first five years they failed to take root. (See Figure 18.2.) Growth rates in 1987 and 1988 were only about 1.5 percent, and agricultural output actually fell in 1988. Only about two-thirds of the state's priority projects

[40] Jerry Hough, *Opening Up the Soviet Economy* (Washington, 1988).

[41] "Economic Reform Stalled in the USSR," *Radio Free Europe* 6, no. 8 (December 10, 1988).

scheduled to be commissioned were actually completed. The backlog of unfinished and abandoned construction grew steadily. Reduced state revenues—combined with rising expenditures for investment, defense, subsidies to unprofitable factories, and Armenian earthquake relief—swelled budget deficits and inflationary pressures. Modernization of industry and real price reforms were postponed, and the USSR lagged technologically even further behind the West and Japan, especially in advanced microcircuits and mainframe computers.

Consumer Complaints Increase

Faced with rising consumer dissatisfaction and bureaucratic obstruction, Gorbachev revised his economic policies, realizing that he could not achieve his goals as quickly as he had hoped. The 1989 plan stressed consumption, cut state investment for the first time since 1945, promised a major reduction in defense outlays, and deferred retail price reforms. Priority went to retooling Soviet plants, proceeding with land leasing, and encouraging the private sector.[42] In 1985 *perestroika* had been launched with a barrage of new regulations, slogans, and resolutions, which often proved contradictory and remained mere verbiage. In several key areas the leadership's efforts to decentralize the economy were emasculated by the bureaucracy or simply abandoned. In November 1989 the government set new production quotas for factories and limited some exports. Although Deputy Premier Leonid Abalkin called such measures "temporary," clearly *perestroika* had stalled as had the Kosygin reforms of 1965. Meeting with economists Gorbachev conceded, "We have a long way to go from formulating a concept to obtaining the goals we have set and changing the quality of our society."[43]

Gorbachev relied heavily on the "human factor" to spur the lagging economy. Many corrupt officials were fired, drastic measures were adopted in 1985 to curb alcohol consumption, and Soviet workers were exhorted to abandon casual attitudes toward work. In September 1988 Gorbachev told representatives of the Soviet media: "We must free the social consciousness from such harmful complexes as the faith in 'a good tsar,' in an omnipotent center, in the idea that someone will impose order and organize *perestroika* from above." Seventy years of Soviet socialism, noted a journalist, had produced a psychology of social dependency: "Give me a free house, cheap meat, and get rid of my neighbor who is working on his own and lives better than I do." Many Soviet citizens responded to Gorbachev's pleas by forming "young peoples' residential complexes," competing to build their own apartment houses with money and materials provided by the state. Cooperatives proliferated in order to provide consumer services, formerly sadly lacking, such as repair facilities and private restaurants, but they encountered the "red-eye" disease of envy by those unwilling to see their fellow citizens prosper, and many cooperatives were burned down.[44] During 1988 Gorbachev retreated, criticizing cooperatives; he rescinded tough anti-alcohol measures after a surge in illegal production (*samogon*) caused losses of state revenue and sugar shortages.

Consumer dissatisfaction during Gorbachev's first five years reflected rising public expectations that the regime failed to satisfy. Per capita consumption remained virtually stagnant. Reduced farm output, inadequate storage facilities, and processing and distribution problems produced serious shortages of some foods. With supplies of meat, fruit, and vegetables sporadic in state stores, prices at collective markets rose considerably, as did those of manufactured goods.[45] Soviet citizens continued to enjoy free health care and education

---

[42] Report by CIA and Defense Intelligence Agency of April 1989, *The Soviet Economy in 1988: Gorbachev Changes Course* (Washington, 1989).

[43] Peter Gumbel, *Wall Street Journal*, November 21, 1989, pp. 1–2.

[44] "Gorbachev Calls for New 'New Soviet Man,'" *Radio Free Europe* 6, no. 6 (November 20, 1988).

[45] CIA report, *The Soviet Economy in 1988.*

while housing and necessities remained heavily subsidized, but overall living standards lagged far behind those of the West. In 1985, almost two-thirds of the United States' GNP went for wages, compared to only 37 percent in the USSR, and the United States was outspending the USSR in education, health care, and social security. In 1985, a typical Soviet family of four with two wage earners spent 59 percent of their income on food, compared with only 15 percent for an American family. Soviet meat consumption per capita was less than city dwellers had consumed in tsarist Russia.[46]

Rapid urbanization added to consumer woes. Urban growth rates approximated 5 percent annually, as the percentage of Soviet citizens living in cities rose from 18 percent in 1917 to 66 percent in 1985. In 1926 only Moscow and Leningrad exceeded 1 million people, but in 1985 there were 21 such cities, and 292 with more than 100,000. Whereas advanced rural and urban planning prevailed in the Baltic states, cities in the Urals and Siberia could not provide adequate services.[47] Under Gorbachev the media published many revealing accounts of drug abuse, a serious and growing problem previously dismissed as nonexistent in the USSR. "Concealing an illness will not make it go away," wrote one newspaper. "We have come to realize that openness is needed in the struggle against drug addiction."[48]

National Security and Foreign Affairs

Introducing dramatic changes in Soviet foreign policy, Gorbachev elaborated a sharply altered view of military power and security. In superpower negotiations the Soviet Union agreed to drastic arms cuts and unprecedentedly intrusive measures of verification. Gorbachev downgraded the military's public role, encouraging civilian defense analysts to propose radical revisions of Soviet military policies. Replacing most of the high command he had inherited, he brought in the obedient General Dmitri Iazov as defense minister and appointed liberal-minded civilians to oversee important aspects of security policy. Most foreign observers viewed Gorbachev's "new political thinking" as constituting a revolution in Soviet security policy.[49]

Some of Gorbachev's statements before 1985 suggest that he had been a defender of Brezhnev's 1970s view that expanded military power, combined with arms control and diplomatic negotiations, would enhance Soviet security. However, beginning in 1983, Gorbachev opposed increased defense spending and expressed mounting concern over the USSR's industrial lag. Once in power he urged "civilized relations" with the West, unveiling in January 1986 a proposal for phased but sweeping arms reductions. At the 27th Congress that followed, he declared that growing East-West interdependence required radical improvements in their relations.[50]

At Gorbachev's accession the Soviet Union remained a garrison state with enormous military forces built up over the previous 15 years at high economic and social cost. The USSR under Brezhnev had relied on military might to provide security at home and to serve as its primary instrument of foreign policy. Under Gorbachev this approach was revised substantially. Even in the early 1980s Soviet marshals had wondered whether a creaking economy could support the highly technological armed forces of the future. Policy changes under Gorbachev proved more far-reaching than at any other time in Soviet history. His "new thinking"

---

[46] "USSR Living Standards Far Below Those of the West," *Radio Free Europe 6*, no. 17, 1989.

[47] George Demko at the Kennan Institute, Washington, DC, October 3, 1988.

[48] John Kramer, "Drug Abuse in the Soviet Union," *Problems of Communism* 37,(March–April 1988), pp. 28–40. In 1988, 52,000 persons reportedly were officially registered in the USSR as drug addicts.

---

[49] Raymond Garthoff, "New Thinking in Soviet Military Doctrine," *Washington Quarterly*, Summer 1988, pp. 131–58.

[50] Bruce Parrott, *The Soviet Union and Ballistic Missile Defense* (Boulder, CO, 1987), pp. 55–56; and "Soviet National Security Under Gorbachev," *Problems of Communism* 37 (November–December 1988), pp. 1–35.

rejected the Brezhnev military buildup as economically prohibitive and politically disastrous. Meanwhile there was growing public criticism of the Soviet military as bloated, expensive, and even morally corrupt. By 1988 some military men questioned the need for a huge standing army.

When two Soviet officers chained themselves to a lamppost outside the Defense Ministry in April 1989, they drew attention to the miseries of Red Army life. To their amazement, the next day they were sitting in Defense Minister Dmitri Iazov's office complaining about poor living conditions, scandalous health care, and insensitive political indoctrination. Although soon discharged from service, they revealed how *glasnost* had uncovered widespread discontent and caused unsettled times in the Soviet military, which were exacerbated by the unpopular war in Afghanistan.[51]

The Soviet economy had been grievously distorted and overstretched by Brezhnev's military buildup. A weak technological base, warned Marshal Nikolai Ogarkov, could not produce new sophisticated weaponry. Advances in high technology elsewhere, he noted, threatened to make obsolete 20 years of Soviet military growth. Discerning Soviet military men realized that problems of high technology could be solved only if the Soviet economy were redirected away from defense.[52] Gorbachev's team viewed Brezhnev's foreign policy, dependent on military power, as a disaster. The invasion of Afghanistan had triggered enormous American rearmament while alienating Japan and China from the USSR. Rejecting Brezhnev's idea of deploying forces that could defeat any combination of foes, Gorbachev accepted the American "zero option" proposal for Intermediate Range Ballistic Missiles even though it required the Soviets to destroy about four warheads for every American one. Gorbachev's

United Nations speech of December 1988, in which he offered to cut Soviet forces unilaterally by 10 percent, reflected this new approach. Discussion on creating a smaller professional Soviet army also proceeded in Moscow.[53]

Supporters of *perestroika* sharply criticized the swollen Soviet military in 1988–1990 as blocking substantive progress on basic economic reforms. Attacks on the military as an institution multiplied. An article by Andrei Sakharov, the dissident scientist, virtually accused the Soviet military of genocide in Afghanistan. Some Red Army officers favored eliminating conscription. An army that had expanded by a million men from 1970 to 1985 was proving too costly to maintain, especially since its traditional Russian core was shrinking. More than one-third of Soviet soldiers were now Muslims who spoke little Russian, creating severe ethnic tensions within the armed forces. A smaller, chiefly Slavic professional army would alleviate such problems.[54]

In a wide-ranging debate in 1989 on national security issues, "new thinkers" advocated a permanent shift away from military means of ensuring security; they proposed channeling most resources into economic development. "Technocrats" favored a short-term shift of resources to militarily relevant sectors of the civilian economy to develop advanced weaponry. "Old thinkers" continued to urge heavy military spending. The "new thinkers," including Gorbachev, generally prevailed and urged an evolution of Soviet foreign policy toward cooperation; they argued that overall economic strength was fundamental to national security. "If we become stronger, more solid economically . . . , the interest of the capitalist world in normal relations with us will grow."[55] This victorious view represented a fundamental

[51] Bill Keller, "Restlessness in Soviet Ranks," *New York Times,* April 21, 1989.

[52] Report for the Joint Economic Committee, *Allocation of Resources in the Soviet Union and China—1986* (Washington, 1989).

[53] Condoleeza Rice, "Gorbachev and the Military: A Revolution in Security Policy Too?" *The Harriman Institute Forum* 2, no. 4 (April 1989), pp. 1–8.

[54] *Radio Free Europe* 6 no. 13 (February 1, 1989).

[55] Matthew Evangelista, "Economic Reform and Military Technology in Soviet Security Policy," *The Harriman Institute Forum* 2, no. 1 (January 1989).

shift away from the rigid, militaristic thinking of the Brezhnev era.

Soviet foreign policy under Gorbachev was transformed. A peaceful international environment, it was hoped, would enable the USSR to realize major domestic reforms without sacrificing its status as a superpower. Gorbachev faced painful decisions over Afghanistan, eastern Europe, and German reunification. Almost immediately he sought to improve Soviet-American relations and mend fences with China so he could trim military expenditures and concentrate on domestic reform. Similarly, Alexander II had sought to maintain Russia's role as a leading European power while achieving major domestic change. Repudiating Brezhnev's policies, Gorbachev blamed his regime for the USSR's declining growth and power. Seeking to demilitarize and stabilize East-West relations, Gorbachev integrated the Soviet Union increasingly into the world capitalist economic order.[56] Defending his innovative foreign policy before the 28th Party Congress, Gorbachev declared:

> I tried to show that only incorrigible "hawks" could see anathema in a policy that did away with hyper-militarization of the country, turned the world back from the nuclear precipice, and created the basis for our integration into the economic and political structures of the world.[57]

Gorbachev's bold policies prompted George F. Kennan, a veteran American diplomat and an architect of the American post–World War II policy of containing the USSR, to urge Washington to negotiate reductions of nuclear and conventional weapons with a liberalizing USSR as steps toward normal relations. Kennan told the Senate Foreign Relations Committee in April 1989:

> What we are witnessing today in Russia is the break-up of much, if not all of the system of power by which that country has been held together and governed since 1917 . . . [especially] in precisely those aspects of Soviet power that have been the most troublesome from the standpoint of Soviet-American relations, namely: the world-revolutionary ideology, rhetoric and political efforts of the early Soviet leadership, . . . [and] the morbid extremism of Stalinist political oppression . . . [whose] remnants are now being dismantled at a pace that renders it no longer a serious impediment to a normal Soviet-American relationship.

Kennan cited three factors that still troubled U.S.-Soviet relations—swollen Soviet armed forces, continued Soviet hegemony over eastern Europe, and the arms race—but he discerned a changing Soviet security policy, military cuts, and a weakening Soviet hold over the Bloc. Declared Kennan prophetically: "So tenuous is the Soviet hold over these [eastern European] countries today that I personally doubt that military intervention . . . would now be a realistic option of Soviet policy." Praising Gorbachev's initiatives on arms control, Kennan concluded that the USSR should no longer be viewed in the United States as an enemy:

> That country should now be regarded essentially as another great power . . . whose aspirations are conditioned outstandingly by its own geographic situation, history and traditions. . . . It ought now to be our purpose to eliminate as soon as possible by amicable negotiations the elements of military tension that have recently dominated Soviet-American relations.[58]

The course of Soviet-American relations from 1985 to 1990 provided a basis for Kennan's optimism. Already in April 1985 Gorbachev in a *Pravda* interview repudiated the former Soviet policy of confrontation. Citing President Reagan's apparent pursuit of military superiority through the Strategic Defense Initiative (SDI), dubbed

---

[56] George Breslauer, "Linking Gorbachev's Domestic and Foreign Policies," *Journal of International Affairs* 65 (Spring 1989), pp. 267–82.

[57] Gorbachev, *Memoirs*, pp. 365–66.

[58] George F. Kennan to the Senate Foreign Relations Committee, April 4, 1989, quoted in the *New York Times*, April 5, 1989.

"Star Wars,"[59] as the chief obstacle to rapprochement with the United States, Gorbachev urged achieving a breakthrough through arms control agreements. In a *Time* magazine interview in August 1985 Gorbachev reiterated the crucial importance of a Soviet-American accord to limit nuclear weapons and ban weapons in outer space. At their Geneva summit meeting that November, after extensive private talks, Reagan and Gorbachev issued a positive joint statement. Soviet newspapers, which had previously depicted Reagan as a trigger-happy cowboy, now described him talking amicably with Gorbachev. Later Gorbachev told the press that their talks, the first between an American and a Soviet leader in more than six years, had been "unquestionably a significant event in international life."

After Geneva both sides moderated their hostile rhetoric. However, Reagan's continued insistence on SDI and his refusal to join with Moscow in a nuclear test ban moratorium slowed progress. Then Gorbachev proposed another summit, and he met with Reagan in Reykjavik, Iceland, in October 1986. They had almost reached agreement to ban all nuclear weapons within a definite time span only to stumble over the issue of testing Reagan's SDI. With Reagan becoming absorbed in the Iran-Contra scandal, Soviet leaders doubted that meaningful agreements could be reached with his administration.

But during 1987 Soviet-American relations moved forward as Reagan moderated his former anti-Soviet stance. In December in Washington he and Gorbachev achieved a major breakthrough by signing a treaty to eliminate medium- and short-range missiles. Scoring a great triumph with the American media and public, Gorbachev announced that the two sides had "emerged from protracted confrontation." The final two

Raisa and Mikhail Gorbachev arrive at Reykjavik, Iceland, in October 1986 for summit talks with U.S. President Reagan.

Gorbachev-Reagan meetings in 1988 produced no major new agreements but deepened their personal relationship. At the largely ceremonial Moscow summit of May 1988 Reagan, who earlier had dubbed the Soviet Union an "evil empire," chatted happily with Soviet citizens and lectured Soviet intellectuals on democracy. Gorbachev's brief meeting with Reagan and President-elect George Bush in New York that December reinforced their rapport and fostered its continuation under the Bush administration.[60] Conferring in Malta in November 1989 against the backdrop of the eastern European democratic revolution, Gorbachev confirmed his resolve not to intervene against it and to continue efforts at arms reduction and European integration. Bush and Gorbachev reached substantial agreement on the difficult

[59] See R. W. Johnson, *Shootdown: Flight 007 and the American Connection* (New York, 1986), pp. 109–10. Johnson describes how Reagan's national security adviser, William Clark, converted the president to the "Star Wars" scheme, keeping this a secret for a month from the secretaries of state and defense.

[60] Gordon Livermore, ed., *Soviet Foreign Policy Today: Reports and Commentaries from the Soviet Union,* 3d ed. (Columbus, OH, 1989), pp. 42–73.

Reuters/Corbis-Bettmann

Soviet President Mikhail Gorbachev smiles as U.S. President George Bush tries on a headphone during their joint press conference at Malta summit meeting, December 1989.

issue of German reunification, which proceeded more rapidly than either of them anticipated.

Fundamental changes in Soviet relations with eastern Europe after 1985 supported Kennan's predictions and fostered improved Soviet-U.S. ties. Late in 1988, as Hungary and Poland liberalized their political and economic policies, Iurii Afanasiev, a liberal Soviet reformer, declared eastern Europe should be free to choose its own path even if that meant abandoning socialism. On a June 1989 visit to France, President Gorbachev expressly repudiated the Brezhnev Doctrine, used earlier to justify the intervention in Czechoslovakia, as outmoded. Instead Soviet officials espoused the "Frank Sinatra Doctrine," or "do it your own way." Praising varying eastern European responses to popular demands for greater freedom, Gorbachev intimated that they were merely implementing *glasnost* and *perestroika* in their own manner.

This major shift in Soviet policy toward the Bloc reflected further development of Khru-

shchev's theme enunciated 30 years earlier of "separate roads to socialism" and of a "socialist commonwealth." However, neither Khrushchev nor Brezhnev would allow Communist regimes to fall, as interventions in Hungary, Czechoslovakia, and Afghanistan confirmed. By contrast, under Gorbachev ideology was largely repudiated in the conduct of foreign policy, permitting eastern Europe to go its own way and enabling the Soviets to withdraw from Afghanistan. By downplaying ideology, Gorbachev enhanced the USSR's image abroad. Meanwhile eastern Europe had lost much of its strategic importance for the USSR because under Communist rule it was draining Soviet resources. Gorbachev, the realist, became willing to cooperate with the West to stabilize eastern Europe on a new basis, although surely he did not anticipate how fast events would move there. During 1988–1989 Communist power was undermined first in Poland and Hungary, then popular movements overturned conservative Communist regimes that lacked popular support in East Germany, Czechoslovakia, Bulgaria, and Romania. This dramatic movement toward political democracy and market economies left only tiny Albania, where the USSR had little influence and no troops, under a Stalinist regime in June 1990. The collapse of the East German Communist regime accelerated the process of German unification and left the Soviet occupation army in East Germany isolated until it was withdrawn beginning in 1991.

Another remarkable shift in Soviet foreign policy was the Soviet military withdrawal from Afghanistan early in 1989. The Communist-led Afghan regime of Najibullah remained to face divided Afghan rebels, but was buttressed with generous Soviet military aid. Soviet withdrawal produced many compensations to the USSR. It helped improve Soviet-American relations, so crucial for Gorbachev. It undermined arguments of American "hawks" that the Afghan intervention had proved the aggressiveness of "Russian imperialism towards the Persian Gulf." Soviet retirement seemed to vindicate those who viewed the Soviet invasion as a product of miscalculation and circumstances.[61] It also allowed relaxation of Soviet tensions with China and a reduction of Soviet forces on China's frontiers and improved the Soviet image in the Muslim world, especially in Iran. Although the war had grown highly unpopular inside the Soviet Union, returning Soviet troops were welcomed home by brass bands and assurances they had accomplished their "international mission."

The Gorbachev regime blamed the Afghan intervention on a small hawkish group in the Politburo surrounding the moribund Brezhnev. Very ill at the time of intervention, Brezhnev reportedly had signed the decision slipped to him hastily by Defense Minister Dmitri Ustinov. The Soviets, affirmed Joseph Collins, had "habitually attempted to pursue their interests in Afghanistan by using the lowest level of resources possible . . . ,

but each rung in this ladder of escalation brought the Soviets into deeper involvement with the Afghan problem."[62] In October 1989 the Kremlin issued a formal apology to the world for the invasion of Afghanistan:

> When more than 100 U.N. members for a number of years were condemning our action, what other evidence did we need to realize that we had set ourselves against all of humanity, violated norms of behavior, ignored universal human values? I am referring of course to our military engagement in Afghanistan. It should teach us a lesson that in this case gross violations of our own laws, intraparty and civil norms and ethics were allowed.[63]

A close parallel was evident between American policies in Vietnam and Soviet intervention in Afghanistan, ending in similar discomfiture for both superpowers. Both cases confirmed the strength of resistance by nationalist guerrillas even against a superpower.

After the Afghan withdrawal, Gorbachev charted a new and promising course in northeast Asia with arms control initiatives and overtures to China, Japan, and South Korea. Moscow sought to alleviate tensions there to permit the USSR to reduce its military forces and outlays, end confrontation with China, and encourage Japanese investment in the Soviet economy. From 1981 to 1988, as Soviet leaders strove to end conflict with China, Sino-Soviet trade increased tenfold. Among the troop reductions announced in Gorbachev's U.N. speech of December 1988 were 200,000 to be cut from Soviet forces in Asia.

Finally, Gorbachev transformed Soviet policy toward the United Nations, reflecting multifaceted efforts to restore the USSR to the civilized world. His article in *Pravda* of September 17, 1988, contained a remarkable agenda: an enhanced role for the secretary general in preventive

---

[61] Mark Urban, *War in Afghanistan* (New York, 1988); Joseph Collins, *The Soviet Invasion of Afghanistan* (Lexington, MA, 1986).

[62] Collins, *The Soviet Invasion*, pp. 124–25.
[63] Eduard Shevardnadze's speech as quoted in the *New York Times*, October 25, 1989.

diplomacy, greater use of U.N. peacekeeping forces in regional conflicts, mandatory acceptance of decisions of the International Court of Justice, a global strategy for environmental protection, and negotiations to make national laws conform to international human rights standards. Previous Soviet leaders had opposed efforts of any secretary general to strengthen U.N. influence and refused to consider third-party arbitration of bilateral disputes. Some Western observers dismissed the new Soviet rhetoric about the United Nations as propaganda and an attempt to make the United States, which under Reagan often failed to pay its dues, look bad. Was Gorbachev, needing many years of external stability to implement *perestroika*, seeking to use the United Nations to help extricate the USSR from overextension abroad? Apparently Gorbachev aimed through the United Nations to make the USSR a major player in world diplomacy, having abandoned class warfare in favor of a new philosophy of international relations to achieve global interdependence and cooperation.[64]

Until his fall, President Gorbachev continued to play a major international role. After seeking unsuccessfully to arrange a peaceful solution of the Persian Gulf crisis, Gorbachev sacrificed the special Soviet position in Iraq and Syria and backed the efforts of the United Nations to force Iraqi strongman Saddam Hussein out of Kuwait. However, the overwhelming American military victory there confirmed the United States as undisputed number one world power. During 1991 the end of the Cold War was confirmed, as the Warsaw Pact dissolved and most Soviet troops withdrew from eastern Europe. At a July summit in Moscow with President Bush, Gorbachev concluded further far-reaching agreements on reducing nuclear armaments.

During his six and one-half years in office, Mikhail S. Gorbachev became a hero in the West for relaxing authoritarian controls in the Soviet Union, permitting eastern Europe to free itself from the Soviet grip, and ending the Cold War. However, Gorbachev became unpopular at home as store shelves emptied and the USSR's economic and political troubles mounted. The Gorbachev regime, noted economist Anders Äslund, took inherited economic stagnation and turned it into drastic and precipitous economic decline. In seeking to reorganize and save the Soviet Union, Gorbachev undermined and finally destroyed it.[65]

InfoTrac® College Edition Search Terms

Enter the search term *Soviet Union* in the Subject Guide, and then go to subdivision *politics and government.*
Enter the search term *Gorbachev* in Keywords.
Enter the search term *glasnost* in Keywords.
Enter the searach term *perestroika* in Keywords.

Suggested Additional Reading

ÄSLUND, A. *Gorbachev's Struggle for Economic Reform . . . 1985–88* (Ithaca, NY, 1989).

BALZER, H., ed. *Five Years That Shook the World: Gorbachev's Unfinished Revolution* (Boulder, CO, 1991).

BARYLSKI, R. V. *The Soldier in Russian Politics . . . Under Gorbachev and Yeltsin* (New Brunswick, NJ, 1998).

BENN, D. W. *From Glasnost to Freedom of Speech: Russian Openness and International Relations* (New York, 1992).

BESCHLOSS, M. R., and S. TALBOTT. *At the Highest Levels: The Inside Story of the End of the Cold War* (Boston, 1993).

BOETTKE, P. J. *Why Perestroika Failed: The Politics and Economics of Socialist Transformation* (New York, 1993).

BOLDIN, V. *Ten Years That Shook the World: The Gorbachev Era as Witnessed by His Chief of Staff,* trans. Evelyn Rossiter (New York, 1994).

BONNER, A. *Among the Afghans* (Durham, NC, 1987).

[64] Richard Gardner at the Harriman Institute (March 23, 1989), "The Soviet Union and the United Nations," *The Harriman Institute Forum* 1, no. 12.

[65] Anders Äslund, *Gorbachev's Struggle for Economic Reform . . . 1985–88* (Ithaca, NY, 1989).

BROWN, A., ed. *New Thinking in Soviet Politics* (New York, 1992).

BROWN, A. *The Gorbachev Factor* (Oxford, 1966).

BRZEZINSKI, Z. *The Grand Failure: The Birth and Death of Communism in the Twentieth Century* (New York, 1989).

BUTLER, W. *Soviet Law,* 2d ed. (London, 1988).

CERF, C., and M. ALBEE, eds. *Small Fires: Letters from the Soviet People to Ogonyok Magazine, 1987–1990* (New York, 1990).

CHERNYAEV, A. S. *My Six Years with Gorbachev,* trans. and ed. Robert English and Elizabeth Tucker (University Park, PA, 2000).

COLLINS, J. *The Soviet Invasion of Afghanistan* (Cambridge, 1986).

CROUCH, M. *Revolution and Evolution: Gorbachev and Soviet Politics* (New York, 1989).

CROZIER, B. *The Gorbachev Phenomenon: Peace and the Secret War* (London, 1990).

DANIELS, R. V. *The End of the Communist Revolution* (New York and London, 1993).

DAVIES, R. W. *Soviet History in the Gorbachev Revolution* (Birmingham, England, 1987, and Bloomington, IN, 1989).

DESAI, P. *Perestroika in Perspective: The Design and Dilemma of Soviet Reform* (Princeton, 1989).

DODER, D., and L. BRANSON. *Gorbachev: Heretic in the Kremlin* (New York, 1991).

DUNSTAN, J., ed. *Soviet Education Under Perestroika* (New York, 1992).

DZIAK, J. *Chekisty: A History of the KGB* (New York, 1988).

FARMER, K. C. *The Soviet Administrative Elite* (New York, 1992).

FREEDMAN, R., ed. *Soviet Jewry in the 1980s* (Durham, NC, 1989).

FRIEDBERG, M., and H. ISHAM, eds. *Soviet Society Under Gorbachev . . .* (Armonk, NY, 1987).

GIBBS, J. *Gorbachev's Glasnost: The Soviet Media in the First Phase of Perestroika* (College Station, TX, 1999).

GLEASON, G. *Federalism and Nationalism: The Struggle for Republican Rights in the USSR* (Boulder, CO, 1990).

GOLDMAN, M. *Gorbachev's Challenge: Economic Reform in the Age of High Technology* (New York, 1987).

———. *What Went Wrong with Perestroika?* (New York, 1991).

GORBACHEV, M., *Memoirs,* trans. Georges Peronansky and Tatjana Varsavsky (New York, 1996).

———. *On My Country and the World* (New York, 1999).

———. *Perestroika: New Thinking for Our Country and the World* (New York, 1987, 1988).

———. *Selected Speeches and Articles,* 2d ed. (Moscow, 1987).

GURTOV, M., ed. *The Transformation of Socialism: Perestroika and Reform in the Soviet Union and China* (Boulder, CO, 1990).

HARLO, V., ed. *Gorbachev and Europe* (New York, 1990).

HAZAN, B. *Gorbachev and His Enemies . . .* (Boulder, CO, 1990).

HIDEN, J., and P. SALMON. *The Baltic Nations and Europe . . . in the 20th Century* (White Plains, NY, 1991).

HILL, K. *The Soviet Union on the Brink: . . . Christianity and Glasnost* (Portland, OR, 1991).

HILL, R. J. *Communist Politics Under the Knife: Surgery or Autopsy?* (London and New York, 1990).

HOSKING, G. *The Awakening of the Soviet Union* (Cambridge, MA, 1990).

HOUGH, J. F. *Democratization and Revolution in the USSR, 1985–1991* (Washington, DC, 1997).

———. *Russia and the West: Gorbachev and the Politics of Reform* (New York, 1988).

ITO, T., ed. *Facing Up to the Past: Soviet Historiography and Perestroika* (Sapporo, Japan, 1989).

JACOBSEN, C. G., ed. *Soviet Foreign Policy: New Dynamics, New Themes* (New York, 1989).

JONES, T. A. *Perestroika: Gorbachev's Social Revolution* (Westview, CT, 1990).

JOYCE, W., et al., eds. *Gorbachev and Gorbachevism* (New York, 1989).

KAGARLITSKY, B. *Farewell Perestroika: A Soviet Chronicle* (London, 1990).

KAISER, R. G. *Why Gorbachev Happened: His Triumphs and His Failures* (New York, 1991). (Excellent summary of Gorbachev's years in power.)

KNIGHT, A. *The KGB: Police and Politics in the Soviet Union* (Boston, 1988).

LANE, D., and C. ROSS. *The Transition from Communism to Capitalism: Ruling Elites from Gorbachev to Yeltsin* (New York, 1999).

LAPIDUS, G. *State and Society in the Soviet Union* (Boulder, CO, 1989).

———, and V. ZASLAVSKY, eds. *From Union to Commonwealth: Nationalism and Separatism in the Soviet Republics* (New York, 1992).

LAQUEUR, W. *Black Hundred: The Rise of the Extreme Right in Russia* (New York, 1994).

LEWIN, M. *The Gorbachev Phenomenon* (Berkeley, 1988).

LIGACHEV, Y. *Inside Gorbachev's Kremlin: The Memoirs of Yegor Ligachev* (Boulder, CO, 1996).

LÖWENHARDT, J., J. OZINGA, and E. VAN REE. *The Rise and Fall of the Soviet Politburo* (New York, 1992).

LUKIN, A. *Political Culture of Russian Democrats* (New York and Oxford, 2000).

MARPLES, D. *Chernobyl and Nuclear Power in the USSR* (New York, 1987).

MAWDSLEY, E. and S. WHITE. *The Soviet Elite from Lenin to Gorbachev* (New York and Oxford, 2000).

MEDVEDEV, R. *The Truth About Chernobyl* (New York, 1991).

MEDVEDEV, Z. *Soviet Agriculture* (New York, 1987).

MELVILLE, A., and G. LAPIDUS. *The Glasnost Papers: Voices on Reform from Moscow* (Boulder, CO, 1990).

MENDELSON, S. E. *Changing Course: Ideas, Politics, and the Soviet Withdrawal from Afghanistan* (Princeton, NJ, 1998).

MIKHEYEV, D. *The Rise and Fall of Gorbachev* (Indianapolis, 1992).

MILLER, J. *Mikhail Gorbachev and the End of Soviet Power* (New York, 1993).

MOSKOFF, W. *Hard Times: Impoverishment and Protest in the Perestroika Years* (Armonk, NY, 1993).

OLIVIER, R. *Islam and Resistance in Afghanistan* (Cambridge, 1986).

PLESSIX, F. DU. *Soviet Women* (New York, 1990).

PRYCE-JONES, D. *The War That Never Was: The Fall of the Soviet Empire, 1985–1991* (London, 1995).

RALEIGH, D. *Soviet Historians and Perestroika: The First Phase* (Armonk, NY, 1990).

RAMET, S., ed. *Religious Policy in the Soviet Union* (New York, 1993).

SAIVETZ, C. R. *The Soviet Union and the Gulf in the 1980s* (Boulder, CO, 1989).

SAKWA, R. *Gorbachev and His Reforms, 1985–1990* (New York and London, 1991).

SENN, A. E. *Gorbachev's Failure in Lithuania* (New York, 1995).

SHANSAB, N. *Soviet Expansion in the Third World* (Silver Spring, MD, 1986).

SHCHERBAK, I. *Chernobyl: A Documentary Story,* trans. Ian Press (New York, 1989).

SMITH, G. *Soviet Politics: Continuity and Contradiction* (New York, 1987).

STERNTHAL, S. *Gorbachev's Reforms: De-Stalinization through Democratization* (Westport, CT, 1997).

TARASULO, I., ed. *Gorbachev and Glasnost: Viewpoints from the Soviet Press* (Wilmington, DE, 1989).

———, ed. *Perils of Perestroika: Viewpoints from the Soviet Press, 1989–1991* (Wilmington, DE, 1992).

URBAN, M. *War in Afghanistan* (New York, 1988).

WHITE, A. *Democratization in Russia under Gorbachev, 1985–91 . . .* (New York, NY, 1999).

WILLERTON, J. P. *Patronage and Politics in the USSR* (New York, 1992).

WOODBY, S. *Gorbachev and the Decline of Ideology in Soviet Foreign Policy* (Boulder, CO, 1989).

YANOV, A. *The Russian Challenge and the Year 2000,* trans. J. Rosenthal (New York, 1987).

ZACEK, J. S. *The Gorbachev Generation: Issues in Soviet Foreign Policy* (New York, 1988).

ZASLAVSKYA, T. *The Second Socialist Revolution . . . ,* trans. S. Davies and J. Warren (Bloomington, IN, 1991).

19

Soviet Culture after Stalin, 1953–1991

The death of Stalin ushered in the first of a series of "thaws" in Soviet culture culminating in the Gorbachev revolution. A largely spontaneous outburst of activity in the arts, coupled with Khrushchev's efforts to rid the Soviet Union of the worst aspects of Stalinism, produced a remarkable cultural revival. Soviet cultural policies under Khrushchev and Brezhnev fluctuated between "thaws" and "freezes," but there was no full-scale return to the Stalin-Zhdanov approach. But until the Gorbachev era, socialist realism persisted as the guiding principle in literature and the arts, and the regime intervened decisively to prevent overt expression of dissident viewpoints—as the careers of Alexander Solzhenitsyn, Boris Pasternak, Andrei Amalrik, and Zhores Medvedev revealed.

The Thaw, 1953–1956

An article of May 1953 deploring the lack of human emotion in Soviet films reflected an initial cautious reaction against Zhdanovism. It decried depersonalized "human machines," standard in

Soviet films, as untrue to life. A heroine agreeing to marry the hero only if he overfulfilled his production norm was a travesty on human feelings, it claimed. Socialist quotas were important for socialist realism, but individual lives amounted to more than that. Such a view could not have been expressed openly in Stalin's final years. In the new, freer air bold ideas found their way into print. The new collective leadership recognized the utter sterility of Soviet culture under Zhdanovism and permitted freer discussion of alternative approaches.

An article that November by composer Aram Khachaturian, "On Creative Boldness and Imagination," directly attacked bureaucratic interference, which had almost destroyed Soviet musical culture: "We must once and for all reject the worthless interference in musical composition as practiced by the musical establishments. Problems of composition cannot be solved bureaucratically." Without repudiating socialist realism, Khachaturian insisted on artistic integrity. "Let the individual artist be trusted more fully, and not be constantly supervised and suspected."[1]

Others joined the burgeoning criticism. The respected poet Alexander Tvardovskii, editor of the prestigious journal *New World,* denounced Soviet literature as "arid, contrived and unreal." Ilia Ehrenburg, a well-known author and former apologist for Stalin, concluded sadly that Russian classics were more popular with the public than contemporary authors because the older works dealt with human emotions and feelings. Could anyone "imagine ordering Tolstoy to write *Anna Karenina*?"[2]

Not everyone shared these liberal views. Stalinist hard-liners had their spokespersons too, and there was some sharp infighting. But party leaders allowed the artistic intelligentsia freer rein. The mood of the times was captured in Ehrenburg's short novel *The Thaw* (1954), which aptly describes these years. Stalinist Russia had been frozen solid, rigid, and somber. The post-Stalin era was an intellectual spring heralded by melting of ice that had prevented growth. Ehrenburg's novel marked a new path for Soviet culture to follow. Writers of "the thaw" stressed recognition of the gulf between the real and the ideal and emphasized truth in all its complexity, rejected tyranny and fear, and expressed concern for human dignity and the individual; they admitted shortcomings in Soviet life. Ehrenburg believed that these fundamental artistic aims could best be achieved within socialist realism. Great enthusiasm about these issues led to an outburst of literary activity from 1954 to 1956. Poetry annuals and literary almanacs appeared without formal approval by the Writers' Union, and new poetic and prose talents emerged.

Despite high optimism among younger Soviet writers and artists in these years, conservative and Stalinist writers fought hard to defend Zhdanovist principles and retain control of literary institutions. At the Second Congress of Soviet Writers in December 1954, A. Surkov, the Stalinist secretary

of the Writers' Union, sharply denounced the new mood and trends and demanded a return to Zhdanovist ideological purity. But others at the congress insisted on even greater freedom, rehabilitation of disgraced writers, recognition of émigré writers, and publication of banned works. Liberals in the Writers' Union looked to Ehrenburg and young writers; conservatives relied on old-line Stalinists who controlled the union. Because party leaders did not intervene, the two factions fought to a stalemate.

At the 20th Party Congress (February 1956) the pendulum swung toward the liberals. Surkov's hard-line diatribe was answered boldly by Mikhail Sholokhov, who denounced literary bureaucrats and hacks who claimed to speak for all Soviet literature. "A writer can learn nothing from Surkov," he concluded. "Why do we need such leaders?" That Sholokhov said this openly at the 20th Party Congress indicates a climate tolerating intellectual debate. Khrushchev's secret speech had compromised many Stalinist writers, temporarily weakening their influence in the Writers' Union. Thus some works sharply critical of aspects of contemporary Soviet life were published. In 1956 *New World* issued Vladimir Dudintsev's novel *Not by Bread Alone,* which exemplified liberal cultural trends. It castigated the exploitation and victimization of talent by arrogant Soviet bureaucrats, outraging literary bureaucrats like Surkov.

Dr. Zhivago and the Refreeze

In this optimistic atmosphere of 1956, Boris Pasternak (1890–1960) submitted his now famous novel *Dr. Zhivago* to *New World.* Pasternak enjoyed the reputation of an outstanding poetic talent even before the Revolution, but had remained largely silent under Stalin, publishing occasional poems, essays, and translations. His extraordinary translations of Shakespeare set a standard for all Soviet translations. Pasternak remained an aloof loner and internal exile, quietly completing his novel in 1955. Revealing his political naiveté, he fully expected *New World* to publish *Dr. Zhivago.* Like Zamiatin and Pilniak 30 years before, he gave

---

[1] Aram Khachaturian, *Sovietskaia Muzyka,* November 1953.
[2] Quoted in E. J. Brown, *Russian Literature Since the Revolution* (New York, 1969), p. 241.

a manuscript copy to an Italian publisher, Feltrinelli, for preparation of an Italian edition after the work appeared in the USSR. To Pasternak's dismay, *New World*'s editors politely refused to publish the novel, but Feltrinelli, despite Surkov's protests, published an Italian translation in November 1957. Soon *Dr. Zhivago* appeared in English, and an original Russian version was published in the West. It was hailed abroad as a masterpiece, and Pasternak was awarded the Nobel Prize for literature in October 1958, but he was pressured by party authorities to reject it. Viciously denounced in the Soviet press,.he was expelled from the Writers' Union and constantly hounded by the authorities, literally to death in 1960, another victim of the Soviet literary inquisition.

The intensely personal *Dr. Zhivago* traces the story of Iurii Zhivago from prerevolutionary times through the Soviet period. Zhivago's life is a shambles; he never uses his medical training. His life's work is a slender volume of poetry included at the end of the novel—Zhivago's legacy to humankind. Pasternak was proclaiming that though he had produced nothing practical, his poetry, like Zhivago's, could stimulate people to think and act creatively. Zhivago's poems, among Pasternak's most profound creations, contain the novel's essence, affirming the constant renewal of life as suggested by Zhivago's name, meaning "living" (*zhivoi*). Pasternak served as a living bridge from the prerevolutionary Russian literary tradition that stressed human spiritual qualities to contemporary Soviet life. In *Dr. Zhivago* Pasternak's essentially religious conception of the future is based on unwavering faith in resurrection and salvation for Zhivago and Russia itself.

Believing the Soviet public unprepared for such a message, party authorities prevented the novel's publication in the USSR. However, "Lara's Theme" from the 1965 film's score became a hit in Moscow, although the film was banned there.

Even before the Pasternak "affair," the pendulum had begun swinging back as the screws tightened again on Soviet culture. Soviet armed intervention in Hungary in October 1956 struck at burgeoning de-Stalinization. The more relaxed atmosphere of the thaw ended as Khrushchev moved decisively to halt a headlong race toward liberalization. He warned students at Moscow University to be careful or they would face the full force of his regime. Two hundred students were expelled and the rest intimidated. Stalinism remained fresh in people's minds.

Culture under Khrushchev

Khrushchev's de-Stalinization campaign had loosened the Soviet grip on the Communist Bloc. Hard-pressed by party conservatives, he adopted a more conventional cultural militancy. The abrupt change in official policy caught many off guard. Late in 1956 the Soviet poet Evgenii Yevtushenko published a provocative poem proclaiming: "Certainly there have been changes; but behind the speeches/Some murky game is being played./ We talk and talk about things we didn't mention yesterday;/ We say nothing about the things we did ourselves." This devastating criticism of party leaders and Khrushchev revealed that the more Stalin's actions were discredited, the more present leaders were implicated in his crimes. Such an attack could not go unchallenged. Yevtushenko was summarily dismissed from the Komsomol (Young Communist League) and stripped of many privileges.

When intellectuals proved slow to respond to Khrushchev's insistence on greater ideological conformity, he personally demanded compliance with his directives. He told Moscow writers at a garden party at his dacha that they were expendable; unless they cooperated, he would use force. Hungary's difficulties in the 1956 revolt could have been avoided, he declared, if intellectuals who had stirred up rebellion had been shot. Khrushchev assured the stunned writers: "My hand will not tremble" [if force is required]. The initial post-Stalin thaw had fallen victim to Khrushchev's political requirements and ambition.

Consolidating his personal power by March 1958, Khrushchev cautiously resumed de-Stalinization and built bridges to the West. Some foreign travel was permitted, and cultural exchanges were negotiated with Western countries, including the United States. The literary thaw resumed. Promising and talented young writers published works that focused more on individual concerns in a complex industrial society rather than on "building socialism." Writers picked up threads of the earlier thaw and wove them into a new, more sophisticated literature. Despite opposition from party conservatives, fearful of liberal works and cultural rapprochement with the West, the liberals regained their ascendancy. Debate, disagreement, innovation, and experimentation were tolerated within limits. At the Third Congress of Soviet Writers in 1959, Khrushchev expressed satisfaction with the cultural atmosphere. He would be liberal, in Soviet terms, if writers supported the party.

Numerous works appearing in the next years testified to the imaginative power of young, unknown Soviet writers such as Aksionov, Nagibin, Kazakov, Tendryakov, and Voinovich. Discarding the literary didacticism and moralizing of much socialist realist literature, their stories and novels revealed a renewed concern for style, psychology, and human emotions. Attracting much popular attention, their works were avidly read and discussed. Taboo subjects were now openly debated. In 1961 Yevtushenko published his famous *Babi Yar*, an extraordinarily powerful poem about the 33,000 Soviet Jews slaughtered by the Nazis in 1941 in Babi Yar ravine near Kiev. Memorializing the innocent Jews, the poem castigated anti-Semitism, whether in fascist or Communist guise. Russian anti-Semitism still "rises in the fumes of alcohol and in drunken conversations." The poem was attacked violently by conservatives as slandering the heroic Russian people who had sacrificed so much to destroy Nazism. Liberals lauded Yevtushenko's courage in confronting squarely a problem deeply rooted in the Russian psyche.

The Soviet film industry received a powerful impetus from Khrushchev's 1956 de-Stalinization speech. As Soviet officials sought to distance themselves from the Stalin era, wider creative latitude and more funding were granted to film-

Michael Curran

Controversial monument to 33,000 Soviet Jews slaughtered by Nazi troops in the Babi Yar ravine near Kiev in 1941.

makers. The Stalin cult of personality had contributed to a deformed cinema in which ordinary people tended to be displaced by panegyrics to the "great leader." A group of remarkable films that broke with stifling wartime restrictions appeared in the late 1950s.

The veteran director Mikhal Kalatozov made *The Cranes Are Flying* in 1957. With innovative hand-held camera work by Sergei Urusevskii and an unusual script that focused on intensely personal portraits of ordinary people coping with the stresses of wartime, this film marked a new beginning for Soviet cinema. The heroine betrays her soldier lover in an act of uncharacteristic human weakness that contrasted markedly with the usual Stalinist emphasis on heroism and sacrifice for the motherland. The film won the Cannes Film Festival's prestigious Grand Prix in 1958, and became a powerful impetus for other filmmakers.

Among the innovative films that followed were Sergei Bondarchuk's *Fate of a Man* (1959), and Grigorii Chukrai's *Ballad of a Soldier* (1959), both cut from the same intensely personal cloth as *The Cranes Are Flying*. These films also focus on the ways in which war fractures human relationships and challenges human values, in contrast to the heroic official versions of the war. With these remarkably creative films, Soviet cinema began to reach new audiences at home and abroad, achieving international recognition and acclaim.

The liberal tendency gained ground elsewhere, too. Early in 1962 the respected art critic Mikhail Alpatov published a defense of modern, abstract art. Others followed, suggesting that "the 20th century is becoming an age of triumphant abstractions." Why was the USSR so backward in appreciating modern art? Moscow's venerable Tretiakov Gallery began cautiously opening its vaults to exhibit some innovative early-20th-century Russian artworks, such as those of Kandinskii and Malevich. The poet Bella Akhmadulina proclaimed optimistically in 1962: "I think the time has become happy for us, that it now runs in our favor. Not only can my comrades work, but they are given every encouragement in their endeavor."[3]

During 1962 the liberals pushed their advantage. In October Yevtushenko's poem "The Heirs of Stalin" appeared in *Pravda*. It was a remarkable commentary on the times: "He [Stalin] has worked out a scheme./ He merely curled up for a nap./ And I appeal to our government with a plea:/ to double,/ and treble/ the guard at his slab,/ so that Stalin will not rise again/ and, with Stalin —the past."[4] Yevtushenko bluntly confronted the possibility of the revival of Stalinism:

No, Stalin has not given up.
He thinks he can outsmart death.
We carried him from the mausoleum.
But how carry Stalin's heirs away from Stalin?

Some of his retired heirs tend roses thinking
in secret
Their enforced leisure will not last. . .

No wonder Stalin's heirs seem to suffer
these days from heart trouble.
They, the former henchmen, hate this era
Of emptied prison camps
And auditoriums full of people listening to poets.[5]

Acknowledging that he had personally authorized publication of Yevtushenko's poem, Khrushchev hinted at a new round of de-Stalinization.

Further confirmation of this came when Khrushchev authorized the unexpurgated publication of Alexander Solzhenitsyn's *One Day in the Life of Ivan Denisovich* in *New World*'s November 1962 issue. Solzhenitsyn's first published work was a powerful portrayal of everyday life in a Stalinist prison camp. Based on his own experiences in the camps, it was understated, dispassionate, and nonpolemical, bringing to life in searing detail one ordinary day in Ivan Denisovich's prison life. It recorded the agony of an inmate reduced to animal level for survival but whose dignity and humanity remain intact. Ivan Denisovich symbolized the indomitable courage of the Russian people in their continuing struggle for freedom and human dignity. *One Day* became an instant sensation, touching millions of Soviet citizens who had experienced years of days like Ivan Denisovich's. Public sentiment about the brutal inhumanity of Stalin's terror was stirred again in apparent preparation for renewed de-Stalinization.

Just as this new campaign began, Khrushchev was immersed in the turbulent political waters of the Cuban missile crisis (October 1962) and an open Sino-Soviet dispute (see Chapter 15). These crises abroad combined with growing economic problems at home again threatened Khrushchev's control of party and state. Sharp consumer price increases that autumn caused outbreaks of violence among workers. All this persuaded Khrushchev to renounce further de-Stalinization.

---

[3] *Literaturnaia Gazeta,* October 2, 1962, p. 4.
[4] Evgenii Yevtushenko, *The Collected Poems, 1952–1990,* ed. A. Todd, trans, G. Reavey (New York, 1991).

[5] Quoted in Priscilla Johnson, *Khrushchev and the Arts,* trans. G. Reavey (Cambridge, MA, 1965), pp. 93–95.

"Stalin's heirs" prepared a counterattack on the cultural front in November 1962. To a retrospective art exhibition, "Thirty Years of Soviet Art," at the huge Manezh Gallery near the Kremlin were added about 75 modernistic canvases and sculptures, apparently as an elaborate "provocation" by cultural conservatives. On December 1 Khrushchev and several Presidium members visited the gallery unannounced. He spent most of his time in three small rooms viewing modernistic works of contemporary Soviet artists. His reaction was what conservatives had anticipated—violent and vulgar. Khrushchev's vicious verbal attack startled liberals, then enjoying a heyday. Pausing before an abstract painting, he remarked:

> I would say this is just a mess. . . . Polyanskii [Presidium member] told me a couple of days ago that when his daughter got married she was given a picture of what was supposed to be a lemon. It consisted of some messy yellow lines that looked . . . as though some child had done his business on the canvas when his mother was away and then spread it around with his hands.

Further on, he lashed out against jazz music: "When I hear jazz, it's as if I had gas on the stomach. I used to think it was static when I heard it on the radio." Proceeding through the exhibition, he declared:

> As long as I am chairman of the Council of Ministers, we are going to support a genuine art. We aren't going to give a kopeck for pictures painted by jackasses.

Speaking to one artist but referring to all modernist painters, Khrushchev fulminated:

> You've either got to get out [of the USSR] or paint differently. As you are, there's no future for you on our soil. . . . Gentlemen, we are declaring war on you.[6]

Hours later began a war for "ideological purity." Press editorials demanded that all unions of writers, artists, composers, and cinema workers be amalgamated in order to prevent nonconformity. The message was clear: centralize and control. Some Stalinist bureaucrats ceased "tending roses" and returned to prominent posts. At a meeting between party authorities and cultural leaders to discuss the current situation, Leonid Ilyichev, the Central Committee's chief ideologist, deplored recent demands by intellectuals to end all Soviet censorship and attacked the inexorable advance of Western "bourgeois" influences on Soviet culture. Following his hard-line speech ensued remarkably candid informal exchanges between party officials and writers and artists. Ehrenburg boldly defended the new freedom, insisting that modern art was not a cover for political reaction. Yevtushenko defended abstract painters, arguing they needed time to straighten out problems in their art. Khrushchev reportedly broke in shouting: "The grave straightens out the hunchback." Unintimidated, Yevtushenko retorted: "Nikita Sergeevich [Khrushchev], we have come a long way since the time when only the grave straightened out hunchbacks."[7] The assembled writers and artists broke into applause with Khrushchev joining in. The intellectuals' unity and sense of common purpose at this meeting provided conservatives with ammunition in the battle against modernism.

The affair of Shostakovich's 13th Symphony further revealed the tense situation. Its first movement was a musical version of Yevtushenko's poem *Babi Yar*. The new symphony was to premiere the evening after the great gathering of party officials and intellectuals. Allegedly, Ilyichev demanded its withdrawal, but Shostakovich refused. At the premiere many musicians and the choir hesitated, fearing reprisals. After a second performance, further performances were canceled. As Moscow's frigid winter descended, a new ideological freeze chilled the intellectual community.

It culminated in March 1963 at a gathering of more than 600 intellectuals. Ilyichev again attacked writers in general and Ehrenburg in par-

---

[6] Johnson, *Khrushchev and the Arts*, pp. 101–105.

[7] Johnson, p. 121.

ticular. Ehrenburg had argued in his memoirs, *People, Years, Life* (1960–1961), that he and others had known full well what was occurring in the USSR in the 1930s but had to remain silent with "clenched teeth." Ilyichev accused Ehrenburg of enjoying special privileges under Stalin and of having frequently praised him hypocritically whereas he (Ilyichev) and his colleagues had flattered Stalin allegedly out of sincere conviction. Ehrenburg considered that Ilyichev's false remarks made a reply unnecessary.

Khrushchev then delivered a devastating speech partially reaffirming Stalin's straightforward, uncomplicated tastes in art and literature and partially rehabilitating Stalin himself. Khrushchev sought to exonerate Stalin's entourage, and himself, of complicity in his crimes. He then realized the dangers of further de-Stalinization, which might raise questions such as "What were you doing during Stalin's criminal rampages?" Ilyichev affirmed he had not known what was happening. Ehrenburg argued that he knew of Stalin's crimes but had remained silent, thus admitting complicity or cowardice. It was clearly better to leave Stalin's ghost alone. De-Stalinization ended as Stalin's conservative heirs used abstract art to dissuade the party from further liberalization. Khrushchev had to yield to mounting pressure within the party, and his personal cultural tastes seemed closer to the conservatives than to the liberals. Anyway, the lid slammed down again. Throughout 1963, at meetings organized by the party, leading cultural figures acknowledged their "errors" and pledged to abide by the party's wise guidance in all matters. Shostakovich, Yevtushenko, Voznesenskii, and many others submitted. Open ferment ended or was submerged. A light frost prevailed with only occasional sunshine.

Culture under Brezhnev

Khrushchev's fall in October 1964 did not herald a new thaw. Brezhnev and Kosygin maintained the status quo: comprehensive cultural controls and inflexible conformity. Writing for "the desk drawer" or painting for "the closet" continued, becoming more widespread after fleeting moments of relative freedom. Literary works in increasing numbers circulated surreptitiously in manuscript copies; artists showed their latest abstract works privately. An organized Soviet counterculture emerged.

New developments in liberal literary circles included *samizdat* and *tamizdat*. *Samizdat*, a play on *Gosizdat*—State Publishing House—meant "self-publication" by authors, not the state. Because individuals lacked access to printing presses, most *samizdat* materials were produced on typewriters or mimeograph machines. Smudged carbon copies circulated from hand to hand; new copies were made when needed. *Tamizdat* referred to materials published abroad—"over there"—that were then smuggled back into the Soviet Union. By these means a considerable body of clandestine literature accumulated in the USSR not subject to official control or censorship.

The Trial of Siniavskii and Daniel

Writing for the desk drawer was often frustrating and unrewarding, so authors sought other means of uncensored expression. Publishing abroad had always been dangerous, as the fate of Zamiatin and Pasternak had shown. Their works had been published abroad out of confusion and misunderstanding, not from conscious intent to evade Soviet censorship. That did not save those authors from vilification and abuse, but neither one was put on trial. Andrei Siniavskii, a distinguished literary critic, and Iuli Daniel, a young writer, consciously evaded party literary controls by smuggling manuscripts out of the USSR for publication abroad under the pseudonyms Abram Tertz (Siniavskii) and Nikolai Arzhak (Daniel), beginning in 1956 when the first thaw ended. For nine years they escaped detection and published stories, short novels, and essays highly critical of Soviet life. These were the first examples of *samizdat* and *tamizdat*.

Siniavskii's publications abroad included a long essay, "On Socialist Realism" (1960), denouncing that doctrine as old-fashioned and inappropriate for the modern USSR. Soviet literature was "a monstrous salad" whose content was distorted by a rigidly imposed form, in which bureaucrats regularly interfered. Siniavskii urged abandoning socialist realism and returning to Mayakovskii's literary experimentation of the 1920s. Also published abroad was *The Trial Begins* (1960), a fictional exposé of Soviet justice as fraudulent, cynical, and arbitrary. Other works poked fun at Soviet foibles or satirized Soviet life. All criticized Soviet institutions, but none was directly anti-Soviet.

Daniel's works were, from a Western perspective, rather harmless literary exercises, less sophisticated than Siniavskii's. Of his four stories published abroad, "This Is Moscow Speaking" and "Hands" are the most interesting. The former is a macabre tale about a Public Murder Day supposedly decreed by the Politburo: On August 10, 1961, all citizens over 16 could kill almost anyone they wished between 6 A.M. and midnight. When people failed to use this license to kill, the party condemned it as sabotage, thus implying that mass terror could be reintroduced in the USSR without much public response. The story "Hands" deals with the psychological impact of terror. A former Cheka officer suffers from chronically shaking hands after being ordered as a young secret policeman to shoot priests accused of counterrevolutionary activities. His friends played a joke on him by loading his pistol with blank cartridges. When the priests implored the young officer not to shoot, advancing with outstretched hands, the officer had shot repeatedly as the priests "miraculously" continued to advance. That experience so unnerved the officer that his hands shook constantly.

The KGB (security police) mounted an intensive campaign to identify Tertz and Arzhak. (Computers analyzed their writing styles.) Finally, Siniavskii and Daniel were arrested in September 1965, accused under the infamous Article 70 of the criminal code of disseminating "slanderous" and "defamatory" inventions about the Soviet system. After the defendants were convicted in the press, a public trial was held in February 1966. Siniavskii received seven years of hard labor (the maximum sentence) and Daniel five years.

The Siniavskii-Daniel trial was unique in Soviet justice. Never before had writers been tried for their writings. Many writers—including Zamiatin, Zoshchenko, and Pasternak—had been publicly denounced and accused of various "crimes," and many more had disappeared during the purges, but none had been tried in open court. A brilliant young Leningrad poet and eventual Nobel laureate, Josef Brodskii, had been tried and convicted in 1964, not for his writings but as a "parasite" lacking gainful employment. (He was a poet but not a member of the Writers' Union.) Unlike defendants in other Soviet public trials, Siniavskii and Daniel defended themselves valiantly.

The harsh sentences shocked Soviet intellectuals. With remarkable unity, liberal intellectuals in the arts and sciences wrote to party authorities to protest the treatment of Siniavskii and Daniel. The only major Soviet writer to support the regime fully over this issue was Mikhail Sholokhov, Nobel Prize laureate, who declared that the sentences were much too mild! Party leaders were unmoved by the storm of protest over the sentences. The trial had aimed to intimidate dissenters. Siniavskii and Daniel were scapegoats for a new "get tough" policy. The trial warned Soviet intellectuals that all works by Soviet citizens were subject to censorship. Succumbing to public pressure would have undermined that aim.

Still, the Siniavskii-Daniel trial backfired, becoming a milestone in a continuing struggle between party leaders and the intellectual elite. From the 1920s onward the literary intelligentsia had been preoccupied with a search for truth based on the conviction that it could be found only in artistic or intellectual freedom. Writers had sought to liberate the creative process from arbitrary party interference. They sought to foster the artistic and moral values of traditional Russian literature: deep concern for the individual, psychological truth, intellectual honesty, and a multi-

ITAR-TASS/SOVFOTO

Andrei Siniavskii (right) and Iuli Daniel at their Moscow trial in February 1966 for allegedly slandering the Soviet system in writings published abroad.

faceted realism. Siniavskii's and Daniel's advocacy of these values led them into direct conflict with the authorities. After their trial, the Soviet intelligentsia realized that the artistic rights they sought could be achieved only with basic political freedoms.

This new consciousness triggered by the Siniavskii-Daniel affair created an unprecedented movement of dissent. Questions were asked about topics previously taboo even in liberal periods of Soviet history. The lack of basic rights, such as freedom from fear and freedom of speech, press, and assembly—all supposedly guaranteed by the Stalin Constitution—was widely discussed by Soviet intellectuals. The realization grew that Soviet citizens' fundamental rights were violated daily. The Constitution did not authorize censorship. How, then, could the party dictate what writers could or could not write or proscribe peaceful protest? These questions deeply disturbed many intellectuals.

Protesting the harsh sentences in the Siniavskii-Daniel trial, four young intellectuals, led by Alexander Ginzburg, collected extensive materials on the trial, including a verbatim transcript. Their aim was to induce the authorities to reopen the case and review the sentences. In January 1967 copies of these materials were sent to the KGB and Supreme Soviet deputies. The official response was to arrest the four young compilers, but a copy of the "white paper" had reached the West and was published. In January 1968 the four were tried and convicted under the notorious Article 70. The sentences of two, Iurii Galanskov and Ginzburg, were harsher than those of Siniavskii and Daniel. The Galanskov-Ginzburg trial evoked unprecedented public protests and triggered a broader civil-rights movement.

Andrei Sakharov, the leading Soviet nuclear physicist and "father of the Soviet H-bomb," organized the Human Rights Movement in 1970. It was designed to protest official policies that violated fundamental individual rights guaranteed by the Soviet Constitution. These freedoms were specified in the UN Declaration on Human Rights, which had been signed by the USSR. Prominent Soviet intellectuals joined in the clamor of protest. The regime responded with further unpublicized arrests and repression. The dissenters sought to inform the public of illegal official actions in *The Chronicle of Current Events,* a remarkable *samizdat* account of arrests, harassments, and exiles. The Brezhnev regime found it increasingly difficult to hide behind a veil of secrecy. The Human Rights Movement aimed not to overthrow the regime or alter the basic Soviet legal structure but merely to have existing laws enforced fairly and uniformly. Its patriotic members sought to have Soviet constitutional provisions observed in practice.

Alexander Solzhenitsyn

Intimately associated with the movement of dissent in the late 1960s and early 1970s was Alexander Solzhenitsyn. His renown grew steadily after publication of his novel *One Day in the Life of Ivan Denisovich* in 1962, though only a few more of his stories were published. Born in 1918, he studied mathematics and physics, became a teacher, and fought valiantly as an artillery officer in World War II. Near the war's end he was arrested and sentenced to the labor camps for referring to Stalin in a personal letter seized by the security police as "the man with the moustache." After eight years in labor camps and three more in exile in Central Asia, Solzhenitsyn in 1956 was considered fully rehabilitated, all charges against him were dismissed as groundless, and his civil rights were restored. *One Day* earned him recognition as a powerful writer and moral authority. Nevertheless, his few published works enraged party conservatives, and under Brezhnev the authorities decided that no more of his works should be published. Despite this decision, Alexander Tvardovskii, editor of *New World,* accepted a major Solzhenitsyn novel, *The Cancer Ward,* for publication there in 1968. The type was already set when the party abruptly ordered Tvardovskii to halt publication. The Galanskov-Ginzburg trial and accompanying

Alexander Isayevich Solzhenitsyn, 1918– , awarded the Nobel Prize for Literature in 1970, expelled from the Soviet Union in 1974 and returned to Russia in 1994.

protests caused the regime to block publication of a novel dealing with repression, abuse of power, and moral decay. Meanwhile a manuscript copy reached the West and was promptly published over Solzhenitsyn's objections. Nonetheless, the Soviet press orchestrated vicious attacks on the author.

The Cancer Ward deals with the terrifying experiences of Rusanov, a high Soviet official. After discovering he has cancer, Rusanov is unable to use his connections to enter an elite clinic and is confined in an ordinary cancer ward, packed with inconsequential, unsympathetic people whom he despises. Rusanov's antithesis is another cancer patient, Kostoglotov, a veteran of the labor camps and exile. He has suffered and survived, but no longer values life nor fears death. With literally nothing to lose, he has much strength to combat cancer. Rusanov, by contrast, has everything to lose—position, wealth, and family—and fear of death makes him desperate. He cannot accept his condition or combat it rationally.

Another Solzhenitsyn novel, *The First Circle,* an extension on a different level of *One Day,* was published in the West in 1968, but not in Brezhnev's USSR. It depicts a prison housing scholars, scientists, and engineers, all convicted of state crimes. Required to work on state scientific projects, they do not feel the physical anguish of Ivan Denisovich; although well-fed and well-housed, they experience a mental anguish more degrading and destructive than physical suffering. Again Solzhenitsyn deals with a central theme that reappears constantly in his works: the indomitable human spirit triumphant over adversity.

Another of Solzhenitsyn's major works is the broad historical panorama *August 1914,* published in the West in 1971, the first of a series of historical works dealing with Russia's travails in World War I and the Revolutions of 1917. Solzhenitsyn contrasts the Russian people's heroic struggle with the tsarist government's criminal incompetence. A historical parallel between Russia in World War I and the Soviet Union in World War II is evident.

Publication in the West of Solzhenitsyn's works led to a mounting campaign of persecution and public vilification against him. His international reputation and the Brezhnev regime's sensitivity to world opinion provided him a security that other dissenters, except for Sakharov, lacked. Like Kostoglotov in *The Cancer Ward,* Solzhenitsyn had suffered all that the Stalin regime could subject him to, and life held no terrors short of physical annihilation; he could not be intimidated or silenced. He spoke out courageously against censorship, repression, and injustice. "No one can bar the road to truth," he proclaimed in a famous letter circulated at the Fourth Congress of Soviet Writers in 1967, "and to advance its cause I am prepared to accept even death." Solzhenitsyn demanded an end to all censorship, insisting on absolute freedom for writers and artists:

> Literature cannot develop in between the categories of "permitted" and "not permitted,"

"about this you may write" and "about this you may not." Literature that is not the breath of contemporary society, that does not transmit the pains and fears of that society, that does not warn in time against threatening moral and social dangers—such literature does not deserve the name of literature; it is only a facade. Such literature loses the confidence of its own people, and its published works are used as wastepaper instead of being read.[8]

In 1970 Solzhenitsyn was awarded the Nobel Prize for literature. The anti-Pasternak scenario of 1958–1959 was reenacted as party hacks attacked Solzhenitsyn as a "leper" and had him expelled from the Writers' Union. This public assault failed to intimidate Solzhenitsyn as it had Pasternak. He proudly accepted the Nobel award but declined to go to Stockholm to receive it for fear of being denied reentry to the USSR. His eloquent Nobel lecture was smuggled to the West and published there in 1972. It was a dignified plea for freedom everywhere and reaffirmed strongly the moral responsibility of the writer and artist "to conquer falsehood." Harassment of Solzhenitsyn intensified in 1973. Fearing for his life, he managed to transmit some key manuscripts to friends in the West to prevent his enemies from silencing him even by death. He instructed his friends to publish them if anything happened to him.

In September 1973 the KGB pressured a Solzhenitsyn typist into revealing the whereabouts of a major underground manuscript she had typed. Solzhenitsyn promptly signaled his Western friends to publish the manuscript, previously smuggled abroad. The first volume of the monumental *The Gulag Archipelago, 1918–1956* was published in Paris in December 1973 and in numerous translations, including English, in 1974. Volumes two and three were issued in 1975. *The Gulag,* a powerfully moving history of the Soviet prison camp system, is dedicated "To all those who did not survive." Solzhenitsyn traces the prison camp system back to Lenin, although it developed into a monstrous structure only under

---

[8] Quoted in *Problems of Communism* 17, no. 5, p. 38.

Stalin. This remarkable account of man's inhumanity to man was based on Solzhenitsyn's personal experiences in the camps and those of hundreds of former prisoners (*zeks*) who shared their stories with him. Publication of *The Gulag Archipelago* in the West provoked an unprecedented campaign of slander and abuse of Solzhenitsyn in the USSR and an equally tremendous international outpouring of support for him. The Brezhnev regime hesitated momentarily in the face of world opinion, but in February 1974 had Solzhenitsyn arrested and charged with treason. The next day he was taken to the Moscow airport and put on a plane for West Germany and involuntary exile. Soon his family joined him and they settled in the United States, where he continued to write and denounce tyranny until his return to Russia in 1994.

In exile Solzhenitsyn identified himself with Russian Orthodoxy and criticized injustice and corruption not only in the Soviet Union but also in the West. He denounced détente, arguing that it helped perpetuate the Soviet dictatorship. Solzhenitsyn grew increasingly strident in his criticisms of the Soviet Union. Like Alexander Herzen, a 19th-century Russian exile in Europe, Solzhenitsyn continued from a Vermont farm his struggle against tyranny in his native land.

Other Soviet Writers

Under Brezhnev significant changes occurred in Soviet culture. While the state continued to determine what would be published officially, writers and artists achieved greater latitude than under Stalin or even under Khrushchev. During the 1970s some literary and artistic experimentation in form was permitted, producing some excellent results. The best Soviet writers created a literature with credible characters in real situations. They wrote about personal conflicts and aspirations, not building communism. Renouncing the reformist political writing of the mid-1950s, they stressed concern with self and everyday problems and shifted away from the novel to the novella and short story. In this genre authors focused on isolated incidents, chance occurrences, and private moods and feelings.

The best writers under Brezhnev walked a tightrope between free literary expression and state-defined aesthetics. Iurii Nagibin's stories portray human love and passion on an intimate level. After visiting the United States, he described his impressions with great insight. Iurii Kazakov's characters have received little from Soviet society and are embittered, frustrated rejects. The characters of talented, youthful Vasili Aksionov often reflect dehumanizing aspects of the Soviet regime and closely resemble the drifters and dreamers of American fiction of the 1950s and 1960s. In the 1970s he examined the macabre, pursuing new directions that ultimately proved officially unacceptable.

The *derevenshchiki* ("village writers") favored contemporary rural settings, often in Siberia, for tightly woven, realistic portrayals of the peasantry and daily life. Valentin Rasputin explored the pathos of peasant life objectively and clearly. His novella *Live and Remember* portrays the tribulations of a peasant deserter from World War II who depends on his wife's wisdom to outwit the authorities. In this simple story of struggle for survival, Rasputin passes no judgments. His gripping tale of rural life, "Money for Maria," describes the problems of a peasant woman managing the village general store. An official audit reveals a large cash shortage for which she is blamed. Respected in the village, she receives much support, but even the entire village cannot cover the shortage. In despair her husband seeks help from a relative in a distant city. Rasputin never reveals whether Maria is exonerated or if the authorities punish her, but the strength and dignity of the peasant community triumphs. Rasputin's timeless story simply ignores the tenets of socialist realism. In the 1980s Rasputin spearheaded the drive to save Lake Baikal from pollution.

Vasili Shukshin's death at age 45 represented a serious loss for Soviet fiction, film, and theater, for he was innovative in all three fields. In his

Michael Curran

Kolkhozniki—collective farm workers. The values of the rural heartland are reflected in works of the *derevenshchiki* writers. These peasant faces reveal those values.

compelling human-interest stories, Shukshin epitomized the *derevenshchiki* movement. His novella *The Red Guelder Rose* treats the formerly taboo subject of the criminal in Soviet society. After serving his sentence, a convict reforms and resolves to labor honestly in a village as an agricultural worker. His ideal world includes wife, family, and socially useful labor, but he cannot discard his criminal past. Eventually the criminals from whom he had sought to escape murder him.

Literary innovation and artistic spontaneity also flourished among non-Russians. The popular stories of Fazil Iskander, a Georgian from Abkhazia, possess a remarkable conversational quality. "Something About Myself" (published in English in 1978) begins:

> Let's just talk . . . about things we don't have to talk about, pleasant things. Let's talk about some of the amusing sides of human nature, as embodied in people we know. There is nothing more enjoyable than discussing certain old habits of our acquaintances. Because, you see,

talking about them makes us aware of our own healthy normality.[9]

Iskander's "talk" is very incisive and symbolic. In "The Thirteenth Labour of Hercules," a parable about the efficacy of humor in facing reality, Iskander argues:

> It seems to me that ancient Rome perished because its emperors in all their marble magnificence failed to realize how ridiculous they were. If they had got themselves some jesters in time (you must hear the truth, if only from a fool), they might have lasted a little longer. But they just went on hoping that the geese would save Rome, and then the barbarians came and destroyed Rome, the emperors and its geese.[10]

Was this intended for an aging Politburo under a moribund Brezhnev? Whatever Iskander's intent, his tales won him a deserved reputation as a gifted

---

[9] Fazil Iskander, "Something About Myself," in *The Thirteenth Labour of Hercules,* trans. R. Dalgish (Moscow, 1978), p. 7.
[10] F. Iskander, *The Thirteenth Labour of Hercules,* p. 51.

storyteller and subtle critic of the Soviet system. His two major works, *Sandro of Chegem* (1983) and *The Gospel According to Chegem* (1984), published in English translation but not in the USSR until recently, capture the spirit of the patriarchal village succumbing to inexorable modernization and Sovietization:

> In my childhood I caught fleeting glimpses of the patriarchal village of Abkhazia and fell in love with it forever. Have I perhaps idealized the vanishing life? Perhaps. A man cannot help ennobling what he loves. We may not recognize it, but in idealizing a vanishing way of life we are presenting a bill to the future. We are saying, "Here is what we are losing; what are you going to give us in exchange?" Let the future think on that if it is capable of thinking at all.[11]

Iskander portrays the modern history of Abkhazia in the Caucasus in stories featuring Uncle Sandro and many other unforgettable characters from Chegem village. Sandro is a fearless, independent spirit, irreverent toward the Soviet regime.

Iskander's digressions as narrator proved unacceptable to Soviet censors. For example:

> With characteristic frankness, Lenin confessed to Gorky . . . that he was humorless. . . . Lenin partially compensated for his deficiency in humor through his magnificent work as an organizer. After Lenin, unfortunately, the Bolsheviks, although they did not possess his genius, decided to follow his lead with respect to humor. . . . They appointed their most unsmiling man [Stalin] to be the country's leader, in the mistaken belief that the most unsmiling man was the most earnest one. This is what revealed the tragedy in the lack of a sense of humor. Yes, he did smile into his moustache with satisfaction, but only later, after 1937 [the Great Purge].[12]

---

[11] F. Iskander, from Foreword to *Sandro of Chegem*, trans. S. Brownsberger (New York, 1983), p. viii.
[12] F. Iskander, *The Gospel According to Chegem*, trans. S. Brownsberger (New York, 1984), pp. 264–65.

Iurii Trifonov (1925–1981) balanced artistic integrity and political acceptability in his short career. His father, an Old Bolshevik, perished in the purges, but Trifonov adapted to party demands: An early novel of his received a Stalin Prize. In middle age, disdaining party approval, he established his reputation with a series of novellas that probed the past and its influence on the present. The past, he suggested, must be confronted in order to free the future from Stalin's savage legacy. *The House on the Embankment* depicts perceptively the impact of the Stalin era: the problems of growing up, seeking meaning in life, and finding a place in Soviet society from World War II to the mid-1970s. Flashbacks allow Trifonov to explore shifting Soviet values. The successes and failures of Glebov, the main character, are chronicled with nostalgia and resignation, symbolizing the ambiguities of Soviet life: "He dreamed of all the things that later came to him—but which brought him no joy because achieving them used up so much of his strength." Was that perhaps the fate of Soviet people struggling for small joys only to discover that their struggle merely entailed more travail? Here is no view of a radiant future, nor the party's triumph over adversity, but only the tribulations of an ordinary, unheroic person. One can pity Glebov and his periodic waverings, but the Soviet authorities failed to find Trifonov's work uplifting.

Trifonov's somber novellas became immensely popular with Soviet readers, who mourned his untimely death in 1981. Trifonov's passing stilled a voice that had spoken appreciatively of ordinary people and everyday experiences, unlike socialist realism's often grandiose portraits, which seemed more and more divorced from Soviet reality. Trifonov's career revealed that genuine talent could flourish to some degree within narrow Soviet confines. Few others negotiated as successfully the delicate boundary between artistic integrity and party dictates.

From a similar background, Vasili Aksionov became an even more famous writer. More politically engaged, he clashed frequently with the authorities until he was forced to emigrate in 1980. Aksionov first won acclaim for his novella *Halfway to the Moon* (1961), recounting experiences of the first generation of Soviet youth to be deeply influenced by the West. His stories, plays, novels, and cinema scripts gained him a reputation as a prolific and outspoken writer.

What triggered Aksionov's expulsion from the USSR (he still resides outside Russia) was his leadership in creating the literary anthology *Metropol,* which relentlessly demanded artistic freedom. Defying censorship, it was published in an edition of only 10 copies! Increasingly frustrated with literary censorship, Aksionov had his explosive novel *The Burn* published in Italy (1980) and the United States (1984) without authorization. Depicting Moscow intellectuals' alienation during the post-Stalin thaw, it became an instant success. Deeply influenced by the contemporary West and derived from Aksionov's experiences as a visting lecturer at UCLA in 1975, it is an intense and generally negative portrait of contemporary Soviet society. In a style reminiscent of Thomas Pynchon, *The Burn* chronicles the adventures of five men with the same name. The novel has a memorable cast of characters, but the plot is weak and poorly developed.

More interesting is Aksionov's *The Island of Crimea,* a fantasy:

> What if Crimea really were an island? What if, as a result, the White Army had been able to defend Crimea from the Reds in 1920? What if Crimea had developed as a Russian, yet Western, democracy alongside the totalitarian mainland?[13]

Aksionov imagines a Crimea resembling contemporary Taiwan or Hong Kong replete with superhighways, neon lights, designer boutiques, and sun-worshipping bathers on beaches all within sight of the totalitarian mainland. Andrei Luchnikov, the main character and son of a White

leader, successfully defends Crimea against the Red Army. Handsome, rich, and powerful, Luchnikov owns a newspaper that leads an unlikely and curious campaign to reunify capitalist Crimea with the Communist mainland. After his emigration, Aksionov's reputation continued to grow both abroad and in the USSR.

Other Cultural Fields

Although leaders in music and art under Brezhnev pushed the regime to the limits of the acceptable, little was produced that openly challenged party authority. The cinema remained largely a wasteland, despite a few exceptional works such as Andrei Tarkovskii's excellent and innovative film *Andrei Rublev,* about the great 15th-century Russian iconographer. Because of its religious theme, it could not be shown widely in the USSR, but it received an award at the Cannes Film Festival. The heroism of the Soviet people in World War II still strongly influenced filmmakers, who found in it a virtually inexhaustible supply of themes.

In music, Dmitrii Shostakovich remained the leading Soviet composer of the Brezhnev era. He continued to produce innovative, rather bitter masterpieces right up to his death in 1975. Both his 13th (*Babi Yar*) and 14th symphonies, whose leitmotifs were death, were works of protest. In this period Soviet classical music underwent a slow but inexorable modernistic evolution and increasingly used Western composition techniques. New composers such as Boris Tishchenko and Rodion Shchedrin imitated Western experimentalism. To the unconcealed disgust of secondrate conservatives such as Tikhon Khrennikov, longtime head of the Composers' Union, they moved ever further from socialist realism's hallowed but deadening tenets. However, under Brezhnev none dared challenge ideological orthodoxy directly. During the 1970s the role of regional composers from various national republics grew significantly more important.

---

[13] V. Aksionov, from Preface to *The Island of Crimea,* trans. M. Heim (New York, 1983), p. ix.

Culture under Gorbachev, 1985–1991

At first the new regime moved cautiously in the cultural realm, until Gorbachev realized that his program of *perestroika* required endorsement and support from the entire country, especially the cultural elite. *Glasnost* greatly widened freedom for all the arts; artists' responses were enthusiastic but wary. Decades of cultural conditioning and conformity could not be discarded overnight. Prior experience taught that "thaws" were followed inevitably by "frosts" or even hard "freezes." However, it soon grew evident that Gorbachev was serious about reform, and bold individuals decided to test *glasnost's* limits. The dissidents had already created bases for a Soviet counterculture. Their ideal—an open, freer cultural atmosphere without state-defined norms—fast became reality. The counterculture surfaced rapidly, as many radical works, formerly considered unacceptable, now appeared, raising questions about censorship. Works that challenged traditional limits became catalysts of free expression. Artists and journalists led this remarkable transformation of Soviet culture.

Cultural organization grew more important as controls shifted from state organs, such as the Ministry of Culture, and as unions won greater influence over culture. But not all unions were dominated by emerging "liberals." The powerful Writers' Union remained under conservative control but grew more tolerant of diverse literary approaches. Innovative leaders prevailed in other unions. Journal editors, historians, and scientists supported *glasnost* ardently.

An outspoken cultural leader was a Ukrainian writer, Vitali Korotich, named editor of the influential journal *Ogonek* (*The Little Flame*) in 1986 and elected to the new Congress of Peoples' Deputies in 1989. He transformed a stodgy, uninteresting journal into a progressive vehicle of opinion, focusing on issues of *glasnost*. Stimulating the new national passion of recapturing the past honestly, Korotich published articles critical of Stalin and Stalinism, openly confronting formerly taboo

social problems such as prostitution, drug abuse, and the Afghan war. His willingness to test *glasnost's* limits made *Ogonek* extremely popular. But Korotich realized that *glasnost* offered no guarantees: "It's like flying. There's a feeling of exhilaration, but you always have the thought in the back of your mind that the plane might crash."[14]

Gorbachev's political reforms and the freedom to criticize, publish, and exhibit sparked a creative renaissance in the USSR. Gorbachev recognized that for his revolution to succeed it had to enlist the country's most creative minds and free them from party-imposed conformity. The USSR had to be opened to outside influences and reintegrated into global culture. Nonetheless, opposition to *glasnost* and *perestroika* persisted, and Gorbachev's critics denounced his policies. At a "conservative" rally in Moscow in February 1988, a Leningrad schoolteacher, Nina Andreeva, warned a wildly cheering crowd that Russia was faced by a "counterrevolution" that threatened to pose grave problems, such as strikes, ethnic violence, and moral degradation. These problems, she argued, stemmed from Gorbachev's efforts to "Westernize" the country and introduce "capitalist exploitation in all our cities."[15]

Literature: New and "Lost" Works

Established authors continued under Gorbachev to publish respectable if unimaginative works with broad appeal. A younger generation of talented, innovative writers emerged, but as of the early 1990s had not really found its true literary voice. *Glasnost* produced a major movement to recapture the portion of Soviet literary tradition long repressed by rigid cultural policies. Works that had languished in desk drawers or circulated in tattered manuscripts were now published at a furious rate, straining press capacity. Among long-suppressed classics finally issued in the USSR were Zamiatin's *We*, Pasternak's *Dr. Zhivago*,

---

[14] *Remaking the Revolution: The Soviet Union 70 Years Later* (Los Angeles, 1988), p. 31.
[15] *New York Times*, February 24, 1988, p. 6.

Akhmatova's *Requiem,* and Solzhenitsyn's *Cancer Ward.* Even Solzhenitsyn's *Gulag Archipelago* was published in 1990. Other long-banned writers were rehabilitated, including Bulgakov, Pilniak, Mandelshtam, and Siniavskii. Soviet readers were introduced to long-forbidden émigré authors and Western writers formerly considered decadent. Works by Nobel laureates Josef Brodskii and Vladimir Nabokov were published, as was James Joyce's *Ulysses.* Recent émigré works such as Aksionov's *The Burn* and Voinovich's *The Life and Extraordinary Adventures of Private Ivan Chonkin* were also issued.

These "lost" works, analyzed in literary journals, were then reintegrated into the USSR's literary legacy. Restrictions on literature brought into the USSR were virtually eliminated. Taboo subjects almost disappeared, as indicated by publication of Anatoli Rybakov's *Children of the Arbat.* Written in the 1960s but set in 1933, this novel boldly records the sinister beginnings of the Great Purges and contains a chilling portrait of Stalin, depicting his callous disregard for human suffering and insatiable lust for power.

An avalanche of works about the Stalin era burst forth, calling attention to the extent of Stalinist repression, which struck the peasantry through collectivization, national minorities through deportation, religious believers through persecution, and the intelligentsia by intimidation. Many of these books had been written decades earlier but had never been published in the USSR. One example is Vasili Grossman's *Life and Fate,* a massive novel about World War II, in scale comparable to Tolstoy's *War and Peace*; it was published in the West in 1985 and in the USSR in 1988. It portrays with devastating honesty the trauma of war in the Soviet Union, especially in the Battle of Stalingrad, which unleashed Russian venality, prejudice, and suspicion. Grossman holds a mirror to Soviet society, which had glossed over negative aspects of the Soviet Union's wartime role. He draws disturbing parallels between Nazi Germany and Stalin's Russia and holds Lenin responsible for Stalinism and other evils in Soviet society.

Completing the novel in 1960, he submitted it to the journal *Znamia* (*The Banner*), which rejected it as "anti-Soviet." The KGB then confiscated the manuscript and harassed Grossman, who died in poverty and isolation in 1964.

Similarly, Vladimir Dudintsev, best known for *Not by Bread Alone* (1956), in 1988 published *White Robes,* a stunning fictional account of the struggle by honest scientists against Trofim Lysenko's perversion of Soviet science under Stalin (see Chapter 36). Daniel Granin's curiously titled *Aurochs* or *Bison* (*Zubr*) depicts the moral dilemma of a Soviet scientist who flees the USSR because of political control of science to pursue his scientific work in Nazi Germany. Such works, questioning the validity of the entire Soviet experience, could not have been published in the USSR prior to Gorbachev.

Also published officially in the USSR was Fazil Iskander's cycle *Sandro of Chegem* and *The Gospel According to Chegem,* which some critics believe may become a 20th-century Russian classic.[16] Anna Akhmatova's poem "Requiem," also published under Gorbachev, is an impassioned solemn chant for her son arrested during the Great Purges:

> Silent flows the Don
> Yellow moon looks quietly on
> Cap askew, looks in the room,
> Sees a shadow in the gloom,
> Sees the woman, sick, at home,
> Sees the woman, all alone,
> Husband buried, then to see
> Son arrested . . . Pray for me.[17]

Georgii Vladimov's novella *Faithful Ruslan,* published in the USSR in 1989 (1979 in the West), is a frightening parable about a loyal and determined trained guard dog at a Siberian forced labor camp. When the camp is closed, Ruslan cannot understand his new role. When the former prison camp becomes a cellulose factory with free workers,

---

[16] Deming Brown, "Literature and Perestroika," *Michigan Quarterly Review* 27, no. 4 (Fall 1989), p. 769.
[17] In *Selected Poems,* ed. Walter Arndt (Ann Arbor, MI, 1976), p. 147.

Ruslan and other guard dogs cannot differentiate them from prisoners and harass the workers as they had once harassed the prisoners. Behavior cannot be changed easily after long conditioning, argues Vladimov. Human beings, like dogs, cannot escape their past.

Such literary archives, once opened, helped Soviet citizens come to grips with their brutal totalitarian past. Under Gorbachev, literary attention focused on that past rather than on new, experimental literary works. Noted the distinguished author and critic Gregorii Baklanov (not to be confused with Oleg Baklanov, a member of the Committee for the State of Emergency, which attempted to overthrow Gorbachev in August 1991) in 1988:

> Three years ago we would never have dreamed of achieving what we have now achieved in the cultural sphere. Nevertheless, we are still lacking a lot . . . because our society is putting all its energy into convalescing.

However, such "convalescing" is essential if former Soviet citizens are to understand massive current changes and place them in accurate context. Another critic, Tatiana Ivanova, wrote in *Ogonek:*

> Our time does not pass in vain. Who can measure the impact of the publication of Grossman's novel [*Life and Fate*] on many thousands of shocked minds? Is it possible for us not to notice the impact of reading *Children of the Arbat,* or *White Robes*? . . . The effect is enormous. . . . We will become different.[18]

A fascinating episode from the Gorbachev era was the national debate over a play not yet produced. The playwright, Mikhail Shatrov, published *On and On and On!* in the journal *Znamia* (*Banner*) in 1988 and overnight became a celebrity. Himself a victim of Stalinism, having lost his parents and close relatives in the purge, and trained as a mining engineer, Shatrov began writing plays in the early 1950s. Some of the early ones were about

Lenin; all were controversial. *The Peace of Brest-Litovsk* (written in 1962, published in 1987) unleashed heated protests. *Pravda* denounced him for "distorting" Soviet history. That was minor compared to the controversy over publication of *On and On and On!,* which raised disturbing questions about the Bolshevik Revolution. His characters ask whether Lenin, had he known the Revolution's outcome, would have led the Bolsheviks in a forceful seizure of power in November 1917. Stalin is portrayed as confronting dilemmas and resolving them violently because of his sadistic, paranoid personality. Shatrov wonders whether Lenin could have intervened successfully to prevent Stalin's rise to power. Exploring alternatives, Shatrov suggests that Stalin's rule was not preordained.

Shatrov's irreverent treatment of the great icons of the Bolshevik Revolution and his questioning of its legitimacy ignited vehement protests. Three historians accused him in *Pravda* of "falsifying" history by portraying Lenin as weak and vacillating. In light of Marxist economic determinism, his critics argued, how could Shatrov suggest that the Bolshevik Revolution was an "accident"? Nina Andreeva castigated Shatrov for spurning socialist realism. Why, she wondered, this obsession with criticizing Stalin? Numerous letters about the play streamed into *Znamia,* mostly praising the play and its publication. A policeman and party member from Irkutsk wrote:

> I want you and Shatrov to know that honest people who value truth and justice are grateful to you for your work which strengthens our belief in the irreversibility of the revolutionary reconstruction of our country.

An unsigned letter from Kiev expressed a very different view:

> Where is your responsibility to the party, your civic honor and simple human dignity when you allow your magazine to publish the vulgarity, anti-Sovietism and political muck pro-

---

[18] Tatiana Ivanova, "Who Risks What?" *Ogonek,* no. 24 (June 11–18, 1988), p. 12.

duced by Shatrov? . . . Whose mouthpiece have you become?[19]

This debate reflected a continuing dispute in Soviet society over *glasnost* and *perestroika.* Shatrov sought above all to help audiences recapture the past and recognize complex truths. Gorbachev's reforms included an effort to "restructure" the past, and Shatrov sought to assist him in *On and On and On!*

Art

Soviet artists too were deeply affected by Gorbachev's reforms. Many artworks hitherto proscribed emerged from closets and cellars into public view. The rigid confines of socialist realism were shattered, and the distinction between "official" and "unofficial" art faded. Soviet artists participated more fully in world art. In July 1989 Sotheby's, a major international art auction house, organized a Moscow auction of 120 contemporary Soviet works. More than 11,000 people attended the preauction exhibition and more than 2,000 the auction itself; receipts, far exceeding expectations, totaled $3.4 million. For many previously unknown artists, such commercial success enabled them to pursue creative work full-time.

Earlier Soviet artist-émigrés staged successful exhibitions in the USSR. Mikhail Chemiakin, a Leningrad artist who had won international acclaim in Paris and New York, held a major retrospective exhibition in Moscow in 1989. While evading the criteria of socialist realism, Chemiakin's art is neither radical nor anti-Soviet. His subject matter comes from traditional Russian culture and history.

Another Soviet artist who won critical applause in the West is Ilia Kabakov. His multipaneled works combine images with text. Dubbed "albums" or "portfolios," his works portray lives of ordinary characters moving through life, as he comments on physical and intellectual activity.

Abstract art was long derided in the USSR as decadent, antisocialist, and devoid of social content, but even before *glasnost* Soviet artists experimented with "unofficial" forms of expression. Under Gorbachev, competing styles and forms were openly accepted. Among well-known Soviet artists who rejected socialist realism in order to continue the earlier abstract tradition of Malevich and others were Boris Sveshnikov and Anatoli Zverev. Soviet abstract painters, winning wider acceptance at home and abroad, sought to enter the mainstream of world art. The enthusiastic response to the first public auction of contemporary Soviet art indicated how far these pioneers had come in only a few years.

Film

The Cinema Workers' and Theater Workers' unions underwent dramatic leadership changes under Gorbachev. The distinguished director Elem Klimov became head of the Cinema Workers, and the liberal Alexander Kamshalov took over Goskino, which supervised the Soviet film industry. Together they opened the film archives and released scores of films repressed over the previous 30 years. Among them, Klimov's own *Agony,* shown in the West as *Rasputin,* portrays the decadence and depravity of the Russian imperial court in the twilight of tsarism. Alexander Askoldov's film *Commissar* (1968), released for showing in 1988, deals with issues such as anti-Semitism, abortion, and child abandonment. It reveals moral dilemmas confronting a young Red Army "commissar" in the Civil War who becomes pregnant, considers abortion, has the child in a poor Jewish home, leaves the child with the family, and then returns to the front.

Glasnost's most celebrated film was *Repentance* (1983, released for viewing in 1987) by the Georgian director Tengiz Abuladze. Surrealistic and filled with symbolism that strikes at the heart of totalitarian dictatorship, the film denounces Stalinism and reaffirms human dignity expressed under the greatest adversity. The film was a sensation, viewed by millions who were deeply affected

---

[19] "Perestroika and Soviet Culture," *Michigan Quarterly Review* 38, no. 4 (Fall 1989), p. 589. *Znamia* reported that the letters ran 5 to 1 in support of the play.

by its humanistic message. The film's final line of dialogue became the key question for many: "What good is a road that does not lead to a church?" In 1988 Abuladze received for *Repentance* the Lenin Prize, the highest state award for creative work; in 1989 the film was recognized at the Cannes Film Festival. Formerly taboo subjects for film, such as alcoholism, family conflicts, and environmental problems, became acceptable. The film *Little Vera* caused a sensation in 1988 because it dealt with sex and drugs and, for the first time in Soviet cinema, featured on-screen nudity.

The Stalinist past provided abundant subject matter for films and documentaries that raised nagging questions about the purges, the betrayals by family and friends, and the issue of responsibility for the past. In documentaries people spoke out about their sufferings in the prison camps, the terror, and people's heroism in combating it. This examination is part of the vital task of accepting the past.

The most confrontive and controversial film to appear was Stanislav Govorukhin's documentary *This Is No Way to Live.* An unrelenting chronicle of more than 70 years of Communist brutality, corruption, criminal activity, and stupidity, the film paints everything a uniform "black," just as former socialist realist films painted everything "rosy." It is, however, yet another vehicle designed to help recapture a lost past, not as a novel or as history, but as a documentary virtually all Soviet citizens could relate to based on their personal experiences. It was, therefore, a powerful tool to wrench Soviet citizens out of their apathetic acceptance of authoritarian misrule. Many cannot understand the decision to allow such a devastating indictment of Communist rule to be shown publicly, but Gorbachev reportedly reviewed the film personally and approved its release. Gradually the former Soviet people were regaining their historical memory, and this film was an important part of that process.

Music

The cult hero of *glasnost* was the deceased young balladeer Vladimir Vysotskii, recognized as a symbol of the triumph over repression that had strangled Soviet culture for decades. Officially Vysotskii was an actor in Iurii Liubimov's famous Taganka Theater in Moscow who also appeared in films. But he was best known as a poet-bard whose bitter, satirical protest songs won him a huge following among youth and members of the intelligentsia. His songs circulated widely in *magnitizdat,* poor-quality homemade recordings made at his many concerts and private songfests. Living in the fast lane, Vysotskii died in 1980 as a widely recognized underground hero. Under *glasnost* he emerged "above ground" to be acknowledged as a "seer" and "legend." His works have sold hundreds of thousands of copies, TV documentaries have recorded his life, and he has achieved huge success in the popular press.

A highly dramatic event associated with musical *glasnost* was the triumphant return to Moscow in February 1990 of the distinguished cellist and conductor Mstislav Rostropovich, who with his wife, the acclaimed soprano Galina Vishnevskaia, was exiled from the USSR in 1974. They had been accused of "acts harmful to the Soviet Union" for offering shelter and support to Solzhenitsyn prior to his own expulsion. Rostropovich's return to the USSR, restoration of his citizenship (revoked in 1978), and the return of his Moscow apartment heralded a new era in Soviet music. The press glorified Rostropovich for his contributions to music and his heroic defense of justice and freedom. Asked about his view of President Gorbachev, Rostropovich commented that Stalin had tried in the 1940s to frighten Prokofiev and Shostakovich into writing more "socialist" music. "I know Gorbachev does not give [music] lessons to my friend, Alfred Schnitke."[20] The distinguished Russian-born

---

[20] Quoted in the *New York Times,* February 14, 1990, p. B1. Schnitke is considered a leading Soviet contemporary composer.

Vladimir Vysotskii (1938–1980), popular Russian poet and balladeer, at a concert in Yaroslavl in February 1979.

pianist Vladimir Horowitz also returned to the Soviet Union for a concert tour in 1986. *Glasnost* thus relaxed controls and provided greater access to the international musical world.

Conclusion

A great artistic revival under Gorbachev contributed mightily to a cultural catharsis in the USSR. Recapturing the past, artists and historians liberated the populace from the deception of Stalinism and the stagnation of the Brezhnev era. The strongest support for Gorbachev's restructuring program came from Soviet artists and writers seeking to energize the nation and generate positive attitudes toward the future.

Alexander Kabakov, a young journalist, published in *Iskusstvo Kino* (*Film Art*) in 1989 a projected script for a science fiction film, *The Non-Returnee.* In this antiutopian film script,

Kabakov portrays a future USSR totally disintegrated and locked in civil war. The country is ruled by roving bands of terrorists, national minorities have all left the Soviet Union, and the economy has sunk to a bare subsistence level. His purpose, stated Kabakov, was to deliver "a stern and sober warning of what could happen if we do not manage to cope with destructive anti-*perestroika* processes present in our society. *Perestroika* may be the last chance."[21] Were Kabakov's views prophetic? Soviet culture has often marched ahead of Soviet politics.

[21] Quoted in *Report on the USSR, Radio Free Europe* . . . 1, no. 33 (August 18, 1989), p. 9.

AP/Wide World Photos

Russian-born pianist Vladimir Horowitz returned triumphantly to the USSR for a concert tour in 1986 after 51 years in exile.

InfoTrac® College Edition Search Terms

Enter the search term *Boris Pasternak* in Keywords. Enter the search term *Solzhenitsyn* in Keywords. Enter the search term *Dmitri Shostakovich* in Keywords.

Suggested Additional Reading

Most works of literature and literary dissent mentioned in this chapter have been translated into English. Consult your library for the most recent editions and anthologies.

KHRUSHCHEV ERA

BARLETT, R. *Shostakovich in Context* (New York and Oxford, 2000).

BETHEA, D. *Joseph Brodsky and the Creation of Exile* (Princeton, 1994).

BROWN, M. C. *Socialist Realist Painting* (New Haven, CT, 1998).

FIELD, A., ed. *Pages from Tarusa: New Voices in Russian Writing* (London, 1964).

GERSTENMAIER, C. *The Voices of the Silent* (New York, 1972).

GIBIAN, G. *Interval of Freedom: Soviet Literature During the Thaw, 1954–1957* (Minneapolis, 1960).

GOLDBERG, A. L., and P. GOLDBERG. *The Thaw Generation: Coming of Age in the Post-Stalin Era* (Pittsburgh, 1993).

GRAHAM, L. R. *What Have We Learned about Science and Technology from the Russian Experience?* (Stanford, CA, 1998).

JOHNSON, P. *Khrushchev and the Arts: The Politics of Soviet Culture, 1962–1964* (Cambridge, MA, 1965).

KARLINSKY, S. *Marina Tsvetaeva . . .* (New York, 1986).

KELLY, C., and SHEPHERD, D., eds. *Russian Cultural Studies: An Introduction* (New York, 1998).

LIVINGSTONE, A. *Pasternak: Dr. Zhivago* (New York, 1989).

LOWE, D. *Russian Writing Since 1953: A Critical Survey* (New York, 1987).

PROKOFIEV, S. *Prokofiev by Prokofiev: A Composer's Memoir,* ed. D. H. Appel, trans. G. Daniels (Garden City, NY, 1979).

REAVEY, GEORGE, ed. and trans. *The New Russian Poets, 1953–1966: An Anthology* (New York, 1966).

ROBIN, R. *Socialist Realism: The Impossible Aesthetic,* trans. C. Porter (Stanford, 1992).

ROTHBERG, A. *The Heirs of Stalin: Dissidence and the Soviet Regime, 1953–1970* (Ithaca, NY, 1972).

SCATTON, L. H. *Mikhail Zoshchenko: Evolution of a Writer* (New York, 1993).

SCHWARZ, B. *Music and Musical Life in Soviet Russia, 1917–1981,* enlarged ed. (Bloomington, IN, 1983).

SJEKLOCHA, P., and I. MEAD. *Unofficial Art in the Soviet Union* (Berkeley, 1967).

SMELIANSKY, A. *The Russian Theatre after Stalin,* trans. Patrick Miles (Brookfield, VT, 1999).

BREZHNEV ERA

AKSYONOV, V. *The Burn* (New York, 1984).

———. *The Island of Crimea* (New York, 1984).

———, et al., eds. *Metropol* (New York, 1983).

AMERT, S. *In a Shattered Mirror: The Late Poetry of Anna Akhmatova* (Stanford, 1992).

BENYON, M. *Life in Russia* (New York, 1983).

BROWN, D. *The Last Years of Soviet Russian Literature: Prose Fiction, 1975–1991* (Cambridge, 1993).

BRUMBERG, A., ed. *In Quest of Justice: Protest and Dissent in the Soviet Union Today* (New York, 1970).

DODGE, M., and A. HILTON, eds. *New Art from the Soviet Union* (Washington, 1977).

DUNLOP, J. B., R. HOUGH, and A. KLIMOFF, eds. *Aleksandr Solzhenitsyn: Critical Essays and Documentary Materials* (Belmont, MA, 1973).

GILLESPIE, D. *Iurii Trifonov: Unity Through Time* (New York, 1993).

HAYWARD, M., ed. *On Trial: The Soviet State Versus "Abram Tertz" and "Nikolai Arzhak"* (New York, 1966).

HOSKING, G. *Beyond Socialist Realism: Soviet Fiction Since Ivan Denisovich* (New York, 1980).

KERBLAY, B. *Modern Soviet Society* (New York, 1983).

KIRK, I. *Profiles in Russian Resistance* (New York, 1975).

KOLESNIKOFF, N. *Yury Trifonov: A Critical Study* (Ann Arbor, MI, 1991).

MEDVEDEV, Z. *The Medvedev Papers: The Plight of Soviet Science Today* (New York, 1971).

MONONOVA, T., ed. *Women and Russia: Feminist Writings from the Soviet Union* (Boston, 1984).

NEPOMNYASHCHY, C. T. *Abram Tertz and the Poetics of Crime* (New Haven, CT, 1995).

OKUDZHAVA, B. *A Taste of Liberty,* trans. Leo Gruliow (Ann Arbor, MI, 1986).

PARTHE, K. *Russian Village Prose: The Radiant Past* (Princeton, 1992).

POLLAK, N., ed. *Mandelshtam: The Reader* (Baltimore, 1995).

POLUKHINA, V. *Joseph Brodsky . . .* (Cambridge, 1989).

REDDAWAY, P., ed. and trans. *Uncensored Russia: Protest and Dissent in the Soviet Union . . .* (New York, 1972).

ROTHBERG, A. *Aleksandr Solzhenitsyn: The Major Novels, 1953–1970* (Ithaca, NY, 1972).

SCAMMELL, M. *Solzhenitsyn: A Biography* (New York, 1984).

SHALAMOV, V. *Kolyma Tales,* trans. J. Glad (New York, 1980).

SHIPLER, D. *Russia: Broken Idols, Solemn Dreams,* 2d ed. (New York, 1989).

SOLZHENITSYN, A., et al. *From Under the Rubble: Essays* (New York, 1975).

TOKES, R., ed. *Dissent in the USSR: Politics, Ideology and People* (Baltimore, 1975).

TRIFONOV, I. *Another Life and House on the Embankment* (New York, 1984).

———. *The Old Man* (New York, 1984).

VISHNEVSKY, P. *Soviet Literary Culture in the 1970s: The Politics of Irony* (Gainesville, FL, 1993).

VOLKOV, S., ed. *Testimony: The Memoirs of Dmitri Shostakovich* (New York, 1979).

WALL, J. *Invented Truth: Soviet Reality and the Literary Imagination of Iurii Trifonov* (Durham, NC, 1991).

GORBACHEV ERA

AITMATOV, C. *The Day Lasts More Than a Hundred Years* (Bloomington, IN, 1983).

AKHMATOVA, A. *The Complete Poems of Anna Akhmatova,* 2 vols., ed. Roberta Reeder, trans. Judith Hemschemeyer (Somerville, MA, 1989).

ANDERSON, R., and P. DEBRECZENY, eds. *Russian Narrative and Visual Art: Varieties of Seeing* (Gainesville, FL, 1993).

BARKER, A. M., ed. *Consuming Russia: Popular Culture, Sex, and Society since Gorbachev* (Durham, NC, 1999).

BARTLETT, R. *Wagner and Russia* (Cambridge, 1995).

BERRY, E., and A. MILLER-POGACAR, eds. *Re-entering the Sign: Articulating New Russian Culture* (Ann Arbor, MI, 1995).

BROWN, D. *The Last Years of Soviet Russian Literature: Prose Fiction, 1975–1991* (New York, 1993).

CHANCES, E. *Andrei Bitov: The Ecology of Inspiration* (New York, 1993).

GARRARD, J., and C. GARRARD. *Inside the Soviet Writers' Union* (New York, 1990).

GROSSMAN, V. *Life and Fate* (New York, 1985).

ISKANDER, F. *Rabbits and Boa Constrictors* (Ann Arbor, MI, 1989).

KETCHIAN, S. *The Poetry of Anna Akhmatova: A Conquest of Time and Space* (Munich, 1986).

LAHUSEN, T., and G. KUPERMAN, eds. *Late Soviet Culture: From Perestroika to Novostroika* (Durham, NC, 1993).

LAWTON, A. *Kinoglasnost: Soviet Cinema in Our Time* (New York, 1993).

LOWELL, S. *The Russian Reading Revolution: Print Culture in the Soviet and Post-Soviet Eras* (New York, 2000).

MUCKLE, J. *Portrait of a Soviet School Under Glasnost* (New York, 1990).

ORLOV, Y. *Memoirs of a Russia Life,* trans. T. Whitney (New York, 1990).

"Perestroika and Soviet Culture," *Michigan Quarterly Review,* 1989. (An extremely valuable collection of essays and translations providing a comprehensive account of Soviet culture under Gorbachev.)

PETRA, S., ed. *Rocking the State: Rock Music and Politics in Eastern Europe and Russia* (Boulder, CO, 1994).

POLOWY, T. *The Novellas of Valentin Rasputin . . . ,* vol. 1 (New York, 1989).

RASPUTIN, V. *Siberia on Fire,* trans. G. Mikkelson and M. Winchell (Dekalb, IL, 1989).

REEDER, R., ed., and J. HEMSCHEMEYER, trans. *The Complete Poems of Anna Akhmatova* (Boston, 1992).

Remaking the Revolution: The Soviet Union 70 Years Later (Los Angeles, 1987). (Selections from the *Los Angeles Times'* coverage of the Soviet Union.)

REEDER, R. *Anna Akhmatova: Poet and Prophet* (New York, 1994).

RIES, N. *Russian Talk: Culture and Conversation during Perestroika* (Ithaca, NY, 1997).

ROSS, D., ed. *Between Spring and Summer: Soviet Conceptual Art in the Era of Late Communism* (Cambridge, MA, 1990).

RUDOVA, L. *Understanding Boris Pasternak* (Columbia, SC, 1997).

RYAN-HAYES, K. L. *Contemporary Russian Satire: A Genre Study* (New York, 1995).

RYBAKOV, A. *Children of the Arbat* (Boston, 1988).

———. *Heavy Sand* (New York, 1983).

SEGEL, H. *Twentieth Century Russian Drama: From Gorkey to the Present* (Baltimore, 1993).

SHALIN, D. N. *Russia's Culture at the Crossroads: Paradoxes of Post Communist Consciousness* (Boulder, CO 1996).

SHNEIDMAN, N. *Soviet Literature in the 1980s . . .* (Toronto, 1989).

SMITH, G. S., ed. and trans. *Contemporary Russian Poetry: A Bilingual Anthology* (Bloomington, IN, 1993.)

SOLOMON, A. *The Irony Tower: Soviet Artists in a Time of Glasnost* (New York, 1990).

TAUBMAN, W., and J. TAUBMAN. *Moscow Spring* (New York, 1989).

THOMAS, D. M. *Solzhenitsyn: A Century in His Lifetime* (New York, 1998).

TUPITSYN, M. *Margins of Soviet Art* (Milan, 1989).

VISHEVSKY, A. *Soviet Literary Culture in the 1970s: The Politics of Irony* (Gainesville, FL, 1993).

VLADIMOV, G. *Faithful Ruslan* (New York, 1979).

JOURNALS

Literaturnaia Gazeta, Moscow. (Now available in English as *The Literary Gazette.*)

Moskovskie Novosti. (English language edition is *Moscow News.*)

Ogonek (*The Little Flame*). (Available only in Russian, ed. Vitali Korotich.)

20

The Collapse of the Soviet Union, 1990–1992

The abortive coup of August 19–21, 1991, led by conservatives appointed to office by President Gorbachev, undermined fatally the already shattered structure of the USSR and destroyed Gorbachev's power. During the last months of 1991 the Soviet empire simply disintegrated into its constituent republics and was finally given a decent burial on December 25. The Soviet Union was succeeded by a loose confederation similar to the European Community and known as the Commonwealth of Independent States, led by Russia, the most powerful by far of the sovereign republics. Meanwhile, the economic situation in the former union grew more and more catastrophic, and ethnic tensions worsened. President Yeltsin of Russia stood forth as the most decisive leader of an extremely difficult transition era. This sudden collapse of a vast multinational empire and superpower was virtually unprecedented in world history. These cataclysmic events proved profoundly traumatic for the peoples of the former Soviet Union and for an anxious world.

Gorbachev Declines, Yeltsin Rises, 1990–1991

By 1990 the Soviet Union—politically, economically, and in national terms—was an empire in crisis and turmoil. Gorbachev had sought unsuccessfully to lead a perilous transition from Brezhnev's authoritarian, centralized system toward pluralism and market socialism. He had moved far beyond Khrushchev in encouraging a pitiless examination of previous Soviet policies and history, inducing many to question sharply the legitimacy of the Soviet regime. Fostering a degree of political debate and change unparalleled since Lenin, Gorbachev threw the party and state into contention, then disintegration.

In the spring and summer of 1990, amid unredeemed promises of drastic economic change, political reform and national disintegration accelerated. Within the Supreme Soviet Boris Yeltsin, favoring radical reform, helped organize a left-wing opposition to Gorbachev, supported on most issues by Andrei Sakharov. Within the party the Democratic Platform group, established in January 1990, advocated ending the party's leading role, electing its officials democratically, and creating a multiparty political system. That group, with Yeltsin as a leader, urged Gorbachev to break with party conservatives led by Egor Ligachev. Ligachev, in turn, accused Gorbachev of straying from Marxism-Leninism and adopting Western social democracy. The conservatives urged restoring Soviet unity under firm, centralized party control. At the Central Committee plenum of February 1990, Yeltsin's 10-point reform program, based on the Democratic Platform group and urging a decentralized, federal party, was rejected.[1] In March the Third Congress of People's Deputies, confirming the end of the Communist Party's political monopoly under Article 6, elected Gorbachev Soviet president. This uncontested "election" triggered public protests that he should have faced a nationwide vote, which he would probably have won. A variety of parties contested spring elections to parliaments in the Christian republics; in the Baltic republics, Georgia, and Armenia the Communists met defeat. Over Gorbachev's opposition, his leftist critic Boris Yeltsin was elected chairman of the Russian parliament. As the republics and regions gained in strength, the central Soviet government steadily lost authority and credibility. That summer Gorbachev and Yeltsin agreed briefly to enact radical economic change embodied in a so-called "500-Day Plan" designed by academician Stanislav Shatalin to introduce a genuine market economy and accelerate privatization of industry and land. However, supported by conservative state and party leaders, Gorbachev soon backed way from its proposals to transfer most economic power to the individual republics.

In the second half of 1990, disturbing extreme conservative trends gathered force in the Soviet Union, foreshadowing the August 1991 coup. In June was formed a "Centrist Bloc" of hard-line elements from the Communist Party, security services, and military demanding a return to cen-

tralized authoritarian rule. Its chief spokesman was the violent Colonel Viktor Alksnis, whose conservative Soiuz faction in the USSR Congress of People's Deputies claimed support from more than one-fourth of its 2,050 deputies. In December the so-called Committee of National Salvation from this bloc pressured Gorbachev to impose a national state of presidential emergency, suspend all political parties, and remove elected officials in the more democratically oriented republics. By the end of 1990 five of these republics—the three Baltic states, Georgia, and Armenia—had declared their independence. Early in 1991 Colonel Alksnis demanded publicly that President Gorbachev be removed from office and that the KGB and Interior Ministry then impose strong centralized rule over the country, by force if necessary. These demands foreshadowed the program of the leaders of the August Coup of 1991.

In the fall of 1990, worried by these trends, Gorbachev veered sharply to the right. He removed a number of top reformers from their positions; others, including Shatalin and Shevardnadze, abandoned him. After Gorbachev replaced Vadim Bakatin, the first Soviet interior minister respectful of the rule of law, with Boris Pugo, a belligerent hard-liner, Foreign Minister Shevardnadze in a dramatic speech on December 20 declared that democrats and reformers were departing and announced his resignation:

> A dictatorship is coming. . . . No one knows what kind of dictatorship it will be and who will come or what the regime will be like. . . . I am resigning. . . . Let this be my contribution, if you like, my protest against the onset of dictatorship.[2]

Believing that hard-line, conservative groups were determined to hold the USSR together by force, Shevardnadze saw Gorbachev yielding to them. The Fourth Congress of People's Deputies, at Gorbachev's urging, elected Genadii Ianaev, a colorless apparatchik, to the new post of vice pres-

---

[1] Jack F. Matlock, Jr., *Autopsy on an Empire: The American Ambassador's Account of the Collapse of the Soviet Union* (New York, 1995), pp. 305–16.

[2] Quoted in Matlock, *Autopsy*, p. 429.

ident of the USSR. After Gorbachev spurned the 500-Day Plan, the Soviet economy underwent a precipitous decline, and all of his promarket economic advisers resigned. The new Soviet premier, Valentin Pavlov, replacing the ill Ryzhkov, introduced an ill-conceived currency reform and invented Western economic conspiracies against the USSR. By early 1991 disgruntled reformers viewed President Gorbachev as an obstacle to necessary fundamental political and economic change.

In January 1991 Gorbachev sought to block Lithuanian independence with an ultimatum and a threat to use force. KGB troops attacked a television complex in Vilnius, killing some civilians. Awakened by his staff, President Gorbachev denied responsibility, but his explanations and those of Interior Minister Pugo were unconvincing. Yeltsin flew to Vilnius and challenged Gorbachev's right to control the Soviet armed forces against the wishes of republic governments. Clearly Gorbachev's authority was shrinking rapidly. Leaving the president's team, economist Nikolai Petrakov attacked Gorbachev openly in a letter:

> A regime in its death throes has made a last-ditch stand: economic reform has been blocked, censorship of the media reinstated, brazen demagogy revived, and an open war on the republics declared. . . . The events in Lithuania [are] criminal.[3]

However, in the spring of 1991 Gorbachev, again shifting course, encouraged decentralization and genuine federalism. Under strong foreign pressure, the independence of the three Baltic republics—Latvia, Lithuania, and Estonia—was approved. In March a nationwide referendum sponsored by Gorbachev favored the preservation of the Soviet Union, but the vote in Ukraine was very close, and six republics refused to participate. Although Gorbachev interpreted this referendum as a victory, it actually revealed dwindling support

Table 20.1
Recent Russian elections, president and legislature

Candidate	Presidential Election, June 12, 1991	
	Votes	% of Total
Boris N. Yeltsin	45,552,041	57.30
Nikolai Ryzhkov	13,395,335	16.85
Vladimir Zhirinovskii	6,211,007	7.81
Iman-Geldy Tuleyev	5,417,464	6.81
Vadim Bakatin	2,719,757	3.42
Albert Makashov	11,136	0.7

for any real union.[4] Nonetheless, on April 23 Gorbachev met with Yeltsin and leaders of eight other republics at a dacha at Novo-Ogarevo near Moscow. They agreed upon terms of a new union treaty that would create a loose federation in place of the old Soviet Union. In June, after a free and vigorous election campaign, Yeltsin was elected president of the Russian Republic on the first ballot, giving him, unlike Gorbachev, an undeniable popular mandate. (See Table 20.1.) On July 20, giving notice of his authoritarian governing style, President Yeltsin ordered the Communist Party excluded from factories and the armed forces. Hard-liners assailed his decree as an illegal move toward dictatorship.

The August Coup

At dawn on August 19, 1991, the eight members of the so-called Committee for the State of Emergency[5] attempted to seize power throughout the Soviet Union and establish a conservative, authoritarian regime.

The roots of the August Coup went back to 1989, when the KGB set up tight surveillance over Yeltsin and leaders of Democratic Russia by tapping their telephone conversations. Reading and

---

[3] Quoted in Matlock, p. 467.

[4] Matlock, p. 494.
[5] The Russian initials for the Committee—GKChP—noted one Muscovite, when pronounced sounded like a cat choking on a hairball!

Members of the Committee for the State of Emergency at a press
conference in Moscow, August 19, 1991. Left to right: Alexander
Tiriakov, Vasili Starodubtsev, Boris Pugo, Gennadii Ianaev
(chairman), and Oleg Baklanov.

commenting on these secret surveillance reports,
President Gorbachev bore full responsibility for
illegal activities that would later be employed
against him. By August 4, 1991, the KGB had
prepared all the documents for the coup, including
the draft of a state of emergency in the USSR. On
August 7 some of the coup leaders began meeting
at a KGB "safe house" in Moscow. Leaving on
vacation August 5, Gorbachev dismissed warnings
from Russian colleagues and the Bush administration of an impending coup.[6]

After ordering President Gorbachev detained at
his summer home in the Crimea, the Emergency
Committee announced that he had been removed
from power temporarily because of illness and had
been replaced by Vice President Gennadii Ianaev.
The conspirators moved swiftly to control the
Russian public media but inexplicably failed to
seize or silence Russian President Yeltsin, who

promptly and unequivocally denounced the
putsch as illegal and unconstitutional.

The Emergency Committee, composed of hard-
line leaders of the Communist Party, the KGB, and
the military, warned in its proclamation to the
Soviet people: "A mortal danger has come to loom
large over our great Motherland." President Gorbachev's reform policies, it claimed, had "entered
a blind alley." Pledged the Committee: "We intend
to restore law and order straight away, end bloodshed, declare a war without mercy on the criminal
world, and eradicate shameful phenomena discrediting our society." The proclamation called on
all loyal Soviet citizens to rally around the Committee and support its efforts "to pull the country
out of its crisis." At a hastily called news conference, Acting President of the USSR Ianaev
declared quizzically:

> Mikhail Gorbachev is now on vacation. He is
> undergoing treatment in the south of our
> country. He is very tired after these many years
> and will need some time to get better, and it is

[6] John B. Dunlop, *The Rise of Russia and the Fall of the Soviet Empire* (Princeton, 1993), pp. 192–93.

our hope that as soon as he feels better, he will take up again his office.[7]

"The great irony of this coup," noted S. Tarasenko, adviser to former Foreign Minister Shevardnadze, "is the fact that those people who demoted Gorbachev are his friends." Gorbachev had appointed all of the "gang of eight" to their posts; now they sought to end his rule and reforms.

What had caused this sudden conservative backlash? The trigger was the scheduled signing on August 20 in Moscow of a new union treaty, dismantling the old Soviet order and transferring many of its hitherto awesome powers to the individual republics. That treaty posed a direct and immediate threat to the power of the institutions represented in the Emergency Committee: the Communist Party, state police agencies, economic technocrats, and some senior military leaders.

Underlying the coup were Gorbachev's efforts to balance off two irreconcilable and uncontrollable forces: a generation of new popular leaders such as Yeltsin and a group of hard-liners and custodians of stability whom Gorbachev had appointed to power. During the previous two years Gorbachev's gyrations between seeking democratic reform and tolerating hard-line crackdowns had grown more and more desperate. Each measure designed to satisfy one side had alienated the other, until he resembled a captain in a storm rushing from port to starboard to keep his ship afloat. The conservative "gang of eight" had thus acted to cancel Gorbachev's political reforms, which threatened the Soviet Empire's cohesiveness and status as a superpower, as well as their own high positions.

In his account of the coup, Gorbachev designated it an inevitable and decisive clash "between the forces of reaction and democracy." Not only was the draft Union Treaty ready for signature, but Gorbachev had called into session the Council of the Federation for August 21 to discuss accelerating economic and financial reforms. "The plotters saw that time was fast running out for them, and so they chose that moment to put their plans into action."

On August 18—the day before the coup—President Gorbachev spoke by telephone with presidents of key republics and with Vice President Ianaev. Just before 5 P.M., told that a group accompanied by a KGB security leader was demanding to see him, Gorbachev discovered that all his telephone lines had just been severed. He promptly resolved to resist any pressure or blackmail, and his family concurred. The delegation of the Emergency Committee demanded that Gorbachev sign a decree transferring power to Vice President Ianaev and the Committee. Refusing pointblank, Gorbachev warned: "You and the people who sent you are irresponsible. You will destroy yourselves, but that is your business and to hell with you. But you will also destroy the country and everything we have already done."[8] Gorbachev was receiving foreign radio reports describing growing public resistance to the coup and support from top world leaders for him and President Yeltsin. Gorbachev's courage and confidence in the Soviet people helped frustrate the coup attempt.

Meanwhile Yeltsin coordinated public opposition. Army vehicles sent into downtown Moscow to enforce the Emergency Committee's decrees were encircled by indignant crowds; soldiers mobilized to disperse them refused to obey orders to fire on the people. Before the parliament of the Russian Republic—the so-called Russian White House—Yeltsin climbed up on an armored truck and appealed for a general strike the next day to protest the coup. By nightfall on August 19 some Russian Republic troops and armored combat vehicles were guarding Yeltsin's headquarters. By then Anatolii Sobchak, mayor of Leningrad (soon to be renamed St. Petersburg), Moscow's deputy mayor, and other republic leaders were openly supporting Yeltsin's defiance of the Committee.

---

[7] *New York Times*, August 20, 1991, p. 9.

[8] Mikhail Gorbachev, *The August Coup* (New York, 1991), pp. 15–22.

President Yeltsin and followers in front of the Russian parliament building, defying the attempted August coup.

On August 20, its second day in power, the Emergency Committee ordered a curfew imposed on Moscow and sent new armored forces into the city. This move provoked clashes with angry civilians, three of whom were killed. Large crowds gathered before the Russian parliament building to protect the defiant Yeltsin. An even larger crowd filled Palace Square in Leningrad to hear Mayor Sobchak denounce the coup and the Committee, whose junta showed increasing signs of disunity and confusion. President Bush, calling Yeltsin on an open telephone line, pledged his support and expressed the view that the poorly prepared coup could be reversed.

On August 21—the third day—the coup collapsed ignominiously, and President Gorbachev returned to Moscow. A key turning point came at dawn, when army tanks under the Emergency Committee's control failed to assault the Russian parliament building guarded by only a handful of defenders. The coup fizzled as Russians rallied behind President Yeltsin and the plotters proved irresolute and divided. Long columns of tanks and

personnel carriers, some decorated with Russian flags, moved out of Moscow to cheers from jubilant Muscovites. A major casualty was communism as a political force. Even the coup leaders failed to wave the drooping flag of Marxism-Leninism. Some Muscovites gloated: "We knew the Communists couldn't do anything right!" Early that day the coup leaders fled the Kremlin; some reached the Crimea, where Gorbachev was quarantined aboard a presidential airplane. "When the plotters turned up at the dacha, I gave orders that they should be arrested," wrote Gorbachev.[9] After President Gorbachev was restored to power, the leaders of the Emergency Committee were arrested or committed suicide.

Why had a coup engineered by the USSR's most formidable military and security agencies failed so ignominiously? The August Coup amazed observers on the scene and abroad by its indecisiveness and incompetence. It was indeed strange that President Yeltsin and other leading

---

[9] Gorbachev, *The August Coup*, p. 36.

democrats had not been arrested, that satellite connections had not been cut, and that foreign correspondents continued reporting freely from Moscow. It was puzzling that KGB chief Vladimir Kriuchkov, a Committee leader who had helped suppress the Hungarian Revolution of 1956, could not even organize a successful coup in Russia. It was a rather stupid attempt, noted American political scientist Jerry Hough, by lackluster leaders who failed to plan ahead or present even a minimally attractive program to the Soviet people.[10] Promising law and order, they failed to establish it and could not even take effective control of the government.

During the 60 hours the junta exercised some control, it sought to halt the process of reform instituted by Gorbachev. Its failure owed something to the public forces unleashed during the previous six years by *glasnost* and *perestroika*. Counting on Russia's authoritarian tradition, public disillusionment with *perestroika*, and a yearning for the "good old days" of order and relative plenty under Brezhnev, the coup leaders miscalculated how the Soviet public would react. Thanks to the efforts of Gorbachev and Yeltsin, no longer was Russia a nation of docile slaves. The methods, timing, and even the language used by the August junta resembled those of Brezhnev and company in ousting Khrushchev in 1964. But unlike the Brezhnev coalition, the Emergency Committee failed to obtain support from commanders of the armed forces, or even from rank-and-file troops. Two new factors in August 1991 were the popular resistance centering in Moscow and Leningrad, and alternative centers of power—Yeltsin's national Russian government, Sobchak's city government in Leningrad, and other republic governments, all of which had greater legitimacy than did the junta. Crucial in the coup's collapse was the split within Soviet military forces; most key commanders either refused to participate or remained on the fence. Such divisions, noted Hough, were mostly generational. The military of

the future—younger leaders such as General Evgenii Shaposhnikov—defeated the army of the past headed by World War II officers such as Marshal Dmitrii Iazov and Sergei Akhromeev (a suicide after the coup failed). Believing that Gorbachev was a traitor for yielding wartime gains, they aimed to suppress democracy and restore a stable Soviet Union.[11]

The Demise of the Soviet Union, 1991–1992

In the immediate aftermath of the failed August Coup, democratic and reform elements in the Soviet Union and world opinion rejoiced. The chief hero of that hour of triumph was Russian President Boris Yeltsin, who had stood stalwartly on a tank before his Moscow headquarters as the symbol of democratic defiance of reaction. While Yeltsin's popularity and power soared, Soviet President Gorbachev returned shaken and shrunken. Initially Yeltsin insulted Gorbachev publicly and, without consulting his own legislature, outlawed the Communist Party in Russia and closed down Communist newspapers. He even threatened to seize Russian-speaking areas of Ukraine and Kazakhstan should they insist on secession. These dictatorial measures alienated some intellectuals and other supporters. Wisely, Yeltsin soon backed away from such arbitrary measures. During the months following the coup Yeltsin took over most of the powers of the former Soviet central government.

President Gorbachev, his authority crumbling, continued to press stubbornly for formation of a federal union, arguing that the republics' outright secession and full independence would lead to catastrophe and even civil war. In September the USSR Congress of People's Deputies granted theoretical power to the republics while vesting considerable authority in a new Soviet State Council chaired by Gorbachev and composed of leaders of the republics. However, that body soon

---

[10] Jerry Hough, "Assessing the Coup," *Current History,* vol. 90 (October 1991).

[11] Hough, "Assessing the Coup."

proved largely impotent because the republics simply ignored its decisions.

The August Coup accelerated the USSR's disintegration into its national components. By discrediting the central agencies—the party, state bureaucracy, and KGB—and by splitting the army, which had previously held the USSR together, the coup transferred most de facto authority to the republics. It remained uncertain whether the vast Russian Republic, containing more than 100 distinct nationalities, would remain united. The mortal blow to the Soviet Union—and to Gorbachev's hopes of preserving the center—was Ukraine's overwhelming vote in the referendum of December 1, 1991, in favor of full independence. Elected as Ukraine's president was Leonid M. Kravchuk, long-time Soviet apparatchik, who underwent a sudden conversion to Ukrainian nationalism only after the August Coup collapsed.

The failed coup dealt a devastating blow to the Communist Party, especially in Russia, where President Yeltsin proclaimed it dissolved and ordered its property seized. Communist elites in some other republics sought to preserve their power by swift proclamations of independence. The KGB, emasculated as an organization, lost its awesome power over the police. With the collapsing Soviet government no longer able to finance them, most of the swollen central ministries were abolished or greatly reduced in personnel. As most army recruits refused to serve outside of their own republics, the new defense chief, General Evgenii Shaposhnikov, advocated a sharply reduced, professional military force. Even before its independence referendum, Ukraine considered constructing its own armed forces. A crucial issue was control of some 27,000 nuclear warheads located in late 1991 in four Soviet republics.

After the coup a question that perplexed Soviet and foreign leaders was whether in the future there would be a single Soviet foreign policy. At first President Gorbachev and foreign supporters such as President Bush insisted that the center would continue to conduct the international business of the Soviet Union. Immediately after the coup Foreign Minister Alexander Bessmertnykh,

implicated in it, was removed by President Gorbachev and replaced by Boris Pankin, the ambassador to Czechoslovakia. When it became evident that Pankin had little international prestige, he was replaced in November by former Soviet Foreign Minister Eduard Shevardnadze, the architect of Gorbachev's "new thinking" in foreign affairs. However, only a month later President Yeltsin abruptly abolished the Soviet foreign ministry and claimed the USSR's permanent seat on the United Nations Security Council for Russia.

The failed coup accelerated the sharp diminution of Soviet power and international influence evident since the collapse in 1989 of eastern European Communist regimes. The Warsaw Treaty organization dissolved and most Soviet troops withdrew from eastern Europe, spurred by generous financial aid from Germany. With the end of the formidable Soviet Bloc in eastern Europe, warmer relations were established between a fading Soviet Union and western European countries, especially Germany. The removal of Soviet power and influence from eastern Europe marked a startling reshuffling of power. The collapse of the coup undermined most remaining Communist regimes worldwide. Cuba's Fidel Castro, still defiantly Communist but isolated and vulnerable, saw Soviet aid to his battered economy disappear. North Korea's aging hard-line dictator, Kim Il-sung, shocked by Gorbachev's overtures to prosperous South Korea, moved toward accommodation with the south. Communist Vietnam, deprived of Soviet aid, turned toward the United States.

After central Soviet ministries were transferred to the control of Yeltsin's Russian government, the formal dissolution of the Soviet Union approached. In the days before his resignation President Gorbachev warned of the dangers ahead if the union were ended, foreseeing ethnic strife, economic chaos, and the disintegration of Russia. Sending a message to the December 21 meeting of republic leaders in Alma-Ata, Kazakhstan, Gorbachev argued for common citizenship and a centralized command to control nuclear weapons. He urged that the USSR Supreme Soviet be convened to dissolve the Soviet Union formally, adding:

> We should begin a new era in the history of the country with dignity and in conformity with standards of legitimacy. . . . We have both the prerequisites and the experience needed to act in the framework of democratic rules.

Earlier Yeltsin had agreed that the Soviet Union should end officially at midnight on December 31, 1991, but then he pressed for an earlier transfer of power. On December 25 Gorbachev delivered his resignation speech on television, then instructed that the nuclear weapons codes be transmitted to General Shaposhnikov representing President Yeltsin.[12] On Christmas Day the Soviet flag, which had flown over the Kremlin for 74 years, was lowered ceremoniously for the last time. The Soviet Union was no more.

The Commonwealth of Independent States

On December 8, 1991, the presidents of the republics of Russia, Ukraine, and Belarus (formerly Byelorussia), meeting in the latter's capital, Minsk, declared that the Soviet Union no longer existed and announced formation of a Commonwealth of Independent States (*Sodruzhestvo Nezavisimykh Gosudarstv*). The leaders of the three Slavic republics, linked historically for centuries, urged establishment of "coordinating bodies" for foreign affairs, defense, and the economy, with their seat in Minsk (in order to meet Ukrainian fears that Russia might dominate any new state). A common "economic space" was to be formed with the ruble as its common currency, and the Commonwealth was to remain open to all former Soviet republics and outside countries "sharing the aims and principles of this agreement." They pledged to fulfill Soviet international obligations and to ensure unified control over Soviet nuclear weapons. The three presidents agreed to carry out "coordinated

radical economic reforms" and create market economies. Soviet President Gorbachev denounced this agreement as "illegal and dangerous," but he was powerless to prevent it.

Two weeks later, at the Alma-Ata meeting, the Commonwealth of Independent States (CIS) was reformed to include central Asian republics, and by the end of December all former Soviet republics had joined it except the three Baltic republics and Georgia, then torn by a violent power struggle between President Zviad Gamsakhurdia and a rebel opposition movement that accused him of dictatorship. On December 25, 1991, President Gorbachev resigned as Soviet chief of state, the Soviet seat at the United Nations was assumed by Russia, and foreign governments recognized the former Soviet republics as independent countries.

Meeting in Minsk on December 30, 1991, the republic leaders agreed to establish governing councils of presidents and prime ministers of their respective states as the chief coordinating bodies of the new CIS. However, they failed to draw up either a political charter for the CIS or a cohesive plan for economic reform, or to establish unified armed forces. Individual republics could form their own armies, declared Yeltsin, although he hoped they would opt for a unified command. Marshal Evgenii Shaposhnikov of Russia would continue indefinitely as interim commander of the CIS's armed forces and its nuclear weapons.

In mid-1992 the former Soviet Empire appeared to be suspended in a vacuum containing the vague and disputatious CIS. Russia was emerging as successor to the old USSR in some ways, as Russian President Yeltsin had supplanted former Soviet President Gorbachev. Russia loomed so much larger territorially, politically, and economically than other republics that it naturally assumed a role of leadership. Thus in January 1992, when Russia introduced its "price liberalization," the other republics partially and hesitantly followed suit. Under the Russian reform consumer prices were to be set by manufacturers, regional authorities, and retailers, not by centralized state

---

[12] Matlock, pp. 645–47.

economic agencies as before. The Russian government maintained price ceilings on basic foods and fuels, allowing them to rise moderately. Most other price controls were lifted, many small businesses were privatized, and the budget deficit was reduced, but privatization of farm property lagged. Increasing numbers of industrial workers were laid off, military plants closed, and exports, imports, and industrial output plummeted, leaving most Russians near or below the poverty level. Other republics continued to follow suit reluctantly.

To alleviate the former Soviet Union's mounting financial crisis, the Group of Seven advanced industrial nations (United States, Germany, Japan, Canada, France, Great Britain, and Italy) on April 1, 1992, announced a $24 billion aid package (mostly credits) for Russia over a three-year period, including $6 billion to stabilize the ruble. Two weeks later an official of the International Monetary Fund (IMF) predicted that other CIS countries would require an additional $20 billion to ensure continued progress toward market economies. "The magnitude of the problem facing the 15 republics is unprecedented," stated an IMF spokesperson. "They go far beyond what is generally understood by the concept of economic transformation. These peoples are creating new nations from scratch and in a very brief period."[13] Soon thereafter Russia and other CIS members were invited to join the IMF. This invitation constituted a major step toward their eventual economic integration with the West, a process begun five years earlier by Gorbachev. Declared President Bush: "The stakes are as high for us now as any that we have faced in this century. . . . Future generations of Americans will thank us for having had the foresight and conviction to stand up for democracy and work for peace."[14]

Meanwhile the former Soviet Army, with some 3.5 million men the largest armed force in the world, survived in a dead empire, "orphaned,

bankrupt, humiliated, demoralized, often for sale."[15] Morale among officers and men plummeted and desertions and draft-dodging were rife, but preserving this army seemed preferable to massive military unemployment. Russian submarines, aircraft, and weapons were being sold to foreign countries to raise cash. Housing was lacking for hundreds of thousands of former Soviet troops withdrawn from Germany and eastern Europe. President Yeltsin of Russia advocated unified Commonwealth armed forces, but President Kravchuk of Ukraine demanded that the 700,000 former Soviet soldiers on its territory swear loyalty to Ukraine. Thousands of long-range nuclear weapons remained in Russia, Ukraine, Kazakhstan, and Belarus.

Controversy between Russia and Ukraine, the two most populous republics, over control of the Black Sea Fleet and possession of Crimea threatened to fragment the infant CIS. On behalf of the Commonwealth's Unified Command, President Yeltsin insisted that the Black Sea Fleet, the smallest of four former Soviet naval fleets, constituted an integral part of the CIS's strategic forces. Some Russian nationalists demanded the retrocession to Russia of Crimea, whose chief city, Sevastopol, was Black Sea Fleet headquarters. Crimea faced a referendum on independence from Ukraine, to which Khrushchev had arbitrarily transferred it from Russia in 1954. After contending over Crimea and the fleet, the presidents of Russia and Ukraine in April 1992 agreed to work out a plan to divide the fleet. "If we are wise enough and calm enough," stated President Kravchuk, "we can solve the [fleet] question in the interest of our states and our people."[16]

After the USSR dissolved, rising national feelings and ethnic tensions threatened also to tear apart the Russian Federation, which contained at least 39 different nationalities. However, President

[13] Steven Greenhouse, "$44 Billion Needed," *New York Times*, April 16, 1992.
[14] Andrew Rosenthal, "Betting on Boris," *New York Times*, April 5, 1992, sec. 4, p. 1.

[15] Serge Schmemann, "The Red Army Fights a Rearguard Action Against History," *New York Times*, March 29, 1992.
[16] Celestine Bohlen, "Black Sea Fleet Dispute Cools," *New York Times*, April 10, 1992.

Yeltsin scored a major success on March 31, when 18 of 20 main subdivisions of the Federation signed a federal treaty creating a new post-Soviet Russian state. While binding them together in a single Russian Federation (or Russia), the treaty accorded local units considerable political and economic autonomy. Although largely Muslim and oil-rich Chechen-Ingushetia (bordering on Georgia) and Tatarstan refused to sign it, the federal treaty nonetheless outlined a way of preserving the Russian Federation intact.

Problem 11

Why Did the Soviet Union Collapse?

How could the apparently powerful and formidable Soviet empire, which had dominated half of Europe since World War II while holding its people in impotent obedience, suddenly disintegrate and collapse in 1991? There has been considerable debate both in the former Soviet empire and in the West since then as to the causes of this sudden death that few anticipated. Did the USSR fall of its own weight from accumulated political, social, and economic imbalances and errors, or was General Secretary Gorbachev responsible by his policies of *glasnost* and *perestroika?* Was this last great world empire bankrupted by excessive military spending under Brezhnev? Were Brezhnev's heavy outlays designed to keep himself in power, or were they a response to major American rearmament by President Reagan? Again is posed the issue: Has Russia's, and the USSR's, fate been determined chiefly by internal or external factors? Should the West—notably the United States—rejoice and take credit for the demise of Soviet communism, its enemy in the Cold War? Was the allegedly false ideology of Marxism-Leninism, based on lies and deception, to blame for the collapse once the Soviet people, partly as a result of foreign radio broadcasts, discovered the truth? Did the West and the United States foster the collapse or seek to prevent it?

Sigmund Krancberg: A Soviet Postmortem

The American scholar, Sigmund Krancberg argues that the "grand failure" of the Soviet system was rooted in the failure of Marxist-Leninist ideology to provide a viable basis for the Soviet regime and its actions.

The degeneration of the Bolshevik dictatorship into "a power that is not limited by any laws, not bound by any rules, and is based directly on force" compromised and impoverished the Communist ideas and plans for social development as an ordered and continuous process of social growth. In the long run, with the lack of legal safeguards against the abuse of power, the sordid reality of Soviet social and political life contributed to the fragility and collapse of the Soviet system—a system that originated "in a utopia that led to its practical failure." Bolshevism—in a massive attempt to substitute ideology for reality—lost in the course of its history the political, moral, and intellectual standing in the countless inhuman excesses of War Communism and forced collectivization, in the extensive purges and Moscow trials, in the Hitler-Stalin pact, and in the autocratic, cruel, and oppressive treatment of the Soviet people after the Second World War. And all these atrocities were committed in the name of a Marxist-Leninist ideology that considered violence as the midwife of history. . . .

. . . The growing recognition of the terrible inefficiencies of the Soviet system, with its social decay and the faltering command economy, was reflected in Gorbachev's catchword of "*perestroika*". . . . Despite its novelty and great significance, *perestroika* failed to alleviate the deepening economic crisis exacerbated by the tradition of rigid planning, poor growth in productivity, and lagging technological performance.[17]

George Urban: American Democracy Aided Communism's Collapse

A former director of Radio Free Europe, George Urban, while agreeing that mistakes and inadequacies of the Soviet system itself were the primary factor in its demise, affirms that the West, and especially the United States, contributed to that result. Urban stresses particularly the impact of broadcasts by Radio Free Europe and Radio Liberty.

In what sense can it be said that we in the West made a contribution to the fall of the Soviet system? We did so, as I see it, in at least three different ways. First, American rearmament under President Reagan, and especially the SDI (Strategic Defense Initiative) project, conjured up for an already declining Soviet economy the prospect of so heavy an extra burden that the Soviet leadership was propelled to surrender Moscow's outposts in the colonial empire as well as its glacis in Central and Eastern Europe. . . . President Reagan had caused the USSR to spend itself into near-bankruptcy; and when bankruptcy began to loom, the USSR sent itself into liquidation.

The second way in which we hastened the demise of the Soviet system has been by example: the mere existence of relatively rich and relatively free capitalist countries, side by side with the Soviet Union and its satellites, carried its own message. The spirit of rebellion grew from nothing more dramatic than geographic proximity. . . . What could be bought in Germany, spoken in France, and printed in Holland could not be bought, spoken or printed in the USSR or Poland. With *glasnost,* the abolition of jamming, growing economic links, cultural cross-fertilization and international

travel, it proved no longer possible to isolate the Soviet system from the rest of the real world. Something had to give—and it did. We can now see why Stalin and the Stalinists were, from their point of view, right to segregate their empire from the rest of humanity. . . .

The third contribution to the fall of the Soviet system has been a deliberate policy of identification with the nations under Communist tutelage. Back in the early 1950s, farsighted Americans recognized the need to equip Western—especially U.S.—foreign policy with a psychological arm to enable us to talk to the peoples of the extended Soviet empire. Radio Free Europe and Radio Liberty . . . turned out to be . . . one of the most successful political investments the U.S. has ever made, for much of World War III was fought and won in terms of ideas and culture.[18]

John P. Maynard: Soviet Communism Collapsed on Its Own

Maynard, a pseudonym for a staff member of the United States Congress, asserts that the West deserves no credit for the USSR's collapse—that, in fact, the United States helped the Soviet Communist Party retain power right to the end by providing economic and technical assistance. Instead the Soviet system collapsed because of the basic flaws of socialism.

It is hard to see how anyone can seriously claim "We won," when we, the West, were primarily responsible for keeping the Soviet Union alive for over seventy years. We did not win. They lost—notwithstanding our efforts to keep them alive!

. . . Franklin Roosevelt came to the aid of the Soviet tyrants many times beginning in 1933 when he extended diplomatic recognition to the Stalinist regime and continuing into World War II . . . in a multitude of ways which we are only now coming to hear about. Most disgraceful was Yalta, when against Churchill's objections, Roosevelt agreed to hand over the entire eastern half of Europe to brutal Marxist depredation under Stalin.

---

[17] Sigmund Krancberg, *A Soviet Postmortem: Philosophical Roots of the "Grand Failure"* (Lanham, MD, 1994), pp. 140–43.

[18] William Barbour and Carol Wekesser, eds., *The Breakup of the Soviet Union: Opposing Viewpoints* (San Diego, 1994), pp. 19–20.

Problem 11 continued

Notwithstanding the Cold War and the U.S. containment policy, every U.S. President since Roosevelt has in some way provided economic and technical assistance which has in effect served to keep communism alive. Most recently, when the "evil empire" began to break up, official U.S. policy was to preserve the Soviet empire intact—denying freedom and self-determination to the various peoples that had been forcibly incorporated into it. George Bush did his best to keep Gorbachev in power. . . .

. . . U.S. financial and technical assistance was undoubtedly used to build up the Soviet military machine. . . . The Soviet economy was aided consciously or unconsciously, by U.S. Presidents and Western industrialists and merchants like Armand Hammer. . . . Ford Motors even constructed and financed the factory that built the large military trucks used by the Soviets in their invasion of Afghanistan. Now our leaders have the gall, the audacity, to say "We won." . . . Socialism collapsed in the USSR under its own weight *despite* the help it constantly received from the West. . . . The collapse of the Soviet Union is a living example of the effects of socialism. . . . The inefficiency, bureaucratic incompetence, inherent nepotism, and the deadening absence of human freedom which kills the soul, were the causes of its collapse.[19]

Michael Mandelbaum: Gorbachev's Reforms Doomed the USSR

A professor of political science at Johns Hopkins University in Baltimore, Mandelbaum argues that it was the well-intentioned but poorly conceived political reforms of a humane Soviet leader, Mikhail Gorbachev, that ultimately destroyed the Soviet system that he had attempted to reform and make freer. However, he praises Gorbachev's humanity and refusal to use violent means to preserve the Soviet empire.

---

[19] John P. Maynard, "What's Sad about the Soviet Collapse," *Conservative Review,* April 1992.

How did it happen that a mighty imperial state, troubled but stable only a few years before, had come to the brink of collapse in 1991? Who and what was responsible? The chief architect of the Soviet collapse was Mikhail Gorbachev himself. During the August 1991 coup, as a prisoner of the junta in his Crimean villa, he was the object of a struggle between the partisans of the old order and the champions of liberal values. But it was Gorbachev who had in the period between his coming to power in 1985 and the fateful days of August 1991, created the conditions that had touched off this struggle.

The Soviet leader had created them unintentionally. His aim had been to strengthen the political and economic system that he inherited, to strip away their Stalinist accretions and make the Soviet Union a modern dynamic state. Instead he had fatally weakened it. Intending to reform Soviet communism he had, rather, destroyed it. The three major policies that he had launched to fashion a more efficient and humane form of socialism—glasnost, democratization, and perestroika—had in the end subverted, discredited, and all but done away with the network of political and economic institutions that his Communist Party had constructed in Russia and surrounding countries since 1917. . . .

Glasnost enabled the people of the Soviet Union to lay claim to the public sphere after seven decades of exile from it. Through democratization they had the opportunity for the first time, to act collectively in that sphere. . . . The experiment in democracy that he launched did not demonstrate, as Gorbachev had hoped, that he enjoyed popular support. . . . Elections discredited the official dictum that the Communist Party had earned public gratitude and support for the "noble farsighted" leadership it had provided since 1917. . . . Democratization also created the opportunity for the beginning of an alternative to the communist political elite to emerge. In Russia its main orientation was anticommunism and Boris Yeltsin became its leading figure. . . .

Glasnost and democratization were for Gorbachev, means to an end. That end was the improvement of Soviet economic performance. Economic reform was the central feature of his program . . . to lift the country out of the economic stagnation into which it had lapsed at the end of

Problem 11 continued

the Brezhnev era. . . . Gorbachev's most enduring and destructive legacy . . . [was] a severe fiscal imbalance. The center's obligations expanded as it poured more and more money into investment and tried to buy public support with generous wage increases. At the same time its income plummeted, as republican governments and enterprises . . . refused to send revenues to Moscow.[20]

John L. H. Keep:
An Element of Chance
Was Involved

John Keep, a leading British scholar, attributes the collapse of the USSR largely to social change over a period of decades and declining economic growth rates. However, he does not view the fall of the Soviet system as inevitable until 1989 and notes elements of chance as well.

In the USSR the accession to power of Mikhail Sergeevich Gorbachev in March 1985 unleashed a chain reaction. Within less than seven years it led to the extinction of the world's number two superpower. Historians are naturally tempted to see such an astonishing development as foreordained, and to try to explain it by the working out of long-term processes. Yet clearly an element of chance was involved as well. . . .

Perhaps the end of Soviet Communism, like its beginnings, can best be explained by weighing up probabilities at successive historical moments. In the earlier case the road led to an increasingly violent catastrophe as various alternative courses of development were successively ruled out. . . . During the Brezhnev era a new generation of Soviet citizens came to the fore who could not be satisfied by the simple certainties of the official ideology. Better educated than their parents or grandparents, and accustomed to a modest level of prosperity, the members of this urban elite sought greater individual autonomy and material well-being. These yearnings evoked a response among writers and

[20] Michael Mandelbaum, "Coup de Grace: The End of the Soviet Union," *Foreign Affairs*, Autumn/Winter 1991–1992.

other intellectuals whose views became widely known, despite the censorship. In this way an informal "second culture" took shape that was potentially as subversive of collectivist values as the "second economy" was of the state-socialist order. By the mid-1980s there were many pointers to impending crisis: falling growth rates, major ecological disasters, and the army's inability to defeat the Afghan *mujaheddin*—to mention only three of the most obvious.

All this made systemic change likely, but not inevitable. Other options were still open. The most plausible scenario was that by embarking on a program of reform the Party would restore its shaken credibility and maintain its rule, perhaps in slightly amended form. This required both a peaceful international environment and an unusual degree of skill on the part of the reformist leaders. They needed to know just where they were heading and to take the people into their confidence. In the event Gorbachev did permit a fair measure of freedom of expression (*glasnost*), but failed to answer clearly the question what *perestroika* (restructuring) really involved or how it was to be achieved. . . . He was basically a pragmatist, but could not shake off a residual Marxist-Leninist dogmatism. . . . He tried to be both Luther and the Pope.

. . . In the face of emerging conservative and radical lobbies he had to take a "centrist" line, advancing or retreating as the constellation of power changed. But each successive tactical shift reduced his area of manoeuvre and added to the ranks of the disaffected. They seized on the new opportunities to make their views known. The greater the amount of liberty conceded, the more difficult it became to check its unwelcome consequences without resorting to coercive methods that had supposedly been abandoned. From 1989 onwards the regime began to lose control.

• • •

Contrary to all earlier expectations, it was Ukraine . . . that would deal the final knife-thrust to the tottering USSR. From mid-1990 onwards there was a fatal weakness at the heart of the empire symbolized by the Yeltsin-Gorbachev dyarchy. The conservative *coup* of August 1991 made it infinitely more difficult to keep the Union together. It was less the cause of the empire's disintegration than a symptom of the cancer that was eating it away. This had its origin in the inability of Communism . . . to

Problem 11 continued

contain centrifugal pressures that had been building up for decades.[21]

Conclusion

Controversy persists whether the chief causes of the sudden collapse of the Soviet Union in 1991 derived from fundamental flaws in a system relying upon a decayed and false ideology, an unfree political setup, and an outdated command economy that could no longer satisfy people's needs, or from pressure applied by the West, notably the United States of President Reagan. The allure of freedom prevalent in the West appears to have contributed to the demise of a system that had long concealed its basic shortcomings from its citizens and from the outside world. The USSR's huge natural resources may have helped prolong its survival until 1991. Was the result inevitable or speeded by a well-meaning President Gorbachev? ■

[21] John L. H. Keep, *Last of the Empires: A History of the Soviet Union 1945–1991* (Oxford and New York, 1995), pp. 331-32, 383. Reprinted by permission of Oxford University Press.

InfoTrac® College Edition Search Terms

Enter the search term *Soviet Union* in the Subject Guide, and then go to subdivision *politics and government*.
Enter the search term *Gorbachev* in Keywords.
Enter the search term *Yeltsin* in the Subject Guide..
Enter the search term *Commonwealth Independent States* in the Subject Guide.

Suggested Additional Reading

ALLISON, G., and G. YAVLINSKY. *Window of Opportunity: The Grand Bargain for Democracy in the Soviet Union* (New York, 1991).

ANDERSON, J. *Religion, State and Politics in the Soviet Union and Successor States* (Cambridge, 1994).

ARNOLD, A. *The Fateful Pebble: Afghanistan's Role in the Fall of the Soviet Empire* (Novato, CA, 1993).

"The August Coup," *New Left Review*, no. 189 (September–October 1991).

BARBOUR, W., and C. WEKNESSER, eds. *The Breakup of the Soviet Union: Opposing Viewpoints* (San Diego, 1994).

BARYSKI, R. V. *The Soldier in Russian Politics: Duty, Dictatorship, and Democracy under Gorbachev and Yeltsin* (New Brunswick, NJ, 1998).

BERMEO, N., ed. *Liberalization and Democratization: Change in the Soviet Union and Eastern Europe* (Baltimore and London, 1992).

BUTTINO, M., ed. *In a Collapsing Empire: Ethnic Conflicts and Nationalism in the Soviet Union* (Milan, 1993).

CASTELLS, M., with E. KISELYOVA. *The Collapse of Soviet Communism: A View from the Information Society* (Berkeley, CA, 1995).

DANIELS, R. *Russia's Transformation: Snapshots of a Crumbling System* (Lanham, MD, 1998).

DUNLOP, J. B. *The Rise of Russia and the Fall of the Soviet Empire* (Princeton, 1993).

D'ENCAUSSE, H. C. *The End of the Soviet Empire: The Triumph of the Nations*, trans. Franklin Philip (New York, 1993).

FESHBACH, M. *Ecological Disaster: Cleaning Up the Hidden Legacy of the Soviet Regime* (New York, 1995).

FOWLES, B. *The Disintegration of the Soviet Union: A Study in the Rise and Triumph of Nationalism* (New York, 1997).

GAIDAR, Y. *Days of Defeat and Victory*, trans. Jane A. Miller (Seattle, 1996).

GILL, G. *The Collapse of a Single Party System: The Disintegration of the Communist Party of the Soviet Union* (Cambridge, 1994).

GORBACHEV, M. *The August Coup: The Truth and the Lessons* (New York, 1991).

GRAHAM, L. R. *The Ghost of the Executed Engineer: Technology and the Fall of the Soviet Union* (Cambridge, MA, 1996).

GWERTZMAN, B., and M. KAUFMAN, eds. *The Collapse of Communism: By the Correspondents of the New York Times,* rev. ed. (New York, 1991).

HEWETT, E. A., and C. G. GADDY. *Open for Business: Russia's Return to the Global Economy* (Washington, 1992).

HOLLANDER, P. *Political Will and Personal Belief: The Decline and Fall of Soviet Communism* (New Haven, CT, 2000).

HOLMES, L. *The End of Communist Power: Anti-Corruption Campaigns and Legitimation Crisis* (New York and Oxford, 1993).

HOUGH, J. F. *Democratization and Revolution in the USSR, 1985–1991* (Washington, DC, 1997).

KOTZ, D. M. with F. WEIR. *Revolution from Above: The Demise of the Soviet System* (New York, 1997).

KRANCBERG, S. *A Soviet Postmortem: Philosophical Roots of the "Grand Failure"* (Lanham, MD, 1994).

KRASNOV, V. *Russia Beyond Communism: A Chronicle of National Rebirth* (Boulder, CO, 1991).

LAPIDUS, G., et al., eds. *From Union to Commonwealth: Nationalism and Separatism in the Soviet Republics* (Cambridge, 1992).

LAUBE, E., ed. *Chronicle of the Soviet Coup, 1990–1992: A Reader in Soviet Politics* (Dubuque, IA, 1992).

LIEVEN, A. *The Baltic Revolution: Estonia, Latvia, Lithuania and the Path to Independence* (New Haven, CT, 1993).

LOORY, S. H., and A. IMSE. *Seven Days That Shook the World: The Collapse of Soviet Communism* (Atlanta, 1991).

MATLOCK, J. F., JR. *Autopsy on an Empire. The American Ambassador's Account of the Collapse of the Soviet Union* (New York, 1995).

MCDANIEL, T. *The Agony of the Russian Idea* (Princeton, NJ, 1996).

MILLAR, J., and S. WOLCHIK, eds. *The Social Legacy of Communism* (Cambridge, 1994).

MORRISON, J. *Boris Yeltsin: From Bolshevik to Democrat* (New York, 1991).

"Moscow, August 1991: The Coup de Grace," *Problems of Communism,* 39 (November–December 1991), pp. 1–62. (Articles on the August Coup.)

ODOM, W. E. *The Collapse of the Soviet Military* (New Haven, CT, 1998).

One Nation Becomes Many: The ACCESS Guide to the Former Soviet Union (Washington, 1992).

PEI, M. *From Reform to Revolution: The Demise of Communism in China and the Soviet Union* (Cambridge, MA, 1994).

REMNICK, D. *Lenin's Tomb: The Last Days of the Soviet Empire* (New York 1993).

REZEN, M., ed. *Nationalism and the Breakup of an Empire: Russia and Its Periphery.* (Westport, CT, 1992).

ROEDER, P. G. *Red Sunset: The Failure of Soviet Politics* (Princeton, 1993).

SMART, C. *The Imagery of Soviet Foreign Policy and the Collapse of the Russian Empire* (Westport, CT, 1995).

SOLCHANYK, R. *Ukraine: From Chernobyl to Sovereignty* (New York, 1992).

SOLOVIEV, V. *Boris Yeltsin: A Political Biography* (New York, 1992).

STENT, A. E. *Russia and Germany Reborn: Unification, the Soviet Collapse, and the New Europe* (Princeton, NJ, 1999).

STOKES, G. *The Walls Come Tumbling Down: The Collapse of Communism in Eastern Europe* (New York and Oxford, 1993).

STRAYER, R. W. *Why Did the Soviet Union Collapse? Understanding Historical Change* (Armonk, NY, 1998).

WALICKI, A. *Marxism and the Leap to the Kingdom of Freedom: The Rise and Fall of the Communist Utopia* (Stanford, CA, 1995).

WALLER, M. *The End of the Communist Power Monopoly* (New York and Manchester, 1994).

WHITE, S., et al., eds. *Development in Soviet and Post-Soviet Politics,* 2d ed. (Durham, NC, 1992).

YELTSIN, B. N. *Against the Grain: An Autobiography,* trans. Michael Glenny (New York, 1990).

21

The Yeltsin Years,
1991–1999

At the end of 1991 most citizens of the former USSR appeared to agree that the Soviet legacy was overwhelmingly negative. The Soviet system, established in November 1917, had proven a colossal failure in virtually every aspect, inducing some to repudiate the November Revolution and its leader, V. I. Lenin, as historical aberrations.

The Legacy of Soviet Communism

Nowhere was Soviet communism's failure more evident than in economics and finance. The centralized economic system outlined by Lenin but created largely by Stalin during the First Five Year Plan, churned out vast amounts of steel, coal, and oil, which made the USSR a leading military power from World War II until 1990, but it was an economy of shortages that provided little for most Soviet consumers. After 1975 most Soviet citizens saw their living standards and buying power fall further and further behind not just the United States and Japan but virtually every European and many Asian countries. The massive heavy industries established in the 1930s became increasingly obsolete under Brezhnev and his successors and caused unprecedented environmental pollution. In agriculture the collective and state farm system, created forcibly under Stalin, had killed or exiled millions of the best Soviet farmers as alleged exploiters (kulaks), enslaving the rest under a 20th-century version of serfdom. Condemning millions to starvation by famine, Stalin disrupted Russian and Ukrainian agriculture, which before 1914 had exported millions of tons of grain. Agriculture became the perpetually backward and inefficient stepchild of Soviet communism, compelling Khrushchev and his successors to import massive amounts of grain from the capitalist West.

During the last years of tsarism Russian workers had enjoyed improving working conditions, rising real wages, and increasing rights to organize and strike. Under the so-called proletarian Soviet dictatorship of Lenin and Stalin they soon lost all these gains and any right to choose their jobs or determine their pay. Low real wages and a cradle-to-grave system of state-provided benefits undermined the Soviet worker's desire to work hard and well. This was summed up in the post-Stalinist quip, "We pretend to work, and they pretend to pay us." The worker's plight was exacerbated by burgeoning corruption, massive stealing from the state, and rampant cynicism. Workers and farmers alike were deprived of any real incentive to strive for quality, and Soviet products were spurned in world markets.

In the 1890s, under Count Witte, Russian state finances were placed on the gold standard and the ruble became fully convertible. Russia prior to World War I enjoyed exemplary credit, which made possible large-scale foreign borrowing to finance advancing industrialization. Under the Soviet regime this progress was totally negated and reversed. By 1991 the USSR had a massive external debt that it could not service and a huge budget deficit. Its currency, the ruble (or better: rubble!), had become virtually worthless inside and outside the country; hyperinflation loomed. The expiring Soviet Union, despite possessing huge quantities of salable raw materials, depended on foreign charity to avert bankruptcy.

Politically, imperial Russia in 1914 was moving, if uncertainly, toward constitutional monarchy, public debate, and the rule of law. It was an empire in which individual minority groups, except for Jews and Poles, enjoyed broader political and cultural rights than in previous centuries. Russia appeared to be following the positive political course taken earlier by western Europe; its links with Europe were growing ever stronger. Then the Soviet regime of Lenin and Stalin imposed a brutal despotism on the peoples of the empire, reintegrating most of them forcibly into a new Soviet empire. The fake federalism embodied in the Stalin Constitution of 1936 left them under Russian rule without real autonomy or decision-making power. Between 1936 and 1953 millions of Russians, but especially non-Russians, were exiled and executed. Entire peoples were uprooted from ancestral homelands and exiled forcibly to Siberia and Central Asia, notably Crimean Tatars, Volga Germans, Chechens, and Baltic peoples. Stalin's minions murdered at least 25 million people of various nationalities, partly to assuage a paranoid dictator.

Soviet foreign policy, after positive beginnings under foreign commissars Chicherin and Litvinov, ended disastrously. Stalin, after helping Hitler achieve power, concluded the Nazi-Soviet Pact in order to dominate eastern Europe; it triggered World War II. Afterward the Stalin regime provoked a lengthy and incredibly costly Cold War with the West. It subjugated eastern Europe, wiping out those who resisted, especially in Poland, imposing by force Soviet-style regimes on its helpless peoples. Thrice the Soviet army intervened with massive force—in East Germany, Hungary, and Czechoslovakia—to suppress popular revolts and perpetuate regimes that lacked local roots. The Cold War saddled the Soviet and Western peoples with huge burdens in order to maintain bloated military forces and huge arsenals of weapons of mass destruction. Soviet foreign policy was based on monstrous lies mouthed by thousands of obedient diplomats or secret police operatives masquerading as diplomats.

Late imperial Russia had seen an unprecedented flowering of creativity in literature, music, and art and had made great contributions to world culture. Russia was becoming increasingly integrated into European civilization. Lenin's Soviet regime severed these promising links, as hundreds of Russian writers, composers, and artists chose exile to escape its tyranny. Many others were later murdered in Stalin's purges. Those who remained in the Soviet Union were subjected to a stifling and pervasive system of state controls euphemistically called "socialist realism," which glorified mediocrity and persecuted originality and creativity. The result, prior to Gorbachev's *glasnost,* was the devastation of the brilliant and creative Russian cultural tradition.

The entire perverted Soviet system rested on the ideology of Marxism-Leninism, based in the USSR on an interlocking network of lies and deceptions. The Soviet people in 1917 had been promised abundance, peace, and freedom under socialism but instead received hardships, shortages, enslavement, and war. In place of a true socialist system based on the equality promised by Marx and Lenin emerged a new class of parasitic apparatchiks and partocrats with special stores and clinics, luxurious dachas, and a myriad of special privileges. That new class exploited the labor of the Soviet masses for its own selfish benefit. Marxist ideology, thoroughly perverted and robbed of all meaning under Stalin, became a mask to conceal massive inequality and injustice. Efforts to liberalize and humanize this corrupt Soviet system under Khrushchev and Gorbachev led instead to its deserved and mostly unlamented destruction in 1991. As had been said of the Roman Empire, the amazing thing was not that it collapsed, but that it persisted so long.

Environmental Problems: A Devastated Land

Among the staggering problems confronting the countries of the former USSR, none is more daunting than their devastated environment. Like other industrialized nations, the Soviet Union ignored environmental consequences as it exploited abundant natural resources to create a massive industrial base. For more than 70 years the USSR assaulted the environment relentlessly and undermined the population's health. The drive to fulfill centrally determined economic plans preempted every other concern. The legacy of that relentless drive has been unprecedented environmental destruction.

However, from the start there were those in Soviet Russia who were aware of the dangers of wantonly disregarding nature. Some Soviet environmentalists were well ahead of European and American colleagues in recognizing the dangers industrial development posed for the environment. They realized that natural resources needed to be expended rationally and husbanded with an eye to their preservation and replenishment.[1]

In the Soviet Union a struggle erupted between "modernizers" advocating rapid technical progress to achieve a modern "heaven on earth" and "preservationists" who believed desecrating nature was an excessive price for "progress." Some Soviet scientists opposed economic bureaucrats advocating human "mastery of nature" and its systematic exploitation by the state. This reflected a struggle between the Communist Party, seeking to monopolize all decision making, and some scientists, especially conservationists, who believed that rational economic progress could be achieved with careful guidance. The latter wished to block development that threatened nature. However, the Bolsheviks proved unwilling to accept any restraints on their decision making, especially in the economic sphere, where socialist construction became the focus of the Soviet regime.

The battle to protect the environment and the people's health was lost during the Stalin era when the party's primacy in scientific and economic decision making went unchallenged; it remained so virtually to the end of Soviet rule. Economic decisions were never subject to debate; one either accepted them or remained silent. Politburo or Central Committee decisions were implemented through the economic ministries without regard for scientific or public opinion. Despite scientists' growing concerns about environmental problems, little could be done about them until the Gorbachev era.

Seeking to demonstrate the socialist system's superiority, from the 1960s on impressive pollution control policies were adopted and Soviet environmental legislation was touted as the world's most stringent. Declared the Soviet Minister of Public Health B. V. Petrovskii in 1968:

> Problems related to air and water pollution are being discussed in a host of capitalist countries. But the capitalist system by its very essence, is incapable of taking radical measures to ensure efficient conservation of nature. In the Soviet Union, however, questions of protecting the environment from pollution by industrial wastes occupy the center of the Party's and government's attention. It is forbidden to put industrial projects into operation if

---

[1] For early Soviet debates on conservation and ecology, see Douglas R. Weiner, *Models of Nature: Ecology, Conservation and Cultural Revolution in Soviet Russia* (Bloomington, IN, 1988), pp. 19–84.

the construction of purification installations has not been completed. The Soviet Union has been the first country in the world to set maximum permissible concentrations of harmful substances in the air of populated areas.[2]

The 1977 Soviet Constitution boasted:

> All necessary steps will be taken to protect and make scientific, rational use of the land and its mineral and water resources, and the plant and animal kingdoms, to preserve the purity of air and water, to ensure reproduction of natural wealth, and to improve the human environment.

Article 42 guaranteed Soviet citizens the right to a healthy environment, and Article 67 obligated them "to protect nature and conserve its riches." At best pious hopes, mostly for international consumption, environmental concern and enforcement were minimal until the end of Soviet rule.

Soviet environmental legislation was so strict that local enforcement was virtually impossible, and the legislation was mostly ignored with impunity. Ultimate responsibility for its enforcement belonged to the Supreme Soviet and the Council of Ministers. The State Planning Committee (Gosplan) was responsible for planning development of the Soviet economy. Environmental aspects of the economic plans were handled by an elaborate structure of ministries and state committees responsible for both conservation and production. Whenever these two conflicted, production prevailed. Noted one American scholar:

> Instead of serving as a referee between polluters and conservationists, government officials usually supported the polluters. . . . The most important criterion for any government official (or factory manager) who seeks promotion or recognition is how much his production has increased in his region (factory), *not* to what extent his rivers have been cleaned up this year. . . . Few government officials (or factory managers) are likely to be particularly

sympathetic to those who threaten the attainment of new production records.[3]

Thus enterprises easily ignored environmental legislation because monitoring agencies were also those responsible for meeting production goals. The economic plan always took precedence over environmental considerations, with tragic results.

Seeking to remedy this sorry state of affairs, Soviet authorities in the late 1970s entrusted power to monitor the environment to the State Committee for Hydrometeorology and Environmental Control *(Gidromet)*. However, it lacked essential powers of enforcement, remained the creature of the economic ministries, and was largely ignored by polluters. After the Chernobyl disaster of 1986 a new agency—the USSR State Committee for Environmental Protection *(Goskompriroda)*—was to supervise the environment, theoretically with broad powers over the ministries, but from the beginning it was underfunded and understaffed and lacked real enforcement authority over the economic ministries. Its chairman was called "a general without an army."

Under Gorbachev a "green movement" flourished briefly and became an outspoken critic of Soviet power. However, with the end of the Soviet Union this movement declined, yielding to pressing problems of economic survival. Environmental concerns, while receiving lip service, have been largely ignored by a Yeltsin government striving to develop a genuine market economy. State funds are lacking even for the most urgent environmental problems. The legacy of Soviet environmental neglect and mismanagement must be ended soon if previous grievous damage to the former Soviet land and people is to be overcome. A full assessment of this damage has yet to be made. Recognizing the problem's dimensions and establishing priorities are urgent for a solution to the area's enormous environmental problems.

---

[2] *Current Digest of the Soviet Press,* July 17, 1968, p. 16.

[3] Marshall I. Goldman, *The Spoils of Progress: Environmental Pollution in the Soviet Union* (Cambridge, MA, 1972), pp. 69–70.

How great was the environmental damage caused by irresponsible Soviet economic policies? Two leading American experts suggest:

> When historians finally conduct an autopsy on the Soviet Union and Soviet Communism, they may reach the verdict of death by ecocide [ecological suicide]. . . . No other great industrial civilization so systematically and so long poisoned its land, air, water and people.[4]

Public health has been so undermined by the polluted environment that in Russia alone among industrialized nations, life expectancy has declined sharply—from 66 in the 1960s to 58 in 1993—and is still declining.[5]

Once boasting majestic stands of forest, pristine lakes and rivers, Russia has become a vast arena of pollution and sickness. While transforming Russia into an urban-industrial giant, Soviet authorities ruthlessly polluted and destroyed rivers and lakes, killed a giant sea, destroyed vast tracts of the world's richest supply of forest, and sacrificed the lives of countless citizens. Five Year Plans created gigantic industrial complexes. Huge industrial centers like Magnitogorsk, Norilsk, and Cheliabinsk churned out millions of tons of iron, steel, and chemicals, relentlessly burning natural resources without regard for pollution of air and water and creating acid rain. With Russia possessing seemingly inexhaustible natural resources, few in the USSR cared about the tremendous waste— that rivers turned purple with oil-well runoff and the sky turned orange in the glow of burning natural gas. Such destruction occurred despite theoretically stringent environmental standards. This wanton disregard of nature is hard to measure and understates the true dimensions of the tragedy. The examples that follow merely suggest the unprecedented damage caused by decades of environmental neglect.

Destruction of the Aral Sea

Once larger than most of the Great Lakes, the Aral Sea east of the Caspian Sea on the Kazakh-Uzbek border has lost two-thirds of its volume and 44 percent of its area. In 1960 it measured 26,000 square miles, but by 1990 11,000 square miles of seabed had become desert. Within a generation it will likely disappear completely.

The destruction of the Aral Sea resulted from decisions made in Moscow, more than 1,000 miles away. Its two primary feeder rivers, the Amu Daria (1,578 miles long) and Syr Daria (1,370 miles long), dumped only one-eighth as much water into the sea in 1990 as in 1960. Cotton consumed these rivers' clear waters as a sacrifice on production's altar. Moscow's central economic planning agencies decided to create a cotton monoculture in Central Asia. Cotton harvests increased 70 percent between 1965 and 1983 following the diversion from the Amu and Syr rivers of huge quantities of water to irrigate almost 18 million acres of cotton.

The water passed into poorly constructed and maintained irrigation ditches, wasting as much as 90 percent of the diverted water before reaching the cotton fields. These waters also carried an increasing chemical runoff from overuse of chemical fertilizers on the cotton crop: phosphates, ammonia, nitrates, and chlorinated hydrocarbons. Virtually all the groundwater in a region of more than 35 million people was poisoned. The Aral Sea's rapid evaporation had unforseen effects on the climate: Temperatures rose in summer and fell in winter to unprecedented extremes. Huge dust storms occurred with increasing frequency as the exposed seabed turned into a great salt desert.

> Yearly in the 1980s the storms carried between 90 and 140 million tons of salt and sand from the 11,000-plus square miles of exposed seabed to Byelorussian farmlands 1,200 miles to the northwest, and half as far southeast to the snowfields of Afghanistan where the Amu Daria rises.[6]

---

[4] Murray Feshbach and Alfred Friendly, Jr., *Ecocide in the USSR: Health and Nature Under Siege* (New York, 1992), p. 1.
[5] See *New York Times,* March 28, 1994, p. A5.

---

[6] Feshbach and Friendly, *Ecocide,* p. 75.

This ecological disaster affected not only the region's soil and water but its people as well. Whole industries were destroyed:

> Once there were 10,000 fishermen working out of Muynak [a center of the fishing industry formerly on the coast and now 65 miles inland], taking pike, perch, and bream as fat as piglets from the Aral. The town produced three percent of the Soviet annual catch. There were 24 native species of fish in the Aral. Today there are none, and the commercial fishing industry is dead.[7]

During the 1980s infant and maternal mortality rates in the region doubled and tripled, respectively. Throat cancers and respiratory and eye diseases have soared from large clouds of gritty salts that clog the air around the Aral Sea. Concluded Feshbach and Friendly: "The sea turning to desert was a symbol of a sixty-year pattern of ecocide by deliberate design."[8]

What of the future? Even heroic measures can never restore the Aral Sea to its condition in 1960. At best the situation might be stabilized so the sea will not disappear completely. But resources to initiate such a stabilization seem unavailable and whatever remains of the Aral Sea will be largely useless, five times saltier than the oceans, a "dead sea."

Air Pollution

Despite stringent air quality norms, air pollution remains a major environmental problem. According to data presented to Soviet prosecutors late in 1990, the life expectancy of Moscow residents—ten years below what it had been in 1970—ranked the metropolis 70th among the world's largest cities. Congenitally deformed children were being born in Moscow one-and-a-half times as often as in the USSR as a whole. With infant mortality two to three times higher in Moscow than in other republic capitals in 1989, "more inhabitants . . .

died than were born."[9] The worst air pollution, however, was in Norilsk, Siberia, above the Arctic Circle, where in 1990 270,000 residents breathed in almost 2.4 million tons of industrial atmospheric pollutants. Sao Paulo, Brazil's largest city, is considered "severely polluted" from 250,000 tons of industrial air pollutants annually, but Norilsk per capita is *222 times* as polluted as Sao Paulo.[10] More than 100 cities in the former USSR have air pollution levels five times or more higher than Soviet standards permitted, exposing millions of people to dangerous respiratory diseases and cancer.

The Chernobyl Accident

The single greatest ecological disaster occurred on April 26, 1986, when Unit Number 4 of the V. I. Lenin Chernobyl Nuclear Power Station was rocked by two explosions, releasing more toxic radioactive material into the atmosphere than the combined bombings of Hiroshima and Nagasaki in World War II.

> A new study suggests that the explosion threw out 100 million curies of dangerous radionuclides, such as cesium 137—twice as much as previous estimates. The World Health Organization reckons that 4.9 million people in Ukraine, Belarus, and Russia were affected. But the consequences, though obviously tragic in some aspects, remain unclear.[11]

The fallout from that accident persists amid growing concern that hasty efforts to seal off reactor 4 were woefully inadequate. Some 180 tons of uranium fuel lie buried inside the sealed-off reactor, and 10 tons of radioactive dust covers everything inside the steel and concrete sarcophagus that encapsulates the damaged reactor, which suffered total meltdown of the core—something originally denied by Soviet authorities. Because the steel and concrete shell is structurally un-

---

[7] William Ellis, "A Soviet Sea Lies Dying," *National Geographic* 177, no. 2 (February 1990), p. 84.
[8] Feshbach and Friendly, p. 75.

[9] Feshbach and Friendly, p. 9.
[10] Feshbach and Friendly, p. 10.
[11] Mike Edwards, "Lethal Legacy: Pollution in the Former USSR," *National Geographic* 186, no. 2 (August 1994), p. 104.

sound, any shifting of debris buried inside could topple the entire structure and high winds could cause it to collapse, releasing a new, lethal cloud of radioactive dust across an already contaminated landscape. It is agreed that the remaining operative reactors on site are unsafe. Because of continuing safety problems at the site, international efforts have been made to have all remaining reactors at Chernobyl shut down. Energy-starved Ukraine has refused—the Chernobyl reactors supply 17 percent of its energy—until alternative sources of energy are on line. In summer 1994 the government ordered reactor 2 restarted.

The full dimensions of the reactor core meltdown are only now emerging. The Chernobyl Union, a citizens group, estimates that at least 5,000 people have died as a direct result of the accident, and the number is increasing each year. More than 30,000 people have been disabled. The spread of cancers and other radiation-related illnesses grows daily; genetic disorders are clearly rising. More than 30,000 square miles of rich farmland have been contaminated, costing billions of dollars. Chernobyl's damage consumes some 15 percent of Ukraine's annual budget, and would cost even more if the government could cope with the growing health problems. Ukraine cannot provide adequate medical diagnosis and treatment, reclamation programs, or adequate measures to prevent future accidents. The future of nuclear power in the CIS states is being publicly debated on local, national, and international levels.

Lake Baikal

For more than 35 years a battle has raged to protect Lake Baikal, the "Pearl of Siberia," from pollution. Battle lines formed between the state bureaucracy and industry, on the one hand, and scientists and public opinion, on the other. That struggle's final outcome remains uncertain, but the efforts to save Lake Baikal have helped define the environmental movement in the former Soviet Union.

Situated in southeastern Siberia, Lake Baikal is the largest body of fresh water on earth—12,200

square miles, up to 5,346 feet deep, a total of 5,520 cubic miles of water. The lake's surface area is about that of Lake Superior, but Baikal holds almost as much fresh water as *all* the Great Lakes combined. Lake Baikal is a natural reservoir for 336 feeder rivers and is drained by a single river, the Angara, flowing northward to the Arctic Ocean. If the water in all the feeder rivers were diverted and the Angara River were allowed to drain the lake, it would take some 400 years to drain it completely.[12] Baikal's waters are so translucent and clear that divers can see clearly to a depth of 150 feet. Baikal comprises a unique ecological system with more than 1,200 forms of unique aquatic life.

Until a century ago, when construction of the Trans-Siberian Railroad intruded, this pristine environment was largely untouched. Even after the railroad appeared, very little development occurred along the lake's extensive perimeter— a few small towns and fishing villages. Serious human challenge to Siberia's "radiant orb" began only in 1957, when Moscow economic planners decided that the lake's pure waters and surrounding stands of timber should be exploited for a very specific purpose, which was revealed only later. In 1979 Ze'ev Wolfson, a knowledgeable Soviet scientist and official, using the pseudonym Boris Komarov, published abroad a devastating account of environmental mismanagement in the USSR. Wrote Komarov:

> At the time [1957], the Ministry of Defense needed new durable cord for heavy bomber tires. Such things are referred to tersely as "strategic interests of the country" and are not subject to discussion even within the Council of Ministers. The immunity of the Baikal projects from any criticism is explained by these "strategic interests." They had sealed Baikal's fate by 1959.[13]

---

[12] Peter Matthiessen, "The Blue Pearl of Siberia," *New York Review of Books* 38, no. 4 (February 14, 1991), p. 37.
[13] Boris Komarov (Ze'ev Wolfson), *The Destruction of Nature in the Soviet Union* (White Plains, NY, 1980), p. 16.

The plan was to build a cellulose-cord processing enterprise at Baikalsk, on the lake's southern shores, and a smaller cardboard manufacturing plant on the major feeder river, the Selenga. Baikal had virtually unlimited supplies of two essential ingredients: pure water and timber. But inasmuch as paper and cellulose manufacturing produce notoriously high levels of toxic wastes, unprecedented opposition developed swiftly to siting the plants in the Baikal region. Outspoken opposition from the scientific community and the public induced the Soviet authorities to compromise by agreeing to install "state-of-the-art" water treatment facilities in order to minimize the dangers to the lake and its environs.

Unfortunately, the plants opened in 1966 before water treatment facilities were available, and loggers began clearing out the vast taiga along the lake's shores. Forest regenerates slowly in the harsh climate, and promised planned reforestation was never initiated. The lakeshore therefore eroded rapidly, and landslides dumped vast quantities of silt into the lake and feeder rivers. Harvested timber was floated down the feeder rivers, and much of it became waterlogged and sank before reaching processing plants. As the timber decayed, bacteria depleted the water's oxygen, destroying fish and aquatic life and the purity of the water in both rivers and lake. Under pressure from scientists and the public, Soviet authorities sought in the 1970s and 1980s to reverse the damage. Logging was banned in a wide belt around the lake, reforestation began, rotting logs were removed from rivers, and log-rafting was banned (logs had to be transported aboard ships).

The worst problem, however, was effluent from more than 100 factories operating on the lake's shores without proper purification facilities. Their untreated wastes were dumped directly into the lake, contaminating it with mercury, lead, zinc, tungsten, and molybdenum. The Baikalsk cellulose factory used enormous amounts of fresh, pure water, discharging it untreated back into the lake.

The factory finally had to install expensive water-purifying equipment to treat badly polluted *intake* water. More than 23 square miles of the lake's floor became a "dead zone," where no life survives. The Intourist hotel at Listvianka, a fishing village on the lakeshore north of the Baikalsk plant, can no longer serve drinking water directly from the lake.[14] Agricultural enterprises send chemical fertilizers directly into the feeder rivers. The largest feeder, the Selenga, carries effluents from the industrial center Ulan Ude, 60 miles upriver. Partially treated and raw sewage and effluent from more than 50 factories pour down the Selenga into the lake.

In a classic case of Soviet mismanagement, it soon became clear that the primary purpose of the Baikalsk and Selenga plants had disappeared. As the plants began operating in 1966, it was discovered that nylon cord was more suitable for bomber tires than super cellulose cord, and far cheaper to produce. Many of the superfluous Baikal plants nonetheless still operate. After almost 30 years in service, defying stringent Soviet and Russian emission standards, the Baikalsk plant alone has dumped almost 2 billion cubic meters of untreated industrial wastes directly into Lake Baikal. Closing the plants has been discussed, but that would cost about 30,000 workers their jobs.

Lake Baikal became the first real battlefield between an incipient "green movement" and Soviet planners. The pollution of Lake Baikal first aroused public interest in state policy formulation and led to questioning the Moscow industrial ministries' arrogant power. Public outcry against the needless destruction of a treasured natural resource finally forced Soviet officials to consider environmental protection as an important component of industry. Not wholly successful, the campaign to save the "Pearl of Siberia" launched a Soviet environmental movement that continues today.

---

[14] Matthiessen, "The Blue Pearl," p. 40.

Conclusion

Few resources are currently available to begin restoring environmental balance in Russia and the CIS states, but public awareness is growing that something must be done to protect the environment and population. One outspoken environmentalist, the Siberian author Valentin Rasputin, is pessimistic:

> I remain gloomy and sad about the environmental prospects. . . . Almost all our country's rivers and lakes, especially in Europe, are polluted to a very high degree . . . and even in Siberia there are regions where the water problem is truly serious. There are many groups trying to save the Aral Sea, the Volga Basin, but it is doubtful they will succeed. It will cost billions of rubles, and nobody has the slightest idea where the money will come from. To be sure ecological consciousness is growing, but many still argue against environmental protection.[15]

Improving environmental quality and public health must remain a top Russian priority into the next decades and beyond. Continued environmental deterioration will further complicate and perhaps even scuttle the reform process. Russia and the CIS states cannot undertake unaided the many tasks of environmental reclamation. A cooperative international program is required, but Russia must take the lead and make the necessary sacrifices to begin the lengthy process of environmental restoration.

Troubled Transitions, The Yeltsin Era

Beginning in 1992, the former Soviet Union underwent an extremely traumatic triple transition: from an autocratic Communist-ruled state toward a decentralized democracy in Russia; from a centralized command economy featuring heavy industry and state-owned land to a consumer-oriented, privatized economy; and from a multina-

tional empire ruled from Moscow to 15 uneasily coexisting and theoretically independent countries. At the end of the nineties it remained uncertain whether this transition could be achieved successfully in Russia and the "near abroad," although considerable economic and political progress had been scored, especially in Russia. The danger remained that this vast area, spanning one-sixth of the globe, could follow the disastrous path taken by former Communist Yugoslavia. Here we will examine key developments there in the realms of politics, economics, and foreign relations during this difficult period.

Politics: Yeltsin vs. the Parliament

Gorbachev's resignation as Soviet president, inevitable with the collapse of the USSR, was the first time a Russian ruler had relinquished power voluntarily. At the insistence of his successor, Boris Yeltsin, Gorbachev was assured a comfortable and secure retirement. During the weeks after the August Coup of 1991, Yeltsin, as president of Russia, had outlined the elements of decommunization as democracy, a market economy, the defense of human rights, private property, and a multiparty political system: "We should aim to do whatever we can to restructure ourselves in a fundamental way so we can follow a civilized road."[16] In October 1991 the Russian Parliament overwhelmingly approved President Yeltsin's reform program, calling for a market economy and democracy. But, only a few months later, as the economic downturn deepened and an anti-reform backlash dominated public opinion, Parliament began to reverse its stance. The privatization program approved by the Parliament on June 11, 1992 was the last reform measure it enacted.

A power struggle between President Yeltsin and Parliament intensified during 1992–93, while Yeltsin's support within it declined. After June 1992, the Duma (lower house) rejected all reform measures proposed by the Yeltsin government. In its duel with Yeltsin the Parliament was directed by

[15] Quoted in Matthiessen, p. 47.

[16] Aron, p. 466.

Ruslan Khasbulatov, a master of political intrigue. At an emergency meeting in March 1993, Parliament sought to curtail the president's powers. The two sides then bickered over a national referendum on Yeltsin's reform policies. Held in April 1993, that referendum approved Yeltsin's reform policies by a narrow margin. Yeltsin then sought a constitutional convention to replace the outdated Brezhnev Constitution, but the Parliament blocked that idea. In the summer of 1993, as the provinces and even some individual cities began declaring themselves independent republics, the Russian Federation seemed about to disintegrate.

In September 1993 the parliament, led by Ruslan Khasbulatov and Vice President A. V. Rutskoi, sought to enact antireform measures and reduce President Yeltsin, who had been issuing numerous authoritarian decrees, to a figurehead. On September 21 Yeltsin responded by ordering parliament dissolved and announcing that new parliamentary elections would be held in December. Parliament then declared Yeltsin "deposed" and "installed" Rutskoi as president of Russia. Yeltsin retaliated by sealing off the "White House" where the parliament convened. Many of those inside it, ironically, were those who with Yeltsin had defied the August 1991 plotters, while the siege was directed by Yeltsin, the chief opponent of the August Coup. At the beginning of October, in an effort to resolve the impasse, negotiations were conducted in Moscow's Danilov Monastery under the auspices of Patriarch Aleksii of the Orthodox Church and Mayor Iurii Luzhkov. When these negotiations failed, Khasbulatov and Rutskoi attempted a military coup on October 4, sending armed detachments to seize the mayor's office and the Ostankino television tower. (See Map 21.1.) Confirming that parliament was controlled by extreme paramilitary groups and hard-line Communists, this resort to force proved a fatal blunder. Yeltsin's government, with army backing, quickly mobilized far greater force, bombarded the "White House," and forced its surrender. The parliamentary leaders were marched off to prison.

Two days after the White House siege ended, President Yeltsin in a television speech proclaimed himself the savior of Russia. On November 10, 1993, with the publication of Yeltsin's draft constitution, a new constitutional structure was established in Russia. A 450-member State Duma was to be elected for two-year terms; the 178 members of the new Federation Council would likewise serve two-year terms. The election of December 12 approved the new constitution by a bare majority, as 45 percent of the electorate abstained and only 31 percent voted yes. Fascists and Communists won a majority of seats in the Duma; almost 25 percent of the party-list votes and about 14 percent of the seats went to the new, misnamed Liberal Democratic Party led by extremist Vladimir Zhirinovskii, who had stressed Russia's national "humiliations." (See Table 21.1.) In part this was a protest vote against rising crime, threatened political chaos, and squabbling reformers. This election nonetheless marked the emergence of political parties and of television as major forces in the new Russian politics. An intriguing new party with much potential influence called itself the New Women of Russia.

Beginning in December 1993, the Yeltsin Constitution created a new, seemingly more stable political framework for Russia with most players abiding by its rules. Noticeable, however, was a rising disillusionment with democracy for failing to produce prosperity and restore Russia's power. By 1994 Russia had a fairly normal parliament, constantly sniping at the government, but a dubious presidency as Yeltsin failed to build a strong political party or movement. Despite a weak and ineffective central government, President Yeltsin dominated a rather featureless political landscape. Almost 10 years after emerging on the national scene, Yeltsin remained a unique, enigmatic, and unpredictable figure. As rumors and reports proliferated about his alleged abuse of alcohol, and between bouts of illness and periodic seclusion, he remained from 1990 the chief agent of Russian political change. From 1989 he had generally, albeit rather inconsistently, supported economic and political reform. Under the 1993 Constitution he obtained strong executive powers backed by a rapidly expanding presidential apparatus. How-

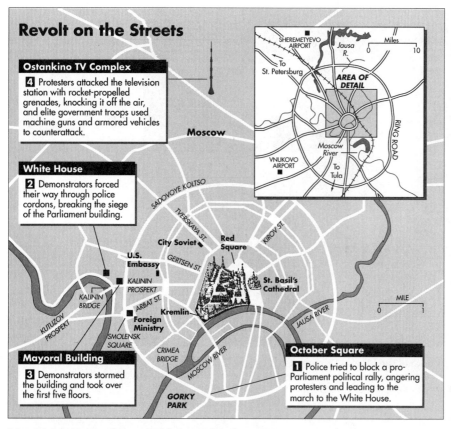

Revolt on the Streets

Ostankino TV Complex

4 Protesters attacked the television station with rocket-propelled grenades, knocking it off the air, and elite government troops used machine guns and armored vehicles to counterattack.

Moscow

White House

2 Demonstrators forced their way through police cordons, breaking the siege of the Parliament building.

SHEREMETYEVO AIRPORT

Jausa R.

Miles

0   10

To St. Petersburg

AREA OF DETAIL

RING ROAD

Moscow River

To Tula

VNUKOVO AIRPORT

SADOVOYE KOLTSO

TVERSKAYA ST.

KIROV ST.

City Soviet

Red Square

U.S. Embassy

GERTSEN ST.

St. Basil's Cathedral

KALININ PROSPEKT

KALININ BRIDGE

ARBAT ST.

Kremlin

Foreign Ministry

KUTUZOV PROSPEKT

SMOLENSK SQUARE

JAUSA RIVER

MILE

0   1

Mayoral Building

3 Demonstrators stormed the building and took over the first five floors.

CRIMEA BRIDGE

MOSCOW RIVER

GORKY PARK

October Square

1 Police tried to block a pro-Parliament political rally, angering protesters and leading to the march to the White House.

Map 21.1 Attempted coup in Moscow, October 1993

SOURCE: *The New York Times*, October 4, 1993. Copyright © 1993 by The New York Times Company. Reprinted by permission.

ever, as his physical health declined, his popularity sank to single-digit levels, making it highly uncertain whether he could achieve reelection in 1996.

In mid-1995 Premier Viktor Chernomyrdin stood as the second most influential Russian political figure until eclipsed by the Communist leader, Gennadii Zyuganov, then by General Alexander Lebed. Chernomyrdin, a former Soviet gas magnate and cautious moderate, showed considerable success in handling Russia's perilous political and economic transition, gaining a personal triumph in June 1995 by negotiating a truce in Russia's ill-advised war in Chechnia (discussed later in this chapter). He stressed stability, a home for Russians wanting "progress without shocks or revolutions,

who are tired of disorder and lies, who are proud of Russian statehood."[16] On the other hand, extreme nationalist Vladimir V. Zhirinovskii, whose influence peaked with the December 1993 parliamentary elections, lost much of his popularity subsequently.

In the elections to the Russian Duma of December 17, 1995, the revived Communist Party led by Zyuganov defeated Chernomyrdin's government party, Our Home Is Russia, more than 2 to 1—roughly 22 to 10 percent. In second place

---

[16] Steven Erlanger, "Russia's Premier: Too Popular for His Own Good?" *New York Times,* June 26, 1995, p. 4.

Vladimir Zhirinovskii, leader of the Liberal Democratic Party of Russia, enthusiastically gestures during a press conference at the Parliament building in Moscow, June 22, 1995.

emerged the ultranationalist and misnamed Liberal Democratic Party of Zhirinovskii. (See Table 21.2.) Seeking to explain this result, Premier Chernomyrdin commented:

> The Communist Party has already been operating for 97 years in Russia and got 20 percent of the vote. Our Home Is Russia has only been working four or five months, and we immediately got almost 10 percent.[17]

The only other political party to win the required 5 percent for admission to the Duma was Grigorii Yavlinskii's liberal Yabloko Party. The extremists' victory provoked speculation that they might form a coalition in the new Duma. However, under the 1993 Constitution the Duma's powers are very limited. Igor M. Kliamkin, director of a Moscow public opinion institute, commented:

> Even together, the Communists and the nationalists cannot really decide anything about the fate of the former Soviet Union from Parliament, but they can foster an imperialistic mood here and further isolate Russia from its neighbors and the West.[18]

The four successful parties filled only half the Duma seats; the remaining 225 seats went to candidates running as individuals. Some observers compared the Russia of 1995 politically with Germany's Weimar Republic before Hitler overthrew it. Others pointed out a resemblance to Charles de

---

[17] Alessandra Stanley, "Communists Lead the Ruling Party," *New York Times,* December 19, 1995, pp. 1, 8.

[18] Stanley, "Communists Lead," p. 8.

Table 21.1 Russian Duma election, December 12, 1993

Parties and Blocs	Party Lists		Single-Member Constituency	Total Seats*
	% of Vote	Seats		
Liberal Democratic Party	22.79	59	5	64
Russia's Choice	15.38	40	18	58
Communist Party of the Russian Federation	12.35	32	16	48
Agrarian Party	7.90	21	12	33
Women of Russia	8.10	21	2	23
Yavlinsky-Boldyrev-Lukin (Yabloko)	7.83	20	2	22
Party of Russian Unity and Accord	6.76	18	1	19
Democratic Party of Russia	5.50	14	1	15
Democratic Russia Movement			5	5
Russian Movement for Democratic Reforms	13.39	—	4	4
Others			153†	153
Total	**100.00**	**225**	**219‡**	**444‡**

*In mid-January 1994, according to Western estimates, the parliamentary factions in the State Duma were as follows: Russia's Choice (76 seats); New Regional Policy (centrist faction comprising independents—65); Liberal Democratic Party (63); Agrarian Party (55); Communist Party of the Russian Federation (45); Party of Russian Unity and Accord (30); Yavlinsky-Boldyrev-Lukin (Yabloko—25); Women of Russia (23); Democratic Party of Russia (15).
†Including 130 members without party affiliations.
‡Totals exclude one deputy from Chechnia and one from the Naberezhnye Chelny district of Tatarstan, where the election was boycotted, and four deputies from the remaining constituencies of Tatarstan (where fewer than 25% of registered voters took part, thereby invalidating the poll). However, in March 1994, in fresh elections in Tatarstan, the five deputies were successfully elected to the State Duma, bringing its total membership to 449.
SOURCE: The Europa World Yearbook 1994, vol. 2, p. 2497.

Gaulle's successful though authoritarian Fifth Republic in France.

President Yeltsin rebounded physically to conduct a vigorous campaign for reelection. In June and July 1996 Russia underwent two dramatic and crucial elections for president that tested its progress toward democracy. In the first round of voting on June 16, with ten competing candidates, including former President Gorbachev, President Yeltsin scored a narrow victory by 35 to 32 percent over his chief rival, Communist Party chief Gennadii Zyuganov. Coming in a surprisingly strong third with 15 percent was retired General Alexander Lebed. Yeltsin promptly recruited him as his new security chief. Yeltsin then arranged for the runoff vote to be held on a weekday, July 3. In that runoff Yeltsin scored a decisive victory, gaining almost 54 percent of the vote against about 40

percent for Zyuganov. (See Table 21.3.) This result was hailed with relief both in Russia and abroad as a great victory for democracy and reform. The victorious Yeltsin promptly reappointed the moderate, Viktor Chernomyrdin, as prime minister, and pledged to continue on the path of reform.

The two year's after his reelection as president in July 1996 were among the most frustrating of Yeltsin's life. While closely engaged in reform efforts, he was severely limited by complex problems and failing health, Initially, he named economic reformer Anatolii Chubais as his chief of staff, indicating that he intended to pursue radical economic policies. In August 1996 Yeltsin redeemed a major promise of his reelection campaign: a truce in Chechnia. Soon thereafter General Aleksandr Lebed and the Chechen leader, Aslan Maskhadov, signed an agreement ending a

Viktor Chernomyrdin. Yeltsin appointed him prime minister in December 1992 and removed him in March 1998.

Gennadii Zyuganov, leader of the Communist Party, addresses an emergency session of the Duma in Moscow, January 11, 1995. Zyuganov was defeated by Yeltsin in the 1996 presidential election and by Vladimir Putin in 2000.

disastrous war and granting Chechnia political autonomy. However, by late August, after over a month's absence from the Kremlin, Yeltsin's grave illness could no longer be concealed. In a national television interview on September 5, Yeltsin announced that he would undergo bypass heart surgery, the first public advance notice of a Russian leader's medical treatment. Yeltsin's quintuple bypass operation on November 5 was followed by a lengthy and uneven recovery. Returning to the Kremlin December 23, Yeltsin two weeks later was again hospitalized with flu and pneumonia.

However, once again Yeltsin rebounded. On March 6, 1997, he confidently delivered his annual "State of Russia" speech to a joint session of Parliament. It contained the most detailed analysis of the status of reforms, major obstacles to economic recovery, and the state's role in a new Russian economy that had ever been given by Yeltsin. The financial and tax systems had to be normalized, he affirmed, and bold decisions made. "I want to hand over to my successor a country with a dynamically growing economy, an effective and fair system of social protection, a country whose citizens are confident of their future."[19]

In March 1997 President Yeltsin's replacement of virtually all cabinet ministers produced the most reformist ministry since Egor Gaidar's resignation in December 1992, and a much more experienced one. Retaining stodgy Viktor Chernomyrdin as premier because a new one would have to be approved by the Duma, Yeltsin appointed the dynamic, popular young former governor of Nizhnii-Novgorod, Boris Nemtsov, and Anatolii Chubais as deputy premiers to carry through "a second economic revolution." The months from April to October 1997 was the most intense period of reform since 1992. Working hard preparing for monthly economic meetings with the premier, Yeltsin signed numerous decrees. Once again he was confident and vigorous, bragging about losing sixty pounds since his operation.

---

[19] Aron, p. 656.

Hermann J. Knipperz/AP/Wide World Photos

General Alexander Lebed, a hero of the Afghan war and a powerful conservative politician, who was elected governor of Krasnoyarsk Region in 1999.

Again relishing the risks of battle, Yeltsin appeared almost daily on television and welcomed foreign dignitaries. When he traveled to the G-7 meeting of leading world powers (which became the G-8 with Russia's addition) in Denver, his fitness, energy and good cheer reflected a newfound respect abroad for Russian democracy and reform. Yeltsin thus contributed to making 1997 the best year so far in Russia's painful and multiple transitions. The combination of peace, freedom, and relative prosperity were virtually unprecedented in Russian history. In summer 1997 Moscow even enjoyed a baby boom, as many people felt better about their lives.

However, prosperity proved very fragile and shortlived; domestic debt ballooned upward. Key provisions of Yeltsin's March 6 reform program fell victim to Duma opposition and delay late that year. As his illness again took over, Yeltsin disappeared completely from public view until mid-January 1998. Then on March 23, 1998, a

convalescent Yeltsin announced on television that he had dismissed Premier Chernomyrdin and his entire cabinet "to make reforms more energetic and effective." As his new premier, Yeltsin appointed 35-year-old Sergei Kirienko, previously energy minister, to head the first truly post-Soviet government representing a new and younger generation. "We have no time to waste," warned Kirienko. That became evident as domestic debt ballooned out of control while the Duma refused to adopt key measures to reduce the deficit by increasing state revenues. By May 1998 one-third of the entire budget went to service the debt. As many workers went unpaid that summer, the federal government was blamed. On July 8 defense industry workers from twenty cities in a rally on Arbat Square in Moscow shouted: "President and Government—resign! Trial for the Yeltsin gang!" Outside the Russian White House miners, demanding their pay, banged their helmets on the ground. A month later, in one of its final acts, the Kirienko government allocated 5 percent of the entire budget to pay their wages. Anxious to destroy a Yeltsin regime it hated, the Duma rejected most of the government's anti-crisis measures.

From February to the end of July 1998, affirms Aron, Yeltsin campaigned intensively for his government and reforms without any summer holiday. Only occasional slurred words, facial grimaces, and lapses of comprehension indicated his struggle with multiple ailments. Attending the belated burial of the remains of Nicholas II and his family in the Cathedral of Sts. Peter and Paul in St. Petersburg, Yeltsin declared: "For many years we were silent about this terrible crime, but we must tell the truth. . . . By burying the remnants of the innocent murdered (Romanovs), we want to expiate the sins of our ancestors."[20] As Russia's financial crisis deepened, Yeltsin was asked everywhere whether the ruble would be devalued. "No, never!" he affirmed. But on August 17 the government abandoned its efforts to support the ruble,

---

[20] Aron, pp. 683–84.

Table 21.2 Russian Duma election, December 17, 1995

Party	Percentage of Party-List Votes	Party-List Seats	Single-Candidate Seats	Total Seats	Seats Won in 1993
Communist Party	22.30%	99	58	157	45
Liberal Democratic Party	11.18	50	1	51	63
Our Home Is Russia	10.13	45	10	55	—
Yabloko	6.89	31	14	45	25
Parties needed a minimum of 5 percent of the vote to win party-list seats.					
Women of Russia	4.61	0	3	3	23
Working Russia	4.53	0	1	1	0
Congress of Russian Communities	4.31	0	5	5	—
Party of Svyatoslav Fyodorov	3.98	0	1	1	—
Democratic Choice of Russia	3.86	0	9	9	76
Agrarian Party	3.78	0	20	20	55
Power to the People	1.61	0	9	9	—
Other parties	Unavailable	0	17	17	—
Independents	—	0	77	77	—

SOURCE: *The New York Times*, December 30, 1995. Copyright © 1995 by The New York Times Company. Reprinted by permission.

which amounted to a devaluation and devastated leading Russian banks. A week later Yeltsin, dismissing the Kirienko cabinet, recalled stolid Viktor Chernomyrdin as premier. Such an obvious retreat under fire amounted to Yeltsin's political suicide. Retreating further, Yeltsin appointed conservative Evgenii Primakov foreign minister. To insure his confirmation, Primakov constantly consulted the Duma, so that the new government became responsible to the parliament rather than the president. Yeltsin's popularity fell to an abysmal 3–5 percent as Russia seemed to have discarded its ailing president.

During the next year, intolerant of challenges to his authority, Yeltsin reshuffled his cabinet repeatedly, running through five premiers, including Chernomyrdin twice. When he named Primakov premier with two communist ministers in September 1998 Yeltsin apparently believed he had created harmony and new support for his policies. Instead, the communists in the Duma pursued their plans to impeach him while Primakov steadily undermined his authority. Then, in May 1999, encircled by communist opponents and

threatened with impeachment, Yeltsin sought once again to become Russia's savior by removing Primakov, the only leader reformers and communists could support following the August 1998 financial collapse. Primakov, claimed Yeltsin, had moved from stabilizing Russia to stagnating it. However, polls then indicated that Primakov was the most trusted and electable Russian politician.

Meanwhile communists in the Duma sought to impeach President Yeltsin, accusing him of five major crimes: dissolving the Soviet Union, destroying the Russian military, waging an illegal war in Chechnia, staging an illegal coup in 1993, and committing genocide against the Russian people whose average lifespan had fallen by several years. Instigating a "criminal war" in Chechnia was the chief charge. However, even if the communists could obtain the required two-thirds vote in both houses of the parliament, impeachment would require approval by both the Constitutional Court and Supreme Court. In any case Yeltsin's term as president was nearing its end. With parliamentary elections scheduled for December 1999 and his own term scheduled to

Table 21.3 Russian presidential election, June 16 and July 3, 1996

Candidate	First ballot	Second ballot
Boris N. Yeltsin	26,665,495	40,200,000*
Gennadii A. Zyuganov	24,211,686	30,110,000*
Alexander I. Lebed	10,974,736	—
Grigorii A. Yavlinskii	5,550,752	—
Vladimir V. Zhirinovskii	4,311,479	—
Svyatoslav N. Fedorov	699,158	—
Mikhail S. Gorbachev	386,069	—
Martin L. Shakkum	277,068	—
Yurii P. Vlasov	151,282	—
Vladimir A. Bryntsalov	123,065	
Total	**74,515,019†**	**73,900,000†**

*Provisional.
† Including votes cast against all candidates and (in the first ballot) 308 votes cast for A. G. Tuleyev, who withdrew from the election after early voting had begun.
SOURCE: *The Europa World Yearbook*, 1996, vol. 2, p. 2688.

end in summer 2000, Yeltsin sought to promote a legacy featuring a developing market economy, political freedom, and Russia's return to the circle of Western democracies.[21]

Economics

Would basic economic reform undermine the Russian Federation's unity? Dismantling the inefficient state sector required active cooperation of regional and local officials, most of whom were members of the former Soviet *nomenklatura*. Would they implement Moscow-ordered reforms or cater to the interests of their own regions? When most prices were freed during 1992, inflation surged. In 1993 consumer and industrial wholesale prices rose by 940 and 1000 percent, respectively. Severe inflation seriously reduced agricultural and industrial output in all CIS countries.[22]

Between 1992 and 1995 privatization proved the most successful aspect of Russian economic

Boris Nemtsov, Russia's First Deputy Premier, former governor of Nizhnii-Novgorod.

reform. (See Figure 21.1.) By October 1, 1992, 150 million privatization vouchers were distributed to the Russian population with a face value of 10,000 rubles each for investment in enterprises or to pay for goods and services. The private sector of the Russian economy expanded rapidly and enormously. During 1992–1993 most small shops and restaurants were privatized; then came the turn of medium- and large-scale enterprises, some 70 percent of which were private by the end of 1994. As the production of larger state firms fell sharply, at the end of 1993 the net material product (the actual production by the economy without counting illegal output) reached only 68 percent of the 1991 level. Entire new branches of business were developed, notably computers, advertising, and insurance. The whole economy was shifting

[21] *New York Times*, May 13, 2000. Michael Wines, "Yeltsin Dismisses His Prime Minister."
[22] John Löwenhardt, *The Reincarnation of Russsia* (Durham, NC, 1995), p. 120.

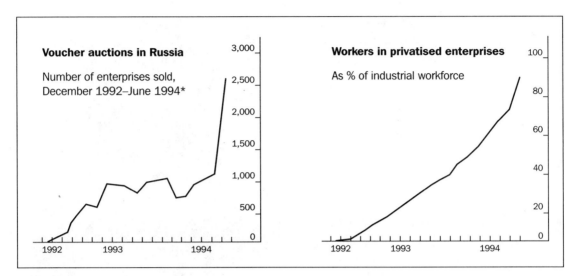

Figure 21.1
Going private

*Sales ended June 1994.

rapidly away from manufacturing to services, from capital goods to consumer products. The private sector was driving Russia inexorably away from the former Soviet command economy and was shaping a future capitalist Russia. By 1995 well over half of all Russian economic activity was in private hands, although few of the inefficient state enterprises had actually closed down. As economist Anders Äslund concluded, "Russia could (and did) reform, and it has become a market economy."[23]

Benefiting from privatization and forming a class of nouveaux riches were primarily former members of the *nomenklatura*. The effects on the bulk of the Russian population were very negative; at least one-third fell below the official subsistence level in 1993. Pensioners and single-parent families suffered the most. In 1993 alone the Russian population declined by 300,000; life expectancy fell

as alcoholism and suicides continued to rise. Heavy industry defended itself vigorously and continued to extract large state subsidies. Resigning in January 1994 after failing to prevent this, Finance Minister Gaidar stated: "Russia never experienced shock therapy. Yes, there were deep reforms in the direction of privatization and price liberalization, but financial policy always remained soft and weak."[24] However, by 1995 Premier Chernomyrdin's team had reined in inflation also.

Organized crime profited greatly from privatization, proliferating throughout Russia and the CIS following the Soviet collapse. By 1994 the territory of the Russian Federation was divided among some 5,000 criminal gangs, and many police and public officials were corrupt. Organized crime controlled major sections of private industry, trade, and banking, accounting for almost one-third of Russia's gross national product.[25] Pene-

---

[23] Anders Äslund, *How Russia Became a Market Economy* (Washington, 1995), p. 316.

[24] Löwenhardt, *Reincarnation of Russia*, p. 55.
[25] Löwenhardt, p. 170.

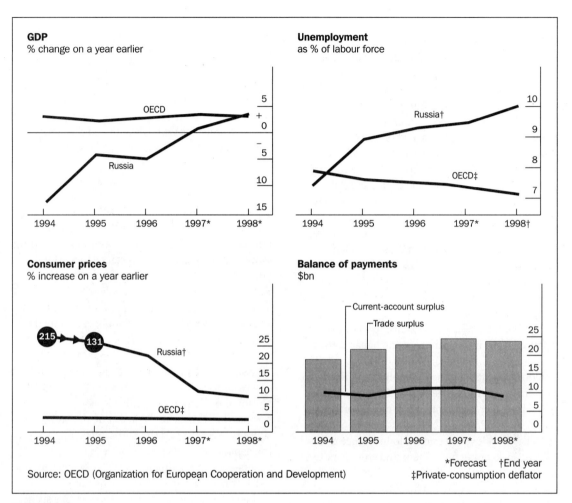

GDP
% change on a year earlier

OECD

Russia

1994   1995   1996   1997*   1998*

Unemployment
as % of labour force

Russia†

OECD‡

1994   1995   1996   1997*   1998†

Consumer prices
% increase on a year earlier

215 → 131

Russia†

OECD‡

1994   1995   1996   1997*   1998*

Balance of payments
$bn

Current-account surplus
Trade surplus

1994   1995   1996   1997*   1998*

*Forecast   †End year
‡Private-consumption deflator

Source: OECD (Organization for European Cooperation and Development)

Figure 21.2
Russian economic trends, 1994–1998

trating every aspect of Russian life, this mafia was usurping political power, taking control of state firms, and engaging in forgery, assault, contract killing, drug running, and arms smuggling. Declared President Yeltsin in 1993: "Corruption is devouring the state from top to bottom."[26] In

order to complete a successful transition to market capitalism, Russia would have to bring this crime wave under control. In mid-1998 that had still not been done. However, Russia in 1998 anticipated its first year of economic growth since the Soviet Union collapsed (see Figure 21.2).

---

[26] Claire Stirling, "Russia's Mafia," *The New Republic,* April 11, 1994, pp. 19–22.

Foreign Relations

After the demise of the Soviet empire, Russia sought to adjust to a new and unfavorable geopolitical situation as the other former Soviet republics became the "near abroad." As of 1992 Russia's new frontiers in Europe resembled those of 1613 after the Time of Troubles. For the first time in centuries Russia lacked borders with Turkey, Iran, or Afghanistan and was without direct contact with the Middle East. The country was deprived of most of its Caspian and Baltic coastlines. Russia's former chief naval base, Sevastopol, now lay in an independent Ukraine. As Muslim separatist movements threatened to fragment the Russian Federation, Russia's relationships with its former colonies and dependencies remained uncertain. Initial hopes that the CIS would become a substitute for the USSR were soon dashed.

Sporadic tension and violence marred Russia's relations with its neighbors in the "near abroad." (See Map 21.2.) In June 1992 a conflict erupted in Moldova involving Russia, Ukraine, and Romania, centering around the newly proclaimed Dniester Moldavian Republic, consisting mostly of Russians. In July President Yeltsin signed an accord with the Moldovan president to introduce a Russian peacekeeping force there. Another disputed issue related to the withdrawal of Russian troops from Estonia and Latvia, which Moscow linked with protecting the rights of their Russian minorities. Potentially the most serious of these crises arose over relations between Russia and Ukraine. The issue of the large Russian minority there became fused with disputes over Crimea and the Black Sea Fleet. The Russian parliament claimed Crimea for Russia, pointing out that roughly 70 percent of its population was Russian. Ukraine and Russia also quarreled over the 400-ship Black Sea Fleet, rotting in its harbors. In August 1992 Presidents Yeltsin and Kravchuk agreed to a joint command for three years, but then in June 1993 agreed to accelerate the splitting of that fleet. Disputes over Crimea and the port of Sevastopol dragged on into 1994, threatening to degenerate into military conflict. It required 14 months of threats and negotiations before a trilateral agreement among Russia, Ukraine, and the United States provided for dismantling and scrapping Ukraine's 1,600 nuclear warheads in Russia in return for security guarantees and some compensation.

These tensions with Ukraine and the status of approximately 25 million Russians living in the "near abroad" soon spurred changes in Russia's foreign policy. Initially, President Yeltsin and Foreign Minister Andrei Kozyrev had pursued a strongly pro-American and pro-Western set of policies and had sought Russia's reintegration into Europe. Late in 1992, however, they began moving away from this pro-Western stance toward the positions adopted by their nationalistic critics. Russian politicians and military leaders increasingly defined Russia's sphere of influence as consisting of all former Soviet republics and much of eastern Europe. During President Yeltsin's visit to Brussels late in 1993, his spokesman declared, "Russia considers itself to be a great power and the successor to the Soviet Union and all its might."[27] During the sharpening conflict in Bosnia-Hercegovina, Russia provided consistent and strong support to Serbia and the Serbs, while opposing the aspirations of its former eastern European clients—Poland, Hungary, and the Czech Republic—to forge closer relations with the West.

Illustrating the dangers threatening Russia in its difficult transition was its war against Chechnia in the Caucasus region. In an earlier era the Muslim leader Shamil had long defied the large army of Emperor Nicholas I. The region was important to Russia because it controlled access to the oil of Azerbaijan. After the Soviet collapse Chechnia became a major center of drug running, arms smuggling, and holdups. In October 1991 General Dzhokar Dudaev forcibly seized power in Grozny, its capital. Stating his intention to break away from Russia, he won the Chechen presidency in disputed elections. For the next three years he

---

[27] Löwenhardt, p. 32.

Map 21.2 Ethnic trouble spots in the Russian Federation

	Income per Person $, Nov. 1994	Population '000 Jan. 1995	% of Russians 1989
Ethnic trouble spots			
6 Chechnia	na	1,006	22.0
Chuvashia	36.3	1,361	26.7
Dagestan	49.1	2,009	9.2
5 Ingushetia	na	228	23.0
3 Kabardino-Balkaria	35.7	787	32.0
2 Karachevo-Cherkassia	35.7	435	42.4
4 North Ossetia	40.5	664	29.9
Tuva	57.4	308	32.0
Resource-rich republics			
Karelia	116.2	789	73.6
Komi	98.7	1,203	57.7
Yakutia (Sakha)	142.6	1,035	50.3
Volga republics			
Bashkortostan	51.8	4,077	39.3
Kalmykia	36.4	320	37.7
Mari-El	41.7	767	47.5
Mordovia	37.0	959	60.8
Tatarstan	48.7	3,754	43.3
Udmurtia	47.9	1,641	58.9
Others			
1 Adygeya	36.2	450	68.0
Altai	70.6	200	60.4
Buryatia	45.2	1,052	70.0
Khakassia	56.9	583	79.5
All Russia	*89.9*	*148,200*	*81.5*

remained head of a semi-independent state, running Chechnia's internal affairs as he wished.

On December 9, 1994, President Yeltsin issued a decree on restoring order and Russian control of Chechnia; on December 11 began a Russian military invasion. Yeltsin later justified this attack by the need to hold the Russian Federation together and to crush organized crime there. Actually the Russian Federation, shaky in 1992, appeared quite solid by late 1994, and Chechen organized crime was declining. The invasion was poorly planned and incompetently carried out by badly trained troops of low morale. Despite the boast by Russian Defense Minister Pavel Grachev that Russian troops could take Grozny in a few hours, initial Russian assaults were repelled. Even after Grozny was finally subdued, Russia faced the difficult task of overcoming Chechen guerrillas in the mountains. The invasion cost Yeltsin the support of many democratic leaders and revealed his shaky control over the Russian military. In May 1996 Yeltsin, in a pre-election move, worked out a ceasefire in Chechnia with the successor of Dudaev in Moscow. That ceasefire was short-lived and the bloody conflict continued into summer 1996. Following Yeltsin's July election victory, his new security chief, General Lebed, worked out an agreement with the Chechens that ended the armed conflict but did not resolve the issue of Chechnia's political status as autonomous or independent. President Yeltsin and the Chechen president signed a peace treaty in Moscow in May 1997.

Russia's use of force in Chechnia, suggests former American ambassador Jack Matlock, may dissuade its leaders from resorting to military action elsewhere. Russia had avoided using military force against its neighbors in recent controversies with Kazakhstan and had handled carefully and peacefully the touchy Crimean issue with Ukraine. Matlock therefore doubted Russia would seek to reabsorb territories of the former USSR: "Russia cannot afford an empire again and the regions will not go along with it."[28] The weak

central government had allowed the de facto development of federalism since 1992. Thus Tatarstan and Sakha (formerly Iakutia), avoiding talk of secession or full sovereignty, had driven hard bargains with the Moscow center. The war in Chechnia revealed a clear need to reform the disintegrating Russian army and police.

Post-Soviet Culture

When the USSR collapsed in 1991, Marxism in Russia was thoroughly discredited. As Russia strives to emerge from the rubble of Communist rule, Russian culture, plagued by chaos and confusion, struggles to reshape itself and to find a new identity. Replacing a controlled Soviet culture will be one more decentralized, diffuse, and dissonant.

Literature

This rupture with the Soviet past is especially evident in literature. The writer/poet in Russia was viewed as society's moral conscience. Literature enjoyed a quasi-religious status, reflecting the popular "soul," as the bearer of truth and justice. During the Soviet era writers were expected to exemplify the regime's moral authority, becoming "engineers of the human soul." Poetry and prose had been among the Soviet regime's most powerful weapons in seeking to legitimize the Communist system and conquer the souls of the people. Osip Mandelshtam, a literary victim of Stalin's Great Purge, declared: "Poetry is respected only in this country—here, people are killed for it. There is no country in which *more* people are killed for it." Clearly, today that is no longer true.

The return of Alexander Solzhenitsyn, the Nobel laureate, to Russia in May 1994 after 20 years of forced exile, mostly in seclusion in Vermont, indicated how dramatically the cultural climate had changed. Abroad Solzhenitsyn was lionized as a great Russian writer like Leo Tolstoy. With his highly publicized return and slow railroad journey from Vladivostok to Moscow, he sought to act as the great Russian writer revitalizing his country by his presence and moral author-

---

[28] Kennan Institute (Washington), *Meeting Report* 12, no. 15, May 1, 1995.

ity. But his homecoming served instead as a graphic example of how greatly the cultural terrain had shifted since the fall of communism.

The idea of a great writer as the nation's conscience had become an anachronism. Educated young Russians were curious about Solzhenitsyn, but few have read his books; they disdain his moral posturing and divorce from post-Communist Russian reality. Gregori Amelin, a young Moscow critic, stated that Solzhenitsyn, "with a Hollywood beard, and a conscience shined to an incredible lustre, fails to realize that his appearance in Russia is shamelessly outdated. Who needs him anyway? No one." In October 1994 Solzhenitsyn excoriated the Russian parliament for its failures and false claims to represent the Russian people. Bemused by his philosophical chastisement, many parliament members considered him entirely out of touch with Russian realities and paid him no heed.

Russian writers no longer epitomize the truth. No longer struggling with the "cursed questions" of society, they are no longer indispensable to the nation's welfare, nor are they now "heroes on the barricades" as before. As writer Alexander Kushner explained to David Remnick, an American journalist:

> The writer in Russia was for so long like an uncrowned prince. Even an unpublished poet had a place of respect. Now this is gone. Why? In those days, literature was the one real door open to people of a certain kind. Now there are lots of doors to walk through. You can go into business, play on the Israeli soccer team, play for a New York hockey team, make your fortune in Greece, or even go into politics, if you should choose. At the same time, literature in the eyes of the people has lost its exceptional importance. Literature will always have a place, as it does in America. Marginal, but important. Small, but beautiful. Of course, if a monster, a fascist, like Vladimir Zhirinovskii, is ever elected President of Russia, literature will have to assume its old role. But for now, no.[29]

---

[29] Quoted in David Remnick, "Exit the Saints," *The New Yorker,* July 18, 1994, p. 52.

Cultural Institutions

The old Soviet cultural institutions have crumbled, and nothing new has appeared to replace them. The Soviet Writers' Union, overseeing and controlling literature for the party, disintegrated after the failed August Coup of 1991. Remaining is the dark, foreboding hulk of the Central House of Writers, formerly an elite Soviet cultural center where Writers' Union members basked in privilege and comfort. The demise of cultural institutions such as the Artists' Union and Composers' Union has left a void in which writers, artists, and composers are drifting. Instead of fretting about the size of editions of their published works, they worry now about survival and the commercial value of the creative process in a highly competitive market. Gone are generous state subsidies and commissions. Like everything else in post-Communist Russia, culture too must find a market. Today bookstores and kiosks bulge with translated Western detective stories, romance novels, and soft-core pornography. Readers demand entertainment, not moralizing or propaganda. The guideline is what sells. Lacking government subsidies, publishers realize that the market will determine their fate, that they must produce commercially successful books.

Literary institutes, cultural think tanks where numerous intellectuals churned out scholarly works about Russian and Soviet literature, have fallen victim to the drought in state subsidies. Literary scholars now find themselves irrelevant, unread, alienated, and preoccupied with mere survival. They have lost their patron and their audience.

Few readers want yet another book about Dostoevskii or Gorkii. Everywhere people read trash novels, books on the occult, or works of long-suppressed authors. Escalating prices have limited public access to the book market. Well-established writers now must write for the market rather than from the heart. Some Russian writers have found a better audience abroad than at home. Andrei Bitov, Vladimir Kushner, Tatiana Tolstaia, Vladimir Sorokhin, and other younger writers are little known in Russia or abroad. Nevertheless, they carry on Russian literary traditions by seeking an audience that will respond positively to their works. They are not cultural heroes like their predecessors under communism.

Music shops contain the latest Western rock music and marginal Russian rock imitators. Radio stations broadcast a steady stream of Russian "top 40" music, drowning out classical. Television features "feel good" pop culture, deplored in the West as vacuous and banal. Cheap, often pirated, cassette tapes of Western and Russian rock music fill music shops and shabby kiosks. Private art galleries have proliferated, filled with various artistic works, many created for the tourist trade or the supposed market.

The painful transition to a market economy has been agonizing for all cultural workers now struggling to survive amid market conditions they do not understand. State funding for the arts, libraries, and educational institutions has been drastically reduced or eliminated. State subsidies are no longer available, and the public cannot afford to support cultural activities. The high cost for Russians of theater and concert tickets denies many Russians access to cultural events. Ticket sales alone cannot sustain theaters and theater companies, concert halls and musicians. Theaters are half empty as the quality of productions deteriorates. Scenery and costumes are shabby and threadbare, as are theaters and concert halls. Even the best productions seem seedy. The best performers and companies, committed to past traditions of excellence, seek opportunities abroad or are driven from their chosen professions. Theater companies and music groups compete for scarce foreign tours in order to meet expenses at home.

Russian cinema features American action films of Arnold Schwarzenegger and Sylvester Stallone and blockbusters like *Jurassic Park* and *Titanic*. Snickers candy bars and Marlboro cigarettes are hawked on many street corners and at corner kiosks. Commercial advertising everywhere has replaced Soviet propaganda slogans. Western designer boutiques, promoting current Western fashions, have replaced many of Moscow's and St. Petersburg's drab shops, but most of their fashionable merchandise is out of reach of most Russians, generating anger and hostility toward the West like that of the Cold War era. These changes have left many Russians confused and resentful of what they perceive as a callous alien cultural invasion.

Maintenance of Russia's cultural heritage is haphazard and inconsistent. Should the Soviet cultural heritage be preserved or destroyed? Despite the natural tendency to discard a discredited past, much produced under communism is worth preserving. Many Soviet monuments remain but without a consensus on what should be destroyed or retained. Meanwhile, monuments of the Communist past deteriorate physically.

Inadequate funding has postponed efforts to preserve most cultural monuments. Without proper scientific supervision, historical monuments and valuable archives are threatened. Currently only minor state resources can be invested in cultural projects. Realizing the dangers facing the Russian cultural heritage, people at the grass roots seek to raise funds at home and abroad to assure survival of the best of Russian and Soviet culture.

Religion

Religion has reemerged to fill a part of the void created by communism's precipitous collapse. The Russian Orthodox Church, existing precariously under Soviet rule, has sought to reestablish itself as a major social force, but not without competition from other religious organizations that view Russia as fertile prosletyzing territory. Major Protestant churches, evangelical and New Age groups, Hare Krishnas and Jehovah's Witnesses compete actively for souls in today's Russia. The Orthodox Church lacks adequate resources to restore its presence among the people. Thousands of churches need restoration or rebuilding; a new generation of priests must be recruited and trained. The Orthodox Church is poorly prepared to manipulate the modern media, utilized so effectively by well-trained, well-funded foreign religious groups. The Church also must refurbish an image tarnished by accusations of collaboration with the Communists and of spying on people for the KGB. It must also compete with the Orthodox Church Abroad, established largely by Russian émigrés, claiming to speak with greater moral authority after its unrelenting, decades-long struggle against communism. Communists carefully controlled the number and assured the political reliability of recruits in Soviet theological schools. The existing Orthodox clergy, insufficient in number, is compromised by complicity with the former regime, tainting its moral authority. All this complicates the Church's ability to compete in the open religious marketplace.

Despite these obstacles, the Orthodox Church is reasserting a central role in society. Churches are reopening, renovation is progressing, often with volunteer labor, Church publications are widely disseminated, and the clergy speaks out on social and economic issues. People are responding as they search for new ethical moorings following Marxism-Leninism's collapse. By far the largest number of believers identify with the Russian Orthodox Church. Currently about 40 percent of Russians consider themselves believers, of whom a majority identify with Orthodoxy. Even nonbelievers feel a historical and cultural affinity for Orthodoxy. With a potentially receptive audience, the Church is thus well situated to exert significant social influence. However, its public influence is being undermined by internal authoritarian and ultranationalist tendencies. The Orthodox hierarchy is divided between conservatives refusing to recognize the legitimacy of other religions and a more ecumenical group that welcomes the cooperation of other denominations in spreading Christian ideas. Patriarch Aleksii II, elected in 1990, while not rejecting Russian religious nationalism, has shown some limited interest in closer ties with other Christian denominations.

The Russian Orthodox Church, like other Russian institutions, is attempting to define its role in the new Russia and in the religiously diverse world beyond Russia's borders. It seeks to minister to the more than 25 million ethnic Russians living outside Russia's borders. How can the Moscow Church assert its authority over these souls and prevent Orthodox hierarchies in other former Soviet republics from declaring independence? Traditionally, national Orthodox churches have been autocephalous, and independent Orthodox churches in Ukraine, Belarus, and Georgia would reduce the status of the Russian church. A large Russian Orthodox diaspora and competition within Russia have stimulated nationalism and intolerance within the Church. Anti-Semitism, long a blot in the Orthodox Church, has revived. The Church faces the daunting task of emancipating itself from its past history, notably its association and compromises with Communist and tsarist regimes. To reassert its moral authority, it must stand above politics, speaking directly to the people's spiritual needs.

Yeltsin's Disputed Legacy

History's verdict on Boris Yeltsin, notes biographer Leon Aron, will be determined by the direction taken eventually by the new Russia he did much to shape. If Russia reverts to authoritarianism, with a corrupt oligarchy ruling a backward and stagnant economy and an impoverished populace, Yeltsin will be remembered as one who missed a unique opportunity to change Russia's destiny. But if Russia becomes peaceful, free, open to the world, and prosperous, Yeltsin will rank high among leaders like Charles de Gaulle and Abraham Lincoln, who took over countries facing catastrophe, held them together, and changed them basically for the better. Yeltsin's own record remains provisional and open to widely differing interpretations.[30]

President Yeltsin, notes Aron, dealt a powerful blow to the 400-year tradition of Russian state-building based upon militarism and imperial expansion by completing an unprecedented peaceful and voluntary contraction of the world's last empire as Russia reverted to frontiers resembling those of 1613. Under Yeltsin, Russian messianism disappeared as the Russian state shrank

---

[30] Aron, pp. 691–97.

and its purpose was demystified. For this, Russian communists and conservative nationalists regard Yeltsin at best as a weakling, at worst as a traitor to the Russian nation. This territorial contraction was paralleled by a demilitarization unprecedented in all of Russian, and probably world, history. When Yeltsin assumed power almost one-third of Russia's gross domestic product was spent on the military. By 1996 this had dropped to 5 percent, and in 1997 Yeltsin promised to reduce the military's share to 3 percent by the year 2000. His reforms ended the Russian military's previously unchallenged claim to Russia's choicest resources, as troop levels shrank from about 4 million in January 1992 to 1.7 million in late 1996. Yeltsin pledged to end military conscription and create an all-volunteer armed force of some 600,000, dealing a final blow to Russian militarism.

A key event in Russia's post-imperial adjustment under Yeltsin was accommodation with an independent Ukraine in a May 1997 treaty of friendship and cooperation that contributed greatly to peace and stability in eastern Europe. His patient, persevering negotiations with this much weaker neighbor, Aron finds, was unprecedented for a Russian leader. After initial protests against NATO expansion into central Europe, Yeltsin chose accommodation and acceptance over a revival of the Cold War. Thus in February 1997 he declared: "It has already happened that we, the East and the West, failed to find a chance to reconcile. This chance must not be missed."[31] Among Yeltsin's main achievements in foreign and security policy were the withdrawal of Russian forces from eastern Europe and the Baltic countries, demilitarizing the economy, and peaceful divorce with Ukraine. Not since the early 16th century has Russia been less of a threat to its neighbors and less belligerent.

Despite a dramatic decline in living standards in the Yeltsin years, Russian democracy survived. From 1993 to 1997 Russians voted in six national elections and referendums, with some two-thirds of eligible voters generally casting ballots. Crucial was the presidential election of 1996 when Yeltsin, though seriously ill, staked everything on a race that at the outset seemed hopeless. A very imperfect but functioning grassroots democracy provided Russia with a degree of political stability. Furthermore, with the tragic exception of Chechnia, Yeltsin avoided a threatened disintegration of the Russian Federation. His Federal Treaty of March 1992 was a first attempt to establish bases for post-Soviet statehood, creating for Russia the new principle of equality between provinces and the center in assigning rights and responsibilities. Believing that Russia could be both democratic and united, Yeltsin told regional leaders in spring 1996: "Russia will have a truly democratic, prosperous, and civilized future only on the basis of the development of federalism."[32] The republics pledged allegiance to the territorial unity of the Russian Federation in return for the right to decide their own internal problems.

A crucial element in Yeltsin's legacy was the 1993 Russian Constitution, which is still in force today. It proclaimed that the chief rights and liberties of citizens were inalienable. Based partly on the United States Constitution and on that of the Fifth French Republic, it featured a powerful presidency while guaranteeing freedom and independence of the press. Yeltsin built upon and greatly extended Gorbachev's legacy of tolerance. Although skewered on television and in the press, he revealed a remarkable tolerance. The amnesty of February 1994, legislated by the Duma and signed by Yeltsin after initial hesitation, was the first time in Russia that the legislature had compelled the president to pardon and grant freedom of action to the regime's violent foes.

The Yeltsin regime promoted the rights and careers of the Jewish minority. Many Jews held top positions under Yeltsin. The end of state-directed anti-Semitism created a situation that most Russian Jews had believed impossible. "Life for Russian Jews has never been better," wrote a *New York*

---

[31] Aron, p. 701.

[32] Aron, pp. 708–09.

Times correspondent in spring 1997. "Nobody is hiding the fact that they are Jewish anymore. . . ." After peaking in 1990–91, Jewish emigration from Russia declined steadily. Emerging in Russia was a middle class independent of the state exercising and strongly defending newly granted rights and freedoms, including that to travel abroad. Promoting legal development, Russian judges were rapidly becoming a self-governing element. Two key elements of the Judicial Reform of 1864 were revived: trials by jury and elected justices of the peace. Finally, Russia under Yeltsin moved far ahead of other post-Soviet states in democratization and market reform, except for the Baltic lands. The stubborn Russian adherence to the democratic ideal promoted by Yeltsin provided much hope for the future.

However, like Russia itself, Yeltsin and his regime proved contradictory and dualistic. Thus in 1994 Yeltsin had ordered Russian troops into Chechnia, prosecuting the war there brutally and incompetently. He eroded the new constitutional system with palace intrigues and by ignoring the newly elected parliament. On the other hand, Yeltsin allowed his worst critics complete freedom, risking all in free elections open to those same critics. Yeltsin left behind a political system still semi-authoritarian, corrupt and mistrusted by society, but governable and with the popular vote. At almost every important juncture Yeltsin moved towards greater political freedom, a free market, and a freer society. Yeltsin, affirmed Aron, made the collapse of Soviet totalitarianism irreversible, dissolved the Russian empire, ended state ownership of the economy, and held together and rebuilt Russia.[33]

London's *Economist* presented a more critical assessment of the Yeltsin legacy. Although unique as Russia's first elected democratic leader and the first to yield power voluntarily and constitutionally to a handpicked successor, Yeltsin also resembled past Russian leaders by seeking to equal the West economically and culturally, but failing as they

had. Sometimes driving change forward, at others just riding the wave, Yeltsin failed to rank with Russia's greatest reformers as a pioneer of change while proving able to accumulate and preserve political authority against all odds. His greatest contribution was not as builder but in destroying a still-potent Communist system by dealing the final blows to the USSR and its ruling Communist Party. From the wreckage of a state-controlled economy he tried to build a semi-capitalist one but never quite succeeded, often being too hesitant or bored to act constructively. At the peak of his career many Russians identified with his bluntness, impulsiveness, and even with his drinking. When Russia badly needed foreign aid, Yeltsin convinced Western leaders to overlook his faults and support him. However, his reputation plunged in his final years, when many Russians believed he had conceded too much to the West.[34] Thus the Yeltsin legacy is a mixed bag of pros and cons.

InfoTrac® College Edition Search Terms

Enter the search term *Yeltsin* in the Subject Guide. Enter the search term *Russia* in the Subject Guide, and then go to subdivision *environmental aspects*. Enter the search term *Russia* in the Subject Guide, and then go to subdivision *economic aspects*. Enter the search term *Russia* in the Subject Guide, and then go to subdivision *economic policy*.

Suggested Additional Reading

A DEVASTATED LAND

FESHBACH, M., and A. FRIENDLY, JR. *Ecocide in the USSR. Health and Nature Under Siege* (New York, 1992).

GOLDMAN, M. I. *The Spoils of Progress: Environmental Pollution in the Soviet Union* (Cambridge, MA, 1972).

KOMAROV, B. *The Destruction of Nature in the Soviet Union* (White Plains, NY, 1980).

---

[33] Aron, pp. 733–35.

[34] *The Economist* (London), January 8, 2000.

MEDVEDEV, Z. *The Legacy of Chernobyl* (New York and London, 1992).

MOORE, J. L., ed. *Legacies of the Collapse of Marxism* (Fairfax, VA, 1994).

PETERSON, D. J. *Troubled Lands: The Legacy of Soviet Environmental Destruction* (Boulder, CO, 1993).

PRYDE, P. *Environmental Management in the Soviet Union* (New York, 1991).

STEWART, J. M. *The Soviet Environment: Problems, Policies and Politics* (New York, 1992).

WEINER, D. R. *Models of Nature: Ecology, Conservation and Cultural Revolution in Soviet Russia* (Bloomington, IN, 1988).

THE YELTSIN YEARS

ARON, L. *Yeltsin: A Revolutioinary Life* (New York, 2000).

ÄSLUND, A. *How Russia Became a Market Economy* (Washington, 1995).

BATALDEN, S., ed. *Seeking God: The Recovery of Religious Identity in Orthodox Russia, Ukraine and Georgia* (DeKalb, IL, 1993).

BEUMERS, B. *Russia on Reels: The Russian Idea in Post-Soviet Cinema* (New York, 2000).

BLUM, D. W., ed. *Russia's Future: Consolidation or Disintegration?* (Boulder, CO, 1994).

BRADY, R. *Kapitalizm: Russia's Struggle to Free Its Economy* (New Haven, 1999).

BREMMER, I., and R. TARAS, eds. *New States, New Politics: Building the Post-Soviet Nations,* 2d ed. (Cambridge, 1996).

BROWN, J. F. *Hopes and Shadows: Eastern Europe After Communism* (Durham, NC, 1994).

BUCKLEY, M. *Post-Soviet Women: From the Baltic to Central Asia* (Cambridge, England, 1997).

BUZGALIN, A. V. *Bloody October in Moscow* (New York, 1994).

COHEN, S. F. *Failed Crusade: America and the Tragedy of Post-Communist Russia* (New York, 2000).

COLTON, T., and R. LEGVOLD, eds. *After the Soviet Union: From Empire to Nations* (New York, 1992).

COOPER, L. *Russia and the World: New State-of-Play on the International Stage* (New York, NY, 1999).

DAVIES, R. W. *Soviet History in the Yeltsin Era* (New York, NY, 1997).

DAWISHA, K. and B. PARROTT, eds. *Democratic Change and Authoritarian Reactions in Russia, Ukraine, Belarus, and Moldova* (Cambridge, England, 1997).

DAWISHA, K., and B. PARROTT. *Russia and the New States of Eurasia: The Politics of Upheaval* (Cambridge, 1994).

DENBER, R., ed. *The Soviet Nationality Reader: The Disintegration in Context* (Boulder, CO, 1992).

DILLER, D. C. *Russia and the Independent States* (Washington, 1993).

DUNLOP, J. B. *Russia Confronts Chechnia: Roots of a Separatist Conflict* (Cambridge, England, 1998).

DUNLOP, J. B. *The Rise of Russia and the Fall of the Soviet Empire* (Princeton, 1993, 1995).

ELLIS, J. *The Russian Orthodox Church: Triumphalism and Defensiveness* (New York, 1996).

ESSIG, L. *Queer in Russia: A Story of Sex, Self, and Other* (Durham, NC, 1999).

FIELD, M. C. and J. L. TWIGG, *Russia's Torn Safety Nets: Health and Social Welfare during the Transition* (New York, 2000).

FREELAND, C. *Sale of the Century: Russia's Wild Ride from Communism to Capitalism* (New York, 2000).

FRIEDMAN, R. I. *Red Mafiya* (New York, 2000).

FUNK, N., and M. MUELLER, eds. *Gender Politics and Post-Communism from Eastern Europe and the Former Soviet Union* (New York, 1993).

GALL, C. and T. de WAAL. *Chechnia: Calamity in the Caucasus* (New York, 1998).

GARDNER, H. *Dangerous Crossroads: Europe, Russia, and the Future of NATO* (Westport, CT, 1997).

GESSEN, M. *Dead Again: The Russian Intelligentsia after Communism* (New York, 1997).

GILL, G., and R. D. MARWICK. *Russia's Stillborn Democracy? From Gorbachev to Yeltsin* (Oxford, UK, 2000).

GINSBURGS, G., et al., eds. *Russia and America: From Rivalry to Reconciliation* (Armonk, NY, 1993).

GOLDENBERG, S. *Pride of Small Nations: The Causasus and Post-Soviet Disorder* (Atlantic Highlands, NJ, 1994).

GOLDMAN, M. I. *Lost Opportunity: What Has Made Economic Reform in Russia So Difficult?* (New York, 1996).

GUSTAFSON, T. *Capitalism Russian-Style* (Cambridge, England, 1999).

HANDELMAN, S. *Comrade Criminal: Russia's New Mafiya* (New Haven, CT, 1995).

HELLBERG-HIRN, E. *Soil and Soul: The Symbolic World of Russianness (Nationalism in Russia)* (Brookfield, VT, 1998).

HERTZ, N. *Russian Business Relationships in the Wake of Reform* (New York, 1997).

HOLDEN, G. *Russia After the Cold War: History and the Nation in Post-Soviet Security Politics* (New York, 1994).

JOHNSON, T., and S. MILLER. *Russian Security After the Cold War: Seven Views From Moscow* (Washington, 1994).

JUVILER, P., et al., eds. *Human Rights for the 21st Century, Foundations for Responsible Hope: A US–Post-Soviet Dialogue* (Armonk, NY, 1993).

JUVILER, P. *Freedom's Ordeal: The Struggle for Human Rights and Democracy in Post-Soviet States* (Philadelphia, PA, 1998).

KAMPFNER, J. *Inside Yeltsin's Russia: Corruption, Conflict, Capitalism* (London, 1994).

KANET, R.E., and A. V. KOZHEMIAKHIN, eds. *The Foreign Policy of the Russian Federation* (New York, 1997).

KARIMOV, I. *Uzbekistan on the Threshold of the Twenty-First Century* (New York, 1998).

KARTSEV, V. *P. Zhirinovsky* (New York, 1995).

KHASBULATOV, R. I. *The Struggle in Russia: Power and Change in the Democratic Revolution* (New York, 1993).

KHAZANOV, A. *After the USSR: Ethnicity, Nationalism, and Politics in the Commonwealth of Independent States* (Madison, WI, 1995).

KIRKOW, P. *Russia's Provinces: Authoritarian Transformation vs. Local Autonomy?* (New York, 1998).

KLEBNIKOV, P. *Godfather of the Kremlin: Boris Berezovsky and the Looting of Russia* (New York, 2000).

KNIGHT, A. *Spies Without Cloaks: The KGB's Successors* (Princeton, 1996).

KUZIO, T. *Ukraine under Kuchma* (New York, 1997).

LAIRD, S. *Voices of Russian Literature: Interviews with Ten Contemporary Writers* (New York, 1999).

LAPIDUS, G., ed. *The New Russia: Troubled Transformation* (Boulder, CO, 1995).

LIEVEN, A. *Chechnya: Tombstone of Russian Power* (New Haven, CT, 1998).

———. *Ukraine and Russia: A Fraternal Rivalry* (Washington, DC, 1999).

LIKHACHEV, D. S. *Reflections on the Russian Soul: A Memoir* (Budapest, 2000).

LLOYD, J. *Rebirth of a Nation: An Anatomy of Russia* (London, 1998).

LOWELL, S. *The Russian Reading Revolution: Print Culture in the Soviet and Post-Soviet Eras* (New York, 2000).

LÖWENHARDT, J. *The Reincarnation of Russia: Struggling with the Legacy of Communism, 1990–1994* (Durham, NC, 1995).

MALIK, H., ed. *Central Asia: Its Strategic Importance and Future Prospects* (New York, 1994).

MARSH, R., ed. *Women in Russia and Ukraine* (New York, 1996).

MCAULEY, M. *Russia's Policy of Uncertainty* (Cambridge, England, 1997).

MCFAUL, M. *Post-Communist Politics: Democratic Prospects in Russia and Eastern Europe* (Washington, 1993).

———. *Russia's 1996 Presidential Election: The End of Polarized Politics* (Stanford, 1997).

———. *The Troubled Birth of Russian Democracy* (Stanford, 1993).

———. *Understanding Russia's Parliamentary Elections: Implications for U.S. Foreign Policy* (Stanford, 1994).

MERRIDALE, C. *Night of Stone: Death and Memory in Russia* (London, 2000).

MICKIEWICZ, E. *Changing Channels: Television and the Struggle for Power in Russia*, rev. ed. (Durham, NC, 1999).

MICHKA, V. *Inside the New Russia* (Broken Arrow, OK, 1994).

MOTYL, A. *Dilemmas of Independence: Ukraine After Totalitarianism* (New York, 1993).

NIMMO, W. F. *Japan and Russia: A Reevaluation in the Post-Soviet Era* (Westport, CT, 1994).

ODOM, W., and R. DUJARRIC. *Commonwealth or Empire? Russia, Central Asia, and the Transcaucasus* (Indianapolis, 1995).

ODOM, W. *The Collapse of the Soviet Military* (New Haven, CT, 1999).

PATTERSON, P., ed. *Socialist Past: The Rise of the Private Sector in Command Economics* (Boulder, CO, 1993).

PIIRAINEN, T. *Toward a New Social Order in Russia* (Brookfield, VT, 1997).

POPOV, N. P. *The Russian People Speak: Democracy at the Crossroads* (Syracuse, NY, 1994).

POSADSKAYA, A., et al., eds. *Women in Russia: A New Era in Russian Feminism* (London and New York, 1994).

RA'ANAN, U., and K. MARTIN, eds. *Russia: A Return to Imperialism?* (New York, 1996).

RA'ANAN, U., et al., eds. *Russian Pluralism—Now Irreversible?* (New York, 1993).

RACIOPPI, L. and K. O'SULLIVAN SEE. *Women's Activism in Contemporary Russia* (Philadelphia, PA, 1997).

RAMET, S. P., ed. *Rocking the State: Rock Music and Politics in Eastern Europe and Russia* (Boulder, CO, 1994).

REDDAWAY, P. and D. GLINSKI. *The Tragedy of Russia's Reforms: Market Bolshevism against Democracy* (Herndon, VA, 2000).

REMNICK, D. *Resurrection: The Struggle for a New Russia* (New York, 1997).

SAIKAL, A., and W. MALEY, eds. *Russia in Search of Its Future* (Cambridge, 1995).

SEDLICKAS, K. S. and R. *The War in Chechnya* (College Station, TX, 1999).

SAIVETZ, C., and A. JONES, eds. *In Search of Pluralism: Soviet and Post-Soviet Politics* (Boulder, CO, 1994).

SERGEYEV, V. M. *The Wild East: Crime and Lawlessness in Post-Communist Russia* (Armonk, NY, 1998).

SESTANOVICH, S., ed. *Rethinking Russia's National Interests* (Washington, 1994).

SHEVTSOVA, L. *Yeltsin's Russia: Myths and Realities* (Washington, DC, 1999).

SHLAPENTOKH, V., et al., eds. *The New Russian Diaspora: Russian Minorities in the Former Soviet Republics* (Armonk, NY, 1994).

SILVERMAN, B. and M. YANOWITCH. *New Rich, New Poor, New Russia: Winners and Losers on the Russian Road to Capitalism* (Armonk, NY, 1997).

SMITH, A. *Russia and the World Economy: Problems of Integration* (New York, 1993).

SMITH, G. B. *Reforming the Russian Legal System* (Cambridge, 1996).

SMITH, G. *The Post-Soviet States: Mapping the Politics of Transition* (London, 1999).

SURASKA, W. *How the Soviet Union Disappeared: An Essay on the Causes of Dissolution* (Durham, NC, 1998).

TROFIMENKO, H. *Russian National Interests and the Current Crisis in Russia* (Brookfield, VT, 1999).

TURPIN, J. *Reinventing the Soviet Self: Media and Social Change in the Former Soviet Union* (Westport, CT, 1995).

VACHNADZE, G. N. *Russia's Hotbeds of Tension* (Commack, NY, 1994).

WANNER, C. *Burden of Dreams: History and Identity in Post-Soviet Ukraine* (University Park, PA, 1998)

WEIGLE, M. A. *Russia's Liberal Project: State-Society Relations in the Transition from Communism* (University Park, PA, 2000).

WHITE, S. *Russia Goes Dry: Alcohol, State and Society* (Cambridge, 1995).

———, et al., eds. *The Politics of Transition: Shaping a Post-Soviet Future* (Cambridge, 1993).

WHITE, S. *Russia's New Politics: The Management of a Postcommunist Society* (Cambridge, UK, 2000).

WILLIAMS, P., ed. *Russian Organized Crime: The New Threat?* (London, 1997).

WILSON, A. *Ukrainian Nationalism in the 1990s: A Minority Faith* (Cambridge, 1996).

YAKOVLEV, A. *The Fate of Marxism in Russia,* trans. Catherine Fitzpatrick (New Haven, CT, 1993).

22

The Putin Presidency

On March 26, 2000, Acting President Vladimir Vladmirovich Putin, age 47, scored a decisive victory in Russia's presidential election over Communist Gennadii Ziuganov. On May 7 Putin formally assumed office as Russia's president in that country's first free and democratic transfer of power. An athlete and former KGB operative, Putin had shot up from obscurity since 1996. As president he affirmed his intention to rule legally and hold together a shaky Russian Federation. What type of leader is the Putin now charged with Russia's destiny? Which policies is he likely to pursue during his four year presidential term? Can Putin move Russia more swiftly and successfully than President Yeltsin through its troubled transitions? Let's take a look at Putin, the man and political leader, and at his views.

Early Life and Career

Vladimir Putin was born on October 7, 1952, in Leningrad (now St. Petersburg) as the only child of a factory foreman and a mother reportedly a decorated war veteran. His paternal grandfather,

born in imperial St. Petersburg, worked as a cook, for a time at one of Stalin's dachas. As a youngster, recalled Putin, "I was a hooligan, not a Pioneer (Communist youth). . . . I really was a bad boy. . . . I got into sports when I was about ten or eleven. . . . It was sports that dragged me off the streets."[1] Like most people in Leningrad then, the Putins lived in a dismal communal flat. By the time Vladimir entered an elite secondary school, he was a top-ranked expert in sambo, which combined judo and wrestling. In a school emphasizing chemistry, he at first planned to become a chemist, then was drawn increasingly to the humanities. Fellow pupils and his teachers recall Putin as the steadiest and hardest working student. In 1970 young Putin enrolled at Leningrad State University, majored in civil law, and studied German, impressing his fellow students with his inner strength and athletic ability. Even in secondary school, recalled Putin, "I wanted to work in intelligence. . . . I wanted to be a spy." Learning that law

---

[1] Putin, V. *First Person.* (New York, NY, 2000), pp. 18–19. An astonishingly frank self-portrait by Russia's President Vladimir Putin.

school would help him achieve that goal, he began to prepare himself for law school: "And nobody could stop me." Athletics remained his sole extracurricular activity. "I became a sambo master black belt after entering university, and then a judo master two years later." Noted a cellist friend, Sergei Roldugin: "Volodya (diminutive of Vladimir) has a very strong character. . . . He's as tenacious as a bulldog."[2]

In 1975 Putin graduated with honors, having acquired at Leningrad University a genuine appreciation of democratic values. Noted Leningrad's mayor Anatolii Sobchak: "The atmosphere at the university was free-thinking, democratic and dissident-like. It is not necessary to convince him [Putin] that we need to have a market economy, to respect private property and the rule of law. It's already his professional credo . . . acquired while he was at the university."[3]

Shortly after graduation, KGB recruiters offered him a job and Putin accepted immediately. He spent most of the next decade in his native Leningrad. In the early 1980s he married Liudmila, a specialist in English and French; they remain happily married with two daughters. In 1985 the KGB sent Putin to communist East Germany where, as Mr. Adarnov, he directed a German-Soviet friendship society in Leipzig while living in nearby Dresden. About his activities there, Putin stated somewhat evasively: "I looked for information about political parties, the tendencies inside these parties, their leaders. . . . It was very routine work."[4]

After East Germany collapsed, and disillusioned with the KGB, Putin returned to Leningrad University intending to embark on an academic career. He began writing a doctoral dissertation for the international affairs department there as a cover for his continued intelligence work. Soon Putin was called in by Leningrad's liberal mayor,

Anatolii Sobchak, who offered him a nice post. When Putin informed the mayor that he was still in the KGB, Sobchak burst out "Screw it!" Sobchak quickly developed great trust in Putin, naming him his external-affairs aide charged with recruiting foreign companies and promoting business. In a city embracing capitalism in the twilight of the Gorbachev era, Putin became the man to see because he got things done. Putin submitted his resignation from the KGB in 1990, but his letter became stalled in the bureaucracy, so that when the August 1991 coup erupted he remained an active KGB officer. During that coup Putin's second letter of resignation was finally accepted. He recalled: "During the days of the [August] coup, all the ideals, all the goals that I had had when I went to work for the KGB had collapsed."[5]

Soon Putin became deputy mayor of St. Petersburg (recovering its traditional name in 1992) and in Sobchak's words, "my most responsible and hard-working assistant." Putin stated that he had quit intelligence work for politics because government service offered a prospect "to make something happen" at a critical time in history. In Sobchak's administration Putin sought to unravel the bureaucracy and foster the building of highways, telecommunications, and hotels in St. Petersburg in order to attract foreign investment. That city's subsequent relative prosperity rests partly upon economic foundations laid by Putin. A senior analyst at the Leontiev Center stated: "Putin was one of the most honest and decent people in the St. Petersburg government."

Then early in 1996 a disaster struck Putin's promising political career. He had shaped Sobchak's political campaign for mayor of St. Petersburg only to have him lose the 1996 election. Alone among Sobchak's aides, Putin promptly resigned his post declaring: "Better to be hanged for loyalty than rewarded for treason."[6]

---

[2] *First Person*, pp. 22, 32–33, 51.
[3] *New York Times*, February 20, 2000. Michael Wines, "Putin Retains Discipline While Steering toward Reform."
[4] *First Person*, p. 67.

[5] Ibid., pp. 83, 90–94; *New York Times*, February 20, 2000. Michael Wines, "Putin Retains Soviet Discipline."
[6] Wines, *op. cit.*

The Road to the Presidency

For a few months after his resignation Putin remained unemployed. Then Pavel Borodin, President Yeltsin's chief of staff, offered him a job in Moscow as deputy to the head of the president's General Affairs Department. "I was in charge of the legal division and Russian property abroad." Putin's political career then took off as he was promoted every year. In 1997 Putin was named head of the Main Control Directorate. Early in 1998 he became first deputy head of the presidential administration responsible for the farflung regions of the Russian Federation. Later that year Putin was appointed director of the Federal Security Service, successor to the sinister KGB. He was not asked whether he wanted that rather thankless position. "The President simply signed a decree," noted Putin, and Premier Kirienko informed him at the airport. Entering that KGB building, Putin felt "as if they were plugging me into an electrical outlet." In his previous Kremlin post, ". . . Nobody controls me. I control everybody else. But at the FSS I reported to the division head and the department head. . . . There was a lot of pressure." In August 1999 President Yeltsin rescued Putin from the security service by nominating him as premier. Recalled Putin, "When I was appointed prime minister, it was interesting and it was an honor. I thought, 'Well, I'll work for a year, and that's fine. If I can help save Russia from collapse, then I'll have something to be proud of.'"[7]

Putin then had no idea he was being groomed as Yeltsin's successor. In mid-December 1999 President Yeltsin, inviting Putin into his office, told him he had decided to resign as president and would name Putin acting president of Russia. "To be honest," responded Putin, "I don't know if I'm ready for this or whether I want it because it is a rather difficult fate."[8] Nonetheless, after some reflection, Putin agreed to serve as acting president. On December 31, 1999 Yeltsin turned over the reins of office to Putin.

That same day, in an initial act as acting president, Putin signed a decree granting retiring President Yeltsin and his family a series of benefits and privileges, including immunity from criminal investigation or prosecution. That apparently was the key to the sudden but smooth transfer of power, and seemingly it had been prepared by Yeltsin's staff.[9] Thereafter, Putin excluded Yeltsin's influential daughter Tatiana Diachenko and several other Yeltsin staff members from the Kremlin.

Vladimir Putin served as acting Russian president until his formal election to that office on March 26, 2000. As a practicing Orthodox Christian he had delivered a sermon on Christmas Eve 1999 to reporters outside a Moscow church. He represented with his team the new people entering the Russian government: "They don't drink or smoke or go hunting. . . . They are entirely different people (from Yeltsin and Chernomyrdin)—not only by age, but by upbringing and behavior."[10] Putin's defining characteristic, noted Wines, seemed to be a passion for order and the desire to see Russia rise from the ashes. A former U.S. Senate aide who had often negotiated with Putin, described him as very tough, mentally swift, excellently prepared, and ingenious in getting through a labyrinthine Russian bureaucracy. "He knows how to get results." Blaming the breakup of the USSR on official laxness, Putin declared: "And if we continue like this, Russia will fall to pieces, and it will happen so quickly you and I cannot even imagine."[11]

During his months as premier and acting president, prosecuting the renewed war in Chechnia, Putin belligerently condemned foreign criticism of Russian behavior there. "Last summer," he stated, "we began a battle, not against the independence of Chechnia, but against the aggressive aspirations that had begun to flourish there. We are not attacking. We are defending ourselves." Putin claimed he had decided to continue the Chechnia operations after the Chechens allegedly blew up

---

[7] *First Person*, pp. 130, 204.
[8] Ibid., p. 204.

[9] *New York Times*, January 2, 2000, Wines, p. 4.
[10] Ibid., February 20 2000, Wines.
[11] Ibid.

apartment houses in Moscow and two other cities. As to future Russian policy in Chechnia, Putin stated:

> First, we have to finish the military operation . . . and break up the major bandit formations. . . . Simultaneously, we need to strengthen the role of law enforcement agencies and restore government agencies. . . . We have to tackle social problems, schools and hospitals . . . , then hold elections.

Direct presidential rule would be needed in Chechnia for a year or two, Putin concluded.[12]

There were various ways of looking at Putin's pledge as acting president to restore strong central government in Russia. In the West that pledge sparked fears of a crackdown on civil liberties and a return to authoritarian rule, fanned by Putin's direction of the war in Chechnia. However, his admirers insisted he wished merely to subjugate a corrupt Russian bureaucracy and economy. Nonetheless, as president Putin would inherit the near dictatorial powers enshrined in Yeltsin's 1993 Constitution. From physical or political infirmity, Yeltsin had never made full use of these. Putin indicated a belief that Russia could not become an advanced nation politically and economically until it rooted out Soviet traditions and bridged an ideological divide pitting a communist third against the democratic remainder. In "Russia at the Turn of the Millenium," published on a Kremlin Internet site, Putin wrote that communism's achievements should be recognized. However, one must "realize the outrageous price our country and its people had to pay for that Bolshevist experiment. Russia needs a strong state power and must have it. But a strong state means a law-based, workable federative state." Crucial in achieving that, Putin continued, were a streamlined, corruption-free bureaucracy, a merit system for hiring and rewarding government workers, a stronger judiciary, and closer ties between Moscow and Russia's regions.[13]

Putin supported his call for serious reforms with sobering statistics. Even if Russia's GDP per person were to rise by 8 percent annually for the next fifteen years, Russia would still only match contemporary Portugal. To achieve the level of Britain or France would require a 10 percent annual growth rate over the same period—and only if Britain and France stood still. Except in the electricity and raw materials industries, individual Russian productivity was only 25 percent that of the United States. Such shortcomings, warned Putin, could be overcome only by a comprehensive plan for Russia's restructuring and recovery. "The paramount word is fast. . . . We have no time for a slow start."[14] What a contrast with traditional Soviet economic boasting!

The London *Economist* confirmed Putin's critical assessment of Russia's economic plight. As the year 2000 began, compared to other well-educated, industrialized countries, Russia was dismally poor. Wages averaged only about $65 per month compared to about $300 in neighboring Estonia. Russia's economy had shrunk almost every year since the Soviet Union's collapse, output falling by 53 percent since 1990, stated official statistics. Except for a few prestige projects in Moscow and St. Petersburg, Russia's physical infrastructure continued to decay. During the 1990s the population had declined by 6 million persons (see Figure 22.1). The political situation was also poor, corruption was blatant, and crime was widespread. The wealthy and powerful stood above the law and, mostly, escaped taxation. Fortunately, there were also recent positive signs. In 1999 the economy had grown by 3.2 percent officially, foreign currency reserves were rising, the ruble was stable, and inflation was under control. Also, more taxes were being collected.[15]

Anatolii Sobchak, Putin's former boss, concluded that he would benefit from his years as an intelligence agent in East Germany in touch with Western governments and businesses. Sobchak

---

[12] *First Person*, pp. 143, 165.
[13] *New York Times*, January 2, 2000, Wines, "A Key to Putin's Plans."

[14] Ibid.
[15] *Economist* (London), April 1, 2000, "Putin's Russia: The Chaos at the Door."

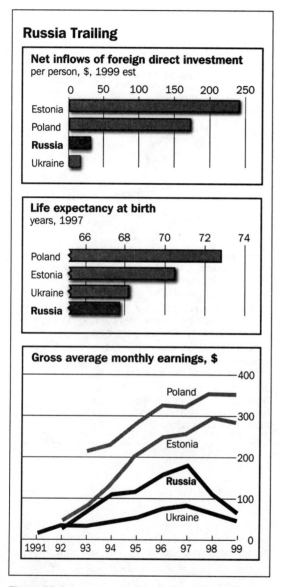

Figure 22.1
Putin's Russia

Source: "Putin's Russia: The Chaos at the Door," *Economist* (London), April 1, 2000. © The Economist Newspaper Group, Inc. Reprinted with permission. Further reproduction prohibited.

expected that Putin would not repeat the mistakes of Russian leaders in the early 1990s by plunging into capitalism without the legal system and governmental regulations required to sustain it.

Instead Sobchak expected Putin to act as had Presidents Theodore and Franklin Roosevelt, who had amassed state power over the economy to shape a modern capitalist system. "I think Putin has a wonderful opportunity to become for Russia what the Roosevelts are for America. And if he does that, he'll become the greatest president in the history of the country."[16]

After the upper house of Russia's Parliament confirmed March 26, 2000, as election day, a brief presidential campaign opened. Putin's presidential prospects had been greatly enhanced by the December 19, 1999, parliamentary elections in which two government parties, buoyed by apparent successes in the war in Chechnia, did surprisingly well. "There are no forces that can stand against Putin today," stated the governor of Saratov province, Dmitrii Aiatsko. "But no one wants succession by acclamation."[17] Putin's prospects were further improved on January 6, 2000, when a group of powerful regional governors abandoned his chief rival, former Premier Primakov, and pledged their support to Putin. Other announced candidates included Grigorii Yavlinskii, leader of the liberal Yabloko Party; Vladimir Zhirinovskii of the semi-fascist Liberal Democratic Party; and the Communist leader, Gennadii Zyuganov (see Figure 22.2). As acting president, Putin called for an election campaign "utterly clean without any mudslinging and aimed at creating equal conditions for all participants."[18]

Putin, like most spies, concealed his motives well, noted *Economist* in January 2000. Was he coming to power as a bottled-up reformer resolved to take Russia into Europe, or did he remain loyal to the ruthless world of the Soviet security services? Currently he enjoyed great power and popularity and had waged war in Chechnia with enthusiasm since becoming

---

[16] *New York Times,* January 2, 2000, Wines, "A Key to Putin's Plans: Intolerance of Corruption," p. 4.
[17] *New York Times,* January 6, 2000, Celestine Bohlen, "Russians to Vote March 26 to Choose a Successor to Yeltsin," p. 8.
[18] Ibid.

Preliminary results for Sunday's elections to the Russian Duma, as of 6:45 p.m. local time Monday with 84% of the vote counted.

% OF VOTE	PARTY	SEATS IN NEW DUMA ■ SEATS IN LAST DUMA ■	% OF NEW DUMA
24.2%	Communist Party	111 / 147	24.7%
23.4	Unity	76	16.9
12.6	Fatherland–All Russia	63	14.0
8.7	Union of Right-Wing Forces	29	6.4
6.1	Yabloko	22 / 46	4.9
6.1	Zhirinovsky bloc	17 / 51	3.8
1.2	Our Home is Russia	7 / 66	1.5

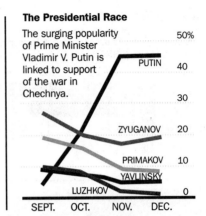

The Presidential Race

The surging popularity of Prime Minister Vladimir V. Putin is linked to support of the war in Chechnya.

Key Figures in the Parties   And how their fortunes have changed:

COMMUNIST PARTY   *Gennadi V. Zyuganov, party leader* Met their expected target of a quarter of the seats, but are unlikely to dominate the new Duma after a pre-election alliance collapsed.

UNITY   *Sergei Shoigu, Emergencies Minister* The success of this newly formed party, backed by Prime Minister Vladimir V. Putin, was helped by frequent, and positive, media coverage of Shoigu.

UNION OF RIGHT-WING FORCES   *Sergei Kiriyenko, former Prime Minister* This coalition of "young reformers," also endorsed by Putin, did well to win 8.7 percent of the vote; many of its key figures are linked to the economic collapse of August 1996.

FATHERLAND–ALL RUSSIA   *Yevgeny M. Primakov, former Prime Minister, and Yuri M. Luzhkov, mayor of Moscow* This left-leaning centrist coalition had expected to do much better but faced fierce attacks from the Kremlin.

ZHIRINOVSKY BLOC   *Vladimir V. Zhirinovsky, party leader* With fewer seats, the ultranationalist Zhirinovsky may not be able to get away with his usual antics.

YABLOKO   *Grigory A. Yavlinsky, party leader* Voters may have tired of Yavllinksy's opposition to the government and his criticism of the war in Chechnya.

OUR HOME IS RUSSIA   *Viktor S. Chernomyrdin, former Prime Minister* Having lost nearly all its seats, and failing to qualify as a party in the new Duma, the party faces an uncertain future.

Figure 22.2
Aftermath of the Russian Parliamentary Elections

Sources: *The New York Times,* Dec. 21, 1999. Copyright © 1999 by the New York Times Co. Reprinted by permission. Based on information from Central Election Commission; Reuters; NTV Russian television; All-Russian/National Center for the Study of Public Opinion (presidential polls).

premier. Flattening opponents in judo, Putin responded to Russian desires for a physically fit, youthful leader. Visiting Chechnia battlefronts in battledress, he had played the role of a military man, but he also appealed to liberals by placing flowers on the grave of their hero, Andrei Sakharov. With his firm grip, Putin might well tackle the lawlessness contributing to Russia's economic misery. His decree of January 6 ordered security forces to crack down on organized crime and terrorism. His background suggested, con-

cluded *Economist,* that Putin was more anxious to modernize Russia than make it democratic.[19]

Putin was emphasizing the urgent need to restore the authority in Russia's 89 regions of a strong central government, noted a *Times* article in early March 2000. During the 1990s, regional leaders had grown used to acting on their own without consulting Moscow. Thus independent-minded Tatarstan had declared its sovereignty in

---

[19] *The Economist,* January 8, 2000, p. 51, "Vladimir Putin, Russia's Post-Cold Warrior."

1990, claimed its oil wealth for itself, and asserted the trappings of statehood with a flag, hymn, and national day. Putin promised to end such freelance federalism. "Regional leaders are very afraid of Putin," stated Elena Mizulina, a Yaroslavl deputy. "He will pressure them—and that is a good thing for Russia—but the key test is how he does it." Already by March 2000 he had begun tightening federal control, having replaced one-quarter of presidential representatives in the regions since January 1.[20]

As the presidential elections approached, the Communists were busily campaigning all across Russia. Their leader, Gennadii Zyuganov, led all other candidates opposing Putin. Although the Communist Party was ridiculed in much of Russia and was weakened by struggles among hardliners, nationalists, and centrists, it remained Russia's largest and best-organized political party. "Yeltsin delivered a major blow to the Communists because he resigned and turned over power to a young guy who is relatively normal," stated Aleksandr Gelman, a playwright and friend of Gorbachev. "Before Yeltsin resigned, it was possi-ble . . . that Communists might come to power." But now, he predicted, Communist influence would slowly decline. However, in the December 1999 parliamentary elections, 24 percent of the voters supported Communist candidates, 2 per-cent more than in 1995.[21]

On the eve of the presidential elections there was great uncertainty in Russia and abroad as to where Putin, if victorious, would take Russia. Early in March Putin met with NATO's Secretary-General and suggested that Russia would eventu-ally join NATO. However, a few days later he stated that Russia had no hope of joining NATO and did not want NATO on its frontiers. Western business interests generally praised Putin's posi-tive emphasis on free trade and open markets and

the need for foreign investment in Russia. He had revealed a clear penchant for order and centralized control. As premier and acting president he had tightened financial controls over the regions while seeking to surround himself with former KGB operatives, noted Nikolai Petrov of the Carnegie Endowment for International Peace. Petrov believed Russia under Putin was headed towards a softened form of dictatorship: "Unfortunately, the majority of [Russians] . . . are ready to give him almost all democracy's achievements to get stabil-ity and security and certain guarantees."[22]

Putin as President

In the presidential election of March 26, 2000, Vladimir Putin won with about 53 percent of the popular vote, while Communist leader Gennadii Zyuganov ran a strong second with almost 30 percent. Grigorii Yavlinskii's poor showing of only 6 percent revealed the disarray of liberal politi-cians. Putin's victory was broadbased: he won majorities in all but six Russian regions. The newly elected president told his cabinet that it needed to concentrate work on a major economic program that he wanted to have ready for his inauguration in early May. That same evening Putin met with ex-President Yeltsin, who praised him warmly. Congratulating Putin, Western leaders expressed hopes for Russia's future. President Clinton in a telephone conversation advised Putin to strengthen democracy and Russia's international ties. President Jiang of China urged him to deepen their "strategic partnership."[23]

Putin's victory drew public attention to an opulent Moscow building named Aleksandr House, where a team of liberal economists and other experts drafted the President's blueprint for Russia. Their leader, German Gref, a leading econ-omist, predicted confidently that by late May Putin

[20] New York Times, March 9, 2000, Celestine Bohlen, "Rus-sian Regions Wary as Putin Tightens Control."
[21] Ibid., March 13, 2000, Patrick Tyler, "Russia's Commu-nists, Still Alive, Await an Opening."
[22] Ibid., March 22, 2000, Michael Wines, "He's Russia's Front-Runner, but His Plans Are a Mystery."
[23] Ibid., March 28, 2000, Patrick Tyler, "Putin Tells Advisors to Prepare 'Weighty' Economic Plan."

would release a plan envisaging radical reforms, from overhauling the tax code to streamlining the bureaucracy. The Aleksandr House team had already established itself as a center of liberal economics within the Putin administration. Stated Boris Nemtsov, a liberal political leader: "A struggle is going on over the strategy for Russia. Either it will be crony capitalism with tycoons, corruption, underground deals, and social polarization, or it will be a Western-style economy." Tycoon Boris Berezovskii dismissed Gref's liberal Aleksandr House as "unprofessional" and its ideas as "naive." The question was whether President Putin could remain independent from competing financial clans and override an entrenched bureaucracy.[24]

Putin's formal installation as president of Russia on May 7, 2000, reminded many of the past. Beneath a gilded sunburst in a gilded palace, his hand on a leather-bound copy of the 1993 Constitution, President Putin swore "to respect and guard the human and civil rights" of Russia. The ceremony was broadcast on all major Russian television networks and was directed with military precision and Hollywood style. As the installation ceremony ended, a choir sang the "Glory" aria from Mikhail Glinka's opera, "A Life for the Tsar" with blessing by Patriarch Aleksy.[25]

An incident that seemed to threaten free expression was the sudden arrest in June 2000 of Vladimir Gusinskii, owner of Media-Most, a leading independent media conglomerate. Russia's leading businessmen promptly condemned this arrest, warning that it imperiled Russia's freedoms. "Until yesterday we believed we lived in a democratic country and today we have serious doubts," wrote seventeen tycoons in a letter to the Russian prosecutor general. This revealed the uneasy relationship of Putin's new government with the power elite. Gusinskii was detained on suspicion

of embezzling millions of dollars in state property, charges that his supporters claimed were trumped up. President Putin initially expressed surprise at the arrest, while Mayor Iurii Luzhkov of Moscow insisted that Gusinskii be released; he was freed after four days.[26]

About the same time, President Putin was welcomed to Berlin by headlines suggesting the hopes Germany placed in a longtime resident of Dresden. "The second German-speaking Russian leader after Lenin," rejoiced the newspaper, *Die Zeit*. Putin's three-day visit to Berlin seemed part of a strategy to link Russia firmly to Western Europe, attract investment, induce Germany to look eastward, and if possible to drive a wedge between Europe and the United States. Putin intimated that his visit was motivated partly by "the special place Germany and its people and culture have in my heart." With over 60 percent of Russia's foreign debt of $150 billion owed to Germany, Putin desired to obtain some debt relief.[27]

In early summer 2000 President Putin flew to Tatarstan, donned a Tatar hat, bobbed for coins, then engaged a Tatar girl in arm wrestling, slamming her arm on the table in a single overpowering move. Observing this on television, Professor Aleksandr Asmolov, a Moscow University psychologist, commented: "This man has a ton of ambition, a mountain, no a cosmos of ambition." Asmolov then wrote Putin urging him to rule more tolerantly. In the months after his election, Putin capitalized on a high voter mandate, favorable opinion polls, and an economy buoyed by high oil prices to begin putting Russia back in order after a decade of wild gyrations under Yeltsin. Putin issued an economic program that won praise from Western governments and pushed a new tax code through a cooperative parliament. He began a major reorganization of the 89 unruly regions, dividing Russia into seven large new administrative areas and installing his

[24] Ibid., April 2, 2000, Celestine Bohlen, "Putin's Team Hammers Out a Plan to Untwist, Level, and Streamline Russia's Economy."
[25] Ibid., May 8, 2000, Michael Wines, "Putin Is Made Russia's President in First Free Transfer of Power."

[26] Ibid., June 15, 2000. Michael Gordon, "Seventeen Russians Protest Fellow Mongul's Arrest."
[27] Ibid., June 15, 2000. Roger Cohen, "Warm Welcome for 'Putin the German'."

Reuters

Boris N. Yeltsin, Vladimir V. Putin, and Patriarch Aleksy II after the inauguration in the Kremlin.

own appointees over them. He humbled auto-cratic governors by siphoning off their power and tax revenues. Putin also began separating the oligarchs from their influence over the Russian government. Firing six senior generals in early August 2000, Putin conferred with his national security council to decide on a major restructuring of the military. Putin seemed more adept than Yeltsin at utilizing his office's enormous powers, but could Russia's fragile democratic institutions resist his authoritarian streak? Can he meld free-dom and discipline into a new structure for Russia while avoiding a slide toward the autocratic Soviet past?[28]

Aleksandr Gelman, a writer working with Gorbachev, declared that Putin had made some mistakes but was seeking a proper balance between freedom and order. However, Sergei Kovalev, a follower of Andrei Sakharov, expressed the view of some intellectuals and dissidents: "The new team [of Putin] is energetically crushing freedom and democracy. . . . He is building . . . a unitary state based on force and trying hard to create the good old Soviet idea: unbroken vertical power from top to bottom." However, Gorbachev, after a lengthy meeting with Putin in August, stated that the president was on the right path. "I support Putin's efforts to strengthen order and responsibility." He warned that, "regionalism is threatening to lead the country to disintegration."[29]

In mid-August 2000 the Russian Orthodox Church canonized Nicholas II and his family for their "humbleness, patience, and meekness" in imprisonment prior to their execution in Ekaterinburg in 1918 on Lenin's orders. This move had long been demanded by powerful right-wing elements. Declared Edvard Radzinskii, biographer of Rasputin: "I predict that it will be a great show, a show of empire, and Mr. Putin will take part in this like a strong guy who remembers strong times."[30]

The sinking of the *Kursk*, one of Russia's newest and most powerful submarines, during naval maneuvers on August 12 in the Barents Sea marked the beginning of the worst ten days of Putin's political life. Putin failed to return immediately from vacation, and official behavior at first was deceitful, even callous. However, as Russia grieved for the 118 seamen lost in this disaster, Putin then moved decisively to reduce the incident's political impact. On national television he took full responsibility for a badly handled and incompetent rescue attempt. Putin declared that family members of the submarine's crew had told him the sinking was his cross to bear as president. The *Kursk* affair temporarily dented Putin's once bulletproof reputation for competence and efficiency, but most Russians, polls showed, still approved of his performance as president. Furthermore, the frank admissions of responsibility by Putin and his aides marked an encouraging move towards openness since previous submarine incidents had simply been hushed up.[31]

One result of the *Kursk* affair was to induce the Putin administration to take a fresh look at reforming Russia's armed forces. Putin told angry relatives of the *Kursk* crew that Russia needed smaller, better equipped and better paid armed forces. On September 8 Defense Minister Marshal Igor Sergeev confirmed the government's decision to reduce the armed forces from 1.2 million to about 850,000 men. Putin had told the *Kursk* relatives that "one has to live according to one's income," and that Russia had wasted money seeking to support the Soviet military structure of the Cold War era. The draft Russian budget for the year 2001 envisaged a considerable increase in expenditures for the military involving higher levels of pay. Russia had inherited a two-million man military when the Soviet Union collapsed, which President Yeltsin had succeeded in reducing to 1.2 million largely by attrition and early retirement."[32]

Tentative Assessment

Is Russia's—and President Putin's—cup half full or half empty? Late in the year 2000 the balance sheet appears largely favorable. As both acting and serving president Putin has carefully preserved and reinforced the fragile Russian Federation by establishing greater control from Moscow over its restive regions. The relationship between the

---

[28] Ibid., August 14, 2000, Patrick Tyler, "Russians Wonder if Putin Accepts Limits to Power."
[29] Ibid.
[30] Ibid., August 15 2000, "Nicolas II and Family Canonized for 'Passion'."

[31] Ibid., August 24, 2000. Michael Wines, "Bereft Russia Hears Putin's mea culpa on Sub Accident"; Economist, August 26, 2000, "The Damage Done," pp. 37–38.
[32] *New York Times*, September 10, 2000, Tyler, "Russia Poised to Cut Military by One-Third."

executive and a formerly rebellious legislature has improved significantly compared with the Yeltsin years. This has enabled the passage of important reform legislation proposed by the Putin regime, especially in regard to the tax code. Russia's economy has definitely been on the upswing, fueled partly by higher world oil prices, partly by higher tax receipts. On the negative side, Russian living standards and life expectancy remain dangerously low. There is concern, notably among liberal intellectuals, that President Putin intends to establish a more authoritarian regime that will restrict freedoms of speech and press. Nonetheless, President Putin represents a new younger, energetic generation divorced from the dictatorial and corrupt Soviet regime.

Culture Under Yeltsin and Putin

Measured against the high hopes and expectations for a "normal life" after the collapse the Soviet Union, most Russians have paid a heavy price for their freedom and liberation from communism. Russia has suffered national decline, economic depression, and social dislocation, disorder, and demographic disruption with a declining birth rate and a rising death rate.

Public Health

Russian health is bad and getting worse. There is a national health crisis in Russia, where life expectancy declined precipitously in the 1990s, to a composite 65.5 years—women 72, men 59.8. Russia is facing a population collapse unprecedented in any country at peace. The Russian population has declined by 6 million people in the past decade. President Putin recently expressed fear that the nation's survival is threatened by declining population. If recent trends persist, it is estimated that Russia will lose about 40 million in population by 2025. Russians are smoking and drinking more than ever, and diseases such as tuberculosis (TB), AIDS, and hepatitis are at epidemic levels. Poor nutrition, alcohol abuse, and uncontrolled smoking, together with a ruined

health care system have left most people at risk. It is estimated that half of Russia's teenage boys will not live to age 60.

The health care system is in shambles. Lack of adequate equipment, modem training for doctors, and few pharmaceutical supplies mean that treatment of illness is slow, antiquated, and in many cases non-existent. Drug-resistant strains of TB have created a serious crisis. Six hundred thousand Russians will be infected with the AIDS virus by the end of 2000. Hepatitis and other infectious diseases are at epidemic levels, with few prophylactic measures being taken by a cash-strapped public health system. Pollution—air, water, and contamination of food products—continues to rob Russians of their health. Russians now consume, on average, about one-half the volume of meat they did a decade ago. The flood of imported food products that began after the collapse of communism ended abruptly with the crash of the ruble in August 1998. Imported products are still available, but at price levels few Russian can afford.

Social Life

Richard Stites has written that it is a mistake to judge Russian life on the basis of observations of the Moscow and St. Petersburg intelligentsia, something common during Soviet times, and common as well today. Russians fortunate enough to live in Moscow and St. Petersburg have many more opportunities than those living in provincial villages, towns, and cities, where the transformation of Russian life is much less evident. Russia at its core is still very much the product of the Soviet legacy. Outside the major centers, despite some superficial changes in the way Russians live, little has changed since the collapse of the Soviet Union. Massive Soviet-built apartment blocks with poor lighting and cramped kitchens and bathrooms, often lacking adequate hot water and heat, remain home to millions of Russians. To be sure, some new buildings have appeared, and large, well-built *dachas*—country homes or summerhouses—outside the major cities have sprung up for the small well-to-do class. Most buildings are in poor repair and little is being done to protect them from further deterioration. Cars proliferate in major cities—2.5 million cars in Moscow—without commensurate improvement in infrastructure to accommodate them.

Russians have always been inveterate gardeners and they still are, growing fruits and vegetables on small garden plots outside urban centers and canning and preserving produce for winter consumption just as they did in Soviet times. Much time and energy are devoted to these pursuits among those lucky enough to have access to small plots. In some heavily polluted areas such as the Kola Peninsula in the far north and around Murmansk even this essential survival practice is impossible without risk of serious illness.

Popular Culture

Moscow and St. Petersburg largely define Russian popular culture in the post-communist era. There are virtually no boundaries that limit or confine Russian popular culture. No ideology dominates popular culture except the idea of freedom of expression. The market rules—what sells in the open market gets printed, performed, screened, recorded, and disseminated. Western culture is still a powerful magnet, but following the economic crisis of summer 1998, Western cultural products have been largely priced out of the market. There is a concerted effort on the part of Russians to rescue their culture from the influx of Western culture in its ubiquitous manifestations.

There is an ongoing effort to Russify things like fast food. McDonald's maintains its presence in a number of Russian cities, but there are now competing chains of fast food purveyors that serve up a version of Russian fast food—meat pies, cabbage rolls, soups, and hot dogs. Coca Cola, that powerful symbol of Western popular culture, established a solid foothold in Russia during *perestroika,* but it is now being challenged by mass distribution of Russian versions of soft drinks, including a resurgence of *kvas*—made from fermented bread and long a staple of Soviet times.

Among young Russians the apparel of choice these days is, as it is everywhere, blue jeans (Levi's or designer jeans), sneakers (Nikes or Reeboks), baseball caps worn backwards, and jackets with sports logos. Drugs and alcohol have also become far more prevalent since the collapse of the Soviet Union, especially among teenagers and generation X-ers. Youth gangs are also a part of the new Russian youth-oriented culture. On the heels of an expanded drug culture, crime has exploded among a young generation with no sense of the civic and social responsibility of Soviet times.

Russian TV provides the most popular form of leisure-time activity in Russia and it is beamed throughout the country. It has sought to find its own voice by producing programming that may be modeled on Western forms but which conveys an entirely Russian content and outlook. Most popular are game shows, talk shows, sit-coms, sports, and news programming, which is controversial, incisive, critical, and ratings conscious. Criticism of the continuing war in Chechnia led to a clash between newly elected President Putin and the oligarch and TV mogul Vladimir Gusinskii, who found himself under arrest, charged with fraud. Putin denied charges that he was attempting to muzzle the free press. Gusinskii's release was won only by his agreement to sell his TV interests. In the TV world, ratings matter, and in the struggle to win viewers, boundaries are pushed to the limit—topless weather reporters and nude interviewers are used to appeal to the prurient interests of viewers.

Russian cinema is rebounding after being overwhelmed by distribution of Western-made films, both in theaters and on video (often in pirated versions sold cheaply on the street). *Titanic* was a titanic hit in Russia, as were the action movies of Arnold Schwarzenegger and Eddie Murphy. Director Nikita Mikhalkov's film *Burnt by the Sun* won an Oscar as best foreign film in 1998 and played to large audiences in Russia. It was an exercise in confronting the past, portraying an episode from the history of the Stalinist purge of military officers during the late thirties. A recent

Mikhalkov film, *The Barber of Siberia,* has been less successful. Mikhalkov's name recognition was sufficient to urge him to consider a run for the Russian presidency.

Rock music rules in Russia. For decades rock music struggled as an underground phenomenon, only grudgingly accepted by Soviet authorities because it could not be controlled or Sovietized as jazz was in an earlier era. Russian rock music is written and performed by Russian groups with energy and enthusiasm that provide an extraordinary intensity and vitality to the search for a Russian cultural idiom on a par with the West. Russian rock bands have followings comparable to the best Western groups. Jazz, with original composers and talented performers, continues to have a large following in Russia, and jazz clubs have proliferated. Classical music, which was a staple during Soviet times, has taken a back seat, although it remains popular with the intelligentsia, especially in Moscow and St. Petersburg. Sale of classical recordings has declined and many well-known orchestras struggle with inadequate funding and half-empty concert halls.

A crumbling infrastructure and inadequate public and private support are threatening much of what is central to Russian culture—theater, classical music, museums, universities, libraries. Russia has a staggering 90,000 officially designated architectural landmarks or historically significant buildings, consisting of churches, palaces, monasteries, and architectural ensembles, some centuries old. Many of these treasures are in danger of disappearing forever. The New York–based World Monument Watch has placed seven Russian sites on its most-endangered list, more than for any other country. Included on that list are Moscow's Bolshoi Theater and St. Petersburg's Hermitage Museum. The federal budget is unable to accommodate necessary assistance to these venerable institutions, and private support is also very scarce. Despite budget shortfalls, the Grand Kremlin Palace recently underwent a massive, $500 million renovation, which has resulted in still unresolved charges of corruption, bribery, and kickbacks. Reconstruction, at enormous expense, of Moscow's Cathedral of Christ the Savior, leveled by the Bolsheviks in 1931, and the lavish renovation of St. Petersburg's Church of the Savior on the Blood have raised questions about the structuring of priorities.

The Bolshoi Theater, a paramount symbol of Russian cultural life, is now 150 years old. It is in danger of collapsing and requires major structural renovation and a completely new electrical system. The Soviet government had promised funds for renovation in 1987, but the project has been on hold ever since and is less likely than ever to receive the necessary government funding to complete renovation. UNESCO is seeking to provide funds for this and several other renovation projects in Russia, including the Hermitage Museum. St. Petersburg's magnificent baroque Winter Palace, which houses the Hermitage's incomparable collection of art is in danger of collapsing because the foundations are sinking, the roof leaks, and heating and cooling systems are archaic and outmoded for a museum of this quality. Historic buildings outside Moscow and St. Petersburg have received even less attention. Rostov Velikii, one of the great religious and cultural centers of medieval Russia, is being assaulted by water and pollution damage.

Nothing brought home more clearly the government's inability to provide leadership and fiscal assistance for revamping infrastructure and strengthening the armed forces than the sinking of the submarine *Kursk* in August 2000 and a fire in the Ostankino TV tower in Moscow the following month. One hundred eighteen Russian sailors lost their lives in the *Kursk* tragedy, and a number of people were killed in the Ostankino fire, which disrupted TV broadcasting in Moscow and across the country.*

---

* The Russian government in spring 2001 contracted with a Dutch firm to raise the *Kursk* from its watery grave.

Science and Education

The physicist A. F. Ioffe became Russia's first Nobel Laureate in more than a decade. Honored for his work on semi-conductors, Ioffe used the occasion of his award to plea for more government support for basic research. Researchers at his institute are paid $80 per month! Russian science, he eloquently argued as an elected member of Russia's Duma, is a key economic resource that is being squandered by a government more interested in oil and natural gas. During Soviet times, government spending on basic science was 7 percent of the national budget. In 1998 the figure was 3.8 percent of a much smaller federal budget, and in 2000 the figure has been reduced to 1.72 percent. One Duma deputy asked: "How is it possible that the finance ministry, which merely consists of bureaucrats, gets one-and-a-half times more money than the entire science sector?"[33]

The educational system, once the pride of the Soviet Union, is struggling to find a way to provide basic education to Russian school-age children. Reports the *Christian Science Monitor,* "While struggling with meager state funding, Russian educators are also wrestling with how to stem a drop in once-enviable standards and debating their fundamental goals.[34] During Soviet times, the state required large numbers of engineers and scientists and the school system provided them. There is no longer such a demand and standards have slipped. Schools are ill-equipped to provide the kind of education required by a free and open society where there is competition among ideas. Educational philosophy is drifting and standards are falling. Unheard of in Soviet times, the problems fostered by an open society have also invaded the schools: drugs, alcohol, violence. Russian teachers are unprepared to cope with them. Moreover, many of the best teachers are leaving to pursue other opportunities. Average teacher salaries are less than $50 per month. Russia's Ministry of Education admits that there is a shortfall of more than 50,000 teachers. No investment is being made in new schools, equipment, and textbooks. An official claims: "Our society will die unless we begin to seriously invest in our schools."[35] One graphic result of this decline is an estimated 10 million illiterates in Russia today.

Conclusion

Declining health, a dangerously low birth rate, crumbling infrastructure, crime, corruption, poverty, and pollution pose enormous problems for Russia at the beginning of a new millennium. The Orthodox Church does not have the moral authority to assume a role of leadership in Russian society. President Putin's government has demonstrated a new energy and sense of direction, and the economy is beginning to show signs of revival, but the Soviet legacy still hangs heavy over the country and old habits inculcated over generations have not disappeared. Putin's response to the sinking of the *Kursk* reveals a government unfamiliar with the need to stand with the people at a time of national tragedy. Russia has made enormous strides since the collapse of communism, but much remains to be done.

InfoTrac® College Edition Search Terms

Enter the search term *Putin* in the Subject Guide. Enter the search term *Russia* in the Subject Guide, and then go to subdivision *economic aspects.* Enter the search term *Russia* in the Subject Guide, and then go to subdivision *economic policy.* Enter the search term *Russia* in the Subject Guide, and then go to subdivision *social aspects.*

[33] *Johnson's Russia List,* #4574, item #1, October 11, 2000.
[34] *Christian Science Monitor,* September 1 2000, p. 1.
[35] Ibid. p. 8.

Appendices

A

Russian and Soviet Leaders, 1801–2001

1. **Russian Tsars:**

Alexander I	1801–1825	Alexander III	1881–1894
Nicholas I	1825–1855	Nicholas II	1894–1917
Alexander II	1855–1881		

2. **Soviet leaders** (all except Lenin were general or first secretaries of the Communist party of the Soviet Union)

V. I. Lenin	1917–1924	L. I. Brezhnev	1964–1982
J. V. Stalin	1924–1953	Iu. V. Andropov	1982–1984
G. M. Malenkov	1953	K. V. Chernenko	1984–1985
N. S. Khrushchev	1953–1964	M. S. Gorbachev	1985–1991

3. **Chairmen of the Council of People's Commissars** (prime ministers after 1946)

V. I. Lenin	1917–1924	N. S. Khrushchev	1958–1964
A. I. Rykov	1924–1930	A. N. Kosygin	1964–1980
V. M. Molotov	1930–1941	N. A. Tikhonov	1980–1985
J. V. Stalin	1941–1953	N. I. Ryzhkov	1985–1990
G. M. Malenkov	1953–1955	V. Pavlov	1991–
N. A. Bulganin	1955–1958		

4. President of Russia (Russian Federation)

Boris N. Yeltsin, 1991–1999
Vladimir V. Putin, 1999–

5. Full members of the Politburo (Presidium, 1952–1966) of the Soviet Communist Party

Name	Years	Name	Years
V. I. Lenin	1919–1924	V. V. Kuznetsov	1952–1953
L. D. Trotskii	1919–1926	V. A. Malyshev	1952–1953
J. V. Stalin	1919–1953	L. G. Melnikov	1952–1953
L. B. Kamenev	1919–1925	N. A. Mikhailov	1952–1953
N. N. Krestinskii	1919–1921	M. G. Pervukhin	1952–1957
G. E. Zinoviev	1921–1926	P. K. Ponomarenko	1952–1953
A. I. Rykov	1922–1930	M. Z. Saburov	1952–1957
M. P. Tomskii	1922–1930	N. M. Shvernik	1952–1953, 1957–1966
N. I. Bukharin	1924–1929		
V. M. Molotov	1926–1957	D. I. Chesnokov	1952–1953
K. E. Voroshilov	1926–1960	M. F. Shkiriatov	1952–1953
M. I. Kalinin	1926–1946	A. I. Kirichenko	1955–1960
Ia. E. Rudzutak	1926–1932	M. A. Suslov	1955–1982
V. V. Kuibyshev	1927–1935	L. I. Brezhnev	1957–1982
L. M. Kaganovich	1930–1957	G. K. Zhukov	June–Oct. 1957
S. M. Kirov	1930–1934	E. A. Furtseva	1957–1961
S. V. Kosior	1930–1938	N. I. Beliaev	1957–1960
G. K. Ordzhonikidze	1930–1937	N. G. Ignatov	1957–1961
A. A. Andreyev	1932–1952	F. R. Kozlov	1957–1964
V. Ia. Chubar	1935–1938	N. A. Mukhitdinov	1957–1961
A. I. Mikoyan	1935–1966	N. V. Podgorny	1960–1977
A. A. Zhdanov	1939–1948	D. S. Polianskii	1960–1976
N. S. Khrushchev	1939–1964	G. I. Voronov	1961–1973
L. P. Beria	1946–1953	A. P. Kirilenko	1962–1981
G. M. Malenkov	1946–1957	A. N. Shelepin	1964–1975
N. A. Voznesenskii	1947–1949	P. E. Shelest	1964–1973
N. A. Bulganin	1948–1958	K. T. Mazurov	1965–1978
A. N. Kosygin	1949–1950, 1960–1980	A. Ia. Pelshe	1966–1983
		V. V. Grishin	1971–1985
V. M. Andrianov	1952–1953	F. D. Kulakov	1971–1978
A. B. Aristov	1952–1953, 1957–1961	D. A. Kunaev	1971–1989
S. D. Ignatiev	1952–1953	V. V. Shcherbitskii	1971–1989
D. S. Korochenko	1952–1953	Iu. V. Andropov	1973–1984
O. V. Kuusinen	1952–1953, 1957–1964	A. A. Gromyko	1973–1988
		D. F. Ustinov	1973–1984
		A. A. Grechko	1973–1976

Full members of the Politburo (Presidium, 1952–1966) of the Soviet
Communist Party (continued)

G. V. Romanov	1976–1985	E. G. Ligachev	1985–1991
K. V. Chernenko	1977–1985	E. A.	
N. A. Tikhonov	1979–1985	Shevarnadze	1985–1991
M. S. Gorbachev	1980–1991	N. I. Ryzhkov	1985–1991
G. A. Aliyev	1982–1987	L. N. Zaikov	1987–1991
M. S.		V. P. Nikonov	1987–1991
Solomentsev	1983–1988	N. I. Sliunkov	1987–1991
V. I. Vorotnikov	1983–1987	A. N. Iakovlev	1987–1991
V. M. Chebrikov	1985–1991		

B

Areas and Populations of Former Soviet Union Republics

Republic	Area (in thousands of square kilometers)	Population (in thousands)	Date	Capital	Population (in thousands)
Armenian SSR	29.8	3,580	1/91	Erivan	1,215
Azerbaijani SSR	86.6	7,145	1/90	Baku	1,757
Belorussian SSR	207.6	10,259	1/90	Minsk	1,612
Estonian SSR	45.1	1,573	1/89	Tallinn	503
Georgian SSR	69.7	5,449	1/89	Tbilisi	1,264
Kazakh SSR	2,717.3	16,690	1/90	Alma-Ata	1,132
Kirghiz SSR	198.5	4,372	1/89	Frunze	626
Latvian SSR	63.7	2,681	1/89	Riga	915
Lithuanian SSR	65.2	3,690	1/89	Vilnius	582
Moldavian SSR	33.7	4,341	1/89	Kishinev	720
Russian SFSR	17,075.4	147,386	1/89	Moscow	8,967
Tadzhik SSR	143.1	5,112	1/89	Dushanbe	604
Turkmen SSR	488.1	3,621	1/90	Ashkhabad	339
Ukrainian SSR	603.7	51,704	1/89	Kiev	2,602
Üzbek SSR	447.4	20,322	1/90	Tashkent	2,079
USSR	22,402.2*	287,925			

*Approximately equivalent to 8.65 million square miles
SOURCE: *Europa World Yearbook* II, (London, 1991), pp. 2679–80.

C

Populations of Principal Cities of the Russian Federation

City	Population (est. 1/1/92)	City	Population (est. 1/1/92)
Moscow	8,746,700	Astrakhan	512,200
St. Petersburg*	4,436,700	Tomsk	504,700
Novosibirsk	1,441,900	Tyumen	496,200
Nizhnii-Novgorod*	1,440,600	Viyatka*	492,500
Ekaterinburg*	1,370,700	Ivanovo	480,400
Samara*	1,239,200	Murmansk	468,300
Omsk	1,168,600	Bryansk	460,500
Chelyabinsk	1,143,000	Lipetsk	463,600
Kazan	1,104,000	Tver*	455,600
Perm	1,098,600	Magnitogorsk	441,200
Ufa	1,097,200	Cheboksary	438,900
Rostov-na-Donu	1,027,100	Nizhnii Tagil	437,400
Volgograd	1,006,100	Kursk	435,200
Krasnoyarsk	925,000	Archangel	413,600
Saratov	909,300	Kaliningrad	410,700
Voronezh	902,200	Groznyi	387,500
Tolyatti	665,700	Chita	376,500
Simbirsk*	656,400	Ulan-Ude	366,000
Izhevsk*	650,700	Kurgan	365,100
Vladivostok	647,800	Vladimir	356,100
Irkutsk	637,000	Smolensk	351,600
Yaroslavl	636,900	Kaluga	346,800
Krasnodar	634,500	Orel	346,600
Khabarovsk	614,600	Sochi	344,200
Barnaul	606,200	Makhachkala	339,300
Novokuznetsk	600,200	Stavropol	331,800
Orenburg	556,500	Vladikavkaz*	324,700
Penza	552,300	Saransk	322,000
Tula	541,400	Komsomolsk-na-Amure	318,600
Ryazan	528,500	Cherepovets	317,100
Kemerovo	520,600	Belgorod	314,200
Naberezhnye Chelny*	515,400	Tambov	310,600

* Some towns that were renamed during the Soviet period have reverted to their former names: St. Petersburg (Leningrad); Nizhnii-Novgorod (Gorkii); Ekaterinburg (Sverdlovsk); Samara (Kuibyshev); Simbirsk (Ulyanovsk); Izhevsk (Ustinov); Naberezhnye Chelny (Brezhnev); Viyatka (Kirov); Tver (Kalinin); Vladikavkaz (Ordzhonikidze).

Sources: UN, *Demographic Yearbook. Europa World Yearbook* II, (London, 1996), p. 2681.

Additional Bibliography

The following brief bibliography contains only major reference works relating to Russian and Soviet history and some key general histories in English emphasizing the modern period. For works on specific periods and topics, see the selected bibliographies at the end of each chapter of this text.

Reference Works

ALLWORTH, E., ed. *Soviet Asia Bibliographies: The Iranian, Mongolian and Turkic Nationalities* (New York, 1973).

American Bibliography of Russian and East European Studies (Bloomington, IN, annually since 1957).

ATTWOOD, LYNNE ET AL., ed. *Red Women on the Silver Screen: Soviet Women and Cinema from the Beginning to the End of the Communist Era* (San Francisco, 1993).

BENNIGSEN, ALEXANDRE, and S. ENDERS WIMBUSH. *Muslims of the Soviet Empire: A Guide* (Bloomington, IN, 1986).

BEZER, C., ed. *Russian and Soviet Studies: A Handbook* (Columbus, OH, 1973).

BRUMFIELD, WILLIAM C. *A History of Russian Architecture* (New York, 1993).

CARPENTER, K. E., comp. *Russian Revolutionary Literature Collection* (New Haven, CT, 1976).

CLARKE, R. A., and D. J. MATKO. *Soviet Economic Facts, 1917–1981* (London, 1983).

CROUCHER, MURLIN, comp. and ed. *Slavic Studies: A Guide to Bibliographies, Encyclopedias and Handbooks*, 2 vols. (Wilmington, DE, 1993).

CRUMMEY, ROBERT, ed. *Reform in Russia and the U.S.S.R.: Past and Prospects* (Champaign, IL, 1990).

DAVIES, R. W. ET AL., ed. *The Economic Transformation of the Soviet Union, 1913–1948* (New York, 1994).

DMYTRYSHYN, BASIL, and FREDERICK COX. *The Soviet Union and the Middle East: A Documentary Record of Afghanistan, Iran and Turkey, 1917–1985* (Princeton, NJ, 1985).

EGAN, DAVID, and M. A. EGAN. *Russian Autocrats from Ivan the Great to the Fall of the Romanov Dynasty: An Annotated Bibliography of English Language Sources to 1985* (Metuchen, NJ, 1987).

EKLOF, BEN, ed. *School and Society in Tsarist and Soviet Russia* (New York, 1993).

The Europa-World Yearbook 1989, 2 vols. (London, 1989).

FLORINSKY, M. T., ed. *McGraw-Hill Encyclopedia of Russia and the Soviet Union* (New York, 1961).

GERON, LEONARD, and ALEX PRAVDA, eds. *Who's Who in Russia and the New States* (London and New York, 1993).

GRAHAM, LOREN. *Science in Russia and the Soviet Union: A Short History* (New York, 1993).

Great Soviet Encyclopedia: A Translation of the Third Edition, 10 vols. (New York, 1973).

GREEN, BARBARA B. *The Dynamics of Russian Politics: A Short History* (Westport, CT, 1994).

GREEN, WILLIAM C., and W. ROBERT REEVES, eds. and trans. *The Soviet Military Encyclopedia: Abridged English Language Edition, Vols.* 1–4 (Boulder, CO 1989).

HAMMOND, T., ed. *Soviet Foreign Relations and World Communism: A Selected Annotated Bibliography of 7,000 Books in 30 Languages* (Princeton, NJ, 1965).

HORAK, S. M. *Junior Slavica: A Selected Annotated Bibliography of Books in English on Russia and Eastern Europe* (Rochester, NY, 1968).

HORECKY, P., ed. *Basic Russian Publications: A Selected and Annotated Bibliography on Russia and the Soviet Union* (Chicago, 1962).

———. *Russia and the Soviet Union: A Bibliographic Guide to Western Language Publications* (Chicago, 1965).

HUSKEY, EUGENE, ed. *Executive Power and Soviet Politics: The Rise and Decline of the Soviet State* (Armonk, NY, 1992).

KATZ, Z. ET AL., eds. *Handbook of Major Soviet Nationalities* (New York, 1975).

KAVASS, IGOR. *Demise of the Soviet Union: A Bibliographic Survey of English Writings on the Soviet Legal System, 1990–1991* (Buffalo, NY, 1992).

KEEFE, E. *Area Handbook for the Soviet Union* (Washington, DC, 1971).

KERNIG, C., ed. *Marxism, Communism and Western Society: A Comparative Encyclopedia*, 8 vols. (New York, 1972).

KUBIJOVYC ET AL., eds. *Ukraine: A Concise Encyclopedia*, 2 vols. (Ottawa, 1971).

LEVIN, NORA. *The Jews in the Soviet Union Since 1917: Paradox of Survival*, 2 vols. (New York and London, 1988).

LEWYTZKYJ, BORYS, ed. *Who's Who in the Soviet Union. A Biographical Encyclopedia of 5,000 Leading Personalities in the Soviet Union* (Munich and New York, 1984).

MAGOCSI, PAUL R. *Ukraine: A Historical Atlas* (Toronto, 1985).

MAICHEL, K. *Guide to Russian Reference Books* (Stanford, CA, 1962).

———. *Guide to Russian Reference Books II: History, Auxiliary Sciences, Ethnography and Geography* (Stanford, CA, 1964).

MARTIANOV, N. N. *Books Available in English by Russians and on Russia* (New York, 1960).

MITCHELL, DONALD W. *A History of Russian and Soviet Sea Power* (New York, 1974).

NATION, R. CRAIG. *A History of Soviet Security Policy, 1917–1991* (Ithaca, NY, 1991).

NERHOOD, H., comp. *To Russia and Return: An Annotated Bibliography of Travelers' English Language Accounts of Russia from the Ninth Century to the Present* (Columbus, OH, 1968).

PEARSON, RAYMOND, ed. *Russia and Eastern Europe: A Bibliographic Guide* (Manchester, England, 1989).

PIERCE, R. *Soviet Central Asia: A Bibliography*, 3 vols. (Berkeley, CA, 1966).

PUSHKAREV, S. G. *A Source Book for Russian History from Early Times to 1917*, ed. A. Ferguson ET AL., 3 vols. (New Haven, CT, 1972).

RAEFF, MARC. *Russia Abroad: A Cultural History of the Russian Emigration, 1919–1939* (New York and Oxford, 1990).

RAGSDALE, HUGH, ed. *Imperial Russian Foreign Policy* (New York, 1993).

RAMET, SABRINA P., ed. *Religious Policy in the Soviet Union* (New York, 1993).

RYAN, MICHAEL, comp. and trans. *Social Trends in Contemporary Russia: A Statistical Source-book* (New York, 1993).

SCHÖPFLIN, G., ed. *The Soviet Union and Eastern Europe: A Handbook* (New York, 1970).

SCHULTHEISS, T., ed. *Russian Studies, 1941–1958: A Cumulation of the Annual Bibliographies from the Russian Review* (Ann Arbor, MI, 1972).

SHAPIRO, D. *A Selected Bibliography of Works in English on Russian History, 1801–1917* (New York and London, 1962).

SHUKMAN, HAROLD, ed. *The Blackwell Encyclopedia of the Russian Revolution* (Oxford, 1988).

SHTEPPA, K. F. *Russian Historians and the Soviet State* (New Brunswick, NJ, 1962).

SMITH, GERALD S., ed. and trans. *Contemporary Russian Poetry: A Bilingual Anthology* (Bloomington, IN, 1993).

STEEVES, PAUL D., ed. *The Modern Encyclopedia of Religions in Russia and the Soviet Union* (Gulf Breeze, FL, 1988–).

SZEFTEL, M. "Russia Before 1917," in *Bibliographical Introduction to Legal History and Ethnology*, ed. J. Glissen (Brussels, 1966).

UTECHIN, S. V. *Everyman's Concise Encyclopedia of Russia* (New York, 1961).

VERNADSKY, GEORGE. *Russian Historiography: A History* (Belmont, MA, 1978).

WHITING, K. *The Soviet Union Today*, rev. ed. (New York, 1966).

WIECZYNSKI, JOSEPH L., ed. *The Modern Encyclopedia of Russian and Soviet History*, 58 vols. (Gulf Breeze, FL, 1976–1994). (Extremely useful.)

WOZNIUK, VLADIMIR. *Understanding Soviet Foreign Policy: Readings and Documents* (New York, 1990).

ZILE, ZIGURDS L., ed. *Ideas and Forces in Soviet Legal History: A Reader on the Soviet State and Law* (New York, 1992).

General Histories

BLACK, CYRIL E. *Understanding Soviet Politics: The Perspective of Russian History* (Boulder, CO, 1986).

DANIELS, ROBERT. *Russia: The Roots of Confrontation* (Cambridge, MA, 1985). (General treatment of Russian and Soviet history.)

DMYTRYSHYN, BASIL. *USSR: A Concise History*, 4th ed. (New York, 1984).

DVORNIK, F. *The Slavs in European History and Civilization* (New Brunswick, NJ, 1975).

DZIEWANOWSKI, M. K. *A History of Soviet Russia*, 4th ed. (Englewood Cliffs, NJ, 1993).

ELLIS, JANE. *The Russian Orthodox Church: A Contemporary History* (Bloomington, IN, 1986).

FLORINSKY, M. T. *Russia: A History and an Interpretation*, 2 vols. (New York, 1953).

———. *Russia: A Short History*, 2d ed. (New York, 1969).

FORSYTH, JAMES. *A History of the Peoples of Siberia: Russia's North Asian Colony, 1581–1990* (New York, 1992).

GADDIS, JOHN L. *Russia, the Soviet Union, and the United States: An Interpretive History*, 2d ed. (New York, 1990).

GRAHAM, LOREN. *Science, Philosophy, and Human Behavior in the Soviet Union* (New York, 1987).

HELLER, MIKHAIL, and A. M. NEKRICH. *Utopia in Power: The History of the Soviet Union from 1917 to the Present* (New York, 1986).

HEYMAN, NEIL M. *Russian History* (New York, 1993).

HINGLEY, R. *A Concise History of Russia* (New York, 1972).

KOCHAN, LIONEL. *The Making of Modern Russia* (New York, 1983).

KORT, M. G. *Soviet Colossus: The Rise and Fall of the USSR* (New York, 1993).

MACKENZIE, DAVID, and MICHAEL CURRAN. *A History of Russia, the Soviet Union, and Beyond*, 6th ed. (Belmont, CA, 2002).

McCLELLAN, WOODFORD. *Russia: The Soviet Period and After*, 3rd ed. (Englewood Cliffs, NJ, 1994).

McNEAL, ROBERT H. *Tsar and Cossack: 1855–1914* (New York, 1987).

MEDISH, VADIM. *The Soviet Union*, 3d ed. (Englewood Cliffs, NJ, 1987).

MILIUKOV, PAUL ET AL. *History of Russia*, trans. C. Markmann, 3 vols. (New York, 1968).

NOGEE, JOSEPH L., and ROBERT DONALDSON. *Soviet Foreign Policy Since World War II*, 4th ed. (New York, 1992).

NOVE, ALEC. *An Economic History of the USSR, 1917–1991*, 3d ed. (New York and London, 1992).

RAEFF, MARC. *Understanding Imperial Russia: State and Society in the Old Regime* (New York, 1984).

RAUCH, GEORG VON. *A History of Soviet Russia*, 6th ed. (New York, 1972).

RIASANOVSKY, N. V. *A History of Russia*, 5th ed. (New York, 1993).

RIHA, T. *Readings in Russian Civilization*, 2d ed., 3 vols. (Chicago, 1969).

ROGGER, HANS. *Russia in the Age of Modernization and Revolution, 1881–1917* (London and New York, 1983, 1988).

SPECTOR, I. *An Introduction to Russian History and Culture*, 5th ed. (Princeton, NJ, 1969).

SUMNER, B. H. *A Short History of Russia* (New York, 1949, 1962).

TREADGOLD, D. W. *Twentieth Century Russia*, 7th ed. (Boulder, CO, 1990)

ULAM, ADAM. *A History of Soviet Russia* (New York, 1976).

WESTWOOD, J. N. *Endurance and Endeavour: Russian History 1812–1992*, 4th ed. (New York, 1992).

WREN, M. C. *The Course of Russian History*, 4th ed. (New York, 1979).

Index